CHILTON BOOK COMPANY

REPAIR & TUNE-UP GUIDE

JEEP®
1945 to
1987

All U.S. and Canadian models of CJ-2A • CJ-3A • CJ-3B •
CJ-5 • CJ-6 • CJ-7 • Scrambler • Wrangler

T3-BPD-268

Sr. Vice President	Ronald A. Hoxter
Publisher and Editor-In-Chief	Kerry A. Freeman, S.A.E.
Managing Editors	Peter M. Conti, Jr. □ W. Calvin Settle, Jr.; S.A.E.
Assistant Managing Editor	Nick D'Andrea
Senior Editors	Richard J. Rivele, S.A.E. □ Ron Webb
Director of Manufacturing	Mike D'Imperio
Manager of Manufacturing	John F. Butler

CHILTON BOOK COMPANY

ONE OF THE DIVERSIFIED PUBLISHING COMPANIES,
A PART OF CAPITAL CITIES/ABC, INC.

SAFETY NOTICE

Proper service and repair procedures are vital to the safe, reliable operation of all motor vehicles, as well as the personal safety of those performing repairs. This book outlines procedures for servicing and repairing vehicles using safe, effective methods. The procedures contain many NOTES, CAUTIONS and WARNINGS which should be followed along with standard safety procedures to eliminate the possibility of personal injury or improper service which could damage the vehicle or compromise its safety.

It is important to note that repair procedures and techniques, tools and parts for servicing motor vehicles, as well as the skill and experience of the individual performing the work vary widely. It is not possible to anticipate all of the conceivable ways or conditions under which vehicles may be serviced, or to provide cautions as to all of the possible hazards that may result. Standard and accepted safety precautions and equipment should be used during cutting, grinding, chiseling, prying, or any other process that can cause material removal or projectiles.

Some procedures require the use of tools specially designed for a specific purpose. Before substituting another tool or procedure, you must be completely satisfied that neither your personal safety, nor the performance of the vehicle will be endangered.

Although the information in this guide is based on industry sources and is as complete as possible at the time of publication, the possibility exists that the manufacturer made later changes which could not be included here. While striving for total accuracy, Chilton Book Company cannot assume responsibility for any errors, changes, or omissions that may occur in the compilation of this data.

PART NUMBERS

Part numbers listed in this reference are not recommendations by Chilton for any product by brand name. They are references that can be used with interchange manuals and aftermarket supplier catalogs to locate each brand supplier's discrete part number.

SPECIAL TOOLS

Special tools are recommended by the vehicle manufacturer to perform their specific job. Use has been kept to a minimum, but where absolutely necessary, they are referred to in the text by the part number of the tool manufacturer. These tools can be purchased under the appropriate part number, from your Jeep dealer or regional distributor or an equivalent tool can be purchased locally from a tool supplier or parts outlet. Before substituting any tool for the one recommended, read the SAFETY NOTICE at the top of this page.

ACKNOWLEDGMENTS

The Chilton Book Company expresses its appreciation to the Jeep Corporation, A Division of American Motors Corporation, Detroit, Michigan for their generous assistance in the preparation of this book.

Copyright © 1987 by Chilton Book Company
All Rights Reserved
Published in Radnor, Pennsylvania 19089 by Chilton Book Company

Manufactured in the United States of America
    0   65432

Chilton's Repair & Tune-Up Guide: Jeep 1945–87
ISBN 0-8019-7675-8 pbk.
Library of Congress Catalog Card No. 85-47977

CONTENTS

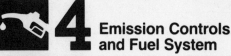

1 General Information and Maintenance

1 How to use this Book
2 Tools and Equipment
17 Routine Maintenance and Lubrication

2 Tune-Up and Performance Maintenance

78 Troubleshooting
81 Tune-Up Specifications
83 Tune-Up Procedures

3 Engine and Engine Overhaul

116 Engine Specifications
120 Engine Electrical System
145 Engine Service
146 Engine Troubleshooting

4 Emission Controls and Fuel System

235 Emission Control System and Service
251 Fuel System Service

5 Chassis Electrical

292 Accessory Service
299 Instruments Panel Service
301 Lights, Fuses and Flashers

284 Chilton's Fuel Economy and Tune-Up Tips

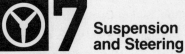

6 Drive Train

306 Manual Transmission
332 Clutch
345 Automatic Transmission
372 Driveshaft and U-Joints
375 Rear Axle

7 Suspension and Steering

398 Suspension
410 Steering

8 Brakes

454 Specifications
471 Disc Brakes
481 Drum Brakes
486 Parking Brake

9 Body and Trim

491 Exterior
507 Interior

520 Mechanic's Data
522 Glossary
528 Abbreviations
530 Index

508 Chilton's Body Repair Tips

Quick Reference Specifications For Your Vehicle

Fill in this chart with the most commonly used specifications for your vehicle. Specifications can be found in Chapters 1 through 3 or on the tune-up decal under the hood of the vehicle.

Tune-Up

Firing Order_____

Spark Plugs:

    Type_____

    Gap (in.)_____

Torque (ft. lbs.)_____

Idle Speed (rpm)_____

Ignition Timing (°)_____

    Vacuum or Electronic Advance (Connected/Disconnected)_____

Valve Clearance (in.)

    Intake_____   Exhaust_____

Capacities

Engine Oil Type (API Rating)_____

    With Filter Change (qts)_____

    Without Filter Change (qts)_____

Cooling System (qts)_____

Manual Transmission (pts)_____

    Type_____

Automatic Transmission (pts)_____

    Type_____

Front Differential (pts)_____

    Type_____

Rear Differential (pts)_____

    Type_____

Transfer Case (pts)_____

    Type_____

FREQUENTLY REPLACED PARTS

Use these spaces to record the part numbers of frequently replaced parts.

PCV VALVE	OIL FILTER	AIR FILTER	FUEL FILTER
Type_____	Type_____	Type_____	Type_____
Part No._____	Part No._____	Part No._____	Part No._____

General Information
and Maintenance

HOW TO USE THIS BOOK

This book covers all model 63, 73, 75, and Maverick utility vehicles, CJ-2A, CJ-3A, CJ-3B, CJ-5, CJ-6, CJ-7, Scrambler and Wrangler models from 1945 through 1987.

The first two chapters will be the most used, since they contain maintenance and tune-up information and procedures. Studies have shown that a properly tuned and maintained Jeep can get at least 10% better gas mileage (which translates into lower operating costs) and periodic maintenance will catch minor problems before they turn into major repair bills. The other chapters deal with the more complex systems of your Jeep. Operating systems from engine through brakes are covered to the extent that the average do-it-yourselfer becomes mechanically involved. This book will not explain such things as rebuilding the differential for the simple reason that the expertise required and the investment in special tools make this task impractical and uneconomical. It will give you the detailed instructions to help you change your own brake pads and shoes, tune-up the engine, replace spark plugs and filters, and do many more jobs that will save you money, give you personal satisfaction and help you avoid expensive problems.

A secondary purpose of this book is a reference guide for owners who want to understand their Jeep and/or their mechanics better. In this case, no tools at all are required. Knowing just what a particular repair job requires in parts and labor time will allow you to evaluate whether or not you're getting a fair price quote and help decipher itemized bills from a repair shop.

Before attempting any repairs or service on your Jeep, read through the entire procedure outlined in the appropriate chapter. This will give you the overall view of what tools and supplies will be required. There is nothing more frustrating than having to walk to the bus stop on Monday morning because you were short one gasket on Sunday afternoon. So read ahead and plan ahead. Each operation should be approached logically and all procedures thoroughly understood before attempting any work. Some special tools that may be required can often be rented from local automotive jobbers or places specializing in renting tools and equipment. Check the yellow pages of your phone book.

All chapters contain adjustments, maintenance, removal and installation procedures, and overhaul procedures. When overhaul is not considered practical, we tell you how to remove the failed part and then how to install the new or rebuilt replacement. In this way, you at least save the labor costs. Backyard overhaul of some components (such as the alternator or water pump) is just not practical, but the removal and installation procedure is often simple and well within the capabilities of the average Jeep owner.

Two basic mechanic's rules should be mentioned here. First, whenever the LEFT side of the Jeep or engine is referred to, it is meant to specify the DRIVER'S side of the Jeep. Conversely, the RIGHT side of the Jeep means the PASSENGER'S side. Second, all screws and bolts are removed by turning counterclockwise, and tightened by turning clockwise. Safety is always the most important rule. Constantly be aware of the dangers involved in working on or around an automobile and take proper precautions to avoid the risk of personal injury or damage to the vehicle. See the section in this chapter, Servicing Your Vehicle Safely, and the SAFETY NOTICE on the acknowledgment page before attempting any service procedures and pay attention to the instructions provided. There are 3 common mistakes in mechanical work:

1. Incorrect order of assembly, disassembly

or adjustment. When taking something apart or putting it together, doing things in the wrong order usually just costs you extra time; however it CAN break something. Read the entire procedure before beginning disassembly. Do everything in the order in which the instructions say you should do it, even if you can't immediately see a reason for it. When you're taking apart something that is very intricate (for example a carburetor), you might want to draw a picture of how it looks when assembled at one point in order to make sure you get everything back in its proper position. We will supply exploded views whenever possible, but sometimes the job requires more attention to detail than an illustration provides. When making adjustments (especially tune-up adjustments), do them in order. One adjustment often affects another and you cannot expect satisfactory results unless each adjustment is made only when it cannot be changed by any other.

2. Overtorquing (or undertorquing) nuts and bolts. While it is more common for overtorquing to cause damage, undertorquing can cause a fastener to vibrate loose and cause serious damage, especially when dealing with aluminum parts. Pay attention to torque specifications and utilize a torque wrench in assembly. If a torque figure is not available remember that, if you are using the right tool to do the job, you will probably not have to strain yourself to get a fastener tight enough. The pitch of most threads is so slight that the tension you put on the wrench will be multiplied many times in actual force on what you are tightening. A good example of how critical torque is can be seen in the case of spark plug installation, especially where you are putting the plug into an aluminum cylinder head. Too little torque can fail to crush the gasket, causing leakage of combustion gases and consequent overheating of the plug and engine parts. Too much torque can damage the threads or distort the plug, which changes the spark gap at the electrode. Since more and more manufacturers are using aluminum in their engine and chassis parts to save weight, a torque wrench should be in any serious do-it-yourselfer's tool box.

There are many commercial chemical products available for ensuring that fasteners won't come loose, even if they are not torqued just right (a very common brand is Loctite®). If you're worried about getting something together tight enough to hold, but loose enough to avoid mechanical damage during assembly, one of these products might offer substantial insurance. Read the label on the package and make sure the product is compatible with the materials, fluids, etc. involved before choosing one.

3. Crossthreading. This occurs when a part such as a bolt is screwed into a nut or casting at the wrong angle and forced, causing the threads to become damaged. Crossthreading is more likely to occur if access is difficult. It helps to clean and lubricate fasteners, and to start threading with the part to be installed going straight in, using your fingers. If you encounter resistance, unscrew the part and start over again at a different angle until it can be inserted and turned several times without much effort. Keep in mind that many parts, especially spark plugs, use tapered threads so that gentle turning will automatically bring the part you're threading to the proper angle if you don't force it or resist a change in angle. Don't put a wrench on the part until it's been turned in a couple of times by hand. If you suddenly encounter resistance and the part has not seated fully, don't force it. Pull it back out and make sure it's clean and threading properly.

Always take your time and be patient; once you have some experience, working on your Jeep will become an enjoyable hobby.

TOOLS AND EQUIPMENT

Naturally, without the proper tools and equipment it is impossible to properly service your vehicle. It would be impossible to catalog each tool that you would need to perform each or every operation in this book. It would also be unwise for the amateur to rush out and buy an expensive set of tools an the theory that he may need one or more of them at sometime.

The best approach is to proceed slowly, gathering together a good quality set of those tools that are used most frequently. Don't be misled by the low cost of bargain tools. It is far better to spend a little more for better quality. Forged wrenches, 10 or 12 point sockets and fine tooth ratchets are by far preferable to their less expensive counterparts. As any good mechanic can tell you, there are few worse experiences than trying to work on a Jeep with bad tools. Your monetary savings will be far outweighed by frustration and mangled knuckles.

Certain tools, plus a basic ability to handle tools, are required to get started. A basic mechanics tool set, a torque wrench, and, for 1976 and later models, a Torx bits set. Torx bits are hexlobular drivers which fit both inside and outside on special Torx head fasteners used in various places on Jeep vehicles.

A special wheel bearing nut socket would be

helpful when removing the front wheel bearings on 4x4 models.

Begin accumulating those tools that are used most frequently; those associated with routine maintenance and tune-up.

In addition to the normal assortment of screwdrivers and pliers you should have the following tools for routine maintenance jobs (your Jeep, depending on the model year, uses both SAE and metric fasteners):

1. SAE/Metric wrenches, sockets and combination open end/box end wrenches in sizes from 1/8" (3mm) to 3/4" (19mm), and a spark plug socket ($^{13}/_{16}$" or 5/8"). If possible, buy various length socket drive extensions. One break in this department is that the metric sockets available in the U.S. will all fit the ratchet handles and extensions you may already have (1/4, 3/8, and 1/2" drive).
2. Jackstands for support
3. Oil filter wrench
4. Oil filter spout for pouring oil
5. Grease gun for chassis lubrication
6. Hydrometer for checking the battery
7. A container for draining oil
8. Many rags for wiping up the inevitable mess.

In addition to the above items there are several others that are not absolutely necessary, but handy to have around. These include oil-dry, a transmission funnel and the usual supply of lubricants, antifreeze and fluids, although these can be purchased as needed. This is a basic list for routine maintenance, but only your personal needs and desires can accurately determine your list of necessary tools.

The second list of tools is for tune-ups. While the tools involved here are slightly more sophisticated, they need not be outrageously expensive. There are several inexpensive tach/dwell meters on the market that are every bit as good for the average mechanic as a $100.00 professional model. Just be sure that it goes to at least 1,200–1,500 rpm on the tach scale and that it works on 4, 6 and 8 cylinder engines. A basic list of tune-up equipment could include:

1. Tach-dwell meter
2. Spark plug wrench
3. Timing light (a DC light that works from the Jeep's battery is best, although an AC light that plugs into 110V house current will suffice at some sacrifice in brightness)
4. Wire spark plug gauge/adjusting tools
5. Set of feeler blades.

Here again, be guided by your own needs. A feeler blade will set the point gap as easily as dwell meter will read dwell, but slightly less accurately. And since you will need a tachometer anyway ... well, make your own decision.

In addition to these basic tools, there are several other tools and gauges you may find useful. These include:

1. A compression gauge. The screw-in type is slower to use, but eliminates the possibility of a faulty reading due to escaping pressure
2. A manifold vacuum gauge
3. A test light
4. An induction meter. This is used for determining whether or not there is current in a wire. These are handy for use if a wire is broken somewhere in a wiring harness.

As a final note, you will probably find a torque wrench necessary for all but the most basic work. The beam type models are perfectly adequate, although the newer click (breakaway) type are more precise, and you don't have to crane your neck to see a torque reading in awkward situations. The breakaway torque wrenches are more expensive and should be recalibrated periodically.

Torque specification for each fastener will be given in the procedure in any case that a specific torque value is required. If no torque specifications are given, use the following values as a guide, based upon fastener size:

Bolts marked 6T
  6mm bolt/nut – 5–7 ft.lb.
  8mm bolt/nut – 12–17 ft.lb.
  10mm bolt/nut – 23–34 ft.lb.
  12mm bolt/nut – 41–59 ft.lb.
  14mm bolt/nut – 56–76 ft.lb.
Bolts marked 8T
  6mm bolt/nut – 6–9 ft.lb.
  8mm bolt/nut – 13–20 ft.lb.
  10mm bolt/nut – 27–40 ft.lb.
  12mm bolt/nut – 46–69 ft.lb.
  14mm bolt/nut – 75–101 ft.lb.

Special Tools

Normally, the use of special factory tools is avoided for repair procedures, since these are not readily available for the do-it-yourself mechanic. When it is possible to perform the job with more commonly available tools, it will be pointed out, but occasionally, a special tool was designed to perform a specific function and should be used. Before substituting another tool, you should be convinced that neither your safety nor the performance of the vehicle will be compromised.

Some special tools are available through your Jeep dealer or major tool manufacturers, such as:

Service Tool Division
Kent-Moore
29784 Little Mack
Roseville, MI 48066-2298

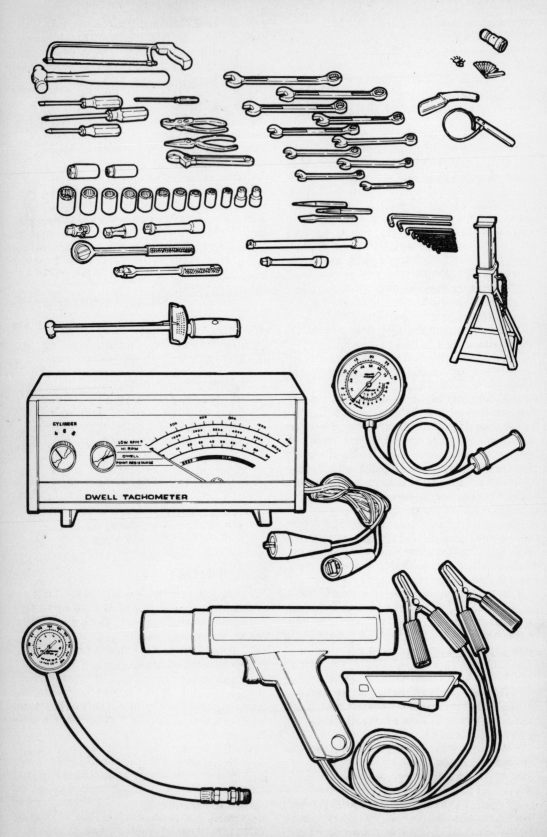

This basic collection of hand tools will handle most of your automotive needs

Miller Special Tools
Utica Tool Co.
32615 Park La.
Garden City, MI 48135

Owatonna Tool Co
Owatonna, MN 55060

Robert Bosch Corp.
2800 S.25th St.
Broadview, IL 60153

Equivalent tools may be purchased at most independent tool dealers or auto parts stores.

SERVICING YOUR VEHICLE SAFELY

It is virtually impossible to anticipate all of the hazards involved with automotive maintenance and service, but care and common sense will prevent most accidents.

The rules of safety for mechanics range from "don't smoke around gasoline," to "use the proper tool for the job." The trick to avoiding injuries is to develop safe work habits and take every possible precaution.

Dos

• Do keep a fire extinguisher and first aid kit within easy reach.

• Do wear safety glasses or goggles when cutting, drilling or prying, even if you have 20–20 vision. If you wear glasses for the sake of vision, they should be made of hardened glass that can also serve as safety glasses, or wear safety goggles over your regular glasses.

• Do shield your eyes whenever you work around the battery. Batteries contain sulphuric acid. In case of contact with the eyes or skin, flush the area with water or a mixture of water and baking soda and get medical attention immediately.

• Do use safety stands for any under-Jeep service. Jacks are for raising vehicles; safety stands are for making sure the vehicle stays raised until you want it to come down. Whenever the vehicle is raised, block the wheels remaining on the ground and set the parking brake.

• Do use adequate ventilation when working with any chemicals. Like carbon monoxide, the asbestos dust resulting from brake lining wear can be poisonous in sufficient quantities.

• Do disconnect the negative battery cable when working on the electrical system. The primary ignition system can contain up to 40,000 volts.

• Do follow manufacturer's directions whenever working with potentially hazardous materials. Both brake fluid and antifreeze are poisonous if taken internally.

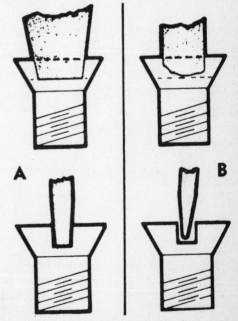

TWO-WIRE CONDUCTOR THIRD WIRE GROUNDING THE CASE

THREE-WIRE CONDUCTOR GROUNDING THRU A CIRCUIT

THREE-WIRE CONDUCTOR ONE WIRE TO A GROUND

THREE-WIRE CONDUCTOR GROUNDING THRU AN ADAPTER PLUG

When using electric tools make sure they are properly grounded

Keep screwdriver tips in good shape. They should fit the slot as shown in "A". If they look like those in "B", they need grinding or replacing

• Do properly maintain your tools. Loose hammerheads, mushroomed punches and chisels, frayed or poorly grounded electrical cords, excessively worn screwdrivers, spread wrenches (open end), cracked sockets, slipping ratchets, or faulty droplight sockets can cause accidents.

If you're using an open end wrench, use the correct size, and position it properly on the nut or bolt

• Do use the proper size and type of tool for the job being done.

• Do when possible, pull on a wrench handle rather than push on it, and adjust your stance to prevent a fall.

• Do be sure that adjustable wrenches are tightly adjusted on the nut or bolt and pulled so that the face is on the side of the fixed jaw.

• Do select a wrench or socket that fits the nut or bolt. The wrench or socket should sit straight, not cocked.

• Do strike squarely with a hammer — avoid glancing blows.

• Do set the parking brake and block the drive wheels if the work requires that the engine be running.

Don'ts

• Don't run an engine in a garage or anywhere else without proper ventilation — EVER! Carbon monoxide is poisonous. It takes a long time to leave the human body and you can build up a deadly supply of it in your system by simply breathing in a little every day. You may not realize you are slowly poisoning yourself. Always use power vents, windows, fans or open the garage doors.

• Don't work around moving parts while wearing a necktie or other loose clothing. Short sleeves are much safer than long, loose sleeves and hard-toed shoes with neoprene soles protect your toes and give a better grip on slippery surfaces. Jewelry such as watches, fancy belt buckles, beads or body adornment of any kind is not safe working around a Jeep. Long hair should be hidden under a hat or cap.

• Don't use pockets for toolboxes. A fall or bump can drive a screwdriver deep into you body. Even a wiping cloth hanging from the back pocket can wrap around a spinning shaft or fan.

• Don't smoke when working around gasoline, cleaning solvent or other flammable material.

• Don't smoke when working around the battery. When the battery is being charged, it gives off explosive hydrogen gas.

• Don't use gasoline to wash your hands! There are excellent soaps available. Gasoline may contain lead, and lead can enter the body through a cut, accumulating in the body until you are very ill. Gasoline also removes all the natural oils from the skin so that bone dry hands will suck up oil and grease.

• Don't service the air conditioning system unless you are equipped with the necessary tools and training. The refrigerant, R-12, is extremely cold and when exposed to the air, will instantly freeze any surface it comes in contact with, including your eyes. Although the refrigerant is normally non-toxic, R-12 becomes a deadly poisonous gas in the presence of an open flame. One good whiff of the vapors from burning refrigerant can be fatal.

HISTORY AND MODEL IDENTIFICATION

The first "Jeep", as we know it today, was the Model MB Military. It was produced from 1941 through 1945. The distinguishing characteristics were an L-head, 4-cylinder engine, no tailgate, a 6 volt(6v) electrical system, split windshield, rear mounted spare tire, and a timing chain.

The next model was the CJ-2A. It was made from 1945 to 1949 and was the first Jeep made available directly to the public. This is the civilian version of the MB Military. The letters CJ stand for Civilian Jeep. The distinguishing characteristics of this model are the L-head, 4-cylinder engine, split windshield, and 6 V electrical system. The civilian version differs from the Model MB Military in that the spare tire is mounted on the side of the vehicle and there is a tailgate.

The CJ-3A was brought out in 1948. The only outward difference between this model and the CJ-2A is that the CJ-3A has a one piece windshield. This model was produced until 1953.

In 1947, Kaiser introduced the Model 2WD and 4WD Truck. This small pick-up was essentially similar to contemporary CJ models, with a 4L–134 engine and 2-piece windshield. it was produced through 1950. At the same time, the Model 4-63 was released. This was a 2-wd station wagon version of the pick-up and was produced through 1950. A distinguishing characteristic was the use of a Planar independent front suspension, using a single transverse leaf spring and upper control arms. In 1949, a 4-wd

1941–45 MB military

1945–49 CJ-2A

1948–53 CJ-3A

1950–51 MC-M38 military

1951–68 MD-M38A1 military

1953–64 CJ-3B

1955–69 CJ-5

1970–81 CJ-5

CJ-6

1976–86 CJ-7

1981–86 Scrambler

1987 Wrangler

version of the 4-63 was introduced, known as the 4x4-63. Conventional front suspension was used. It too was produced through 1950. In 1950, a 6-cylinder version was introduced, known as the 6-73, equipped with the 6–226 engine. It was produced only in 1950.

In 1950 the Models 4-73 and 4x4-73 were introduced in both pick-up and station wagon configurations. They used the 4F-134 and 6–226 engines The were produced through 1951.

The military services received a new model Jeep in 1950: the Model MC-M38 Military. This Jeep had a 24v electrical system, a 4-cylinder L-head engine, no tailgate, brush guards over the headlights, a one piece windshield, and a rear mounted spare tire. This model was produced only until 1951.

In 1951 the Model MF-M38A1 Military replaced the Model MC-M38 Military. The newer model had rounded front fenders and was made until 1968.

A new civilian Jeep, the Model CJ-3B, was introduced in 1953. It can be distinguished by its high flat hood but also had a 4-cylinder, F-head engine, side mounted spare tire, one piece windshield, tailgate, angular fenders (like all of the earlier models), and a 6v or 12v electrical system. The CJ-3B was made until 1964.

In 1956, the model 4-75 4x4 Utility Wagon was introduced. It used the 4F–134, 6–226 and 6–230 engines. It was produced through 1964.

In 1958, a 2-wd version of the 4-75 was introduced, named the Maverick. It had "captive air" tires and a 4F–134 engine. It was produced only in 1958.

The CJ-5, a civilian version of the MD-38A1 was released in 1955. It had a tailgate, a 6v or 12v electrical system, and rounded fenders. Two engines were offered for the first time in the Universal series with this introduction. The traditional 4-cylinder F-head was offered as well as the V6 Buick engine. The V6 was available from 1965 through 1971. The CJ-5's spare is usually mounted on the side. In 1972 the wheelbase of the CJ-5 was lengthened from 81 to 84" to accommodate the larger American Motors engines.

A longer version of the CJ-5 was also introduced in 1955. This was the CJ-6 with a wheelbase of 101" It was identical to the CJ-5 except for the longer wheelbase. The CJ-6 also had its wheelbase elongated (to 104") in 1972 to accommodate the larger American Motors engines.

For the 1976 model year, the CJ-6 was discontinued in the U.S. and Canada, although still exported. A new model, CJ-7, featuring an optional one piece removable plastic hardtop, automatic transmission, steel side doors with roll up windows and the full time 4WD system, Quadra-Trac® was introduced. The CJ-7 has a wheelbase of 93.5".

In mid-year 1981 Jeep introduced its newest model, the Scrambler. Designed for rugged dependability and good fuel economy, the Scrambler is both a work and recreational vehicle.

The standard engine is a GM built 151 cid 4-cylinder with an American Motors 6–258 an an option. A manual 4-speed transmission is standard with automatic as an option. The standard transfer case is the 2-speed Dana 300.

For 1984 the CJ-5 was discontinued. The 4–151 was replaced by an AMC 4–150.

For 1987, the CJ series was discontinued entirely, and replaced by the Wrangler series. The Wrangler utilizes Dana axles, an AISIN or Peugeot 5-speed as standard equipment, the Chrysler 999 automatic and the 4–150 as the standard engine, with the 6–258 as the option.

SERIAL NUMBER IDENTIFICATION

Vehicle

1945–70

The vehicle serial number is located on a metal plate mounted on the firewall under the hood. It is on the left side on CJ-5, and CJ-6 models and on the right on CJ-3B models. Identification of a specific vehicle requires a prefix plus a serial number. The following chart identifies the Jeep model by the serial number prefix.

Any prefix that is not given here indicates that yours is a special vehicle with differences that are not covered in this book.

1971–87

When American Motor Corporation took over the Jeep Corporation, the numbering system

1945–70 Model Identification by Serial Number

All Models have a 5 or 6 digit serial number

Model	Prefix
CJ-2A	no prefix
CJ-3A	no prefix
	451-GB1
	452-GB1
	453-GB1
CJ-3B	453-GB2
	454-GB2
	57348
	8105
CJ-5	57548
	8305
CJ-5A	8322
CJ-6	57648
	8405
CJ-6A	8422

was changed to the American Motors 13 digit (through 1980) or 17 digit (1981 and later) alpha-numerical Vehicle Identification Number (VIN).

This number is stamped on a metal plate on the left side of the firewall.

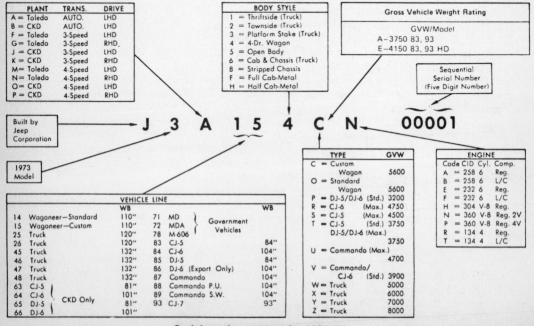

Serial number system for 1971–74

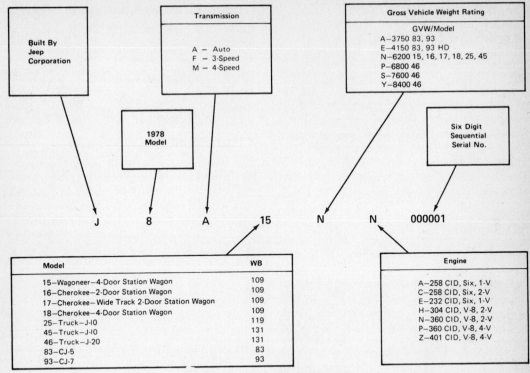

Serial number code system for 1975–80

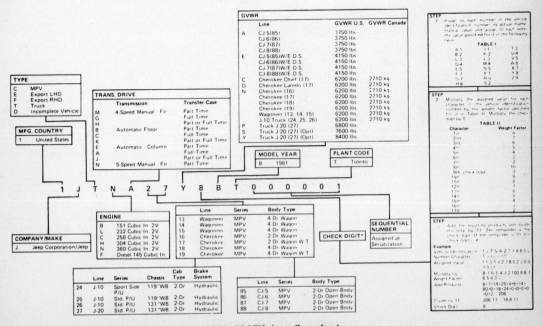

1981–86 VIN decoding chart

A metal identification plate is riveted to the driver side of the dash panel in the engine compartment.

1. Order number
2. Paint gun number
3. Vehicle identification number (VIN)
4. Vehicle deviation or special sales request and order (SSR & O)
5. Trim option number
6. Paint option number

1981–86 vehicle identification plate

CJ-2A, CJ-3A, CJ-3B serial number plate location

CJ-5, CJ-6, CJ-7 and Scrambler serial number plate location

Engine

4–134

The engine serial number for the Willys built F-Head 4 cylinder engine is located on the water pump boss at the front of the engine. It consists of a 5 or 6 digit number. The engine code prefix for the F-Head is 4J.

4-134 engine serial number

It is sometimes necessary to machine oversize or undersize clearances for cylinder blocks and crankshafts. If your engine is equipped with oversized or undersized parts, it is necessary to order parts that will match the old parts. To find out if your engine is one with odd-sized parts, check the engine code letter or the engine code number itself—which in some cases is followed by a letter or a series of letters. The following chart explains just what the letters indicate:

• Letter A (10001-A) indicates 0.010" (0.254mm) undersized main and connecting rod bearings.
• Letter B (10001-B) indicates 0.010" (0.254mm) oversized cylinder bore.
• Letter AB (l0001-AB) indicates the combination of A and B above.
• Letter C (10001-C) indicates 0.002" (0.0508mm) undersized piston pin.
• Letter D (10001-D) indicates 0.010" (0.254mm) undersized main bearing journals.
• Letter E (10001-E) indicates 0.010" (0.254mm) undersized connecting rod bearing journals.

4–150

The engine serial number for the American Motors built 4–150 is located on a machined pad at the rear right side of the block, just below the head.

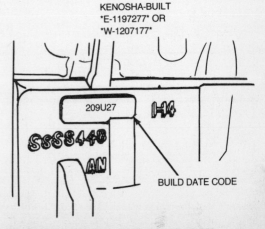

Engine serial number location for the 4-150

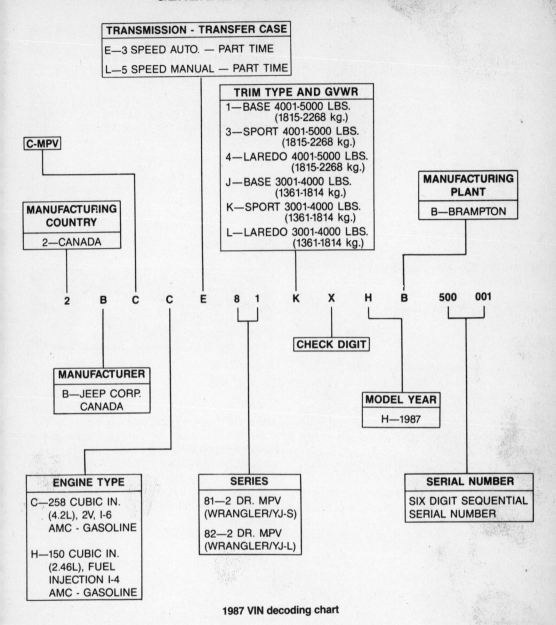

TRANSMISSION - TRANSFER CASE

E—3 SPEED AUTO. — PART TIME

L—5 SPEED MANUAL — PART TIME

TRIM TYPE AND GVWR

1—BASE 4001-5000 LBS.
(1815-2268 kg.)

3—SPORT 4001-5000 LBS.
(1815-2268 kg.)

4—LAREDO 4001-5000 LBS.
(1815-2268 kg.)

J—BASE 3001-4000 LBS.
(1361-1814 kg.)

K—SPORT 3001-4000 LBS.
(1361-1814 kg.)

L—LAREDO 3001-4000 LBS.
(1361-1814 kg.)

C-MPV

MANUFACTURING PLANT

B—BRAMPTON

MANUFACTURING COUNTRY

2—CANADA

2 B C C E 8 1 K X H B 500 001

CHECK DIGIT

MANUFACTURER

B—JEEP CORP.
CANADA

MODEL YEAR

H—1987

ENGINE TYPE

C—258 CUBIC IN.
(4.2L), 2V, I-6
AMC - GASOLINE

H—150 CUBIC IN.
(2.46L), FUEL
INJECTION I-4
AMC - GASOLINE

SERIES

81—2 DR. MPV
(WRANGLER/YJ-S)

82—2 DR. MPV
(WRANGLER/YJ-L)

SERIAL NUMBER

SIX DIGIT SEQUENTIAL
SERIAL NUMBER

1987 VIN decoding chart

Also on the block, just above the oil filter, is the oversized/undersized component code. The codes are explained as follows:

B: cylinder bores 0.010" (0.254mm) over

C: camshaft bearing bores 0.010" (0.254mm)over

M: main bearing journals 0.010" (0.254mm)under

P: connecting rod journals 0.010" (0.254mm) under

4–151

In 1980, a General Motors 151 cid, 4-cylinder engine became standard equipment on all CJ models. A three character code is stamped into

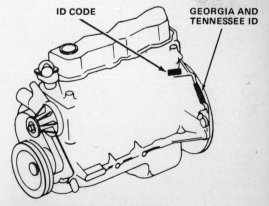

ID CODE

GEORGIA AND TENNESSEE ID

1980–83 4-151 engine ID number

The parts size letter code is on the boss directly above the oil filter on inline sixes

the left rear top corner of the block. Additionally, engines built for sale in Georgia and Tennessee have a non-repeating number stamped into the left rear block flange.

6–225

The engine number for the Buick built V6–225 engine is located on the right side of the engine, on the crankcase, just below the head. The code is KLH. The codes RU and RV, included in the engine number of 1965 and 1966 engines, indicate manual or automatic transmission, respectively.

It is sometimes necessary to machine oversize or undersize clearances for cylinder blocks and crankshafts. If your engine is equipped with oversized or undersized parts, it is necessary to order parts that will match the old parts. To find out if your engine is one with odd-sized parts, check the engine code letter or the engine code number itself—which in some cases is followed by a letter or a series of letters. The following chart explains just what the letters indicate:

Letter A (10001-A) indicates 0.010″ (0.254mm) undersized main and connecting rod bearings.

Letter B (10001-B) indicates 0.010″ (0.254mm) oversized cylinder bore.

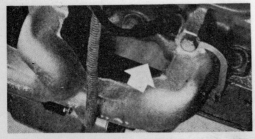

6-225 engine serial number location

Letter AB (l0001-AB) indicates the combination of A and B above.

Letter C (10001-C) indicates 0.002″ (0.0508mm) undersized piston pin.

Letter D (10001-D) indicates 0.010″ (0.254mm) undersized main bearing journals.

Letter E (10001-E) indicates 0.010″ (0.254mm) undersized connecting rod bearing journals.

6–226

The 6–226 engine serial number is stamped on a machined surface near the left front corner of the block, above the generator. The serial number will have a prefix, FW, followed by a 5 digit number.

Engine serial number location on the 6-226

6–230

The 6–230 engine serial number is stamped on a machined surface on the right front of the block, just behind the ignition coil. The serial number prefixes are:

NS60C: 2-wheel drive, manual trans., 1-bbl carburetor

TS60C: 4-wheel drive, manual trans., 1-bbl carburetor

ND60C: 2-wheel drive, manual trans., 2-bbl carburetor

TD60C: 4-wheel drive, manual trans., 2-bbl carburetor

AD60C: Automatic Transmission

A suffix A, indicates 0.010″ (0.254mm) oversized main and rod bearings; B indicates 0.010″ (0.254mm) oversized pistons; AB is a combination of both.

6–232 and 6–258

The American Motors engine code is, of course, found in the identification plate on the firewall. The second location is on a machined surface of the block between number 2 and 3

6-232, 258 engine serial number location

spark plugs. For further identification, the displacement is cast into the side of the block. The letter in the code identifies the engine by displacement (cu. in.), carburetor type and compression ratio.

On vehicles equipped with the 6–232 made prior to 1971, the engine code number is located on a machined surface, adjacent to the distributor. The letter contained in the code number denotes the cu. in. displacement of the engine. The letter, L, denotes 232 cu in. 8.5:1 compression ratio. The engine code letter is located on a boss directly above the oil filter.

On 6–232 engines built before 1971, the size code is stamped on a tag located on the left front side of the baffle above the intake manifold below the build date, and on the boss above the oil filter. The following chart explains just what the letters indicate on the 232 sixes made prior to 1971:

First Digit – Size of the bore: A, B, or C

Second Digit – Size of the main bearings: A, B, or C

Third Digit – Size of the connecting rod bearings: A, B, or C

A - Standard; B - 0.010″ (0.254mm) undersized; C - 0.010″ (0.254mm) oversized

All of the engines made after 1971 have the same undersize/oversize letter codes, located on the boss directly above the oil filter. The parts size code is as follows:

Letter B indicates 0.010″ (0.254mm) oversized cylinder bore.

Letter M indicates 0.010″ (0.254mm) undersized main bearings.

Letter P indicates 0.010″ (0.254mm) undersized connecting rod bearings.

Letter C indicates 0.010″ (0.254mm) oversized camshaft block bores.

8–304

On the American Motors built 8–304 engines, the number is located on a tag attached to the right valve cover. For further identification, the displacement is cast into the side of the block. The letter in the code identifies the en-

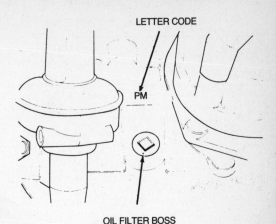

LETTER CODE

PM

OIL FILTER BOSS

4-150 oversized/undersized component code location

gine by displacement (cu. in.), carburetor type and compression ratio.

All of the engines made after 1971 have the same undersize/oversize letter codes, located on a tag next to the engine number. The parts size code is as follows:

Letter B indicates 0.010″ (0.254mm) oversized cylinder bore.

Letter M indicates 0.010″ (0.254mm) undersized main bearings.

Letter P indicates 0.010″ (0.254mm) undersized connecting rod bearings.

Letters PM indicate a combination of the above specifications for P and M.

Letter C indicates 0.010″ (0.254mm) oversized camshaft block bores.

Transmission

There is a tag attached to the transmission case that identifies the manufacturer and model of the transmission. It is necessary to have the information on this tag before ordering parts. When reassembling the transmission, be sure that this tag is replaced on the transmission case so identification can be made in the future.

In some cases, the transmission identification number may be embossed on the transmission housing.

8-304 engine serial number location

ROUTINE MAINTENANCE

See the Maintenance Intervals Chart in this chapter for the recommended maintenance intervals for the components covered here.

Engine Application Chart

Engine	Actual Displacement			Type	Mfg. by	Years	Models
	Cu. In.	CC	Liters				
4-134	134.21	2,199.3	2.2	L-Head	Kaiser	1945–53	CJ-2A, CJ3A
4-134	134.21	2,199.3	2.2	F-Head	Kaiser	1953–69	CJ-3B, CJ-5, CJ-6
4-150	150.45	2,465.4	2.5	OHV	AMC	1984–87	CJ-5, CJ-7, Scrambler, Wrangler
4-151	150.78	2,470.8	2.5	OHV	Chevrolet	1980–83	CJ-5, CJ-7 Scrambler
6-225	225.29	3,691.8	3.7	OHV	Buick	1966–71	CJ-5, CJ-6
6-226	226.15	3,705.9	3.7	L-Head	Kaiser	1950–60	Utility
6-230	230.41	3,775.6	3.8	OHC	Continental	1960–64	Utility
6-232	231.91	3,800.3	3.8	OHV	AMC	1972–78	CJ-5, CJ-6
6-258	258.08	4,229.2	4.2	OHV	AMC	1972–87	CJ-5, CJ-6, CJ-7, Scrambler, Wrangler
8-304	303.92	4,980.3	5.0	OHV	AMC	1976–81	CJ-5, CJ-6

Manual Transmission Application Chart

Transmission Types	Years	Models
AISIN AX5 5-sp**	1987	Standard on some models
Peugeot BA 10/5 5-sp**	1987	Standard on some models
Tremec T-150 3-sp	1976–79	Standard on all models
Tremec T-176 4-sp	1980	All CJ-5 and CJ-7 w/8-304
	1981	Some CJ-5, CJ-7 w/6-258
		All models w/8-304
	1982–83	All models w/6-258
	1984–86	Standard on some models with 6-258
Warner SR-4 4-sp	1980	CJ-7 w/6-258
	1981	All CJ-5, CJ-7 w/4-151
		Some CJ-5 and CJ-7 w/6-258
Warner T-4 4-sp	1982–83	Standard on all models w/4-151
	1984–86	Standard on all models w/4-150
		Standard on some models w/6-258
Warner T-5 5-sp	1982–83	Optional on CJ-5 w/4-151
		Optional on CJ-7 and Scrambler w/6-258
	1984–86	Optional on all models
Warner T-14A 3-sp	1972–75	Standard on all models
Warner T-18 4-sp	1971–75	Optional on all models
Warner T-18A 4-sp	1976–79	Optional on all models
Warner T-86 4-sp OD	1947–58	Optional on 2-wd Utility models w/6-226 engine
Warner T-86AA 3-sp	1955–71	Standard on all V6 models
Warner T-90 3-sp	1947–58	Standard on 4-wd models w/4-134 engine
Warner T-90C* 3-sp	1945–71	Standard on all models
Warner T-90J 3-sp	1947–58	Standard on 4-wd Utility models w/6-226 engine
Warner T-96 4-sp OD	1947–58	Optional on 2-wd Utility models w/4-134 engine
Warner T-98A 4-sp	1955–71	Optional on all models

*On CJ-2A models up to serial #38221, the transmission has external linkage.
**Which transmission is in your vehicle is determined by availability at the time of production.
OD: Equipped with a Warner R-10B overdrive

Transfer Case Application Chart

Transfer Case Type	Years	Models
Dana 300	1980–86	All models
New Process NP-207	1987	All models
Spicer 18	1945–71	All models
Spicer 20	1972–79	All models
Warner Quadra-Trac®	1976–79	Standard on CJ-7 w/automatic trans.

Automatic Transmission Application Chart

Transmission Type	Years	Models
Turbo Hydra-Matic 400	1976–79	CJ-7
Chrysler 904	1981	CJ-7 w/4-151
Chrysler 999	1980–81	CJ-7 w/6-258 and 8-304
	1982–86	CJ-7 and Scrambler w/6-258
	1987	Wrangler w/6-258

Front Drive Axle Application Chart

Axle Type	Years	Models
Spicer 25	1945–53	CJ-2A, CJ-3A
	1947–64	Utility Models
Dana 27	1954–71	CJ-3B, CJ-5, CJ-6
Dana 27A	1954–71	CJ-3B, CJ-5, CJ-6
Dana 30	1971–87	All models

Air Cleaner

OIL BATH TYPE

To service the oil bath type air cleaner on the L4–134, F4–134, 6–226 or 6–230, first unscrew the oil cup clamp and remove the oil cup from the cleaner body. Remove the oil from the cup and scrape out all the dirt inside, on the bottom. Wash the cup with a safe solvent. Refill the oil cup and replace it on the air cleaner body. Use the same viscosity of oil as you use in the engine crankcase.

To service the air cleaner body (less the oil cup), loosen the hose clamp and remove the hose form the cleaner. Detach the breather hose from the fitting on the cleaner. Remove the two wing nuts and lift the cleaner from the vehicle. Agitate the cleaner body thoroughly in a cleaning solution to clean the filtering element and then dry the element with compressed air. Reinstall the air cleaner body and replace the oil cup. The air cleaner should be serviced every 2,000 miles.

To service the oil bath type air cleaner on V6 engines, first remove the air cleaner from the engine by unscrewing the wing nut on top of the air cleaner. Remove the oil cup from the body of the air cleaner and remove all of the oil from the oil cup. Remove all of the dirt from the inside of the coil cup with a safe solvent. Wash the filter element in solvent, air dry it, and then fill the oil cup to the indicated level with clean oil. Assemble the air cleaner element to the oil cup, making sure that the gasket is in place between the two pieces. Mount the air cleaner assembly in the carburetor, making sure that the gasket between the air cleaner and the carburetor is in place and making a good seal. Secure the air cleaner to the carburetor with the wing nut.

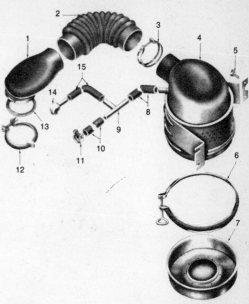

1. Horn
2. Flexible connector
3. Hose clamp
4. Body
5. Wing nut
6. Clamp
7. Oil cup
8. Hose
9. Hose tee
10. Hose
11. Hose clamp
12. Clamp
13. Gasket
14. Elbow
15. Hose

Exploded view of an oil bath air cleaner for the 4-134

Rear Axle Application Chart

Axle Type	Years	Models
AMC 7^9/$_{16}$" ring gear	1984–86	All models
AMC 8⅞" ring gear	1973–83	All models
Dana/Spicer 23-2	1945–49	CJ-2A before serial #13453
Dana/Spicer 27	1955–64	DJ-3A
Dana 35C	1987	All models
Dana/Spicer 41-2	1945–49	CJ-2A after serial #13453
Dana/Spicer 44	1947–64	Utility Models w/3700 lb GVW
	1948–72	CJ-3A, CJ-3B, CJ-5, CJ-6
Dana/Spicer 53	1947–64	Utility Models w/4500 lb GVW

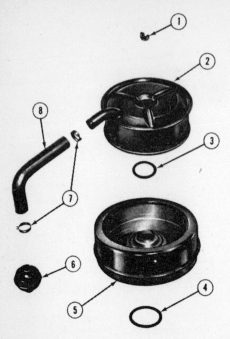

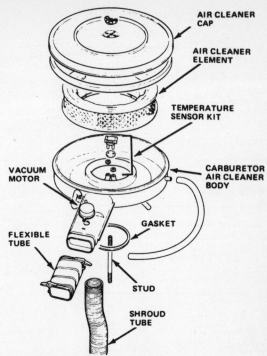

1. Wing nut
2. Cover
3. Rubber gasket
4. Cork gasket
5. Oil cup
6. Breather
7. Clamps
8. Vent tube

Exploded view of an oil bath air cleaner for the 6-225

8 cylinder air cleaner assembly

PAPER ELEMENT TYPE

Remove the wing nut or hex nuts on top of the cover. On 4–151 and V8s, remove the cover and lift out the element. On sixes, detach the

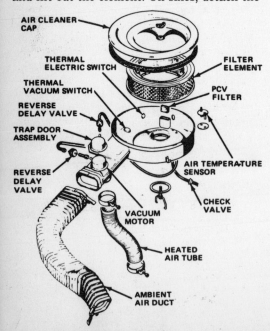

6-232, 258 air cleaner assembly

Polyurethane and paper element air cleaner

rubber hose from the engine rocker arm (valve) cover and set the cover aside, being careful not to damage the large diameter hose or hoses to the air cleaner inlet.

If the filter element has a foam wrapper, remove the wrapper and wash it in detergent or a safe solvent. Squeeze and blot dry. Wet the wrapper in engine oil and squeeze it tightly in an absorbent towel or rag to remove the excess.

Clean the dirt from the paper element by rapping it gently against a flat surface. Replace the element as necessary.

Clean the housing and the cover. Replace the oiled wrapper, if any, on the element and reinstall the element in the housing, placing it 180 degrees from its original position.

NOTE: *The oiled foam wrapper element is a factory option for some years. It should be available through Jeep parts. There are also aftermarket variations on this, both dry and oiled.*

Fuel Filter

REPLACEMENT

Early 4–134 and all 6–226

Most of these engines have a fuel pump with a bowl containing a replaceable filter element. Some have only a mesh strainer in the fuel pump.

Late 4–134, 1984–86 4–150, 6–225, 6–230, 6–232, 6–258, 8–304

All these engines have a throwaway cartridge filter in the line between the fuel pump and the carburetor. To replace it:

1. Remove the air cleaner as necessary.
2. Put an absorbent rag under the filter to catch spillage.
3. Remove the hose clamps.
4. Remove the filter and short attaching hoses.
5. Remove the hoses if they are to be reused.
6. Assemble the new filter and hoses.

NOTE: *The original equipment wire hose clamps should be replaced with screw type band clamps for the best results.*

7. 1975 V8 and all 1976 and later filters have two outlets. The extra one is to return fuel vapors and bubbles to the tank so as to prevent vapor lock. The tank line outlet must be up.
8. Install the filter, tighten the clamps, start the engine, and check for leaks. Discard the rag and old filter safely.

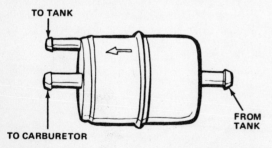

TO TANK

FROM TANK

TO CARBURETOR

Fuel filter used on late model American Motors built engines

1987 4–150

The filter is located behind a protective shield on the left frame rail, just in front of the shock absorber.

CAUTION: *Wear protective goggles to prevent fuel from spraying into your eyes. Have the new filter handy to install immediately.*

1. Raise and support the rear end on jackstands.

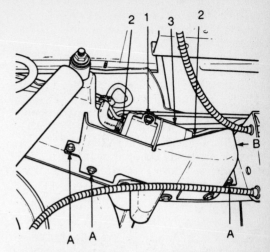

1. Filter retaining bolt
2. Hose clamps
3. Filter

a. Filter shield bolts
b. Filter shield

1987 4-150 fuel filter

2. Remove the protective shield bolts (A) and remove the shield.
3. Remove the filter retaining strap bolt, (1).
4. Clamp shut the hose on the inlet side of the filter to prevent fuel from draining once the filter is removed.
5. Remove the hose clamps, (2).
6. Remove the filter.
7. Installation is the reverse of removal.

4–151

The filter is located behind the large inlet nut in the carburetor. It is a small, paper, throwaway type.

CAUTION: *DO NOT perform a filter change on a hot engine!*

1. Place an absorbent rag under the carburetor inlet nut.

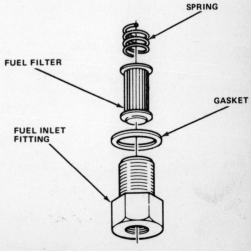

SPRING

FUEL FILTER

GASKET

FUEL INLET FITTING

4-151 fuel filter

2. Hold the inlet nut with one wrench, while loosening the fuel line fitting with another. Remove the fuel line.

3. Unscrew the inlet nut and remove the nut, washer, spring and filter.

4. Installation is the reverse of removal. It's always best to use a new washer. Coat the threads of the inlet nut with a non-hardening, fuel-proof gasket cement. DO NOT OVERTIGHTEN THE INLET NUT! The threads are easily stripped in the carburetor. Hold the inlet nut with a wrench while tightening the fuel line fitting.

PCV Valve

The PCV valve, which is the heart of the positive crankcase ventilation system, should be free of dirt and residue and in working order. As long as the valve is kept clean and is not showing signs of becoming damaged or

6-232, 258 PCV air filter

gummed up, it should work properly. When the valve cannot be cleaned sufficiently or becomes sticky and will not operate freely, it should be replaced.

The PCV filter, which is located at the air filter housing on some 6-cylinder models, should be checked along with the PCV valve. Just blow out the screen with compressed air in the reverse direction of the normal air flow. Check to see that the screen forms a good seal around the edges of the air cleaner housing so no dirt can pass. If the screen is torn or clogged, or if it is seated improperly and cannot be repaired, replace it.

On 4–151 and V8 engines, the air being drawn into the PCV system passes through a polyurethane foam filter located in the oil filler cap. The filler cap is vented only by a hose connected to the air cleaner. The foam filter in the oil filler cap should be cleaned with safe solvent.

The PCV valve is in the right rocker arm (valve) cover on the V6, in the intake manifold

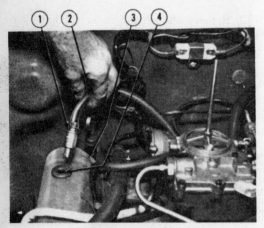

1. Ventilation valve
2. Hose to Carburetor Inlet
3. Right rocker cover
4. Grommet

Removing the PCV valve on 6-225 engines

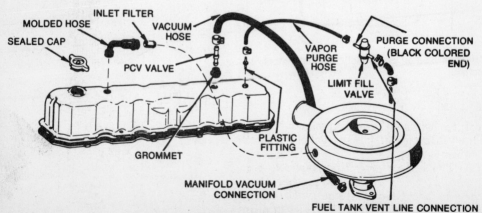

PCV valve location on the 6-232, 258

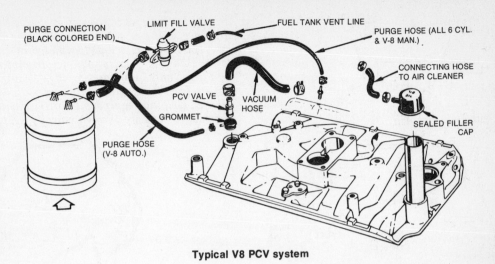

PURGE CONNECTION
(BLACK COLORED END)

LIMIT FILL VALVE

FUEL TANK VENT LINE

PURGE HOSE (ALL 6 CYL.
& V-8 MAN.)

CONNECTING HOSE
TO AIR CLEANER

PCV VALVE

VACUUM
HOSE

GROMMET

SEALED FILLER
CAP

PURGE HOSE
(V-8 AUTO.)

Typical V8 PCV system

on the four, in the intake manifold behind the carburetor on the V8, and in the rocker arm cover on the inline sixes.

Heat Riser

The heat riser is a thermostatically operated valve in the exhaust manifold. It closes when the engine is cold, to direct hot exhaust gases to the intake manifold, in order to preheat the incoming fuel/air mixture. If it sticks closed, the result will be a rough idle after the engine warms up. If it sticks open, there will be frequent stalling during warmup, especially in cold and damp weather.

On the V6 and V8, the valve is between the exhaust manifold and the exhaust pipe. On the inline sixes, it is an integral part of the exhaust manifold. The heat riser counterweight

should move freely. If it sticks, apply Jeep Heat Valve Lubricant or something similar (engine cool) to the ends of the shaft. Sometimes rapping the end of the shaft sharply with a hammer (engine hot) will break it loose. If this fails, parts must be removed for repair or replacement.

Evaporative Canister

All Wagoneers and Commandos equipped with American Motors V8s, and 1973 and later 4- and 6-cylinder engines, have fuel evaporative emission control systems which include an evaporative storage canister. The purpose of this charcoal canister is to store gasoline vapors until they can be drawn into the engine and burned along with the air/fuel mixture.

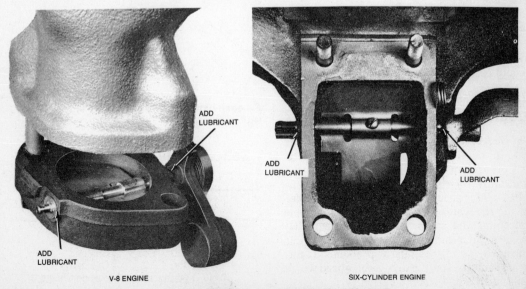

ADD
LUBRICANT

ADD
LUBRICANT

ADD
LUBRICANT

ADD
LUBRICANT

V-8 ENGINE

SIX-CYLINDER ENGINE

Heat riser lubrication points (shown detached)

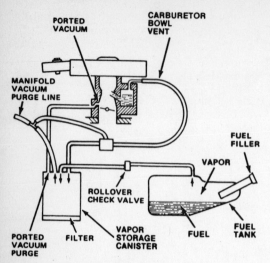

Typical fuel vapor control system

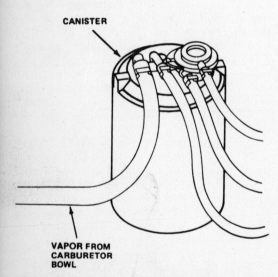

Fuel vapor storage canister and hoses

The air filter in the bottom of the canister should be replaced every 15,000 miles.

Battery

ELECTROLYTE LEVEL

The correct level should be at the bottom of the well inside each cell opening. The surface of the electrolyte should appear distorted, not flat. Only colorless, odorless, preferably distilled, water should be added. It is a good idea to add the water with a squeeze bulb to avoid splashing and spills. If water is frequently needed, the most likely cause is overcharging, caused by voltage regulator problems. If any acid should escape, it can be neutralized with a baking soda and water solution.

CAUTION: *Avoid sparks and smoking*

around the battery! It gives off explosive hydrogen gas. If you get acid on your skin or eyes, rinse it off immediately with lots of water. See a doctor if got in your eyes. In winter, add water only before driving to prevent the battery from freezing and cracking.
NOTE: *Original equipment batteries with the ganged caps are often chronically wet on*

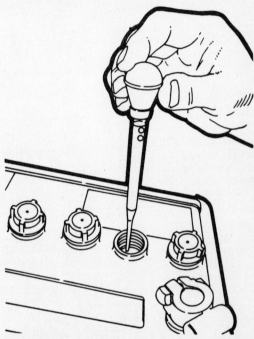

The specific gravity of the battery can be checked with a simple float-type hydrometer

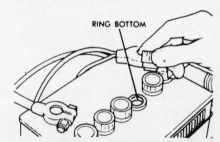

Fill each battery cell to the bottom of the split ring with distilled water

Battery State of Charge at Room Temperature

Specific Gravity Reading	Charged Condition
1.260–1.280	Fully Charged
1.230–1.250	¾ Charged
1.200–1.220	½ Charged
1.170–1.190	¼ Charged
1.140–1.160	Almost no Charge
1.110–1.130	No Charge

top, *causing a lot of corrosion in the battery tray. The problem is insufficient venting. Solve it by removing the caps and drilling a tiny vent hole for each cell through the top of the cap.*

At least once a year check the specific gravity of the battery. It should be between 1.20–1.26 at room temperature. Clean and tighten the terminal clamps and apply a thin coating of petroleum jelly to the terminals. This will help to retard corrosion. The terminals can be cleaned with a stiff wire brush or with a terminal cleaner made for the purpose. These are inexpensive and can be purchased in most any decently equipped parts store.

If water is added during freezing weather, the truck should be driven several miles to al-

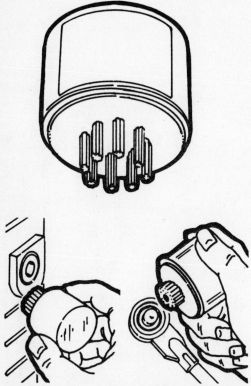

Cleaning the inside of the cable end

Special tools are available for cleaning the terminals and cable clamps on side terminal batteries

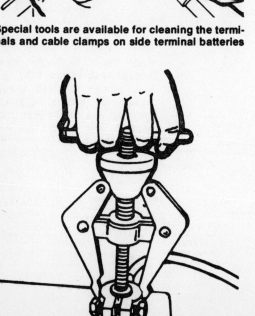

Use a small puller to remove the battery cables

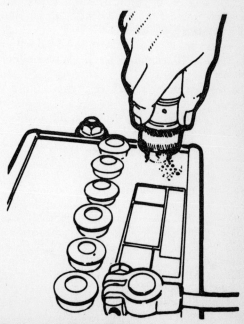

Cleaning the battery terminal

JUMP STARTING A DEAD BATTERY

The chemical reaction in a battery produces explosive hydrogen gas. This is the safe way to jump start a dead battery, reducing the chances of an accidental spark that could cause an explosion.

Jump Starting Precautions

1. Be sure both batteries are of the same voltage.
2. Be sure both batteries are of the same polarity (have the same grounded terminal).
3. Be sure the vehicles are not touching.
4. Be sure the vent cap holes are not obstructed.
5. Do not smoke or allow sparks around the battery.
6. In cold weather, check for frozen electrolyte in the battery. Do not jump start a frozen battery.
7. Do not allow electrolyte on your skin or clothing.
8. Be sure the electrolyte is not frozen.
CAUTION: *Make certain that the ignition key, in the vehicle with the dead battery, is in the OFF position. Connecting cables to vehicles with on-board computers will result in computer destruction if the key is not in the OFF position.*

Jump Starting Procedure

1. Determine voltages of the two batteries; they must be the same.
2. Bring the starting vehicle close (they must not touch) so that the batteries can be reached easily.
3. Turn off all accessories and both engines. Put both cars in Neutral or Park and set the handbrake.
4. Cover the cell caps with a rag—do not cover terminals.
5. If the terminals on the run-down battery are heavily corroded, clean them.
6. Identify the positive and negative posts on both batteries and connect the cables in the order shown.
7. Start the engine of the starting vehicle and run it at fast idle. Try to start the car with the dead battery. Crank it for no more than 10 seconds at a time and let it cool off for 20 seconds in between tries.
8. If it doesn't start in 3 tries, there is something else wrong.
9. Disconnect the cables in the reverse order.
10. Replace the cell covers and dispose of the rags.

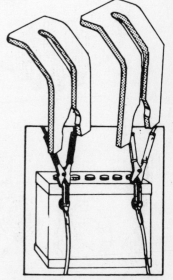

Side terminal batteries occasionally pose a problem when connecting jumper cables. There frequently isn't enough room to clamp the cables without touching sheet metal. Side terminal adaptors are available to alleviate this problem and should be removed after use.

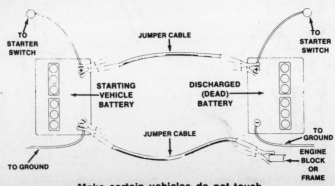

Make certain vehicles do not touch

This hook-up for negative ground cars only

low the water to mix with the electrolyte. Otherwise the battery could freeze.

If the battery becomes corroded, a mixture of baking soda and water will neutralize the corrosion. This should be washed off after making sure that the caps are tight and securely in place. Rinse the solution off with cold water.

If a fast charger is used to charge the battery while the battery is in the truck, disconnect the battery first.

NOTE: *Keep flame or sparks away from the battery! It gives off explosive hydrogen gas, while it is being charged.*

Windshield Wipers

For maximum effectiveness and longest element life, the windshield and wiper blades should be kept clean. Dirt, tree sap, road tar and so on will cause streaking, smearing and blade deterioration if left on the windshield. It is advisable to wash the windshield carefully with a commercial glass cleaner at least once a month. Wipe off the rubber blades with a wet rag afterwards. Do not attempt to move the wipers back and forth by hand! Damage to the motor and drive mechanism will result.

If the blades are found to be cracked, broken or torn they should be replaced immediately. Replacement intervals will vary with usage, although ozone deterioration usually limits blade lift to about one year. If the wiper pattern is smeared or streaked, or if the blade chatters across the glass, the blades should be replaced. It is easiest and most sensible to replace them in pairs.

There are basically three different types of wiper blade refills, which differ in their method of replacement. One type has two release buttons, approximately ⅓ of the way up from the ends of the blade frame. Pushing the buttons down releases a lock and allows the rubber blade to be removed from the frame. The new blade slides back into the frame and locks in place.

The second type of refill has two metal tabs which are unlocked by squeezing them together. The rubber blade can then be withdrawn from the frame jaws. A new one is installed by inserting it into the front frame jaws and sliding it rearward to engage the remaining frame jaws. There are usually four jaws. Be certain when installing that the refill is engaged in all of them. At the end of its travel, the tabs will lock into place on the front jaws of the wiper blade frame.

The third type is a refill made from polycarbonate. The refill has a simple locking device at one end which flexes downward out of the groove into which the jaws of the holder fit, allowing easy release. By sliding the new refill through all the jaws and pushing through the slight resistance when it reaches the end of its travel, the refill will lock into position.

Regardless of the type of refill used, make sure that all of the frame jaws are engaged as the refill is pushed into place and locked. The metal blade holder and frame will scratch the glass if allowed to touch it.

Belts

INSPECTION

The belts which drive the engine accessories such as the alternator or generator, the air pump, power steering pump, air conditioning compressor and water pump are of either the V-belt design or flat, serpentine design. Older belts show wear and damage readily, since their basic design was a belt with a rubber casing. As the casing wore, cracks and fibers were readily apparent. Newer design, caseless belts do not show wear as readily, and many untrained people cannot distinguish between a good, serviceable belt and one that is worn to the point of failure.

It is a good idea, therefore, to visually inspect the belts regularly and replace them, routinely, every two to three years.

ADJUSTING

Belts are normally adjusted by loosening the bolts of the accessory being driven and moving that accessory on its pivot points until the proper tension is applied to the belt. The accessory is held in this position while the bolts are tightened. To determine proper belt tension, you can purchase a belt tension gauge or simply use the deflection method. To determine deflection, press inward on the belt at the midpoint of its longest straight run. The belt should deflect (move inward) ⅜ to ½″ (9.525–12.7mm). Some long V-belts and most serpentine belts have idler pulleys which are used for adjusting purposes. Just loosen the idler pulley and move it to take up tension on the belt.

REMOVAL AND INSTALLATION

To remove a drive belt, simply loosen the accessory being driven and move it on its pivot point to free the belt. Then, remove the belt. If an idler pulley is used, it is often necessary, only, to loosen the idler pulley to provide enough slack the remove the belt.

It is important to note, however, that on engines with many driven accessories, several or all of the belts may have to be removed to get at the one to be replaced.

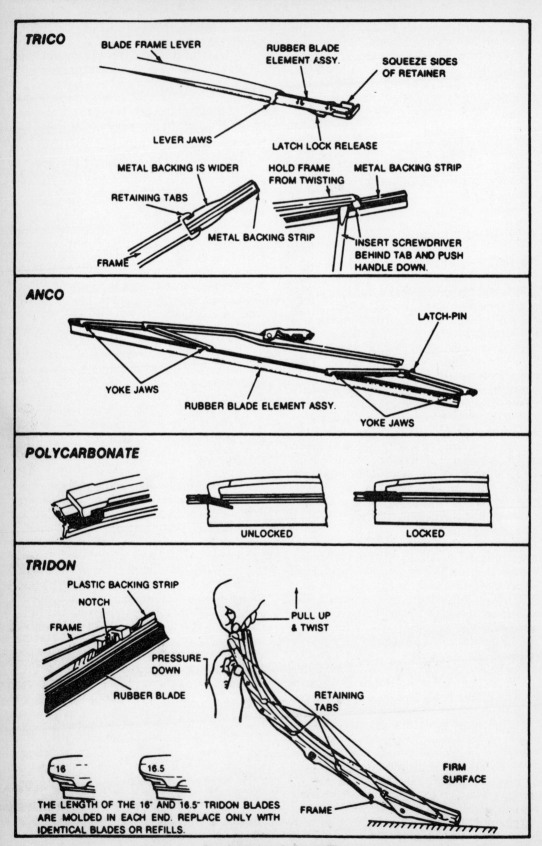

TRICO

BLADE FRAME LEVER

RUBBER BLADE ELEMENT ASSY.

SQUEEZE SIDES OF RETAINER

LEVER JAWS

LATCH LOCK RELEASE

METAL BACKING IS WIDER

HOLD FRAME FROM TWISTING

METAL BACKING STRIP

RETAINING TABS

METAL BACKING STRIP

FRAME

INSERT SCREWDRIVER BEHIND TAB AND PUSH HANDLE DOWN.

ANCO

LATCH-PIN

YOKE JAWS

RUBBER BLADE ELEMENT ASSY.

YOKE JAWS

POLYCARBONATE

UNLOCKED

LOCKED

TRIDON

PLASTIC BACKING STRIP

NOTCH

FRAME

PULL UP & TWIST

PRESSURE DOWN

RUBBER BLADE

RETAINING TABS

16

16.5

FIRM SURFACE

THE LENGTH OF THE 16" AND 16.5" TRIDON BLADES ARE MOLDED IN EACH END. REPLACE ONLY WITH IDENTICAL BLADES OR REFILLS.

FRAME

Popular styles of wiper refills

HOW TO SPOT WORN V-BELTS

V-Belts are vital to efficient engine operation—they drive the fan, water pump and other accessories. They require little maintenance (occasional tightening) but they will not last forever. Slipping or failure of the V-belt will lead to overheating. If your V-belt looks like any of these, it should be replaced.

Cracking or weathering

This belt has deep cracks, which cause it to flex. Too much flexing leads to heat build-up and premature failure. These cracks can be caused by using the belt on a pulley that is too small. Notched belts are available for small diameter pulleys.

Softening (grease and oil)

Oil and grease on a belt can cause the belt's rubber compounds to soften and separate from the reinforcing cords that hold the belt together. The belt will first slip, then finally fail altogether.

Glazing

Glazing is caused by a belt that is slipping. A slipping belt can cause a run-down battery, erratic power steering, overheating or poor accessory performance. The more the belt slips, the more glazing will be built up on the surface of the belt. The more the belt is glazed, the more it will slip. If the glazing is light, tighten the belt.

Worn cover

The cover of this belt is worn off and is peeling away. The reinforcing cords will begin to wear and the belt will shortly break. When the belt cover wears in spots or has a rough jagged appearance, check the pulley grooves for roughness.

Separation

This belt is on the verge of breaking and leaving you stranded. The layers of the belt are separating and the reinforcing cords are exposed. It's just a matter of time before it breaks completely.

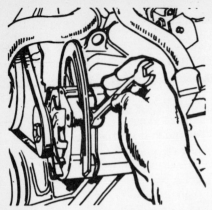

To adjust belt tension or to replace belts, first loosen the component's mounting and adjusting bolts slightly

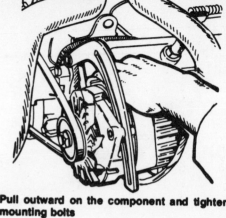

Pull outward on the component and tighten the mounting bolts

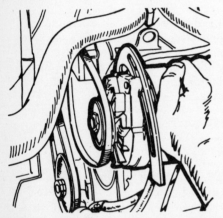

Push the component toward the engine and slip off the belt

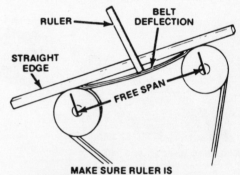

Measuring belt deflection

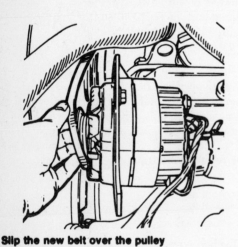

Slip the new belt over the pulley

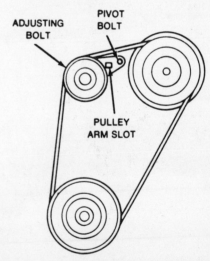

Some pulleys have a rectangular slot to aid in moving the accessories to be tightened

Hoses

REMOVAL AND INSTALLATION

Radiator hoses are generally of two constructions, the preformed (molded) type, which is custom made for a particular application, and the spring-loaded type, which is made to fit several different applications. Heater hoses are all of the same general construction.

Hoses are retained by clamps. To replace a hose, loosen the clamp and slide it down the

HOW TO SPOT BAD HOSES

Both the upper and lower radiator hoses are called upon to perform difficult jobs in an inhospitable environment. They are subject to nearly 18 psi at under hood temperatures often over 280°F., and must circulate nearly 7500 gallons of coolant an hour—3 good reasons to have good hoses.

Swollen hose

A good test for any hose is to feel it for soft or spongy spots. Frequently these will appear as swollen areas of the hose. The most likely cause is oil soaking. This hose could burst at any time, when hot or under pressure.

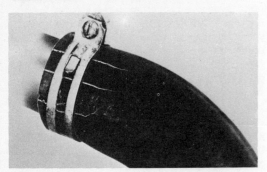

Cracked hose

Cracked hoses can usually be seen but feel the hoses to be sure they have not hardened; a prime cause of cracking. This hose has cracked down to the reinforcing cords and could split at any of the cracks.

Frayed hose end (due to weak clamp)

Weakened clamps frequently are the cause of hose and cooling system failure. The connection between the pipe and hose has deteriorated enough to allow coolant to escape when the engine is hot.

Debris in cooling system

Debris, rust and scale in the cooling system can cause the inside of a hose to weaken. This can usually be felt on the outside of the hose as soft or thinner areas.

hose, away from the attaching point. Twist the hose from side to side until it is free, then pull it off. Before installing the new hose, make sure that the outlet fitting is as clean as possible. Coat the fitting with non-hardening sealer and slip the hose into place. Install the clamp and tighten it.

Air Conditioning System

Air conditioning was first offered on CJ models in 1977. This system remained unchanged through 1980. The compressor used was the vertical, 2-cylinder Tecumseh model.

For the 1981 model year, all Jeep vehicles built for sale in California, and equipped with the 6–258 engine, utilized a Japanese made Sankyo, 5-cylinder axial compressor. All non-California 6–258 engines and all 8–304 engines utilized the Tecumseh compressor.

In 1982, the Sankyo became the only compressor used on CJ models.

All systems utilize a sight glass for system inspection.

NOTE: *This book contains simple testing and charging procedures for your Jeep's air conditioning system. More comprehensive testing, diagnosis and service procedures may be found in CHILTON'S GUIDE TO AIR CONDITIONING SERVICE AND REPAIR, book part number 7580, available at your local retailer.*

GENERAL SERVICING PROCEDURES

The most important aspect of air conditioning service is the maintenance of pure and adequate charge of refrigerant in the system. A refrigeration system cannot function properly if a significant percentage of the charge is lost. Leaks are common because the severe vibration encountered in an automobile can easily cause a sufficient cracking or loosening of the air conditioning fittings. As a result, the extreme operating pressures of the system force refrigerant out.

The problem can be understood by considering what happens to the system as it is operated with a continuous leak. Because the expansion valve regulates the flow of refrigerant to the evaporator, the level of refrigerant there is fairly constant. The receiver-drier stores any excess of refrigerant, and so a loss will first appear there as a reduction in the level of liquid. As this level nears the bottom of the vessel, some refrigerant vapor bubbles will begin to appear in the stream of liquid supplied to the expansion valve. This vapor decreases the capacity of the expansion valve very little as the valve opens to compensate for its presence. As the quantity of liquid in the condenser decreases, the operating pressure will drop there and throughout the high side of the system. As the R-12 continues to be expelled, the pressure available to force the liquid through the expansion valve will continue to decrease, and,

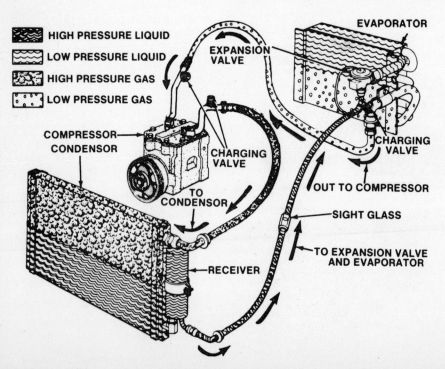

Basic air conditioning system components and flow diagram, showing the Tecumseh 2-cylinder compressor

Troubleshooting Basic Air Conditioning Problems

Problem	Cause	Solution
There's little or no air coming from the vents (and you're sure it's on)	• The A/C fuse is blown • Broken or loose wires or connections • The on/off switch is defective	• Check and/or replace fuse • Check and/or repair connections • Replace switch
The air coming from the vents is not cool enough	• Windows and air vent wings open • The compressor belt is slipping • Heater is on • Condenser is clogged with debris • Refrigerant has escaped through a leak in the system • Receiver/drier is plugged	• Close windows and vent wings • Tighten or replace compressor belt • Shut heater off • Clean the condenser • Check system • Service system
The air has an odor	• Vacuum system is disrupted • Odor producing substances on the evaporator case • Condensation has collected in the bottom of the evaporator housing	• Have the system checked/repaired • Clean the evaporator case • Clean the evaporator housing drains
System is noisy or vibrating	• Compressor belt or mountings loose • Air in the system	• Tighten or replace belt; tighten mounting bolts • Have the system serviced

Sight glass condition
  Constant bubbles, foam or oil streaks
  Clear sight glass, but no cold air
  Clear sight glass, but air is cold
  Clouded with milky fluid
	• Undercharged system
	
	• No refrigerant at all
	• System is OK
	• Receiver drier is leaking dessicant
		• Charge the system
		
		• Check and charge the system
		
		• Have system checked

Large difference in temperature of lines	• System undercharged	• Charge and leak test the system
Compressor noise	• Broken valves • Overcharged • Incorrect oil level • Piston slap • Broken rings • Drive belt pulley bolts are loose	• Replace the valve plate • Discharge, evacuate and install the correct charge • Isolate the compressor and check the oil level. Correct as necessary. • Replace the compressor • Replace the compressor • Tighten with the correct torque specification
Excessive vibration	• Incorrect belt tension • Clutch loose • Overcharged • Pulley is misaligned	• Adjust the belt tension • Tighten the clutch • Discharge, evacuate and install the correct charge • Align the pulley
Condensation dripping in the passenger compartment	• Drain hose plugged or improperly positioned • Insulation removed or improperly installed	• Clean the drain hose and check for proper installation • Replace the insulation on the expansion valve and hoses
Frozen evaporator coil	• Faulty thermostat • Thermostat capillary tube improperly installed • Thermostat not adjusted properly	• Replace the thermostat • Install the capillary tube correctly • Adjust the thermostat
Low side low—high side low	• System refrigerant is low • Expansion valve is restricted	• Evacuate, leak test and charge the system • Replace the expansion valve
Low side high—high side low	• Internal leak in the compressor—worn	• Remove the compressor cylinder head and inspect the compressor. Replace the valve plate assembly if necessary. If the compressor pistons, rings or

Troubleshooting Basic Air Conditioning Problems (cont.)

Problem	Cause	Solution
Low side high—high side low (cont.)		cylinders are excessively worn or scored replace the compressor
	• Cylinder head gasket is leaking	• Install a replacement cylinder head gasket
	• Expansion valve is defective	• Replace the expansion valve
	• Drive belt slipping	• Adjust the belt tension
Low side high—high side high	• Condenser fins obstructed	• Clean the condenser fins
	• Air in the system	• Evacuate, leak test and charge the system
	• Expansion valve is defective	• Replace the expansion valve
	• Loose or worn fan belts	• Adjust or replace the belts as necessary
Low side low—high side high	• Expansion valve is defective	• Replace the expansion valve
	• Restriction in the refrigerant hose	• Check the hose for kinks—replace if necessary
	• Restriction in the receiver/drier	• Replace the receiver/drier
	• Restriction in the condenser	• Replace the condenser
Low side and high side normal (inadequate cooling)	• Air in the system	• Evacuate, leak test and charge the system
	• Moisture in the system	• Evacuate, leak test and charge the system

eventually, the valve's orifice will prove to be too much of a restriction for adequate flow even with the needle fully withdrawn.

At this point, low side pressure will start to drop, and severe reduction in cooling capacity, marked by freeze-up of the evaporator coil, will result. Eventually, the operating pressure of the evaporator will be lower than the pressure of the atmosphere surrounding it, and air will be drawn into the system wherever there are leaks in the low side.

Because all atmospheric air contains at least some moisture, water will enter the system and mix with the R-12 and the oil. Trace amounts of moisture will cause sludging of the oil, and corrosion of the system. Saturation and clogging of the filter-drier, and freezing of the expansion valve orifice will eventually result. As air fills the system to a greater and greater extend, it will interfere more and more with the normal flows of refrigerant and heat.

A list of general precautions that should be observed while doing this follows:

1. Keep all tools as clean and dry as possible.

2. Thoroughly purge the service gauges and hoses of air and moisture before connecting them to the system. Keep them capped when not in use.

3. Thoroughly clean any refrigerant fitting before disconnecting it, in order to minimize the entrance of dirt into the system.

4. Plan any operation that requires opening the system beforehand in order to minimize the length of time it will be exposed to open air. Cap or seal the open ends to minimize the entrance of foreign material.

5. When adding oil, pour it through an extremely clean and dry tube or funnel. Keep the oil capped whenever possible. Do not use oil that has not been kept tightly sealed.

6. Use only refrigerant 12. Purchase refrigerant intended for use in only automotive air conditioning system. Avoid the use of refrigerant 12 that may be packaged for another use, such as cleaning, or powering a horn, as it is impure.

7. Completely evacuate any system that has been opened to replace a component, other than when isolating the compressor, or that has leaked sufficiently to draw in moisture and air. This requires evacuating air and moisture with a good vacuum pump for at least one hour.

If a system has been open for a considerable length of time it may be advisable to evacuate the system for up to 12 hours (overnight).

8. Use a wrench on both halves of a fitting that is to be disconnected, so as to avoid placing torque on any of the refrigerant lines.

ADDITIONAL PREVENTIVE MAINTENANCE CHECKS

Antifreeze

In order to prevent heater core freeze-up during A/C operation, it is necessary to maintain permanent type antifreeze protection of

+ 15°F. or lower. A reading of –15°F. is ideal since this protection also supplies sufficient corrosion inhibitors for the protection of the engine cooling system.

NOTE: *The same antifreeze should not be used longer than the manufacturer specified.*

Radiator Cap

For efficient operation of an air conditioned car's cooling system, the radiator cap should have a holding pressure which meets manufacturer's specifications. A cap which fails to hold these pressure should be replaced.

Condenser

Any obstruction of or damage to the condenser configuration will restrict the air flow which is essential to its efficient operation. It is therefore, a good rule to keep this unit clean and in proper physical shape.

NOTE: *Bug screens are regarded as obstructions.*

Condensation Drain Tube

This single molded drain tube expels the condensation, which accumulates on the bottom of the evaporator housing, into the engine compartment.

If this tube is obstructed, the air conditioning performance can be restricted and condensation buildup can spill over onto the vehicle's floor.

SAFETY PRECAUTIONS

Because of the importance of the necessary safety precautions that must be exercised when working with air conditioning systems and R-12 refrigerant, a recap of the safety precautions are outlined.

1. Avoid contact with a charged refrigeration system, even when working on another part of the air conditioning system or vehicle. If a heavy tool comes into contact with a section of copper tubing or a heat exchanger, it can easily cause the relatively soft material to rupture.

2. When it is necessary to apply force to a fitting which contains refrigerant, as when checking that all system couplings are securely tightened, use a wrench on both parts of the fitting involved, if possible. This will avoid putting torque on refrigerant tubing. (It is advisable, when possible, to use tube or line wrenches when tightening these flare nut fittings.)

3. Do not attempt to discharge the system by merely loosening a fitting, or removing the service valve caps and cracking these valves. Precise control is possibly only when using the service gauges. Place a rag under the open end of the center charging hose while discharging the system to catch any drops of liquid that might escape. Wear protective gloves when connecting or disconnecting service gauge hoses.

4. Discharge the system only in a well ventilated area, as high concentrations of the gas can exclude oxygen and act as an anesthesia. When leak testing or soldering, this is particularly important, as toxic gas is formed when R-12 contacts any flame.

5. Never start a system without first verifying that both service valves are backseated, if equipped, and that all fittings are throughout the system are snugly connected.

6. Avoid applying heat to any refrigerant line or storage vessel. Charging may be aided by using water heated to less than 125°F to warm the refrigerant container. Never allow a refrigerant storage container to sit out in the sun, or near any other source of heat, such as a radiator.

7. Always wear goggles when working on a system to protect the eyes. If refrigerant contacts the eye, it is advisable in all cases to see a physician as soon as possible.

8. Frostbite from liquid refrigerant should be treated by first gradually warming the area with cool water, and then gently applying petroleum jelly. A physician should be consulted.

9. Always keep refrigerant can fittings capped when not in use. Avoid sudden shock to the can which might occur from dropping it, or from banging a heavy tool against it. Never carry a can in the passenger compartment of a car.

10. Always completely discharge the system before painting the vehicle (if the paint is to be baked on), or before welding anywhere near the refrigerant lines.

TEST GAUGES

Most of the service work performed in air conditioning requires the use of a set of two gauges, one for the high (head) pressure side of the system, the other for the low (suction) side.

The low side gauge records both pressure and vacuum. Vacuum readings are calibrated from 0 to 30 inches and the pressure graduations read from 0 to no less than 60 psi.

The high side gauge measures pressure from 0 to at last 600 psi.

Both gauges are threaded into a manifold that contains two hand shut-off valves. Proper manipulation of these valves and the use of the attached test hoses allow the user to perform the following services:

1. Test high and low side pressures.

2. Remove air, moisture, and contaminated refrigerant.

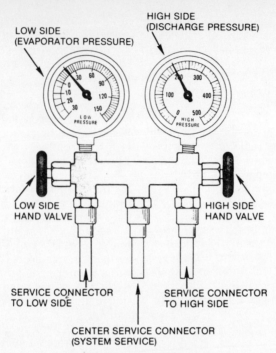

LOW SIDE
(EVAPORATOR PRESSURE)

HIGH SIDE
(DISCHARGE PRESSURE)

LOW SIDE
HAND VALVE

HIGH SIDE
HAND VALVE

SERVICE CONNECTOR
TO LOW SIDE

SERVICE CONNECTOR
TO HIGH SIDE

CENTER SERVICE CONNECTOR
(SYSTEM SERVICE)

Typical manifold gauge set

3. Purge the system (of refrigerant).

4. Charge the system (with refrigerant).

The manifold valves are designed so that they have no direct effect on gauge readings, but serve only to provide for, or cut off, flow of refrigerant through the manifold. During all testing and hook-up operations, the valves are kept in a close position to avoid disturbing the refrigeration system. The valves are opened only to purge the system or refrigerant or to charge it.

INSPECTION

CAUTION: *The compressed refrigerant used in the air conditioning system expands into the atmosphere at a temperature of –21.7°F (–29.833°C) or lower. This will freeze any surface, including your eyes, that it contacts. In addition, the refrigerant decomposes into a poisonous gas in the presence of a flame. Do not open or disconnect any part of the air conditioning system.*

Sight Glass Check

You can safely make a few simple checks to determine if your air conditioning system needs service. The tests work best if the temperature is warm (about 70°F [21.1°C]).

NOTE: *If your vehicle is equipped with an aftermarket air conditioner, the following system check may not apply. You should contact the manufacturer of the unit for instructions on systems checks.*

1. Place the automatic transmission in Park or the manual transmission in Neutral. Set the parking brake.

2. Run the engine at a fast idle (about 1,500 rpm) either with the help of a friend or by temporarily readjusting the idle speed screw.

3. Set the controls for maximum cold with the blower on High.

4. Locate the sight glass in one of the system lines. Usually it is on the left alongside the top of the radiator.

5. If you see bubbles, the system must be recharged. Very likely there is a leak at some point.

6. If there are no bubbles, there is either no refrigerant at all or the system is fully charged. Feel the two hoses going to the belt-driven compressor. If they are both at the same temperature, the system is empty and must be recharged.

7. If one hose (high-pressure) is warm and the other (low-pressure) is cold, the system may be all right. However, you are probably making these tests because you think there is something wrong, so proceed to the next step.

8. Have an assistant in the car turn the fan control on and off to operate the compressor clutch. Watch the sight glass.

9. If bubbles appear when the clutch is disengaged and disappear when it is engaged, the system is properly charged.

10. If the refrigerant takes more than 45 seconds to bubble when the clutch is disengaged,

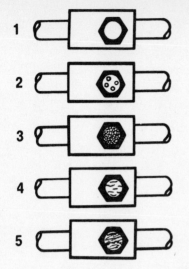

1   Clear sight glass — system correctly charged or over-charged

2   Occasional bubbles — refrigerant charge slightly low

3   Oil streaks on sight glass — total lack of refrigerant

4   Heavy stream of bubbles — serious shortage of refrigerant

5   Dark or clouded sight glass — contaminent present

Sight glass inspection

the system is overcharged. This usually causes poor cooling at low speeds.

CAUTION: *If it is determined that the system has a leak, it should be corrected as soon as possible. Leaks may allow moisture to enter and cause a very expensive rust problem.*

NOTE: *Exercise the air conditioner for a few minutes, every two weeks or so, during the* cold months. This avoids the possibility of the compressor seals drying out from lack of lubrication.

TESTING THE SYSTEM

1. Connect a gauge set.
2. Close (clockwise) both gauge set valves.
3. Mid-position both service valves.

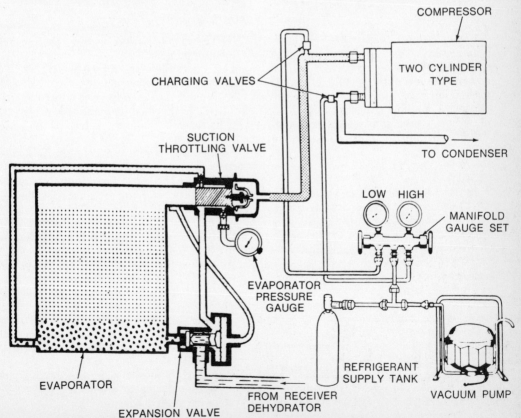

Gauge connections on the Tecumseh compressor

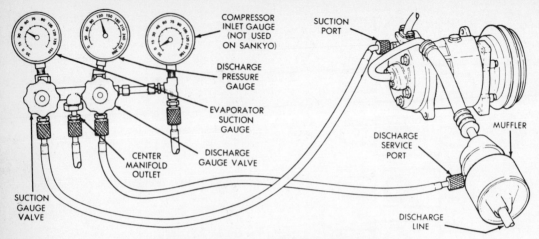

Gauge connections on the Sankyo compressor

4. Park the Jeep in the shade. Start the engine, set the parking brake, place the transmission in NEUTRAL and establish an idle of 1,500 rpm.

5. Run the air conditioning system for full cooling, but NOT in the MAX or COLD mode.

6. Insert a thermometer into the center air outlet.

7. Use the accompanying performance chart for a specifications reference. If pressures are abnormal, refer to the accompanying Pressure Diagnosis Chart.

ISOLATING THE COMPRESSOR

It is not necessary to discharge the system for compressor removal. The compressor can be isolated from the rest of the system, eliminating the need for recharging.

1. Connect a manifold gauge set.

2. Close both gauge hand valves and mid-position (crack) both compressor service valves.

3. Start the engine and turn on the air conditioning.

4. Turn the compressor suction valve slowly clockwise towards the front-seated position. When the suction pressure drops to zero, stop the engine and turn off the air conditioning. Quickly front-seat the valve completely.

5. Front-seat the discharge service valve.

6. Loosen the oil level check plug to remove any internal pressure.

The compressor is now isolated and the service valves can now be removed.

DISCHARGING THE SYSTEM

1. Connect the manifold gauge set.

2. Turn both manifold gauge set hand valves to the full open (counterclockwise) position.

3. Open both service valve slightly, from the backseated position, and allow the refrigerant to discharge *slowly*.

NOTE: *If you allow the refrigerant to rush out, it will take some refrigerant oil with it!*

EVACUATING THE SYSTEM

NOTE: *This procedure requires the use of a vacuum pump.*

1. Connect the manifold gauge set.

2. Discharge the system.

3. Connect the center service hose to the inlet fitting of the vacuum pump.

4. Turn both gauge set valves to the wide open position.

5. Start the pump and note the low side gauge reading.

6. Operate the pump for a minimum of 30 minutes after the lowest observed gauge reading.

7. Leak test the system. Close both gauge set valves. Turn off the pump and note the low side gauge reading. The needle should remain stationary at the point at which the pump was turned off. If the needle drops to zero rapidly, there is a leak in the system which must be repaired.

8. If the needle remains stationary for 3 to 5

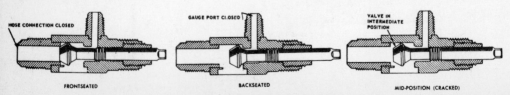

Manual service valve positions

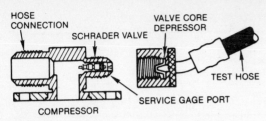

HOSE CONNECTION

SCHRADER VALVE

VALVE CORE DEPRESSOR

TEST HOSE

SERVICE GAGE PORT

COMPRESSOR

Schrader valve

minutes, open the gauge set valves and run the pump for at least 30 minutes more.

9. Close both gauge set valves, stop the pump and disconnect the gauge set. The system is now ready for charging.

LEAK TESTING

Some leak tests can be performed with a soapy water solution. There must be at least a ½lb charge in the system for a leak to be detected. The most extensive leak tests are performed with either a Halide flame type leak tester or the more preferable electronic leak tester.

In either case, the equipment is expensive, and, the use of a Halide detector can be **extremely** hazardous!

CHARGING THE SYSTEM

1. Connect the gauge set.
2. Close (clockwise) both gauge set valves.
3. Mid-position the service valves.
4. Connect the center hose to the refrigerant can opener valve.
5. Make sure the can opener valve is closed, that is, the needle is raised, and connect the valve to the can. Open the valve, puncturing the can with the needle.
6. Loosen the center hose fitting at the pressure gauge, allowing refrigerant to purge the hose of air.

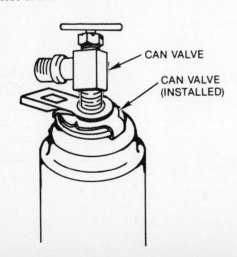

CAN VALVE

CAN VALVE (INSTALLED)

One pound R-12 can with opener valve connected

7. Open the low side gauge set valve and the can valve.

8. Start the engine and turn the air conditioner to the maximum cooling mode. The compressor will operate and pull refrigerant gas into the system.

NOTE: *To help speed the process, the can may be placed, upright, in a pan of warm water, not exceeding 125°F.*

9. If more than one can of refrigerant is needed, close the can valve and gauge set low side valve when the can is empty and connect a new can to the opener. Repeat the charging process until the sight glass indicates a full charge. The frost line on the outside of the can will indicate what portion of the can has been used.

10. When the charging process has been completed, close the gauge set valve and can valve. Run the system for at least five minutes to allow it to normalize.

11. Back-seat (turn fully counterclockwise) both service valves.

12. Loosen both service hoses at the gauges to allow any refrigerant to escape. Remove the gauge set and install the dust caps on the service valves.

NOTE: *Multi-can dispensers are available which allow a simultaneous hook-up of up to four 1 lb. cans of R-12.*

CAUTION: *Never exceed the recommended maximum charge for the system. The maximum charge for systems using the 2-cylinder Tecumseh compressor is 2½ lb.; 2 lb. for those systems using the 5-cylinder Sankyo compressor.*

Front Hub and Wheel Bearings

ADJUSTMENT

NOTE: *Sodium-based grease is not compatible with lithium-based grease. Read the package labels and be careful not to mix the two types. If there is any doubt as to the type of grease used, completely clean the old grease from the bearing and hub before replacing.*

Before handling the bearings, there are a few things that you should remember to do and not to do.

Remember to DO the following:

• Remove all outside dirt from the housing before exposing the bearing.

• Treat a used bearing as gently as you would a new one.

• Work with clean tools in clean surroundings.

• Use clean, dry canvas gloves, or at least clean, dry hands.

Normal Operating Temperature and Pressures*

Relative Humidity (percent)	Surrounding Air Temperature (°F)	Maximum Desirable Center Register Discharge Air Temp. (°F)	Suction Pressure PSI (REF)	Head Pressure PSI (+25 PSI)
20	70	40	11	177
	80	41	15	208
	90	42	20	226
	100	43	23	255
30	70	40	12	181
	80	41	16	214
	90	42	22	234
	100	44	26	267
40	70	40	13	185
	80	42	18	220
	90	43	23	243
	100	44	26	278
50	70	40	14	189
	80	42	19	226
	90	44	25	251
	100	46	27	289
60	70	41	15	193
	80	43	21	233
	90	45	25	259
	100	46	28	300
70	70	41	16	198
	80	43	22	238
	90	45	26	267
	100	46	29	312
80	70	42	18	202
	80	44	23	244
	90	47	27	277
	100	—	—	—
90	70	42	19	206
	80	47	24	250
	90	48	28	284
	100	—	—	—

*Operate engine with transmission in neutral. Keep vehicle out of direct sunlight.

Pressure Diagnosis

Condition	Possible Cause	Correction
Low side low— High side low	System refrigerant low	Evacuate, leak test, and charge system
Low side high— High side low	Internal leak in compressor—worn	Remove compressor cylinder head and inspect compressor. Replace valve plate assembly if necessary. If compressor pistons, rings, or cylinders are excessively worn or scored, replace compressor.
	Head gasket leaking	Install new cylinder head gasket
	Expansion valve	Replace expansion valve
	Drive belt slipping	Set belt tension
Low side high— High side high	Clogged condenser fins	Clean out condenser fins
	Air in system	Evacuate, leak test, and charge system
	Expansion valve	Replace expansion valve
	Loose or worn fan belts	Adjust or replace belts as necessary
Low side low— High side high	Expansion valve	Replace expansion valve
	Restriction in liquid line	Check line for kinks—replace if necessary
	Restriction in receiver	Replace receiver
	Restriction in condenser	Replace condenser
Low side and high side normal (inadequate cooling)	Air in system	Evacuate, leak test, and charge system
	Moisture in system	Evacuate, leak test, and charge system.

• Clean solvents and flushing fluids are a must.

• Use clean paper when laying out the bearings to dry.

• Protect disassembled bearings from rust and dirt. Cover them up.

• Use clean rags to wipe bearings.

• Keep the bearings in oil-proof paper when they are to be stored or are not in use.

• Clean the inside of the housing before replacing the bearing.

Do NOT do the following:

• Don't work in dirty surroundings.

• Don't use dirty, chipped or damaged tools.

• Try not to work on wooden work benches or use wooden mallets.

• Don't handle bearings with dirty or moist hands.

• Do not use gasoline for cleaning. Use a safe solvent.

• Do not spin-dry bearings with compressed air. They will be damaged.

• Do not spin dirty bearings.

• Avoid using cotton waste or dirty cloths to wipe bearings.

• Try not to scratch or nick bearing surfaces.

• Do not allow the bearing to come in contact with dirt or rust at any time.

1945–86

4-WD

1. Raise the front of the vehicle and place jackstands under the axle.

2. Remove the wheel.

3. Remove the front hub grease cap and driving hub snapring. On models equipped with locking hubs, remove the retainer knob hub ring, agitator knob, snapring, outer clutch retaining ring and actuating cam body.

4. Remove the splined driving hub and the pressure spring. This may require slight prying with a screwdriver.

5. Remove the external snapring from the sindle shaft and remove the hub shaft drive gear.

6. Remove the wheel bearing locknut, lockring, adjusting nut and inner lockring.

7. On vehicles with drum brakes, remove the hub and drum assembly. This may require that the brake adjusting wheel be backed off a few turns. The outer wheel bearing and spring retainer will come off with the hub.

8. On vehicles with disc brakes, remove the caliper and suspend it out of the way by hanging it from a suspension or frame member with a length of wire. Do not disconnect the brake

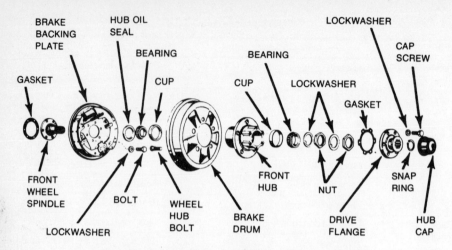

Typical front wheel hub and bearings, with drum brakes

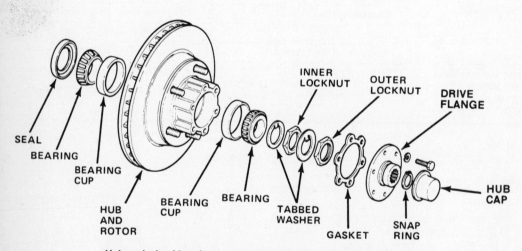

Hub and wheel bearings on models with disc brakes through 1979

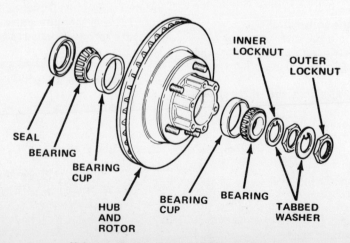

Hub and wheel bearings on 1980–86 models

hose, and be careful to avoid stretching the hose. Remove the rotor and hub assembly. The outer wheel bearing and, on vehicles with locking hubs, the spring collar, will come off with the hub.

9. Carefully drive out the inner bearing and seal from the hub, using a wood block.

10. Inspect the bearing races for excessive wear, pitting or grooves. If they are cracked or grooved, or if pitting and excess wear is present, drive them out with a drift or punch.

11. Check the bearing for excess wear, pitting or cracks, or excess looseness.

NOTE: *If it is necessary to replace either the bearing or the race, replace both. Never replace just a bearing or a race. These parts wear in a mating pattern. If just one is replaced, premature failure of the new part will result.*

12. If the old parts are retained, thoroughly clean them in a safe solvent and allow them to dry on a clean towel. Never spin dry them with compressed air.

13. On vehicles with drum brakes, cover the spindle with a cloth and thoroughly brush all dirt from the brakes. Never blow the dirt off the brakes, due to the presence of asbestos in the dirt, which is harmful to your health when inhaled.

14. Remove the cloth and thoroughly clean the spindle.

15. Thoroughly clean the inside of the hub.

16. Pack the inside of the hub with EP wheel bearing grease. Add grease to the hub until it is flush with the inside diameter of the bearing cup.

17. Pack the bearing with the same grease. A needle-shaped wheel bearing packer is best for this operation. If one is not available, place a large amount of grease in the palm of your hand and slide the edge of the bearing cage through the grease to pick up as much as possible, then work the grease in as best you can with your fingers.

18. If a new race is being installed, very carefully drive it into position until it bottoms all around, using a brass drift. Be careful to avoid scratching the surface.

19. Place the inner bearing in the race and install a new grease seal.

20. Place the hub assembly onto the spindle and install the inner lockring and outer bearing. Install the wheel bearing nut and torque it to 50 ft.lb. while turning the wheel back and forth to seat the bearings. Back off the nut about ¼ turn (90°) maximum.

21. Install the lockwasher with the tab aligned with the keyway in the spindle and turn the inner wheel bearing adjusting nut until the peg on the nut engages the nearest hole in the lockwasher.

22. Install the outer locknut and torque it to 50 ft.lb.

23. Install the spring collar, drive flange, snapring, pressure spring, and hub cap.

24. Install the caliper over the rotor.

1947–64

2-WD

1. Raise the front of the vehicle and place jackstands under the axle.

2. Remove the wheel.

3. Remove the front hub grease cap.

4. Remove the cotter pin and locknut.

5. Pull out on the brake drum slightly to free the outer bearing and remove the bearing.

6. Remove the drum and hub.

7. Using an awl, puncture the inner seal and pry it out. Discard the seal.

8. Remove the inner bearing.

9. Inspect the bearing races for excessive wear, pitting or grooves. If they are cracked or grooved, or if pitting and excess wear is present, drive them out with a drift or punch.

1. Steering knuckle
2. Brake
3. Hub grease seal
4. Inner bearing cone
5. Inner bearing cup
6. Hub and drum
7. Outer bearing cup
8. Outer bearing cone
9. Tongued washer
10. Nut
11. Cotter pin
12. Grease cap
13. Nut
14. Lockwasher
15. Bolt

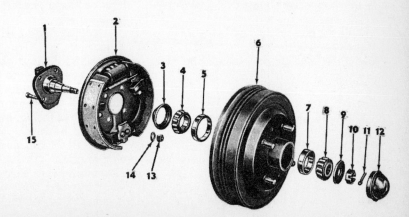

2-wd front hub and wheel bearings

10. Check the bearing for excess wear, pitting or cracks, or excess looseness.

NOTE: *If it is necessary to replace either the bearing or the race, replace both. Never replace just a bearing or a race. These parts wear in a mating pattern. If just one is replaced, premature failure of the new part will result.*

11. If the old parts are retained, thoroughly clean them in a safe solvent and allow them to dry on a clean towel. Never spin dry them with compressed air.

12. On vehicles with drum brakes, cover the spindle with a cloth and thoroughly brush all dirt from the brakes. Never blow the dirt off the brakes, due to the presence of asbestos in the dirt, which is harmful to your health when inhaled.

13. Remove the cloth and thoroughly clean the spindle.

14. Thoroughly clean the inside of the hub.

15. Pack the inside of the hub with EP wheel bearing grease. Add grease to the hub until it is flush with the inside diameter of the bearing cup.

16. Pack the bearing with the same grease. A needle-shaped wheel bearing packer is best for this operation. If one is not available, place a large amount of grease in the palm of your hand and slide the edge of the bearing cage through the grease to pick up as much as possible, then work the grease in as best you can with your fingers.

17. If a new race is being installed, very carefully drive it into position until it bottoms all around, using a brass drift. Be careful to avoid scratching the surface.

18. Place the inner bearing in the race and install a new grease seal.

19. Place the hub assembly onto the spindle and install the outer bearing. Install the wheel bearing nut and tighten it until the hub binds while turning. Back off the nut about $1/6$–$1/4$ turn to free the bearings. Install a new cotter pin.

20. Install the grease cap.

21. Install the wheel.

22. Lower the vehicle and install the hub cap.

1987

1. Raise and support the front end on jackstands.

2. Remove the wheel.

3. Dismount the caliper and suspend it out of the way.

4. Remove the rotor.

5. Remove the hub nut pin, cap and nut.

6. Remove the hub.

7. The hub and bearings are usually replaced as a unit. The hub and bearing carrier may, however, be disassembled and the bearings replaced as a set. Once the hub and bearing carrier have been separated, the bearings should not be reused.

8. Pack the hub cavity and bearings with wheel bearing grease and install the hub on the axle shaft. If the carrier was separated from the hub, make sure you install a new carrier seal and inner bearing seal.

9. Install the hub washer and nut. Torque the nut to 175 ft.lb. and instal the cap and new cotter pin.

10. Install the rotor, caliper and wheel.

Locking Hub Service

Jeep vehicles through 1979 were not factory equipped with locking hubs. Locking hubs were a dealer installed option or installed by the owner after purchase. Beginning in 1980, factory installed hubs were offered.

1945–79

The following is a general service procedure that should apply to all types. Locking hubs should be lubricated at least once a year and as soon as possible if running for extended periods submerged in water. The same type of grease should be used in the locking hubs as is used on the wheel bearings. EP lithium based chassis lube is preferred.

1. Remove the lockout screws and washers.

2. Remove the hub ring and knob.

3. Remove the internal snapring from the groove in the hub.

4. Remove the cam body ring and clutch retainer from the hub and disassemble the parts.

5. Remove the axle shaft snapring. It may be necessary to push in on the gear and pull out on the axle with a bolt to make the snapring removal easier.

6. Remove the drive gear and clutch gear. A slight rocking of the hub may make them slide out easier.

7. Remove the coil spring and spring retainer.

8. Clean all the components in a safe solvent. Wipe out the hub with a clean cloth.

9. Grease the inside of the hub liberally.

10. Install the spring retainer ring with the undercut area facing inwards. Be sure it seats against the bearing.

11. Install the coil spring with the large end going in first.

12. Install the axle shaft sleeve and ring and the inner clutch ring with the teeth of both components meshed together in a locked position. It may be necessary to rock the hub to mesh the splines of the axle with those of the

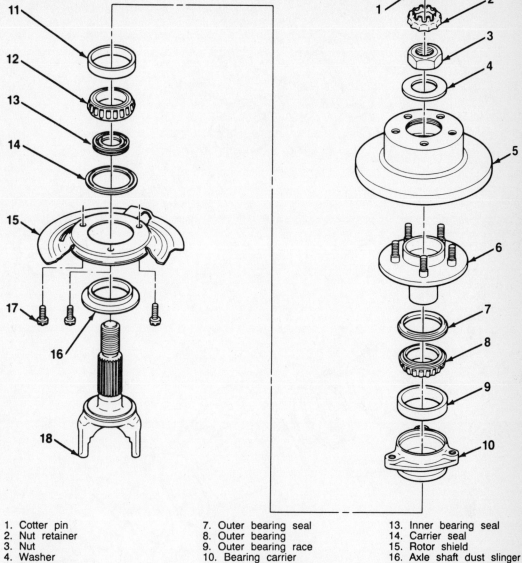

1. Cotter pin	7. Outer bearing seal
2. Nut retainer	8. Outer bearing
3. Nut	9. Outer bearing race
4. Washer	10. Bearing carrier
5. Brake rotor	11. Inner bearing race
6. Hub	12. Inner bearing

13. Inner bearing seal
14. Carrier seal
15. Rotor shield
16. Axle shaft dust slinger
17. Bearing carrier bolts
18. Axle shaft

1987 front hub and bearings

axle shaft sleeve and ring. Keep the two gears locked in position.

13. Install the axle shaft snapring. Push in on the gear and pull out on the axle with a bolt to allow the snapring to go into the groove.

14. Install the actuating cam body ring into the outer clutch retaining ring and install them in the hub.

15. Install the internal snapring.

16. Apply a small amount of Lubriplate® grease to the ears of the cam.

17. Assemble the knob in the hub ring and assemble them to the axle with the knob in the locked position. Tighten the screws and wash-ers evenly and alternately, making sure the retainer ring is not cocked in the hub.

18. Torque the screws to 40 in.lb.

1980–86

1. Remove the bolts and lockwashers attaching the hub body to the axle.

2. Remove the hub body and discard the gasket.

CAUTION: *Do not turn the hub control dial after removed.*

3. Remove the retaining ring from the axle shaft.

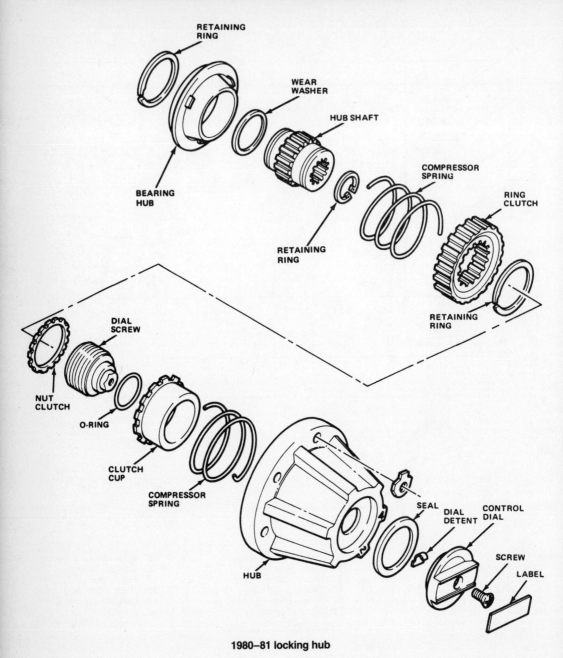

1980–81 locking hub

4. Remove the hub clutch and bearing assembly.

5. Clean and inspect all parts.

6. Lubricate all parts with chassis lubricant. DO NOT PACK THE HUB WITH GREASE!

7. Install in reverse of removal. Torque the retaining nuts to 30 ft.lb.

Tires and Wheels

Inspect the tire treads for cuts, bruises and other damage. Check the air valves to be sure that they are tight. Replace any missing valve caps.

The tires should be checked frequently for proper air pressure. A chart in the glove compartment or on the driver's door pillar gives the recommended inflation pressure. Pressures can increase as much as 6 psi due to heat buildup. It is a good idea to have your own accurate gauge, and to check pressures weekly. Not all gauges on service station air pumps can be trusted.

Inspect tires for uneven wear that might indicate the need for front end alignment or tire

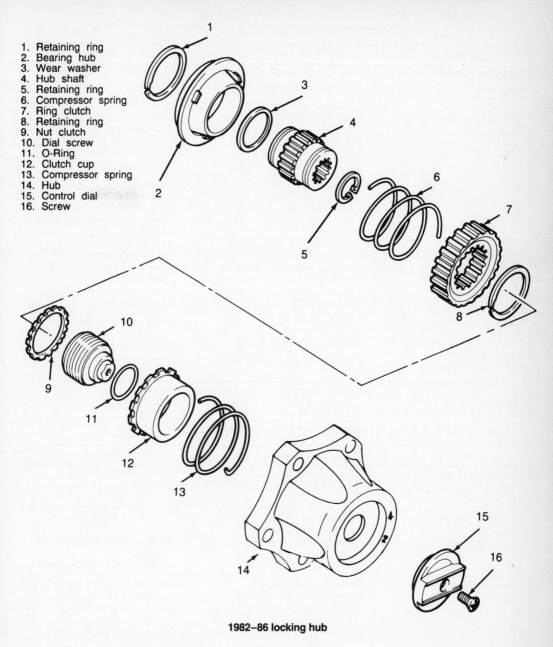

1. Retaining ring
2. Bearing hub
3. Wear washer
4. Hub shaft
5. Retaining ring
6. Compressor spring
7. Ring clutch
8. Retaining ring
9. Nut clutch
10. Dial screw
11. O-Ring
12. Clutch cup
13. Compressor spring
14. Hub
15. Control dial
16. Screw

1982–86 locking hub

rotation. Tires should be replaced when a tread wear indicator appears as a solid band across the tread.

When you buy new tires, give some thought to these points, especially if you are switching to larger tires or to another profile series (50, 60, 70, 78):

1. All four tires should be the same. Four wheel drive requires that all tires be the same size, type, and tread pattern to provide even traction on loose surfaces, to prevent driveline bind when conventional part time four wheel drive is used, and to prevent excessive wear on the center differential with full time four wheel drive.

2. The wheels must be the correct width for the tire. Tire dealers have charts of tire and rim compatibility. A mismatch can cause sloppy handling and rapid tread wear. The old rule of thumb is that the tread width should match the rim width (inside bead to inside bead) within an inch. For radial tires, the rim width should be 80% or less of the tire (not tread) width.

3. The height (mounted diameter) of the new tires can greatly change speedometer ac-

Troubleshooting Basic Wheel Problems

Problem	Cause	Solution
The car's front end vibrates at high speed	• The wheels are out of balance • Wheels are out of alignment	• Have wheels balanced • Have wheel alignment checked/adjusted
Car pulls to either side	• Wheels are out of alignment • Unequal tire pressure • Different size tires or wheels	• Have wheel alignment checked/adjusted • Check/adjust tire pressure • Change tires or wheels to same size
The car's wheel(s) wobbles	• Loose wheel lug nuts • Wheels out of balance • Damaged wheel • Wheels are out of alignment • Worn or damaged ball joint • Excessive play in the steering linkage (usually due to worn parts) • Defective shock absorber	• Tighten wheel lug nuts • Have tires balanced • Raise car and spin the wheel. If the wheel is bent, it should be replaced • Have wheel alignment checked/adjusted • Check ball joints • Check steering linkage • Check shock absorbers
Tires wear unevenly or prematurely	• Incorrect wheel size • Wheels are out of balance • Wheels are out of alignment	• Check if wheel and tire size are compatible • Have wheels balanced • Have wheel alignment checked/adjusted

Troubleshooting Basic Tire Problems

Problem	Cause	Solution
The car's front end vibrates at high speeds and the steering wheel shakes	• Wheels out of balance • Front end needs aligning	• Have wheels balanced • Have front end alignment checked
The car pulls to one side while cruising	• Unequal tire pressure (car will usually pull to the low side) • Mismatched tires • Front end needs aligning	• Check/adjust tire pressure • Be sure tires are of the same type and size • Have front end alignment checked
Abnormal, excessive or uneven tire wear See "How to Read Tire Wear"	• Infrequent tire rotation • Improper tire pressure • Sudden stops/starts or high speed on curves	• Rotate tires more frequently to equalize wear • Check/adjust pressure • Correct driving habits
Tire squeals	• Improper tire pressure • Front end needs aligning	• Check/adjust tire pressure • Have front end alignment checked

curacy, engine speed at a given road speed, fuel mileage, acceleration, and ground clearance. Tire makers furnish full measurement specifications. Speedometer drive gears are available from Jeep parts for correction.

NOTE: *Dimensions of tires marked the same size may vary significantly, even among tires from the same maker.*

4. The spare tire should be usable, at least for low speed operation, with the new tires.

You will probably have to remove the side mounted spare for clearance. This is especially true on 1972 and later models, since they have a wider tread and minimal tire-to-spare clearance.

5. There shouldn't be any body interference when loaded, on bumps, or in turning.

The only sure way to avoid problems with these points is to stick to tire and wheel sizes available as factory options.

How to Read Tire Wear

The way your tires wear is a good indicator of other parts of your car. Abnormal wear patterns are often caused by the need for simple tire maintenance, or for front end alignment.

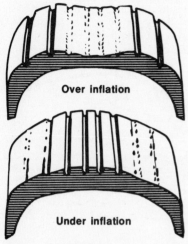

Over inflation

Excessive wear at the center of the tread indicates that the air pressure in the tire is consistently too high. The tire is riding on the center of the tread and wearing it prematurely. Occasionally, this wear pattern can result from outrageously wide tires on narrow rims. The cure for this is to replace either the tires or the wheels.

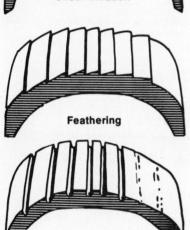

Under inflation

This type of wear usually results from consistent under-inflation. When a tire is under inflated, there is too much contact with the road by the outer treads, which wear prematurely. When this type of wear occurs, and the tire pressure is known to be consistently correct, a bent or worn steering component or the need for wheel alignment could be indicated.

Feathering

Feathering is a condition when the edge of each tread rib develops a slightly rounded edge on one side and a sharp edge on the other. By running your hand over the tire, you can usually feel the sharper edges before you'll be able to see them. The most common causes of feathering are incorrect toe-in setting or deteriorated bushings in the front suspension.

One side wear

When an inner or outer rib wears faster than the rest of the tire, the need for wheel alignment is indicated. There is excessive camber in the front suspension, causing the wheel to lean too much putting excessive load on one side of the tire. Misalignment could also be due to sagging springs, worn ball joints, or worn control arm bushings. Be sure the vehicle is loaded the way it's normally driven when you have the wheels aligned.

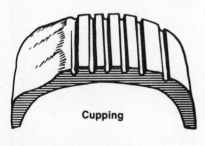

Cupping

Cups or scalloped dips appearing around the edge of the tread almost always indicate worn (sometimes bent) suspension parts. Adjustment of wheel alignment alone will seldom cure the problem. Any worn component that connects the wheel to the car can cause this type of wear. Occasionally, wheels that are out of balance will wear like this, but wheel imbalance usually shows up as bald spots between the outside edges and center of the tread.

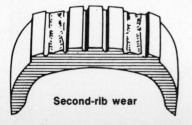

Second-rib wear

Second-rib wear is normally found only in radial tires, and appears where the steel belts end in relation to the tread. Normally, it can be kept to a minimum by paying careful attention to tire pressure and frequently rotating the tires. This is frequently considered normal wear but excessive amounts indicate that the tires are too wide for the wheels.

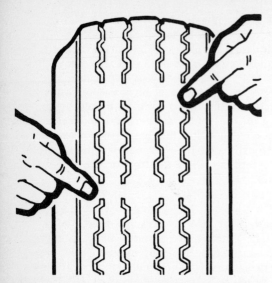

Tread wear indicators are built into all new tires. When they appear, it's time to replace the tires

Tread depth can be checked with a penny; when the top of Lincoln's head is visible, it's time for new tires

TIRE ROTATION

Tire rotation is recommended to obtain maximum tread wear. The pattern you use depends on personal preference, and whether or not you have a usable spare. Radial tires should not be cross-switched. They last longer if their direction of rotation is not changed. Truck type tires sometimes have directional tread indicated by

Tread depth can also be checked with an inexpensive gauge made for the purpose

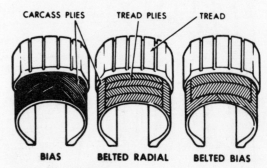

Types of tire construction

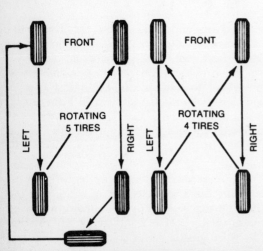

Bias/Bias-Belted Tire Rotation

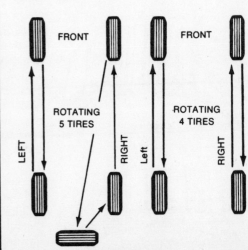

Radial Tire Rotation

Tire rotation

arrows on the sidewalls. The arrow shows the direction of rotation. They will wear very rapidly if reversed. Studded snow tires will lose their studs if their rotation direction is reversed.

NOTE: *Mark the wheel position or direction of rotation on radial, or studded snow tires before removing them.*

CAUTION: *Avoid overtightening the lug nuts to prevent damage to the brake disc or drum. Alloy wheels can also be cracked by overtightening. Use of a torque wrench is highly recommended. Tighten the lug nuts in a criss-cross sequence shown to 85 ft.lb.*

FLUIDS AND LUBRICANTS

Fuel and Oil Recommendations

FUEL

All models through 1974 are designed to use a regular grade of gasoline. All 1975 and later models must use unleaded gasoline.

ENGINE OIL

Many factors help to determine the proper oil for your Jeep. The big question is what viscosity to use and when. The whole question of viscosity revolves around the lowest anticipated ambient temperature to be encountered before your next oil change. The recommended viscosity ratings for temperatures ranging from below 0°F (–18°C) to above + 32°F (0°C) are listed in the accompanying chart. They are broken down into multiviscosities and single viscosities. Multiviscosity oils are recommended because of their wider range of acceptable temperatures and driving conditions.

The SAE grade number indicates the viscosity of the engine oil, or its ability to lubricate under a given temperature. The lower the SAE grade number, the lighter the oil. The lower

Lowest Air Temperature Anticipated	Multiviscosity Engine Oil
Above 40°F	SAE 10W-30, 40, 50 or 20W-40, 50
Above 32°F	SAE 10W-30 or 10W-40
Above 0°F	SAE 10W-30 or 10W-40
Below 0°F	SAE 5W-20 or 5W-30
	Single-Viscosity Engine Oil
Above 40°F	SAE 30 or 40
Above 32°F	SAE 20W-20
Above 0°F	SAE 20
Below 0°F	SAE 10W

Engine oil viscosity selection chart

the viscosity, the easier it is to crank the engine in cold weather.

The API (American Petroleum Institute) designation indicates the classification of engine oil for use under given operating conditions. For gasoline engines, only oils designated for Service SE/SF, or just SF, should be used. You can find the SE or SF marking either on the top or on the side of the container. The viscosity rating should be in the same place. Select the viscosity rating to be used by your type of driving and the temperature range anticipated before the next oil change.

The multiviscosity oils offer the advantage of being adaptable to temperature extremes. They allow easy starts at low temperatures, yet still give good protection at high speeds and warm temperatures.

Engine

OIL LEVEL CHECK

Make sure that your vehicle is on a level surface to ensure an accurate reading. Then, raise

This is the oil's SAE viscosity grade. The numbers followed by a 'W' indicate an oil with low temperature performance characteristics and the 'non-W' numbers describe an oil with high temperature characteristics. If there is one number, it is a single grade. Two or more numbers indicate a 'multi-viscosity' oil which has both low and high temperature characteristics.

This means that the oil will protect expensive engine components. Even if your car is no longer under warranty, it indicates that the oil is of good quality.

This is the manufacturer's brand name.

These letters generally mean that the oil meets or exceeds established standards for use in gasoline (indicated by 'S' and a following letter) and diesel and commercial engines (indicated by 'C' and a following letter). These designations replace the older classifications which may be called for in some owners' manuals. The SF rating is the highest standard for gasoline automobiles.

The top of the oil can will tell you all you need to know about the oil

the hood, position the holdup rod, and measure the oil with the dipstick which is on the left side of 4-cylinder and V8 engines and on the right of 6-cylinder engines. Add oil through the filler pipe on the right side of 4–134 engines, through the valve cover filler hole on 4–150, 4–151, 6–225, 232 and 258, through the filler pipe on the left side of the 6–226 and 6–230, and through the filler pipe at the front of the engine on V8s.

If the oil is below the ADD mark, add a quart of oil, then recheck the level. If the level is still not reading full, add only a half of a quart at a time, until the dipstick reads FULL. Do not overfill the engine. When you check the oil, make sure that you allow sufficient time for all

of the oil to drain back into the crankcase after stopping the engine. A minute or so should be enough time.

OIL AND FILTER CHANGE

Before draining the oil, make sure that the engine is at operating temperature. Hot oil will hold more impurities in suspension and will flow better, removing more oil and dirt.

Drain the oil into a suitable receptacle. After the drain plug is loosened, unscrew the plug with your fingers, using a rag to shield your fingers from the heat. Push in on the plug as you unscrew it so you can feel when all of the screw threads are out of the hole. You can then

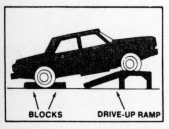

1. Warm the car up before changing your oil. Raise the front end of the car and support it on drive-on ramps or jackstands.

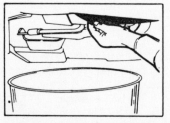

2. Locate the drain plug on the bottom of the oil pan and slide a low flat pan of sufficient capacity under the engine to catch the oil. Loosen the plug with a wrench and turn it out the last few turns by hand. Keep a steady inward pressure on the plug to avoid hot oil from running down your arm.

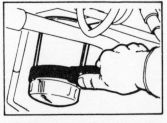

3. Remove the oil filter with a filter wrench. The filter can hold more than a quart of oil, which will be hot. Be sure the gasket comes off with the filter and clean the mounting base on the engine.

4. Lubricate the gasket on the new filter with clean engine oil. A dry gasket may not make a good seal and will allow the filter to leak.

5. Position a new filter on the mounting base and spin it on by hand. Do not use a wrench. When the gasket contacts the engine, tighten it another ½–1 turn by hand.

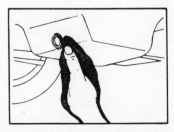

6. Using a rag, clean the drain plug and the area around the drain hole in the oil pan.

7. Install the drain plug and tighten it finger-tight. If you feel resistance, stop and be sure you are not cross-threading the plug. Finally, tighten the plug with a wrench.

8. Locate the oil cap on the valve cover. An oil spout is the easiest way to add oil, but a funnel will do just as well.

9. Start the engine and check for leaks. The oil pressure warning light will remain on for a few seconds; when it goes out, stop the engine and check the level on the dipstick.

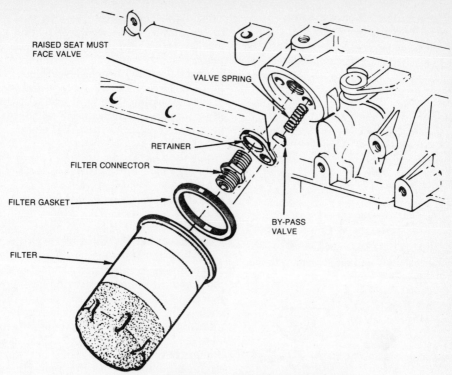

RAISED SEAT MUST
FACE VALVE

VALVE SPRING

RETAINER

FILTER CONNECTOR

FILTER GASKET

BY-PASS
VALVE

FILTER

Spin-on oil filter used on inline sixes and V8

remove the plug quickly with the minimum amount of oil running down your arm. You will also have the plug in your hand and not in the bottom of a pan of hot oil.

Change the oil filter every time you change the oil. The engine should be at operating temperature. On the older L4–134 and F4–134 and all 6–226 engines, the oil filter is located on the right side forward part of the engine. To change the element, remove the bolt, remove the lid, and remove and discard the element. Clean out the cup with a clean, dry cloth and flushing oil or clean, light viscosity engine oil. Clean the lid in the same manner and remove and discard the old gasket. Replace it with a new one. Do not use a solvent that could get into the oil and dilute it. Place the new filter element in the cup. Place the lid on the cup and the bolt down through the center. Tighten the bolt to 10–15 ft.lb. Start the engine and look for leaks. If a leak does develop, turn off the engine and remove the oil filter lid. Inspect the gasket to see if it is seated properly. Adjust the gasket if needed. Replace the lid, start the engine, and check for leaks. if the leak persists, tighten the bolt further.

On the newer F4–134, 4–150, 4–151, 6–225, 6–230, 6–232, 6–258, and 8–304 engines, the oil filter is the spin-on type. On the F4–134 engines, the filter is in the same place as the former cartridge type filter. On the V6 engine, the filter is on the right side of the engine just

below the alternator. On the 6–232 and 258, the filter is located on the lower, center right side of the engine. On the 6–230, it is at the lower left front of the block.

To replace the filter, you will need an oil filter wrench. Loosen the filter with the filter wrench. With a rag wrapped around the filter, unscrew the filter from the oil pump housing. Be careful of hot oil that might run down the side of the filter, especially on the straight sixes and V8s. On the F4–134 engines, the filter is mounted with the open side facing downward so you won't have to worry about oil running down on your hand. Make sure that you have a pan under the filter before you start to remove it from the engine so you won't make a mess and, if some of the hot oil does happen to get on you, you will have a place to dump the filter in a hurry. Wipe the base of the mounting plate with a clean, dry cloth. When you install the new filter, smear a small amount of oil on the gasket with your finger, just enough to coat the entire surface where it comes in contact with the mounting plate. When you tighten the filter, turn it only a quarter of a turn after it comes in contact with the mounting plate.

Manual Transmission
FLUID LEVEL CHECK

The level of lubricant in the transmission should be maintained at the filler hole on all

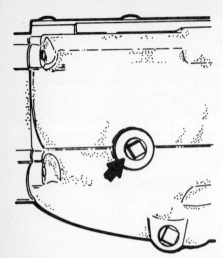

Manual transmission fill and drain plugs with the drain plug at the bottom center

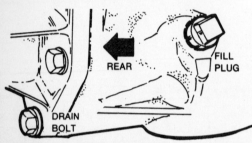

Manual transmission fill and drain plugs, using a tailshaft bolt as the drain plug

manual transmissions. This hole is on the right side. When you check the level in the transmission, make sure that the vehicle is level so that you get a true reading. When you remove the filler plug, lubricant should run out of the hole. Replace the plug quickly for a minimum loss of lubricant. If lubricant does not run out of the hole when the plug is removed, lubricant should be added until it does. Replace the plug as soon as the lubricant reaches the level of the hole.

FLUID CHANGE

Remove the drain plug which is at the bottom of the transmission or else on the side near the bottom. Allow all the lubricant to run out before replacing the plug. Replace the case with the correct viscosity oil. All manual transmissions, except the T4 & T5, use SAE 80W-90 gear oil. The T4 & T5 use Dexron®II automatic transmission fluid.

Automatic Transmission
FLUID LEVEL CHECK

The fluid level in automatic transmissions is checked with a dipstick in the filler pipe at the right rear of the engine. The fluid level should be maintained between the ADD and FULL marks on the end of the dipstick with the automatic transmission fluid at normal operating temperatures. To raise the level from the ADD mark to the FULL mark, requires the addition of one pint of fluid. The fluid level with the fluid at room temperature (75°F) should be approximately ¼" below the ADD mark.

NOTE: *In checking the automatic transmission fluid, insert the dipstick in the filler tube with the markings toward the center of the vehicle. Also, remember that the FULL mark on the dipstick is calibrated for normal operating temperature. This temperature is obtained only after at least 15 miles of expressway driving or the equivalent of city driving.*

1. With the transmission in Park, the engine running at idle speed, the foot brake applied and the vehicle resting on level ground, move the transmission gear selector through each of the gear positions, including Reverse, allowing time for the transmission to engage. Return the shift selector to the Park position and apply the parking brake. Do not turn the engine off, but leave it running at idle speed.

2. Clean all dirt from around the transmission dipstick cap and the end of the filler tube.

3. Pull the dipstick out of the tube, wipe it off with a clean cloth, and push it back into the tube all the way, making sure that it seats completely.

4. Pull the dipstick out of the tube again and read the level of the fluid on the stick. The level should be between the ADD and FULL marks. If fluid must be added, add enough fluid through the tube to raise the level to between the ADD and FULL marks. Do not overfill the transmission because this will cause foaming and loss of fluid through the vent.

NOTE: *Use only Dexron® or Dexron®II transmission fluid.*

DRAIN, FILTER SERVICE AND REFILL

If, when the transmission fluid level is checked, the fluid is noticed to be discolored from a clear red to brown, has a burned smell, or contains water, it should be changed immediately.

1. Drive the vehicle for at least 20 minutes at expressway speeds or the equivalent to raise the temperature of the fluid to its normal operating range.

2. Drain the automatic transmission fluid into an appropriate container before it has cooled. The fluid is drained by loosening the transmission pan and allowing the fluid to run out around the edges. It is best to loosen only one corner of the pan and allow most of the fluid to drain out.

3. Remove the remaining pan screws, and remove the pan and pan gasket.

4. Remove the strainer and discard it.

5. Remove the O-ring seal from the pickup pipe and discard it.

6. Install a new O-ring seal on the pickup pipe and install the new strainer and pipe assembly.

7. Thoroughly clean the bottom pan and position a new gasket on the pan mating surface.

8. Install the pan and tighten the attaching screws to 10–13 ft.lb.

9. Pour about 5 qts. of Dexron® or Dexron®II automatic transmission fluid down the dipstick tube. Make sure that the funnel, container, hose or any other item used to assist in filling the transmission is clean.

10. Start the engine with the transmission in Park. Do NOT race it. Allow the engine to idle for a few minutes.

11. After the engine has been running for a few minutes, move the selector lever through all of the gears.

12. With the selector lever in Park, check the transmission fluid level and adjust as necessary. Remember the transmission fluid must be warm when at the Full mark.

NOTE: *On some 1977–79 models, fluid may overflow through the filler pipe, or vent tube. If this condition occurs:*

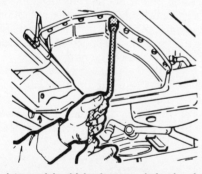

Many late model vehicles have no drain plug. Loosen the pan bolts and allow one corner of the pan to hang, so that the fluid will drain out

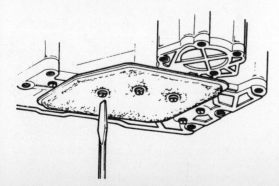

Removing automatic transmission filter

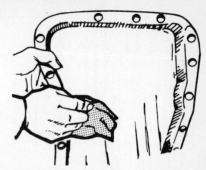

Clean the pan thoroughly with a safe solvent and allow it to air dry

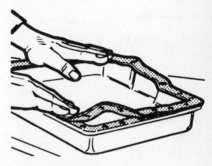

Install a new pan gasket

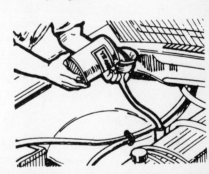

Fill the transmission with the required amount of fluid. Do not overfill. Start the engine and run the selector through all the shift points. Check the fluid and add as necessary

1. Insert a length of stiff wire into the vent tube. If the tube is restricted, clean of replace it.

2. If the tube is not restricted, make sure that the fluid level is correct. If the fluid level is correct perform a road test. If the fluid overflows during the road test.

3. Raise and support the vehicle on jackstands.

4. Loosen the vacuum modulator adapter retaining bolt. Pull the modulator outward about ½–1″. Drain off about 1 pint of fluid. Seat the modulator and tighten the attaching bolt. Lower the vehicle and road test. Check the fluid level and file a new mark on the dipstick for the new fill level.

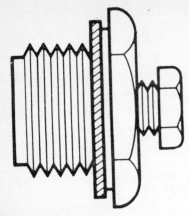

2-piece NP-207 drain plug

Part Time Transfer Case
FLUID LEVEL CHECK

The transfer case should be checked in the same manner as the manual transmission. The level should be up to the filler hole. Use the same viscosity oil as in the transmission. The filler hole is on the right side. Check the oil level at the top hole. The bottom one is for draining.

> NOTE: *Some NP-207 models have a two piece fill plug, i.e., a small threaded plug inside a larger one. If your transfer case is so equipped, the fluid level is checked at the bottom of the smaller plug. To remove the smaller plug, hold the larger one firmly with a wrench while removing the smaller plug.*

DRAIN AND REFILL

All manual transfer cases are to be serviced at the same time and in the same manner as the manual transmissions. The transfer case has its own drain plug which should be opened. Do not rely on the transmission drain plug to completely drain the transfer case, even if they are interconnected. Once the transfer case has been drained, replace the drain plug, remove the fill plug and fill the transfer case. The Dana/Spicer 18 and 20 used SAE 80W-90 gear oil. The NP-207 uses Dexron®II. The Dana 300 uses SAE 85W-90 gear oil. Replace the fill plug.

Quadra-Trac® Full Time Transfer Case
FLUID LEVEL CHECK

Fluid levels in the Quadra-Trac® transfer case and low range reduction unit, if so equipped, should be checked at the same time. The lubricant levels are checked at the filler plug holes. The filler plug holes are located on the rear side of the transfer case assembly, just below center in the middle of the case housing and to the right of center of the reduction unit housing. The lubricant should be level with each filler plug hole. If not, replenish with Quadra-Trac® lubricant.

DRAIN AND REFILL

Remove the filler plugs from both the transfer case and the optional low range reduction unit. Remove the transfer case drain plug and allow the unit to drain. Replace the plug. Loosen the five bolts on the reduction unit (it has no drain plug) and pull it out slightly. Add one pint of Quadra-Trac® lubricant to the reduction unit and install the filler plug. Fill the transfer case to the filler hole level with Quadra-Trac® lubricant and replace the plug.

> CAUTION: *Don't overtighten the filler and drain plugs in the aluminum case. The correct torque is 10–25 ft.lb.*

After changing the fluid, it may be necessary to drive the vehicle in figure 8s for about

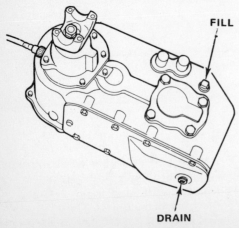

Dana 300 transfer case drain and fill plugs

FILL

DRAIN

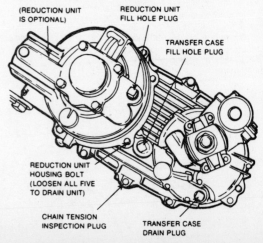

(REDUCTION UNIT IS OPTIONAL)

REDUCTION UNIT FILL HOLE PLUG

TRANSFER CASE FILL HOLE PLUG

REDUCTION UNIT HOUSING BOLT (LOOSEN ALL FIVE TO DRAIN UNIT)

CHAIN TENSION INSPECTION PLUG

TRANSFER CASE DRAIN PLUG

Typical Quadra-Trac external components

fifteen minutes to work the fresh lubricant into the clutches in the transfer case differential.

CAUTION: *Don't hold the steering wheel on full lock for more than about five seconds at a time during these maneuvers. The power steering fluid can overheat and cause pump and gear damage.*

NOTE: *The Quadra-Trac® in some Jeep vehicles may develop a low frequency, pulsating noise or grating or rasping which sometimes occurs in low speed cornering or parking. This is caused by the brake cones releasing suddenly after sticking. The condition is known as stick-slip. As a remedy, AMC/Jeep has introduced a new lubricant, part number 8130444, which must be used in a drain and refill procedure. However, this new lubricant is especially prone to water contamination, so a new vent kit must be installed. The kit is part number 81030445. On vehicles that do not exhibit this problem, the original lubricant, part number 5358652 may be used. Directions for installing the vent kit are supplied with the kit.*

Brake and Clutch Master Cylinders

On models through 1971, the master cylinder is located under the floor. To check the level of the brake fluid remove the floor plate. Clean the area of all dirt so that, when you remove the cover, no dirt will fall in and contaminate the brake fluid. Dirt in the hydraulic system could score the inside of the master cylinder or wheel cylinders and cause leakage or brake failure. Unscrew the lid of the master cylinder with a wrench. The fluid level should be within ½" from the top of the reservoir chamber. Use only heavy duty brake fluid and keep it away from any other fluids or vapors that could contaminate it.

On 1972 and later Jeep vehicles, the master cylinder is located under the hood, on the left side of the firewall. To check the fluid, use a screwdriver to pry off the retaining clip from the lid of the reservoir. The fluid level should be within ¼" of the top of the reservoir.

If the master cylinder is less than half full, there is probably a leak somewhere in the hydraulic system. Investigate the problem before driving the vehicle.

Coolant

COOLANT LEVEL CHECK

The coolant level should be maintained about ½" below the filler neck of the radiator with 4L–134, 4F–134, 6–226 and 6–230 engines.

On the American Motor and GM engines (4, 6, and V8), the coolant level should be maintained 1½–2" below the bottom of the filler cap when the engine is cold. Since operating temperatures reach as high as +205°F (+96°C) for the four and six, and +190°F (+88°C) for the V8s, coolant could be forced out of the radiator if it is filled too high. The radiator coolant level should be checked regularly, such as every time you fill the vehicle with gas. Never open the radiator cap of an engine that hasn't had sufficient time to cool or the pressure can blow off the cap and send out a spray of scalding water.

On systems with a coolant recovery tank, maintain the coolant level at the level marks on the recovery bottle.

For best protection against freezing and overheating, maintain an approximate 50%

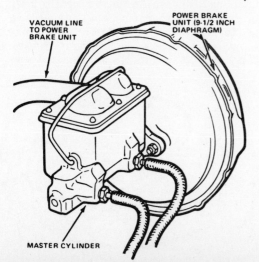

VACUUM LINE TO POWER BRAKE UNIT

POWER BRAKE UNIT (9-1/2 INCH DIAPHRAGM)

MASTER CYLINDER

Typical 1972 and later master cylinder mounting

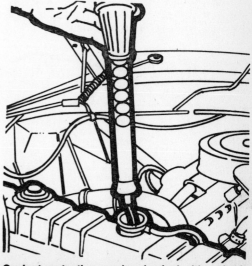

Coolant protection can be checked with a simple float-type tester

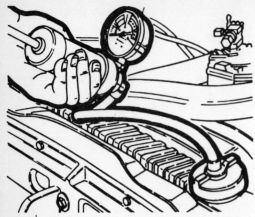

The system should be pressure tested once a year

water and 50% ethylene glycol antifreeze mixture in the cooling system. Do not mix different brands of antifreeze to avoid possible chemical damage to the cooling system.

Avoid using water that is known to have a high alkaline content or is very hard, except in emergency situations. Drain and flush the cooling system as soon as possible after using such water.

CAUTION: *Cover the radiator cap with a thick cloth before removing it from a radiator in a vehicle that is hot. Turn the cap counterclockwise slowly until pressure can be heard escaping. Allow all pressure to escape from the radiator before completely removing the radiator cap. It is best to allow the engine to cool if possible, before removing the radiator cap.*

NOTE: *Never add cold water to an overheated engine while the engine is not running.*

After filling the radiator, run the engine until it reaches normal operating temperature, to make sure that the thermostat has opened and all the air is bled from the system.

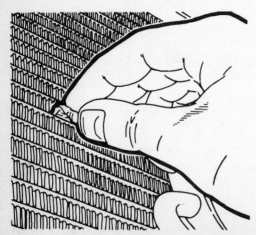

Keep the radiator fins clear for maximum cooling

DRAINING, FLUSHING AND REFILLING

CAUTION: *When draining the coolant, keep in mind that cats and dogs are attracted by the ethylene glycol antifreeze, and are quite likely to drink any that is left in an uncovered container or in puddles on the ground. This will prove fatal in sufficient quantity. Always drain the coolant into a sealable container. Coolant should be reused unless it is contaminated or several years old.*

To drain the cooling system, allow the engine to cool down **BEFORE ATTEMPTING TO REMOVE THE RADIATOR CAP**. Then turn the cap until it hisses. Wait until all pressure is off the cap before removing it completely.

CAUTION: *To avoid burns and scalding, always handle a warm radiator cap with a heavy rag.*

1. At the dash, set the heater TEMP control lever to the fully HOT position.

2. With the radiator cap removed, drain the radiator by loosening the petcock at the bottom of the radiator. Locate any drain plugs in the block and remove them. Flush the radiator with water until the fluid runs clear.

3. Close the petcock and replace the plug(s), then refill the system with a 50/50 mix of ethylene glycol antifreeze. Fill the system to ¾–1¼" (19.05–31.75mm) from the bottom of the filler neck. Reinstall the radiator cap.

NOTE: *If equipped with a fluid reservoir tank, fill it up to the MAX level.*

4. Operate the engine at 2,000 rpm for a few minutes and check the system for signs of leaks.

Radiator Cap Inspection

Allow the engine to cool sufficiently before attempting to remove the radiator cap. Use a rag to cover the cap, then remove by pressing down and turning counterclockwise to the first stop. If any hissing is noted (indicating the release of pressure), wait until the hissing stops com-

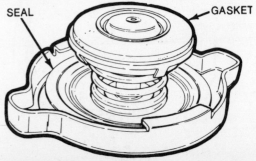

Check the radiator cap's rubber gasket and metal seal for deterioration at least once a year

pletely, then press down again and turn counterclockwise until the cap can be removed.

CAUTION: *DO NOT attempt to remove the radiator cap while the engine is hot. Severe personal injury from steam burns can result.* Check the condition of the radiator cap gasket and seal inside of the cap. The radiator cap is designed to seal the cooling system under normal operating conditions which allows the build up of a certain amount of pressure (this pressure rating is stamped or printed on the cap). The pressure in the system raises the boiling point of the coolant to help prevent overheating. If the radiator cap does not seal, the boiling point of the coolant is lowered and overheating will occur. If the cap must be replaced, purchase the new cap according to the pressure rating which is specified for your vehicle.

Prior to installing the radiator cap, inspect and clean the filler neck. If you are reusing the old cap, clean it thoroughly with clear water. After turning the cap on, make sure the arrows align with the overflow hose.

Axles

FLUID LEVEL CHECK

The standard front and rear axle differentials use SAE 80W/90 gear oil. Either is acceptable for use in the differential housing. Powr-Lok® differentials use only Jeep Powr-Lok® Lubricant or its equivalent. In Trac-Lok® axles, use any limited slip gear oil meeting SAE 75W/90, 80W/90 or 85W/90 specifications. Check the level of the oil in the differential housing every 5,000 miles under normal driving conditions and every 3,000 miles if the vehicle is used in severe driving conditions. The level should be up to the filler hole. When you remove the filler plug, the oil should start to run out. If it does not, replenish the supply until it does.

The lubricant should be changed every 30,000 miles. If running in deep water, change the lubricant daily.

DRAIN AND REFILL

1. Remove the axle differential housing cover and allow the lubricant to drain out into a proper container.

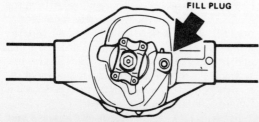

AMC axle fill plug location

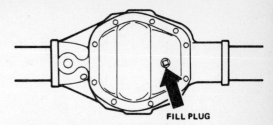

Dana/Spicer axle fill plug location

2. Install the differential housing cover and a new gasket.

3. Tighten the cover attaching bolts to 15–25 ft.lb.

4. Remove the fill plug and add new lubricant to the fill hole level.

5. Replace the fill plug.

NOTE: *Trac-Lok® (limited-slip) differentials may be cleaned only by disassembling the unit and wiping with clean, lint-free rags.*

Manual Steering Gear

FLUID LEVEL CHECK

Through 1971

There is a fill plug on top of the steering gear box. The level should be maintained at the bottom of the fill plug hole. The correct lubricant is SAE 80W/90 gear oil.

1972 and Later

These models use a steering box which is packed with grease. There is normally no need to add lubricant. However, the cover bolt opposite the adjuster may be removed for filling.

Power Steering Reservoir

The level of the fluid should be at the correct point on the dipstick attached to the inside of the lid of the power steering pump. Replenish the supply with DEXRON®II automatic transmission fluid.

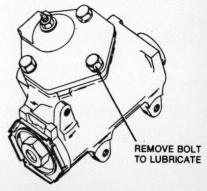

Manual steering gear fill hole

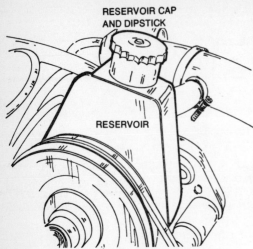

RESERVOIR CAP
AND DIPSTICK

RESERVOIR

Power steering pump dipstick location

Steering Knuckle

The axle shaft universal joints on models through 1971 are located in the steering knuckle and are bathed in oil as they turn. To check the fluid level in the steering knuckle, remove the filler plug from the inside of the knuckle. The fluid should be at the level of the hole. If it is not, replenish the supply. Examine the knuckle for leaks if the level is abnormally low. A leak should be readily visible.

NOTE: *This does not apply to 1972 and later models.*

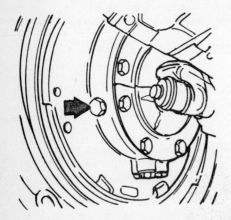

Front axle steering knuckle fill plug location

OUTSIDE VEHICLE MAINTENANCE

Lock Cylinders

Apply graphite lubricant sparingly through the key slot. Insert the key and operate the lock several times to be sure that the lubricant is worked into the lock cylinder.

Door Hinges and Hinge Checks

Spray a silicone lubricant on the hinge pivot points to eliminate any binding conditions. Open and close the door several times to be sure that the lubricant is evenly and thoroughly distributed.

Tailgate

Spray a silicone lubricant on all of the pivot and friction surfaces to eliminate any squeaks or binds. Work the tailgate to distribute the lubricant

Body Drain Holes

Be sure that the drain holes in the doors and rocker panels are cleared of obstruction. A small screwdriver can be used to clear them of any debris.

PUSHING AND TOWING

To push start your vehicle, (manual transmission only) follow the procedures below. Check to make sure that the bumpers of both vehicles are aligned so neither will be damaged. Be sure that all electrical system components are turned off (headlights, heater blower, etc.). Turn on the ignition switch. Place the shift lever in second or third and push in the clutch pedal. At about 15 mph (24 kmh), signal the driver of the pushing vehicle to fall back, depress the accelerator pedal, and release the clutch pedal slowly. The engine should start.

When you are doing the pushing or pulling, make sure that the two bumpers match so you won't damage the vehicle you are to push. Another good idea is to put an old tire in between the two vehicles. If the bumpers don't match, perhaps you should tow the other vehicle. Try to keep your Jeep right up against the other vehicle while you are pushing. If the two vehicles do separate, stop and start over again instead of trying to catch up and ramming the other vehicle. Also try, as much as possible, to avoid riding or slipping the clutch.

If you have to tow the other vehicle, make sure that the tow chain or rope is sufficiently long and strong, and that it is attached securely to both vehicles at a strong place. Attach the chain at a point on the frame or as close to it as possible. Once again, go slowly and tell the other driver to do the same. Warn the other driver not to allow too much slack in the line when he gains traction and can move under his own power. Otherwise he may run over the tow line and damage both vehicles.

If your Jeep must be towed, follow these guidelines:

1. A Jeep with a manual transmission can be towed with either all four wheels or either axle on the ground for any distance at a safe speed with both the transmission and transfer case in Neutral.

2. To tow a Jeep with an automatic transmission and Quadra-Trac*, the driveshaft to the axle(s) remaining on the ground must be disconnected. Be sure to index mark the driveshafts and yoke flanges for alignment upon assembly. Also, the driveshafts must be tied securely up out of the way or removed completely while the vehicle is being towed.

3. A Jeep equipped with an automatic transmission and Quadra-Trac® with the optional low range reduction unit can be towed with all four wheels on the ground without disconnecting the driveshafts. Place the transmission shift lever in Park, the low range reduction unit shift lever in Neutral, and the emergency drive control knob in the Normal position. If the emergency drive system was engaged when the engine was shut down, it will have to be restarted and the emergency drive control knob turned to the Normal position to disengage the system since the control mechanism is vacuum operated.

CAUTION: *Never tow the Jeep with the emergency drive system engaged or the reduction unit in low range.*

In all cases, unnecessary wear and tear can be avoided by disconnecting the driveshafts at the differentials and either tying them up out of the way or removing them altogether. Be sure to index mark the driveshafts and yoke flanges for proper alignment during assembly. If the Jeep is equipped with free running front hubs (manual transmission only), there is no need to remove the front driveshaft, simply disengage the hubs.

TRAILER TOWING

Jeep vehicles have long been popular as trailer towing vehicles. Their strong construction, 4-wheel drive and wide range of engine/transmission combinations make them ideal for towing campers, boat trailers and utility trailers.

Factory trailer towing packages are available on most Jeep vehicles. However, if you are installing a trailer hitch and wiring on your Jeep, there are a few thing that you ought to know.

Trailer Weight

Trailer weight is the first, and most important, factor in determining whether or not your vehicle is suitable for towing the trailer you have

in mind. The horsepower-to-weight ratio should be calculated. The basic standard is a ratio of 35:1. That is, 35 pounds of GVW for every horsepower.

To calculate this ratio, multiply you engine's rated horsepower by 35, then subtract the weight of the vehicle, including passengers and luggage. The resulting figure is the ideal maximum trailer weight that you can tow. One point to consider: a numerically higher axle ratio can offset what appears to be a low trailer weight. If the weight of the trailer that you have in mind is somewhat higher than the weight you just calculated, you might consider changing your rear axle ratio to compensate.

Hitch Weight

There are three kinds of hitches: bumper mounted, frame mounted, and load equalizing.

Bumper mounted hitches are those which attach solely to the vehicle's bumper. Many states prohibit towing with this type of hitch, when it attaches to the vehicle's stock bumper, since it subjects the bumper to stresses for which it was not designed. Aftermarket rear step bumpers, designed for trailer towing, are acceptable for use with bumper mounted hitches.

Frame mounted hitches can be of the type which bolts to two or more points on the frame, plus the bumper, or just to several points on the frame. Frame mounted hitches can also be of the tongue type, for Class I towing, or, of the receiver type, for classes II and III.

Load equalizing hitches are usually used for large trailers. Most equalizing hitches are welded in place and use equalizing bars and chains to level the vehicle after the trailer is hooked up.

The bolt-on hitches are the most common, since they are relatively easy to install.

Check the gross weight rating of your trailer. Tongue weight is usually figured as 10% of gross trailer weight. Therefore, a trailer with a maximum gross weight of 2,000 lb. will have a maximum tongue weight of 200 lb. Class I tarilers fall into this category. Class II trailers are those with a gross weight rating of 2,000–3,500 lb., while Class III trailers fall into the 3,500–6,000 lb. category. Class IV trailers are those over 6,000 lb. and are for use with fifth wheel trucks, only.

When you've determined the hitch that you'll need, follow the manufacturer's installation instructions, exactly, especially when it comes to fastener torques. The hitch will subjected to a lot of stress and good hitches come with hardened bolts. Never substitute an inferior bolt for a hardened bolt.

Recommended Equipment Checklist

Equipment	Class I Trailers Under 2,000 pounds	Class II Trailers 2,000-3,500 pounds	Class III Trailers 3,500-6,000 pounds	Class IV Trailers 6,000 pounds and up
Hitch	Frame or Equalizing	Equalizing	Equalizing	Fifth wheel Pick-up truck only
Tongue Load Limit**	Up to 200 pounds	200-350 pounds	350-600 pounds	600 pounds and up
Trailer Brakes	Not Required	Required	Required	Required
Safety Chain	3/16″ diameter links	1/4″ diameter links	5/16″ diameter links	—
Fender Mounted Mirrors	Useful, but not necessary	Recommended	Recommended	Recommended
Turn Signal Flasher	Standard	Constant Rate or heavy duty	Constant Rate or heavy duty	Constant Rate or heavy duty
Coolant Recovery System	Recommended	Required	Required	Required
Transmission Oil Cooler	Recommended	Recommended	Recommended	Recommended
Engine Oil Cooler	Recommended	Recommended	Recommended	Recommended
Air Adjustable Shock Absorbers	Recommended	Recommended	Recommended	Recommended
Flex or Clutch Fan	Recommended	Recommended	Recommended	Recommended
Tires	***	***	***	***

NOTE: The information in this chart is a guide. Check the manufacturer's recommendations for your car if in doubt.

*Local laws may require specific equipment such as trailer brakes or fender mounted mirrors. Check your local laws. Hitch weight is usually 10-15% of trailer gross weight and should be measured with trailer loaded.

**Most manufacturer's do not recommend towing trailers of over 1,000 pounds with compacts. Some intermediates cannot tow Class III trailers.

***Check manufacturer's recommendations for your specific car/ trailer combination.

—Does not apply

Wiring

Wiring the car for towing is fairly easy. There are a number of good wiring kits available and these should be used, rather than trying to design your own. All trailers will need brake lights and turn signals as well as tail lights and side marker lights. Most states require extra marker lights for overwide trailers. Also, most states have recently required back-up lights for trailers, and most trailer manufacturers have been building trailers with back-up lights for several years.

Additionally, some Class I, most Class II and just about all Class III trailers will have electric brakes.

Add to this number an accessories wire, to operate trailer internal equipment or to charge the trailer's battery, and you can have as many as seven wires in the harness.

Determine the equipment on your trailer and buy the wiring kit necessary. The kit will contain all the wires needed, plus a plug adapter set which included the female plug, mounted on the bumper or hitch, and the male plug, wired into, or plugged into the trailer harness.

When installing the kit, follow the manufacturer's instructions. The color coding of the wires is standard throughout the industry.

One point to note, some domestic vehicles, and most imported vehicles, have separate turn signals. On most domestic vehicles, the brake lights and rear turn signals operate with the same bulb. For those vehicles with separate turn signals, you can purchase an isolation unit so that the brake lights won't blink whenever the turn signals are operated, or, you can go to your local electronics supply house and buy four diodes to wire in series with the brake and turn signal bulbs. Diodes will isolate the brake and turn signals. The choice is yours. The isolation units are simple and quick to install, but far more expensive than the diodes. The diodes, however, require more work to install properly, since they require the cutting of each bulb's wire and soldering in place of the diode.

One, final point, the best kits are those with a spring loaded cover on the vehicle mounted socket. This cover prevent dirt and moisture from corroding the terminals. Never let the vehicle socket hang loosely. Always mount it securely to the bumper or hitch.

Cooling
ENGINE

One of the most common, if not THE most common, problems associated with trailer towing is engine overheating.

With factory installed trailer towing packages, a heavy duty cooling system is usually included. Heavy duty cooling systems are available as optional equipment on most Jeep vehicles, with or without a trailer package. If you have one of these extra-capacity systems, you shouldn't have any overheating problems.

If you have a standard cooling system, without an expansion tank, you'll definitely need to get an aftermarket expansion tank kit, preferably one with at least a 2 quart capacity. These kits are easily installed on the radiator's overflow hose, and come with a pressure cap designed for expansion tanks.

Another helpful accessory is a Flex Fan. These fan are large diameter units are designed to provide more airflow at low speeds, with blades that have deeply cupped surfaces. The blades then flex, or flatten out, at high speed, when less cooling air is needed. These fans are far lighter in weight than stock fans, requiring less horsepower to drive them. Also, they are far quieter than stock fans.

If you do decide to replace your stock fan with a flex fan, note that if your Jeep has a fan clutch, a spacer between the flex fan and water pump hub will be needed.

Aftermarket engine oil coolers are helpful for prolonging engine oil life and reducing overall engine temperatures. Both of these factors increase engine life.

While not absolutely necessary in towing Class I and some Class II trailers, they are recommended for heavier Class II and all Class III towing.

Engine oil cooler systems consist of an adapter, screwed on in place of the oil filter, a remote filter mounting and a multi-tube, finned heat exchanger, which is mounted in front of the radiator or air conditioning condenser.

TRANSMISSION

An automatic transmission is usually recommended for trailer towing. Modern automatics have proven reliable and, of course, easy to operate, in trailer towing.

The increased load of a trailer, however, causes an increase in the temperature of the automatic transmission fluid. Heat is the worst enemy of an automatic transmission. As the temperature of the fluid increases, the life of the fluid decreases.

It is essential, therefore, that you install an automatic transmission cooler.

The cooler, which consists of a multi-tube, finned heat exchanger, is usually installed in front of the radiator or air conditioning compressor, and hooked inline with the transmission cooler tank inlet line. Follow the cooler manufacturer's installation instructions.

Select a cooler of at least adequate capacity, based upon the combined gross weights of the Jeep and trailer.

Cooler manufacturers recommend that you use an aftermarket cooler in addition to, and not instead of, the present cooling tank in your Jeep radiator. If you do want to use it in place of the radiator cooling tank, get a cooler at least two sizes larger than normally necessary.

NOTE: *A transmission cooler can, sometimes, cause slow or harsh shifting in the transmission during cold weather, until the fluid has a chance to come up to normal operating temperature. Some coolers can be purchased with or retrofitted with a temperature bypass valve which will allow fluid flow through the cooler only when the fluid has reached operating temperature, or above.*

JACKING AND HOISTING

Scissors jacks or hydraulic jacks are recommended for all Jeep vehicles. To change a tire, place the jack beneath the spring plate, below the axle, near the wheel to be changed.

Make sure that you are on level ground, that the transmission is in Reverse or with automatic transmissions, Park; the parking brake is set, and the tire diagonally opposite to the one to be changed is blocked so that it will not roll. Loosen the lug nuts before you jack the wheel to be changed completely free of the ground.

If you use a hoist, make sure that the pads of the hoist are located in such a way as to lift on the Jeep frame and not on a shock absorber mount, floor boards, oil pan, or any other part that cannot support the full weight of the vehicle.

HOW TO BUY A USED TRUCK

Many people believe that a two or three year old, or older, truck is a better buy than a new one. This may be true. The new truck suffers the heaviest depreciation in the first few years, but is not old enough to present a lot of costly repairs. Whatever the age of the used truck you want to buy, this section and a little patience will help you select one that should be safe and dependable.

Shopping Tips

1. First, decide what model you want and how much you want to spend.

2. Check the used car lots and your local newspaper ads. Privately owned trucks are usually less expensive, however, you will not get a warranty that, in most cases, comes with a used truck purchased from a dealer.

3. Never shop at night. The glare of the lights makes it easy to miss defects in the paint and faults in the body caused by accident or rust repair.

4. Once you've found a truck that you're interested in, try to get the name and phone number of the previous owner. Contact that person for details about the truck. If he or she refuses information about the truck, shop elsewhere. A private seller can tell you about the truck and its maintenance history, but there are few laws requiring honesty from private citizens who are selling used vehicles. There are laws forbidding the tampering with or turning back a vehicle's odometer mileage reading. These laws apply to both a private seller as well commercial dealers. The law also requires that the seller, or anyone transferring ownership of a vehicle, must provide the buyer with a signed statement indicating the mileage on the odometer at the time of transfer.

5. Write down the year, model and serial number of the truck before you buy it. Then, dial 1–800–424–9393, the toll-free number of the National Highway Traffic Safety Administration, and ask if the truck has ever been included on any manufacturer's recall list. If so, make sure the necessary repairs were made.

6. Use the Used Truck Checklist in this section, and check all the items on the used truck that you are considering. Some items are more important than others. You've already determined how much money you can afford for repairs, and, depending on the price of the truck, you should consider doing some of the needed repairs yourself. Beware, however, of trouble in areas involving operation, safety or emissions. Problems in the Used Truck Checklist are arranged as follows:

1–8: Two or more problems in this segment indicate a lack of maintenance. You should reconsider your selection.

9–13: Indicates a lack of proper care, however, these can usually be corrected with a tune-up or relatively simple parts replacement.

14–17: Problems in the engine or transmission can be very expensive. Walk away from any truck with problems in these areas.

7. If you are satisfied with the apparent condition of the truck, take it to an independent diagnostic center or mechanic for a complete checkout. If your state has a state inspection program, have it inspected immediately before purchase, or specify on the invoice that purchase is conditional on the truck's passing a state inspection.

8. Road test the truck. Refer to the Road Test Checklist in this section. If your original evaluation, and the road test agree, the rest is up to you.

Used Truck Checklist

NOTE: *The numbers on the illustration correspond to the numbers in this checklist.*

1. *Mileage:* Average mileage is about 12,000 miles per year. More than average may indicate hard usage. Catalytic converter equipped models may need converter service beyond the 50,000 mile mark.

2. *Paint:* Check around the tailpipe, molding and windows for overspray, indicating that the truck has been repainted.

3. *Rust:* Check fenders, doors, rocker panels, window moldings, wheelwells, flooring and in the bed, for signs of rust. Any rust at all will be a problem. There is no way to stop the spread of rust, except to replace the part or panel.

4. *Body Appearance:* Check the moldings, bumpers, grille, vinyl roof, glass, doors, tail gate and body panels for overall condition. Check for misalignment, loose holddown clips, ripples, scratches in the glass, rips or patches in the top. Mismatched paint, welding in the bed, severe misalignment of body panels or ripples may indicate crash work.

5. *Leaks:* Get down under the truck and take a good look. There are no "normal" leaks, other than water from the air conditioning condenser drain tube.

6. *Tires:* Check the tire air pressure. A common trick is to pump the tires up hard to make the truck roll more easily. Check the tread wear and the spare tire condition. Uneven wear is a sign that the front end is, or was, out of alignment. See the Troubleshooting Chapter for indications of treadwear.

7. *Shock Absorbers:* Check the shocks by forcing downward sharply on each corner of the truck. Good shocks will not allow the truck to rebound more than twice after you let go.

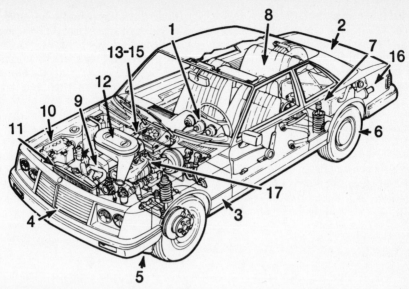

You should check these points when buying a used truck. The "Used Car Checklist" gives an explanation of the numbered items

8. *Interior:* Check the entire interior. You're looking for an interior condition that agrees with the overall condition of the truck. Reasonable wear can be expected, but be suspicious of new seatcovers on sagging seats, new pedal pads, and worn armrests. These indicate an attempt to cover up hard usage. Pull back the carpets and/or mats and look for signs of water leaks or flooding. Look for missing hardware, door handles, control knobs, etc. Check lights and signal operations. Make sure that all accessories, such as air conditioner, heater, radio, etc., work. Air conditioning, especially automatic temperature control units, can be very expensive to repair. Check the operation of the windshield wipers.

9. *Belts and Hoses:* Open the hood and check all belts and hoses for wear, cracks, or weak spots. Check around hose connections for stains, indicating leaks.

10. *Battery:* Low electrolyte level, corroded terminals and/or a cracked battery case, indicate a lack of maintenance.

11. *Radiator:* Look for corrosion or rust in the coolant, indicating a lack of maintenance.

12. *Air Filter:* A dirty air filter element indicates a lack of maintenance.

13. *Spark Plug Wires:* Check the wires for cracks, burned spots or wear. Worn wires will have to be replaced.

14. *Oil Level:* If the level is low, chances are that the engine either uses an excessive amount of oil, or leaks. If the oil on the dipstick appears foamy or tan in color, a leakage of coolant into the oil is indicated. Stop here, and go elsewhere for your truck. If the oil appears thin or has the smell of gasoline, stop here and go elsewhere for your truck.

15. *Automatic Transmission:* Pull the transmission dipstick out when the engine is running in PARK. If the fluid is hot, the dipstick should read FULL. If the fluid is cold, the level will show about one pint low. The fluid itself should be bright red and translucent, with no burned odor. Fluid that is brown or black and has a burned odor is a sign that the transmission needs major repairs.

16. *Exhaust:* Check the color of the exhaust smoke. Blue smoke indicates excessive oil usage, usually due to major internal engine problems. Black smoke can indicate burned valves or carburetor problems. Check the exhaust system for leaks. A leaky system is dangerous and expensive to replace.

17. *Spark Plugs:* Remove one of the spark plugs. An engine in good condition will have spark plugs with a light tan or gray deposit on the electrodes. See the color Tune-Up section for a complete analysis of spark plug condition.

Road Test Check List

1. *Engine Performance:* The truck should have good accelerator response, whether cold or warm, with adequate power and smooth acceleration through the gears.

2. *Brakes:* Brakes should provide quick, firm stops, with no squealing, pulling or fade.

3. *Steering: Sure control with no binding, harshness or looseness, and no shimmy in the wheel should be encountered. Noise or vibration from the steering wheel means trouble.*

4. *Clutch:* Clutch action should be quick and

smooth with easy engagement of the transmission.

5. *Manual Transmission:* The transmission should shift smoothly and crisply with easy change of gears. No clashing and grinding should be evident. The transmission should not stick in gear, nor should there be any gear whine evident at road speed.

6. *Automatic Transmission:* The transmission should shift rapidly and smoothly, with no noise, hesitation or slipping. The transmission should not shift back and forth, but should stay in gear until an upshift or downshift is needed.

7. *Differential:* No noise or thumps should be present. No external leakage should be present.

8. *Driveshaft, Universal Joints:* Vibration and noise could mean driveshaft problems. Clicking at low speed or coast conditions means worn U-joints.

9. *Suspension:* Try hitting bumps at different speeds. A truck that bounces has weak shock absorbers. Clunks mean worn bushings or ball joints.

10. *Frame:* Wet the tires and drive in a straight line. Tracks should show two straight lines, not four. Four tire tracks indicates a frame bent by collision damage. If the tires can't be wet for this purpose, have a friend drive along behind you and see if the truck appears to be traveling in a straight line.

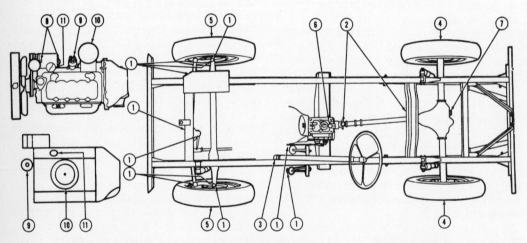

1. Chassis bearings
2. Universal joints
3. Steering gear
4. Rear wheel bearings
5. Front wheel bearings
6. Transmission
7. Differential
8. Generator
9. Distributor
10. Air cleaner
11. Engine oil

DJ series lubrication chart

Capacities Chart

Model	Engine	Crank-case Incl. Filter (qt)	Transmission (pt.)*				Transfer Case (pt.)		Drive Axle (pt.)		Fuel Tank (gal.)	Cooling System (qt)	
			3-sp	4-sp	5-sp	Auto	Man.	Auto	Front	Rear		w/AC	wo/AC
2WD, 4WD	4-134	5.0	3.5	—	—	—	3.50	—	2.5	2.75	10.5	—	12.0
4-63, 4x4-63	4-134	5.0	3.5	—	—	—	3.50	—	2.5	2.75	10.5	—	12.0
6-63	6-226	6.0	(11)	6.75	—	—	(12)	—	3.0	3.0	22.0	—	12.0
4-73	4-134	5.0	3.5	—	—	—	3.50	—	2.5	2.75	10.5	—	12.0
	6-226	6.0	(11)	6.75	—	—	(12)	—	3.0	3.0	22.0	—	12.0
4-75	4-134	5.0	3.5	—	—	—	3.50	—	2.5	2.75	10.5	—	12.0
	6-226	6.0	(11)	6.75	—	—	(12)	—	3.0	3.0	22.0	—	12.0
	6-230	6.0	2.75	6.5	—	—	3.25	—	(13)	3.0	20.0	—	12.0
CJ-2A	4-134	5.0	3.5	—	—	—	3.50	—	2.5	2.75	10.5	—	12.0
CJ-3A	4-134	5.0	3.5	—	—	—	3.50	—	2.5	2.75	10.5	—	12.0
CJ-3B	4-134	5.0	3.0	—	—	—	3.50	—	2.5	2.50	10.5	—	12.0
CJ-5	4-134	5.0	3.0	6.75	—	—	3.50	—	2.5	2.50	10.5	—	12.0
	4-151	3.0	—	3.00	—	—	4.00	—	2.5	4.8	14.8	7.8	7.8
	6-225	4.0	3.0	6.75	—	—	3.50	—	2.5	2.5	10.5	10.0	—
	6-232	5.0	2.5(1)	6.5	—	—	3.25	—	2.5	(2)	16.0	10.5	—
	6-258	5.0	2.5(1)	(3)	4.5	—	(4)	—	2.5	(2)	(5)	10.5	12.0
	8-304	5.0	2.5(1)	(3)	4.5	—	(4)	—	2.5	(2)	(5)	14.0	15.5
CJ-6	4-134	5.0	3.0	6.75	—	—	3.5	—	2.5	2.5	10.5	12.0	—
	6-225	4.0	3.0	6.75	—	—	3.5	—	2.5	2.5	10.5	12.0	—
	6-232	5.0	2.5(1)	6.5	—	—	3.25	—	2.5	(2)	16.0	10.5	—
	6-258	5.0	2.5(1)	(3)	4.5	—	(4)	—	2.5	(2)	(5)	10.5	12.0
	8-304	5.0	2.75	(3)	—	—	3.25	—	2.5	2.5	16.0	10.5	12.0

Capacities Chart (cont.)

Model	Engine	Crankcase Incl. Filter (qt)	Transmission (pt.)*				Transfer Case (pt.)		Drive Axle (pt.)		Fuel Tank (gal.)	Cooling System (qt)	
			3-sp	4-sp	5-sp	Auto	Man.	Auto	Front	Rear		w/AC	wo/AC
CJ-7	4-150	4.0	—	3.9	4.5	—	4.0	—	2.5	4.8	20.0	7.8	7.8
	4-151	3.0	—	3.0	4.5	17.0	4.0	—	2.5	4.8	14.8	7.8	7.8
	6-232	5.0	2.8	6.5	—	—	3.25	—	2.5	4.8	16.0	10.5	—
	6-258	5.0	2.8	③	4.5	⑥	3.25	⑦	2.5	4.8	⑤	10.5	12.0
	8-304	5.0	2.8	③	—	17.0	3.25	⑦	2.5	4.8	⑤	13.0	14.5
Scrambler	4-150	4.0	—	3.9	4.5	17.0	4.0	—	2.5	4.8	20.0	7.8	7.8
	4-151	3.0	—	③	4.5	17.0	4.0	—	2.5	4.8	16.0	7.8	7.8
	6-258	5.0	—	③	4.5	17.0	4.0	—	2.5	4.8	⑧	10.5	12.0
Wrangler	4-150	4.0	—	—	⑨	—	4.5	—	2.5	2.5	⑩	9.0	9.0
	6-258	6.0	—	—	⑨	17.0	4.5	—	2.5	2.5	⑩	10.5	10.5

*The automatic transmission figure is for total capacity. For drain and refill only, use about one half this amount, then run the engine until the fluid is warm and add as much as necessary to bring the level to the full mark on the dipstick.

① 1976 and later: 3.0
② Dana rear: 3.0
AMC 7 9/16" rear: 4.0
AMC 8 7/8" rear: 4.8
③ T-18 6.5
SR-4: 3.0
T-176: 3.5
T-4: 3.9
④ 1972–79: 3.25
1980–83: 4.0
⑤ 1972–79: 16.0
1980 and later: 14.8
⑥ 1976–79: 22.0
1980 and later: 17.0
⑦ Without reduction unit: 3.5
With reduction unit: 4.5
⑧ 1981–83: 16.0
1984–86: 20.0
⑨ AISIN AX5: 7.0
Peugeot BA10/5: 3.5
⑩ Standard: 15.0
Optional: 20.0
⑪ Transmission and transfer case are filled together, sharing a common sump. Total capacity for the 3-speed with transfer case is 6.5 pts.
⑫ Transfer case capacity on vehicles with the optional 4-speed transmission is 3.5 pts.
⑬ Dana 27: 2.5
Dana 44: 3.0

Preventive Maintenance Chart

1945–50

Interval	Item	Service
Every 1,000 miles	Steering linkage	EP chassis lube
	U-Joints	EP chassis lube
	Spring shackles w/fittings	EP chassis lube
	Steering gear level	Check
	Rear wheel bearings w/fittings	Lubricate sparingly
	Manual transmission	Check level
	Transfer case	Check level
	Front axle	Check level
	Rear axle	Check level
	Distributor oiler	Lubricate w/engine oil
	Distributor wick and pivot	Lubricate w/engine oil
	Distributor cam	2cc of silicone grease
	Generator	2–4 drops of engine oil
	6-cyl. heat riser	Lubricate
Every 2,000 miles	Change oil and filter	See oil viscosity chart
	Air cleaner	Clean and refill with engine oil
Every 6,000 miles	Front wheel bearings	Clean and repack
	Fuel filter	Replace
	Oil filler cap	Clean
	Timing and dwell	Check
	Heat riser	Lubricate
	Point, condenser, rotor	Replace
	Spark plugs	Replace
	Drive belts	Check
	Rear wheel bearings wo/fittings	Clean and repack
Every 10,000 miles	Manual transmission	Change fluid
	Transfer case	Change fluid
	Front axle	Change fluid
	Rear axle	Change fluid
Every 12,000 miles	Steering knuckles	Change lubricant
	Speedometer cable	Lubricate
Every 24,000 miles	Engine coolant	Flush and change
	Spark plug wires	Change
Every 300 hours	Power take off	Drain and refill

1951–61

Interval	Item	Service
Every 2,000 miles	Steering linkage	EP chassis lube
	U-joints	EP chassis lube
	Spring shackles w/fittings	EP chassis lube
	Steering gear level	Check
	Rear wheel bearings w/fittings	Lubricate sparingly
	Manual transmission	Check level
	Transfer case	Check level
	Front axle	Check level
	Rear axle	Check level
	Distributor oiler	Lubricate w/engine oil
	Distributor wick and pivot	Lubricate w/engine oil
	Distributor cam	2cc of silicone grease
	Generator	2–4 drops of engine oil
	Change oil and filter (4-134)	See oil viscosity chart
	4-134 air cleaner	Clean and refill with engine oil
Every 6,000 miles	Front wheel bearings	Clean and repack
	Rear wheel bearings wo/fittings	Clean and repack

Preventive Maintenance Chart (cont.)

Interval	Item	Service
Every 10,000 miles	Manual transmission	Change fluid
	Transfer case	Change fluid
	Front axle	Change fluid
	Rear axle	Change fluid
Every 12,000 miles	Steering knuckles	Change lubricant
	Speedometer cable	Lubricate
	Fuel filter	Replace
	PCV valve	Replace
	Oil filler cap	Clean
	Timing and dwell	Check
	Heat riser	Lubricate
	Point, condenser, rotor	Replace
	Spark plugs	Replace
Every 24,000 miles	Spark plug wires	Change
Once a year	Engine coolant	Flush and change

*Severe service

1962–69

Interval	Item	Service
Every 4,000 miles	Engine oil and filter	Change
Every 6,000 miles	Steering gear	Check level
	Differentials	Check level
	King pins	Chassis lube
	Manual transmission	Check level
	Transfer case	Check level
	Clutch cross shaft	Chassis lube
	Air cleaner, dry type	Change filter
	Drive belts	Check
	Air cleaner, oil bath type	Clean and refill
Every 12,000 miles	All chassis lube fittings	EP chassis lube
	Front and rear wheel bearings	Clean and repack
	U-joints	EP chassis lube
	Fuel filter	Replace
	PCV valve	Replace
	Oil filler cap	Clean
	Timing and dwell	Check
	Heat riser	Lubricate
	Point condenser, rotor	Replace
	Spark plugs	Replace
Every 30,000 miles	Differentials	Change fluid
	Manual transmission	Change fluid
	Transfer case	Change fluid
	Spark plug wires	Change

1970–73

Interval	Item	Service
Every 6,000 miles	Engine oil and filter	Change
	Steering gear	Check level
	Differentials	Check level
	Manual transmission	Check level
	Transfer case	Check level
	Drive belts	Check
	Air cleaner	Change filter
Every 12,000 miles	All chassis lube fittings	EP chassis lube
	Front and rear wheel bearings	Clean and repack
	U-joints	EP chassis lube

Preventive Maintenance Chart (cont.)

Interval	Item	Service
Every 12,000 miles	Fuel filter	Replace
	PCV valve	Replace
	Oil filler cap	Clean
	Timing and dwell	Check
	Heat riser	Lubricate
	Point condenser, rotor	Replace
	Spark plugs	Replace
Every 30,000 miles	Differentials	Change fluid
	Manual transmission	Change fluid
	Spark plug wires	Change
	Transfer case	Change fluid

1974–76

Interval	Item	Service
Every 5,000 miles	Engine oil and filter	Change
	Steering gear	Check level
	Power steering reservoir	Check level
	Heat riser	Lubricate
	Differentials	Check level
	Manual transmission	Check level
	Transfer case	Check level
	Automatic transmission	Check level
	All chassis lube fittings	EP chassis lube
	Drive belts	Check
	Air cleaner	Change filter
Every 10,000 miles	Driveshaft splines	EP chassis lube
Every 15,000 miles	Front and rear wheel bearings	Clean and repack
	U-joints	EP chassis lube
	Fuel filter	Replace
	PCV valve	Replace
	Oil filler cap	Clean
	Timing and dwell	Check
	Point, condenser, rotor	Replace
	Spark plugs	Replace
	EGR valve port	Clean
Every 25,000 miles	Automatic transmission	Change fluid and filter
Every 30,000 miles	Differentials	Change fluid
	Manual transmission	Change fluid
	Spark plug wires	Change
	Model 20 transfer case	Change fluid

1977–79

Interval	Item	Service
Every 5,000 miles	Engine oil and filter	Change
	Steering gear	Check level
	Power steering reservoir	Check level
	Heat riser	Lubricate
	Differentials	Check level
	Manual transmission	Check level
	Transfer case	Check level
	Automatic transmission	Check level
	Air cleaner	Change filter
	Drive belts	Check
Every 10,000 miles	Driveshaft splines	EP chassis lube

1977–79 (cont.)

Interval	Item	Service
Every 15,000 miles	All chassis lube fittings	EP chassis lube
	U-joints	EP chassis lube
	Fuel filter	Replace
	PCV valve	Replace
	Oil filler cap	Clean
	Timing and dwell	Check
	Point, condenser, rotor	Replace
	Spark plugs	Replace
	EGR valve port	Clean .
Every 25,000 miles	Automatic transmission	Change fluid and filter
Every 30,000 miles	Differentials	Change fluid
	Manual transmission	Change fluid
	Model 20 transfer case	Change fluid
	Spark plug wires	Change
	Front wheel bearings	Clean and repack

1980–86

Interval	Item	Service
Every 5,000 miles	Engine oil and filter	Change
	Steering gear	Check level
	Power steering reservoir	Check level
	Heat riser	Lubricate
	Differentials	Check level
	Manual transmission	Check level
	Transfer case	Check level
	Automatic transmission	Check level
	Air cleaner	Change filter
	Drive belts	Check
Every 10,000 miles	Driveshaft splines	EP chassis lube
Every 15,000 miles	All chassis lube fittings	EP chassis lube
	U-joints	EP chassis lube
	Fuel filter	Replace
	PCV valve	Replace
	Oil filler cap	Clean
	Spark plugs	Replace
	EGR valve port	Clean
Every 25,000 miles	Automatic transmission	Change fluid and filter
Every 30,000 miles	Differentials	Change fluid
	Manual transmission	Change fluid
	Spark plug wires	Change
	Front wheel bearings	Clean and repack
	Transfer case	Change fluid

1987

Interval	Item	Service
Every 5,000 miles	Engine oil and filter	Change
	Steering gear	Check level
	Power steering reservoir	Check level
	Differentials	Check level
	Manual transmission	Check level
	Transfer case	Check level
	Automatic transmission	Check level
	Air cleaner	Change filter
	Drive belts	Check
Every 15,000 miles	All chassis lube fittings	EP chassis lube
	U-joints	EP chassis lube
	Fuel filter	Replace
	PCV valve	Replace
	Oil filler cap	Clean
	Spark plugs	Replace
Every 30,000 miles	Spark plug wires	Change
	Front wheel bearings	Clean and repack
Every 48,000 miles	Manual transmission	Change fluid
	Differentials	Change fluid
	Automatic transmission	Change fluid and filter
	Transfer case	Change fluid

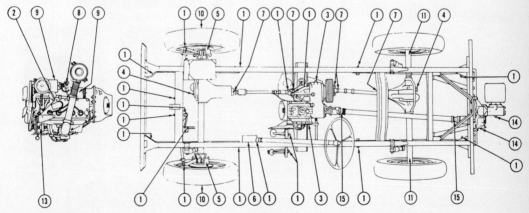

1. Chassis bearings
2. Engine
3. Transmission and transfer case
4. Differentials
5. Front axle U-joints
6. Steering gear
7. Drive shaft U-joints
8. Distributor:
   Oiler
   Wick
   Pivot
   Cam
9. Generator and starter
10. Front wheel bearings
11. Rear wheel bearings
13. Governor
14. Power Take-off (PTO)
15. PTO U-joints

CJ-2A and CJ-3A lubrication chart

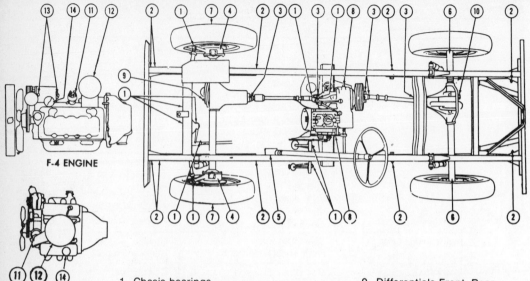

F-4 ENGINE

V-6 ENGINE

1. Chasis bearings
2. Spring shackle bushings
   Spring pivot bolt bushings
   Universal joints
3. Driveshafts
4. Front axle shaft
5. Steering gear housing
6. Rear wheel bearings
7. Front wheel bearings
8. 3 Speed transmission and transfer case
   4 Speed transmission and transfer case[1]

9. Differentials Front, Rear
10. Speedometer cable
11. Distributor
    Oiler
    Wick
    Picot
    Cam
12. Air cleaner
13. Generator
14. Engine

CJ-3B, CJ-5, CJ-6 lubrication chart through 1971

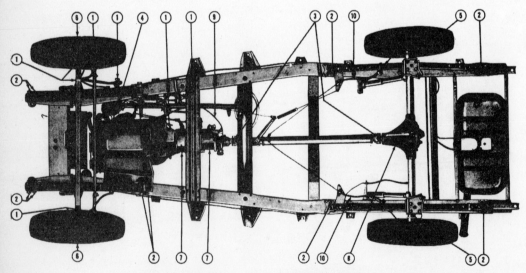

1. Chassis bearings
2. Spring shackle bushings
   Spring pivot bushings
3. Universal joints
4. Steering gear
5. Rear wheels

6. Front wheels
7. Transmission
   Overdrive
8. Differential
9. Speedometer cable
10. Handbrake cable

4-cylinder, 2-wd Utility lubrication chart

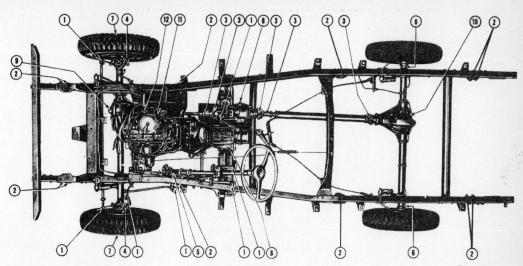

1. Chassis bearings
2. Spring shackle bushings
   Spring pivot bushings
3. Universal joints
4. Front axle shaft
5. Steering gear

6. Rear wheels
7. Front wheels
8. Transmission
   Transfer case
9. Front differential
10. Rear differential

11. Distributor
    Oiler
    Wick
    Pivot
    Cam
12. Air cleaner

4-cylinder, 4-wd Utility lubrication chart

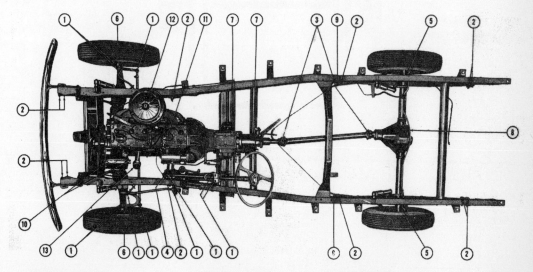

1. Chassis bearings
2. Spring shackle bushings
   Spring pivot bushings
3. Universal joints
4. Steering gear

5. Rear wheels
6. Front wheels
7. Transmission
   Overdrive
8. Differential

9. Handbrake cable
10. Generator
11. Distributor
    Oiler
    Wick

Pivot
Cam
12. Air cleaner
13. Engine oil

6-cylinder, 2-wd Utility lubrication chart

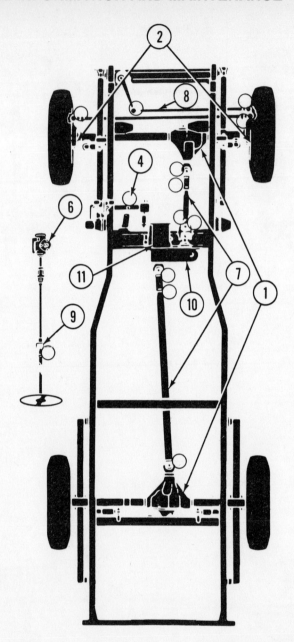

○ LUBRICATION POINTS

1. Differentials
2. Front wheel bearings
3. Not used
4. Clutch lever and linkage
5. Not used
6. Manual steering gear
7. Driveshafts
8. Steering linkage
9. Steering shaft U-joint
10. Transfer case
11. Transmission

1972 and later lubrication chart

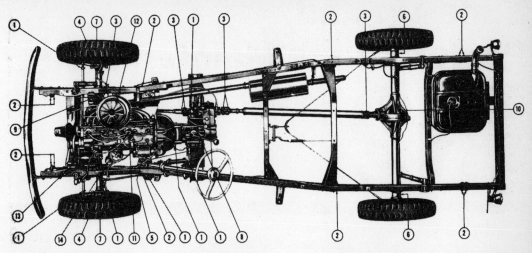

1. Chassis bearings	5. Steering gear	9. Front differential	Pivot
2. Spring shackle bushings	6. Rear wheels	10. Rear differential	Cam
Spring pivot bushings	7. Front wheels	11. Distributor	12. Air cleaner
3. Universal joints	8. Transmission	Oiler	13. Generator
4. Front axle shaft	Transfer case	Wick	14. Engine oil

6-cylinder, 4-wd Utility lubrication chart

Tune-Up and Performance Maintenance

T2

Troubleshooting Engine Performance

Problem	Cause	Solution
Hard starting (engine cranks normally)	• Binding linkage, choke valve or choke piston	• Repair as necessary
	• Restricted choke vacuum diaphragm	• Clean passages
	• Improper fuel level	• Adjust float level
	• Dirty, worn or faulty needle valve and seat	• Repair as necessary
	• Float sticking	• Repair as necessary
	• Faulty fuel pump	• Replace fuel pump
	• Incorrect choke cover adjustment	• Adjust choke cover
	• Inadequate choke unloader adjustment	• Adjust choke unloader
	• Faulty ignition coil	• Test and replace as necessary
	• Improper spark plug gap	• Adjust gap
	• Incorrect ignition timing	• Adjust timing
	• Incorrect valve timing	• Check valve timing; repair as necessary
Rough idle or stalling	• Incorrect curb or fast idle speed	• Adjust curb or fast idle speed
	• Incorrect ignition timing	• Adjust timing to specification
	• Improper feedback system operation	• Refer to Chapter 4
	• Improper fast idle cam adjustment	• Adjust fast idle cam
	• Faulty EGR valve operation	• Test EGR system and replace as necessary
	• Faulty PCV valve air flow	• Test PCV valve and replace as necessary
	• Choke binding	• Locate and eliminate binding condition
	• Faulty TAC vacuum motor or valve	• Repair as necessary
	• Air leak into manifold vacuum	• Inspect manifold vacuum connections and repair as necessary
	• Improper fuel level	• Adjust fuel level
	• Faulty distributor rotor or cap	• Replace rotor or cap
	• Improperly seated valves	• Test cylinder compression, repair as necessary
	• Incorrect ignition wiring	• Inspect wiring and correct as necessary
	• Faulty ignition coil	• Test coil and replace as necessary
	• Restricted air vent or idle passages	• Clean passages
	• Restricted air cleaner	• Clean or replace air cleaner filler element
	• Faulty choke vacuum diaphragm	• Repair as necessary

Troubleshooting Engine Performance (cont.)

Problem	Cause	Solution
Faulty low-speed operation	• Restricted idle transfer slots	• Clean transfer slots
	• Restricted idle air vents and passages	• Clean air vents and passages
	• Restricted air cleaner	• Clean or replace air cleaner filter element
	• Improper fuel level	• Adjust fuel level
	• Faulty spark plugs	• Clean or replace spark plugs
	• Dirty, corroded, or loose ignition secondary circuit wire connections	• Clean or tighten secondary circuit wire connections
	• Improper feedback system operation	• Refer to Chapter 4
	• Faulty ignition coil high voltage wire	• Replace ignition coil high voltage wire
	• Faulty distributor cap	• Replace cap
Faulty acceleration	• Improper accelerator pump stroke	• Adjust accelerator pump stroke
	• Incorrect ignition timing	• Adjust timing
	• Inoperative pump discharge check ball or needle	• Clean or replace as necessary
	• Worn or damaged pump diaphragm or piston	• Replace diaphragm or piston
	• Leaking carburetor main body cover gasket	• Replace gasket
	• Engine cold and choke set too lean	• Adjust choke cover
	• Improper metering rod adjustment (BBD Model carburetor)	• Adjust metering rod
	• Faulty spark plug(s)	• Clean or replace spark plug(s)
	• Improperly seated valves	• Test cylinder compression, repair as necessary
	• Faulty ignition coil	• Test coil and replace as necessary
	• Improper feedback system operation	• Refer to Chapter 4
Faulty high speed operation	• Incorrect ignition timing	• Adjust timing
	• Faulty distributor centrifugal advance mechanism	• Check centrifugal advance mechanism and repair as necessary
	• Faulty distributor vacuum advance mechanism	• Check vacuum advance mechanism and repair as necessary
	• Low fuel pump volume	• Replace fuel pump
	• Wrong spark plug air gap or wrong plug	• Adjust air gap or install correct plug
	• Faulty choke operation	• Adjust choke cover
	• Partially restricted exhaust manifold, exhaust pipe, catalytic converter, muffler, or tailpipe	• Eliminate restriction
	• Restricted vacuum passages	• Clean passages
	• Improper size or restricted main jet	• Clean or replace as necessary
	• Restricted air cleaner	• Clean or replace filter element as necessary
	• Faulty distributor rotor or cap	• Replace rotor or cap
	• Faulty ignition coil	• Test coil and replace as necessary
	• Improperly seated valve(s)	• Test cylinder compression, repair as necessary
	• Faulty valve spring(s)	• Inspect and test valve spring tension, replace as necessary
	• Incorrect valve timing	• Check valve timing and repair as necessary
	• Intake manifold restricted	• Remove restriction or replace manifold
	• Worn distributor shaft	• Replace shaft
	• Improper feedback system operation	• Refer to Chapter 4

Troubleshooting Engine Performance (cont.)

Problem	Cause	Solution
Misfire at all speeds	• Faulty spark plug(s)	• Clean or replace spark plug(s)
	• Faulty spark plug wire(s)	• Replace as necessary
	• Faulty distributor cap or rotor	• Replace cap or rotor
	• Faulty ignition coil	• Test coil and replace as necessary
	• Primary ignition circuit shorted or open intermittently	• Troubleshoot primary circuit and repair as necessary
	• Improperly seated valve(s)	• Test cylinder compression, repair as necessary
	• Faulty hydraulic tappet(s)	• Clean or replace tappet(s)
	• Improper feedback system operation	• Refer to Chapter 4
	• Faulty valve spring(s)	• Inspect and test valve spring tension, repair as necessary
	• Worn camshaft lobes	• Replace camshaft
	• Air leak into manifold	• Check manifold vacuum and repair as necessary
	• Improper carburetor adjustment	• Adjust carburetor
	• Fuel pump volume or pressure low	• Replace fuel pump
	• Blown cylinder head gasket	• Replace gasket
	• Intake or exhaust manifold passage(s) restricted	• Pass chain through passage(s) and repair as necessary
	• Incorrect trigger wheel installed in distributor	• Install correct trigger wheel
Power not up to normal	• Incorrect ignition timing	• Adjust timing
	• Faulty distributor rotor	• Replace rotor
	• Trigger wheel loose on shaft	• Reposition or replace trigger wheel
	• Incorrect spark plug gap	• Adjust gap
	• Faulty fuel pump	• Replace fuel pump
	• Incorrect valve timing	• Check valve timing and repair as necessary
	• Faulty ignition coil	• Test coil and replace as necessary
	• Faulty ignition wires	• Test wires and replace as necessary
	• Improperly seated valves	• Test cylinder compression and repair as necessary
	• Blown cylinder head gasket	• Replace gasket
	• Leaking piston rings	• Test compression and repair as necessary
	• Worn distributor shaft	• Replace shaft
	• Improper feedback system operation	• Refer to Chapter 4
Intake backfire	• Improper ignition timing	• Adjust timing
	• Faulty accelerator pump discharge	• Repair as necessary
	• Defective EGR CTO valve	• Replace EGR CTO valve
	• Defective TAC vacuum motor or valve	• Repair as necessary
	• Lean air/fuel mixture	• Check float level or manifold vacuum for air leak. Remove sediment from bowl.
Exhaust backfire	• Air leak into manifold vacuum	• Check manifold vacuum and repair as necessary
	• Faulty air injection diverter valve	• Test diverter valve and replace as necessary
	• Exhaust leak	• Locate and eliminate leak
Ping or spark knock	• Incorrect ignition timing	• Adjust timing
	• Distributor centrifugal or vacuum advance malfunction	• Inspect advance mechanism and repair as necessary
	• Excessive combustion chamber deposits	• Remove with combustion chamber cleaner
	• Air leak into manifold vacuum	• Check manifold vacuum and repair as necessary
	• Excessively high compression	• Test compression and repair as necessary

Troubleshooting Engine Performance (cont.)

Problem	Cause	Solution
Ping or spark knock (cont.)	• Fuel octane rating excessively low • Sharp edges in combustion chamber • EGR Valve not functioning properly	• Try alternate fuel source • Grind smooth • Test EGR System and replace as necessary
Surging (at cruising to top speeds)	• Low carburetor fuel level • Low fuel pump pressure or volume • Metering rod(s) not adjusted properly (BBD Model Carburetor) • Improper PCV valve air flow • Air leak into manifold vacuum • Incorrect spark advance • Restricted main jet(s) • Undersize main jet(s) • Restricted air vents • Restricted fuel filter • Restricted air cleaner • EGR valve not functioning properly • Improper feedback system operation	• Adjust fuel level • Replace fuel pump • Adjust metering rod • Test PCV valve and replace as necessary • Check manifold vacuum and repair as necessary • Test and replace as necessary • Clean main jet(s) • Replace main jet(s) • Clean air vents • Replace fuel filter • Clean or replace air cleaner filter element • Test EGR System and replace as necessary • Refer to Chapter 4

Tune-up Specifications

Engine	Years	Spark Plugs		Distributor		Ignition Timing (deg.)		Valve * Clearance		Idle Speed	
		Type	Gap (in.)	Point Gap (in.)	Dwell (deg.)	Man. Trans.	Auto. Trans.	In.	Exh.	Man. Trans.	Auto. Trans.
4-134	1945–52	J-8	0.030	①	②	5B	—	0.016	0.016	600	—
	1953–77	J-8	0.030	①	②	5B	—	0.018	0.016	600	—
4-150	1984–86	RFN-14LY	0.035	Electronic		③	—	Hyd.	Hyd.	750	—
	1987	RC-12LYC	0.035	Electronic		④	—	Hyd.	Hyd.	⑤	—
4-151	1980	R44TSX	0.060	Electronic		10B	—	Hyd.	Hyd.	900	—
	1981	R44TSX	0.060	Electronic		10B	12B	Hyd.	Hyd.	900	700
	1982–83	R44TSX	0.060	Electronic		12B	—	Hyd.	Hyd.	900	—
6-225	1965–71	44S	0.035	0.016	30	5B	—	Hyd.	Hyd.	550	—
6-226	1950–60	J-8	0.030	㉘	㉙	5B	—	0.014	0.014	550	—
6-230	1960–64	L-12Y	0.030	0.020	38	5B	—	0.008	0.008	600	—
6-232	1972	N-12Y	0.035	0.016	32	5B	—	Hyd.	Hyd.	675	—
	1973	N-12Y	0.035	0.016	32	5B	—	Hyd.	Hyd.	700	—
	1974	N-12Y	0.035	0.016	32	5B	—	Hyd.	Hyd.	600	—
	1975	N-12Y	0.035	Electronic		5B	—	Hyd.	Hyd.	700	—
	1976	N-12Y	0.035	Electronic		8B	—	Hyd.	Hyd.	600	—
	1977	N-12Y	0.035	Electronic		⑥	—	Hyd.	Hyd.	⑦	—
	1978	N-13L	0.035	Electronic		⑥	—	Hyd.	Hyd.	⑦	—

Tune-up Specifications (cont.)

Engine	Years	Spark Plugs Type	Gap (in.)	Distributor Point Gap (in.)	Dwell (deg.)	Ignition Timing (deg.) Man. Trans.	Auto. Trans.	Valve* Clearance In.	Exh.	Idle Speed Man. Trans.	Auto. Trans.
6-258	1972–73	N-12Y	0.035	0.016	32	3B	—	Hyd.	Hyd.	700	—
	1974	N-12Y	0.035	0.016	32	3B	—	Hyd.	Hyd.	600	—
	1975	N-12Y	0.035	Electronic		3B	—	Hyd.	Hyd.	600	—
	1976	N-12Y	0.035	Electronic		6B	8B	Hyd.	Hyd.	600	⑧
	1977	N-12Y	0.035	Electronic		⑨	⑩	Hyd.	Hyd.	⑪	⑧
	1978	N-13L	0.035	Electronic		⑫	⑩	Hyd.	Hyd.	⑪	550
	1979	N-13L	0.035	Electronic		6B	4B	Hyd.	Hyd.	700	600
	1980	N-14LY	0.035	Electronic		⑬	⑭	Hyd.	Hyd.	700	600
	1981	RFN-14LY	0.035	Electronic		⑮	⑬	Hyd.	Hyd.	650	550
	1982–83	RFN-14LY	0.035	Electronic		⑯	⑯	Hyd.	Hyd.	⑰	⑱
	1984–87	RFN-14LY	0.035	Electronic		⑲	⑲	Hyd.	Hyd.	⑳	㉑
8-304	1972–74	N-12Y	0.035	0.016	32	5B	—	Hyd.	Hyd.	750	—
	1975	N-12Y	0.035	Electronic		5B	—	Hyd.	Hyd.	750	—
	1976	N-12Y	0.035	Electronic		5B	10B	Hyd.	Hyd.	750	700
	1977–78	N-12Y	0.035	Electronic		5B	㉒	Hyd.	Hyd.	750	700
	1979	N-12Y	0.035	Electronic		5B	8B	Hyd.	Hyd.	⑬	600
	1980	N-12Y	0.035	Electronic		㉔	㉕	Hyd.	Hyd.	700	600
	1981	N-12Y	0.035	Electronic		㉖	10B	Hyd.	Hyd.	⑰	600

NOTE: *The specifications on the underhood sticker often reflect changes made during production. If the specifications on your vehicle's sticker disagree with the specifications in this chart, use the sticker specifications.*

*Valve clearance is set on a cold engine.

① Autolite distributor: 0.020
  Delco distributor: 0.022
② Autolite distributor: 42
  Delco distributor: 25–34
③ All except high altitude: 12B
  High altitude: 19B
④ Set by computer; not adjustable
⑤ Not adjustable
⑥ Except high altitude: 5B
  High altitude: 10B
⑦ Except high altitude: 850
  High altitude: 600
⑧ Except Calif.: 550
  Calif.: 700
⑨ Except Calif. and high altitude: 3B
  Calif.: 6B
  High altitude: 10B
⑩ Except high altitude: 8B
  High altitude: 10B
⑪ Except high altitude: 850
  High altitude: 600
⑫ Except Calif. and high altitude: 3B
  Calif.: 8B
  High altitude: 10B
⑬ Except Calif.: 8B
  Calif.: 6B
⑭ Except Calif.: 10B
  Calif.: 8B
⑮ Except Calif.: 8B
  Calif.: 4B

⑯ Except Calif.: 6B
  Calif.: 13B
⑰ Except Calif.: 600
  Calif.: 650
⑱ Except Calif.: 500
  Calif.: 550
⑲ Except high altitude: 9B
  High altitude: 16B
⑳ Except high altitude: 680
  High altitude: 700 [±] 70
㉑ Except high altitude: 600
  High altitude: 650 [±] 70
㉒ Except Calif.: 10B
  Calif.: 5B
㉓ Except Calif.: 700
  Calif.: 750
㉔ Except Calif.: 8B
  Calif.: 5B
㉕ Except Calif.: 12B
  Calif.: 10B
㉖ Except high altitude: 8B
  High altitude: 12B
㉗ Except high altitude: 600
  High altitude: 700
㉘ Autolite distributor: 0.020
  Delco distributor: 0.022
㉙ Autolite distributor: 39
  Delco distributor: 31–37

TUNE-UP PROCEDURES

In order to extract the full measure of performance and economy from your engine it is essential that it be properly tuned at regular intervals. A regular tune-up will keep your vehicle's engine running smoothly and will prevent the annoying minor breakdowns and poor performance associated with an untuned engine.

A complete tune-up should be performed every 12,000 miles or twelve months, whichever comes first. This interval should be halved if the vehicle is operated under severe conditions, such as trailer towing, prolonged idling, continual stop and start driving, or if starting or running problems are noticed. It is assumed that the routine maintenance described in Chapter 1 has been kept up, as this will have a decided effect on the results of a tune-up. All of the applicable steps of a tune-up should be followed in order, as the result is a cumulative one.

If the specifications on the tune-up sticker in the engine compartment disagree with the Tune-Up Specifications chart in this chapter, the figures on the sticker must be used. The sticker often reflects changes made during the production run.

Spark Plugs

Spark plugs ignite the air and fuel mixture in the cylinder as the piston reaches the top of the compression stroke. The controlled explosion that results forces the piston down, turning the crankshaft and the rest of the drive train.

The average life of a spark plug is dependent on a number of factors; the mechanical condition of the engine; the type of fuel; driving conditions; and the driver.

When you remove the spark plugs, check their condition. They are a good indicator of the condition of the engine.

A small deposit of light tan or gray material on a spark plug that has been used for any period of time is to be considered normal. Additives in unleaded fuels may give a number of unusual color indications; for instance, MMT (a manganese anti-knock compound) will cause rust red deposits.

The gap between the center electrode and the side or ground electrode can be expected to increase not more than 0.001" (0.0254mm) every 1,000 miles under normal conditions.

When a spark plug is functioning normally or, more accurately, when the plug is installed in an engine that is functioning properly, the plugs can be taken out, cleaned, regapped, and reinstalled in the engine without doing the engine any harm.

When, and if, a plug fouls and begins to misfire, you will have to investigate, correct the cause of the fouling, and either clean or replace the plug.

There are several reasons why a spark plug will foul and you can learn which reason by just looking at the plug. A few of the most common reasons for plug fouling, and a description of the fouled plug's appearance, is listed in the "Color Insert" section which also offers solutions to the problems.

SPARK PLUG HEAT RANGE

Spark plug heat range is the ability of the plug to dissipate heat. The longer the insulator (or the farther it extends into the engine), the hotter the plug will operate; the shorter the insulator the cooler it will operate. A plug that absorbs little heat and remains too cool will quickly accumulate deposits of oil and carbon since it is not hot enough to burn them off. This leads to plug fouling and consequently to misfiring. A plug that absorbs too much heat will have no deposits, but, due to the excessive heat, the electrodes will burn away quickly and in some instances, preignition may result. Preignition takes place when plug tips get so hot that they glow sufficiently to ignite the fuel/air mixture before the actual spark occurs. This early ignition will usually cause a pinging during low speeds and heavy loads.

The general rule of thumb for choosing the correct heat range when picking a spark plug is: if most of your driving is long distance, high speed travel, use a colder plug; if most of your driving is stop and to, use a hotter plug. Original equipment plugs are compromise plugs, but most people never have occasion to change their plugs from the factory-recommended heat range.

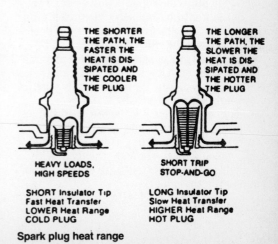

THE SHORTER THE PATH, THE FASTER THE HEAT IS DISSIPATED AND THE COOLER THE PLUG

THE LONGER THE PATH, THE SLOWER THE HEAT IS DISSIPATED AND THE HOTTER THE PLUG

HEAVY LOADS, HIGH SPEEDS

SHORT TRIP STOP-AND-GO

SHORT Insulator Tip
Fast Heat Transfer
LOWER Heat Range
COLD PLUG

LONG Insulator Tip
Slow Heat Transfer
HIGHER Heat Range
HOT PLUG

Spark plug heat range

REMOVAL

1. Remove the wires one at a time and number them so you won't cross them when you replace them.

2. Remove the wire from the end of the spark plug by grasping the wire by the rubber boot. If the boot sticks to the plug, remove it by twisting and pulling at the same time. Do not pull the wire itself or you will most certainly damage the core, or tear the connector.

3. Use a spark plug socket to loosen all of the plugs about two turns.

4. If compressed air is available, blow off the area around the spark plug holes. Otherwise, use a rag or a brush to clean the area. Be careful not to allow any foreign material to drop into the spark plug holes.

5. Remove the plugs by unscrewing them the rest of the way from the engine.

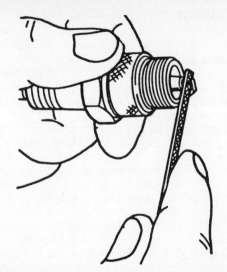

Plugs that are in good condition can be filed and re-used

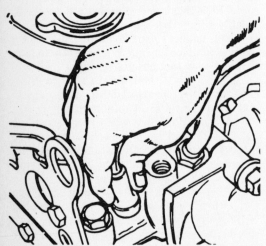

Twist and pull on the rubber boot to remove the spark plug wires; never pull on the wire itself

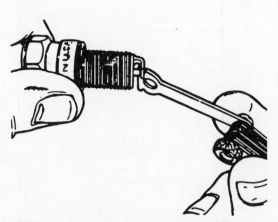

Adjust the electrode gap by bending the side electrode

INSPECTION

Check the plugs for deposits and wear. If they are not going to be replaced, clean the plugs thoroughly. Remember that any kind of deposit will decrease the efficiency of the plug. Plugs can be cleaned on a spark plug cleaning machine, which can sometimes be found in service stations, or you can do an acceptable job of cleaning with a stiff brush.

Check spark plug gap before installation. The ground electrode must be aligned with the center electrode and the specified size wire gauge should pass through the gap with a slight drag. If the electrodes are worn, it is possible to file them level.

INSTALLATION

1. Insert the plugs in the spark plug hole and tighten them hand tight. Take care not to crossthread them.

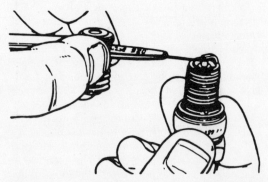

Always use a wire gauge to check the electrode gap

2. Tighten the plugs to 11 ft.lb. on the 4–151; 25–30 ft.lb. on all other engines.

3. Install the spark plug wires on their plugs. Make sure that each wire is firmly connected to each plug.

CHECKING AND REPLACING SPARK PLUG CABLES

Visually inspect the spark plug cables for burns, cuts, or breaks in the insulation. Check the spark plug boots and the nipples on the distributor cap and coil. Replace any damages wiring. If no physical damage is obvious, the wires can be checked with an ohmmeter for excessive resistance.

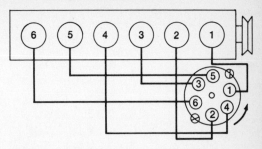

Distributor wiring and firing order: 6-230

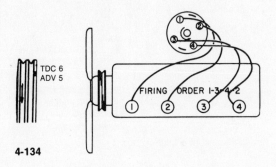

4-134

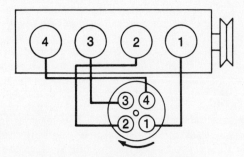

Distributor wiring and firing order: 4-150

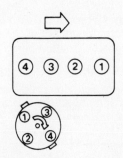

4-151

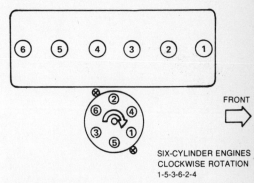

SIX-CYLINDER ENGINES
CLOCKWISE ROTATION
1-5-3-6-2-4

Inline six cylinder engines through 1974 (point-type ignition)

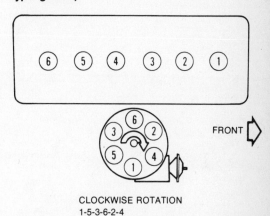

CLOCKWISE ROTATION
1-5-3-6-2-4

SIX-CYLINDER ENGINES

Inline six cylinder engines starting 1975 (electronic ignition)

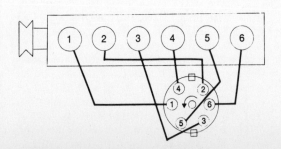

Distributor wiring and firing order: 6-226

V6

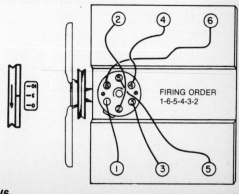

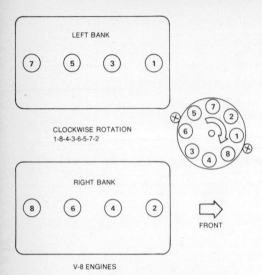

V8 engines through 1974 (point-type ignition)

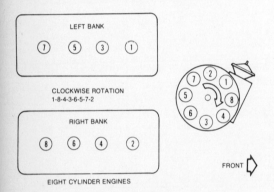

V8 engines starting 1975 (electronic ignition)

When installing a new set of spark plug cables, replace the cables one at a time so there will be no mixup. Start by replacing the longest cable first. Install the boot firmly over the spark plug. Route the wire exactly the same as the original. Insert the nipple firmly into the tower on the distributor cap. Repeat the process for each cable.

HEI Plug Wire Resistance Chart

Wire Length (inches)	Minimum Ohms	Maximum Ohms
Up to 15	3,000	10,000
15–25	4,000	15,000
25–35	6,000	20,000
Over 35		25,000

Breaker Points and Condenser

When you replace a set of points, always replace the condenser at the same time.

NOTE: *These components are not used in electronic ignition systems (1975 and later).*

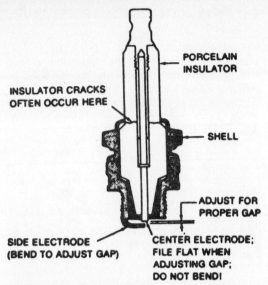

Cross section of a spark plug

When you change the point gap or the dwell, you will also have changed the ignition timing. So, if the point gap or dwell is changed, the ignition timing must be adjusted.

There are two ways to check the breaker point gap; it can be done with a feeler gauge or a dwell meter. Either way you set the amount of time that the points remain closed or open. The time is measured in degrees of gap between the breaker points with a feeler gauge, you are setting the maximum amount the points will open when the rubbing block on the points is on a high point of the distributor cam. When you adjust the points with a dwell meter, you are adjusting the number of degrees that the points will remain closed before they start to open as a high point of the distributor cam approaches the rubbing block.

INSPECTION OF THE POINTS

1. Disconnect the high tension wire from the top of the distributor and the coil, and unsnap the distributor retaining caps.

2. Remove the distributor cap by prying off the spring clips on the L- or F-head, or depressing and turning the holddown screws on the side of the cap on all other engines.

3. Remove the rotor from the distributor shaft by pulling it straight up. On the 304 cu in. V8 and 225 cu. in. V6, the rotor is attached to the distributor shaft by screws. Remove the screws to remove the rotor. Examine the condition of the rotor. If it is cracked or the metal tip is excessively worn or burned, it should be replaced.

4. Pry open the contact points with a screwdriver and check the condition of the contacts. If they are excessively worn, burned, or pitted, they should be replaced.

TROUBLESHOOTING BASIC POINT-TYPE IGNITION SYSTEM PROBLEMS

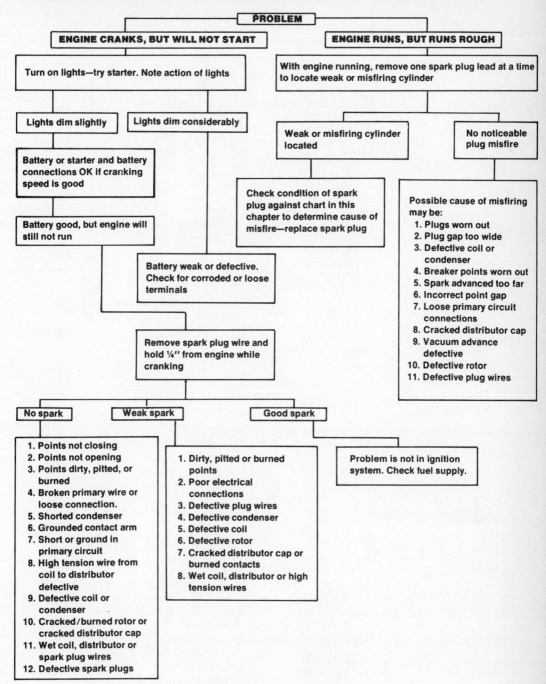

5. If the points are in good condition, adjust them, and replace the rotor and the distributor cap. If the points need to be replaced, follow the replacement procedure below.

REPLACEMENT OF THE BREAKER POINTS AND CONDENSER

NOTE: *Most 1945–71 vehicles were equipped with Autolite ignition systems.*

However, beginning in 1954, some were equipped with Delco systems. Never interchange parts during replacement.

1. Remove the coil high tension wire from the top of the distributor cap. Remove the distributor cap from the distributor and place it out of the way. Remove the rotor from the distributor shaft.

2. Remove the dust cover that is in the top of

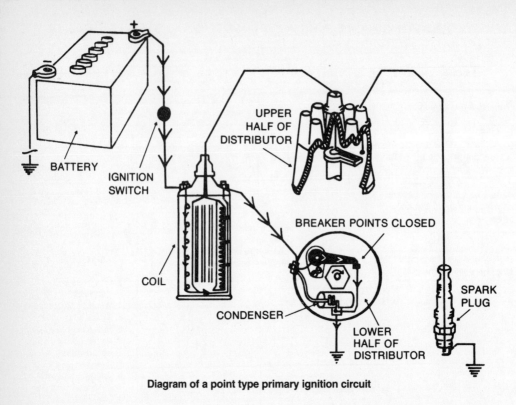

Diagram of a point type primary ignition circuit

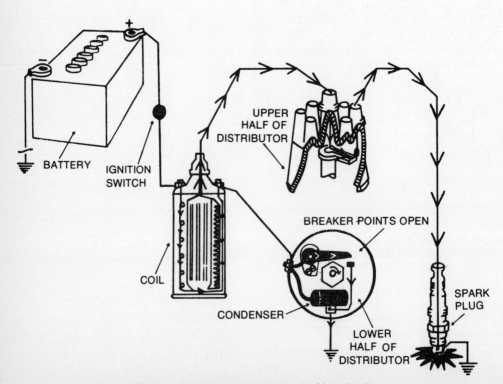

Diagram of a point type secondary ignition circuit

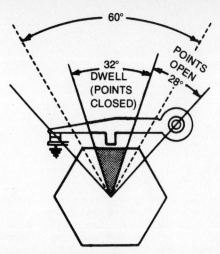

Typical breaker point dwell

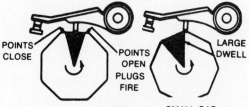

NORMAL DWELL-NORMAL GAP

SMALL GAP EXCESSIVE DWELL

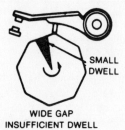

WIDE GAP INSUFFICIENT DWELL

Dwell angle functions

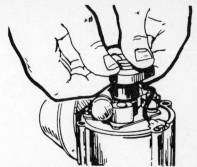

Removing the rotor, except Delco V6 and V8

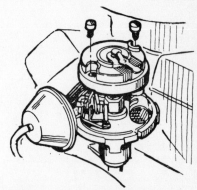

Removing trhe rotor from Delco V6 or V8

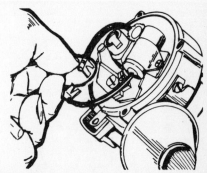

Removing the wires from the points on all but Delco V6 or V8

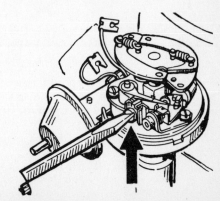

Removing the wires from the points on Delco V6 or V8

the distributor on some models, covering the points. It is pressed in handtight.

3. Loosen the screw that holds the condenser lead to the body of the breaker points. Remove the condenser from the points.

4. Remove the screw that holds and grounds the condenser to the distributor body. Remove the condenser from the distributor and discard it.

5. Remove the points assembly attaching screws and adjustment lockscrews. A screwdriver with a holding mechanism will come in handy so you don't drop a screw into the distributor and have to remove the entire distributor to retrieve it.

6. Remove the points by lifting them straight up off the locating dowel on the plate. Wipe off the cam and apply new cam lubricant. Discard the old set of points.

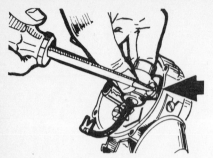

Removing the condenser from all but the Delco V6 or V8

Removing the point set holddown screws from all but Delco V6 or V8

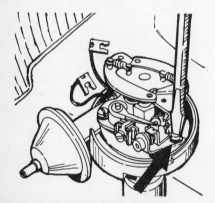

On the Delco V6 and V8 distributors, loosen, but don't remove the point set holddown screws. Slide the point set out from under the screws

7. Slip the new set of points onto the locating dowel and install the screws that hold the assembly onto the plate. Do not tighten them all the way.

8. Attach the new condenser to the plate with the ground screw.

9. Attach the condenser lead to the points at the proper place. On American Motors engines, and the V6, the primary wire from the coil must now be attached to the points also. Make sure that the connectors for these two

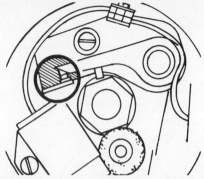

Once the points are installed, make certain that the contact surfaces are properly aligned. If there is misalignment, correct it by bending the STATIONARY arm, NOT THE MOVING ARM! Use a pair of needle-nosed pliers to bend the arm.

wires do not touch the body of the distributor; they will short out the primary circuit of the ignition if they do.

10. Apply a small amount of cam lubricant to the shaft where the rubbing block of the points touches.

ADJUSTMENT OF THE BREAKER POINTS WITH A FEELER GAUGE

1. If the contact points of the assembly are not parallel, bend the stationary contact so they make contact across the entire surface of the contacts. Bend only the bracket part of the point assembly, not the contact surface.

2. Turn the engine until the rubbing block of the points is on one of the high points of the distributor cam. You can do this by either turning the ignition switch to the start position and releasing it quickly or by using a wrench on the bolt that holds the crankshaft pulley to the crankshaft.

3. Place the correct size feeler gauge between the contacts. Make sure it is parallel with the contact surfaces.

4. With your free hand, insert a screwdriver into the notch provided for adjustment or into the eccentric adjusting screw, and then twist the screwdriver to either increase or decrease the gap to the proper setting. V6 and V8 engines have to be adjusted at the adjusting screw with an allen wrench.

5. Tighten the adjustment lockscrew and recheck the contact gap to make sure that it didn't change when the lockscrew was tightened.

6. Replace the rotor, distributor cap, and the high tension wire that connects the top of the distributor and the coil. Make sure that the rotor if firmly seated all the way onto the distributor shaft and that the tab of the rotor is aligned with the notch in the shaft. Align the

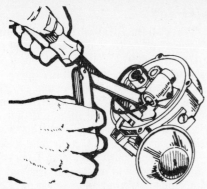

Adjusting the points on all but Delco V6 and V8

Adjusting the points on the Delco V6 and V8

tab in the base of the distributor cap with the notch in the distributor body. Make sure that the cap is firmly seated on the distributor and that the retainers are in place. Make sure that the end of the high tension wire is firmly placed in the top of the distributor and the coil.

ADJUSTMENT OF THE BREAKER POINTS WITH A DWELL METER

NOTE: *Some early models have 6v ignition systems. Make sure your dwell meter has a 6v capability.*

1. Adjust the points with a feeler gauge as described above.

2. Connect the dwell meter to the ignition circuit as according to the manufacturer's instructions. One lead of the meter is to be connected to a ground and the other lead is to be connected to the distributor post on the coil. An adapter is usually provided for this purpose.

3. If the dwell meter has a set line on it, adjust the meter to zero the indicator.

4. Start the engine.

NOTE: *Be careful when working on any vehicle while the engine is running. Make sure that the transmission is in neutral and that the parking brake is on. Keep hands, cloth-*

ing, tools, and the wires of the test instruments clear of the rotating fan blades.

5. Observe the reading on the dwell meter. If the meter does not have a scale for 4-cylinder engines, multiply the 8-cylinder reading by two. If the reading is within the specified range, turn off the engine and remove the dwell meter.

6. If the reading is above the specified range, the breaker point gap is too small. If the reading is below the specified range, the gap is too large. In either case, the engine must be stopped and the gap adjusted in the manner previously covered.

NOTE: *On the V6 engine and V8 engines, it is possible to adjust the dwell while the engine is running.*

7. Start the engine and check the reading on the dwell meter. When the correct reading is obtained, disconnect the dwell meter.

8. Check the adjustment of the ignition timing.

American Motors Breakerless Inductive Discharge Ignition System

During the years 1975 through 1977, all American Motors built engines were equipped with the Breakerless Inductive Discharge (BID) ignition system. The system consists of an electronic ignition control unit, a standard type ignition coil, a distributor that contains an electronic sensor and trigger wheel instead of a cam, breaker points and condenser, and the usual high tension wires and spark plugs. There are no contacting (and thus wearing) surfaces between the trigger wheel and the sensor. The dwell angle remains the same and never requires adjustment. The dwell angle is determined by the control unit and the angle between the trigger wheel spokes.

NOTE: *This book contains simple testing procedures for your Jeep's electronic ignition. More comprehensive testing on this system and other electronic control systems on your Jeep can be found in CHILTON'S GUIDE TO ELECTRONIC ENGINE CONTROLS, book part number 7535, available at your local retailer.*

COMPONENTS

The AMC breakerless inductive discharge (BID) ignition system consists of five components:

Control unit
Coil
Breakerless distributor
Ignition cables
Spark plugs

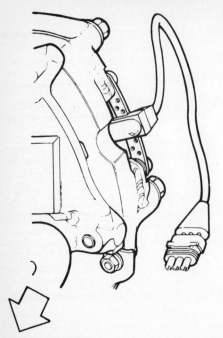

BID distributor sensor

The control unit is a solid state, epoxy sealed module with waterproof connectors. The control unit has a built-in current regulator, so no separate ballast resistor or resistance wire is needed in the primary circuit. Battery voltage is supplied to the ignition coil positive (+) terminal when the ignition key is turned to the ON or START position; low voltage coil primary current is also supplied by the control unit.

In place of the points, cam, and condenser, the distributor has a sensor and trigger wheel. The sensor is a small coil which generates an electromagnetic field when excited by the oscillator in the control unit. This system was last used in 1977.

OPERATION

When the ignition switch is turned on, the control unit is activated. The control unit then sends an oscillating signal to the sensor, which cause the sensor to generate a magnetic field. When one of the trigger wheel teeth enters this field, the strength of the oscillation in the sensor is reduced. One the strength drops to a predetermined level, a demodulator circuit operates the control unit's switching transistor. The switching transistor is wired in series with the coil primary circuit; it switches the circuit off, inducing high voltage in the coil secondary winding when it gets the demodulator signal. From this point on, the BID ignition system works in the same manner as a conventional system.

SYSTEM TEST

1. Check all the BID ignition system electrical connections.

2. Disconnect the coil-to-distributor high tension lead from the distributor cap.

3. Using insulated pliers and a heavy glove, hold the end of the lead ½" (12.7mm) away from a ground. Crank the engine. If there is a spark, the trouble is not in the ignition system. Check the distributor cap, rotor, and wires.

4. Replace the spark plug lead. Turn the ignition switch off and disconnect the coil high tension cable from the center tower on the distributor cap. Place a paper clip around the cable ½–¾" (12.7–19.05mm) from the metal end. Ground the paper clip to the engine. Crank the engine. If there is spark, the distributor cap or rotor may be at fault.

5. Turn the ignition switch off and replace the coil wire. Make the spark test of Step 3 again. If there is no spark, check the coil high tension wire with an ohmmeter. It should show 5–10,000Ω resistance. If not, replace it and repeat the spark test.

6. Detach the distributor sensor lead wire plug. Check the wire connector by trying a no. 16 (0.177") drill bit for a snug fit in the female terminals. Apply a light coat of Silicone Dielectric Compound or its equivalent to the male terminals. Fill the female cavities ¼ full. Reconnect the plug.

7. Repeat the test of Step 4.

8. If there was a spark in Step 7, detach the sensor lead plug and try a replacement sensor. Try the test again. If there is a spark, the sensor was defective.

9. Connect a multitester with a volt scale, between the coil positive terminal and an engine ground. With the ignition switch on, the volt scale should read battery voltage. If it is lower, there is a high resistance between the battery (through the ignition switch) and the coil.

10. Connect the multitester between the coil negative terminal and an engine ground. With the ignition switch on, the voltage should be 5–8. If not, replace the coil. If you get a battery voltage reading, crank the engine slightly to move the trigger wheel tooth away from the sensor; voltage should drop to 5–8.

11. Check the sensor resistance by connecting an ohmmeter to its leads. Resistance should be 1.6–2.4Ω.

COIL TESTING

Test the coil with a conventional coil checker or an ohmmeter. Primary resistance should be 1.25–1.40Ω and secondary resistance should be 9–12KΩ. The open output circuit should be more than 20 kilovolts. Replace the coil if it doesn't meet specifications.

DISTRIBUTOR OVERHAUL

NOTE: *If you must remove the sensor from the distributor for any reason, it will be necessary to have the special sensor positioning gauge in order to align it properly during installation.*

Disassembly

1. Scribe matchmarks on the distributor housing, rotor, and engine block. Disconnect the leads and vacuum lines from the distributor. Remove the distributor. Unless the cap is to be replaced, leave it connected to the spark plug cables and position it out of the way.
2. Remove the rotor and dust cap.
3. Place a small gear puller over the trigger wheel, so that its jaws grip the inner shoulders of the wheel and not its arms. Place a thick washer between the gear puller and the distributor shaft to act as a spacer; do not press against the smaller inner shaft.
4. Loosen the sensor holddown screw with a small pair of needlenosed pliers; it has a tamper proof head. Pull the sensor lead grommet out of the distributor body and pull out the leads from around the spring pivot pin.
5. Release the sensor securing spring by lifting it. Make sure that it clears the leads. Slide the sensor off the bracket. Remember, a special gauge is required for sensor installation.
6. Remove the vacuum advance unit securing screw. Slide the vacuum unit out of the distributor. Remove it only if it is to be replaced.
7. Clean the vacuum unit and sensor brackets. Lubrication of these parts is not necessary.

Assembly

1. Install the vacuum unit, if it was removed.
2. Assemble the sensor, sensor guide, flat washer, and retaining screw. Tighten the screw only far enough to keep the assembly together; don't allow the screw to project below the bottom of the sensor.
NOTE: *Replacement sensors come with a slotted head screw to aid in assembly. If the original sensor is being used, replace the tamperproof screw with a conventional one. Use the original washer.*
3. Secure the sensor on the vacuum advance unit bracket, making sure that the tip of the sensor is placed in the notch on the summing bar.
4. Position the spring on the sensor and route the leads around the spring pivot pin. Fit the sensor lead grommet into the slot on the distributor body. Be sure that the lead can't get caught in the trigger wheel.
5. Place the special sensor positioning gauge over the distributor shaft, so that the flat on the shaft is against the large notch on the gauge. Move the sensor until the sensor core fits into the small notch on the gauge. Tighten the sensor securing screw with the gauge in place (through the round hole in the gauge).
6. It should be possible to remove and install the gauge without any side movement of the sensor. Check this and remove the gauge.
7. Position the trigger wheel on the shaft. Check to see that the sensor core is centered between the trigger wheel legs and that the legs don't touch the core.
8. Bend a piece of 0.050" (1.27mm) gauge wire, so that it has a 90^0 angle and one leg ½" (12.7mm) long. Use the gauge to measure the clearance between the trigger wheel legs and the sensor boss. Press the trigger wheel on the shaft until it just touches the gauge. Support the shaft during this operation.
9. Place 3 to 5 drops of SAE 20 oil on the felt lubricator wick.
10. Install the dust shield and rotor on the shaft.
11. Install the distributor on the engine using the matchmarks made during removal and adjust the timing. Use a new distributor mounting gasket.

American Motors Solid State Ignition (SSI) System

AMC introduced Solid State Ignition (SSI) as a running change on some 1977 Canadian models. It is standard equipment on all 1978 and later American Motors built engines, except the 1987 4–150.

The system consists of a sensor and toothed trigger wheel inside the distributor, and a permanently sealed electronic control unit which determines dwell, in addition to the coil, ignition wires, and spark plugs.

The trigger wheel rotates on the distributor shaft. As one of its teeth nears the sensor magnet, the magnetic field shifts toward the tooth. When the tooth and sensor are aligned, the magnetic field is shifted to its maximum, signaling the electronic control unit to switch off the coil primary current. This starts an electronic timer inside the control unit, which allows the primary current to remain off only long enough for the spark plug to fire. The timer adjusts the amount of time primary current is off according to conditions, thus automatically adjusting dwell. There is also a special circuit within the control unit to detect and ignore spurious signals. Spark timing is adjusted by both mechanical (centrifugal) and vacuum advance.

A wire of 1.35Ω resistance is spliced into the ignition feed to reduce voltage to the coil during running conditions. The resistance wire is bypassed when the engine is being started so that full battery voltage may be supplied to the coil. Bypass is accomplished by the I-terminal on the solenoid.

SECONDARY CIRCUIT TEST

1. Disconnect the coil wire from the center of the distributor cap.

NOTE: *Twist the rubber boot slightly in either direction, then grasp the boot and pull straight up. Do not pull on the wire, and do not use pliers.*

2. Hold the wire ½" (12.7mm) from a ground with a pair of insulated pliers and a heavy glove. As the engine is cranked, watch for a spark.

3. If a spark appears, reconnect the coil wire. Remove the wire from one spark plug, and test for a spark as above.

CAUTION: *Do not remove the spark plug wires from cylinder 3 on the 4–150, or cylinder 3 or 5 on a 1977–79 6–258 or 1 or 5 on a 1980 and later 6–258, or cylinders 3 or 4 of an 8–360, when performing this test, as sensor damage could occur.*

3. If a spark occurs, the problem is in the fuel system or ignition timing. If no spark occurs, check for a defective rotor, cap, or spark plug wires.

4. If no spark occurs from the coil wire in Step 2, test the coil wire resistance with an ohmmeter. It should be $7,700–9,300\Omega$ at $+75°F$ (24°C) or $12,000\Omega$ maximum at $+93°F$ (34°C).

COIL PRIMARY CIRCUIT TEST

1. Turn the ignition On. Connect a multitester to the coil positive (+) terminal and a ground. If the voltage is 5.5–6.5 volts, go to Step 2. If above 7 volts, go to Step 4. If below 5.5 volts, disconnect the condenser lead and measure. If the voltage is now 5.5–6.5 volts, replace the condenser. If not, go to Step 6.

2. With the multitester connected as in Step 1, read the voltage with the engine cranking. If battery voltage is indicated, the circuit is okay. If not, go to Step 3.

3. Check for a short or open in the starter solenoid I-terminal wire. Check the solenoid for proper operation.

4. Disconnect the wire from the starter solenoid I-terminal, with the ignition On and the multitester connected as in Step 1. If the voltage drops to 5.5–6.5 volts, replace the solenoid.

If not, connect a jumper between the coil negative (–) terminal and a ground. If the voltage drops to 5.5–6.5 volts, go to Step 5. If not, repair the resistance wire.

5. Check for continuity between the coil (–) terminal and D4, and D1 to ground. If the continuity is okay, replace the control unit. If not, check for an open wire and go back to Step 2.

6. Turn ignition Off. Connect an ohmmeter between the + coil terminal and dash connector AV. If above 1.40Ω, repair the resistance wire.

7. With the ignition Off, connect the ohmmeter between connector AV and ignition switch terminal 11. If less than 0.1 ohm, replace the ignition switch or repair the wire, whichever is the cause. If above 0.1 ohm, check connections, and check for defective wiring.

COIL TEST

1. Check the coil for cracks, carbon tracks, etc., and replace as necessary.

2. Connect an ohmmeter across the coil + and – terminals, with the coil connector removed. If $1.13–1.23\Omega$ @ 75°F (24°C), the coil is okay. If not, replace it.

CONTROL UNIT AND SENSOR TEST

1. With the ignition On, remove the coil high tension wire from the distributor cap and hold ½" (12.7mm) from ground with insulated pliers. Disconnect the 4-wire connector at the control unit. If a spark occurs (normal), go to Step 2. If not, go to Step 5.

2. Connect an ohmmeter to D2 and D3. If the resistance is $400–800\Omega$ (normal), go to Step 6. If not, go to Step 3.

3. Disconnect and reconnect the 3-wire connector at distributor. If the reading is now $400–800\Omega$, go to Step 6. If not, disconnect the 3-wire connector and go to Step 4.

4. Connect the ohmmeter across B2 and B3. If $300–800\Omega$, repair the harness between the 3-wire and 4-wire connectors. If not, replace the sensor.

5. Connect the ohmmeter between D1 and the battery negative terminal. If the reading is 0 (0.002 or less), go to Step 2. If above 0.002Ω, there is a bad ground in the cable or at the distributor. Repair the ground and retest.

6. Connect a multitester across D2 and D3. Crank the engine. If the needle fluctuates, the system is okay. If not, either the trigger wheel is defective, or the distributor is not turning. Repair or replace as required.

IGNITION FEED TO CONTROL UNIT TEST

NOTE: *Do not perform this test without first performing the Coil Primary Circuit Test.*

1. With the ignition On, unplug the 2-wire

connector at the module. Connect a multitester between F2 and ground. If the reading is battery voltage, replace the control unit and go to Step 3. If not, go to Step 2.

2. Repair the cause of the voltage reduction: either the ignition switch or a corroded dash connector. Check for a spark at the coil wire. If okay, stop. If not, replace the control unit and check for proper operation.

3. Reconnect the 2-wire connector at the control unit, and unplug the 4-wire connector at the control unit. Connect an ammeter between C1 and ground. If it reads 0.9–1.1 amps, the system is okay. If not, replace the module.

American Motors Solid State (Renix) Ignition System for 1987 4–150 Engines

These engines are equipped with electronically controlled fuel injection. Therefore, the electronic ignition system is different from that used on carbureted engines.

The system consists of:
- a solid state ignition control module (ICM)
- an electronic control module (ECU)
- a forty tooth rotor in the distributor
- TDC sensor mounted at the rear of the engine on the flywheel housing

The control module consists of a solid state ignition circuit and an integrated ignition coil each of which can be removed and serviced separately. Spark timing control is determined by the ignition control module. Signals fromn the ECU relay information about engine load and other driving conditions to both the ICM and fuel injection system electronic control components.

Electrical feed to the ICM is through terminal A of connector 1 (see illustration). Electrical feed occurs only when the ignition switch is in the START and RUN positions. Terminal B of connector 1 is grounded at the engine oil dipstick bracket, along with the ECU ground wire and the O_2 sensor ground.

DIAGNOSIS

Primary System

Primary system diagnosis is made through the diagnostic connector, using the appropriate diagnostic computer. Primary circuit tests are made at (D1–2) B+ after ignition; tachometer voltage is at D1–1; vehicle ground is at D1–3.

Secondary System

1. Remove the center wire from the distributor cap.

2. Using insulated pliers, hold the terminal end about ½" (12.7mm) from the engine head and crank the engine.

3. If a spark jumps from the wire to the head, reconnect the wire and remove a wire from one of the spark plugs.

4. Make a metal extension to insert in the spark plug wire boot, and, holding the wire and extension about ½" (12.7mm) from the head, crank the engine.

5. If a spark occurs, check ECU sensors using tester MS 1700, or equivalent. If the sensors check out okay, the problem is probably in the fuel system.

6. If no spark occurs, The rotor, distributor cap or spark plug wires are defective.

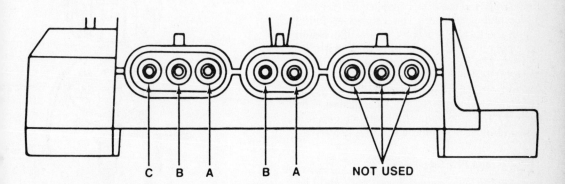

C B A   B A   NOT USED

CONNECTOR 1:
A - Ignition (+)
B - Ground (−)
C - Tach Signal Diagnostic Connector
   D1 - Pin 1

CONNECTOR 2:
A - Not Used
B - ECU Square Wave Output
   Ignition Coil Interface

4-150 ignition control module

Delco High Energy Ignition (HEI) System — 4–151

The General Motors HEI system is a pulse triggered, transistor controlled, inductive discharge ignition system. The entire HEI system is contained within the distributor cap.

The distributor, in addition to housing the mechanical and vacuum advance mechanisms, contains the ignition coil (except on some inline six engines), the electronic control module, and the magnetic triggering device. The magnetic pick-up assembly contains a permanent magnet, a pole piece with internal teeth, and a pick-up coil (not to be confused with the ignition coil).

In the HEI system, as in other electronic ignition systems, the breaker points have been replaced with an electronic switch—a transistor, which is located within the control module. This switching transistor performs the same function the points did in a conventional ignition system; it simply turns coil primary current on and off at the correct time. Essentially then, electronic and conventional ignition systems operate on the same principle.

The module which houses the switching transistor is controlled (turned on and off) by a magnetically generated impulse induced in the pick-up coil. When the teeth of the rotating timer align with the teeth of the pole piece, the induced voltage in the pick-up coil signals the electronic module to open the coil primary circuit. The primary current then decreases, and a high voltage is induced in the ignition coil secondary windings, which is then directed through the rotor and spark plug wires to fire the spark plugs.

In essence, then, the pick-up coil module system simply replaces the conventional breaker points and condenser. The condenser found within the distributor is for radio suppression purposes only and has nothing to do with the ignition process. The module automatically controls the dwell period, increasing it with increasing engine speed. Since dwell is automatically controlled, it cannot be adjusted. The module itself is non-adjustable and non-repairable and must be replaced if found defective.

HEI SYSTEM PRECAUTIONS

Before going on to troubleshooting, it might be a good idea to take note of the following precautions.

Timing Light Use

Inductive pick-up timing lights are the best kind to use with HEI. Timing lights which connect between the spark plug and the spark

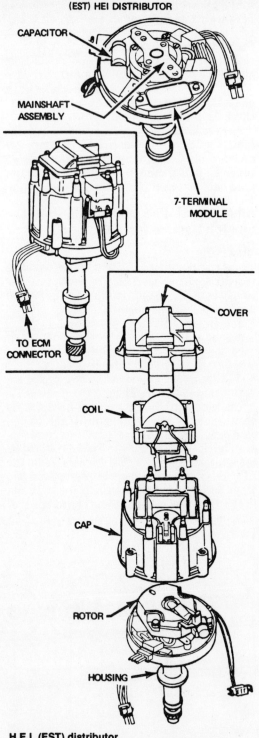

H.E.I. (EST) distributor

plug wire occasionally (not always) give false readings.

Spark Plug Wires

The plug wires used with HEI systems are of a different construction than conventional wires. When replacing them, make sure you get the correct wires, since conventional wires won't carry the voltage. Also handle them carefully to avoid cracking or splitting them and never pierce them.

Tachometer Use

Not all tachometers will operate or indicate correctly when used on an HEI system. While some tachometers may give a reading, this does not necessarily mean the reading is correct. In addition, some tachometers hook up differently from others. If you can't figure out whether or not your tachometer will work on your truck, check with the tachometer manufacturer. Dwell readings have no significance at all.

HEI System Testers

Instruments designed specifically for testing HEI systems are available from several tool manufacturers. Some of these will even test the module itself. However, the test given in the following section will require only a multitester with volt and ohm scales.

TROUBLESHOOTING THE HEI SYSTEM

The symptoms of a defective component within the HEI system are exactly the same as those you would encounter in a conventional system. Some of these symptoms are:

Hard or no starting
Rough idle
Poor fuel economy
Engine misses under load or while accelerating

If you suspect a problem in the ignition system, there are certain preliminary checks which you should carry out before you begin to check the electronic portions of the system.

First, it is extremely important to make sure that the vehicle's battery is in good condition. A defective or poorly charged battery will cause the various components of the ignition system to read incorrectly when tested.

Second, make sure all of the wiring connections are clean and tight, not only at the battery, but also at the distributor cap, coil and module.

Since the major difference between electronic and point type ignition systems is in the distributor area, it is imperative to check the secondary ignition wires first. If the secondary system checks out okay, then the problem is probably not in the ignition system. To check the secondary system, perform a simple spark test. Remove on of the spark plug wires from the plug and insert a makeshift extension made of conductive metal, in the wire boot. Hold the wire and extension about ¼"

(6.35mm) away from the block and crank the engine. If a normal spark occurs, then the problem is most likely not in the ignition system. Check for fuel system problems, or fouled spark plugs.

If, however, there is no spark or a weak spark, then further ignition system testing will have to be done. Troubleshooting techniques fall into two categories, depending on the nature of the problem. The categories are (1) Engine cranks, but won't start, and (2) Engine runs, but runs rough or cuts out.

Engine Fails to Start

If the engine won't start, perform a spark test as described earlier. If no spark occurs, check for the presence of normal battery voltage at the battery (BAT) terminal in the distributor cap. The ignition switch must be in the on position for this test. Either a multitester or a test light may be used for this test. Connect the test light wire to ground and the probe end to the BAT terminal at the distributor. If the light comes on, you have voltage to the distributor. If the light fails to come on, this indicates an open circuit in the ignition primary wiring leading to the distributor. In this case, you will have to check wiring continuity back to the ignition switch using test light. If there is battery voltage at the BAT terminal, but no spark at the plugs, then the problem lies within the distributor assembly. Go on to the distributor components test section.

Engine Runs, but Runs Roughly or Cuts Out

1. Make sure the plug wires are in good shape first. There should be no obvious cracks or breaks. You can check the plug wires with an ohmmeter, but do not pierce the wires with a probe. Check the chart for the correct plug wire resistance.

2. If the plug wires are okay, remove the cap assembly, and check for moisture, cracks, chips, or carbon tracks, or any other high voltage leaks or failures. Replace the cap if you find any defects. Make sure the timer wheel rotates when the engine is cranked. If everything is all right so far, go on to the distributor components test section.

HEI Plug Wire Resistance Chart

Wire Length (inches)	Minimum Ohms	Maximum Ohms
Up to 15	3,000	10,000
15–25	4,000	15,000
25–35	6,000	20,000
Over 35		25,000

Distributor Components Testing

If the trouble has been narrowed down to the units within the distributor, the following tests can help pinpoint the defective component. An ohmmeter with both high and low ranges should be used. These tests are made with the cap assembly removed and the battery wire disconnected.

1. Connect an ohmmeter between the TACH and BAT terminals in the distributor cap. The primary coil resistance should be less than one ohm (zero or nearly zero).

2. To check the coil secondary resistance, connect an ohmmeter between the rotor button and the BAT terminal. Then connect the ohmmeter between the ground terminal and the rotor button. The resistance in both cases should be between 6,000 and 30,000Ω.

3. Replace the coil only if the readings in steps 1 and 2 are infinite.

NOTE: *These resistance checks will not disclose shorted coil windings. This condition can be detected only with scope analysis or a suitably designed coil tester. If these instruments are unavailable, replace the coil with a known good coil as a final coil test.*

4. To test the pick-up coil, first disconnect the white and green module leads. Set the ohmmeter on the high scale and connect it between a ground and either the white or green lead. Any resistance measurement less than infinity requires replacement of the pick-up coil.

5. Pick-up coil continuity is tested by connecting the ohmmeter (on low range) between the white and green leads. Normal resistance is between 500 and 1500Ω. Move the vacuum

advance arm while performing this test. This will detect any break in coil continuity. Such a condition can cause intermittent misfiring. Replace the pick-up coil if the reading is outside the specific limits.

6. If no defects have been found at this time, and you still have a problem, then the module will have to be checked. If you do not have access to a module tester, the only possible alternative is a substitution test. If the module fails the substitution test, replace it.

COMPONENT REPLACEMENT

Integral Ignition Coil

1. Disconnect the feed and module wire terminal connectors from the distributor cap.

2. Remove the ignition set retainer.

3. Remove the 4 coil cover-to-distributor cap screws and coil cover.

4. Remove the 4 coil-to-distributor cap screws.

5. Using a blunt drift, press the coil wire spade terminals up out of distributor cap.

6. Lift the coil up out of the distributor cap.

7. Remove and clean the coil spring, rubber seal washer and coil cavity of the distributor cap.

8. Coat the rubber seal with a dielectric lubricant furnished in the replacement ignition coil package.

9. Reverse the above procedures to install.

Distributor Cap

1. Remove the feed and module wire terminal connectors from the distributor cap.

2. Remove the retainer and spark plug wires from the cap.

3. Depress and release the 4 distributor cap-to-housing retainers and lift off the cap assembly.

4. Remove the 4 coil cover screws and cover.

5. Using a finger or a blunt drift, push the spade terminals up out of the distributor cap.

6. Remove all 4 coil screws and lift the coil, coil spring, and rubber seal washer out of the cap coil cavity.

7. Using a new distributor cap, reverse the above procedures to assembly, being sure to clean and lubricate the rubber seal washer with dielectric lubricant.

Rotor

1. Disconnect the feed and module wire connectors from the distributor.

2. Depress and release the 4 distributor cap to housing retainers and lift off the cap assembly.

3. Remove the two rotor attaching screws and rotor.

4. Reverse the above procedure to install.

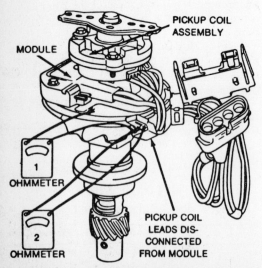

PICKUP COIL ASSEMBLY

MODULE

1 OHMMETER

2 OHMMETER

PICKUP COIL LEADS DISCONNECTED FROM MODULE

Ohmmeter 1 shows the connections for testing the pick-up coil. Ohmmeter 2 shows the connections for testing the pick-up coil continuity

Vacuum Advance

1. Remove the distributor cap and rotor as previously described.

2. Disconnect the vacuum hose from the vacuum advance unit.

3. Remove the two vacuum advance retaining screws, pull the advance unit outward, rotate, and disengage the operating rod from its tang.

4. Reverse the above procedure to install.

Module

1. Remove the distributor cap and rotor as previously described.

2. Disconnect the harness connector and pick-up coil spade connectors from the module. Be careful not to damage the wires when removing the connector.

3. Remove the two screws and module from the distributor housing.

4. Coat the bottom of the new module with dielectric lubricant supplied with the new module. Reverse the above procedure to install.

Ignition Timing

Ignition timing is the measurement, in degrees of crankshaft rotation, of the point at which the spark plugs fire in each of the cylinders. It is measured in degrees before or after Top Dead Center (TDC) of the compression stroke. Ignition timing is controlled by turning the distributor in the engine.

Ideally, the air/fuel mixture in the cylinder will be ignited by the spark plug just as the pis-

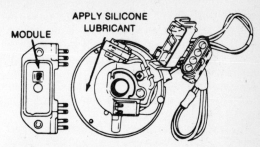

Module replacement; be sure to coat the mating surfaces with silicone lubricant

ton passes TDC of the compression stroke. If this happens, this piston will be beginning the power stroke just as the compressed and ignited air/fuel mixture starts to expand. The expansion of the air/fuel mixture then forces the piston down on the power stroke and turns the crankshaft.

Because it takes a fraction of a second for the spark plug to ignite the gases in the cylinder, the spark plug must fire a little before the piston reaches TDC. Otherwise, the mixture will not be completely ignited as the piston TDC and the full benefit of the explosion will not be used by the engine. The timing measurement is given in degrees of crankshaft rotation before the piston reaches TDC (BTDC). If the setting for the ignition timing is 5 degrees BTDC, the spark plug must fire 5 degrees before that piston reaches TDC. This only holds true, however, when the engine is at idle speed.

As the engine speed increases, the pistons go faster. The spark plugs have to ignite the fuel even sooner if it is to be completely ignited when the piston reaches TDC. To do this, the distributor has a means to advance the timing

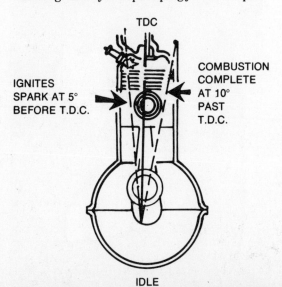

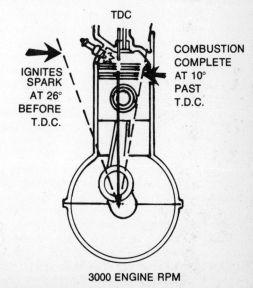

Ignition timing at idle and at 3,000 rpm

of the spark as the engine speed increases. In some Jeep vehicles that were made before 1972, the advancing of the spark in the distributor was accomplished by weights alone. Others have a vacuum diaphragm to assist the weights. It is necessary to disconnect the vacuum line to the distributor when the engine is being timed.

If the ignition is set too far advanced (BTDC), the ignition and expansion of the fuel in the cylinder will occur too soon and tend to force the piston down while it is still traveling up. This causes engine ping. If the engine is too far retarded after TDC (ATDC), the piston will have already passed TDC and started on its way down when the fuel is ignited. This will cause the piston to be forced down for only a portion of its travel. This will result in poor engine performance and lack of power.

The timing is best checked with a timing light. This device is connected in series with the no. 1 spark plug. The current that fires the spark plug also causes the light to flash.

There is a notch on the front of the crankshaft pulley on the 4–134 engine. There are also marks to indicate TDC and 5° BTDC on the timing gear cover that will assist you in setting ignition timing.

On the 6–232 and 6–258, there is a mark on the crankshaft pulley and a scale divided into degrees. The 8–304, 8–350, 8–360, and 8–401 have the same mark and scale arrangement.

The 6–225, and the 6–226 have the scale on the crankshaft pulley and the pointer mark on the engine.

When the engine is running, the timing light is aimed at the marks on the engine and crankshaft pulley.

There are three basic types of timing lights available. The first is a simple neon bulb with two wire connections. One wire connects to the spark plug terminal and the other plugs into the end of the spark plug wire for the No. 1 cylinder, thus connecting the light in series with the spark plug. This type of light is pretty dim and must be held very close to the timing marks to be seen. Sometimes a dark corner has to be sought out to see the flash at all. This type of light is very inexpensive. The second type operates from the car battery – two alligator clips connect to the battery terminals, while an adapter enables a third clip to be connected to the No. 1 spark plug and wire. This type is a bit more expensive, but it provides a nice bright flash that you can see even in bright sunlight. It is the type most often seen in professional shops. The third type replaces the battery power source with 110 volt current.

NOTE: *Connect a tachometer to the BID or SSI ignition system in the conventional way; to the negative (distributor) side of the coil and to a ground. HEI distributor caps have a Tach terminal. Some tachometers may not work with a BID, SSI, or HEI ignition system and there is a possibility that some could be damaged. Check with the manufacturer of the tachometer to make sure it can be used.*

Timing should be checked at each tune-up and any time the points are adjusted or replaced. The timing marks consist of a notch on the rim of the crankshaft pulley and a graduated scale attached to the engine front (timing) cover. A stroboscopic flash (dynamic) timing light must be used, as a static light is too inaccurate for emission controlled engines.

IGNITION TIMING ADJUSTMENT

Point Type Ignition

NOTE: *Some early engines have 6v ignition systems. Make sure your tach/dwell and timing light have 6v capability.*

1. Locate the timing marks on the pulley and on the front of the engine, or on the flywheel on CJ-2A and early CJ-3A engines.

2. Clean off the timing marks so you can see them.

3. Mark the timing marks with a piece of chalk or white paint. Mark the one on the engine that will indicate correct timing when it is aligned with the mark on the pulley or flywheel.

4. Attach a tachometer to the engine.

5. Attach a timing light according to the manufacturer's instructions. If the timing

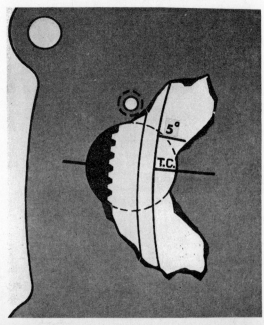

Timing marks on CJ-2A and early CJ-3A flywheel

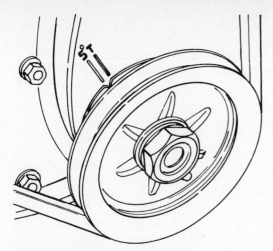

Late CJ-3A and later 4-134 timing marks

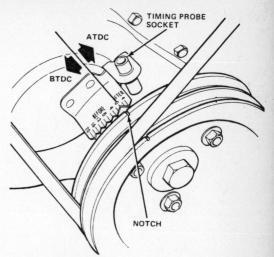

4-151 timing marks

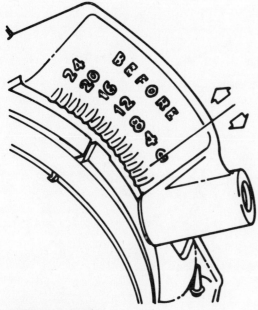

4-150 timing marks

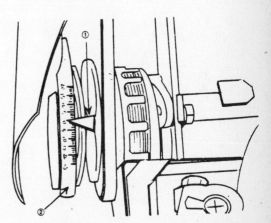

1. Timing pointer   2. Vibration damper

6-226 timing marks

1. Generator mounting bracket
2. Timing scale
3. Notch on the damper

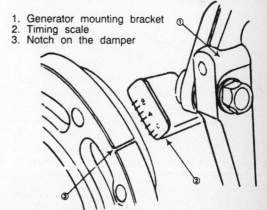

6-230 timing marks

light has three wires, one is attached to the no. 1 spark plug lead with an adapter. The other two are connected to the battery. The red one goes to the positive side of the battery and the black one to the negative terminal.

6. Disconnect the vacuum line to the distributor at the distributor. Plug the end of the hose.

7. Check to make sure that all of the wires clear the fan and then start the engine.

8. If there is an idle speed solenoid, disconnect it.

9. Aim the timing light at the timing marks. If the marks that you put on the pulley and the engine are aligned, the timing is correct. Turn off the engine and remove the ta- chometer and the timing light. If the marks are not in alignment, proceed to the following steps.

10. Turn off the engine.

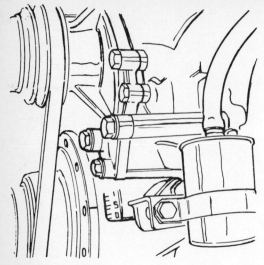

V6-225 timing marks

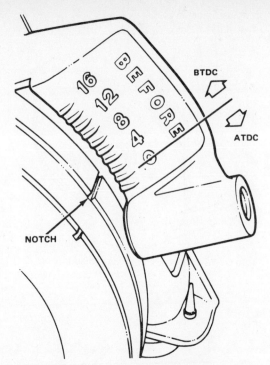

6-258 timing marks with electronic ignition

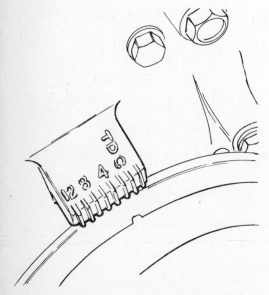

6-232, 258 timing marks with point type ignition

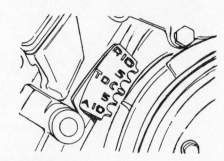

8-304 timing marks

11. Loosen the distributor lockbolt just enough so that the distributor can be turned with a little effort.

12. Start the engine. Keep the cords of the timing light clear of the fan.

13. With the timing light aimed at the pulley and the marks on the engine, turn the distributor in the direction of rotor rotation to retard the spark, and in the opposite direction of rotor rotation to advance the spark. Line up the marks on the pulley and the engine.

14. When the marks are aligned, tighten the distributor lockbolt and recheck the timing with the timing light to make sure that the distributor did not move when you tightened the distributor lockbolt.

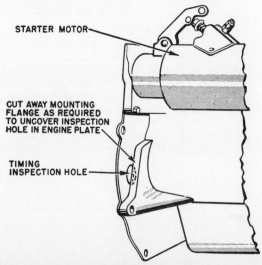

Covered timing hole on CJ-3A engines

15. Turn off the engine and remove the timing light.

NOTE: *On CJ-3A models beginning with engine #130859, a 4½" (114.3mm) starter motor was used. To use the larger starter, it was necessary to increase the width of the cylinder block flange, partially covering the flywheel hole. This makes it impossible to use the hole for timing purposes. In this event, use the timing marks on the crankshaft pulley. If a replacement block is installed with the later design in a vehicle originally equipped with the earlier design timing marks, it will be necessary to cut away enough of the flange to allow a view of the timing marks, as no other timing marks exist on these early engines.*

Electronic Ignition

1. Warm up the engine to normal operating temperature. Stop the engine and connect the timing light to the No. 1 (left front on V8, front on four or six) spark plug wire. Clean off the timing marks and mark the pulley notch and timing scale with white chalk.

2. Disconnect and plug the vacuum line at the distributor. This is done to prevent any distributor vacuum advance.

3. Start the engine and adjust the idle to 500 rpm with the carburetor idle speed screw on 1975–77 Jeep vehicles. On 1978 and later models, set the idle speed to the figure shown on the underhood sticker. This is done to prevent any distributor centrifugal advance. If there is a throttle stop solenoid, disconnect it electrically.

4. Aim the timing light at the pointer marks. Be careful not to touch the fan, because it may appear to be standing still. If the pulley notch isn't aligned with the proper timing mark (refer to the Tune-Up Specifications chart), the timing will have to be adjusted.

NOTE: *TDC or Top Dead Center corresponds to 0 degrees. B, or BTDC, or Before Top Dead Center, may be shown as A for Advanced on a V8 timing scale. R on a V8 timing scale means Retarded, corresponding to ATDC, or After Top Dead Center.*

5. Loosen the distributor clamp locknut. You can buy trick wrenches that make this task a lot easier. Turn the distributor slowly to adjust the timing, holding it by the base and not the cap. Turn counterclockwise to advance timing (toward BTDC), and clockwise to retard (toward TDC or ATDC).

6. Tighten the locknut. Check the timing again, in case the distributor moved slightly as you tightened it.

7. Replace the distributor vacuum line and correct the idle speed to that specified in the Tune-Up Specifications chart.

8. Stop the engine and disconnect the timing light.

VALVE LASH ADJUSTMENT

Valve lash determines how far the valves enter into the cylinder and how long they stay open and closed.

If the valve clearance is too large, part of the lift of the camshaft will be used in removing the excessive clearance. The valve will, consequently, not be opening as far as it should. This condition has two effects; the valve train components will emit a tapping sound as they take up the excessive clearance and the engine will perform poorly. If the valve clearance is too small, the intake valves and the exhaust valves will open too far and they will not fully seat on the cylinder head when they close. When a valve seats itself on the cylinder head, it does two things; it seals the combustion chamber so that none of the gases in the cylinder escape and it cools itself by transferring some of the heat it absorbs from the combustion in the cylinder to the cylinder head and to the engine's cooling system. If the valve clearance is too small, the engine will run poorly because of the gases escaping from the combustion chamber. The valves will also become overheated and will warp, since they cannot transfer heat unless they are touching the valve seat in the cylinder head.

NOTE: *While all valve adjustments must be made as accurately as possible, it is better to have the valve adjustment slightly loose than slightly tight, as burned valves may result from overly tight adjustments.*

The 4–134 F-Head, 6–226 L-head, and the 6–230 OHC engines have adjustable valves. All other engines have hydraulic valve lifters which maintain a zero clearance.

4-134 Engine

The L4-134 has all the valves in the block. Adjustment procedure is the same for all valves. Rotor type exhaust valves were not original equipment, however, some repair kits did supply these. In those cases, follow the specifications for F4-134 engines.

NOTE: *The engine must be cold when the valves are adjusted.*

1. On the F4–134, remove the valve cover. Check all the cylinder head bolts to make sure they are tightened to the correct torque specifications.

2. Remove the valve side cover.

3. Turn the engine until the lifter for the

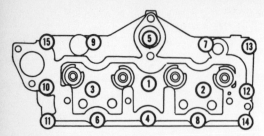

F-head cylinder head torque sequence; L-head is similar

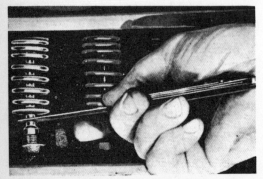

L- and F-head exhaust valve adjustment

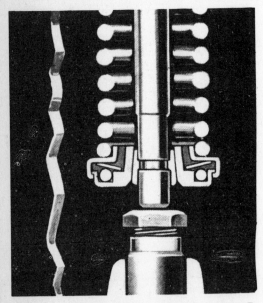

L-head intake and exhaust valve adjustment; F-head exhaust valve adjustment screw

front intake valve is down as far as it will go. The lifter should be resting on the center of the heel (back) of the cam lobe for that valve. You can observe the position of the lifter by looking through the side valve spring cover opening. Put the correct size feeler gauge between the rocker arm and the valve stem. There should be a very slight drag on the feeler gauge when it is pulled through the gap. If there is a slight

drag, the valve is at the correct setting. If the feeler gauge cannot pass between the rocker arm and the valve stem, the gap between them is too small and must be increased. If the gauge can be passed through the gap without any drag, the gap is too large and must be decreased. Loosen the locknut on the top of the rocker arm (pushrod side) by turning it counterclockwise. Turn the adjusting screw clockwise to lessen the gap and counterclockwise to increase the gap. When the gap is correct, turn the locknut clockwise to lock the adjusting screw. Follow this procedure for all of the intake valves, making sure that the lifter is all the way down for each adjustment.

4. Turn the engine so that the first exhaust valve is completely closed and the lifter that operates that particular valve is all of the way down and on the heel of the cam lobe that operates it.

5. Insert the correct size feeler gauge between the valve stem of the exhaust valve and the adjusting screw. This is done through the side of the engine in the space that is exposed when the side valve spring cover is removed. If there is a slight drag on the feeler gauge, you can assume that the gap is correct. If there is too much drag or not enough, turn the adjusting screw clockwise to increase the gap and counterclockwise to decrease the gap.

6. When all of the valves have been adjusted to the proper clearance, replace the covers with new gaskets.

6–226 L-Head

NOTE: *Valves should be adjusted with the engine cold.*

1. Remove the fuel pump.
3. Remove the valve cover.
3. Clearance is adjusted by holding the tap-

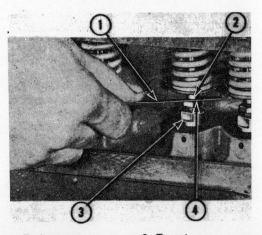

1. Feeler gauge
2. Valve stem
3. Tappet
4. Tappet adjusting screw

Check the 6-226 valve clearance

1. Tappet wrenches

Adjusting the 6-226 valves

pet with one wrench and turning the tappet adjuster with another wrench. Check the clearance with a feeler gauge inserted between the tappet and the end of valve stem. Use the following guide to determine the sequence of valve adjustment. Tappets and valves are numbered consecutively from the front of the engine to the back.

6-226 Tappet Adjustment Sequence

With These Valves Fully Raised	Adjust These Tappets
1 & 3	10 & 12
8 & 9	4 & 5
2 & 6	7 & 11
10 & 12	1 & 3
4 & 5	8 & 9
7 & 11	2 & 6

6–230 OHC

Rocker arm adjustment may be made with the engine hot or cold, but the preferred method is with the engine hot and running. The best way of differentiating between the intake and exhaust valves is to simply note which ones are adjacent to the intake manifold tubes and which are adjacent to the exhaust manifold tubes.

COLD METHOD

1. Run the engine to normal operating temperature, then shut it off.
2. Remove the valve cover.
3. Turn the engine by hand until the first cam lobe points to the 6 o'clock position.
4. Insert a feeler gauge between the rocker arm and the top of the valve stem. Check the Tune-Up Specifications chart for the correct valve clearance.

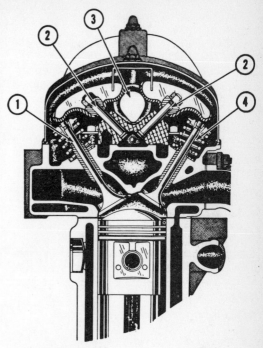

| 1. Exhaust valve | 3. Cam lobe |
| 2. Rocker arm stud | 4. Intake valve |

6-230 valve train

1. Socket wrench   2. Feeler gauge

Adjusting valve clearance on the 6-230

5. Use a socket wrench to turn the adjusting nut until the correct clearance is obtained. A slight drag should be felt on the feeler gauge when you try to remove it.
6. Do each valve in turn, in this manner, turning the engine so that each cam lobe is in the 6 o'clock position.
7. Replace the valve cover, using a new gasket coated with gasket sealer.

HOT METHOD

1. Run the engine to normal operating temperature, then shut it off.
2. Remove the valve cover.
3. Start the engine and let it idle. If the vehicle is equipped with automatic transmission,

set the parking brake, block the wheels and place it in Drive.

4. Proceeding from front to rear, slide the appropriate thickness feeler gauge (see the Tune-Up Specifications chart) between the rocker arm and the top of the valve stem. A slight drag should be felt when withdrawing the gauge. Turn the rocker arm adjusting nut with a socket wrench to give the specified clearance. This is a tricky procedure when done the first time, but it is the most precise way of adjusting the valves.

FUEL SYSTEM

This section contains only tune-up adjustment procedures for fuel systems. Descriptions, adjustments, and overhaul procedures for fuel system components can be found in the Fuel System section of Chapter 4.

IDLE SPEED ADJUSTMENT 1945–74

1. Start the engine and run it until it reaches operating temperature.
2. If it hasn't already been done, check and adjust the ignition timing. After you have set the timing, turn off the engine.
3. Attach a tachometer to the engine.

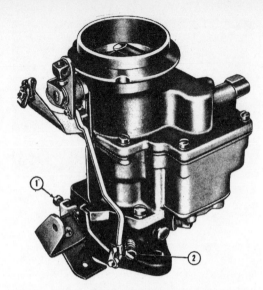

1. Idle speed screw
2. Mixture screw

Early model Cater YF used on the 4-134 and 6-226

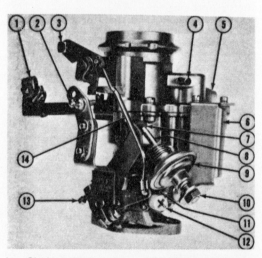

1.	Choke cable bracket	8,9.	Dashpot plunger
2,7.	Throttle lever	10.	Locknut
3.	Choke shaft	11.	Stop pin
4.	Bowl vent	12.	Idle mixture limiter
5.	Fuel inlet	13.	Idle speed screw
6.	Dashpot bracket	14.	Fast idle rod

Late model Carter YF: 4-134

4. Remove the air cleaner, except on 1971 and later model engines. Leave the air cleaner on these models. Turn on the headlights to high beam.
5. Start the engine and, with the transmission in Neutral or Park, check the idle speed on the tachometer. If the reading on the tachometer is correct, turn off the engine and remove the tachometer. If it is not correct, proceed to the following steps.
6. Turn the idle adjusting screw at the bot-

1. Curb idle speed adjusting screw
2. Idle mixture adjusting screw

Carter YF938D carburetor used on CJ-3B models. The adjustment points on CJ-2A and CJ-3A models are similar

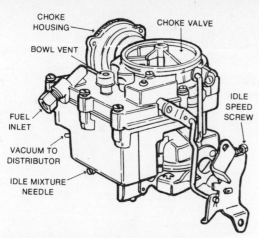

Rochester 2GC carburetor adjustment points

tom of the carburetor with a screwdriver—clockwise to increase idle speed and counterclockwise to decrease it.

MIXTURE ADJUSTMENT 1945–74

The idle mixture screw is located at the very bottom of the carburetor.

1. Turn the screw until it is all the way in. Do not force the screw in any further because it is very easy to damage the needle valve and its seat by screwing the adjusting screw in too tightly.

2. Turn the screw out ¾ to 1¾ turns. This should be the normal adjustment setting. For a richer mixture, turn the screw out. The ideal setting for the mixture adjustment screw results in the maximum engine rpm.

NOTE: *Limiter caps are installed on all carburetors on all 1971 and later American Motors engines and some pre-1971 engines. These caps limit the amount of adjustment that can be made and should not be removed, if possible. If a satisfactory idle cannot be obtained, however, they can be removed by installing a sheet metal screw in the center of the screw and turning clockwise. After removing the caps, adjust the carburetor in the same manner as was used without the caps. There are special service limiter caps available to replace the ones removed. Install the service limiter caps with the ears positioned against the full rich stops. Be careful not to disturb the idle setting while installing the caps. Press the caps squarely and firmly into place.*

IDLE SPEED AND MIXTURE ADJUSTMENTS

1975–78

CAUTION: *On vehicles equipped with a catalytic converter, do not idle the engine over three minutes at a time. If the adjustments* are not completed within three minutes, run the engine at 2000 rpm for one minute.

1. Turn the idle screw(s) to the full rich position. Note the position of the screw head slot inside the limiter cap slots.

2. Remove the limiter cap(s) carefully with a pair of needlenosed pliers. Reset the idle speed screws to the approximate position before cap removal.

3. Connect an accurate tachometer to the engine according to the manufacturer's instructions.

4. Run the engine to operating temperature.

5. Adjust the idle to 30 rpm above the recommended idle speed.

NOTE: *On V8 engines with automatic transmissions, the throttle stop solenoid is used to adjust the idle speed. Use the following procedure for these vehicles:*

a. With the solenoid wire connected, loos-

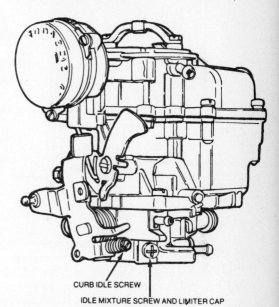

Carter YF used on the 6-232 and 6-258

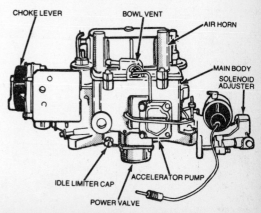

Autolite/Motorcraft 2100 right side

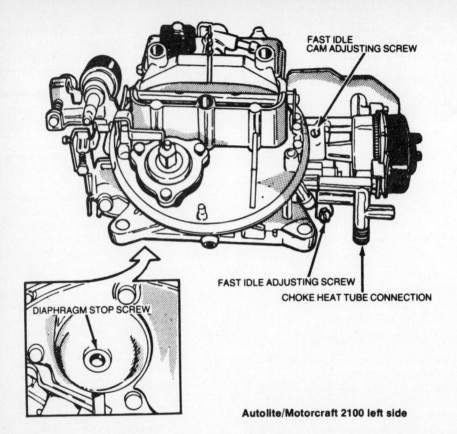

FAST IDLE
CAM ADJUSTING SCREW

DIAPHRAGM STOP SCREW

FAST IDLE ADJUSTING SCREW
CHOKE HEAT TUBE CONNECTION

Autolite/Motorcraft 2100 left side

en the locknut and turn the solenoid in or out to obtain the specified rpm.

b. Tighten the solenoid bracket.

c. Disconnect the solenoid wire and adjust the idle speed screw to 500 rpm. Connect the wire.

6. Starting from the full rich stop position (established before the limiters were removed), turn the mixture screws clockwise (leaner) until a slight rpm drop is indicated.

7. Turn the mixture screws counterclockwise until the highest rpm reading is obtained

at the best lean idle setting. On carburetors with two screws, turn them evenly in alternating equal increments.

NOTE: *If the idle speed changed more than 30 rpm during the adjustment, reset it to 30 rpm above the specified rpm and repeat the adjustment.*

1979–80

The procedure for adjusting the idle speed and mixture is called the lean drop procedure and is made with the engine operating at normal operating temperature and the air cleaner in place as follows:

1. Turn the mixture screws to the full rich position with the tabs on the limiters against the stops. Note the position of the screw head slot inside the limiter cap slots.

2. Remove the idle limiter caps by threading a sheet metal screw in center of the cap and turning clockwise. Discard the limiter caps.

3. Reset the adjustment screws to the same position noted before the limiter caps were removed.

4. Start the engine and allow it to reach normal operating temperature.

5. Adjust the idle speed to 30 rpm above the specified rpm. See the Tune-Up Specifications chart. On 6-cylinder engines with a throttle stop solenoid, turn the solenoid in or out to ob-

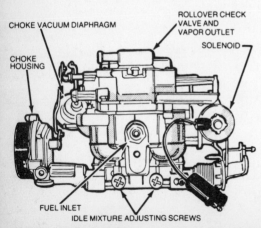

CHOKE VACUUM DIAPHRAGM

ROLLOVER CHECK
VALVE AND
VAPOR OUTLET

SOLENOID

CHOKE
HOUSING

FUEL INLET
IDLE MIXTURE ADJUSTING SCREWS

BBD 2-bbl adjustments

tain the specified rpm. On V8 engines with a throttle stop solenoid, turn the hex screw on the throttle stop solenoid carriage to obtain the specified rpm. This is done with the solenoid wire connected. Tighten the solenoid locknut, if so equipped. Disconnect the solenoid wire and adjust the curb idle speed screw to obtain an idle speed of 500 rpm. Reconnect the solenoid wire.

6. Starting from the full rich stop position, as was determined before the limiter caps were removed, turn the mixture adjusting screws clockwise (leaner) until a loss of engine speed is noticed.

7. Turn the screws counterclockwise (richer) until the highest rpm reading is obtained at the best lean idle setting. The best lean idle setting is on the lean side of the highest rpm setting without changing rpm.

8. If the idle speed changed more than 30 rpm during the mixture adjustment procedure, reset the idle speed to 30 rpm above the specified rpm with the idle speed adjusting screw or the throttle stop solenoid and repeat the mixture adjustment.

9. Install new limiter caps over the mixture adjusting screws with the tabs positioned against the full rich stops. Be careful not to disturb the idle mixture setting while installing the caps.

1981–82

Idle mixture screws on these carburetors are sealed with plugs or dowel pins. A mixture adjustment must be undertaken ONLY when the carburetor is overhauled, the throttle body replaced, or the engine does not meet required emission standards. Since expensive testing equipment is needed to properly set the mixture, only the idle speed adjusting procedure is given below.

NOTE: *The adjustment is made with the manual transmission in neutral and the automatic in drive. Therefore, make certain that the vehicle's parking brake is set firmly, and that the wheels are blocked. It may be a good idea to have someone in the vehicle with their foot on the brake.*

1. Connect a tachometer, start engine and warm it to normal operating temperature. The choke and intake manifold heater (6-cylinder engine only) must be off.

2. If the engine speed is not within the OK range, turn the curb idle adjustment screw to obtain the specified curb idle rpm.

3. For the 6-cylinder engine (BBD carburetor): Disconnect the vacuum hose from the vacuum actuator and holding solenoid wire connector. Adjust the curb (slow) idle speed adjustment screw to obtain the specified curb

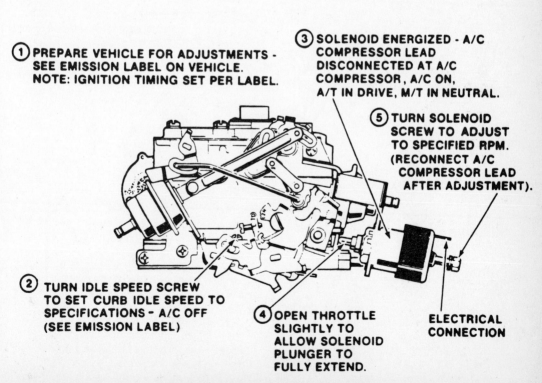

① PREPARE VEHICLE FOR ADJUSTMENTS - SEE EMISSION LABEL ON VEHICLE. NOTE: IGNITION TIMING SET PER LABEL.

③ SOLENOID ENERGIZED - A/C COMPRESSOR LEAD DISCONNECTED AT A/C COMPRESSOR, A/C ON, A/T IN DRIVE, M/T IN NEUTRAL.

⑤ TURN SOLENOID SCREW TO ADJUST TO SPECIFIED RPM. (RECONNECT A/C COMPRESSOR LEAD AFTER ADJUSTMENT).

② TURN IDLE SPEED SCREW TO SET CURB IDLE SPEED TO SPECIFICATIONS - A/C OFF (SEE EMISSION LABEL)

④ OPEN THROTTLE SLIGHTLY TO ALLOW SOLENOID PLUNGER TO FULLY EXTEND.

ELECTRICAL CONNECTION

Idle Speed Adjustment—without A/C—E2SE

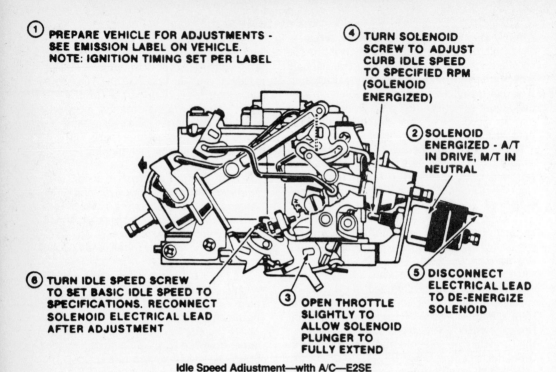

① PREPARE VEHICLE FOR ADJUSTMENTS - SEE EMISSION LABEL ON VEHICLE. NOTE: IGNITION TIMING SET PER LABEL

④ TURN SOLENOID SCREW TO ADJUST CURB IDLE SPEED TO SPECIFIED RPM (SOLENOID ENERGIZED)

② SOLENOID ENERGIZED - A/T IN DRIVE, M/T IN NEUTRAL

⑥ TURN IDLE SPEED SCREW TO SET BASIC IDLE SPEED TO SPECIFICATIONS. RECONNECT SOLENOID ELECTRICAL LEAD AFTER ADJUSTMENT

③ OPEN THROTTLE SLIGHTLY TO ALLOW SOLENOID PLUNGER TO FULLY EXTEND

⑤ DISCONNECT ELECTRICAL LEAD TO DE-ENERGIZE SOLENOID

Idle Speed Adjustment—with A/C—E2SE

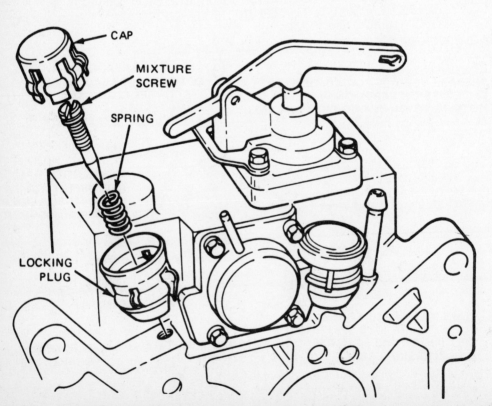

CAP

MIXTURE SCREW

SPRING

LOCKING PLUG

Some 1980 and later 2150 models have 2-piece metal plugs and caps in place of plastic limiter caps on the idle mixture adjusting screws. They should be carefully removed before attempting any adjustments.

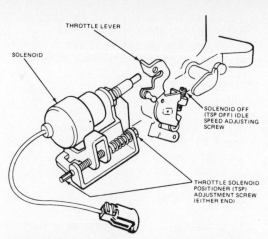

THROTTLE LEVER

SOLENOID

SOLENOID OFF
(TSP OFF) IDLE
SPEED ADJUSTING
SCREW

THROTTLE SOLENOID
POSITIONER (TSP)
ADJUSTMENT SCREW
(EITHER END)

Location of the idle speed adjustment on the Motor-craft/Autolite 2100, 2150

(slow) idle rpm, if it is not within the OK range. Refer to the Emission Control Information label, and the Tune-Up Specifications Chart. Apply a direct source of vacuum to the vacuum actuator. Turn the vacuum actuator adjustment screw on the throttle lever until the specified rpm is obtained (900 rpm for manual transmissions, and 800 rpm for automatic transmissions). Disconnect the manifold vacuum source from the vacuum actuator. With the jumper wire, apply battery voltage (12v) to energize the holding solenoid. Turn the A/C on, if equipped.

NOTE: *The throttle must be opened manually to allow the Sol-Vac throttle positioner to be extended.*

With the Sol-Vac throttle positioner extended, the idle speed should be 650 rpm for automatic transmission equipped vehicles and 750 rpm for manual transmission equipped vehicles. If the idle speed is not within tolerance, adjust the Sol-Vac (hex-head adjustment screw) to obtain the specified rpm. Remove the jumper wire from the Sol-Vac holding solenoid wire connector. Connect the Sol-Vac holding solenoid wire connector. Connect the original hose to the vacuum actuator.

4. For four and eight cylinder engines (2SE, E2SE or 2150 carburetor), turn the nut on the solenoid plunger or the hex screw on the solenoid carriage to obtain the specified idle rpm. Tighten the locknut, if equipped. Disconnect the solenoid wire connector and adjust the curb idle screw to obtain a 500 rpm idle speed. Connect the solenoid wire connector. If the model 2150 carburetor (8-cylinder engine), is equipped with a dashpot, fully depress the dashpot stem with the throttle at the curb idle position, and measure the clearance between the stem and throttle lever. The clearance

should be 0.032″ (0.8128mm). Adjust it by loosening the locknut and turning the dashpot.

1983–84
4–150

1. Fully warm up the engine.
2. Check the choke fast idle adjustment: Disconnect and plug the EGR valve vacuum hose. Position the fast idle adjustment screw on the second step of the fast idle cam with the transmission in neutral. Adjust the fast idle speed to 2,000 rpm for manual transmission and 2,300 rpm for automatic transmission. Allow the throttle to return to normal curb idle and reconnect the EGR vacuum hose.
3. To adjust the Sol-Vac Vacuum Actuator: Remove the vacuum hose from the vacuum actuator and plug the hose. Connect an external vacuum source to the actuator and apply 10–15 inches Hg. of vacuum to the actuator. Shift the transmission to Neutral. Adjust the idle speed to the following rpm using the vacuum actuator adjustment screw on the throttle lever: 850 rpm for automatic transmission 950 rpm for manual transmission. The adjustment is made with all accessories turned off.

NOTE: *The curb idle should always be adjusted after vacuum actuator adjustment.*

4. To adjust the curb idle: Remove the vacuum hose from the Sol-Vac vacuum actuator and plug the hose. Shift the transmission into Neutral. Adjust the curb idle using the ¼″ (6.35mm) hex-head adjustment screw on the end of the Sol-Vac unit. Set the speed to 750 rpm for manual transmission, 700 rpm for automatic transmission. Reconnect the vacuum hose to the vacuum actuator.

NOTE: *Engine speed will vary 10–30 rpm during this mode due to the closed loop fuel control.*

5. To adjust the TRC (Anti-Diesel): The TRC screw is preset at the factory and should not require adjustment. However, to check adjustment, the screw should be ¾ turn from closed throttle position.

6–258

SOL-VAC VACUUM ACTUATOR ADJUSTMENT

1. Disconnect and plug the vacuum hose to the Sol-Vac vacuum actuator.
2. Disconnect the Sol-Vac electrical connector. Connect an external vacuum source to the vacuum actuator and apply 10–15 inches (Hg.) of vacuum.
3. Open throttle for at least 3.0 seconds (1200 rpm); then close throttle.
4. Set the speed using the vacuum actuator adjustment screw on the throttle lever to obtain specified rpm.

5. Disconnect the external vacuum source. Reconnect the Sol-Vac vacuum hose and electrical connector.

SOL-VAC HOLDING SOLENOID ADJUSTMENT

NOTE: *The Sol-Vac vacuum actuator adjustment should always precede the Sol-Vac solenoid adjustment.*

1. Disconnect and plug the vacuum hose at the Sol-Vac vacuum actuator.

2. Disconnect the Sol-Vac electrical connector.

3. Energize the Sol-Vac holding solenoid with either of the two following methods:

    a. Apply battery voltage (12v) to the solenoid, or,

    b. Reconnect the Sol-Vac electrical connector and turn on the rear window defogger or turn on the air conditioner with the compressor disconnected.

4. Open throttle for at least 3.0 seconds (1,200 rpm) to allow the Sol-Vac holding solenoid to fully extend.

5. Set the speed using the ¼" (6.35mm) hex-head adjustment screw on the end of the Sol-Vac unit to obtain the specified rpm.

6. Reopen the throttle above 1,200 rpm to insure the correct holding position and reset the speed if necessary. Reconnect the vacuum hose to the Sol-Vac actuator. Reconnect the Sol-Vac electrical connector if disconnected.

1985–86

4-150 W/YFA CARBURETOR

1. The TRC (anti-Diesel) adjustment screw is statically set at ¾ of turn from the throttle valve closed position during factory assembly and does not normally require readjustment. Should this adjustment be required, turn the adjustment screw counterclockwise to the throttle plate closed position and then turn the screw clockwise ¾ turn.

2. Connect a tachometer to the ignition coil TACH wire connector.

3. Place the transmission in NEUTRAL and lock the parking brake.

4. Start the engine and allow it to reach normal operating temperature.

5. Connect an external vacuum source to the Sol-Vac vacuum actuator and apply 10–15 in.Hg. of vacuum. Plug the engine vacuum hose.

6. Adjust the vacuum actuator until an engine speed of approximately 1,000 rpm is achieved.

NOTE: *Refer to the Vehicle Emission Control Information Label for the latest specifica-*

tions for the particular engine being adjusted.

7. Remove the vacuum source from the vacuum actuator and retain the plug in the vacuum hose from the engine.

8. Turn the hex-head curb idle speed adjustment screw until the speed of 500 rpm is obtained.

NOTE: *Refer to the Vehicle Emission Control Label for the latest specifications for the particular engine being adjusted.*

9. Stop the engine and connect the engine vacuum hose to the vacuum actuator.

10. Remove the tachometer from the engine.

4-150 W/THROTTLE BODY FUEL INJECTION

Adjustments are not possible on this unit, as all functions are computer controlled.

6-258

NOTE: *The carburetor choke and intake manifold heater must be off. This occurs when the engine coolant heats to approximately +160°F (71°C).*

1. Have the engine at normal operating temperature. Connect a tachometer to the ignition coil negative (TACH) terminal.

2. Remove the vacuum hose from the Sol-Vac vacuum actuator unit. Plug the vacuum hose. Disconnect the holding solenoid wire connector.

3. Adjust the curb (slow) idle speed screw to obtain the correct curb idle speed. Refer to the specifications under Idle Speed or refer to the Emission Information label, under the hood, for the correct curb idle engine rpm.

4. Apply a direct source of vacuum to the vacuum actuator, using a hand vacuum pump or its equivalent. When the Sol-Vac throttle positioner is fully extended, turn the vacuum actuator adjustment screw on the throttler lever until the specified engine rpm is obtained. Disconnect the vacuum source from the vacuum actuator.

5. With a jumper wire, apply battery voltage (12v) to energize the holding solenoid.

NOTE: *The holding wire connector can be installed and either the rear window defroster or the air conditioner (with the compressor clutch wire disconnected) can be turned on to energize the holding solenoid.*

6. Hold the throttle open manually to allow the throttle positioner to fully extend.

NOTE: *Without the vacuum actuator, the throttle must be opened manually to allow the Sol-Vac throttle positioner to fully extend.*

7. If the holding solenoid idle speed is not within specifications, adjust the idle using the

¼" (6.35mm) hex-headed adjustment screw on the end of the Sol-Vac unit. Adjust to specifications.

8. Disconnect the jumper wire from the Sol-Vac holding solenoid wire connector, if used. Connect the wire connector to the Sol-Vac unit, if not connected. Install the original vacuum hose to the vacuum actuator.

9. Remove the tachometer and if disconnected, connect the compressor clutch wire. Install any other component that was previously removed.

Engine and
Engine Overhaul

Generator and Regulator Specifications

6 Volt

	Generator				Regulator			
Manufacturer	Model No.	Output amps	Brush Spring Tension (oz.)		Model No.	Regulated Voltage	Regulated Amperage	Cutout Relay Closing Voltage
Autolite	GDZ 4817 GDZ 6001	35	35–53		VRP-6003 VPR-4007 VBO-4601	7.1–7.3	49	6.3–6.8
	GGW 4801 GGW 7404	45	35–53 18–36		VBO-4601C VBE-6105A	7.1–7.3	49	6.3–6.8
Delco-Remy	1102811	45	28		1972063	6.9–7.4	42–47	5.9–6.7

12 Volt

	Generator				Regulator			
Manufacturer	Model No.	Output amps	Brush Spring Tension (oz.)		Model No.	Regulated Voltage	Regulated Amperage	Cutout Relay Closing Voltage
Autolite	GJP-7202B GJP-7202A	35	18–36		VRX-6009B VBO-4201E-4E	14.3–14.7	39	12.6–13.6
Delco-Remy	1102096	35	28		197229	13.8–14.8	27–33	11.8–13.5

Alternator and Regulator Specifications

		Alternator			Regulator	
Engine	Year	Manufacturer	Field Current @ 12v (amps)	Output (amps)	Manufacturer	Volts @ 75°F
4-134	1966–71	Motorola	1.2–1.7	35	Motorola	14.2–14.6
4-150	1984–87	Delco-Remy	4.0–5.0	56 ①	Delco-Remy	13.9–14.9
4-151	1980–83	Delco-Remy	4.0–5.0	42 ②	Delco-Remy	12.0–15.5
6-225	1966–71	Motorola	1.2–1.7	35	Delco-Remy	14.2–14.6
6-230	1960–64	Motorola	1.2–1.7	35 ⑥	Motorola	14.2–14.6
6-232, 258	1972–74	Motorola	1.8–2.5	37	Motorola	13.7–14.2

Alternator and Regulator Specifications (cont.)

Engine	Year	Alternator			Regulator	
		Manufacturer	Field Current @ 12v (amps)	Output (amps)	Manufacturer	Volts @ 75°F
6-232, 258	1975	Delco-Remy	1.8–2.5	37 ③	Delco-Remy	13.7–14.2
	1976–79	Delco-Remy	4.0–5.0	37 ②	Delco-Remy	12.0–15.5
6-258	1980–86	Delco-Remy	4.0–5.0	42 ②	Delco-Remy	13.9–14.9
8-304	1972–74	Motorola	1.8–2.5	37 ④	Motorola	13.7–14.2
	1975	Motorola	1.8–2.5	37 ④	Motorola	12.7–15.3
	1976–77	Motorcraft	2.5–3.0	40 ⑤	Motorcraft	13.1–14.8
	1978–79	Delco-Remy	4.0–5.0	37 ②	Delco-Remy	12.0–15.5
	1980–81	Delco-Remy	4.0–5.0	42 ②	Delco-Remy	12.0–15.5

① Optional 68 and 78
② Optional 56, 63, 78 and 85
③ Optional 55 and 63
④ Optional 51 and 62
⑤ Optional 60
⑥ Optional 40 amp

Starter Specifications

Engine	Year	Manufacturer	Lock Test		Torque (ft. lb.)	No-Load Test			Brush Spring Tension (oz.)
			Amps	Volts		Amps	Volts	RPM	
4-134	1945–65	Autolite 6v	335	2.0	6.0	65	5.0	4,300	42–53
		Autolite 12v	280	4.0	6.2	50	10.0	5,300	31–47
		Delco 6v	600	3.0	15.0	60	5.0	6,000	35 min.
		Delco 12v	435	5.8	10.5	75	10.3	6,900	24 min.
	1966–71	Autolite	①	4.0	②	50	10.0	4,400	31–47
		Delco	435	5.8	1.5	75	10.3	6,900	24 min.
		Prestolite	405	N.A.	9.0	50	10.0	5,300	32–40
4-150	1984	Delco	Not Recommended			67	12.0	8,500	30–40
	1985–87	Motorcraft	Not Recommended			67	12.0	8,368	N.A.
		Bosch	120	9.6	N.A.	75	12.5	2,900	N.A..
6-225	1966–71	Delco	Not Recommended			75	10.6	6,200	32–40
6-226	1950–60	Autolite 6v	335	2.0	6.0	65	5.0	4.300	42–53
		Autolite 12v	280	4.0	6.2	50	10.0	5,300	31–47
		Delco 6v	600	3.0	15.0	60	5.0	6,000	35 min.
		Delco 12v	435	5.8	10.5	75	10.3	6,900	24 min.
6-230	1960–64	Prestolite	405	4.0	9.0	60	10.0	4,200	42–53
6-232, 6-258	1972–78	Autolite	600	3.4	13.0	65	12.0	9,250	35–40
6-258	1979–81	Motorcraft	Not Recommended			77	12.0	9,250	35–40
	1982–87	Motorcraft	Not Recommended			67	12.0	7,868	35–40
8-304	1972–81	Autolite	600	3.4	13.0	65	12.0	9,250	35–40

N.A.: Information Not Available
min.: minimum
① Starter #MDU7004: 280   ② Starter #MDU7004: 6.2
   All others: 170   All others: 1.5

General Engine Specifications

Engine	Years	Fuel System Type	SAE net Horsepower @ rpm	SAE net Torque ft. lb. @ rpm	Bore x Stroke	Comp. Ratio	Oil Press. (psi.) @ 2000 rpm
4-134	1945–52	1-bbl	60 @ 4,000	105 @ 2,000	3.125 x 4.375	7.0:1	35
	1953–67	1-bbl	75 @ 4,000	114 @ 2,000	3.125 x 4.375	7.4:1	35
	1968–71	1-bbl	75 @ 4,000	114 @ 2,000	3.125 x 4.375	6.7:1	35
4-150	1984–86	1-bbl	83 @ 4,200	116 @ 2,600	3.876 x 3.188	9.2:1	40
	1987	TBI	117 @ 5,000	135 @ 3,000	3.876 x 3.188	9.2:1	40
4-151	1980–83	2-bbl	90 @ 4,400	128 @ 2,400	4.000 x 3.000	8.24:1	38
6-225	1965–71	2-bbl	160 @ 4,200	235 @ 3,500	3.750 x 3.400	9.0:1	33
6-226	1950–60	1-bbl	105 @ 3,600	190 @ 1,400	3.312 x 4.375	6.86:1	35
6-230	1960–64	1-bbl	140 @ 4,400	210 @ 1,750	3.343 x 4.375	8.5:1	45
6-232	1972–78	1-bbl	100 @ 3,600	185 @ 1,800	3,750 x 3.500	8.0:1	50
6-258	1972–76	1-bbl	110 @ 3,500	195 @ 2,000	3.750 x 3.895	8.0:1	50
	1977–86	2-bbl	114 @ 3,600	196 @ 2,000	3.750 x 3.895	8.0:1	50
	1987	2-bbl	112 @ 3,000	210 @ 2,000	3.750 x 3.895	8.6:1	50
8-304	1972–81	2-bbl	150 @ 4,200	245 @ 2,500	3,750 x 3.753	8.4:1	50

TBI: Throttle Body Injection
1-bbl: one barrel carburetor
2-bbl: two barrel carburetor

Camshaft Specifications
(All specifications in inches)

Engine	Journal Diameter					Bearing Clearance	Lobe Lift		End Play
	1	2	3	4	5		Int.	Exh.	
4-134 L-Head	2.1860–2.1855	2.1225–2.1215	2.0600–2.0590	1.6230–1.6225	—	0.0010–0.0025	0.3510	0.3510	0.004 0.007
4-134 F-Head	2.1860–2.1855	2.1225–2.1215	2.0600–2.0590	1.6230–1.6225	—	0.0010–0.0025	0.2600	0.3510	0.004–0.007
4-150	2.0300–2.0290	2.0200–2.0190	2.0100–2.0009	2.0000–1.9990	—	0.0010–0.0030	0.2650	0.2650	0
4-151	1.8690	1.8690	1.8690	—	—	0.0007–0.0027	0.3980	0.3980	0.0015–0.0050
6-225	1.7560–1.7550	1.7260–1.7250	1.6960–1.6950	1.6660–1.6650	—	0.0015–0.0040	N.A.	N.A.	N.A.
6-226	1.8725–1.8735	1.8095–1.8105	1.7472–1.7485	1.2475–1.2485	—	0.0010–0.0030	0.2840	0.2840	0.003–0.007
6-230	1.9975–1.9965	1.8725–1.8715	1.7505–1.7495	1.3755–1.3745	—	0.0020–0.0040	0.3750	0.3750	0.007–0.008
6-232	2.0300–2.0290	2.0200–2.0190	2.0100–2.0090	2.0000–1.9990	—	0.0010–0.0030	0.2540	0.2540	0
6-258	2.0300–2.0290	2.0200–2.0190	2.0100–2.0090	2.0000–1.9990	—	0.0010–0.0030	0.2540 ①	0.2540 ①	0
8-304	2.1205–2.1195	2.0905–2.0895	2.0605–2.0595	2.0305–2.0295	2.0005–1.9995	0.0010–0.0030	0.2660	0.2660	0

N.A.: Information not available
① 1985–87: 0.2531

Valve Specifications

Engine	Seat Angle (deg)	Face Angle (deg)	Spring Test Pressure (lbs. @ in.)	Spring Installed Height (in.)	Stem to Guide Clearance (in.)		Stem Diameter (in.)	
					Intake	Exhaust	Intake	Exhaust
4-134 L-Head	45	45	120 @ 1.750	2.109	0.0007–0.0022	0.0025–0.0045	0.3730	0.3715
4-134 F-Head	45	45	①	1.660	0.0007–0.0022	0.0025–0.0045	0.3733–0.3738	0.3710–0.3720
4-150	45	44	212 @ 1.203	1.625	0.0010–0.0030	0.0010–0.0030	0.3110–0.3120	0.3110–0.3120
4-151	46	45	176 @ 1.250	1.660	0.0010–0.0027	0.0010–0.0027	0.3422	0.3422
6-225	45	45	168 @ 1.260	1.640	0.0012–0.0032	0.0015–0.0035 ②	0.3415–0.3427	0.3402–0.3412
6-226	⑨	⑩	107 @ 1.312	1.672	0.0012–0.0030	0.0032–0.0050	0.3402–0.3410	0.3382–0.3390
6-230	45	45	130 @ 0.886	1.260	0.0010–0.0030	0.0025–0.0045	0.3400–0.3410	0.3385–0.3395
6-232	③	④	⑤	⑥	0.0010–0.0030	0.0010–0.0030	0.3715–0.3725	0.3715–0.3725
6-258	③	④	⑦	⑧	0.0010–0.0030	0.0010–0.0030	0.3715–0.3725	0.3715–0.3725
8-304	③	④	218 @ 1.359	1.812	0.0010–0.0030	0.0010–0.0030	0.3715–0.3725	0.3715–0.3725

① Intake: 153 @ 1.400
Exhaust: 120 @ 1.750
② Measured at the top
③ Intake: 30
Exhaust: 44½
④ Intake: 29
Exhaust: 44
⑤ With rotators: 219 @ 1.875
Without rotators: 195 @ 1.437
⑥ Intake: 1.786
Exhaust: 2.110

⑦ 1972–76: with rotators, 218 @ 1.875
without rotators: 195 @ 1.437
1977–78: 208 @ 1.386
1979–87: Intake, 195 @ 1.411
Exhaust, 220 @ 1.188
⑧ 1972–78: 1.786
1979–84: Intake, 1.786
Exhaust, 1.625
1985–87: 1.786

⑨ Intake: 30
Exhaust: 45
⑩ Intake: 60
Exhaust: 45

Crankshaft and Connecting Rod Specifications
(All specifications in inches)

Engine	Crankshaft				Connecting Rod		
	Main Bearing Journal Dia.	Main Bearing Oil Clearance	Shaft End Play	Thrust on No.	Journal Dia.	Oil Clearance	Side Clearance
4-134	2.3331–2.3341	0.0003–0.0029	0.0040–0.0060	1	1.9375–1.9383	0.0001–0.0019	0.004–0.010
4-150	2.4996–2.5001	0.0010–0.0025	0.0015–0.0065	2	2.0934–2.0955	0.0010–0.0030	0.010–0.019
4-151	2.2988	0.0005–0.0022	0.0035–0.0085	5	1.8690	0.0007–0.0027	0.006–0.022
6-225	2.4993–2.4997	0.0005–0.0021	0.0040–0.0080	2	1.9998–2.0002	0.0020–0.0023	0.006–0.017
6-226	2.3740–2.3750	0.0008–0.0028	0.0030–0.0070	4	2.0623	0.0007–0.0025	0.006–0.011
6-230	2.3747–2.3755	0.0005–0.0025	0.0030–0.0070	4	2.0619–2.0627	0.0006–0.0025	Snug
6-232	2.4986–2.5001	0.0010–0.0020	0.0015–0.0065	3	2.0934–2.0955	0.0010–0.0020	0.005–0.014
6-258	2.4986–2.5001	①	0.0015–0.0065	3	2.0934–2.0955	②	③
8-304	2.4986–2.5001 ④	⑤	0.0030–0.0080	3	2.0934–2.0955	0.0010–0.0020	0.006–0.018

① 1972–73: 0.0010–0.0020
1974–80: 0.0010–0.0030
1981: #1—0.0005–0.0026
#2, 3, 4, 5, 6—0.0005–0.0030
#7—0.0011–0.0035
1982–87: 0.0010–0.0025

② 1972–73: 0.0010–0.0020
1974–76: 0.0010–00.030
1977–81: 0.0010–0.0025
1982–87: 0.0010–0.0030

③ 1972–80: 0.005–0.014
1981–87: 0.010–0.019

④ #1, 2, 3, 4: 2.7474–2.7489
#5: 2.7464–2.7479

⑤ #1, 2, 3, 4,—0.0010–0.0020
#5—0.0020–0.0030

Piston and Ring Specifications
(All specifications in inches)

Engine	Ring Gap			Ring Side Clearance			Piston * Clearance
	#1 Compr.	#2 Compr.	Oil Control	#1 Compr.	#2 Compr.	Oil Control	
4-134	0.0070– 0.0170	0.0070– 0.0170	0.0070– 0.0170	0.0020– 0.0040	0.0015– 0.0035	0.0010– 0.0025	0.0025– 0.0045
4-150	0.0100– 0.0200	0.0100– 0.0200	0.0100– 0.0250	0.0017– 0.0032	0.0017– 0.0032	0.0010 0.0080	0.0009– 0.0017
4-151	0.0027– 0.0033	0.0090– 9.0190	0.0150– 0.0550	0.0025– 0.0033	0.0025– 0.0033	0.0025– 0.0033	0.0025– 0.0033
6-225	0.0100– 0.0200	0.0100– 0.0200	0.0150– 0.0350	0.0020– 0.0035	0.0030– 0.0050	0.0015– 0.0085	0.0005– 0.0011
6-226	0.0080– 0.0180	0.0080– 0.0160	0.0080– 0.0160	0.0020– 0.0040	0.0030– 0.0070	0.0060– 0.0100	0.0007– 0.0017
6-230	0.0100– 0.0450	0.1000– 0.0450	0.0150– 0.0550	0.0020– 0.0031	0.0020– 0.0031	Snug	0.0007– 0.0017
6-232	0.0100– 0.0200	0.0100– 0.0200	0.0150– 0.0550	0.0015– 0.0030	0.0015– 0.0030	0.0010– 0.0080	0.0009– 0.0017
6-258	0.0100– 0.0200	0.0100– 0.0200	①	②	②	0.0010– 0.0080	0.0009– 0.0017
8-304	0.0100– 0.0200	0.0100– 0.0200	0.0100– 0.0250	0.0015– 0.0030	0.0015– 0.0030	0.0011– 0.0080	0.0010– 0.0018

* Measured at the skirt
① 1972–73: 0.0150–0.0550
   1974–87: 0.0100–0.0250
② 1972–80: 0.0015–0.0030
   1981–87: 0.0017–0.0032

Torque Specifications
(All specifications in ft. lb.)

Engine	Cyl. Head	Conn. Rod	Main Bearing	Crankshaft Damper	Flywheel	Manifold	
						Intake	Exhaust
4-134	60–70	35–45	65–75	65–75	35–41	29–35 ①	20–35
4-150	80–90	30–35	75–85	75–85	50 ②	20–25	20–25
4-151	93–97	28–32	63–67	155–165	53–57	Bolt: 40 Nut: 30	Bolt: 40 Nut: 30
6-225	65–85	30–40	85–95	140–150	50–65	45–55	14–20
6-226	35–45	40–45	85–95	100–130	35–40	30–35	
6-230	80–95	40–45	85–95	100–130	40–45	15–20	35–40
6-232	100–110	25–30	75–85	50–60	100–110	40–45	23–28
6-258	③	30–35	75–85	75–85	100–110	20–25	④
8-304	100–110	25–30	95– 105	53–58	100–110	40–45	23–27

① L-Head only
② Plus a 60° turn
③ 1972–80: 105
   1981–87: 85
④ 1972–79: 23
   1980 and later (see illustration in text): Bolts #1 thru 11: 23
                                  Bolts #12 & 13: 50

ENGINE ELECTRICAL

NOTE: *CJ-2A, CJ-3A and some CJ-3B, CJ-5 and CJ-6 models are equipped with 6 volt electrical systems. The easiest way to tell which system your Jeep has is to look at the battery. A 6 volt battery has three cell caps; a 12 volt battery has six cell caps. All systems are negative ground.*

Ignition Coil

REMOVAL AND INSTALLATION

All Except the 4–151 and 1987 4–150

1. Disconnect the battery ground.
2. Disconnect the two small and one large wire from the coil.
3. Disconnect the condenser connector from the coil, if equipped.

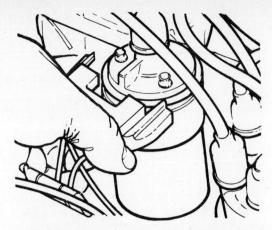

Typical coil used on all engines except the 4-151 and 1987 4-150. Earlier models had separate wires, rather than the slip-on connector

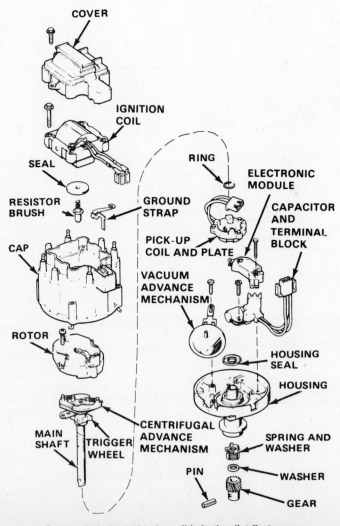

On the 1980–81 4-151, the coil is in the distributor cap

4. Unbolt and remove the coil.
5. Installation is the reverse of removal.

4–151

1980–81

1. Remove the distributor cap.
2. Remove the three coil cover attaching screws and lift off the cover.
3. Remove the four coil attaching screws and lift off the coil.
4. Installation is the reverse of removal.

1982–83

1. Disconnect the harness at the coil.
2. Pulling on the boot, only, pull the coil-to-distributor cap wire from the coil.
3. Remove the three coil mounting screws and lift off the coil.
4. Installation is the reverse of removal.

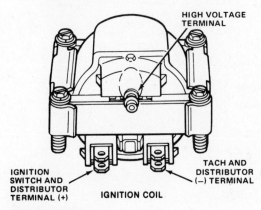

1982–83 4-151 coil

1987 4–150

The coil is an integral part of the Ignition Control Module (ICM), mounted to the left of the battery on the firewall. The coil can, however, be removed for separate replacement.

Ignition Module
REMOVAL AND INSTALLATION

The ignition module is mounted next to the battery on all models. It is a sealed, weatherproof unit on all models, except the 1987 4–150. The 1987 4–150 incorporates the coil in the control module. The coil, on these models, can be removed separately.

Removing the module, on all models, is a matter of simply removing the fasteners that attach it to the fender or firewall and pulling apart the connectors. When unplugging the connectors, pull them apart with a firm, straight pull. NEVER PRY THEM APART! To pry them will cause damage. When reconnect-

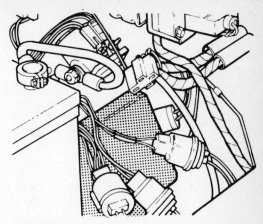

Ignition control module used on all but the 1987 4-150

ing them, coat the mating ends with silicone dielectric grease to waterproof the connection. Press the connectors together firmly to overcome any vacuum lock caused by the grease.

NOTE: *If the locking tabs weaken or break, don't replace the unit. Just secure the connection with electrical tape or tie straps.*

Distributor
REMOVAL

All, Except the 6–226

1. Remove the high-tension wires from the distributor cap terminal towers, noting their positions to assure correct reassembly. For diagrams of firing orders and distributor wiring, refer to the tune-up and troubleshooting section.
2. Remove the primary lead from the terminal post at the side of the distributor.

NOTE: *The wire connector on 1978 and later models will contain a special conductive grease. Do not remove it. The same grease will also be found on the metal parts of the rotor.*

3. Disconnect the vacuum line if there is one.
4. Remove the two distributor cap retaining hooks or screws and remove the distributor cap.
5. Note the position of the rotor in relation to the base. Scribe a mark on the base of the distributor and on the engine block to facilitate reinstallation. Align the marks with the direction the metal tip of the rotor is pointing.
6. Remove the bolt that holds the distributor to the engine.
7. Lift the distributor assembly from the engine.

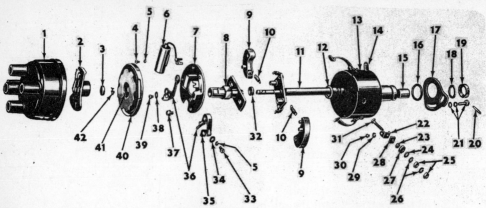

1. Cap
2. Rotor
3. Cam oiling wick
4. Condenser mounting screw
5. Lockwasher
6. Condenser
7. Breaker plate
8. Cam and stop plate
9. Governor weight
10. Governor spring
11. Driveshaft
12. Thrust washer
13. Base
14. Oiler

15. Bearing
16. Rubber O-ring
17. Advance arm
18. Lower thrust washer
19. Driveshaft collar
20. Collar rivet
21. Screw and washers
22. Connector
23. Bushing
24. Terminal washer
25. Terminal nut
26. Terminal lockwasher
27. Insulating washer
28. Terminal insulation

29. Connector lockwasher
30. Connector screw
31. Terminal post
32. Cam spacer
33. Breaker arm spring clip screw
34. Spring clip screw washer
35. Spring clip
36. Distributor points
37. Breaker plate screw
38. Washer
39. Locking screw
40. Plate seal
41. Felt washer
42. Snapring

4-134 distributor

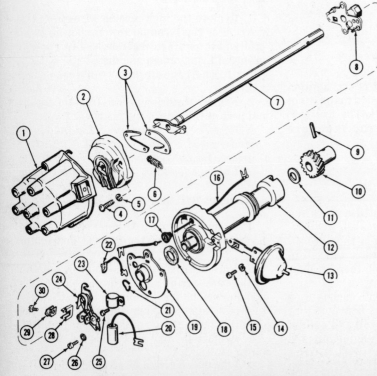

1. Cap assembly
2. Rotor
3. Governor weight
4. Rotor mounting screw
5. Lockwasher
6. Weight spring (governor)
7. Shaft
8. Cam assembly
9. Gear pin
10. Drive gear
11. Spacer washer
12. Housing
13. Vacuum control
14. Lockwasher
15. Control mounting screw
16. Primary lead
17. Lead grommet
18. Washer
19. Breaker plate
20. Condenser
21. Retaining spring
22. Ground lead
23. Condenser clamp
24. Contact set
25. Clamp screw
26. Lockwasher
27. Contact screw
28. Insulator
29. Spring clip
30. Screw

6-225 distributor

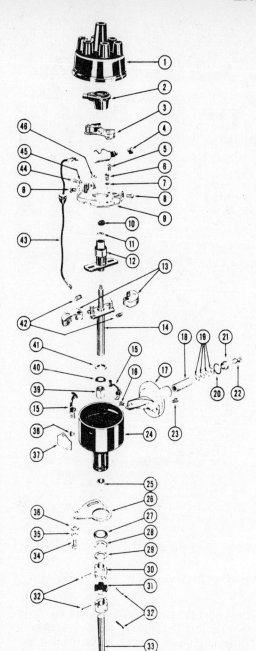

1. Cap
2. Rotor
3. Breaker points
4. Condenser
5. Breaker point adjustment lockscrew
6. Condenser mounting screw
7. Washer
8. Breaker plate mounting screw
9. Breaker plate
10. Felt cam wick
11. Cam retaining ring
12. Cam-and-stop plate
13. Governor weights
14. Driveshaft
15. Holddown clips
16. Diaphragm housing mounting screw
17. Diaphragm housing
18. Spring
19. Spacers
20. Gasket
21. Reducer bushing
22. Elbow
23. Diaphragm housing
24. Distributor housing
25. Bushing
26. Advance arm
27. Washer
28. Washer
29. Insulated washer
30. Coupling
31. Bushing
32. Coupling rivet
33. Driveshaft
34. Bolt
35. Washer
36. Washer
37. Identification plate
38. Grease cap
39. Bushing
40. Washer
41. Washer
42. Governor weight springs
43. Low tension lead
44. Terminal
45. Washer
46. Vacuum arm retaining ring

6-230 distributor

6-226

1. Remove the vacuum line and primary lead from the distributor.

2. Remove the distributor cap.

3. Note the position of the rotor in relation to the base. Scribe a mark on the base of the distributor and on the engine head to facilitate installation. Align the marks with the direction the metal tip of the rotor is pointing.

3. Remove the bolt and lockwasher which retain the advance arm to the adapter. Lift out the distributor.

INSTALLATION

All Except the 4–150

1. Insert the distributor shaft and assembly into the engine. Line up the mark on the distributor and the one on the engine with the metal tip of the rotor. Make sure that the vacuum advance diaphragm is pointed in the same

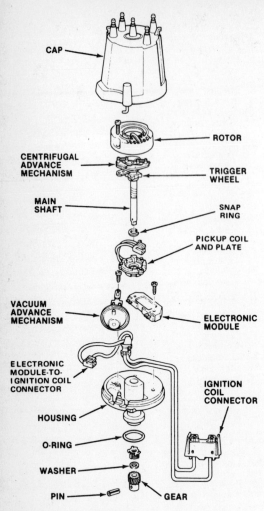

CAP

ROTOR

CENTRIFUGAL
ADVANCE
MECHANISM

TRIGGER
WHEEL

MAIN
SHAFT

SNAP
RING

PICKUP COIL
AND PLATE

VACUUM
ADVANCE
MECHANISM

ELECTRONIC
MODULE

ELECTRONIC
MODULE-TO-
IGNITION COIL
CONNECTOR

IGNITION
COIL
CONNECTOR

HOUSING

O-RING

WASHER

PIN

GEAR

1982–83 4-151 distributor

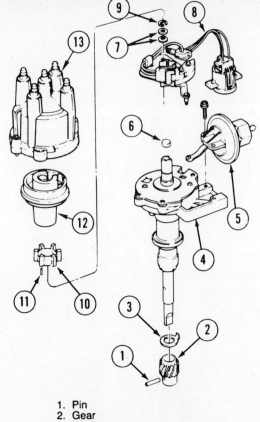

1. Pin
2. Gear
3. Washer
4. Distributor body
5. Vacuum advance mechanism
6. Wick
7. Washers
8. Pick-up coil
9. Retainer
10. Trigger wheel
11. Pin
12. Rotor
13. Cap

1984–86 4-150 distributor

direction as it was pointed originally. This will be done automatically if the marks on the engine and the distributor are line up with the rotor.

NOTE: *On the 6–225, 6–226 and F4–134, the distributor shaft fits into a slot in the end of the oil pump shaft. Therefore, the rotor won't turn when the distributor is pressed into place.*

2. Install the distributor holddown bolt and clamp. Leave the screw loose enough so that you can move the distributor with heavy hand pressure.

3. Connect the primary wire to the distributor side of the coil. Install the distributor cap on the distributor housing. Secure the distributor cap with the spring clips or the screw type retainers, whichever is used.

4. Install the spark plug wires. Make sure that the wires are pressed all of the way into the top of the distributor cap and firmly onto the spark plugs.

5. Adjust the point cam dwell and set the ignition timing. Refer to the tune-up section.

If the engine was turned while the distributor was removed, or if the marks were not drawn, it will be necessary to initially time the engine. Follow the procedure below.

NOTE: *Design of the V6 engine requires a special form of distributor cam. The distributor may be serviced in the regular way and should cause no more problems than any other distributor, if the firing plan is thoroughly understood. The distributor cam is not ground to standard six cylinder indexing intervals. This particular form requires that the original pattern of spark plug wiring be used. The engine will not run in balance if number one spark plug wire is inserted into number six distributor cap tower, even*

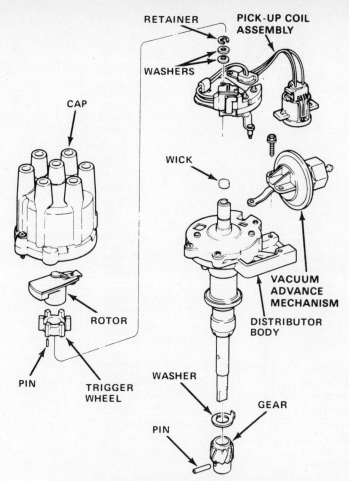

RETAINER   PICK-UP COIL
            ASSEMBLY

WASHERS

CAP

WICK

VACUUM
ADVANCE
MECHANISM

ROTOR

DISTRIBUTOR
BODY

PIN   TRIGGER
       WHEEL

WASHER

GEAR

PIN

SSI distributor. 6-cylinder is shown; the V8 is similar

*though each wire in the firing sequence is ad-
vanced to the next distributor tower. There is
a difference between the firing intervals of
each succeeding cylinder through the 720°
engine cycle.*

INSTALLATION, ENGINE ROTATED

All Except the 4–150

1. If the engine has been rotated while the
distributor was out, you'll have to first put the
engine on No. 1 cylinder at Top Dead Center
firing position. You can either remove the
valve cover or No. 1 spark plug to determine
engine position. Rotate the engine with a socket wrench on the nut at the center of the front
pulley in the normal direction of rotation. Either feel for air being expelled forcefully
through the spark plug hole or watch for the
engine to rotate up to the Top Center mark
without the valves moving (both valves will be
closed). Stop turning F4–134 engines when either the 5 degree mark on the flywheel is in

the middle of the flywheel inspection opening,
or the marks on the crankshaft pulley and the
timing gear cover are in alignment. If the
valves are moving as you approach TDC or
there is no air being expelled through the plug
hole, turn the engine another full turn until
you get the appropriate indication as the engine approaches TDC position.

2. Start the distributor into the engine with
the matchmarks between the distributor body
and the engine lined up. Turn the rotor slightly until the matchmarks on the bottom of the
distributor body and the bottom of the distributor shaft near the gear are aligned.

NOTE: *On the 4–134, 6–225 and 6–226, the
distributor shaft indexes with the oil pump
driveshaft.*

Then, insert the distributor all the way into
the engine. If you have trouble getting the distributor and camshaft gears to mesh, turn the
rotor back and forth very slightly until the distributor can be inserted easily. If the rotor is
not now lined up with the position of No. 1 plug
terminal, you'll have to pull the distributor

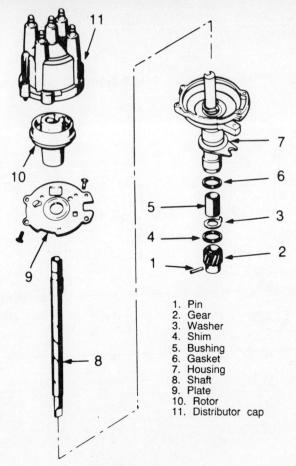

1. Pin
2. Gear
3. Washer
4. Shim
5. Bushing
6. Gasket
7. Housing
8. Shaft
9. Plate
10. Rotor
11. Distributor cap

1987 4-150 distributor

back out slightly, shift the position of the rotor appropriately, and then reinstall it.

3. Align the matchmarks between the distributor and engine. Install the distributor mounting bolt and tighten it finger tight. Reconnect the vacuum advance line and distributor wiring connector, and reinstall the gasket and cap. Reconnect the negative battery cable. Adjust the ignition timing as described in Chapter 2. Then, tighten the distributor mounting bolt securely.

NOTE: *A CJ-5 and CJ-6 F4-134 distributor (IAD 4041) is identical to the distributor of the CJ-3B (IAD 4008A) except for the holddown arm. The CJ-5 and CJ-6 distributor originally installed in the CJ-3B. It is necessary to remove the oil pump in order to install the newer distributor in the CJ-3B. Place the distributor in the correct timing position and install the holddown screw. Engage the distributor drive and carefully mesh the gears without disturbing the correct timing position of the distributor, and then replace the oil pump.*

INSTALLATION

4-150

1. Rotate the engine until the No. 1 piston is at TDC compression.

2. Using a flat bladed screwdriver, in the distributor hole, rotate the oil pump gear so that the slot in the oil pump shaft is slightly past the 3:00 o'clock position, relative to the length of the engine block.

3. With the distributor cap removed, install the distributor with the rotor at the 5:00

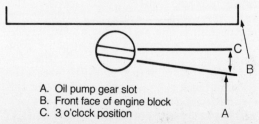

A. Oil pump gear slot
B. Front face of engine block
C. 3 o'clock position

Positioning the oil pump shaft for distributor installation on the 4-150

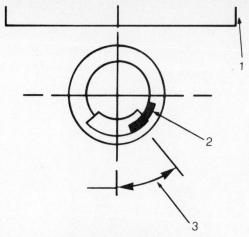

1. Front face of engine block
2. Rotor pre-positioned
3. 5 o'clock position (approx.)

Positioning the distributor rotor and shaft for installation, on the 4-150

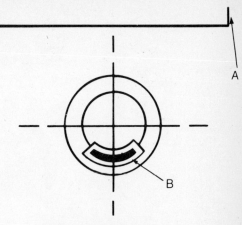

A. Front face of engine block
B. Rotor position when properly installed

Rotor position with the distributor properly installed on the 4-150

o'clock position, relative to the oil pump gear shaft slot. When the distributor is comnpletely in place, the rotor should be at the 6:00 o'clock position. If not, remove the distributor and perform the entire procedure again.

4. Tighten the lockbolt.

Alternator and Generator

All Jeep vehicles through 1964 had DC generators. In 1965, alternators were installed on the Tuxedo Park versions of the CJ-5 and CJ-6. These models were known respectively as the CJ-5A and CJ-6A. Starting 1966, all Jeep vehicles came with alternators.

An alternator differs from a conventional DC shunt generator in that the armature is stationary, and is called the stator, while the field rotates and is called the rotor. The higher current values in the alternator's stator are conducted to the external circuit through fixed leads and connections, rather than through a rotating commutator and brushes as in a DC generator. This eliminates a major point of maintenance.

Troubleshooting Basic Charging System Problems

Problem	Cause	Solution
Noisy alternator	• Loose mountings • Loose drive pulley • Worn bearings • Brush noise • Internal circuits shorted (High pitched whine)	• Tighten mounting bolts • Tighten pulley • Replace alternator • Replace alternator • Replace alternator
Squeal when starting engine or accelerating	• Glazed or loose belt	• Replace or adjust belt
Indicator light remains on or ammeter indicates discharge (engine running)	• Broken fan belt • Broken or disconnected wires • Internal alternator problems • Defective voltage regulator	• Install belt • Repair or connect wiring • Replace alternator • Replace voltage regulator
Car light bulbs continually burn out— battery needs water continually	• Alternator/regulator overcharging	• Replace voltage regulator/alternator
Car lights flare on acceleration	• Battery low • Internal alternator/regulator problems	• Charge or replace battery • Replace alternator/regulator
Low voltage output (alternator light flickers continually or ammeter needle wanders)	• Loose or worn belt • Dirty or corroded connections • Internal alternator/regulator problems	• Replace or adjust belt • Clean or replace connections • Replace alternator or regulator

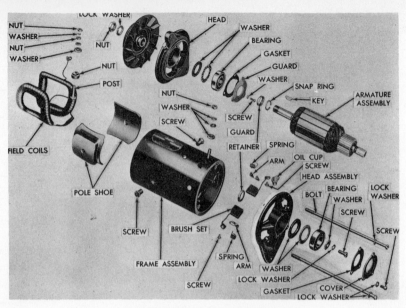

Exploded view of the generator

The alternator employs a 3-phase stator winding. The rotor consists of a field coil encased between 6-poled, interleaved sections, producing a 12-pole magnetic field with alternating north and south poles. By rotating the rotor inside the stator, and alternating current is induced in the stator windings. This alternating current is changed to direct current by diodes and is routed out of the alternator through the output terminal. Diode rectifiers act as one way electrical valves. Half of the diodes have a negative polarity and are grounded. The other half of the diodes have a positive polarity and are connected to the output terminal.

Since the diodes have a high resistance to the flow of current in one direction, and a low resistance in the opposite direction, they are connected in a manner which allows current to flow from the alternator to the battery in the low resistance direction.

The high resistance in the other direction prevents the flow of current from the battery to the alternator. Because of this feature, there is

1. Auxiliary terminal
2. Output terminal
3. Auxiliary terminal
4. Field terminal
5. Ground terminal
6. Ground terminal

Motorola alternator used through 1971

1972–75 Prestolite alternator

Delcotron alternator used on 1976 and later Jeep

no need for a circuit breaker between the alternator and the battery.

Residual magnetism in the rotor field poles is minimal. The starting field current must, therefore, be supplied by the battery. It is connected to the field winding through the ignition switch and the charge indicator lamp or ammeter.

As in the DC shunt generator, the alternator voltage is regulated by varying the field current. This is accomplished electronically in the transistorized voltage regulator. No current regulator is required because all alternators have self limiting current characteristics.

An alternator is better that a conventional, DC shunt generator because it is lighter and more compact, because it is designed to supply the battery and accessory circuits through a wide range of engine speeds, and because it eliminates the necessary maintenance of replacing brushes and servicing commutators.

The transistorized voltage regulator is an electronic switching device. It senses the voltage at the auxiliary terminal of the alternator and supplies the necessary field current for maintaining the system voltage at the output terminal. The output current is determined by the battery electrical load, such as operating headlights or heater blower.

The transistorized voltage regulator is a sealed unit that has no adjustments and must be replaced as a complete unit when it ceases to operate.

ALTERNATOR PRECAUTIONS

To prevent damage to the alternator and regulator, the following precautionary measures must be taken when working with the electrical system.

1. Never reverse battery connections. Always check the battery polarity visually. This is to be done before any connections are made to be sure that all of the connections correspond to the battery ground polarity of the Jeep.

2. Booster batteries for starting must be connected properly. Make sure that the positive cable of the booster battery is connected to the positive terminal of the battery that is getting the boost. This applies to both negative and ground cables.

3. Disconnect the battery cables before using a fast charger. The charger has a tendency to force current through the diodes in the opposite direction for which they were designed. This burns out the diodes.

4. Never use a fast charger as a booster for starting the vehicle.

5. Never disconnect the voltage regulator while the engine is running.

6. Do not ground the alternator output terminal.

7. Do not operate the alternator on an open circuit with the field energized.

8. Do not attempt to polarize an alternator.

REMOVAL AND INSTALLATION

1. Remove all of the electrical connections from the alternator or generator. Label all of the wires so that you can install them correctly.

2. Remove all of the attaching nuts, bolts and washers noting different sized threads or nuts and bolts that go in certain holes.

3. Remove the alternator carefully.

4. To install, reverse the above procedure and adjust the belt as described below. Torque the mounting bolts to 25–30 ft.lb.; the sliding adjuster bolt to 20 ft.lb.

BELT TENSION ADJUSTMENT

The fan belt drives the generator/alternator and the water pump. If it is too loose, it will slip and the generator/alternator will not be able to produce the rated current. if the belt is too loose, the water pump would not be driven and the engine could overheat. Check the tension of the fan belt by pushing your thumb down on the longest span of belt midway between the pulleys. If the belt flexes more than ½" (12.7mm), it should be tightened. Loosen the bolt on the adjusting bracket and pivot bolt and move the alternator or generator away from the engine to tighten the belt. Do not apply pressure to the rear of the case aluminum housing of an alternator; it might break. Tighten the adjusting bolts when the proper tension is reached.

Regulator

The voltage regulators that are used with alternators are transistorized and cannot be serviced. If the voltage regulator is not operating properly, it must be replaced.

The voltage regulators that are used with shunt type generators are serviceable and can be adjusted. These regulators have three units: the circuit breaker, the voltage regulator and the current limiting regulator. Each has a separate function.

VOLTAGE REGULATOR

The function of the voltage regulator unit is to hold the generated voltage at a predetermined value as long as the circuit values allow the voltage to build to the operating load.

The electromagnet of the voltage regulator unit has a winding of many turns of fine wire and is connected across the charging circuit so that the system voltage controls the amount of magnetism. The contacts of the voltage regulator unit are connected in the generator field circuit so that the field circuit is completed through the contacts when they are closed and through a resistor when the contacts are opened.

When the voltage rises to a predetermined amount, there is sufficient magnetism created by the regulator winding to pull the armature down. This opens the contacts and inserts resistance in the field circuit of the generator, thus reducing the field current. The generated voltage immediately drops, reducing the pull on the armature to the point where the spring closes the contacts. The output again rises and the cycle is repeated.

These cycles occur at sufficiently high frequencies to hold the generated voltage at a constant level and they will continue as long as the voltage of the circuit is high enough to keep the voltage regulator unit in operation. When there is a current load that is great enough to lower the battery voltage below the operating voltage of the voltage regulating unit, the contacts will remain closed and the generator will maintain a charging rate that is limited by its speed and capacity output.

CURRENT LIMITING REGULATOR

The function of the current limiting regulator is to limit the output of the generator to its maximum safe output.

The electromagnet of the current regulator unit consists of a winding of heavy wire connected in a series with the generator output. When the generator output reaches a predetermined level, the current in the winding produces enough magnetism to overcome spring tension and pull the armature down. This opens the contacts and inserts resistance in the field circuit of the generator. With the field current reduced by the resistance, the generator output falls and there is no longer sufficient magnetism to hold the contacts open. As soon as the spring closes the contacts, the output and the cycle is repeated. These cycles occur at a high enough frequency to limit the output to a minimum fluctuation.

VOLTAGE TESTS AND ADJUSTMENTS

Circuit Breaker

The circuit breaker is the unit with the heavy wire windings and is located on the end of the unit.

1. Connect an ammeter in series with the regulator B (battery) terminal and the lead that is removed from that terminal. Connect a voltmeter from the regulator A (armature) terminal to the regulator base.

2. Disconnect the field lead from the regulator F terminal and insert a variable resistance between the lead and the regulator terminal.

3. Run the generator at about 1,000 generator rpm. Insert all of the resistance in the field circuit. Slowly reduce the resistance, noting the voltage reading just before the change caused by the closing of the circuit breaker. In-

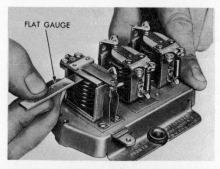

Adjusting the air gap on an Autolite regulator

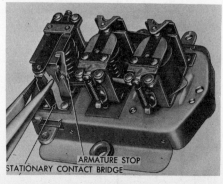

Adjusting the point gap on an Autolite regulator

Bending the spring hanger to adjust the voltage on an Autolite regulator

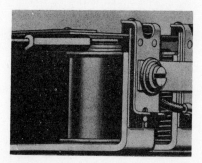

Adjusting the air gap on the voltage unit in the Autolite regulator

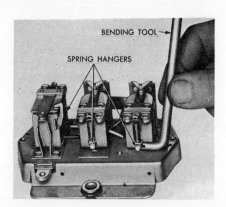

BENDING TOOL ➞

SPRING HANGERS

Adjusting the voltage unit setting in the Autolite regulator

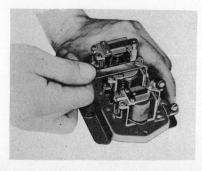

Cleaning the Autolite regulator current regulator points

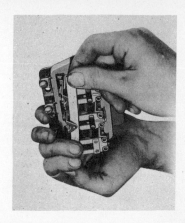

Using tape to clean the current regulator points on an Autolite regulator

PIN GAUGE

ADJUSTING SCREW

Adjusting the current regulator air gap on the Autolite regulator

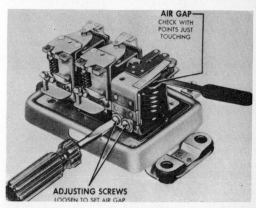

AIR GAP
CHECK WITH
POINTS JUST
TOUCHING

ADJUSTING SCREWS
LOOSEN TO SET AIR GAP

Measuring the cutout air gap on the Delco regulator

crease the charging rate to the figure specified for the regulator being tested, then reduce the charging rate by inserting resistance into the field circuit. Note the charging rate just before the circuit breaker opens and the ammeter reading drops to zero. The closing voltage and the opening voltage or current should be within the limits specified.

4. To adjust the closing voltage, change the

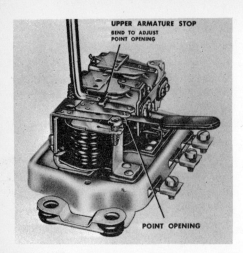

Adjusting the cutout point opening on the Delco regulator

Adjusting the voltage unit setting on Delco regulators

Adjusting the cutout closing voltage on the Delco regulator

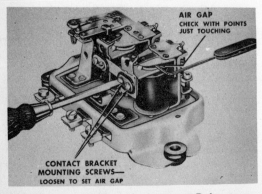

Adjusting the voltage unit air gap on Delco regulators

armature spring tension by bending the hanger at the lower end of the spring. Increase the spring tension to raise the closing voltage or decrease the tension to lower the voltage. To adjust the opening voltage, raise or lower the stationary contact, keeping the contacts perfectly aligned. Increasing the contact gap lowers the opening voltage. Change the contact gap by expanding or contracting the contact gap by expanding or contracting the stationary contact bracket, keeping the contacts aligned. Do not adjust the gap between the contacts to less than the specified minimum.

Voltage Regulator

The voltage regulator unit is the one with the fine wire winding.

1. Connect the ammeter as noted above and connect the voltmeter from the regulator B terminal to the regulator base. Remove the variable resistance from the field circuit.

2. Run the generator at one half maximum output for 15 minutes to make sure the regulator is at normal temperature. Have the cover on the unit during this warmup period and also when taking the readings.

3. Stop the engine, then bring it to approximately 2,500 generator rpm. Adjust the amperage to one half of the maximum output by turning on lights or accessories and then note the voltmeter reading. This reading should be within the limits specified for the voltage regulator.

4. To adjust the operating voltage, change the armature spring tension by bending the hanger at the lower end of the armature spring. After each adjustment, stop the engine

and then restart it. Bring it up to speed and adjust the current before taking a reading. The clicks of the opening and closing of the contacts should be regular and clear without irregularities. If the tone is not clear and regular, remove the regulator cover and inspect the contacts. The contacts should be flat and not burned excessively, and should be aligned to make full face contact. Refer to the section on cleaning the contacts if necessary.

Current Regulator

The current regulator is the unit in the middle of the unit with the heavy wire winding.

1. Connect the regulator and instruments as described above for the voltage regulator and run the generator at approximately 3,000 generator rpm. Turn on lights and accessories so the generator must charge at its maximum rate. The ammeter should show a reading within the specified limits.

2. To adjust the opening amperage, change the armature spring tension by bending the hanger at the lower end of the armature spring. Stop the engine after each adjustment and then restart it. Bring the engine to speed and take an ammeter reading. Keep the cover on the unit when taking the readings. The clocks of the points closing and opening should be clear in tone and regular in frequency without irregularities or misses. If this is not the case, the contacts will have to be serviced.

Contacts

The contacts should be inspected on all three of the units inside the cover of the voltage regulator. The contacts will become grayed and slightly worn during normal use. If the contacts are burned or dirty, or if they are not smooth or aligned properly, they should be adjusted and cleaned. File the contacts smooth. Just file enough so that there is a smooth surface presented to each contact. It is not necessary to file out every trace of pitting. After filing, dampen a clean cloth with carbon tetrachloride and pull the cloth between the contacts of each of the three units. Repeat with a clean dry cloth.

NOTE: *Keep in mind that after filing the points, the gap might have been changed enough to affect the performance of the three units. Check the three units and perform the adjustments. It might be a good idea to examine the contacts before making any adjustments. If the contacts need to be serviced, do it before adjusting spring tensions, etc.*

REMOVAL AND INSTALLATION

If the voltage regulator still does not function properly, after all of the checks and adjustments, replace the entire unit. Follow the procedure below.

1. Remove all of the electrical connections. Label them as you remove them so you can replace them in the correct order on the replacement unit.

2. Remove all of the holddown screws and then remove the unit from the vehicle.

3. Install the new voltage regulator using the holddown screws from the old one, or new ones if they are provided with the replacement regulator. Tighten down the holddown screws.

4. Connect the armature lead to the armature terminal of the voltage regulator.

5. Connect the battery lead to the battery terminal of the voltage regulator.

6. Momentarily touch the field lead to the battery terminal of the voltage regulator. This polarizes the generator and voltage regulator so they have the same polarization as the rest of the electrical system. This has to be done every time all of the leads are disconnected from the generator voltage regulator.

7. Connect the field lead to the field terminal of the voltage regulator.

Starter

REMOVAL AND INSTALLATION

The starter on the L4–134, F4–134 and 6–226 engines can be removed from the top of the engine. The starter motor on all other engines must be removed from beneath the vehicle.

1. Disconnect the battery ground.

2. Raise and support the vehicle on jackstands.

3. Remove all wires from the starter and tag them for installation.

4. Remove all but one upper attaching bolt, support the starter (it's heavier than it looks) and remove the last bolt.

5. Pull the starter from the engine.

6. Installation is the reverse of removal. Torque the mounting bolts to:

4–134, 6–225, 6–232, 6–258, 8–304: 25 ft.lb.
4–150: 17 ft.lb.
6–226, 6–230: 30 ft.lb.

STARTER DRIVE REPLACEMENT
Autolite

1. Remove the cover of the starter drive's actuating lever arm. Remove the through bolts, starter drive gear housing, and the return spring of the driver gear's actuating lever.

2. Remove the pivot pin which retains the starter gear actuating lever and remove the lever and armature.

3. Remove the stopring retainer. Remove and discard the stopring which holds the drive

Troubleshooting Basic Starting System Problems

Problem	Cause	Solution
Starter motor rotates engine slowly	• Battery charge low or battery defective	• Charge or replace battery
	• Defective circuit between battery and starter motor	• Clean and tighten, or replace cables
	• Low load current	• Bench-test starter motor. Inspect for worn brushes and weak brush springs.
	• High load current	• Bench-test starter motor. Check engine for friction, drag or coolant in cylinders. Check ring gear-to-pinion gear clearance.
Starter motor will not rotate engine	• Battery charge low or battery defective	• Charge or replace battery
	• Faulty solenoid	• Check solenoid ground. Repair or replace as necessary.
	• Damage drive pinion gear or ring gear	• Replace damaged gear(s)
	• Starter motor engagement weak	• Bench-test starter motor
	• Starter motor rotates slowly with high load current	• Inspect drive yoke pull-down and point gap, check for worn end bushings, check ring gear clearance
	• Engine seized	• Repair engine
Starter motor drive will not engage (solenoid known to be good)	• Defective contact point assembly	• Repair or replace contact point assembly
	• Inadequate contact point assembly ground	• Repair connection at ground screw
	• Defective hold-in coil	• Replace field winding assembly
Starter motor drive will not disengage	• Starter motor loose on flywheel housing	• Tighten mounting bolts
	• Worn drive end busing	• Replace bushing
	• Damaged ring gear teeth	• Replace ring gear or driveplate
	• Drive yoke return spring broken or missing	• Replace spring
Starter motor drive disengages prematurely	• Weak drive assembly thrust spring	• Replace drive mechanism
	• Hold-in coil defective	• Replace field winding assembly
Low load current	• Worn brushes	• Replace brushes
	• Weak brush springs	• Replace springs

gear to the armature shaft and then remove the drive gear assembly.

To install the unit:

1. Lightly Lubriplate® the armature shaft splines and install the starter drive gear assembly on the shaft. Install a new stopring and stopring retainer.

2. Position the starter drive gear actuating lever to the frame and starter drive assembly. Install the pivot pin.

3. Fill the starter drive gear housing one quarter full of grease.

4. Position the drive actuating lever return spring and the drive gear housing to the frame, then install and tighten the through bolts. Be sure that the stopring retainer is properly seated in the drive housing.

Delco-Remy

1. Remove the through bolts.

2. Remove the starter drive housing.

3. Slide the two piece thrust collar off the end of the armature shaft.

4. Slide a standard ½″ (12.7mm) pipe coupling, or other spacer, onto the shaft so the end of the coupling butts against the edge of the retainer.

5. Tap the end of the coupling with a hammer, driving the retainer toward the armature end of the snapring.

6. Remove the snapring from its groove in the shaft with pliers. Slide the retainer and the starter drive from the armature.

To install the unit:

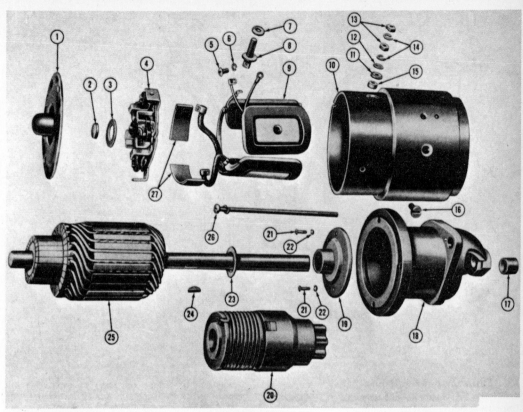

1. End plate	10. Frame	19. Intermediate bearing
2. Plug	11. Insulating washer	20. Bendix drive
3. Thrust washer	12. Washer	21. Screw
4. Brush plate assembly	13. Nut	22. Lockwasher
5. Screw	14. Lockwasher	23. Thrust washer
6. Lockwasher	15. Insulating bushing	24. Key
7. Insulating washer	16. Pole shoe screw	25. Armature
8. Terminal	17. Sleeve bearing	26. Thru-bolt
9. Field coil and pole shoe set	18. Drive end frame	27. Insulator

4-134 starter motor

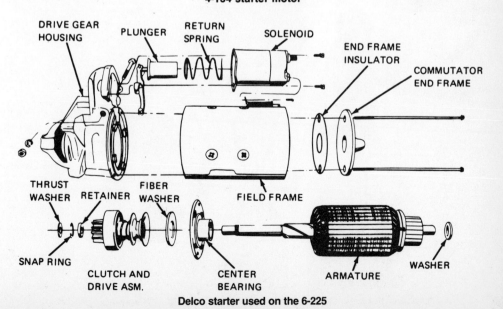

Delco starter used on the 6-225

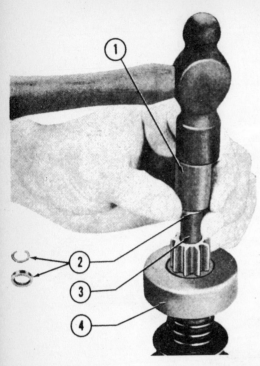

1. ½ in. pipe coupling   3. Armature shaft
2. Snap ring and retainer   4. Drive assembly

Removing the starter drive assembly from the armature shaft

1. Lubricate the drive end of the shaft with silicone lubricant.

2. Slide the drive gear assembly onto the shaft, with the gear facing outward.

3. Slide the retainer onto the shaft with the cupped surface facing away from the gear.

4. Stand the whole starter assembly on a block of wood with the snapring positioned on the upper end of the shaft. Drive the snapring down with a small block of wood and a hammer. Slide the snapring into its groove.

5. Install the thrust collar onto the shaft with the shoulder next to the snapring.

6. With the retainer on one side of the snapring and the thrust collar on the other side, squeeze them together with a pair of pliers until the ring seats in the retainer. On models without a thrust collar, use a washer. Remember to remove the washer before installing the starter in the engine.

Prestolite

1. Slide the thrust collar off the armature shaft.

2. Using a standard ½″ (12.7mm) pipe connector, drive the snapring retainer off the shaft.

3. Remove the snapring from the groove, and then remove the drive assembly.

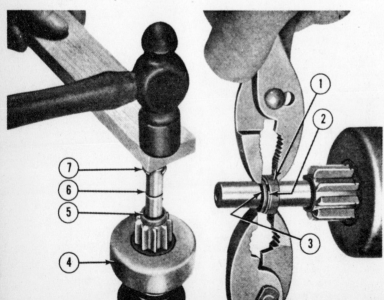

1. Retainer
2. Snap ring
3. Thrust collar
4. Drive assembly
5. Retainer
6. Groove in the armature shaft
7. Snap ring

Installing the pinion stop retainer and thrust collar on the armature shaft

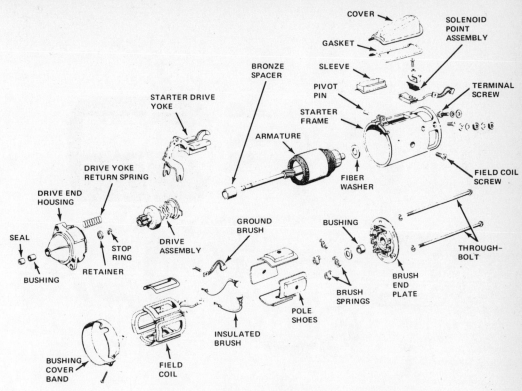

1972–77 starter motor

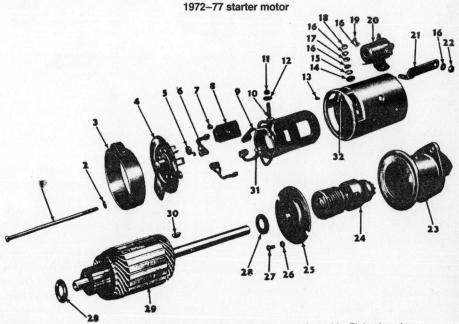

1. Thru bolt
2. Lockwasher
3. Band cover
4. Commutator end head
5. Brush spring
6. Brush set
7. Pole shoe screw
8. Shoe pole
9. Field coil
10. Terminal stud
11. Terminal stud insulator bushing
12. Terminal stud insulator inner washer
13. Rd. head ground screw
14. Terminal stud insulator outer washer
15. Plain washer
16. Terminal stud lockwasher
17. Terminal stud hex. nut
18. Terminal stud hex. nut
19. Rd. head switch mounting screw
20. Solenoid switch
21. Connector
22. Hex. nut
23. Pinion housing
24. Bendix drive
25. Bronze intermediate bearing
26. Ground lockwasher
27. Rd. head internal bearing screw
28. Thrust washer
29. Armature
30. Woodruff key
31. Equalizer
32. Dowel pin

Starter motor used on the 6-226

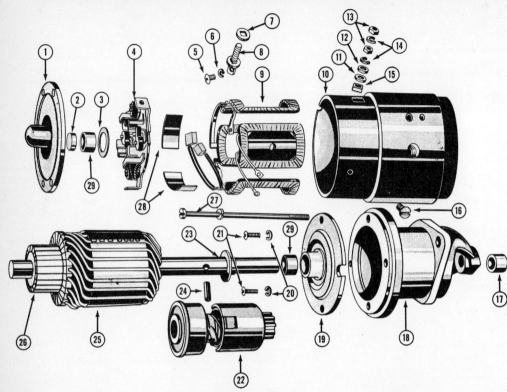

1. Commutator endplate
2. Plug
3. Thrust washer
4. Brush holder
5. Screw
6. Lockwasher
7. Washer
8. Terminal stud
9. Field coil and pole shoe
10. Motor frame
11. Washer
12. Insulator washer
13. Terminal stud nut
14. Lockwasher
15. Insulator washer
16. Screw
17. Bearing
18. Drive end frame
19. Intermediate bearing plate
20. Lockwasher
21. Screw
22. Bendix Folo-Thru® drive
23. Thrust washer
24. Holding pin
25. Armature
26. Commutator
27. Through bolt
28. Insulator
29. Bushing

6-230 starter motor

To install the unit:

1. Lubricate the drive end and splines with Lubriplate®.

2. Install the clutch assembly onto the shaft.

3. Install the snapring retainer with the cupped surface facing toward the end of the shaft.

4. Install the snapring into the groove. Use a new snapring if necessary.

5. Install the thrust collar onto the shaft with the shoulder against the snapring.

6. Force the retainer over the snapring in the same manner as was used for the Delco-Remy starters.

SOLENOID OR RELAY REPLACEMENT

Autolite

On the early CJ-2A, CJ-3A, CJ-3B, CJ-5, and CJ-6 with Autolite starters, there were no solenoids or relays to activate the starter drive. The starter drive activated itself by the cen-

trifugal force of the starter motor and deactivated itself in the normal way (by the centrifugal force of the engine's flywheel).

Autolite starters were installed with solenoids mounted on the starter housing beginning in 1960.

To remove the solenoid from the starter, remove all of the leads to the solenoid, remove the connecting lever, and remove the attaching bolts that hold the solenoid assembly to the starter housing. Remove the solenoid assembly from the starter housing.

To install the solenoid assembly, reverse the above procedure.

Delco-Remy

Remove the leads from the solenoid. Remove the drive housing of the starter motor. Remove the shift lever pin and bolt from the shift lever. Remove the attaching bolts that hold the solenoid assembly to the housing of the starter mo-

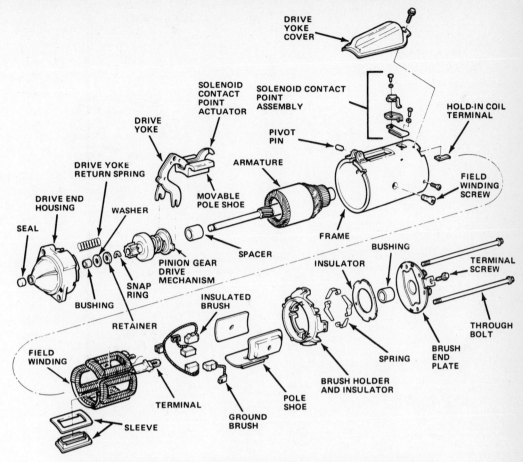

Starter motor used on all 1978–86 engines, except the 4-150 and 4-151

tor. Remove the starter solenoid from the starter housing. To install the solenoid, reverse the above procedure.

Prestolite

1. Remove the leads from the solenoid assembly.
2. Remove the attaching bolts that hold the solenoid to the starter housing.
3. Remove the bolt form the shift lever.
4. Remove the solenoid assembly from the starter housing.
5. Reverse the procedure for installation.

STARTER OVERHAUL

Autolite/Motorcraft

DISASSEMBLY

1. Remove the cover screw, the cover through-bolts, the starter drive end housing and the starter drive plunger lever return spring.
2. Remove the starter gear plunger lever pivot pin, the lever and the armature. Remove the stop ring retainer and the stop ring from

the armature shaft (discard the ring), then the starter drive gear assembly.

3. Remove the brush end plate, the insulator assembly and the brushes from the plastic holder, then lift out the brush holder. For reassembly, note the position of the brush holder with respect to the end terminal.
4. Remove the two ground brush-to-frame screws.
5. Bend up the sleeve's edges which are inserted in the frame's rectangular hole, then remove the sleeve and the retainer. Detach the field coil ground wire from the copper tab.
6. Remove the three coil retaining screws. Cut the field coil connection at the switch post lead, then remove the pole shoes and the coils from the frame.
7. Cut the positive brush leads from the field coils (as close to the field connection point as possible).
8. Check the armature and the armature windings for broken or burned insulation, open circuits or grounds.
9. Check the commutator for runout. If it is rough, has flat spots or is more than 0.005"

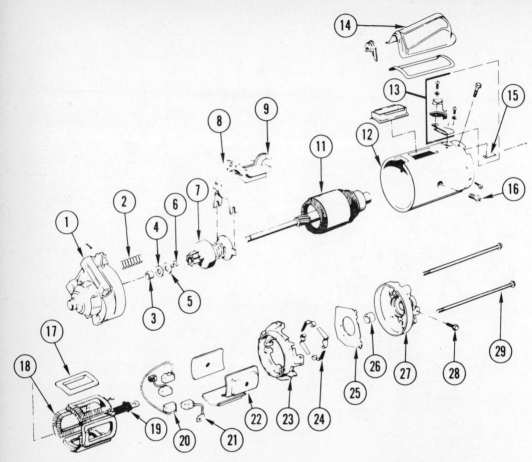

1. Drive end housing
2. Drive yoke return spring
3. Bushing
4. Washer
5. Retainer
6. Snapring
7. Pinion gear drive mechanism
8. Drive yoke
9. Solenoid contact point actuator
10. Moveable pole shoe
11. Armature
12. Frame
13. Solenoid contact point assembly
14. Drive yoke cover
15. Hold-in coil terminal
16. Field winding screw
17. Sleeve
18. Field winding
19. Terminal
20. Insulated brush
21. Ground brush
22. Pole shoe
23. Brush holder and insulator
24. Springs
25. Insulator
26. Bushing
27. Brush end plate
28. Terminal screw
29. Through bolt

Starter motor used on the 1984–86 4-150

(0.127mm) out of round, reface the commutator face.

10. Inspect the armature shaft and the two bearings for scoring and excessive wear, then replace (if necessary).

11. Inspect the starter drive. If the gear teeth are pitted, broken or excessively worn, replace the starter drive.

NOTE: *The factory brush length is ½" (12.7mm); the wear limit is ¼" (6.35mm).*

ASSEMBLY

1. Install the starter terminal, the insulator, the washers and the nut in the frame.

NOTE: *Be sure to position the screw slot perpendicular to the frame end surface.*

2. Position the coils and the pole pieces, with the coil leads in the terminal screw slot, then install the screws. When tightening the pole screws, strike the frame with several sharp hammer blows to align the pole shoes, then stake the screws.

3. Install the solenoid coil and the retainer, then bend the tabs to hold the coils to the frame.

4. Using resin-core solder and a 300 watt iron, solder the field coils and the solenoid wire to the starter terminal. Check for continuity and ground connections of the assembled coils.

5. Position the solenoid coil ground terminal over the nearest ground screw hole and the ground brushes-to-starter frame, then install the screws.

6. Apply a thin coating of Lubriplate* on

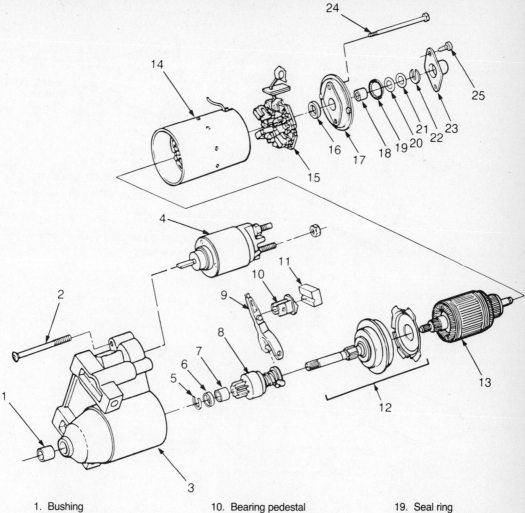

1. Bushing
2. Screw
3. Shield
4. Solenoid switch
5. Retainer
6. Stop ring
7. Bushing
8. Overrunning clutch drive
9. Fork
10. Bearing pedestal
11. Sealing rubber
12. Planetary gear system
13. Armature
14. Stator frame
15. Brush holder
16. Gasket
17. Commutator end shield
18. Bushing
19. Seal ring
20. Shim
21. Shim
22. Retaining washer
23. Closure cap
24. Hexagon screw
25. Screw

Starter motor used on the 1987 4-150

the armature shaft splines. Install the starter motor drive gear assembly-to-armature shaft, followed by a new stop ring and retainer. Install the armature in the starter frame.

7. Position the starter drive gear plunger lever to the frame and the starter drive assembly, then install the pivot pin. Place some grease into the end housing bore. Fill it about ¼ full, then position the drive end housing to the frame.

8. Install the brush holder and the brush springs. The positive brush leads should be positioned in their respective brush holder slots, to prevent grounding problems.

9. Install the brush end plate. Be certain that the end plate insulator is in the proper position on the end plate. Install the two starter frame through-bolts and torque them to 55–75 in.lb.

10. Install the starter drive plunger lever cover and tighten the retaining screw.

Delco-Remy

Disassembly

1. Detach the field coil connectors from the motor solenoid terminal.

NOTE: *If equipped, remove solenoid mounting screws.*

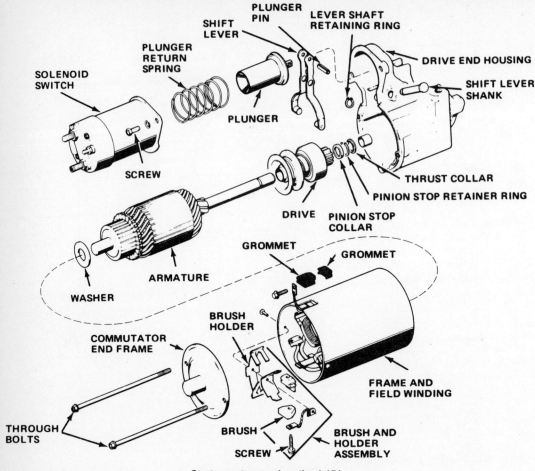

Starter motor used on the 4-151

2. Remove the through-bolts, the commutator end frame, the field frame and the armature assembly from drive housing.

3. Remove the overrunning clutch from the armature shaft as follows:

    a. Slide the two piece thrust collar off the end of the armature shaft.

    b. Slide a standard ½" (12.7mm) pipe coupling or other spacer onto the shaft, so that the coupling end butts against the retainer edge.

    c. Using a hammer, tap the coupling end, driving the retainer towards the armature end of the snapring.

    d. Using snapring pliers, remove the snapring from its groove in the shaft, then slide the retainer and the clutch from the shaft.

4. Disassemble the field frame brush assembly by releasing the V-spring and removing the support pin. The brush holders, the brushes and the springs can now be pulled out as a unit and the leads disconnected.

NOTE: *On the integral frame units, remove*

the brush holder from the brush support and the brush screw.

5. If equipped, separate the solenoid from the lever housing.

Cleaning And Inspection

1. Clean the parts with a rag. Do not immerse the parts in a solvent.

CAUTION: *Immersion in a solvent will dissolve the grease that is packed in the clutch mechanism. It will damage the armature and the field coil insulation.*

2. Test the overrunning clutch action. The pinion should turn freely in the overrunning direction but must not slip in the cranking direction. Check that the pinion teeth have not been chipped, cracked or excessively worn. Replace the unit (if necessary).

3. Inspect the armature commutator. If the commutator is rough or out of round, it should be machined and undercut.

NOTE: *Undercut the insulation between the commutator bars by $\frac{1}{32}$" (0.79375mm). The undercut must be the full width of the insula-*

tion and flat at the bottom. A triangular groove will not be satisfactory. Most late model starter motor use a molded armature commutator design. No attempt to undercut the insulation should be made or serious damage may result to the commutator.

Assembly

1. Install the brushes into the holders, then install solenoid (if equipped).

2. Assemble the insulated and the grounded holder together. Using the V-spring, position and assemble the unit on the support pin. Push the holders and the spring to bottom of the support, then rotate the spring to engage the slot in the support. Attach the ground wire to the grounded brush and the field lead wire to the insulated brush, then repeat this procedure for other brush sets.

3. Assemble the overrunning clutch to the armature shaft as follows:

   a. Lubricate the drive end of the shaft with silicone lubricant.

   b. Slide the clutch assembly onto the shaft with the pinion outward.

   c. Slide the retainer onto the shaft with the cupped surface facing away from the pinion.

   d. Stand the armature up on a wood surface with the commutator downward. Position the snapring on the upper end of the shaft and drive it onto the shaft with a small block of wood and a hammer, then slide the snapring into groove.

   e. Install the thrust collar onto the shaft with the shoulder next to snapring.

   f. With the retainer on one side of the snapring and the thrust collar on the other side, squeeze two sets together (with pliers) until the ring seats in the retainer. On models without a thrust collar use a washer. Remember to remove the washer before continuing.

4. Lubricate the drive end bushing with silicone lubricant, then slide the armature and the clutch assembly into place, while engaging the shift lever with the clutch.

NOTE: *On the non-integral starters, the shift lever may be installed in the drive gear housing first.*

5. Position the field frame over the armature and apply sealer (silicone) between the frame and the solenoid case. Position the frame against the drive housing, making sure the brushes are not damaged in the process.

6. Lubricate the commutator end bushing with silicone lubricant, place a washer on the armature shaft and slide the commutator end frame onto the shaft. Install the through-bolts and tighten.

7. Reconnect the field coil connections to the solenoid motor terminal. Install the solenoid mounting screws (if equipped).

8. Check the pinion clearance. It should be 0.010–0.140" (0.254–3.556mm) with the pinion in the cranking position, on all models.

Bosch

DISASSEMBLY

1. Disconnect the field coil wire from the solenoid terminal.

2. Remove the solenoid and work the plunger off the shift fork.

3. Remove the two end shield bearing cap screws, the cap and the washers.

4. Remove the two commutator end frame cover through-bolts, the cover, the two brushes and the brush plate.

5. Slide the field frame off over the armature. Remove the shift lever pivot bolt, the rubber gasket and the metal plate.

6. Remove the armature assembly and the shift lever from the drive end housing. Press the stop collar off the snapring, then remove the snapring, the clutch assembly, the clutch assembly and the drive end housing from the armature.

INSPECTION AND SERVICE

1. The brushes that are worn more than ½ the length of new brushes or are oil-soaked, should be replaced. The new brushes are $^{11}/_{16}$" (17.4625mm) long.

2. Do not immerse the starter clutch unit in cleaning solvent. Solvent will wash the lubricant from the clutch.

3. Place the drive unit on the armature shaft, then, while holding the armature, rotate the pinion.

NOTE: *The drive pinion should rotate smoothly in one direction only. The pinion may not rotate easily but as long as it rotates smoothly it is in good condition. If the clutch unit does not function properly or if the pinion is worn, chipped or burred, replace the unit.*

ASSEMBLY

1. Lubricate the armature shaft and the splines with SAE 10W or 30W oil.

2. Fit the drive end housing onto the armature, then install the clutch, the stop collar and the snapring onto the armature.

3. Install the shift fork pivot bolt, the rubber gasket and the metal plate. Slide the field frame into position and install the brush holder and the brushes.

4. Position the commutator end frame cover and the through-bolts.

5. Install the shim and the armature shaft

lock. Check the endplay, which should be 0.002–0.012″ (0.05–0.30mm), then install the bearing cover.

6. Assemble the plunger to the shift fork, then install the solenoid with its mounting bolts. Connect the field wire to the solenoid.

Prestolite

DISASSEMBLY AND ASSEMBLY

1. To remove the solenoid, remove the screw from the field coil connector and solenoid mounting screws. Rotate the solenoid 90° and remove it along with the plunger return spring.

2. For further service, remove the two through-bolts, then remove the commutator end frame and washer.

3. To replace the clutch and drive assembly proceed as follows:

 a. Remove the thrust washer or the collar from the armature shaft.

 b. Slide a ⅝″ (15.875mm) deep socket or a piece of pipe of suitable size over the shaft and against the retainer as a driving tool. Tap the tool to remove the retainer off the snapring.

 c. Remove the snapring from the groove in the shaft. Check and make sure the snapring isn't distorted. If it is, it will be necessary to replace it with a new one upon reassembly.

 d. Remove the retainer and clutch assembly from the armature shaft.

4. The shift lever may be disconnected from the plunger at this time by removing the roll pin.

5. On models with the standard starter, the brushes may be removed by removing the brush holder pivot pin which positions one insulated and one grounded brush. Remove the brush and spring and replace the brushes as necessary.

6. On models with the smaller 5MT starter, remove the brush and holder from the brush support, then remove the screw from the brush holder and separate the brush and holder. Replace the brushes as necessary.

7. Installation is the reverse of removal. Assemble the armature and clutch and drive assembly as follows:

 a. Lubricate the drive end of the armature shaft and slide the clutch assembly onto the armature shaft with the pinion away from the armature.

 b. Slide the retainer onto the shaft with the cupped side facing the end of the shaft.

 c. Install the snapring into the groove on the armature shaft.

 d. Install the thrust washer on the shaft.

 e. Position the retainer and thrust washer with the snapring in between. Using two pliers, grip the retainer and thrust washer or collar and squeeze until the snapring is forced into the retainer and is held securely in the groove in the armature shaft.

 f. Lubricate the drive gear housing bushing.

 g. Engage the shift lever yoke with the clutch and slide the complete assembly into the drive gear housing.

NOTE: *When the starter motor has been disassembled or the solenoid has been replaced, it is necessary to check the pinion clearance. Pinion clearance must be correct to prevent the buttons on the shift lever yoke from rubbing on the clutch collar during cranking.*

CHECKING PINION CLEARANCE

1. Disconnect the motor field coil connector from the solenoid motor terminal and insulate it carefully.

2. Connect one 12 volt battery lead to the solenoid switch terminal and the other to the starter frame.

3. Flash a jumper lead momentarily from the solenoid motor terminal to the starter frame. This will shift the pinion into cranking position and it will remain there until the battery is disconnected.

4. Push the pinion back as far as possible to take up any movement, and check the clearance with a feeler gauge. The clearance should be 0.010–0.140″ (0.254–3.556mm).

5. There is no means for adjusting pinion clearance on the starter motor. If clearance does not fall within the limits, check for improper installation and replace all worn parts.

Battery

REMOVAL AND INSTALLATION

1. Remove the holddown screws from the battery box. Loosen the nuts that secure the cable ends to the battery terminals. Lift the battery cables from the terminals with a twisting motion.

2. If there is a battery cable puller available, make use of it. Lift the battery from the vehicle.

3. Before installing the battery in the vehicle, make sure that the battery terminals are clean and free from corrosion. Use a battery terminal cleaner on the terminals and on the inside of the battery cable ends. If a cleaner is not available, use a heavy sandpaper to remove the corrosion. A mixture of baking soda and water will neutralize any acid. Place the battery in the vehicle. Install the cables on the terminals. Tighten the nuts on the cable ends.

Smear a light coating of grease on the cable ends and the tops of the terminals. This will prevent buildup of oxidized acid on the terminals and the cable ends. Install and tighten the nuts of the battery box.

ENGINE MECHANICAL

Design

L-HEAD 4-CYLINDER

The model L4–134 engine is an L-head 4-cylinder engine. The cylinder block and crankcase are cast integrally. Both intake and exhaust valves are mounted in the cylinder block with through water jacketing to provide effective cooling. The valves are operated by conventional valve tappets. The engine is equipped with a fully counterbalanced crankshaft supported by three main bearings. To better control balance, the counterweights are independently forged and permanently attached to the crankshaft with dowels and capscrews that are tack welded. Crankshaft end play is adjusted by shims placed between the crankshaft thrust shims placed between the crankshaft thrust washer and the shoulder on the crankshaft.

Aluminum pistons, forged steel connecting rods, and replaceable main and connecting rod bearings are used in this engine. The camshaft on current production engines is gear driven from the crankshaft (chain driven on early production engines).

The water pump is mounted on the front of the cylinder block, and is belt driven by the crankshaft. Circulation of the coolant is controlled by a thermostat installed in the water outlet which is mounted on top of the cylinder head.

The engine is pressure lubricated. An oil pump, gear driven by the camshaft, is mounted externally on the left side of the crankcase. The pump forces the lubricant through oil channels and drilled passages in the crankshaft to efficiently lubricate the main and connecting rod bearings. Lubricant is also force fed to the camshaft bearings and timing gears. Cylinder walls and piston pins are lubricated from spurt holes in the "follow" side of the connecting rods.

The carburetor is mounted on top of the intake manifold. The intake and exhaust manifolds are mounted on the left side of the cylinder block. A thermostatically controlled valve in the exhaust manifold controls the temperature of fuel/air mixture in the intake manifold.

F-HEAD 4 CYLINDER

The F4–134, 4-cylinder engine is of a combination valve-in-head and valve-in-block construction. The intake valves are mounted in the head and are operated by pushrods through rocker arms. The intake manifold is cast as an integral part of the cylinder head and is completely water jacketed. This type of construction transfers heat from the cooling system to the intake passages and assists in vaporizing the fuel when the engine is cold. Therefore, there is no heat control valve (heat riser) needed in the exhaust manifold.

The exhaust valves are mounted in the block with thorough water jacketing to provide effective cooling of the valves.

The engine is pressure lubricated. An oil pump which is driven by the camshaft forces the lubricant through oil channels and drilled passages in the crankshaft to efficiently lubricate the main and connecting rod bearings. Lubricant is also force fed to the camshaft bearings, rocker arms, and timing gears. Cylinder walls and piston pins are lubricated from spurt holes in the "follow" side of the connecting rods.

The circulation of the coolant is controlled by a thermostat in the water outlet elbow which is cast as part of the cylinder head.

The engine is equipped with a fully counterbalanced crankshaft that is supported by three main bearings. The counterweights of the crankshaft are independently forged and are permanently attached to the crankshaft with dowels and cap screws that are tack welded. Crankshaft endplay is adjusted by placing shims between the crankshaft thrust washer and the shoulder on the crankshaft.

The pistons have an extra groove directly above the top ring which acts as a heat dam or insulator.

The engine was available in compression ratios ranging from 6.3:1 to 7.8:1. This permits the use of regular octane gas. The displacement of the F4–134 engine is 134.2 cu. in.

4–150

The 4–150 engine used in 1984 and later models is a new design, developed from existing technology at work in the venerable 6–258. It is a four cylinder, overhead valve configuration with cast iron head and block. The crankshaft rides in 5 main bearings. Both manifolds are on the left side of the engine. The engine is thoroughly conventional in all respects. 1987 models utilize a throttle body fuel injection system, replacing the 2-bbl carburetor.

4–151

The 151 cid General Motors built, overhead valve, four cylinder engine has a crossflow cylinder head, five main crankshaft bearings, hydraulic lifters, conventional ball socket rocker

Troubleshooting Engine Mechanical Problems

Problem	Cause	Solution
External oil leaks	• Fuel pump gasket broken or improperly seated	• Replace gasket
	• Cylinder head cover RTV sealant broken or improperly seated	• Replace sealant; inspect cylinder head cover sealant flange and cylinder head sealant surface for distortion and cracks
	• Oil filler cap leaking or missing	• Replace cap
	• Oil filter gasket broken or improperly seated	• Replace oil filter
	• Oil pan side gasket broken, improperly seated or opening in RTV sealant	• Replace gasket or repair opening in sealant; inspect oil pan gasket flange for distortion
	• Oil pan front oil seal broken or improperly seated	• Replace seal; inspect timing case cover and oil pan seal flange for distortion
	• Oil pan rear oil seal broken or improperly seated	• Replace seal; inspect oil pan rear oil seal flange; inspect rear main bearing cap for cracks, plugged oil return channels, or distortion in seal groove
	• Timing case cover oil seal broken or improperly seated	• Replace seal
	• Excess oil pressure because of restricted PCV valve	• Replace PCV valve
	• Oil pan drain plug loose or has stripped threads	• Repair as necessary and tighten
	• Rear oil gallery plug loose	• Use appropriate sealant on gallery plug and tighten
	• Rear camshaft plug loose or improperly seated	• Seat camshaft plug or replace and seal, as necessary
	• Distributor base gasket damaged	• Replace gasket
Excessive oil consumption	• Oil level too high	• Drain oil to specified level
	• Oil with wrong viscosity being used	• Replace with specified oil
	• PCV valve stuck closed	• Replace PCV valve
	• Valve stem oil deflectors (or seals) are damaged, missing, or incorrect type	• Replace valve stem oil deflectors
	• Valve stems or valve guides worn	• Measure stem-to-guide clearance and repair as necessary
	• Poorly fitted or missing valve cover baffles	• Replace valve cover
	• Piston rings broken or missing	• Replace broken or missing rings
	• Scuffed piston	• Replace piston
	• Incorrect piston ring gap	• Measure ring gap, repair as necessary
	• Piston rings sticking or excessively loose in grooves	• Measure ring side clearance, repair as necessary
	• Compression rings installed upside down	• Repair as necessary
	• Cylinder walls worn, scored, or glazed	• Repair as necessary
	• Piston ring gaps not properly staggered	• Repair as necessary
	• Excessive main or connecting rod bearing clearance	• Measure bearing clearance, repair as necessary
No oil pressure	• Low oil level	• Add oil to correct level
	• Oil pressure gauge, warning lamp or sending unit inaccurate	• Replace oil pressure gauge or warning lamp
	• Oil pump malfunction	• Replace oil pump
	• Oil pressure relief valve sticking	• Remove and inspect oil pressure relief valve assembly
	• Oil passages on pressure side of pump obstructed	• Inspect oil passages for obstruction
	• Oil pickup screen or tube obstructed	• Inspect oil pickup for obstruction
	• Loose oil inlet tube	• Tighten or seal inlet tube

Troubleshooting Engine Mechanical Problems (cont.)

Problem	Cause	Solution
Low oil pressure	• Low oil level • Inaccurate gauge, warning lamp or sending unit • Oil excessively thin because of dilution, poor quality, or improper grade • Excessive oil temperature • Oil pressure relief spring weak or sticking • Oil inlet tube and screen assembly has restriction or air leak • Excessive oil pump clearance • Excessive main, rod, or camshaft bearing clearance	• Add oil to correct level • Replace oil pressure gauge or warning lamp • Drain and refill crankcase with recommended oil • Correct cause of overheating engine • Remove and inspect oil pressure relief valve assembly • Remove and inspect oil inlet tube and screen assembly. (Fill inlet tube with lacquer thinner to locate leaks.) • Measure clearances • Measure bearing clearances, repair as necessary
High oil pressure	• Improper oil viscosity • Oil pressure gauge or sending unit inaccurate • Oil pressure relief valve sticking closed	• Drain and refill crankcase with correct viscosity oil • Replace oil pressure gauge • Remove and inspect oil pressure relief valve assembly
Main bearing noise	• Insufficient oil supply • Main bearing clearance excessive • Bearing insert missing • Crankshaft end play excessive • Improperly tightened main bearing cap bolts • Loose flywheel or drive plate • Loose or damaged vibration damper	• Inspect for low oil level and low oil pressure • Measure main bearing clearance, repair as necessary • Replace missing insert • Measure end play, repair as necessary • Tighten bolts with specified torque • Tighten flywheel or drive plate attaching bolts • Repair as necessary
Connecting rod bearing noise	• Insufficient oil supply • Carbon build-up on piston • Bearing clearance excessive or bearing missing • Crankshaft connecting rod journal out-of-round • Misaligned connecting rod or cap • Connecting rod bolts tightened improperly	• Inspect for low oil level and low oil pressure • Remove carbon from piston crown • Measure clearance, repair as necessary • Measure journal dimensions, repair or replace as necessary • Repair as necessary • Tighten bolts with specified torque
Piston noise	• Piston-to-cylinder wall clearance excessive (scuffed piston) • Cylinder walls excessively tapered or out-of-round • Piston ring broken • Loose or seized piston pin • Connecting rods misaligned • Piston ring side clearance excessively loose or tight • Carbon build-up on piston is excessive	• Measure clearance and examine piston • Measure cylinder wall dimensions, rebore cylinder • Replace all rings on piston • Measure piston-to-pin clearance, repair as necessary • Measure rod alignment, straighten or replace • Measure ring side clearance, repair as necessary • Remove carbon from piston
Valve actuating component noise	• Insufficient oil supply	• Check for: (a) Low oil level (b) Low oil pressure (c) Plugged push rods (d) Wrong hydraulic tappets

Troubleshooting Engine Mechanical Problems (cont.)

Problem	Cause	Solution
Valve actuating component noise (cont.)		(e) Restricted oil gallery (f) Excessive tappet to bore clearance
	• Push rods worn or bent	• Replace worn or bent push rods
	• Rocker arms or pivots worn	• Replace worn rocker arms or pivots
	• Foreign objects or chips in hydraulic tappets	• Clean tappets
	• Excessive tappet leak-down	• Replace valve tappet
	• Tappet face worn	• Replace tappet; inspect corresponding cam lobe for wear
	• Broken or cocked valve springs	• Properly seat cocked springs; replace broken springs
	• Stem-to-guide clearance excessive	• Measure stem-to-guide clearance, repair as required
	• Valve bent	• Replace valve
	• Loose rocker arms	• Tighten bolts with specified torque
	• Valve seat runout excessive	• Regrind valve seat/valves
	• Missing valve lock	• Install valve lock
	• Push rod rubbing or contacting cylinder head	• Remove cylinder head and remove obstruction in head
	• Excessive engine oil (four-cylinder engine)	• Correct oil level

Troubleshooting the Cooling System

Problem	Cause	Solution
High temperature gauge indication— overheating	• Coolant level low	• Replenish coolant
	• Fan belt loose	• Adjust fan belt tension
	• Radiator hose(s) collapsed	• Replace hose(s)
	• Radiator airflow blocked	• Remove restriction (bug screen, fog lamps, etc.)
	• Faulty radiator cap	• Replace radiator cap
	• Ignition timing incorrect	• Adjust ignition timing
	• Idle speed low	• Adjust idle speed
	• Air trapped in cooling system	• Purge air
	• Heavy traffic driving	• Operate at fast idle in neutral intermittently to cool engine
	• Incorrect cooling system component(s) installed	• Install proper component(s)
	• Faulty thermostat	• Replace thermostat
	• Water pump shaft broken or impeller loose	• Replace water pump
	• Radiator tubes clogged	• Flush radiator
	• Cooling system clogged	• Flush system
	• Casting flash in cooling passages	• Repair or replace as necessary. Flash may be visible by removing cooling system components or removing core plugs.
	• Brakes dragging	• Repair brakes
	• Excessive engine friction	• Repair engine
	• Antifreeze concentration over 68%	• Lower antifreeze concentration percentage
	• Missing air seals	• Replace air seals
	• Faulty gauge or sending unit	• Repair or replace faulty component
	• Loss of coolant flow caused by leakage or foaming	• Repair or replace leaking component, replace coolant
	• Viscous fan drive failed	• Replace unit
Low temperature indication— undercooling	• Thermostat stuck open	• Replace thermostat
	• Faulty gauge or sending unit	• Repair or replace faulty component

Troubleshooting the Cooling System (cont.)

Problem	Cause	Solution
Coolant loss—boilover	• Overfilled cooling system	• Reduce coolant level to proper specification
	• Quick shutdown after hard (hot) run	• Allow engine to run at fast idle prior to shutdown
	• Air in system resulting in occasional "burping" of coolant	• Purge system
	• Insufficient antifreeze allowing coolant boiling point to be too low	• Add antifreeze to raise boiling point
	• Antifreeze deteriorated because of age or contamination	• Replace coolant
	• Leaks due to loose hose clamps, loose nuts, bolts, drain plugs, faulty hoses, or defective radiator	• Pressure test system to locate source of leak(s) then repair as necessary
	• Faulty head gasket	• Replace head gasket
	• Cracked head, manifold, or block	• Replace as necessary
	• Faulty radiator cap	• Replace cap
Coolant entry into crankcase or cylinder(s)	• Faulty head gasket	• Replace head gasket
	• Crack in head, manifold or block	• Replace as necessary
Coolant recovery system inoperative	• Coolant level low	• Replenish coolant to FULL mark
	• Leak in system	• Pressure test to isolate leak and repair as necessary
	• Pressure cap not tight or seal missing, or leaking	• Repair as necessary
	• Pressure cap defective	• Replace cap
	• Overflow tube clogged or leaking	• Repair as necessary
	• Recovery bottle vent restricted	• Remove restriction
Noise	• Fan contacting shroud	• Reposition shroud and inspect engine mounts
	• Loose water pump impeller	• Replace pump
	• Glazed fan belt	• Apply silicone or replace belt
	• Loose fan belt	• Adjust fan belt tension
	• Rough surface on drive pulley	• Replace pulley
	• Water pump bearing worn	• Remove belt to isolate. Replace pump.
	• Belt alignment	• Check pully alignment. Repair as necessary.
No coolant flow through heater core	• Restricted return inlet in water pump	• Remove restriction
	• Heater hose collapsed or restricted	• Remove restriction or replace hose
	• Restricted heater core	• Remove restriction or replace core
	• Restricted outlet in thermostat housing	• Remove flash or restriction
	• Intake manifold bypass hole in cylinder head restricted	• Remove restriction
	• Faulty heater control valve	• Replace valve
	• Intake manifold coolant passage restricted	• Remove restriction or replace intake manifold

NOTE: *Immediately after shutdown, the engine enters a condition known as heat soak. This is caused by the cooling system being inoperative while engine temperature is still high. If coolant temperature rises above boiling point, expansion and pressure may push some coolant out of the radiator overflow tube. If this does not occur frequently it is considered normal.*

Troubleshooting the Serpentine Drive Belt

Problem	Cause	Solution
Tension sheeting fabric failure (woven fabric on outside circumference of belt has cracked or separated from body of belt)	• Grooved or backside idler pulley diameters are less than minimum recommended • Tension sheeting contacting (rubbing) stationary object • Excessive heat causing woven fabric to age • Tension sheeting splice has fractured	• Replace pulley(s) not conforming to specification • Correct rubbing condition • Replace belt • Replace belt
Noise (objectional squeal, squeak, or rumble is heard or felt while drive belt is in operation)	• Belt slippage • Bearing noise • Belt misalignment • Belt-to-pulley mismatch • Driven component inducing vibration • System resonant frequency inducing vibration	• Adjust belt • Locate and repair • Align belt/pulley(s) • Install correct belt • Locate defective driven component and repair • Vary belt tension within specifications. Replace belt.
Rib chunking (one or more ribs has separated from belt body)	• Foreign objects imbedded in pulley grooves • Installation damage • Drive loads in excess of design specifications • Insufficient internal belt adhesion	• Remove foreign objects from pulley grooves • Replace belt • Adjust belt tension • Replace belt
Rib or belt wear (belt ribs contact bottom of pulley grooves)	• Pulley(s) misaligned • Mismatch of belt and pulley groove widths • Abrasive environment • Rusted pulley(s) • Sharp or jagged pulley groove tips • Rubber deteriorated	• Align pulley(s) • Replace belt • Replace belt • Clean rust from pulley(s) • Replace pulley • Replace belt
Longitudinal belt cracking (cracks between two ribs)	• Belt has mistracked from pulley groove • Pulley groove tip has worn away rubber-to-tensile member	• Replace belt • Replace belt
Belt slips	• Belt slipping because of insufficient tension • Belt or pulley subjected to substance (belt dressing, oil, ethylene glycol) that has reduced friction • Driven component bearing failure • Belt glazed and hardened from heat and excessive slippage	• Adjust tension • Replace belt and clean pulleys • Replace faulty component bearing • Replace belt
"Groove jumping" (belt does not maintain correct position on pulley, or turns over and/or runs off pulleys)	• Insufficient belt tension • Pulley(s) not within design tolerance • Foreign object(s) in grooves • Excessive belt speed • Pulley misalignment • Belt-to-pulley profile mismatched • Belt cordline is distorted	• Adjust belt tension • Replace pulley(s) • Remove foreign objects from grooves • Avoid excessive engine acceleration • Align pulley(s) • Install correct belt • Replace belt
Belt broken (Note: identify and correct problem before replacement belt is installed)	• Excessive tension • Tensile members damaged during belt installation • Belt turnover • Severe pully misalignment • Bracket, pulley, or bearing failure	• Replace belt and adjust tension to specification • Replace belt • Replace belt • Align pulley(s) • Replace defective component and belt

Troubleshooting the Serpentine Drive Belt (cont.)

Problem	Cause	Solution
Cord edge failure (tensile member exposed at edges of belt or separated from belt body)	• Excessive tension • Drive pulley misalignment • Belt contacting stationary object • Pulley irregularities • Improper pulley construction • Insufficient adhesion between tensile member and rubber matrix	• Adjust belt tension • Align pulley • Correct as necessary • Replace pulley • Replace pulley • Replace belt and adjust tension to specifications
Sporadic rib cracking (multiple cracks in belt ribs at random intervals)	• Ribbed pulley(s) diameter less than minimum specification • Backside bend flat pulley(s) diameter less than minimum • Excessive heat condition causing rubber to harden • Excessive belt thickness • Belt overcured • Excessive tension	• Replace pulley(s) • Replace pulley(s) • Correct heat condition as necessary • Replace belt • Replace belt • Adjust belt tension

arms, exceptionally long pushrods, a gear driven camshaft and a coolant heated aluminum intake manifold.

V6–225

The V6 engine has a displacement of 225 cu. in. and a compression ratio of 9.0:1 which permits the use of regular octane gas.

It has two banks of three cylinders each of which are opposed to one another at a 90 degree angle. The left bank of cylinders, as viewed from the driver's seat, is set forward of the right bank so that the connecting rods of opposite pairs of pistons and rods can be attached to the same crankpin.

The crankshaft counterbalance weights are cast as an integral part of the crankshaft. All of the crankshaft bearings are identical in diameter, except for no. 2 bearing which is the thrust bearing. It is larger than the rest.

The cast iron heads are interchangeable. The camshaft, which is located above the crankshaft, between the two banks, operates hydraulic valve lifters. The rocker arms are not adjustable.

6–226 L-Head

This Kaiser-built engine is used in the Utility Series trucks. It is of the valve-in-block, or flathead, design. The head and block are cast iron. With this arrangement, there are no moving parts in the cylinder head. The crankshaft is supported by four main bearings.

6–230

The overhead camshaft 6–230, built by the Continental Engine Corp. was a fairly radical design for its day, incorporating features found in more modern engines. The camshaft has only six cams, with the same cam operating both intake and exhaust valves on each cylinder. The cylinders and crankcase are integrally cast, forming a rigid unit. The fully balanced crankshaft is supported by four, unusually large, main bearings. The head employs a cross-flow design with hemispherical combustion chambers.

6–232, 258

The American Motors 6-cylinder engines are inline sixes with overhead intake and exhaust valves. The valves are operated by paired bridged pivot rocker arms in 1973 and 1975–79 models. The rockers are mounted on a common shaft in most 1972 and 1974 models. None of the rocker arms are adjustable. The 232 was last used in the 1978 model year.

8–304

The 304 V8 has two banks of four cylinders each which are opposed to each other at a 90 degree angle. The camshaft is located above the crankshaft, between the two banks. It operates the valves through the use of hydraulic lifters, pushrods, and separately mounted rocker arms on 1972 models. The rocker arms are mounted in pairs on bridged pivots on 1973–79 models. A two barrel carburetor is used.

Engine Overhaul Tips

Most engine overhaul procedures are fairly standard. In addition to specific parts replacement procedures and complete specifications for your individual engine, this chapter also is a guide to accept rebuilding procedures. Examples of standard rebuilding practice are shown and should be used along with specific details concerning your particular engine.

Competent and accurate machine shop services will ensure maximum performance, reliability and engine life.

In most instances it is more profitable for the do-it-yourself mechanic to remove, clean and inspect the component, buy the necessary parts and deliver these to a shop for actual machine work.

On the other hand, much of the rebuilding work (crankshaft, block, bearings, piston rods, and other components) is well within the scope of the do-it-yourself mechanic.

TOOLS

The tools required for an engine overhaul or parts replacement will depend on the depth of your involvement. With a few exceptions, they will be the tools found in a mechanic's tool kit (see Chapter 1). More in-depth work will require any or all of the following:
• a dial indicator (reading in thousandths) mounted on a universal base
• micrometers and telescope gauges
• jaw and screw-type pullers
• scraper
• valve spring compressor
• ring groove cleaner
• piston ring expander and compressor
• ridge reamer
• cylinder hone or glaze breaker
• Plastigage®
• engine stand
The use of most of these tools is illustrated in this chapter. Many can be rented for a one-time use from a local parts jobber or tool supply house specializing in automotive work.

Occasionally, the use of special tools is called for. See the information on Special Tools and Safety Notice in the front of this book before substituting another tool.

INSPECTION TECHNIQUES

Procedures and specifications are given in this chapter for inspecting, cleaning and assessing the wear limits of most major components. Other procedures such as Magnaflux® and Zyglo® can be used to locate material flaws and stress cracks. Magnaflux® is a magnetic process applicable only to ferrous materials. The Zyglo® process coats the material with a fluorescent dye penetrant and can be used on any material Check for suspected surface cracks can be more readily made using spot check dye. The dye is sprayed onto the suspected area, wiped off and the area sprayed with a developer. Cracks will show up brightly.

OVERHAUL TIPS

Aluminum has become extremely popular for use in engines, due to its low weight. Observe the following precautions when handling aluminum parts:
• Never hot tank aluminum parts (the caustic hot tank solution will eat the aluminum.
• Remove all aluminum parts (identification tag, etc.) from engine parts prior to the tanking.
• Always coat threads lightly with engine oil or antiseize compounds before installation, to prevent seizure.
• Never overtorque bolts or spark plugs especially in aluminum threads.
Stripped threads in any component can be repaired using any of several commercial repair kits (Heli-Coil®, Microdot®, Keenserts®, etc.).

When assembling the engine, any parts that will be frictional contact must be prelubed to provide lubrication at initial start-up. Any product specifically formulated for this purpose can be used, but engine oil is not recommended as a prelube.

When semi-permanent (locked, but removable) installation of bolts or nuts is desired, threads should be cleaned and coated with Loctite® or other similar, commercial non-hardening sealant.

REPAIRING DAMAGED THREADS

Several methods of repairing damaged threads are available. Heli-Coil® (shown here), Keenserts® and Microdot® are among the most widely used. All involve basically the same principle—drilling out stripped threads, tapping the hole and installing a prewound insert—making welding, plugging and oversize fasteners unnecessary.

Two types of thread repair inserts are usually supplied: a standard type for most Inch Coarse, Inch Fine, Metric Course and Metric Fine thread sizes and a spark lug type to fit most spark plug port sizes. Consult the individual manufacturer's catalog to determine

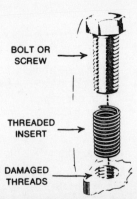

BOLT OR SCREW

THREADED INSERT

DAMAGED THREADS

Damaged bolt holes can be repaired with thread repair inserts

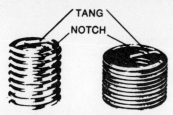

Standard thread repair insert (left) and spark plug thread insert (right)

Drill out the damaged threads with specified drill. Drill completely through the hole or to the bottom of a blind hole

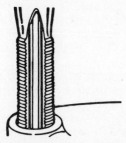

With the tap supplied, tap the hole to receive the thread insert. Keep the tap well oiled and back it out frequently to avoid clogging the threads

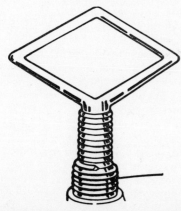

Screw the threaded insert onto the installation tool until the tang engages the slot. Screw the insert into the tapped hole until it is ¼–½ turn below the top surface. After installation break off the tang with a hammer and punch

exact applications. Typical thread repair kits will contain a selection of prewound threaded inserts, a tap (corresponding to the outside diameter threads of the insert) and an installation tool. Spark plug inserts usually differ because they require a tap equipped with pilot threads and a combined reamer/tap section. Most manufacturers also supply blister-packed thread repair inserts separately in addition to a master kit containing a variety of taps and inserts plus installation tools.

Before effecting a repair to a threaded hole, remove any snapped, broken or damaged bolts or studs. Penetrating oil can be used to free frozen threads. The offending item can be removed with locking pliers or with a screw or stud extractor. After the hole is clear, the thread can be repaired, as follows:

Checking Engine Compression

A noticeable lack of engine power, excessive oil consumption and/or poor fuel mileage measured over an extended period are all indicators of internal engine war. Worn piston rings, scored or worn cylinder bores, blown head gaskets, sticking or burnt valves and worn valve seats are all possible culprits here. A check of each cylinder's compression will help you locate the problems.

As mentioned in the Tools and Equipment section of Chapter 1, a screw-in type compression gauge is more accurate that the type you simply hold against the spark plug hole, although it takes slightly longer to use. It's worth it to obtain a more accurate reading. Follow the procedures below.

1. Warm up the engine to normal operating temperature.

2. Remove all spark plugs.

3. Disconnect the high tension lead from the ignition coil.

4. On fully open the throttle either by operating the carburetor throttle linkage by hand or by having an assistant floor the accelerator pedal.

The screw-in type compression gauge is more accurate

5. Screw the compression gauge into the no.1 spark plug hole until the fitting is snug.

NOTE: *Be careful not to crossthread the plug hole. On aluminum cylinder heads use extra care, as the threads in these heads are easily ruined.*

6. Ask an assistant to depress the accelerator pedal fully on both carbureted and fuel injected Jeep vehicles. Then, while you read the compression gauge, ask the assistant to crank the engine two or three times in short bursts using the ignition switch.

7. Read the compression gauge at the end of each series of cranks, and record the highest of these readings. Repeat this procedure for each of the engine's cylinders. Compare the highest reading of each cylinder to the compression pressure specification in the Tune-Up Specifications chart in Chapter 2. The specs in this chart are maximum values.

A cylinder's compression pressure is usually acceptable if it is not less than 80% of maximum. The difference between any two cylinders should be no more than 12–14 pounds.

8. If a cylinder is unusually low, pour a tablespoon of clean engine oil into the cylinder through the spark plug hole and repeat the compression test. If the compression comes up after adding the oil, it appears that the cylinder's piston rings or bore are damaged or worn. If the pressure remains low, the valves may not be seating properly (a valve job is needed), or the head gasket may be blown near that cylinder. If compression in any two adjacent cylinders is low, and if the addition of oil doesn't help the compression, there is leakage past the head gasket. Oil and coolant water in the combustion chamber can result from this problem. There may be evidence of water droplets on the engine dipstick when a head gasket has blown.

Engine
REMOVAL AND INSTALLATION
L4–134

1. Drain the cooling system by opening the drain cocks on the bottom of the radiator and the lower right side of the block.

CAUTION: *When draining the coolant, keep in mind that cats and dogs are attracted by the ethylene glycol antifreeze, and are quite likely to drink any that is left in an uncovered container or in puddles on the ground. This will prove fatal in sufficient quantity. Always drain the coolant into a sealable container. Coolant should be reused unless it is contaminated or several years old.*

2. Disconnect the battery.

3. Remove the upper and lower radiator hoses and the heater hoses.

4. Remove the four bolts securing the fan hub and blades.

5. Remove the four radiator attaching screws and lift out the radiator.

6. Disconnect the fuel line and the windshield wiper hose at the fuel pump.

7. Remove the air cleaner from the carburetor.

8. Disconnect the choke and throttle controls.

9. Disconnect the cables at the starter and remove the starter.

10. Disconnect the generator wires.

11. Disconnect the wires from the coil, oil pressure sender and temperature sender.

12. Disconnect the exhaust pipe from the manifold.

13. Place a jack under the crankshaft pulley, disconnect and remove the two front engine supports, and slightly lower the engine. This will allow access to the two top bolts on the bell housing.

14. Install a lifting sling and shop crane on the engine and take up all slack.

15. Unbolt the engine from the bell housing.

16. Pull the engine forward or roll the vehicle backwards until the clutch clears the bell housing. Then, lift the engine up and out of the vehicle.

17. Lower the engine into the vehicle. Push the engine backwards until the clutch enters the bell housing.

18. Bolt the engine to the bell housing.

19. Let the engine down, onto the two front supports.

20. Bolt the engine to the supports.

21. Connect the exhaust pipe to the manifold.

22. Connect the wires to the coil, oil pressure sender and temperature sender.

23. Connect the generator wires.

24. Install the starter and connect the cables at the starter.

25. Connect the choke and throttle controls.

26. Install the air cleaner on the carburetor.

27. Connect the fuel line, and the windshield wiper hose at the fuel pump.

28. Install the radiator.

29. Install the four bolts securing the fan hub and blades.

30. Install the upper and lower radiator hoses and the heater hoses.

31. Connect the battery.

32. Fill the cooling system.

F4–134

1. Drain the cooling system by opening the draincocks at the bottom of the radiator and the lower right side of the cylinder block.

Standard Torque Specifications and Fastener Markings

In the absence of specific torques, the following chart can be used as a guide to the maximum safe torque of a particular size/grade of fastener.

- There is no torque difference for fine or coarse threads.
- Torque values are based on clean, dry threads. Reduce the value by 10% if threads are oiled prior to assembly.
- The torque required for aluminum components or fasteners is considerably less.

U.S. Bolts

SAE Grade Number	1 or 2			5			6 or 7		
Number of lines always 2 less than the grade number.									
Bolt Size (Inches)—(Thread)	Ft./Lbs.	Kgm	Nm	Ft./Lbs.	Kgm	Nm	Ft./Lbs.	Kgm	Nm
¼ — 20	5	0.7	6.8	8	1.1	10.8	10	1.4	13.5
— 28	6	0.8	8.1	10	1.4	13.6			
⁵⁄₁₆ — 18	11	1.5	14.9	17	2.3	23.0	19	2.6	25.8
— 24	13	1.8	17.6	19	2.6	25.7			
⅜ — 16	18	2.5	24.4	31	4.3	42.0	34	4.7	46.0
— 24	20	2.75	27.1	35	4.8	47.5			
⁷⁄₁₆ — 14	28	3.8	37.0	49	6.8	66.4	55	7.6	74.5
— 20	30	4.2	40.7	55	7.6	74.5			
½ — 13	39	5.4	52.8	75	10.4	101.7	85	11.75	115.2
— 20	41	5.7	55.6	85	11.7	115.2			
⁹⁄₁₆ — 12	51	7.0	69.2	110	15.2	149.1	120	16.6	162.7
— 18	55	7.6	74.5	120	16.6	162.7			
⅝ — 11	83	11.5	112.5	150	20.7	203.3	167	23.0	226.5
— 18	95	13.1	128.8	170	23.5	230.5			
¾ — 10	105	14.5	142.3	270	37.3	366.0	280	38.7	379.6
— 16	115	15.9	155.9	295	40.8	400.0			
⅞ — 9	160	22.1	216.9	395	54.6	535.5	440	60.9	596.5
— 14	175	24.2	237.2	435	60.1	589.7			
1 — 8	236	32.5	318.6	590	81.6	799.9	660	91.3	894.8
— 14	250	34.6	338.9	660	91.3	849.8			

Metric Bolts

Relative Strength Marking	4.6, 4.8			8.8		
Bolt Markings						
Bolt Size Thread Size x Pitch (mm)	Ft./Lbs.	Kgm	Nm	Ft./Lbs.	Kgm	Nm
6 x 1.0	2–3	.2–.4	3–4	3–6	.4–.8	5–8
8 x 1.25	6–8	.8–1	8–12	9–14	1.2–1.9	13–19
10 x 1.25	12–17	1.5–2.3	16–23	20–29	2.7–4.0	27–39
12 x 1.25	21–32	2.9–4.4	29–43	35–53	4.8–7.3	47–72
14 x 1.5	35–52	4.8–7.1	48–70	57–85	7.8–11.7	77–110
16 x 1.5	51–77	7.0–10.6	67–100	90–120	12.4–16.5	130–160
18 x 1.5	74–110	10.2–15.1	100–150	130–170	17.9–23.4	180–230
20 x 1.5	110–140	15.1–19.3	150–190	190–240	26.2–46.9	160–320
22 x 1.5	150–190	22.0–26.2	200–260	250–320	34.5–44.1	340–430
24 x 1.5	190–240	26.2–46.9	260–320	310–410	42.7–56.5	420–550

CAUTION: *When draining the coolant, keep in mind that cats and dogs are attracted by the ethylene glycol antifreeze, and are quite likely to drink any that is left in an uncovered container or in puddles on the ground. This will prove fatal in sufficient quantity. Always drain the coolant into a sealable container. Coolant should be reused unless it is contaminated or several years old.*

2. Disconnect the battery at the positive terminal to avoid the possibility of a short circuit.

3. Remove the air cleaner horn from the carburetor and disconnect the breather hose at the oil filler pipe.

4. Disconnect the carburetor choke and throttle controls by loosening the clamp bolts and setscrews.

5. Disconnect the fuel tank-to-fuel pump line at the fuel pump by unscrewing the connecting nut.

6. Plug the fuel line to prevent leakage. Disconnect the windshield wiper vacuum hose at the fuel pump.

7. Remove the radiator stay bar on the CJ-3B.

8. Remove the upper and lower radiator hoses. Remove the heater hoses, if so equipped, from the water pump and the rear of the cylinder head.

9. Remove the fan hub and fan blades.

10. Remove the four radiator attaching screws and remove the radiator and shroud as one unit.

11. Remove the starter motor cables and remove the starter motor.

12. Disconnect the wires from the alternator or the generator. Disconnect the ignition primary wire at the ignition coil.

13. Disconnect the oil pressure and temperature sending unit wires at the units.

14. Disconnect the exhaust pipe at the exhaust manifold by removing the stud nuts.

15. Remove the spark plug wires from the cable bracket that is mounted to the rocker arm cover. Remove the cable bracket by removing the stud nuts.

16. Remove the rocker arm cover by removing the attaching stud nuts.

17. Attach a lifting bracket to the engine using the head bolts. Be sure that the bolts selected will hold the engine with the weight balanced. Attach the lifting bracket to a boom hoist, or other lifting device, and take up all of the slack.

18. Remove the two nuts and bolts from each front engine support. Disconnect the engine ground strap. Remove the engine supports. Lower the engine slightly to permit access to the two top bolts on the flywheel housing.

19. Remove the bolts that attach the flywheel housing to the engine.

20. Pull the engine forward, or roll the vehicle backward, until the clutch clears the flywheel housing. Lift the engine from the vehicle.

21. Lower the engine into the vehicle. Push the engine backwards until the clutch enters the bell housing.

22. Bolt the engine to the bell housing.

23. Let the engine down, onto the two front supports.

24. Bolt the engine to the supports.

25. Install the rocker arm cover.

26. Install the spark plug wires on the cable bracket that is mounted to the rocker arm cover. Install the cable bracket by installing the stud nuts.

27. Connect the exhaust pipe at the exhaust manifold by installing the stud nuts.

28. Connect the oil pressure and temperature sending unit wires at the units.

29. Connect the wires from the alternator or the generator. Connect the ignition primary wire at the ignition coil.

30. Install the starter motor and install the starter motor cables.

31. Install the radiator and shroud as one unit.

32. Install the fan hub and fan blades.

33. Install the upper and lower radiator hoses. Install the heater hoses, if so equipped, on the water pump and the rear of the cylinder head.

34. Install the radiator stay bar on the CJ-3B.

35. Connect the windshield wiper vacuum hose at the fuel pump.

36. Connect the fuel tank-to-fuel pump line at the fuel pump.

37. Connect the carburetor choke and throttle controls.

38. Install the air cleaner horn on the carburetor and connect the breather hose at the oil filler pipe.

39. Connect the battery at the positive terminal.

40. Fill the cooling system.

4–150

1. Disconnect the battery ground cable.
2. Remove the air cleaner.
3. Remove the hood.
4. Drain the coolant.

CAUTION: *When draining the coolant, keep in mind that cats and dogs are attracted by the ethylene glycol antifreeze, and are quite likely to drink any that is left in an uncovered container or in puddles on the ground. This*

will prove fatal in sufficient quantity. Always drain the coolant into a sealable container. Coolant should be reused unless it is contaminated or several years old.

5. Remove the lower radiator hose.

6. Remove the upper radiator hose.

7. Disconnect the coolant recovery hose.

8. Remove the fan shroud.

9. Disconnect the automatic transmission coolant lines.

10. Discharge the refrigerant system. See Chapter 1.

CAUTION: *Do this CAREFULLY, or let someone with experience do it for you. GREAT PERSONAL INJURY CAN OCCUR WHEN MISHANDLING REFRIGERANT GAS!*

11. Disconnect and remove the condenser. Cap all openings at once!

12. Remove the radiator.

13. Remove the fan and install a $5/16''$ x $1/2''$ (7.9375mm x 12.7mm) capscrew through the pulley and into the water pump flange to maintain the pulley-to-pump alignment.

14. Disconnect the heater hoses.

15. Disconnect the throttle linkage.

16. Disconnect the cruise control linkage.

17. Disconnect the oil pressure sending unit wire.

18. Disconnect the temperature sending unit wire.

19. Disconnect and tag all vacuum hoses connected to the engine.

20. Remove the air conditioning compressor.

21. Remove the power steering hoses at the gear.

22. Drain the power steering reservoir.

23. Remove the power brake vacuum check valve from the booster.

24. Raise and support the front end on jackstands.

25. Disconnect and tag the starter wires.

26. Remove the starter.

27. Disconnect the exhaust pipe at the manifold.

28. Remove the flywheel housing access cover.

29. On vehicles equipped with automatic transmission, matchmark the converter and flywheel and remove the attaching bolts.

30. Remove the upper flywheel housing-to-engine bolts and loosen the lower ones.

31. Remove the engine mount cushion-to-engine compartment bolts.

32. Attach a shop crane to the lifting eyes on the engine.

33. Raise the engine off the front supports.

34. Place a floor jack under the flywheel housing.

35. Remove the remaining flywheel housing bolts.

36. Lift the engine out of the vehicle.

37. Mount the engine on a work stand or cradle. Never let it rest on the oil pan.

To install the engine:

38. Lower the engine into place in the vehicle.

39. Lubricate the manual transmission input shaft with chassis lube before insertion into clutch splines.

40. Install the flywheel housing bolts. Torque the top flywheel housing-to-engine bolts to 27 ft.lb. and the bottom ones to 43 ft.lb.

41. Install the engine mount cushion-to-engine compartment bolts. Torque the front bracket support bolts to 33 ft.lb.

42. Remove the shop crane.

43. On vehicles equipped with automatic transmission, install the converter attaching bolts.

44. Install the flywheel housing access cover.

45. Connect the exhaust pipe at the manifold.

46. Install the starter.

47. Connect the wires.

48. Raise and support the front end on jackstands.

49. Install the power brake vacuum check valve on the booster.

50. Fill the power steering reservoir.

51. Connect the power steering hoses at the gear.

52. Install the air conditioning compressor.

53. Connect all vacuum hoses.

54. Connect all wires.

55. Connect the throttle linkage.

56. Connect the cruise control linkage.

57. Connect the heater hoses.

58. Install the fan.

59. Install the radiator.

60. Install the condenser.

61. Evacuate and charge the refrigerant system. See Chapter 1.

CAUTION: *Do this CAREFULLY, or let someone with experience do it for you. GREAT PERSONAL INJURY CAN OCCUR WHEN MISHANDLING REFRIGERANT GAS!*

62. Install the fan shroud.

63. Connect the automatic transmission coolant lines.

64. Install the upper radiator hose.

65. Connect the coolant recovery hose.

66. Install the lower radiator hose.

67. Fill the cooling system.

68. Install the hood.

69. Install the air cleaner.

70. Connect the battery ground cable.

4–151

1. Disconnect the battery.
2. Remove the air cleaner.
3. Jack up the vehicle and support it on jackstands.
4. Disconnect the exhaust pipe from the manifold.
5. Disconnect the oxygen sensor.
6. Disconnect the wires from the starter.
7. Unbolt the starter and remove it from the vehicle.
8. Disconnect the wires from the distributor and oil pressure sending unit.
9. Remove the engine mount nuts.
10. On vehicles with manual transmission, remove the clutch slave cylinder and flywheel inspection plate.
11. Remove the clutch or converter housing-to-engine bolts.
12. On vehicle with automatic transmission, disconnect the converter from the drive plate.
13. Lower the vehicle.
14. Support the transmission with a jack.
15. Tag all hoses at the carburetor and remove them.
16. Disconnect the mixture control solenoid wire from the carburetor, (not all vehicles have these).
17. Disconnect the wires from the alternator.
18. Disconnect the throttle cable from the bracket and the carburetor.
19. Disconnect the choke and solenoid wires at the carburetor.
20. Disconnect the temperature sender wire.
21. Drain the radiator at the drain cock, then remove the lower hose.

CAUTION: *When draining the coolant, keep in mind that cats and dogs are attracted by the ethylene glycol antifreeze, and are quite likely to drink any that is left in an uncovered container or in puddles on the ground. This will prove fatal in sufficient quantity. Always drain the coolant into a sealable container. Coolant should be reused unless it is contaminated or several years old.*

22. Remove the upper radiator hose and the heater hoses.
23. Remove the fan shroud, and radiator.
24. Remove the power steering hoses at the pump.
25. Attach a shop crane to the engine and lift it out of the vehicle.

NOTE: *The manual transmission may have to be raised slightly to allow a smooth separation.*

26. Lower the engine into the truck.
27. On vehicle with automatic transmission, Connect the converter to the drive plate.
28. Install the clutch or converter housing-to-engine bolts. Torque the bolts to 35 ft.lb.
29. On vehicles with manual transmission, Install the clutch slave cylinder and flywheel inspection plate. Torque the slave cylinder bolts to 18 ft.lb.
30. Install the engine mount nuts. Torque them to 34 ft.lb.
31. Connect the wires to the distributor and oil pressure sending unit.
32. Install the starter. Torque the mounting bolts to 27 ft.lb.; the bracket nut to 40 in.lb.
33. Connect the wires to the starter.
34. Connect the oxygen sensor.
35. Connect the exhaust pipe at the manifold. Torque the nuts to 35 ft.lb.
36. Install the power steering hoses at the pump.
37. Install the fan shroud, and radiator.
38. Install the upper radiator hose and the heater hoses.
39. Connect the temperature sender wire.
40. Connect the choke and solenoid wires at the carburetor.
41. Connect the throttle cable at the bracket and the carburetor.
42. Connect the wires to the alternator.
43. Connect the mixture control solenoid wire at the carburetor, (not all vehicles have these).
44. Install all hoses at the carburetor.
45. Lower the vehicle.
46. Install the air cleaner.
47. Connect the battery.
48. Fill the cooling system.

6–225

1. Remove the hood.
2. Disconnect the battery ground cable from the engine and the battery.
3. Remove the air cleaner.
4. Drain the coolant from the radiator and engine.

CAUTION: *When draining the coolant, keep in mind that cats and dogs are attracted by the ethylene glycol antifreeze, and are quite likely to drink any that is left in an uncovered container or in puddles on the ground. This will prove fatal in sufficient quantity. Always drain the coolant into a sealable container. Coolant should be reused unless it is contaminated or several years old.*

5. Disconnect the alternator wiring harness from the connector at the regulator.
6. Disconnect the upper and lower radiator hoses from tne engine.
7. Remove the right and left radiator support bars.
8. Remove the radiator from the vehicle.
9. Disconnect the engine wiring harnesses

from the connectors which are located on the firewall.

10. Disconnect the battery cable and wiring from the engine starter assembly.

11. Remove the starter assembly from the engine.

12. Disconnect the engine fuel hoses from the fuel lines at the right fame rails.

13. Plug the fuel lines.

14. Disconnect the throttle linkage and the choke cable from the carburetor and remove the cable support bracket that is mounted on the engine.

15. Disconnect the exhaust pipes from the right and left sides of the engine.

16. Place a jack under the transmission and support the weight of the transmission.

17. Remove the bolts that secure the engine to the front motor mounts.

18. Attach a suitable sling to the engine lifting eyes and, using a hoist, lift the engine just enough to support its weight.

19. Remove the bolts that secure the engine to the flywheel housing.

20. Raise the engine slightly and slide the engine forward to remove the transmission main shaft form the clutch plate splines.

NOTE: *The engine and the transmission must be raised slightly to release the spline from the clutch plate while sliding the engine forward.*

21. When the engine is free of the transmission shaft, raise the engine and remove it from the vehicle.

22. Lower the engine into the vehicle.

23. Slide the engine rearward to install the transmission main shaft in the clutch plate splines.

24. Install the bolts that secure the engine to the flywheel housing. Torque the bolts to 30–40 ft.lb.

25. Install the bolts that secure the engine to the front motor mounts. Torque the bolts to 75 ft.lb.

26. Connect the exhaust pipes to the right and left sides of the engine.

27. Connect the throttle linkage and the choke cable to the carburetor and Install the cable support bracket that is mounted on the engine.

28. Connect the engine fuel hoses to the fuel lines at the right fame rails.

29. Install the starter assembly on the engine. Torque the starter-to-block bolts to 30–40 ft.lb.; the bracket bolts to 10–12 ft.lb.

30. Connect the battery cable and wiring to the engine starter assembly.

31. Connect the engine wiring harnesses to the connectors which are located on the firewall.

32. Install the radiator.

33. Install the right and left radiator support bars.

34. Connect the upper and lower radiator hoses to the engine.

35. Connect the alternator wiring harness to the connector at the regulator.

36. Fill the cooling system.

37. Install the air cleaner.

38. Connect the battery ground cable to the engine and the battery.

39. Install the hood.

6–226

1. Drain the cooling system.

CAUTION: *When draining the coolant, keep in mind that cats and dogs are attracted by the ethylene glycol antifreeze, and are quite likely to drink any that is left in an uncovered container or in puddles on the ground. This will prove fatal in sufficient quantity. Always drain the coolant into a sealable container. Coolant should be reused unless it is contaminated or several years old.*

2. Remove the hood.

3. Remove the radiator and heater hoses, and all other cooling system hoses.

4. Remove the radiator.

5. Disconnect the battery.

6. Remove the coolant surge tank.

7. Remove the air cleaner and air cleaner bracket.

8. Remove the rear heater hose support bracket.

9. Remove the vacuum line which runs between the carburetor and distributor.

10. Tag and remove the spark plug wires from the distributor.

11. Remove the coil lead from the distributor.

12. Remove the distributor cap.

13. Rotate the engine so that the no.1 cylinder is at TDC of the compression stroke.

13. Mark the relationship of the rotor and distributor body.

14. Mark the relationship of the distributor body and head.

15. Remove the holddown clamp.

16. Remove the distributor.

17. Disconnect the choke cable and wire.

18. Disconnect the throttle control wire at the carburetor.

19. Disconnect the accelerator cable at the distributor adapter.

20. Disconnect the fuel line at the carburetor.

21. Remove the carburetor.

22. Remove the oil filler tube by pulling it straight out of the block.

23. Tag the coil wires and disconnect them.

24. Remove the ignition coil.

25. Disconnect the oil filter hoses.

26. Remove the filter and bracket.

27. Disconnect the wire at the temperature sending unit.

28. Disconnect the wires at the starter. Tag them.

29. Remove the generator housing.

30. Remove the generator and bracket.

31. Remove the generator idler pulley and bracket.

32. Remove the fan belt.

33. Remove the fan.

NOTE: *Early models used a four-bladed fan. Willys recommended that owners of these vehicles replace the fan with the later six-bladed unit. If the original fan was attached with hex nuts and lockwashers, the new fan should be installed using elastic stop nuts.*

34. Disconnect the radiator brace at the engine mount and swing it out of the way.

35. Disconnect the vacuum line at the fuel pump.

36. Disconnect the fuel lines at the fuel pump.

37. Disconnect the exhaust pipe at the manifold.

38. Disconnect the transfer case linkage.

39. Disconnect the wire at the oil pressure sending unit.

40. Disconnect the engine ground strap.

41. Disconnect the transmission shift rods at the transmission and secure them out of the way.

42. Disconnect the clutch cable at the cross shaft.

43. Remove the cross shaft.

44. Disconnect the hand brake release spring.

45. Disconnect the hand brake cable and conduit and move it out of the way.

46. Disconnect the front driveshaft at the transfer case and axle.

47. Disconnect the rear driveshaft at the transfer case.

48. Disconnect the speedometer cable at the transfer case.

49. Attach a lifting bracket, using existing head bolts.

50. Take up the weight of the engine with a shop crane.

51. Support the transmission with a jackstand.

52. Remove the front engine mount bolts.

53. Place a floor jack under the rear engine support crossmember.

54. Remove the crossmember attaching bolts.

55. Remove the engine-to-bell housing attaching bolts.

56. Raise the engine slightly to free it from the front mounts.

57. Remove the floor jack.

58. Slide the engine forward to free it from the transmission.

59. Raise the engine clear of the truck.

60. Place the engine on a work stand or dolly. Never let it rest on the oil pan.

61. Lower the engine into the truck.

62. Slide the engine rearward to engage the transmission.

63. Lower the engine onto the front mounts.

64. Install the engine-to-bell housing attaching bolts. Torque them to 40 ft.lb.

65. Install the crossmember attaching bolts. Torque them to 30 ft.lb.

66. Install the front engine mount bolts. Torque them to 50 ft.lb.

67. Connect the speedometer cable at the transfer case.

68. Connect the front driveshaft at the axle and transfer case.

69. Connect the rear driveshaft at the transfer case.

70. Connect the hand brake cable and conduit.

71. Connect the hand brake release spring.

72. Install the cross shaft.

73. Connect the clutch cable at the cross shaft

74. Connect the transmission shift rods at the transmission.

75. Adjust the linkage.

76. Connect the engine ground strap.

77. Connect the wire at the oil pressure sending unit.

78. Connect the transfer case linkage.

79. Connect the exhaust pipe at the manifold. Torque the nuts to 50 ft.lb.

80. Connect the vacuum line and fuel lines at the fuel pump.

81. Connect the radiator brace at the engine mount.

82. Install the fan and belt.

83. Adjust the belt.

84. Install the generator idler pulley and bracket.

85. Install the generator and bracket. Torque the bolts to 25 ft.lb.

86. Install the generator housing.

87. Connect the wires at the starter.

88. Connect the wire at the temperature sending unit.

89. Install the filter and bracket.

90. Connect the oil filter hoses.

91. Install the ignition coil.

92. Install the oil filler tube.

93. Install the carburetor.

94. Connect the fuel line at the carburetor.

95. Connect the throttle control wire at the carburetor.

96. Connect the accelerator cable at the distributor adapter.

97. Connect the choke cable and wire.

98. Install the distributor, aligning all the matchmarks.

99. Install the distributor cap and connect all the wires.

100. Install the vacuum line which runs between the carburetor and distributor.

101. Install the rear heater hose support bracket.

102. Install the air cleaner and air cleaner bracket.

103. Install the coolant surge tank.

104. Connect the battery.

105. Install the radiator.

106. Install the radiator and heater hoses, and all other cooling system hoses.

107. Install the hood.

108. Fill the cooling system.

6–230

1. Raise and support the truck on jackstands.

2. Drain the oil from the engine.

3. Remove the oil filter.

4. Drain the coolant.

CAUTION: *When draining the coolant, keep in mind that cats and dogs are attracted by the ethylene glycol antifreeze, and are quite likely to drink any that is left in an uncovered container or in puddles on the ground. This will prove fatal in sufficient quantity. Always drain the coolant into a sealable container. Coolant should be reused unless it is contaminated or several years old.*

5. Disconnect the hydraulic line at the clutch slave cylinder.

6. Remove the hood.

7. Remove the upper and lower radiator hoses.

8. Disconnect the automatic transmission cooler lines.

9. Remove the heater hoses.

10. Remove the radiator.

11. Disconnect and tag all wires attached to the engine.

12. Disconnect and tag any remaining hoses attached to the engine.

13. Remove the drive belts.

14. Remove the alternator.

15. Remove the fan and spacer.

16. Remove the battery and tray.

17. Unbolt the exhaust pipe from the manifold.

18. Remove the exhaust pipe from the bracket at the clutch housing.

19. Remove the carburetor.

20. Disconnect the fuel line at the frame.

21. Remove the front engine support bolts.

22. Take up the weight of the engine with a shop crane.

23. Remove the transfer case.

24. Remove the transmission.

25. Raise the engine slightly, pull it forward to clear the firewall and lift it out of the vehicle.

26. Lower the engine into the vehicle and slide it rearward slightly.

27. Install the front engine support bolts. Torque the engine mount bolts to 25–30 ft.lb.

28. Install the transmission. Torque the bellhousing-to-engine bolts to 40–50 ft.lb.

29. Install the transfer case.

30. Remove the shop crane.

31. Connect the fuel line at the frame.

32. Install the carburetor. Torque the nuts to 12–15 ft.lb.

33. Install the exhaust pipe to the bracket at the clutch housing.

34. Connect the hydraulic line at the clutch slave cylinder.

35. Connect the exhaust pipe to the manifold.

36. Install the battery and tray.

37. Install the fan and spacer.

38. Install the alternator. Torque mounting bolts to 40–45 ft.lb.; the adjusting bolt to 12–15 ft.lb.

39. Install the drive belts.

40. Install the radiator.

41. Install the heater hoses.

42. Install the upper and lower radiator hoses.

43. Connect the automatic transmission cooler lines.

44. Connect any remaining hoses to the engine.

45. Connect all wires to the engine.

46. Fill the cooling system.

47. Install the oil filter.

48. Fill the cranckcase.

49. Install the hood.

6–232, 6–258, 8–304

1. Remove the air cleaner.

2. Drain the cooling system.

CAUTION: *When draining the coolant, keep in mind that cats and dogs are attracted by the ethylene glycol antifreeze, and are quite likely to drink any that is left in an uncovered container or in puddles on the ground. This will prove fatal in sufficient quantity. Always drain the coolant into a sealable container. Coolant should be reused unless it is contaminated or several years old.*

3. Disconnect the upper and lower radiator hoses.

4. If equipped with an automatic transmis-

sion, disconnect the cooler lines from the radiator.

5. Remove the radiator and the fan. If the Jeep has air conditioning, evacuate the system, remove the condenser and cap all openings immediately. See Chapter 1.

6. If so equipped, remove the power steering pump and the drive belt, and place the unit aside. Do not remove the power steering hoses. Remove the battery and tray if equipped with the 1972–75 8–304.

7. If the vehicle has air conditioning, remove the compressor.

8. Disconnect all wires, lines, linkage, and hoses that are connected to the engine. Remove the oil filter on the Sixes.

9. Remove both of the engine front support cushion-to-frame retaining nuts.

10. Disconnect the exhaust pipe, or pipes if equipped with the V8, at the support bracket and exhaust manifold.

11. Support the weight of the engine with a lifting device.

12. Remove the front support cushion and bracket assemblies from the engine.

13. Remove the transfer case shift lever boot and the transmission access cover.

14. If equipped with an automatic transmission, remove the upper bolts securing the transmission bellhousing to the engine. If equipped with a manual transmission, remove the upper bolts that secure the clutch housing to the engine.

15. Remove the starter motor.

16. If the vehicle is equipped with an automatic transmission:

a. Remove the engine to transmission adapter plate inspection covers.

b. Mark the assembled position of the converter and flex plate and remove the converter-to-flex plate retaining screws.

c. Remove the remaining bolts securing the transmission bellhousing to the engine.

17. If equipped with a manual transmission, remove the lower cover of the clutch housing and the remaining bolts that secure the clutch housing to the engine.

18. Support the transmission with a floor jack.

19. Attach a suitable sling to the engine and using a hoist, lift the engine upward and forward at the same time, removing it from the vehicle.

20. Lower the engine into the vehicle and slide it rearward to engage the transmission.

21. If equipped with an automatic transmission, install the upper bolts securing the transmission bellhousing to the engine. Torque them to 27 ft.lb. If equipped with a manual transmission, install the upper bolts that se-

cure the clutch housing to the engine. Torque them to 27 ft.lb.

22. If equipped with a manual transmission, install the lower cover of the clutch housing and the remaining bolts that secure the clutch housing to the engine. Torque the clutch housing spacer-to-bolts to 12–15 ft.lb. Torque the clutch housing lower bolts to 43 ft.lb.

23. If the vehicle is equipped with an automatic transmission:

a. Install the remaining bolts securing the transmission bellhousing to the engine. Torque the bellhousing lower bolts to 43 ft.lb.

b. Mark the assembled position of the converter and flex plate and install the converter-to-flex plate retaining screws. Torque the bolts to 20–25 ft.lb.

c. Install the engine to transmission adapter plate inspection covers.

24. Install the starter motor. Torque the mounting bolts to 18 ft.lb.

25. Install the transfer case shift lever boot and the transmission access cover.

26. Install the front support cushion and bracket assemblies from the engine.

27. Remove the shop crane.

28. Connect the exhaust pipe, or pipes if equipped with the V8, at the support bracket and exhaust manifold. Torque the nuts to 20 ft.lb.

29. Install both of the engine front support cushion-to-frame retaining nuts. Torque them to 35 ft.lb.

30. Connect all wires, lines, linkage, and hoses that are connected to the engine.

31. Install the oil filter on the Sixes.

32. If so equipped, install the power steering pump and the drive belt.

33. Install the battery and tray if equipped with the 1972–75 8–304.

NOTE: *If the vehicle has air conditioning, mount and connect the air conditioning compressor. See Chapter 1.*

34. Install the radiator and the fan, and the condenser.

35. Evacuate, charge and leak test the refrigerant system.

36. If equipped with an automatic transmission, connect the cooler lines to the radiator.

37. Connect the upper and lower radiator hoses.

38. Fill the cooling system.

39. Install the air cleaner.

Rocker Shafts and Rocker Studs
REMOVAL AND INSTALLATION
F4–134

1. Remove the rocker arm cover attaching bolts and remove the rocker arm cover.

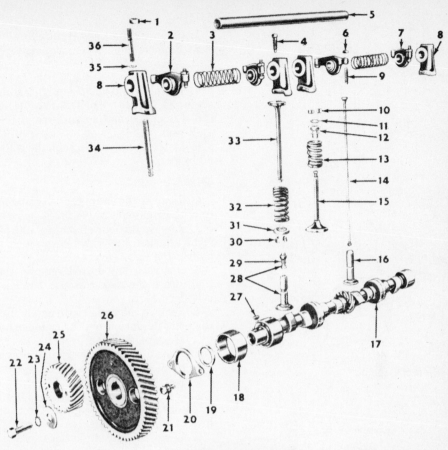

F4-134 valve train

1. Nut
2. Left rocker arm
3. Rocker arm shaft spring
4. Rocker shaft lock screw
5. Rocker shaft
6. Nut
7. Right rocker arm
8. Rocker arm shaft bracket
9. Intake valve tappet adjusting screw
10. Intake valve upper retainer lock
11. Oil seal
12. Intake valve spring upper retainer
13. Intake valve spring
14. Intake valve push rod
15. Intake valve
16. Intake valve tappet
17. Camshaft
18. Camshaft front bearing
19. Camshaft thrust plate spacer
20. Camshaft thrust plate
21. Bolt and lock washer
22. Bolt
23. Lockwasher
24. Camshaft gear washer
25. Crankshaft gear
26. Camshaft gear
27. Woodruff key No. 9
28. Exhaust valve tappet
29. Tappet adjusting screw
30. Spring retainer lock
31. Roto cap assembly
32. Exhaust valve spring
33. Exhaust valve
34. Rocker shaft support stud
35. Washer
36. Rocker arm cover stud

2. Remove the nuts from the rocker arm shaft support studs.

3. Remove the intake valve pushrods from the engine.

4. Install in the reverse order. Tighten the rocker arm retaining bolts to 30–33 ft.lb.

4–150

1. Remove the rocker arm cover. The cover seal is RTV sealer. Break the seal with a clean putty knife or razor blade. Don't attempt to remove the cover until the seal is broken. To remove the cover, pry where indicated at the bolt holes.

2. Remove the two capscrews at each bridge and pivot assembly. It's best to remove the cap-screws alternately, a little at a time each to avoid damage to the bridge.

3. Remove the bridges, pivots and rocker arms. Keep them in order.

4. Install the rocker arms and bridge and pivot assemblies. Tighten the capscrews to 19 ft.lb.

5. Clean the mating surfaces of the cover and head.

6. Run a ⅛" (3.175mm) bead of RTV sealer around the mating surface of the head. Install the cover within 10 minutes! Don't allow any of the RTV material to drop into the engine! In the engine it will form and set and possibly block and oil passage. Torque the cover bolts to 36–60 in.lb.

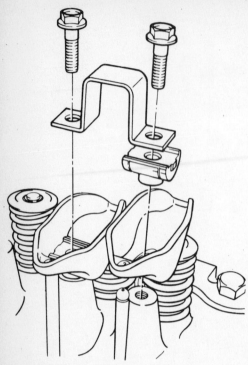

4-150 rocker arm assembly

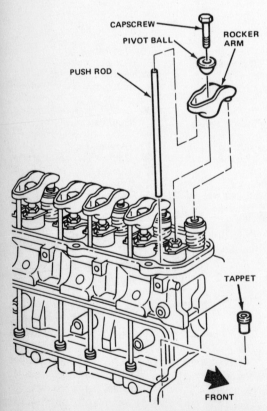

4-151 rocker arm and pushrod removal and installation

4-151

1. Remove the rocker arm cover.
2. Remove the rocker arm capscrew and ball.
3. Remove the rocker arm.
4. Install rocker arms. Tighten the capscrews to 20 ft.lb. DO NOT OVERTORQUE!
5. Clean the mating surfaces of the cover and head.
6. Install the cover. Tighten the bolts to 36–60 in.lb.

6-225

1. Remove the crankcase ventilator valve from the right side valve cover.
2. Remove the four attaching bolts from the right and left side valve covers and remove both of the valve covers.
3. Unscrew, but do not remove, the bolts that attach the rocker arm assemblies to the cylinder heads.
4. Remove the rocker arm assemblies, with the bolts in place, from the cylinder heads.
5. Mark each of the pushrods so that they can be installed in their original positions.
6. Remove the pushrods.
7. Install the pushrods.
8. Install the rocker arm assemblies. Install in the reverse order. Tighten the bolts to 30 ft.lb., a little at a time.
9. Clean the mating surfaces of the covers and heads.
10. Install the valve covers using new gaskets. Torque the bolts to 36–60 in.lb.
11. Install the crankcase ventilator valve from the right side valve cover.

6-230

1. Remove the camshaft cover.
2. Remove the rocker arm-to-stud nuts and lift off the rocker arms and balls.
3. Install the rocker arm and ball on the stud.
4. Install, but do not tighten, the rocker arm nut.
5. When all removed arms are installed, adjust the valves, BEING VERY CAREFUL TO PRECISELY ALIGN THE ROCKER ARMS WHILE TIGHTENING THE NUT!
6. Clean the mating surfaces of the cam cover and head.
7. Install the cam cover, using a new gasket. Torque the bolts to 36–60 in.lb.

1972 and 1974 6-232, 6-258

1. Remove the valve cover by removing the six valve cover attaching screws.
2. Loosen, but do not remove, the six bolts that attach the rocker arm assembly to the cylinder head.

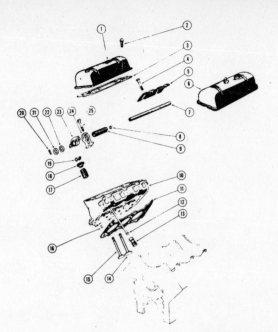

1. Right rocker arm cover
2. Rocker arm cover bolt
3. Gasket
4. Bolt
5. Baffle
6. Left rocker arm cover
7. Rocker arm shaft
8. Plug
9. Rocker arm spring
10. Cylinder head
11. Head gasket
12. Pushrod
13. Valve lifter
14. Intake valve
15. Exhaust valve
16. Dowel pin
17. Valve spring
18. Valve spring cap
19. Valve spring cap key
20. Cotter pin
21. Rocker arm shaft end washer
22. Rocker arm shaft spring
23. Rocker arm
24. Rocker arm shaft bracket
25. Bolt

6-225 valve train

1. Exhaust valve
2. Valve guide
3. Valve guide seal
4. Valve spring
5. Valve spring retainer
6. Rocker arm
7. Rocker arm stud
8. Rocker arm ball
9. Rocker arm guide
10. Camshaft
11. Cam bearing support deck
12. Rocker arm
13. Rocker arm cover
14. Oil tube
15. Valve spring retainer
16. Valve spring
17. Valve guide seal
18. Valve guide
19. Intake valve
20. Intake manifold

6-230 valve installation arrangement

3. Lift the whole rocker arm assembly off the head with the bolts in place.

4. Identify each of the pushrods so that they can be replaced in their original positions.

5. Remove the pushrods.

6. Install the rocker arm assembly. Tighten bolts, working evenly, from the center outward, to 22 ft.lb.

7. Clean the mating surfaces of the valve cover and head.

8. Install the valve cover, using a new gasket. Torque the bolts to 36–60 ft.lb.

1973, 1975–78 6–232
1975–87 6–258
1973–81 8–304

On these engines the rocker arms pivot on a bridged pivot that is secured with two capscrews. The bridged pivots maintain proper rocker arm-to-valve tip alignment.

1. Remove the rocker cover and gasket.

2. Remove the two capscrews at each bridged pivot, backing off each capscrew one turn at a time to avoid breaking the bridge.

3. Remove each bridged pivot and corre-

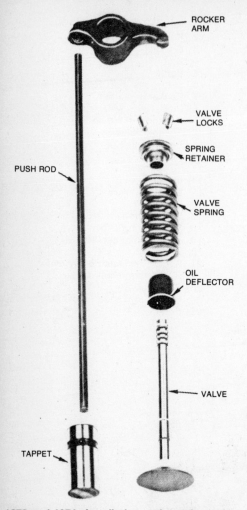

1972 and 1974 six cylinder engine valve train

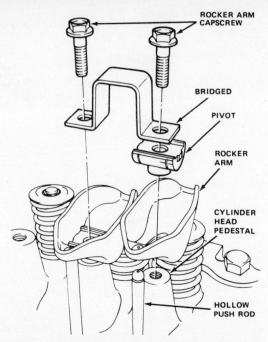

Rocker arm assembly used on the 1973, 1975–78 6-232, 1975–87 6-258, 1973–81 8-304

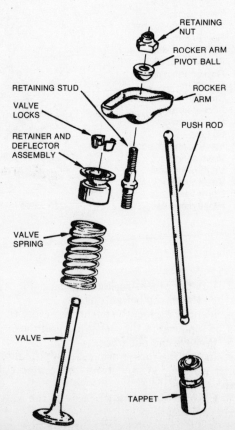

1972 V8 valve train

sponding pair of rocker arms and place them on a clean surface in the same order as they are removed.

NOTE: *Bridged pivots, capscrews, rockers, and pushrods must all be reinstalled in their original positions.*

4. Clean all the parts in a suitable solvent and use compressed air to blow out the oil passages in the pushrods and the rocker arms. Replace any excessively worn parts.

5. Install rocker arms, pushrods and bridged pivots in the same positions from which they were removed.

NOTE: *Be sure that the bottom end of each pushrod is centered in the plunger which they were removed. Be sure that the bottom end of each pushrod is centered in the plunger cap of each hydraulic valve tappet.*

6. Install the capscrews and tighten them one turn at a time, alternating between the two screws on each bridge. Tighten the capscrews to 21 ft.lb. on the Sixes and 10 ft.lb. on the 304 V8.

7. Install the rocker cover(s) with new gasket(s).

1972 8–304

The 1972 8–304 has each rocker arm individually mounted on a separate stud. Each rocker assembly consists of the following: a rocker arm retaining stud, a rocker arm pivot ball, a rocker arm, and a retaining stud. Each assembly is removed and installed separately. To remove:

1. Unscrew the rocker retaining nut from the stud and lift off the rocker arm and its pivot ball.
2. Remove the stud from the block with a wrench.
3. Label the pushrods so that they can be installed in their original positions and remove them from the block.
4. When installing the rocker arm retaining studs, use caution not to cross thread them. They are designed to cause an interference fit. Lubricate the studs with high pressure grease before installing them in the head. Install the rocker arm assemblies in the reverse order of removal. Tighten the rocker arm retaining nuts to 23 ft.lb.

Thermostat

REMOVAL AND INSTALLATION

The thermostat is located in the water outlet housing at the front or on top of the engine. On the V6 and the 304 V8 the water outlet housing is located in the front of the intake manifold.

CAUTION: *When draining the coolant, keep in mind that cats and dogs are attracted by the ethylene glycol antifreeze, and are quite likely to drink any that is left in an uncovered container or in puddles on the ground. This will prove fatal in sufficient quantity. Always drain the coolant into a sealable container. Coolant should be reused unless it is contaminated or several years old.*

To remove the thermostats from all of these engines, first drain the cooling system. It is not necessary to disconnect or remove any of the hoses. Remove the two attaching screws and lift the housing from the engine. Remove the thermostat and the gasket. To install, place the thermostat in the housing with the spring inside the engine. Install a new gasket with a small amount of sealing compound applied to both sides. Install the water outlet and tighten the attaching bolts to 30 ft.lb. Refill the cooling system.

Intake Manifold

REMOVAL AND INSTALLATION

L4–134

The intake and exhaust manifolds are bolted together and are easiest removed as an assembly.

1. On models so equipped, remove the crankcase ventilator tube which runs from the ventilator valve mounted in the intake manifold to an elbow mounted on the valve cover plate.
2. Remove the seven nuts from the manifold-to-block studs.
3. Pull the manifolds off the studs. Discard the gasket.
4. If the studs were removed for replacement, coat the new studs with a sealer such as Permatex® No. 2, prior to installation.
5. Place a new gasket in position on the studs and carefully slide the manifolds on. Torque to 29–35 ft.lb. in a circular pattern from the ends toward the center.

F4–134

On the F4–134 engine the intake manifold is cast as an integral part of the head.

4–150

NOTE: *It may be necessary to remove the carburetor or the throttle body from the intake manifold before the manifold is removed.*

1. Disconnect the negative battery cable. Drain the radiator.

CAUTION: *When draining the coolant, keep in mind that cats and dogs are attracted by*

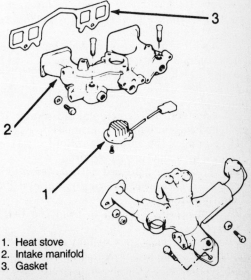

1. Heat stove
2. Intake manifold
3. Gasket

4-150 manifolds

the ethylene glycol antifreeze, and are quite likely to drink any that is left in an uncovered container or in puddles on the ground. This will prove fatal in sufficient quantity. Always drain the coolant into a sealable container. Coolant should be reused unless it is contaminated or several years old.

2. Remove the air cleaner. Disconnect the fuel pipe. Remove the carburetor or the throttle body, as required.

3. Disconnect the coolant hoses from the intake manifold.

4. Disconnect the throttle cable from the bellcrank.

5. Disconnect the PCV valve vacuum hose from the intake manifold.

6. If equipped, remove the vacuum advance CTO valve vacuum hoses.

7. Disconnect the system coolant temperature sender wire connector (located on the intake manifold). Disconnect the air temperature sensor wire, if equipped.

8. Disconnect the vacuum hose from the EGR valve.

9. On vehicles equipped with power steering remove the power steering pump and its mounting bracket. Do not detach the power steering pump hoses.

10. Disconnect the intake manifold electric heater wire connector, as required.

11. Disconnect the throttle valve linkage, if equipped with automatic transmission.

12. Disconnect the EGR valve tube from the intake manifold.

13. Remove the intake manifold attaching screws, nuts and clamps. Remove the intake manifold. Discard the gasket.

14. Clean the mating surfaces of the manifold and cylinder head.

NOTE: *If the manifold is being replaced, ensure all fittings, etc., are transferred to the replacement manifold.*

15. Install the intake manifold. Install the intake manifold attaching screws, nuts and clamps. Torque manifold fasteners to 23 ft.lb.

16. Connect the EGR valve tube to the intake manifold.

17. Connect the throttle valve linkage, if equipped with automatic transmission.

18. Connect the intake manifold electric heater wire connector, as required.

19. On vehicles equipped with power steering install the power steering pump and its mounting bracket.

20. Connect the vacuum to from the EGR valve.

21. Connect the system coolant temperature sender wire connector (located on the intake manifold). Connect the air temperature sensor wire, if equipped.

22. If equipped, install the vacuum advance CTO valve vacuum hoses.

23. Install the carburetor or the throttle body. Torque the carburetor or throttle body mounting bolts to 14 ft.lb.

24. Connect the PCV valve vacuum hose to the intake manifold.

25. Connect the throttle cable to the bellcrank.

26. Connect the fuel pipe.

27. Connect the coolant hoses to the intake manifold.

28. Install the air cleaner.

29. Connect the negative battery cable.

30. Fill the cooling system.

4–151

1. Remove the negative cable.

2. Remove the air cleaner and the PCV valve hose.

CAUTION: *DO NOT remove the block drain plugs or loosen the radiator draincock the with system hot and under pressure because serious burns from the coolant can occur.*

3. Drain the cooling system.

CAUTION: *When draining the coolant, keep in mind that cats and dogs are attracted by the ethylene glycol antifreeze, and are quite likely to drink any that is left in an uncovered container or in puddles on the ground. This will prove fatal in sufficient quantity. Always drain the coolant into a sealable container. Coolant should be reused unless it is contaminated or several years old.*

4. Tag and remove the vacuum hoses (ensure the distributor vacuum advance hose is removed).

5. Disconnect the fuel pipe and electrical wire connections from the carburetor.

6. Disconnect the carburetor throttle linkage. Remove the carburetor and the carburetor spacer.

7. Remove the bellcrank and throttle link-

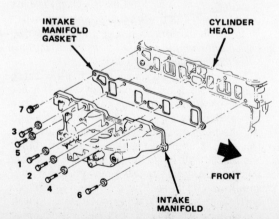

4-151 intake manifold bolt tightening sequence

age brackets and move them to one side for clearance.

8. Remove the heater hose at the intake manifold.

9. Remove the alternator. Note the position of spacers for installation.

10. Remove the manifold-to-cylinder head bolts and remove the manifold.

11. Position the replacement gasket and install the replacement manifold on the cylinder head. Start all bolts.

12. Tighten all bolts with 37 ft.lb.

13. Connect the heater hose to the intake manifold.

14. Install the bellcrank and throttle linkage brackets.

15. Connect the carburetor throttle linkage to the brackets and bellcrank.

16. Install the carburetor spacer and tighten the bolts with 15 ft.lb.

17. Install the carburetor and gasket. Tighten the nuts with 15 ft.lb.

18. Install the fuel pipe and electrical wire connections. Install the vacuum hoses.

19. Install the battery negative cable.

CAUTION: *Use extreme caution when the engine is operating. Do not stand in a direct line with the fan. Do not put your hands near pulleys, belts or fan. Do not wear loose clothing.*

20. Refill the cooling system. Start the engine and inspect for leaks.

21. Install the air cleaner and the PCV valve hose.

6-225

1. Drain the cooling system.

CAUTION: *When draining the coolant, keep in mind that cats and dogs are attracted by the ethylene glycol antifreeze, and are quite likely to drink any that is left in an uncovered container or in puddles on the ground. This will prove fatal in sufficient quantity. Always drain the coolant into a sealable container.*

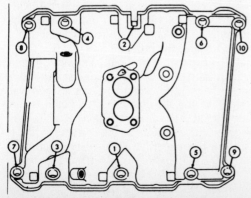

6-225 intake manifold tightening sequence

Coolant should be reused unless it is contaminated or several years old.

2. Disconnect the crankcase vent hose, distributor vacuum hose, and the fuel line from the carburetor.

3. Disconnect the two distributor leads from the coil.

4. Disconnect the wire from the temperature sending unit.

5. Remove the ten cap bolts that hold the intake manifold to the cylinder head. They must be replaced in their original location.

6. Remove the intake manifold assembly and gasket from the engine.

7. Reverse the above procedure for installation. Tighten the bolts to the correct torque, and in the proper sequence.

6-226

NOTE: *The intake and exhaust manifolds are removed as a unit, then separated.*

1. Remove the engine cover and housing.

2. Remove the air cleaner and carburetor.

3. Disconnect the exhaust pipe at the manifold.

4. Unbolt and remove the manifolds.

5. Installation is the reverse of removal. Retainers are used under the retaining nuts on all studs except the top ends and lower center. Plain washer are used under these nuts. It is possible, if you're not careful, to install the manifold assembly so that it interferes with the fit of the valve chamber cover at the upper rear corner of the cover. Leakage would result in this case. Torque the nuts, from the center towards the ends, to 30–35 ft.lb.

6-230

1. Disconnect and tag any hoses, wires or cables attached to the manifold or carburetor.

2. Remove the air cleaner.

3. Remove the carburetor.

4. Remove the nut and lockwasher that attaches the manifold and dipstick tube to the lower center stud on the head.

5. Remove the dipstick and tube.

6. Support the manifold and remove the four remaining nuts and lockwashers that attach it to the head and manifold.

7. Discard the gasket and thoroughly clean the mating surfaces of the head and manifold.

8. Installation is the reverse of removal. Always use a new gasket. Note that the gasket overlaps the intake port openings slightly. This is a calculated overlap designed to assist in air/fuel distribution. Do not attempt to cut the gasket to make it larger. Torque the manifold nuts to 15–20 ft.lb.

6-232, 6-258

The intake manifold and exhaust manifold are mounted externally on the left side of the engine and are attached to the cylinder head. The intake and exhaust manifolds are removed as a unit. On some engines, an exhaust gas recirculation valve is mounted on the side of the intake manifold.

1. Remove the air cleaner and carburetor.
2. Disconnect the accelerator cable from the accelerator bellcrank.
3. Disconnect the PCS vacuum hose from the intake manifold.
4. Disconnect the distributor vacuum hose and electrical wires at the TCS solenoid vacuum valve.
5. Remove the TCS solenoid vacuum valve and bracket from the intake manifold. In some cases it might not be necessary to remove the TCS unit.
6. If so equipped, disconnect the EGR valve vacuum hoses.
7. Remove the power steering mounting bracket and pump and set it aside without disconnecting the hoses.
8. Remove the EGR valve, if so equipped.
9. Disconnect the exhaust pipe from the manifold flange. Disconnect the spark CTO hoses and remove the oxygen sensor.
10. Remove the manifold attaching bolts, nuts and clamps.
11. Separate the intake manifold and exhaust manifold from the engine as an assembly. Discard the gasket.
12. If either manifold is to be replaced, they should be separated at the heat riser area.
13. Clean the mating surfaces of the manifolds and the cylinder head before replacing the manifolds. Replace them in reverse order of the above procedure with a new gasket. Tighten the bolts and nuts to the specified torque in the proper sequence.
14. Connect the exhaust pipe to the manifold flange. Torque the nuts to 20 ft.lb. Connect the spark CTO hoses and install the oxygen sensor.

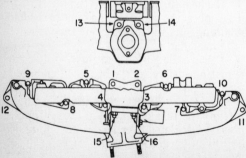

6-232, 258 intake manifold tightening sequence

15. Install the EGR valve, if so equipped.
16. Install the power steering mounting bracket and pump.
17. If so equipped, connect the EGR valve vacuum hoses.
18. Install the TCS solenoid vacuum valve and bracket to the intake manifold.
19. Connect the distributor vacuum hose and electrical wires at the TCS solenoid vacuum valve.
20. Connect the PCS vacuum hose to the intake manifold.
21. Connect the accelerator cable to the accelerator bellcrank.
22. Install the air cleaner and carburetor.

8-304

1. Drain the coolant from the radiator.
CAUTION: *When draining the coolant, keep in mind that cats and dogs are attracted by the ethylene glycol antifreeze, and are quite likely to drink any that is left in an uncovered container or in puddles on the ground. This will prove fatal in sufficient quantity. Always drain the coolant into a sealable container. Coolant should be reused unless it is contaminated or several years old.*
2. Remove the air cleaner assembly.
3. Disconnect the spark plug wires. Remove the spark plug wire brackets from the valve covers, and the bypass valve bracket.
4. Disconnect the upper radiator hose and the by-pass hose from the intake manifold. Disconnect the heater hose from the rear of the manifold.
5. Disconnect the ignition coil bracket and lay the coil aside.
6. Disconnect the tCS solenoid vacuum valve from the right side valve cover.
7. Disconnect all lines, hoses, linkages and wires from the carburetor and intake manifold and TCS components as required.
8. Disconnect the air delivery hoses at the air distribution manifolds.
9. Disconnect the air pump diverter valve and lay the valve and the bracket assembly, including the hoses, forward of the engine.
10. Remove the intake manifold after removing the cap bolts that hold it in place. Remove and discard the side gaskets and the end seals.
11. Clean the mating surfaces of the intake manifold and the cylinder head before replacing the intake manifold. Use new gaskets and tighten the cap bolts to the correct torque. Install in reverse order of the above procedure.
NOTE: *There is no specified tighten sequence for this intake manifold. Start at the center bolts and work outward.*
12. Connect the air pump diverter valve.

13. Connect the air delivery hoses at the air distribution manifolds.

14. Connect all lines, hoses, linkages and wires to the carburetor and intake manifold and TCS components as required.

15. Install the TCS solenoid vacuum valve to the right side valve cover.

16. Install the ignition coil bracket.

17. Connect the upper radiator hose and the by-pass hose to the intake manifold. Connect the heater hose to the rear of the manifold.

18. Connect the spark plug wires. Install the spark plug wire brackets on the valve covers, and the bypass valve bracket.

19. Install the air cleaner assembly.

20. Fill the cooling system.

Exhaust Manifold

REMOVAL AND INSTALLATION

L4–134

See Intake Manifolds

F4–134

1. Remove the air delivery hose from the air injection tube assembly if the engine is so equipped. If not, proceed to step two.

2. Remove the five nuts from the manifold studs.

3. Pull the manifold from the mounting studs. Be careful not to damage the air injection tubes if the engine is equipped with an air pump.

4. Remove the gaskets from the cylinder block.

5. If the exhaust manifold is to be replaced it will be necessary to remove the air injection tubes from the exhaust manifold. The application of heat may be necessary to aid removal.

6. Use new gaskets when replacing the exhaust manifold. Make sure that the cylinder head are clean. Tighten the attaching nuts to the correct torque specification.

7. If the exhaust manifold was be replaced, install the air injection tubes. The application of heat may be necessary to aid installation.

8. Install the air delivery hose on the air injection tube assembly if the engine is so equipped.

4–150

1. Remove the intake manifold.

2. Disconnect the EGR tube.

3. Disconnect the exhaust pipe at the manifold.

4. Disconnect the oxygen sensor wire.

5. Support the manifold and remove the nuts from the studs.

6. If a new manifold is being installed,

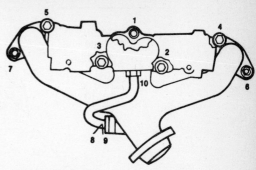

4-150 exhaust manifold torque sequence

transfer the oxygen sensor. Torque the sensor to 35 ft.lb.

7. Thoroughly clean the gasket mating surfaces of the manifold and head.

8. Install the manifold, using a new gasket. Torque the nuts to 23 ft.lb.

9. Connect the oxygen sensor wire.

10. Connect the exhaust pipe at the manifold.

11. Connect the EGR tube.

12. Install the intake manifold.

NOTE: *On some 1984–85 4–150 engines, the manifold end studs can be bent or broken if the manifold is misaligned. To remedy this:*

a. Remove the manifold.

b. Replace any bent or broken studs.

c. Using a straightedge, check the flatness of the manifold mating surface. If a 0.015″ (0.38mm) flat feeler gauge can be inserted between the straightedge and the manifold, at any point, replace the manifold.

d. Modify the original or replacement manifold by grinding the mounting flanges as shown in the accompanying illustration.

e. Install the manifold

4–151

1. Remove the air cleaner and heated air tube.

2. Remove the engine oil dipstick tube attaching bolt.

3. Remove the oxygen sensor, if equipped.

4. Raise the vehicle and disconnect the exhaust pipe from the manifold. Lower the vehicle.

5. Remove the exhaust manifold bolts and remove the manifold and gasket.

6. Install the replacement gasket and the exhaust manifold on the cylinder head. Tighten all bolts to 39 ft.lb.

7. Install the dipstick tube attaching bolts.

6–225

1. Remove the five attaching screws, one nut, and exhaust manifold from the side of the cylinder head.

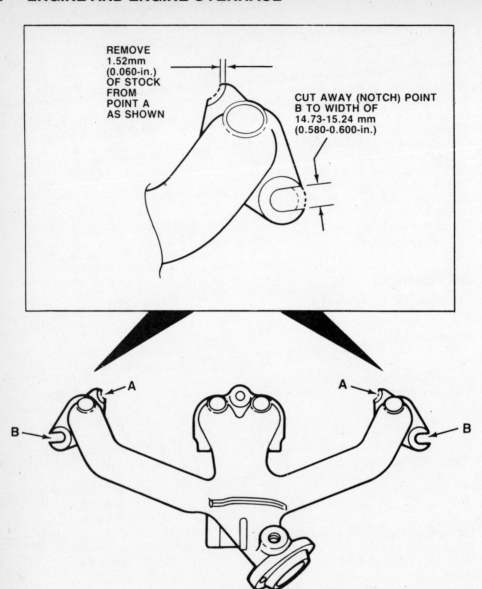

REMOVE
1.52mm
(0.060-in.)
OF STOCK
FROM
POINT A
AS SHOWN

CUT AWAY (NOTCH) POINT
B TO WIDTH OF
14.73-15.24 mm
(0.580-0.600-in.)

Exhaust manifold modification on the 4-150

6-225 exhaust manifold bolts

2. Use a new gasket when replacing the exhaust manifolds. Make sure that the mating surfaces of the manifold and the cylinder head are clean. Tighten the manifold nuts and bolts to the correct torque.

6–226

The exhaust manifold is removed as an assembly, with the intake manifold. See the appropriate procedure, above.

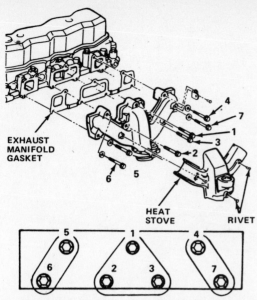

EXHAUST
MANIFOLD
GASKET

HEAT
STOVE   RIVET

4-151 exhaust manifold bolt tightening sequence

6-230

1. Disconnect the exhaust pipe at the manifold.

2. Remove the ten nuts, eight flat washers and two retainers that attach the manifold to the head.

3. Lift off the manifold and remove and discard the gasket.

4. Clean the mating surfaces thoroughly and install the manifold, using a new gasket. Torque the nuts to 35–40 ft.lb.

5. Attach the exhaust pipe.

6-232, 6-258

The intake and exhaust manifolds of the 232 and 258 cu. in. Sixes must be removed together. See the procedure for removing and installing the intake manifold.

8-304

1. Disconnect the spark plug wires.

2. Disconnect the air delivery hose at the distribution manifold.

3. Remove the air distribution manifold and the injection tubes.

4. Disconnect the exhaust pipe at the manifold.

5. Remove the exhaust manifold attaching bolts and washers along with the spark plug shields.

6. Separate the exhaust manifold from the cylinder head.

7. Install in reverse order of the above procedure. Clean the mating surfaces and tighten the attaching bolts to the correct torque.

Air Conditioning Compressor
REMOVAL AND INSTALLATION

6-258

1977–80 ALL
1981, EXCEPT CALIF.

1. Isolate the compressor. See Chapter 1.

2. Remove both service valves and cap the valves and compressor ports immediately.

3. Remove the alternator belt and adjusting bolt.

4. Remove the upper alternator mounting bolt and loosen the lower mounting bolt.

5. Remove the idler pulley.

6. Disconnect the compressor clutch wire. Remove the compressor mounting nuts and lift out the compressor. BE CAREFUL; IT'S HEAVY!

7. For installation, install the compressor, alternator and belt, idler pulley, and adjust the drive belts.

8. Install the service valves and purge the compressor of air. Open the valves.

9. Connect the clutch wire.

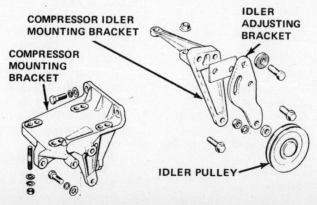

COMPRESSOR IDLER
MOUNTING BRACKET

IDLER
ADJUSTING
BRACKET

COMPRESSOR
MOUNTING
BRACKET

IDLER PULLEY

Compressor mounting on the 6-258 for 1977–80 all, and 1981, except Calif.

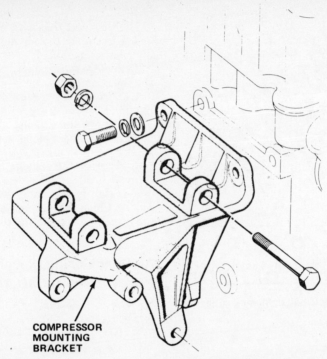

COMPRESSOR
MOUNTING
BRACKET

Compressor mounting on the 1981 California 6-258 and all 1982–87 models

1981 CALIFORNIA MODELS
1982–87 ALL MODELS

1. Isolate the compressor. See Chapter 1.
2. Disconnect the battery ground.
3. Remove the discharge and suction hoses from the compressor and cap all openings immediately.
4. Loosen the alternator and remove the drive belts.
5. Remove the alternator from its brackets and set it out of the way.
6. Unbolt and remove the compressor.
7. For installation, install the compressor and alternator, connect the hoses and install and tension the drive belts. Connect the compressor clutch wire. Open the valves.

8–304

1. Isolate the compressor. See Chapter 1.
2. Remove both service valves and cap the valves and compressor ports immediately.
3. Loosen the alternator and remove the drive belts.
4. Remove the alternator mounting bracket.
5. Remove the compressor clutch wire.
6. Remove the compressor and mounting bracket as an assembly.
7. For installation, install the compressor and mounting bracket, install the alternator

bracket, connect the clutch wire, install the belts, idler pulley, and adjust the drive belts.
8. Install the service valves and purge the compressor of air. Open the valves.

Radiator
REMOVAL AND INSTALLATION

1. Drain the radiator by opening the drain cock and removing the radiator pressure cap.
CAUTION: *When draining the coolant, keep in mind that cats and dogs are attracted by the ethylene glycol antifreeze, and are quite likely to drink any that is left in an uncovered container or in puddles on the ground. This will prove fatal in sufficient quantity. Always drain the coolant into a sealable container. Coolant should be reused unless it is contaminated or several years old.*
2. Remove the upper and lower hose clamps and hoses at the radiator.
3. Disconnect the automatic transmission oil cooler lines at the radiator, if so equipped. Remove the radiator shroud from the radiator, if so equipped.
4. Remove all attaching screws that secure the radiator to the radiator body support.
5. Remove the radiator.
6. Replace in reverse order of the above procedure.

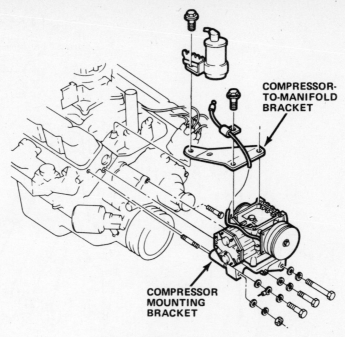

**COMPRESSOR-
TO-MANIFOLD
BRACKET**

**COMPRESSOR
MOUNTING
BRACKET**

8-304 compressor mounting

Water Pump
REMOVAL AND INSTALLATION

4–134 L- and F-Head

1. Drain the cooling system.
CAUTION: *When draining the coolant, keep in mind that cats and dogs are attracted by the ethylene glycol antifreeze, and are quite likely to drink any that is left in an uncovered container or in puddles on the ground. This will prove fatal in sufficient quantity. Always drain the coolant into a sealable container. Coolant should be reused unless it is contaminated or several years old.*
2. Disconnect the hoses at the pump.
3. Remove the fan belt.
4. Unbolt the fan and hub assembly.
5. Unbolt and remove the pump.
6. Installation is the reverse of removal. Torque the pump bolts to 17 ft.lb. Always use a new gasket coated with sealer.

4–150

NOTE: *Some 4–150 engines with air conditioning are equipped with a serpentine drive belt and have a reverse rotating water pump coupled with a viscous fan drive assembly. The components are identified by the words REVERSE stamped on the cover of the viscous drive and on the inner side of the fan. The word REV is also cast into the body of the water pump.*
1. Drain the cooling system.

CAUTION: *When draining the coolant, keep in mind that cats and dogs are attracted by the ethylene glycol antifreeze, and are quite likely to drink any that is left in an uncovered container or in puddles on the ground. This will prove fatal in sufficient quantity. Always drain the coolant into a sealable container. Coolant should be reused unless it is contaminated or several years old.*
2. Disconnect the hoses at the pump.
3. Remove the drive belts.
4. Remove the power steering pump bracket.
5. Remove the fan and shroud.
6. Unbolt and remove the pump.
7. Clean the mating surfaces thoroughly.
8. Using a new gasket, install the pump and torque the bolts to 13 ft.lb.
9. Install all other parts in reverse order of removal.

4–151

1. Remove the fan belt.
2. Remove the fan and hub assembly.
3. Drain the cooling system.
CAUTION: *When draining the coolant, keep in mind that cats and dogs are attracted by the ethylene glycol antifreeze, and are quite likely to drink any that is left in an uncovered container or in puddles on the ground. This will prove fatal in sufficient quantity. Always drain the coolant into a sealable container.*

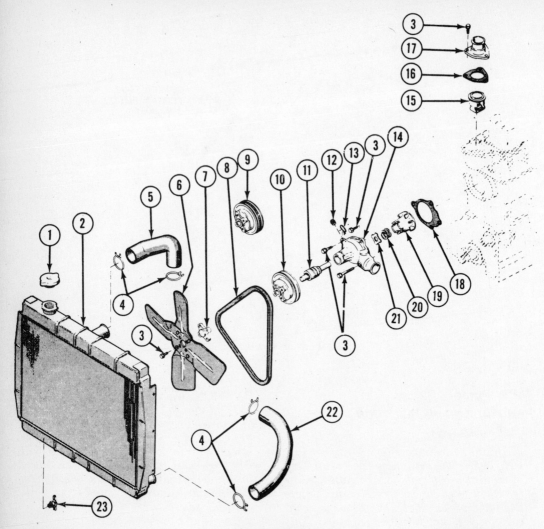

1. Radiator pressure cap
2. Radiator
3. Bolt
4. Hose clamp
5. Upper hose
6. Fan
7. Fan spacer
8. Fan and alternator belt
9. Pulley (double groove)
10. Pulley (single groove)
11. Bearing and shaft
12. Pipe plug
13. Bearing retainer spring
14. Pump body
15. Thermostat
16. Gasket
17. Water outlet fitting
18. Gasket
19. Impeller
20. Pump seal
21. Seal washer
22. Lower hose
23. Drain cock

4-134 cooling system components

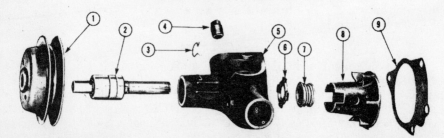

1. Fan and pump pulley
2. Bearing and shaft
3. Bearing retainer spring
4. Pipe plug
5. Pump body
6. Seal washer
7. Pump seal
8. Impeller
9. Gasket

4-134 water pump

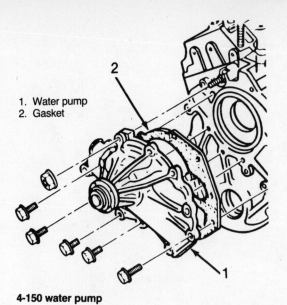

1. Water pump
2. Gasket

4-150 water pump

Coolant should be reused unless it is contaminated or several years old.

4. Disconnect the hoses at the pump.

5. Unbolt and remove the pump.

6. Installation is the reverse of removal. Always use a new gasket coated with sealer. Torque the water pump bolts to 25 ft.lb. Tighten the fan and hub bolts to 18 ft.lb.

6–225

1. Drain the cooling system.

CAUTION: *When draining the coolant, keep in mind that cats and dogs are attracted by the ethylene glycol antifreeze, and are quite likely to drink any that is left in an uncovered container or in puddles on the ground. This will prove fatal in sufficient quantity. Always drain the coolant into a sealable container. Coolant should be reused unless it is contaminated or several years old.*

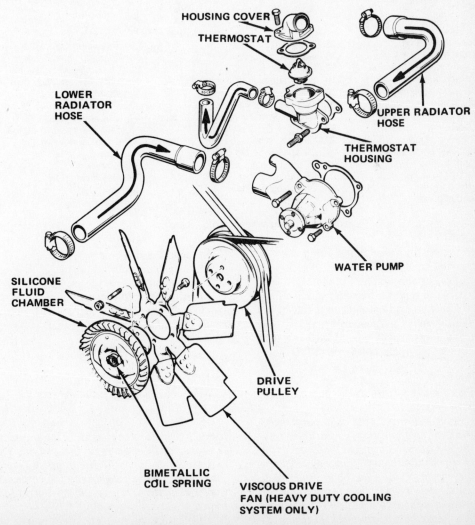

4-151 water pump and related components

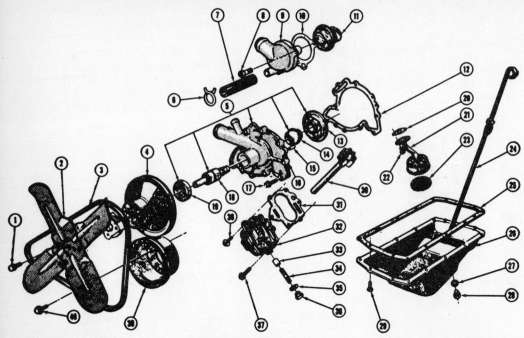

1. Bolt and lock washer
2. Fan assembly
3. Fan and alternator belt
4. Fan driven pulley
5. Water pump assembly
6. Hose clamp
7. Thermostat by-pass hose
8. Hex head bolt
9. Water outlet elbow
10. Water outlet elbow gasket
11. Thermostat
12. Water pump gasket
13. Impeller and insert, water pump
14. Water pump seal
15. Dowel pin
16. Water pump cover
17. Bolt
18. Water pump shaft and bearing
19. Fan hub
20. Oil suction pipe gasket
21. Oil suction housing, pipe and flange
22. Bolt
23. Oil pump screen
24. Oil dipstick
25. Oil pan gasket
26. Oil pan assembly
27. Drain plug gasket
28. Drain plug
29. Screw and lockwasher
30. Oil pump shaft and gear
31. Oil pump cover gasket
32. Valve by-pass and cover assembly
33. Oil pressure valve
34. Valve by-pass spring
35. Oil pressure valve cap gasket
36. Oil pressure valve cap
37. Screw
38. Screw
39. Fan driving pulley
40. Hex head bolt

6-225 cooling system components

2. Disconnect all hoses at the pump.
3. Remove the drive belts.
4. Remove the fan and hub assembly.
5. Unbolt and remove the water pump along with the alternator adjustment bracket.
6. Installation is the reverse of removal. Always use a new gasket coated with sealer. Torque the water pump bolts to 6–8 ft.lb.

6–226

1. Disconnect the hoses at the pump. Drain the cooling system.
CAUTION: *When draining the coolant, keep in mind that cats and dogs are attracted by the ethylene glycol antifreeze, and are quite likely to drink any that is left in an uncovered container or in puddles on the ground. This will prove fatal in sufficient quantity. Always drain the coolant into a sealable container. Coolant should be reused unless it is contaminated or several years old.*

2. Remove the fan belt.
3. Remove the fan and hub.
4. Unbolt and remove the pump.
5. Installation is the reverse of removal. Always use a new gasket coated with sealer. Torque the pump bolts to 17 ft.lb.

6–230

1. Drain the cooling system.
CAUTION: *When draining the coolant, keep in mind that cats and dogs are attracted by the ethylene glycol antifreeze, and are quite likely to drink any that is left in an uncovered container or in puddles on the ground. This will prove fatal in sufficient quantity. Always drain the coolant into a sealable container. Coolant should be reused unless it is contaminated or several years old.*

2. Disconnect the hoses at the pump.
3. Remove the fan and pulley.

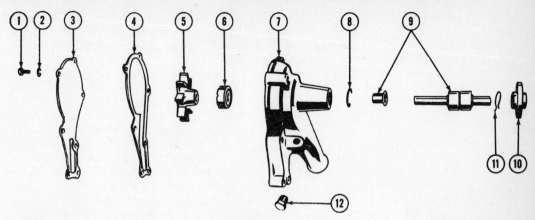

1. Bolt
2. Lockwasher
3. Cover
4. Gasket
5. Impeller
6. Seal
7. Body
8. Snap ring
9. Drive shaft and flinger
10. Pulley hub
11. Retainer
12. Plug

6-226 water pump

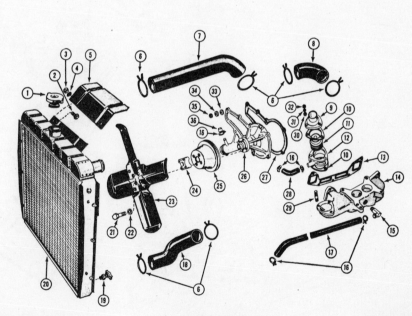

1. Radiator pressure cap
2. Bolt
3. Nut
4. Lockwasher
5. Shroud
6. Hose clamp
7. Upper radiator hose
8. Water hose
9. Water outlet elbow
10. Thermostat gasket
11. Thermostat
12. Thermostat housing
13. Intake manifold gasket
14. Intake manifold
15. Elbow
16. Hose clamp
17. Water hose
18. Lower radiator hose
19. Drain cock
20. Radiator
21. Bolt
22. Lockwasher
23. Cooling fan
24. Spacer
25. Fan drive pulley
26. Water pump
27. Water pump gasket
28. Bypass hose
29. Stud
30. Flat washer
31. Lockwasher
32. Nut
33. Flat washer
34. Lockwasher
35. Nut
36. Cap

6-230 cooling system components

4. Unbolt and remove the pump. Discard the gasket.

5. Clean the gasket mating surfaces thoroughly. Coat both sides of the new gasket with sealer. Install the pump and torque the mounting bolts to 15–20 ft.lb. Install all other parts in reverse order of removal.

6–232, 258

1. Drain the cooling system.

CAUTION: *When draining the coolant, keep in mind that cats and dogs are attracted by the ethylene glycol antifreeze, and are quite likely to drink any that is left in an uncovered container or in puddles on the ground. This will prove fatal in sufficient quantity. Always drain the coolant into a sealable container. Coolant should be reused unless it is contaminated or several years old.*

2. Disconnect all hoses at the pump.
3. Remove the drive belts.
4. Remove the fan shroud attaching screws.

5. Unbolt the fan and fan drive assembly and remove along with the shroud. On some models it may be easier to turn the shroud ½ turn.

6. Unbolt and remove the pump.

NOTE: *Engines built for sale in California having a single, serpentine drive belt and viscous fan drive, have a reverse rotating pump and drive. These components are identified by the word REVERSE stamped on the drive cover and inner side of the fan, and REV cast into the water pump body. Never interchange standard rotating parts with these.*

7. Installation is the reverse of removal. Always use a new gasket coated with sealer. Torque the water pump bolts to 13 ft.lb.; the fan bolts to 18 ft.lb.

8–304

1. Drain the cooling system.

CAUTION: *When draining the coolant, keep in mind that cats and dogs are attracted by*

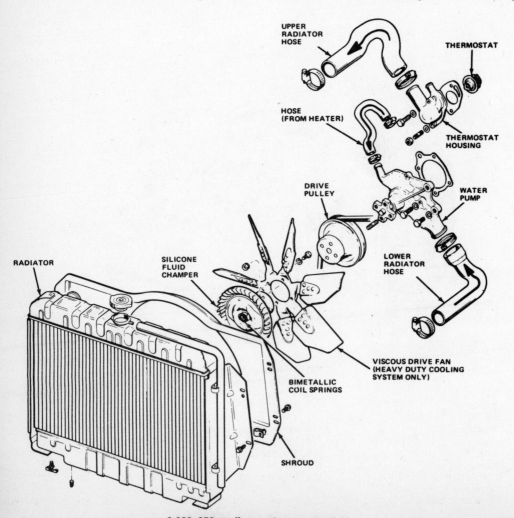

6-232, 258 cooling system components

1. Radiator upper hose
2. Thermostat housing cover
3. Gasket
4. Thermostat
5. Gasket
6. Drive pulley
7. Viscous drive fan
8. Coolant recovery bottle
9. Radiator
10. Shroud
11. Bimetallic coil spring
12. Silicone fluid chamber
13. Stud
14. Hose (from heater)
15. Water pump
16. Bypass hose

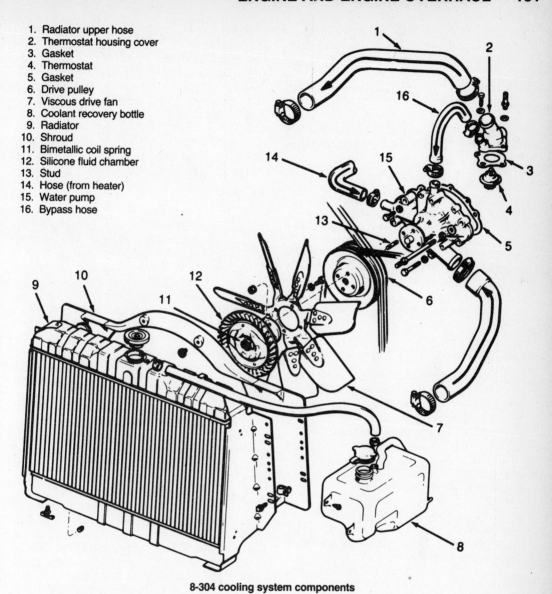

8-304 cooling system components

the ethylene glycol antifreeze, and are quite likely to drink any that is left in an uncovered container or in puddles on the ground. This will prove fatal in sufficient quantity. Always drain the coolant into a sealable container. Coolant should be reused unless it is contaminated or several years old.

2. Disconnect all hoses at the pump.

3. Loosen all drive belts.

4. Remove the shroud, but reinsert one bolt to hold the radiator.

5. Remove the fan and hub.

6. If the vehicle is equipped with A/C install a double nut on the compressor bracket-to-water pump stud and remove the stud.

7. Remove, but do not disconnect the alternator and bracket.

8. If so equipped, remove the nuts that attach the power steering pump to the rear half of the pump bracket.

9. Remove the two bolts that attach the front half to the rear half of the bracket.

10. Remove the remaining upper screw from the inner air pump support bracket, loosen the lower bolt and drop the bracket away from the power steering front bracket.

11. Remove the front half of the power steering bracket from the water pump mounting stud.

12. Unbolt and remove the water pump.

13. Install the pump. Always use a new gasket coated with sealer. Torque the pump-to-timing case bolts to 48 in.lb. and the pump-to-block bolts to 25 ft.lb.

14. Install the front half of the power steering bracket to the water pump mounting stud. Torque the power steering pulley nut to 60 ft.lb.

15. Install the upper screw from the inner air pump support bracket, and tighten the lower bolt.

16. If so equipped, install the nuts that attach the power steering pump to the rear half of the pump bracket.

17. Install the two bolts that attach the front half to the rear half of the bracket.

18. Install the alternator and bracket.

19. If the vehicle is equipped with A/C install a double nut on the compressor bracket-to-water pump stud and install the stud.

20. Install the fan and hub.

21. Install the shroud.

22. Adjust all drive belts.

23. Connect all hoses at the pump.

24. Fill the cooling system.

Cylinder Head

REMOVAL AND INSTALLATION

NOTE: *It is important to note that each engine has its own head bolt tightening sequence and torque. Incorrect tightening procedure may cause head warpage and compression loss. Correct sequence and torque for each engine model is shown in this chapter.*

L4–134

1. Remove the spark plugs.

2. Drain the cooling system.

CAUTION: *When draining the coolant, keep in mind that cats and dogs are attracted by the ethylene glycol antifreeze, and are quite likely to drink any that is left in an uncovered container or in puddles on the ground. This will prove fatal in sufficient quantity. Always drain the coolant into a sealable container. Coolant should be reused unless it is contaminated or several years old.*

3. Remove the temperature sending unit.

4. Remove the head nuts.

5. Lift the head from the block.

NOTE: *Do not use a sharp instrument such as a chisel or screwdriver to break the head*

from the block. If the head sticks, screw lifting hooks into the #1 and 4 spark plug holes.

6. Thoroughly clean the gasket mating surfaces. Remove all traces of old gasket material. Remove all carbon deposits from the combustion chambers. Lay a straightedge across the head and check for flatness. Total deviation should not exceed 0.001″ (0.0254mm).

7. Install the head, using a new gasket. Make sure the head and block surfaces are clean. Torque the head to 60–70 ft.lb.

F4–134

1. Drain the coolant.

CAUTION: *When draining the coolant, keep in mind that cats and dogs are attracted by the ethylene glycol antifreeze, and are quite likely to drink any that is left in an uncovered container or in puddles on the ground. This will prove fatal in sufficient quantity. Always drain the coolant into a sealable container. Coolant should be reused unless it is contaminated or several years old.*

2. Remove the upper radiator hose.

3. Remove the carburetor.

4. On early engines remove the by-pass hose on the front of the cylinder head.

5. Remove the rocker arm cover.

6. Remove the rocker arm attaching stud nuts and rocker arm shaft assembly.

7. Remove the cylinder head bolts. One of the bolts is located below the carburetor mounting, inside the intake manifold.

8. Lift off the cylinder head.

9. Thoroughly clean the gasket mating surfaces. Remove all traces of old gasket material. Remove all carbon deposits from the combustion chambers. Lay a straightedge across the head and check for flatness. Total deviation should not exceed 0.001″ (0.0254mm).

10. Reverse the procedure to install the cylinder head. Tighten the head bolts first to 40 ft.lb. then to the specified torque in the correct sequence.

F-head cylinder head torque sequence

4–150

1. Disconnect the battery ground.

2. Drain the cooling system.

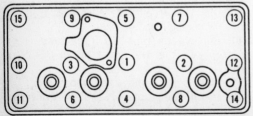

4-134 L-head cylinder head bolt tightening sequence

CAUTION: *When draining the coolant, keep in mind that cats and dogs are attracted by the ethylene glycol antifreeze, and are quite likely to drink any that is left in an uncovered container or in puddles on the ground. This will prove fatal in sufficient quantity. Always drain the coolant into a sealable container. Coolant should be reused unless it is contaminated or several years old.*

3. Disconnect the hoses at the thermostat housing.

4. Remove the air cleaner.

5. Remove the rocker arm cover. The cover seal is RTV sealer. Break the seal with a clean putty knife or razor blade. Don't attempt to remove the cover until the seal is broken. To remove the cover, pry where indicated at the bolt holes.

6. Remove the rocker arms. Keep them in order!

7. Remove the pushrods. Keep them in order!

8. Remove the power steering pump bracket.

9. Suspend the pump out of the way.

10. Remove the intake and exhaust manifolds.

11. Remove the air conditioning compressor drive belt.

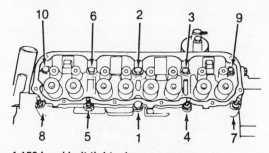

4-150 head bolt tightening sequence

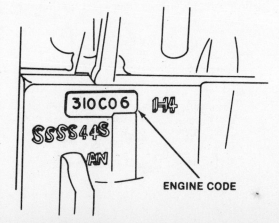

Engine code location

12. Loosen the alternator drive belt.

13. Remove the compressor/alternator bracket mounting bolt.

14. Unbolt the compressor and suspend it out of the way. DO NOT DISCONNECT THE REFRIGERANT LINES!

15. Remove the spark plugs.

16. Disconnect the temperature sending unit wire.

17. Remove the head bolts.

18. Lift the head off the engine and place it on a clean workbench.

19. Remove the head gasket.

NOTE: *Some head bolts used on the spark plug side of the 1984 4-150 were improperly hardened and may break under the head during service or at head installation while torquing the bolts. Engines with the defective bolts are serial numbers 310U06 through 310U14. Whenever a broken bolts is found, replace all bolts on the spark plug side of the head with bolt #400 6593.*

20. Thoroughly clean the gasket mating surfaces. Remove all traces of old gasket material. Remove all carbon deposits from the combustion chambers. Lay a straightedge across the head and check for flatness. Total deviation should not exceed 0.001" (0.0254mm).

21. Do not apply sealant to the head or block. Coat both sides of the gasket with sealer. The gasket should be stamped TOP for installation. Place the gasket on the block.

22. Install the head on the block.

23. Coat the bolt labeled 8 in the torque sequence illustration, with Permatex #2, or equivalent. Install all the bolts. Tighten the bolts in three equal steps, in the sequence shown, to 85 ft.lb. Torque #8 to 75 ft.lb.

24. Connect the temperature sending unit wire.

25. Install the spark plugs.

26. Install the compressor.

27. Install the compressor/alternator bracket mounting bolt.

28. Adjust the alternator drive belt.

29. Install the air conditioning compressor drive belt.

30. Install the intake and exhaust manifolds.

31. Install the power steering pump bracket.

32. Install the pushrods. Keep them in order!

33. Install the rocker arms. Keep them in order!

34. Thoroughly clean the mating surfaces of the head and rocker cover. Run a ⅛" (3.175mm) bead of RTV sealer along the length of the sealing surface of the head. Position the cover on the head within 10 minutes of applying the sealer. Torque the cover bolts, in a crisscross pattern, to 55 in.lb.

35. Install the air cleaner.

36 Connect the hoses at the thermostat housing.

37. Connect the battery ground.

38. Fill the cooling system.

4-151

NOTE: *The 4-151 rocker cover is sealed with RTV silicone gasket material. Do not use a conventional gasket.*

1. Drain the cooling system and disconnect the hoses at the thermostat housing.

CAUTION: *When draining the coolant, keep in mind that cats and dogs are attracted by the ethylene glycol antifreeze, and are quite likely to drink any that is left in an uncovered container or in puddles on the ground. This will prove fatal in sufficient quantity. Always drain the coolant into a sealable container. Coolant should be reused unless it is contaminated or several years old.*

2. Remove the cylinder head cover (valve cover), the gasket, the rocker arm assembly, and the pushrods.

3. Remove the intake and exhaust manifold from the cylinder head.

4. Disconnect the spark plug wires and remove the spark plugs to avoid damaging them.

5. Disconnect the temperature sending unit wire, ignition coil and bracket assembly and battery ground cable from the engine.

6. Remove the cylinder head bolts, the cylinder head and gasket from the block.

7. Thoroughly clean the gasket mating surfaces. Remove all traces of old gasket material. Remove all carbon deposits from the combustion chambers. Lay a straightedge across the head and check for flatness. Total deviation should not exceed 0.001" (0.0254mm).

8. Thoroughly clean the mating surfaces of the head and rocker cover. Run a 1/8" (3.175mm) bead of RTV sealer along the length of the sealing surface of the head, inboard of the bolt holes. Position the cover on the head within 10 minutes of applying the sealer. Torque the cover bolts, in a crisscross pattern, to 55 in.lb.

9. Do not apply sealant to the head or block. Coat both sides of the gasket with sealer. The gasket should be stamped TOP for installation. Place the gasket on the block.

10. Install the head on the block. Insert the bolts and tighten them, in sequence, to the proper torque.

11. Install the pushrods and the rocker arm assembly.

12. Install the intake and exhaust manifold on the cylinder head.

13. Install the spark plugs and connect the spark plug wires.

14. Connect the temperature sending unit wire, ignition coil and bracket assembly and battery ground cable at the engine.

15. Connect the hoses at the thermostat housing.

16. Fill the cooling system.

6-225

1. Drain the cooling system.

CAUTION: *When draining the coolant, keep in mind that cats and dogs are attracted by the ethylene glycol antifreeze, and are quite likely to drink any that is left in an uncovered container or in puddles on the ground. This will prove fatal in sufficient quantity. Always drain the coolant into a sealable container. Coolant should be reused unless it is contaminated or several years old.*

2. Remove the intake manifold.

3. Remove the rocker cover.

4. Remove the exhaust pipes at the flanges.

5. Remove the alternator in order to remove the right head.

6. Remove the dipstick and power steering pump, if so equipped, in order to remove the left head.

7. Remove the valve cover and the rocker assemblies. Mark these parts so that they can be reinstalled in exactly the same positions.

8. Unbolt the head bolts and lift off the cylinder head(s). It is very important that the inside of the engine be protected from dirt. The hydraulic lifters are particularly susceptible to being damaged by dirt.

9. Thoroughly clean the gasket mating sur-

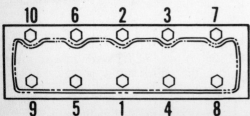

4-151 cylinder head torque sequence

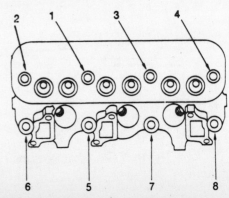

V6-225 cylinder head torque sequence

faces. Remove all traces of old gasket material. Remove all carbon deposits from the combustion chambers. Lay a straightedge across the head and check for flatness. Total deviation should not exceed 0.001" (0.0254mm).

10. Do not apply sealant to the head or block. Coat both sides of the gasket with sealer. The gasket should be stamped TOP for installation. Place the gasket on the block.

11. Install the head on the block. Insert the bolts and tighten them, in sequence, to the 65–85 ft.lb., in three progressive passes.

12. Install the rocker assemblies and the valve covers. Torque the rocker arm assemblies to 25–35 ft.lb.; the valve covers to 36–60 in.lb.

13. Install the dipstick and power steering pump, if so equipped.

14. Install the alternator. Torque the bracket-to-head bolts to 30–40 ft.lb.; the bracket to water pump bolts to 18–25 ft.lb.

15. Install the exhaust pipes at the flanges. Torque the nuts to 20 ft.lb.

16. Install the intake manifold. Torque the bolts to 45–55 ft.lb.

17. Fill the cooling system.

6–226

1. Remove the hood.
2. Remove the carburetor.
3. Remove the intake and exhaust manifold assembly.
4. Drain the cooling system.

CAUTION: *When draining the coolant, keep in mind that cats and dogs are attracted by the ethylene glycol antifreeze, and are quite likely to drink any that is left in an uncovered container or in puddles on the ground. This will prove fatal in sufficient quantity. Always drain the coolant into a sealable container. Coolant should be reused unless it is contaminated or several years old.*

5. Remove the water pump.
6. Remove the surge tank, water outlet and thermostat.
7. Remove the distributor and plug wires. Tag the wires for installation.
8. Remove the oil filter and bracket and position it out of the way.
9. Remove the coil.
10. Unbolt the oil filler tube from the head.
11. Remove and tag any wires connected to the head.
12. Remove the head bolts. There is a partially hidden head bolt next to the distributor adapter.
13. Lift off the head. Discard the head gasket.
14. Inspect the head for cracks, leaks or other damage. Replace leaky core plugs. Lay a

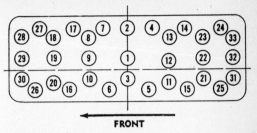

6-226 head bolt torque sequence

straightedge across the head and check for flatness. Total deviation should not exceed 0.031" (0.7874mm). Localized deviation, between any two points, should not exceed 0.010" (0.254mm). Unevenness between the head and block, at any given point should not exceed 0.015" (0.381mm). If deviation is not within acceptable limits, the head should be replaced.

15. Thoroughly clean the mating surfaces of the head and block.

16. Check the head bolt holes for proper depth. To do this, place the head on the block, without the gasket. Insert the bolts into the holes, without the washers. Turn each bolt down, by hand. The bolts should be free enough to be turned all the way down by hand. The head of each bolt must tighten down on the head surface. If a bolt does not turn freely, clean and/or retap the hole as necessary. If a bolt will not turn all the way down, check for foreign matter in the hole. If there is no foreign matter, the hole will have to be deepened by retapping.

17. Obtain two bolts which are the thread size as the head bolts, but are at least 5 inches (127mm) longer. Cut the heads off the bolts and file screwdriver slots in each one. Install these bolts in positions 24 and 26, in the illustration.

18. Coat both sides of the new gasket with sealer. Position the gasket on the block. Make sure that the bolt holes line up.

19. Lower the head onto the block, using the guide bolts.

20. Coat the threads of the head bolts with sealer and install them. Turn the bolts down snugly, in the proper sequence. Remove the guide bolts and install bolts 24 and 26. Torque all bolts, in the proper sequence, to 45 ft.lb.

21. Install any wires connected to the head.
22. Attach the oil filler tube to the head.
23. Install the coil.
24. Install the oil filter and bracket.
25. Install the distributor and plug wires.
26. Install the surge tank, water outlet and thermostat.
27. Install the water pump.
28. Install the intake and exhaust manifold assembly.

29. Install the carburetor.
30. Install the hood.
31. Fill the cooling system.
32. Start the engine and let it reach normal operating temperature. Shut off the engine and retorque the bolts to 45 ft.lb., in sequence. Recheck the bolt torque at 500 miles and 1,000 miles after service.

6–230

NOTE: *This procedure requires a special tool.*
1. Remove the camshaft cover.
2. Install camshaft sprocket remover W-268, or its equivalent, as shown. Tighten the nut to relieve tension on the camshaft.
3. Remove the capscrew, lockwasher, flat washer and fuel pump eccentric from the camshaft sprocket.
4. Pull forward on the sprocket to remove it from the shaft. With the sprocket still engaged in the chain, release the tension on the tool by loosening the nut. Gently allow the sprocket to rest on the bosses in the cover.
NOTE: *Do not rotate the crankshaft while the camshaft sprocket is removed in this manner. Do not attempt to remove the camshaft sprocket from the chain.*
5. Disconnect the lubrication tube from the head and block.
6. Remove the two timing chain cover-to-head bolts.
7. Remove the head bolts. Note that there are three short head bolts and eleven long ones. All bolts have flat washers.
8. Lift off the head and discard the gasket.
9. Inspect the head for cracks, leaks or other damage. Replace leaky core plugs. Lay a straightedge across the head and check for flatness. Total deviation should not exceed 0.003" (0.0762mm).

1. Nut   2. Tool W-268   3. Camshaft sprocket

Camshaft sprocket removal and installation tool installed on the engine

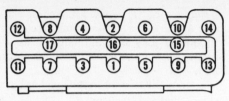

6-230 cylinder head tightening sequence

10. Thoroughly clean the mating surfaces of the head and block. Remove all carbon from the combustion chambers and tops of pistons. Clean all water and oil gallery holes.
11. Coat both sides of the new gasket with sealer. Position the gasket on the block. Make sure that the bolt holes line up.
12. Obtain two bolts which are the thread size as the head bolts, but are at least 5½" (139.7mm). Cut the heads off the bolts and file screwdriver slots in each one.
13. Using a hoist, lower the head to within ¼" (6.35mm) of the block.
14. Install the two modified bolts in bolt holes 12 and 14 in the head (see the torque sequence illustration) and screw them into the block to act as guide pins. This procedure is important, as these guide pins will prevent damage to the timing cover, chain and sprocket.
15. Lower the head into position and install the head bolts, with the exception of the #12 and 14 bolts, finger tight. Leave the guide pins in holes 12 and 14.
16. Start the timing cover-to-head bolts into the head.
17. Torque the 12 installed head bolts, in the sequence illustrated, to 35 ft.lb. Then, remove the guide pins and install the two head bolts in their places. Torque them to 35 ft.lb. also.
NOTE: *Late production engines have zinc-plated bolts for these two locations. Make sure that these special bolts are used.*
18. Torque all bolts, in the sequence shown, to 95 ft.lb.
19. Connect the lubrication tube from the head and block.
20. Install the camshaft sprocket and chain.
21. Install the capscrew, lockwasher, flat washer and fuel pump eccentric on the camshaft sprocket.
22. Remove camshaft sprocket tool W-268.
23. Install the camshaft cover.

6–232, 6–258

1. Drain the cooling system and disconnect the hoses at the thermostat housing.
CAUTION: *When draining the coolant, keep in mind that cats and dogs are attracted by the ethylene glycol antifreeze, and are quite likely to drink any that is left in an uncovered container or in puddles on the ground. This*

will prove fatal in sufficient quantity. Always drain the coolant into a sealable container. Coolant should be reused unless it is contaminated or several years old.

2. Remove the cylinder head cover (valve cover), the gasket, the rocker arm assembly, and the pushrods.

NOTE: *The pushrods must be replaced in their original positions.*

3. Remove the intake and exhaust manifold from the cylinder head.

4. Disconnect the spark plug wires and the spark plugs to avoid damaging them.

5. Disconnect the temperature sending unit wire, ignition coil and bracket assembly from the engine.

6. Remove the cylinder head bolts, the cylinder head and gasket from the block.

7. Thoroughly clean the gasket mating surfaces. Remove all traces of old gasket material. Remove all carbon deposits from the combustion chambers. Lay a straightedge across the head and check for flatness. Total deviation should not exceed 0.001″ (0.0254mm).

8. Do not apply sealant to the head or block. Coat both sides of the gasket with sealer. The gasket should be stamped TOP for installation. Place the gasket on the block.

9. Install the head on the block. Insert the bolts and tighten them, in sequence, to the proper torque, in three progressive passes. Torque all bolts to 85 ft.lb., except #11 in the torque sequence, which should be coated with sealer and torqued to 75 ft.lb.

NOTE: *Some head bolts used on the spark plug side of the 1984 6–258 were improperly hardened and may break under the head during service or at head installation while torquing the bolts. Engines with the defective bolts are serial numbers 310C06 through 310C14. Whenever a broken bolts is found,* replace all seven bolts on the spark plug side of the head with bolt #400 6593.

10. Connect the temperature sending unit wire, ignition coil and bracket assembly at the engine.

11. Install the spark plugs and connect the spark plug wires.

12. Install the intake and exhaust manifold on the cylinder head.

13. Install the the rocker arm assembly, and the pushrods.

NOTE: *The pushrods must be replaced in their original positions.*

14. Install the cylinder head cover (valve cover) and the gasket.

15. Connect the hoses at the thermostat housing.

16. Fill the cooling system

8–304

1. Drain the cooling system and cylinder block.

CAUTION: *When draining the coolant, keep in mind that cats and dogs are attracted by the ethylene glycol antifreeze, and are quite likely to drink any that is left in an uncovered container or in puddles on the ground. This will prove fatal in sufficient quantity. Always drain the coolant into a sealable container. Coolant should be reused unless it is contaminated or several years old.*

2. When removing the right cylinder head, it may be necessary to remove the heater core housing from the firewall.

3. Remove the valve cover(s) and gasket(s).

4. Remove the rocker arm assemblies and the pushrods.

NOTE: *The valve train components must be replaced in their original positions.*

5. Remove the spark plugs to avoid damaging them.

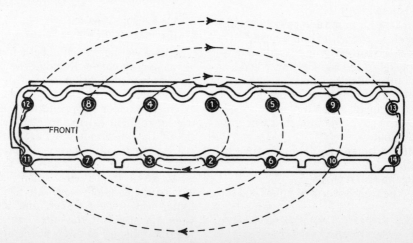

6-232, 258 head torque sequence

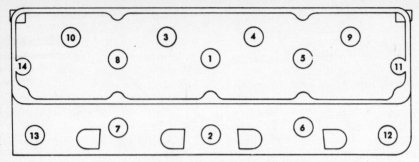

V8 cylinder head torque sequence

6. Remove the intake manifold with the carburetor still attached.

7. Remove the exhaust pipes at the flange of the exhaust manifold. When replacing the exhaust pipes it is advisable to install new gaskets at the flange.

8. Loosen all of the drive belts.

9. Disconnect the battery ground cable and alternator bracket from the right cylinder head.

10. Disconnect the air pump and power steering pump brackets from the left cylinder head.

11. Remove the cylinder head bolts and lift the head(s) from the cylinder block.

12. Remove the cylinder head gasket from the head or the block.

13. Thoroughly clean the gasket mating surfaces. Remove all traces of old gasket material. Remove all carbon deposits from the combustion chambers. Lay a straightedge across the head and check for flatness. Total deviation should not exceed 0.001" (0.0254mm).

14. Do not apply sealant to the head or block. Coat both sides of the gasket with sealer. The gasket should be stamped TOP for installation. Place the gasket on the block.

15. Install the head on the block. Insert the bolts and tighten them, in sequence, to the proper torque, in three progressive passes. Torque all bolts to 80 ft.lb.

16. Connect the air pump and power steering pump brackets to the left cylinder head.

17. Connect the battery ground cable and alternator bracket to the right cylinder head.

18. Adjust all of the drive belts.

19. Install the exhaust pipes at the flange of the exhaust manifold. When replacing the exhaust pipes it is advisable to install new gaskets at the flange.

20. Install the intake manifold with the carburetor still attached.

21. Install the spark plugs.

22. Install the rocker arm assemblies and the pushrods.

NOTE: *The valve train components must be replaced in their original positions.*

23. Install the valve cover(s) and gasket(s).

24. Install the heater core housing on the firewall.

25. Fill the cooling system and cylinder block.

Valves and Springs

NOTE: *Fabricate a valve arrangement board to use when you remove the valves, which will indicate the port in which each valve was originally installed (and which cylinder head on V6 and V8 models). Also note that the valve keys, rotators, caps, etc. should be arranged in a manner which will allow you to install them on the valve on which they were originally used.*

REMOVAL

All Except the F4–134 Exhaust Valves and all L4–134 and 6–226 Valves

1. The head must be removed from the engine. In all but the 4–134, all the valves are in the head. In the 4–134, just the intakes are in the head. The exhaust valves are in the block.

2. Remove the rocker arm assemblies.

3. Using a spring compressor, compress the valve springs and remove the keepers (locks). Relax the compressor and remove the washers or rotators, the springs, and the lower washers (on some engines). Keep all parts in order.

F4–134 Exhaust Valves
L4–134 Intake and Exhaust Valves

1. Remove the attaching bolts from the side valve spring cover. Remove the side valve spring cover and gasket.

2. Use rags to block off the three holes in the exhaust chamber to prevent the valve retaining locks from falling into the crankcase, should they be accidentally dropped.

3. Using a valve spring compressor, compress the valve springs only on those valves which are in the closed position (valve seated against the head). Remove the valve spring retainer locks, the retainer, and the exhaust valve spring. Close the other valves by rotating the camshaft and repeat the above operation for the remaining valves.

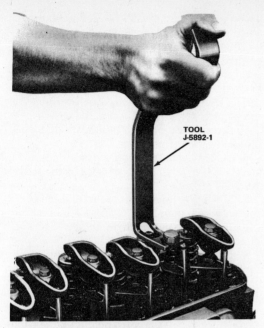

Using a valve spring compressor

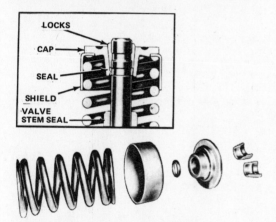

Typical upper valve train components

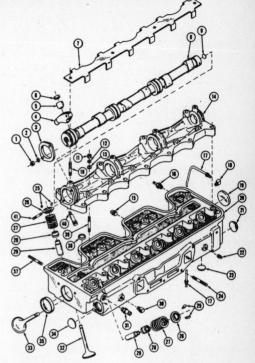

1. Nut	21. Expansion plug
2. Lockwasher	22. Plug
3. Cam shaft retainer	23. Expansion plug
4. Rocker arm	24. Stud
5. Rocker arm ball	25. Valve locks
6. Rocker arm nuts	26. Valve spring retainer
7. Rocker arm guide	27. Valve spring
8. Cam shaft	28. Valve guide seal
9. Plug	29. Valve guide
10. Stud	30. Elbow
11. Nut	31. Hose adapter
12. Lockwasher	32. Exhaust valve
13. Flat washer	33. Intake valve
14. Cam bearing support deck	34. Expansion plug
15. Plug	35. Expansion plug
16. Temperature sending unit	37. Stud
17. Oil tube	38. Plug
18. Elbow	39. Stud
19. Expansion plug	40. Rocker arm stud
20. Cylinder head	41. Stud

6-230 cylinder head

4. Lift all of the valves from the cylinder block. If the valve cannot be removed from the block, pull the valve upward as far as possible and remove the spring. Lower the valve and remove any carbon deposits from the valve stem. This will permit removal of the valve.

6–226

1. Remove the cylinder head.
2. Remove the valve chamber cover from the side of the block. Look for evidence of oil seepage past the cover bolt seals.
3. Remove the two valve tappet oil shields. They are held in place by spring clips and may be lifted out with your fingers, or pried out.
4. Use shop rags to block off the holes in the valve chamber, to prevent the valve locks from falling into the crankcase.

5. Using a spring compressor on those valves which are closed, compress the valve springs and remove the locks. Relax the compressor and remove the retainer and spring. Lift the valve from the block and mark it for assembly. Rotate the crankshaft and close each valve in turn, performing the removal procedure.

INSPECTION AND REFACING

1. Clean the valves with a wire wheel.
2. Inspect the valves for warping, cracks or wear.

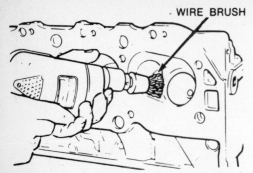

Remove the carbon from the cylinder head with a wire brush and electric drill

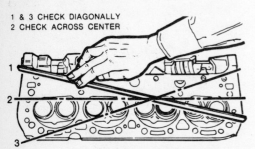

Check the cylinder head for warpage

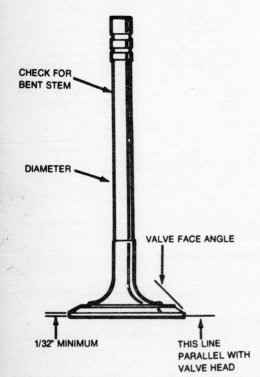

Critical valve dimensions

3. The valves may be refaced if not worn or pitted excessively.

4. Using a valve guide cleaner chucked into a drill, clean all of the valve guides. Check the valve stem diameter and the guide diameter with micrometers. Valve guides on the 4–134, 6–226 and 6–230 are replaceable. On the other engines, the guide must be reamed and an insert pressed in, or they may be knurled to bring up interior metal, restoring their diameter. Oversized valve stems are available to compensate for wear.

5. Install each valve into its respective port (guide) of the cylinder head.

6. Mount a dial indicator so that the stem is at 90° to the valve stem, as close to the valve guide as possible.

7. Move the valve off its seat, and measure the valve guide-to-stem clearance by rocking the stem back and forth to actuate the dial indicator.

8. In short, the refacing of valves and other such head work is most easily done at a machine shop. The quality and time saved easily justifies the cost.

9. Inspect the springs for obvious signs of wear. Check their installed height and tension using the values in the Valve Specifications Chart in this chapter.

REFACING

Using a valve grinder, resurface the valves according to specifications in this chapter.
NOTE: *All machine work should be performed by a competent, professional machine shop.*
CAUTION: *Valve face angle is not always identical to valve seat angle.*
A minimum margin of $\frac{1}{32}$" (0.79375mm) should remain after grinding the valve. The valve stem top should also be squared and resurfaced, by placing the stem in the V-block of the grinder, and turning it while pressing lightly against the grinding wheel. Be sure to chamfer the edge of the tip so that the squared edges don't dig into the rocker arm or cam.

LAPPING

This procedure should be performed after the valves and seats have been machined, to insure that each valve mates to each seat precisely.

1. Invert the cylinder head, lightly lubricate the valve stems, and install the valves in the head as numbered.

2. Coat valve seats with fine grinding compound, and attach the lapping tool suction cup to a valve head.
NOTE: *Moisten the suction cup.*

3. Rotate the tool between your palms, changing position and lifting the tool often to prevent grooving.

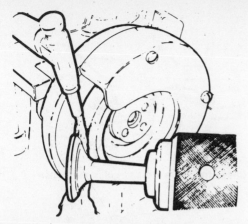

Refacing a valve. Any well equipped machine shop can do this job

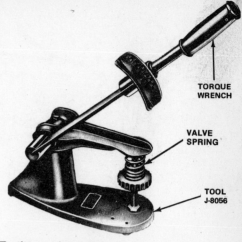

Testing a valve spring

Lapping the valves by hand

NOT MORE THAN 5/64"

CLOSED COIL END DOWNWARD

Check the valve spring free length and squareness

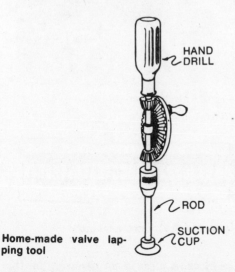

HAND DRILL

ROD

SUCTION CUP

Home-made valve lapping tool

4. Lap the valve until a smooth, polished seat is evident.

5. Remove the valve and tool, and rinse away all traces of grinding compound.

VALVE SPRING TESTING

Place the spring on a flat surface next to a square. Measure the height of the spring, and rotate it against the edge of the square to measure distortion. If spring height varies (by comparison) by more than $\frac{1}{16}$" (1.5875mm) or if distortion exceeds $\frac{1}{16}$" (1.5875mm), replace the spring.

In addition to evaluating the spring as above, test the spring pressure at the installed and compressed (installed height minus valve lift) height using a valve spring tester. Spring pressure should be ± 1 lb. of all other springs in either position.

INSTALLATION

1. Coat all parts with clean engine oil. Install all parts in their respective locations. The spring is installed with the closely wound coils toward the valve head. Always use new valve seals.

2. Use a spring compressor to install the keepers and slowly release the compressor after the keepers are in place.

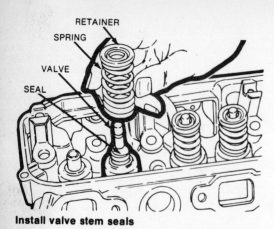

Install valve stem seals

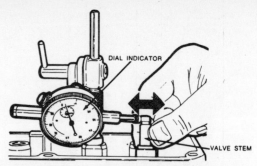

Check the valve stem-to-guide clearance

Check valve spring installed height:

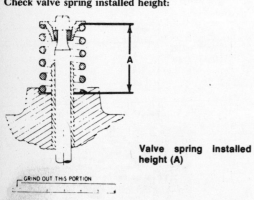

Valve spring installed height (A)

NOTE: *Coat the locks, on the 6–226, with chassis grease to hold them in place until you release the spring compressor.*

3. Release the spring compressor. Tap the end of the stem with a wood mallet to insure that the keepers are securely in place.

4. Install all other parts in reverse order of removal.

Valve Guides

REMOVAL AND INSTALLATION

4–134, 6–230

NOTE: *A press is used for removal and installation of guides.*

1. Place the head in the press and press the old guide out through the bottom and the new one in through the top. On the 6–230, all the guides are the same. On the 4–134, the only guides in the head are the intakes.

2. Once the new guide is in place, check its protrusion. On the 6–230, the guide should protrude 0.45″ (11.43mm) above the head surface. On the 4–134, the guide should be flush with the head surface.

3. The exhaust valve guides on the 4–134 are also replaceable. These guides are located

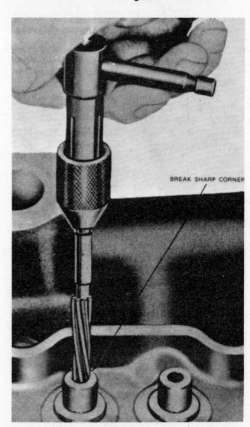

Close-up of a hand reamer

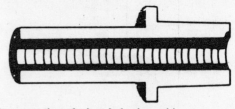

Cross section of a knurled valve guide

in the block. A press is not necessary for this procedure. The engine should be removed from the vehicle. The head, oil pan and crankshaft should be removed. The guides are driven out of their bores from above, with a driver made

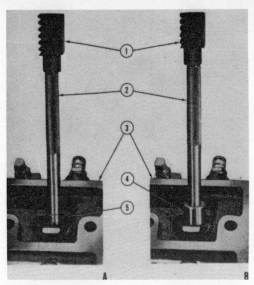

1. Arbor press   4. Stop
2. Driver   5. Valve guide
3. Cylinder head

Removing and installing a valve guide

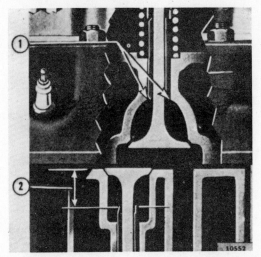

1. Flush at this point   2. One inch [25.4 mm.]

4-134 valves

for the purpose. The new guides are then driven in with the same tool, until their tops are 1 inch below the block surface.

4. On all three engines, after the guides are in place, they must be reamed:

6–230: 0.342–0.343″ (8.6868–8.7122mm)

4–134: Intake, 0.3740–0.3760″ (9.4996–9.5504mm)

Exhaust, 0.3735–0.3765″ (9.4869–9.5631mm)

6–226

NOTE: *A press is not necessary for this procedure. The engine should be removed from*

the vehicle. The head, and oil pan should be removed.

1. The guides are pulled out of their bores from above, with a tool made for the purpose.

2. Check the valve guide bore and the outside diameter of the new guide. Ream the bore, if necessary, to obtain a 0.0005–0.0030″ (0.0127–0.0762mm) press fit. Guides are available in 0.0005″ (0.0127mm) and 0.0055″ (0.1397mm) oversizes.

3. The new guides are then pulled into place with the same tool, until their tops are $1\frac{7}{32}$″ (30.95625mm) below the block surface.

4. Ream the new guides to a diameter of 0.3423–0.3432″ (8.694–8.717mm).

Valve Seats
INSPECTION AND REFACING

The exhaust valve seats on the 4–134 and 6–226 are replaceable. All others have integral seats. Check the condition of the seats for excessive wear, pitting or cracks. Remove all traces of deposits from the seats. The seats may be refaced with a special grinding tool, to the dimensions shown in the Valve Specifications Chart.

You can replace the exhaust valve seats by driving them out from the bottom with a driver made for the purpose. This requires removal of the engine from the truck. Removal of the

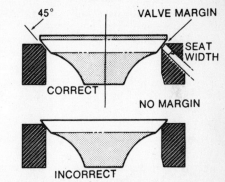

Valve seat width and centering

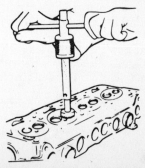

Reaming a valve seat with a hand reamer

Checking valve seat concentricity with a dial gauge

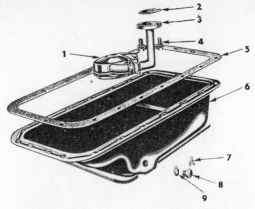

1. Floating oil intake
2. Gasket
3. Oil float support
4. Screw and lockwasher
5. Oil pan gasket
6. Oil pan
7. Bolt and lockwasher
8. Drain plug
9. Drain plug gasket

4-134 oil pan

1. Front seal
2. Rear seal
3. Gaskets

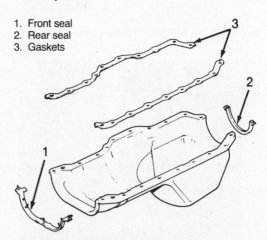

4-150 oil pan gasket and seal positioning

head, crankshaft, camshaft and pistons and rods. The new seats should be chilled with dry ice and installed immediately. They are driven into place with a seat installation tool. After installation, they should be ground to a 45° angle.

Oil Pan

REMOVAL AND INSTALLATION

L4-134, F4-134, 6-225

To remove the oil pan on these engines, remove the oil pan attaching bolts and remove the oil pan. Clean all of the attaching surfaces and install new gaskets.

4-150

1. Disconnect the battery ground.
2. Raise and support the truck on jackstands.
3. Drain the oil.
4. Disconnect the exhaust pipe at the manifold.
5. Remove the starter.
6. Remove the bellhousing access plate.
7. Unbolt and remove the oil pan.
8. Clean the gasket surfaces thoroughly.
9. Install a replacement seal at the bottom of the timing case cover and at the rear bearing cap.
10. Using new gaskets coated with sealer, install the pan and torque the bolts to 10 ft.lb.
11. Install all other parts in reverse order of removal.

4-151

1. Disconnect the battery ground.
2. Raise the vehicle and support it on jackstands.
3. Drain the oil.

4. Remove the starter.
5. Unbolt and remove the oil pan.
6. Clean all gasket surfaces, and remove all sludge and deposits from the pan.
7. Install the rear pan gasket in the main bearing cap and apply a small amount of RTV sealant in the depressions where the pan gasket contacts the block.
8. Position the gasket on the pan. Apply a 1/8 x 1/4" (3.175mm x 6.35mm) bead of RTV sealant at the split lines of the front and side gaskets.
9. Position the pan on the block carefully to avoid gasket misalignment. Install the bolts and tighten them to 45 in.lb.
10. Install the starter. Tighten the bolts to 17 ft.lb.; the nut to 40 in.lb.
11. Connect the starter cables, lower the vehicle, fill the crankcase and run the engine to operating temperature, checking for leaks.

1. Oil dipstick
2. Oil pan baffle
3. Oil pan gasket
4. Oil pan
5. Drain plug gasket
6. Drain plug
7. Oil pump screen
8. Oil suction housing, pipe and flange
9. Oil suction pipe gasket
10. Oil pump idler gear
11. Valve by-pass and cover assembly
12. Oil pressure valve
13. Spring
14. Gasket
15. Oil pressure valve cap
16. Oil filter
17. Oil pump cover gasket
18. Oil pump shaft and gear

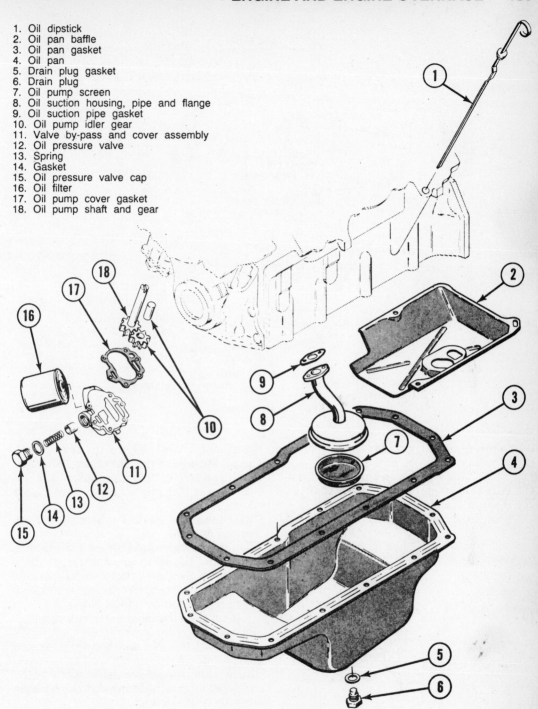

6-225 oil pan and pump

6–226

1. Remove the engine from the truck.

2. Place the engine on a work stand and turn it upside down.

3. Remove the oil pan attaching bolts and remove the oil pan.

4. Clean all the mating surfaces and install a new gasket coated with sealer on the pan.

5. Position the oil pan, install the bolts and tighten them to 9 ft.lb.

6. Install the engine.

6–230

1. Unbolt and remove the pan.

2. Pull the ends of the pan gasket from the front and rear filler blocks.

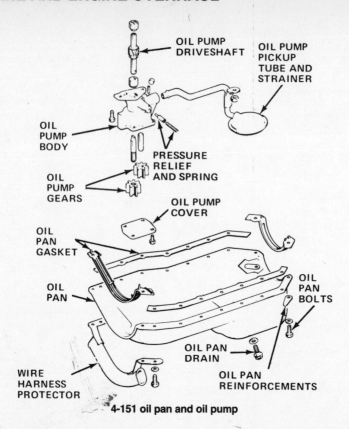

4-151 oil pan and oil pump

3. Insert gasket aligning dowels in the holes on each side of the block at the front.

4. Place the new gasket on top of the old gasket. With the gaskets held in place by the dowels, make a cut through both gaskets, $\frac{3}{32}$" (2.38mm) from the front filler block, or $\frac{5}{16}$"

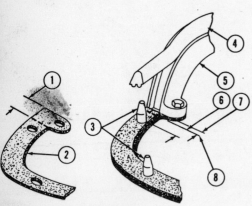

1. 1¼" dimension
2. New gasket
3. Locating dowels
4. Rubber filler block gasket
5. Front filler block
6. ⁵⁄₁₆" dimension
7. ³⁄₃₂" dimension
8. Cut old and new gasket

6-230 oil pan gasket replacement

(7.9375mm) from the edge of the nearest hole. The cut must be so that the triangular end of the oil pan seal will cover the splice.

5. Remove both gaskets and discard the old one.

6. Clean the gasket mating surfaces thoroughly.

7. Coat both sides of the new gaskets with sealer, and the splice near the front filler block. With the dowels in the holes, position the gaskets on the block. Replace the ends of the oil pan seal at both filler blocks.

8. Coat the filler block seals with clean engine oil.

9. Install the pan and hand-tighten the bolts.

10. Working from the center bolts toward the ends, and alternating from side to side, torque the bolts to 12–15 ft.lb.

6–232, 6–258, 8–304

1. Raise the vehicle and drain the engine oil.

2. Remove the starter motor.

3. Place a jack under the transmission bell housing. Disconnect the engine right support cushion bracket from the block and raise the engine to allow sufficient clearance for oil pan removal.

4. Remove the oil pan attaching bolts and remove the oil pan.

5. Remove the oil pan front and rear neoprene oil seals and the side gaskets. Thoroughly clean the gasket surfaces of the oil pan and the engine block. Remove all of the sludge and dirt from the oil pan sump.

6. Apply a generous amount of RTV silicone to the end tabs of a new oil pan front seal and install the seal to the timing case cover.

7. Cement new oil pan side gaskets into position on the engine block and apply a generous amount of RTV silicone to the side gasket contacting surface of the seal end tabs.

8. Install the seal in the recess of the rear main bearing cap, making sure that it is fully seated.

9. Coat the oil pan contacting surface of the front and rear oil pan seals with engine oil.

10. Install the oil pan and assemble the engine mount in the reverse order of removal.

Oil Pump

REMOVAL AND INSTALLATION

L- and F-Head

1. Set number one piston at TDC in order to reinstall the oil pump without disturbing the ignition timing.

2. Remove the distributor cover and note the position of the rotor. Keep the rotor in that position when the oil pump is installed.

3. Remove the cap screws and lockwashers that attach the oil pump to the cylinder block. Carefully slide the oil pump and its driveshaft out of the cylinder block.

The oil pump is driven by the camshaft by means of a spiral gear. The distributor in turn is driven by the oil pump by means of a tongue on the end of the distributor shaft which engages a slot in the end of the oil pump shaft. Because the tongue and the slot are both machined off center, the two shafts can be meshed in only one position. Since the position of the distributor shaft determines the timing of the engine, and is controlled by the oil pump shaft, the position of the oil pump shaft with respect to the camshaft is important. If only the oil pump has been removed, install it so that the slot in the end of the shaft lines up with the tip of the distributor shaft and allows that shaft to slip into it without disturbing the the original position of the distributor. If the engine has been disturbed or both the distributor and the oil pump have been removed, follow the procedure given below.

1. Turn the crankshaft to align the timing marks on the crankshaft and camshaft timing gears.

2. Install the oil pump gasket on the pump.

3. With the wider side of the slot on top, start the oil pump driveshaft into the opening in the cylinder keeping the mounting holes in the body of the pump in alignment with the holes in the cylinder block.

1. Cover screw
2. Cover
3. Cover gasket
4. Shaft and rotors
5. Body assembly
6. Driven gear
7. Pump gasket
8. Gear retaining pin
9. Relief valve retainer
10. Relief valve retainer gasket
11. Relief valve spring
12. Relief valve plunger

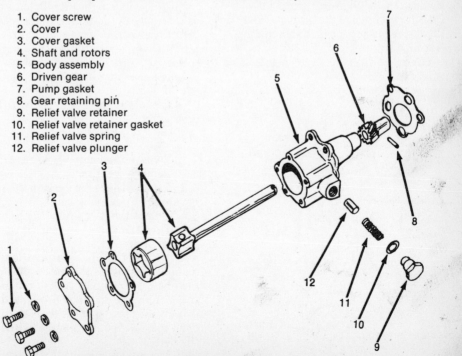

Oil pump used on late L-head and all F-head engines

4. Insert a long blade screwdriver into the distributor shaft opening in the side of the cylinder block and engage the slot in the oil pump shaft. Turn the shaft so that the slot is positioned at what would be roughly the nine thirty position on a clock face.

5. Remove the screwdriver and observe the position of the slot in the end of the oil pump shaft to make certain it is properly positioned.

6. Replace the screwdriver and, while turning the screwdriver clockwise to guide the oil pump driveshaft gear into engagement with the camshaft gear, press against the oil pump to force it into position.

7. Remove the screwdriver and again observe the position of the slot. If installation was properly made, the slot will be in a position roughly equivalent to the 11 o'clock position on the face of a clock, with the wider side of the slot still on the top. If the slot is improperly positioned, remove the oil pump and repeat the operation.

8. Coat the threads of the capscrews with gasket cement and secure the oil pump in place.

4–150

1. Disconnect the battery ground.
2. Raise and support the Jeep on jackstands.
3. Drain the oil.
4. Disconnect the exhaust pipe at the manifold.
5. Remove the starter.
6. Remove the bellhousing access plate.
7. Unbolt and remove the oil pan.
8. Clean the gasket surfaces thoroughly.
9. Install a replacement seal at the bottom of the timing case cover and at the rear bearing cap.
10. Using new gaskets coated with sealer, in-

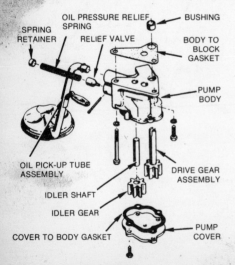

4-150 and 6-232, 258 oil pump

stall the pan and torque the bolts to 10 ft.lb.

11. Install all other parts in reverse order of removal.

4–151

1. Drain the oil and remove the oil pan.
2. Remove the oil pump retaining screws and separate the oil pump and gasket from the engine block.
3. Install in reverse order of the above procedure.

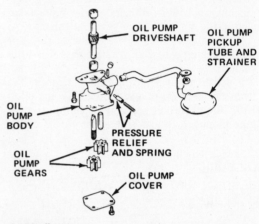

4-151 oil pump

6–225

1. Remove the oil filter.
2. Disconnect the wire from the oil pressure indicator switch in the filter by-pass pump cover assembly to the timing chain cover.
3. Remove the screws that attach the oil pump cover assembly to the timing chain cover.
4. Remove the cover assembly and slide out the oil pump.
5. Install in reverse order of the above procedure.

6–226

1. Remove the engine from the truck.
2. Remove the oil pan.
3. Remove the lockwire from the rear intermediate main bearing bolts.
4. Unbolt the pump from the bearing cap.
5. Turn the engine so that no.1 piston is at TDC compression.
6. Install the distributor. Rotate the oil pump driveshaft so that when the oil pump is installed, the pump driveshaft tongue engages the slot in the lower end of the distributor driveshaft. The slot at the top of the distributor shaft must be roughly parallel with the side of the block.
7. Install the pump and torque the attaching nuts to 35 ft.lb.

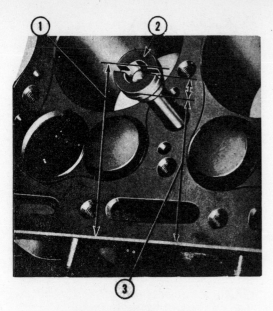

1. Approximately parallel
2. Distributor main drive shaft
3. Narrow side of distributor drive shaft

6-226 oil pump driveshaft positioning

6-230

1. Remove the fan.

2. Remove the three nuts that attach the pump to the timing case cover.

3. Pull the pump straight up and out of the cover. Discard the gasket.

4. Prime the pump with clean engine oil prior to installation. Always use a new gasket.

5. If the engine was not rotated during pump removal, simply install the pump, engaging the drive slots.

6. If the engine was rotated, turn the crankshaft until #1 piston is at TDC compression and the pointer on the timing marks is aligned with the 0 mark.

7. Position the pump and gasket on the mounting studs. Do not install the pump far enough to engage the drive gear. Insert a long screwdriver into the distributor shaft opening in the opposite side of the cover and engage the slot in the oil pump shaft. Turn the shaft so that the slot is in the 4 & 10 o'clock position with the narrow side of the shaft up. Remove the screwdriver and, with a light, look in the hole to see if the slot is properly positioned. Install the screwdriver again, and turn the screwdriver counterclockwise to guide the oil pump drive gear into engagement with the crankshaft. Press against the pump gear to force it into engagement. Remove the screwdriver and again observe the slot. If correctly positioned, it will be in the 3 & 9 o'clock posi-

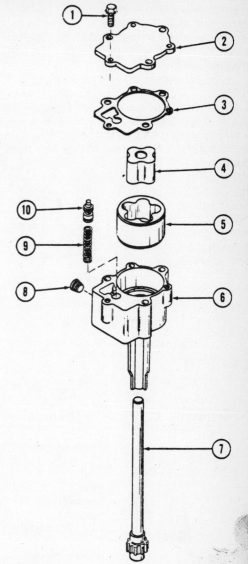

1. Screw
2. Cover
3. Cover gasket
4. Inner rotor
5. Outer rotor
6. Pump body
7. Drive shaft
8. Plug
9. Relief valve spring
10. Relief valve

6-230 oil pump

tion, with the narrow side still on top. Install the nuts.

6-232, 6-258

1. Drain the oil and remove the oil pan.

2. Remove the oil pump retaining screws and separate the oil pump and gasket from the engine block.

NOTE: *Do not disturb the position of the oil pick-up tube and screen assembly in the pump body. If the tube is moved within the pump body, a new assembly must be installed to assure an airtight seal.*

3. Installation is the reverse of removal. Torque the short bolts to 10 ft.lb.; the long bolts to 17 ft.lb.

8-304

Remove the retaining screws and separate the oil pump cover, gasket and oil filter as an assembly from the pump body (timing chain cover). Install in reverse order with a new filter and gasket.

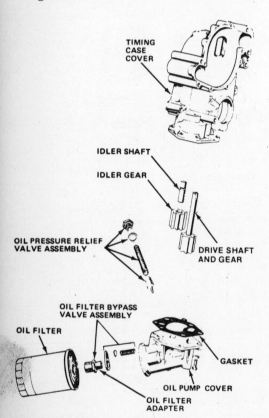

8-304 oil pump

Crankshaft Pulley (Vibration Damper)

REMOVAL AND INSTALLATION

1. Remove the fan shroud, as required. If necessary, drain the cooling system and remove the radiator. Remove drive belts from pulley.

CAUTION: *When draining the coolant, keep in mind that cats and dogs are attracted by the ethylene glycol antifreeze, and are quite likely to drink any that is left in an uncovered container or in puddles on the ground. This will prove fatal in sufficient quantity. Always drain the coolant into a sealable container.*

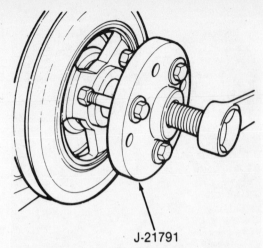

J-21791

Using a puller to remove the crankshaft damper

Coolant should be reused unless it is contaminated or several years old.

2. On those engines with a separate pulley, remove the retaining bolts and separate the pulley from the vibration damper.

3. Remove the vibration damper/pulley retaining bolt from the crankshaft end.

4. Using a puller, remove the damper/pulley from the crankshaft.

5. Upon installation, align the key slot of the pulley hub to the crankshaft key. Complete the assembly in the reverse order of removal. Torque the retaining bolts to specifications.

Timing Gear Cover

TIMING GEAR COVER AND OIL SEAL REPLACEMENT

L4–134 and F4–134

1. Remove the drive belts and crankshaft pulley.

2. Remove the attaching bolts, nuts and lock washers that hold the timing gear cover to the engine.

3. Remove the timing gear cover.

4. Remove the timing pointer.

5. Remove the timing gear cover gasket.

6. Remove and discard the crankshaft oil seal from the timing gear cover.

7. Replace in reverse order of the above procedure. Replace the crankshaft oil seal. Use a new timing gear cover gasket.

4–150

NOTE: *Special tools are needed for this job.*

1. Remove the drive belts and fan shroud.

2. Unscrew the vibration damper bolts and washer.

3. Using a puller, remove the vibration damper.

1. Pulley
2. Timing cover
3. Seal

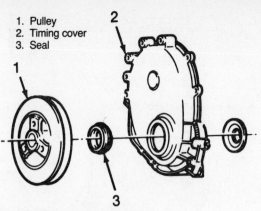

4-150 timing cover assembly

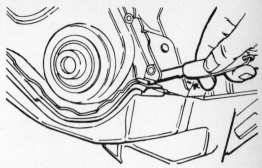

Cutting the pan gasket

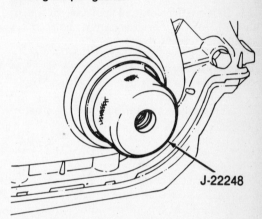

Timing cover centering tool installed on a 4-150

4. Remove the fan assembly. If the fan is equipped with a fan clutch DO NOT LAY IT DOWN! If you lay it down, the fluid will leak out of the clutch and irreversibly damage the fan.

5. Disconnect the battery ground.

6. Remove the air conditioning compressor/alternator bracket assembly and lay it out of the way. DO NOT DISCONNECT THE REFRIGERANT LINES!

7. Unbolt the cover from the block and oil pan. Remove the cover and front seal.

8. Cut off the oil pan side gasket end tabs and oil pan front seal tabs.

9. Clean all gasket mating surfaces thoroughly.

10. Remove the seal from the cover.

11. Apply sealer to both sides of the new case cover gasket and position it on the block.

12. Cut the end tabs off the new oil pan side gaskets corresponding to those cut off the orig-

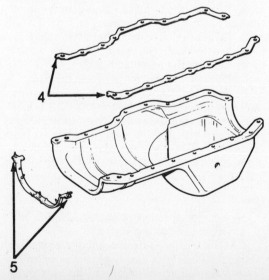

4-150 oil pan and gaskets

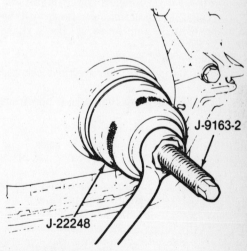

Oil seal installation tool

inal gasket and attach the tabs to the oil pan with gasket cement.

13. Coat the front cover seal end tab recesses generously with RTV sealant and position the side seal in the cover.

14. Apply engine oil to the seal-to-pan contact surface.

15. Position the cover on the block.

16. Insert alignment tool J-22248 into the crankshaft opening in the cover.

17. Install the cover bolts. Tighten the cover-to-block bolts to 5 ft.lb.; the cover-to-pan bolts to 11 ft.lb.

18. Remove the alignment tool and position the new front seal on the tool with the seal lip facing outward. Apply a light film of sealer to the outside diameter of the seal. Lightly coat the crankshaft with clean engine oil.

19. Position the tool and seal over the end of the crankshaft and insert the Draw Screw J-9163-2 into the installation tool.

20. Tighten the nut until the tool just contacts the cover.

21. Remove the tools and apply a light film of engine oil on the vibration damper hub contact surface of the seal.

22. With the key inserted in the keyway in the crankshaft, install the vibration damper, washer and bolt. Lubricate the bolt and tighten it to 108 ft.lb.

23. Install all other parts in reverse order of removal.

4-151

1. Disconnect the battery ground.
2. Remove the crankshaft pulley hub.
3. Remove the alternator bracket.
4. Remove the fan and radiator shroud.
5. Remove the oil pan-to-timing case cover bolts.
6. Pull the cover forward just enough to allow cutting the oil pan front seal flush with the block on both sides of the cover. Use a sharp knife or razor.
7. Remove the front cover.
8. Clean the gasket surface on the block and cover.
9. Cut the tabs from the new oil pan front seal.
10. Install the seal on the cover, pressing the tips into the holes provided in the cover.
11. Coat a new gasket with sealer and place on the cover.
12. Apply a 1/8" (3.175mm) bead of RTV sealant to the joint formed at the oil pan and block.
13. Install an aligning tool such as tool J-23042 in the timing case cover seal.

NOTE: *It is important that an aligning tool is used to avoid seal damage and to ensure a tight, even seal fit.*

14. Position the cover on the block and partially retighten the two oil pan-to-cover bolts.
15. Install the remaining bolts, and tighten all bolts to 45 in.lb.
16. Install all other parts in reverse order of removal. Torque the fan assembly bolts to 18 ft.lb.

6-225

1. Remove the water pump and crankshaft pulley.

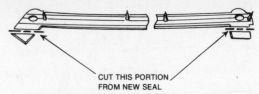

CUT THIS PORTION FROM NEW SEAL

4-151 oil pan seal modification

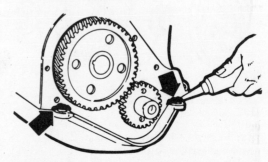

Applying RTV sealant on 4-151 engines

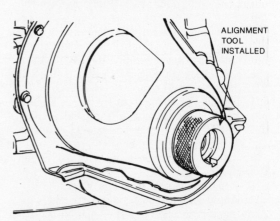

ALIGNMENT TOOL INSTALLED

Timing case cover alignment tool installed on 4-151 engines

2. Remove the two bolts that attach the oil pan to the timing chain cover.

3. Remove the five bolts that attach the timing chain cover to the engine block.

4. Remove the cover and gasket.

5. Remove the crankshaft front oil seal.

6. From the rear of the timing chain cover, coil new packing around the crankshaft hole in the cover so that the ends of the packing are at the top. Drive in the new packing with a punch. It will be necessary to ream out the hole to obtain clearance for the crankshaft vibration damper hub.

6-226

NOTE: *Special tools are needed for this job.*
1. Drain the cooling system.
CAUTION: *When draining the coolant, keep in mind that cats and dogs are attracted by the ethylene glycol antifreeze, and are quite likely to drink any that is left in an uncovered container or in puddles on the ground. This*

Water pump and timing chain cover bolts location 6-225

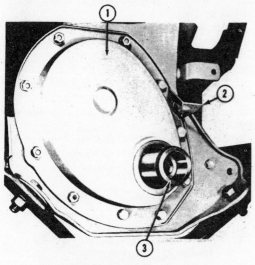

1. Timing chain cover
2. Timing pointer
3. Oil seal installing sleeve

6-226 timing cover installation

will prove fatal in sufficient quantity. Always drain the coolant into a sealable container. Coolant should be reused unless it is contaminated or several years old.

2. Remove the radiator.

3. Remove the vibration damper and timing pointer.

4. Unbolt and remove the cover. Discard the gasket.

5. Brace the cover and drive out the old seal.

6. Drive the new seal into place, making sure that it is flush and not cocked. Lubricate the inner seal surface with clean engine oil.

7. Coat both sides of a new gasket with sealer and position it on the block.

8. Position the cover on the block, and if one is available, use an aligning tool to aid in positioning the cover.

9. Install the bolts and tighten them to 15 ft.lb.

10. Install all other parts in reverse order of removal. Fill the cooling system.

6–230

NOTE: *Special tools are needed for this job.*

1. Remove the fan, hub and drive pulley.
2. Remove the water pump.
3. Remove the oil pump.
4. Remove the distributor.
5. Remove the thermostat and housing.
6. Remove the bolt and pilot washer that attach the vibration damper to the crankshaft. Later model engines have a lock plate on the damper.
7. Using a puller, remove the damper from the crankshaft.
8. Using seal remover W-286, pull the front seal from the case.
9. Remove the hose from the water port of the cover.
10. Unbolt and remove the cover from the front plate.
11. Make sure that the mating surfaces of the cover and block are clean.
12. Coat both sides of the new gaskets with sealer and position them on the block.
13. Place the cover on the block and install and tighten the bolts. Torque the $\frac{5}{16}''$ (7.9375mm) bolts to 12–15 ft.lb. and the $\frac{3}{8}''$ (9.525mm) bolts to 15–20 ft.lb.
14. Using a seal driver, install a new front seal. Apply sealer to the outer rim of the seal and clean engine oil to the seal lips prior to installation.
15. Install all other parts in reverse order of removal. The vibration damper may be pressed on by reversing the removal tool. Torque the

1. Oil seal   2. Puller W-270 or W-286

Removing the 6-230 front oil seal

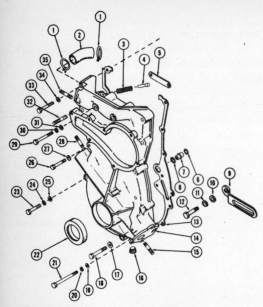

1. Hose clamp
2. Water hose
3. Push rod springs
4. Fuel pump push rod
5. Gasket
6. O-ring
7. Sleeve
8. O-ring
9. Alternator bracket
10. Washer
11. Lock washer
12. Bolt
13. Gasket
14. Timing chain cover
15. Stud
16. Plug
17. Lockwasher
18. Bolt
19. Flatwasher
20. Lockwasher
21. Bolt
22. Crankshaft front oil seal
23. Bolt
24. Lockwasher
25. Flatwasher
26. Bolt
27. Lockwasher
28. Stud
29. Bolt
30. Lockwasher
31. Flatwasher
32. Stud
33. Bolt
34. Flatwasher
35. Stud

6-230 timing chain cover

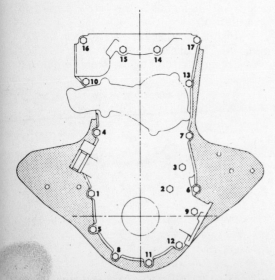

6-230 timing chain cover bolt tightening sequence

damper bolt to 100–130 ft.lb. If a damper lock is used, torque the bolts to 40–50 ft.lb.

6–232, 6–258

COVER REMOVED

1. Remove the drive belts, engine fan and hub assembly, the accessory pulley, and vibration damper.

2. Remove the oil pan to timing chain cover screws and the screws that attach the cover to the block.

3. Raise the timing chain cover just high enough to detach the retaining nibs of the oil pan neoprene seal from the bottom side of the cover. This must be done to prevent pulling the seal end tabs away from the tongues of the oil pan gaskets which would cause a leak.

4. Remove the timing chain cover and gasket from the engine.

5. Use a razor blade to cut off the oil pan seal end tabs flush with the front face of the cylinder block and remove the seal. Clean the timing chain cover, oil pan, and cylinder block surfaces.

6. Apply seal compound (Perfect Seal, or equivalent) to both sides of the replacement timing case cover gasket and position the gasket on cylinder block.

7. Cut the end tabs off the replacement oil pan gasket corresponding to the pieces cut off the original gasket. Cement these pieces on the oil pan.

8. Coat the oil pan seal end tabs generously with Permatex® No. 2 or equivalent, and position the seal on the timing case cover.

Trim the timing gear cover gasket as indicated before installation on 6-232, 258

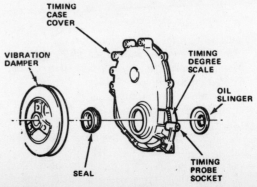

6-232, 258 timing cover and seal

9. Position the timing case cover on the engine. Place Timing Case Cover Alignment Tool and Seal Installer J-22248 in the crankshaft opening of the cover.

10. Install the cover-to-block screws and oil pan-to-cover screws. Tighten the cover-to-block screws to 60 in.lb. and the oil pan-to-cover screws to 11 ft.lb.

11. Remove the cover aligning tool and position the replacement oil seal aligning tool in the case. Position the replacement oil seal on the tool with the seal lip facing outward. Apply a light film of Perfect Seal, or equivalent, on the outside diameter of the seal.

12. Insert the draw screw from Tool J-9163 into the seal installing tool. Tighten the nut against the tool until the tool contacts the cover.

13. Remove the tools and apply a light film of engine oil to the seal lip.

14. Install the vibration damper and tighten the retaining screw to 80 ft.lb.

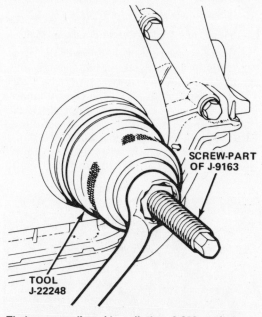

Timing case oil seal installation, 6-258 engines

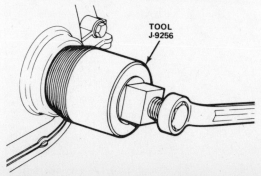

6-258 timing case cover oil seal removal

15. Install the damper pulley. Tighten the capscrews to 20 ft.lb.

16. Install the engine fan and hub assembly.

17. Install the drive belt(s).

COVER INSTALLED

1. Remove the drive belts.
2. Remove the vibration damper pulley.
3. Remove the vibration damper.
4. Remove the oil seal with Tool J-9256.
5. Position the replacement oil seal on the Timing Case Cover Alignment Tool and Seal Installer J-22248 with the seal lip facing outward. Apply a light film of Perfect Seal, or equivalent, to the outside diameter of the seal.
6. Insert the draw screw from Tool J-9163 into the seal installing tool. Tighten the nut against the tool until the tool contacts the cover.
7. Remove the tools. Apply a light film of engine oil to the seal lip.
8. Install the vibration damper and tighten the retaining bolt to 80 ft.lb.
9. Install the damper pulley. Tighten the capscrews to 20 ft.lb.
10. Install the drive belt(s).

8–304

1. Remove the negative battery cable.
2. Drain the cooling system and disconnect the radiator hoses and by-pass hose.

CAUTION: *When draining the coolant, keep in mind that cats and dogs are attracted by the ethylene glycol antifreeze, and are quite likely to drink any that is left in an uncovered container or in puddles on the ground. This will prove fatal in sufficient quantity. Always drain the coolant into a sealable container. Coolant should be reused unless it is contaminated or several years old.*

3. Remove all of the drive belts and the fan and spacer assembly.
4. Remove the alternator and the front portion of the alternator bracket as an assembly.
5. Disconnect the heater hose.
6. Remove the power steering pump and/or the air pump, and the mounting bracket as an assembly. Do not disconnect the power steering hoses.
7. Remove the distributor cap and note the position of the rotor. Remove the distributor. (See the Engine Electrical Section.)
8. Remove the fuel pump.
9. Remove the vibration damper and pulley.
10. Remove the two front oil pan bolts and the bolts which secure the timing chain cover to the engine block.

NOTE: *The timing gear cover retaining bolts vary in length and must be installed in the*

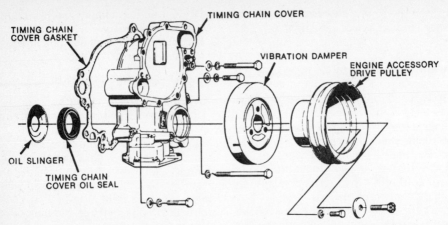

8-304 timing case, cover and seal. The unit for engines through 1976 is shown. 1977 and later engines are identical, except for the location of the seal

same locations from which they were removed.

11. Remove the cover by pulling forward until it is free of the locating dowel pins.

12. Clean the gasket surface of the cover and the engine block.

13. Pry out the original seal from inside the timing chain cover and clean the seal bore.

14. Drive the new seal into place from the inside with a block of wood until it contacts the outer flange of the cover.

15. Apply a light film of motor oil to the lips of the new seal.

16. Before reinstalling the timing gear cover, remove the lower locating dowel pin from the engine block. The pin is required for correct alignment of the cover and must either be reused or a replacement dowel pin installed after the cover is in position.

17. Cut both sides of the oil pan gasket flush with the engine block with a razor blade.

18. Trim a new gasket to correspond to the amount cut off at the oil pan.

19. Apply sealer to both sides of the new gasket and install the gasket on the timing case cover.

20. Install the new front oil pan seal.

21. Align the tongues of the new oil pan gasket pieces with the oil pan seal and cement them into place on the cover.

22. Apply a bead of sealer to the cutoff edges of the original oil pan gaskets.

23. Place the timing case cover into position and install the front oil pan bolts. Tighten the bolts slowly and evenly until the cover aligns with the upper locating dowel.

24. Install the lower dowel through the cover and drive it into the corresponding hole in the engine block.

25. Install the cover retaining bolts in the same locations from which they were removed. Tighten to 25 ft.lb.

26. Assemble the remaining components in the reverse order of removal.

Timing Chain or Gears and Tensioner

REMOVAL AND INSTALLATION

L4–134 in CJ-2A Models Before Engine #175402

1. Remove the timing chain cover.

2. Pull the sprocket forward alternately and evenly until they are free.

3. On installation, align the timing marks on the sprockets. Check the end float between the crankshaft sprocket and the thrust plate. Clearance should be 0.004–0.008″ (0.1016–0.2032mm). Camshaft gear-to-thrust plate clearance is 0.003–0.055″ (0.0762–1.397mm).

Timing gear alignment on 4-134 engines before engine #175402

Both clearances are adjustable by shim packs. Check, also, the running clearances between the gears. Proper clearance is 0-0.002″ (0–0.0508mm).

4. Turn the crankshaft so that Nos. 1 & 4 piston are at TDC as indicated by the TC mark on the flywheel seen through the timing hole in the right side of the flywheel housing.

5. Place the camshaft sprocket on the shaft and turn the shaft until the punch mark on the rim of the sprocket faces the punchmark on the crankshaft sprocket.

6. Remove the camshaft sprocket and install the sprocket and timing chain. Timing is correct when a line drawn through the sprocket centers, intersects the timing marks on both sprockets.

L4–134 After Engine #175402 and All F4–134

1. Remove the timing gear cover.

2. Use a puller to remove both the crankshaft and the camshaft gear from the engine after removing all attaching nuts and bolts.

3. Remove the Woodruff keys.

Installation is as follows:

1. Install the Woodruff key in the longer of the two keyways on the front end of the crankshaft.

2. Install the crankshaft timing gear on the front end of the crankshaft with the timing mark facing away from the cylinder block.

3. Align the keyway in the gear with the Woodruff key and then drive or press the gear onto the crankshaft firmly against the thrust washer.

4. Turn the camshaft or the crankshaft as necessary so that the timing marks on the two gears will be together after the camshaft gear is installed.

5. Install the Woodruff key in the keyway on the front of the camshaft.

6. Start the large timing gear on the camshaft with the timing mark facing out.

1. Puller   2. Camshaft gear

Pulling the 4-134 valve timing gears for engines after #175402

4-134 timing gear alignment for engines after #175402

NOTE: *Do not drive the gear onto the camshaft as the camshaft may drive the plug out of the rear of the engine and cause an oil leak.*

7. Install the camshaft retaining screw and torque it to 30–40 ft.lb. This will draw the gear onto the camshaft as the screw is tightened. Standard running tolerance between the timing gears is 0.000 to 0.002″ (0.05mm).

8. Install the timing gears with the marks aligned as shown.

9. Set the intake valve clearance to 0.020″ (0.5mm) on the #1 cylinder.

10. Rotate the crankshaft until the #1 cylinder intake valve is ready to open as indicated by the IO mark on the flywheel. The mark should be centered in the hole.

NOTE: *Some later models do not have an IO mark. TC and 5 degrees are the only marks. On these engines, the intake valve opens at 9 degrees BTC. To estimate valve opening, measure the distance between TC and 5 degrees and measure about that distance further on. On CJ-3A models beginning with engine #130859, a 4½″ (114.3mm) starter motor was used. To use the larger starter, it was necessary to increase the width of the cylinder block flange, partially covering the flywheel hole. This makes it impossible to use the hole for timing purposes. In this event, use the timing marks on the crankshaft pulley. If a replacement block is installed with the later design in a vehicle originally equipped with the earlier design timing marks, it will be necessary to cut away enough of the flange to allow a view of the timing marks, as no other timing marks exist on the these early engines.*

4-150

1. Remove the timing case cover.

2. Rotate the crankshaft so that the timing

marks on the cam and crank sprockets align next to each other, as illustrated.

3. Remove the oil slinger from the crankshaft.

4. Remove the cam sprocket retaining bolt and remove the sprocket and chain. The crank sprocket may also be removed at this time. If the tensioner is to be removed, the oil pan must be removed. first.

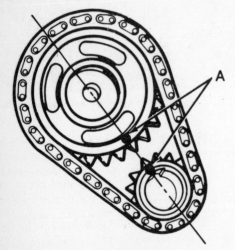

4-150 valve timing mark alignment

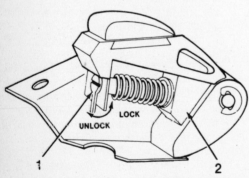

4-150 timing chain tensioner. 1 is the tensioner lever, 2 is the block

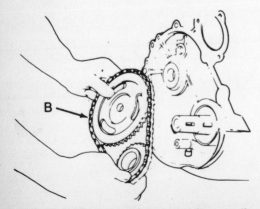

Installing the timing chain and sprockets on the 4-150

5. Prior to installation, turn the tensioner lever to the unlock (down) position.

6. Pull the tensioner block toward the tensioner to compress the spring. Hold the block and turn the tensioner lever to the lock (up) position. The camshaft sprocket bolt should be torqued to 50 ft.lb. on 1984–86 models; 80 ft.lb. on 1987 models.

7. Install the sprockets and chain together, as a unit. Make sure the timing marks are aligned.

To verify that the timing chain is correctly installed:

   a. Turn the crankshaft to place the **camshaft** timing mark at approximately the one o'clock position.

   b. At this point, there should be a tooth on the **crankshaft** sprocket meshed with the chain at the three o'clock position.

   c. Count the number of timing chain pins between the two timing marks on the right side (your right, facing the engine). There should be 20 pins.

8. Install the oil pan, slinger and timing cover.

4–151

NOTE: *Removal of the camshaft gear requires a special adapter #J-971 and the use of a press. Camshaft removal is necessary.*

1. Place the adapter on the press and place the camshaft through the opening.

2. Press the shaft out of the gear using a socket or other suitable tool.

CAUTION: *The thrust plate must be in position so that the woodruff key does not damage the gear when the shaft is pressed out.*

3. To install the gear firmly support the shaft at the back of the front journal in an arbor press using pressplate adapters J-21474-13 or J-21795-1.

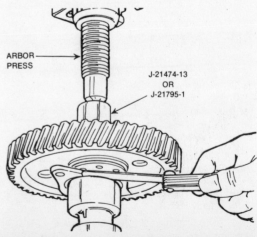

Installing 4-151 camshaft timing gear and measuring thrust plate end clearance

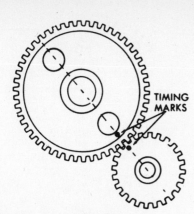

TIMING MARKS

4-151 timing mark alignment

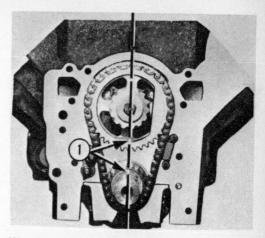

V6 valve timing sprocket alignment

4. Place the gear spacer ring and thrust plate over the end of the shaft, and install the woodruff key in the shaft keyway.

5. Install the camshaft gear and press it onto the shaft until it bottoms against the gear spacer ring. The end clearance of the thrust plate should be 0.0015–0.0050″ (0.0381–0.127mm). If less than 0.0015″ (0.0381mm), the spacer ring should be replaced.

6–225

1. Remove the timing chain cover.

2. Make sure that the timing marks on the crankshaft and the camshaft sprockets are aligned. This will make installing the parts easier.

NOTE: *It is not necessary to remove the timing chain dampers (tensioners) unless they are worn or damaged and require replacement.*

3. Remove the front crankshaft oil slinger.

4. Remove the bolt and the special washer that hold the camshaft distributor drive gear and fuel pump eccentric at the forward end of the camshaft. Remove the eccentric and the gear from the camshaft.

5. Alternately pry forward the camshaft sprocket and then the crankshaft sprocket until the camshaft sprocket is pried from the camshaft.

6. Remove the camshaft sprocket, sprocket key, and timing chain from the engine.

7. Pry the crankshaft sprocket from the crankshaft.

Install as follows:

1. If the engine has not been disturbed proceed to step Number 4 for installation procedures.

2. If the engine has been disturbed turn the crankshaft so that number one piston is at top dead center.

3. Temporarily install the sprocket key and the camshaft sprocket on the camshaft. Turn the camshaft so that the index mark of the

sprocket is downward. Remove the key and sprocket from the camshaft.

4. Assemble the timing chain and sprockets. Install the keys, sprockets, and chain assembly on the camshaft and crankshaft so that the index marks of both the sprockets are aligned.

NOTE: *It will be necessary to hold the spring loaded timing chain damper out of the way while installing the timing chain and sprocket assembly.*

5. Install the front oil slinger on the crankshaft with the inside diameter against the sprocket (concave side toward the front of the engine).

6. Install the fuel pump eccentric on the camshaft and the key, with the oil groove of the eccentric forward.

7. Install the distributor drive gear on the camshaft. Secure the gear and eccentric to the camshaft with the retaining washer and bolt.

8. Torque the bolt to 40–55 ft.lb.

6–226

1. Remove the timing chain cover.

2. Before removing the parts, check for timing chain stretch. Press inward on the chain at a point midway between the gears. If the chain deflects more than ½″ (12.7mm), it is overly stretched and must be discarded.

3. Bend up the locktabs and the camshaft gear retaining bolt and remove the bolt.

4. Pry, alternately, behind each gear until both are free.

5. Inspect both gears. If either appears to be excessively worn, or if either are chipped or cracked, both gears and the chain must be replaced. If only the chain is defective, then, only the chain needs replacement. Inspect the cover. If it is bent or damaged, replace it.

6. Place the two gears into the chain so that

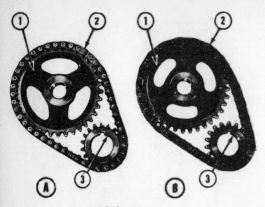

A. Link belt
B. Morse chain
1. Camshaft timing gear
2. Timing gear chain
3. Crankshaft timing gear

The two types of timing chains used on the 6-226, and their relative keyway positioning

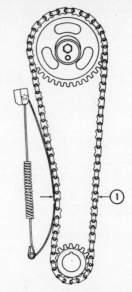

1. 3.38″ minimum at narrowest point

6-230 timing chain measurement

there are exactly nine links, or ten pins, between the timing marks on the gears.

7. If either the camshaft or crankshaft was rotated while the gears were off, position the shafts so that the keways are positioned as illustrated.

8. Slide the gears onto the shafts. If everything is aligned properly, the gears should slip into place with finger pressure.

9. If the camshaft has to be tapped into place, check that the camshaft bearing journals are not contacting the sides of nos. 1, 5, or 9 tappets. This sometimes occurs when the camshaft is pushed backwards during gear installation. If this does occur, hold the camshaft forward to prevent tappet damage.

10. When the gears are fully seated, place the lockplate on the camshaft, with the tab in the hole of the gear.

11. Install the camshaft gear nut and torque it to 40 ft.lb. Bend the lockplate to secure the nut.

12. Install the oil slinger on the crankshaft.

13. Install the remaining parts in reverse order of removal.

6-230

NOTE: *Special tools are needed for this job.*

1. Remove the timing chain cover. Measure across the gap between the chain sides. If the gap is less than 3.38″ (85.85mm), the chain is stretched and should be replaced.

2. Install the cam sprocket remover tool as shown under Cylinder Head Removal and Installation.

3. Remove the sprocket with the tool as described in Cylinder Head.

4. Slide the chain from the sprocket.

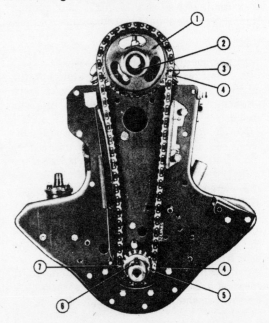

1. Camshaft sprocket	5. Timing mark
2. Drive dowel	6. Key
3. Timing mark	7. Timing chain
4. Copper link	

6-230 timing chain installed

5. Remove the chain tensioner pin to release tension on the tensioner blade. Remove the blade assembly and spring.

6. Remove the chain guide bracket.

7. The crank sprocket may now be removed.

8. Install the tensioner bracket on the front plate with the rubber covered leg positioned between the chain and the front plate.

9. Install the two capscrews and washers and two new $5/16-24$ seal nuts. Hold these seal nuts from turning when tightening the bolts.

10. Position the tensioner blade assembly and spring on the anchor stud on the front engine plate. Bend the blade so that the hook at the upper end of the spring is aligned with the notch in the top of the blade.

11. Insert the tensioner pin so that it engages the spring and blade. Position the top of the tensioner in the bracket.

12. Rotate the engine so that No. 1 piston is at TDC compression. Air will be forced out the spark plug hole when this occurs.

13. With the engine at TDC #1, the keyways in the crankshaft should be in the 12 o'clock position.

14. Temporarily install the camshaft sprocket and turn the camshaft until the nose of the #1 cam lobe, and the dowel hole on the camshaft, are pointing downward to the 6 o'clock position. Remove the sprocket.

15. Install a key in the crankshaft keyway nearest the block.

16. Install the cam sprocket remover tool as before.

17. Position the chain on the sprockets so that the keyway of the crank sprocket is up and the keyway of the cam sprocket is down. The copper links of the chain should be aligned with the timing marks on the sprockets. When properly assembled, there should be 1½ chain units, comprising 31 steel links between the copper links.

18. Lift the assembled chain and sprockets and slide the crank sprocket into position until it is fully seated.

19. Using the cam sprocket tool, tighten the nut to pull tension on the chain and align the sprocket with the end of the shaft. Push the sprocket off the tool and onto the shaft, aligning the key and key slot.

20. Position the fuel pump eccentric on the camshaft sprocket. Install the capscrew, lockwasher and flat washer.

21. Remove the camshaft tool.

6-232, 6-258

1. Remove the drive belts, engine fan and hub assembly, accessory pulley, vibration damper and timing chain cover.

2. Remove the oil seal from the timing chain cover.

3. Remove the camshaft sprocket retaining bolt and washer.

4. Rotate the crankshaft until the timing mark on the crankshaft sprocket is closest to and in a center line with the timing pointer of the camshaft sprocket.

5. Remove the crankshaft sprocket, cam-

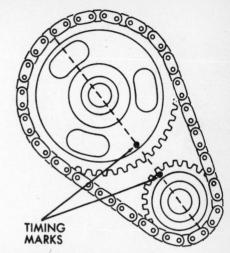

TIMING MARKS

6-232, 258 timing mark alignment

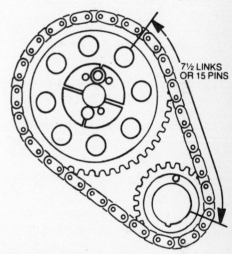

7½ LINKS OR 15 PINS

6-232, 258 alignment verification

shaft sprocket and timing chain as an assembly. Disassemble the chain and sprockets.

Installation is as follows:

1. Assemble the timing chain, crankshaft sprocket and camshaft sprocket with the timing marks aligned.

2. Install the assembly to the crankshaft and the camshaft.

3. Install the camshaft sprocket retaining bolt and washer and tighten to 45-55 ft.lb.

4. Install the timing chain cover and a new oil seal.

5. Install the vibration damper, accessory pulley, engine fan and hub assembly and drive belts. Tighten the belts to the proper tension.

8-304

1. Remove the timing chain cover and gasket.

2. Remove the crankshaft oil slinger.

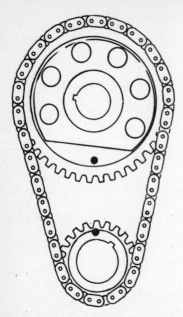

Timing gear alignment on 8-304 engines

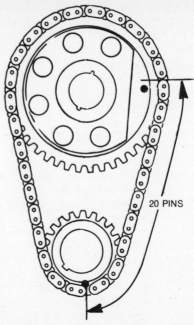

Correct timing chain installation verification, 8-304

3. Remove the camshaft sprocket retaining bolt. and washer, distributor drive gear and fuel pump eccentric.

4. Rotate the crankshaft until the timing mark on the crankshaft sprocket is adjacent to, and on a center line with, the timing mark on the camshaft sprocket.

5. Remove the crankshaft sprocket, cam-shaft sprocket and timing chain as an assembly.

6. Clean all of the gasket surfaces.

Installation is as follows:

1. Assemble the timing chain, crankshaft sprocket and camshaft sprocket with the timing marks on both sprockets aligned.

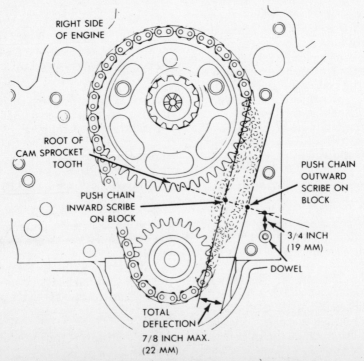

Measuring timing chain deflection on 8-304 engines

2. Install the assembly to the crankshaft and the camshaft.

3. Install the fuel pump eccentric, distributor drive gear, washer and retaining bolt. Tighten the bolt to 25–35 ft.lb.

4. Install the crankshaft oil slinger.

5. Install the timing chain cover using a new gasket and oil seal.

NOTE: *In mid-year 1979, a new timing chain, camshaft sprocket and crankshaft sprocket were phased into production on all 8–304 engines. These are offered as replacement parts for older engines. When installing any one of these parts on an older engine, all three parts must be installed. None of the new parts is usable in conjunction with the older parts. They must be installed as a set. To determine the necessity for a replacement of an older chain, perform the following deflection test:*

1. Remove the timing case cover.

2. Rotate the sprockets until all slack is removed from the right side of the chain.

3. Locate the dowel on the lower left side of the engine and measure up ¾″ (19.05mm). Make a mark.

4. Measure across the chain with a straightedge from the mark to a point at the bottom of the camshaft sprocket.

5. Grab the chain at the point where the straightedge crosses it. Push the chain left (inward) as far as it will go. Make a mark on the block at this point. Push the chain to the right as far as it will go. Make another mark. Measure between the two marks. Total deflection should not exceed ⅞″ (22.23mm).

6. Replace the chain and sprockets if deflection is not within specifications.

7. Replace the timing case cover.

Valve Timing

L4–134 IN CJ-2A MODELS BEFORE ENGINE #175402

1. Turn the crankshaft so that Nos. 1 & 4 piston are at TDC as indicated by the TC mark on the flywheel seen through the timing hole in the right side of the flywheel housing.

2. Place the camshaft sprocket on the shaft and turn the shaft until the punch mark on the rim of the sprocket faces the punchmark on the crankshaft sprocket.

3. Remove the camshaft sprocket and install the sprocket and timing chain. Timing is correct when a line drawn through the sprocket centers, intersects the timing marks on both sprockets.

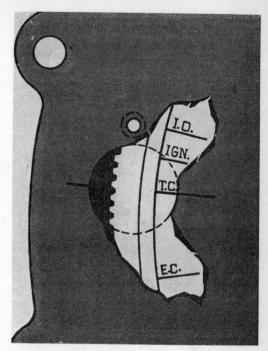

Flywheel timing marks on CJ-2A engines before engine #175402

L4–134 AFTER ENGINE #175402 AND ALL F4–134

1. Install the timing gears with the marks aligned as shown.

2. Set the intake valve clearance to 0.020″ (0.5mm) on the #1 cylinder.

3. Rotate the crankshaft until the #1 cylinder intake valve is ready to open as indicated

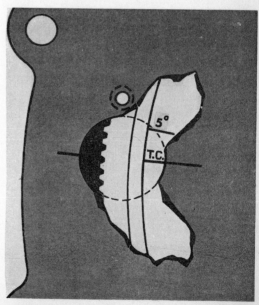

Flywheel timing marks on CJ-2A engines after engine #175402

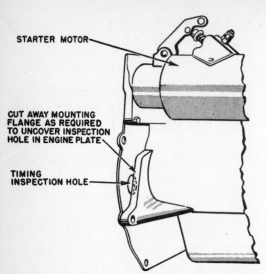

STARTER MOTOR

CUT AWAY MOUNTING FLANGE AS REQUIRED TO UNCOVER INSPECTION HOLE IN ENGINE PLATE

TIMING INSPECTION HOLE

Uncovering timing inspection hole on CJ-3A engines

by the IO mark on the flywheel. The mark should be centered in the hole.

NOTE: *Some later models do not have an IO mark. TC and 5 degrees are the only marks. On these engines, the intake valve opens at 9 degrees BTC. To estimate valve opening, measure the distance between TC and 5 degrees and measure about that distance further on. On CJ-3A models beginning with engine #130859, a 4½" (114.3mm) starter motor was used. To use the larger starter, it was necessary to increase the width of the cylinder block flange, partially covering the flywheel hole. This makes it impossible to use the hole for timing purposes. In this event, use the timing marks on the crankshaft pulley. If a replacement block is installed with the later design in a vehicle originally equipped with the earlier design timing marks, it will be necessary to cut away enough of the flange to allow a view of the timing marks, as no other timing marks exist on the these early engines.*

Camshaft

REMOVAL AND INSTALLATION

NOTE: *Caution must be taken when performing this procedure. Camshaft bearings are coated with babbit material, which can be damaged by scraping the cam lobes across the bearing.*

L4–134, F4–134

1. Remove the engine.
2. Remove the exhaust manifold.
3. Remove the oil pump and the distributor.
4. Remove the crankshaft pulley.
5. Remove the cylinder head.
6. Remove the exhaust valves.
7. Remove the timing gear cover and the crankshaft and camshaft timing gears.
8. Remove the front end plate.
9. Push the intake and exhaust valve lifters into the cylinder block as far as possible so that the ends of the lifters are not in contact with the camshaft.
10. Secure each tappet in the raised position by installing a clip type clothes pin on the shank of each tappet or tie them up in the plate and spacer.
11. Remove the crankshaft thrust plate attaching screws. Remove the camshaft thrust plate and spacer.
12. Pull the camshaft forward out of the cylinder block being careful to prevent damage to the camshaft bearing surfaces.
13. Slide the camshaft into the cylinder block being careful to prevent damage to the camshaft bearing surfaces.
14. Install the crankshaft thrust plate attaching screws. Install the camshaft thrust plate and spacer.
15. Remove the clothes pins.
16. Install the front end plate.
17. Install the timing gear cover and the crankshaft and camshaft timing gears.
18. Install the exhaust valves.
19. Install the cylinder head.
20. Install the crankshaft pulley.
21. Install the oil pump and the distributor.
22. Install the exhaust manifold.
23. Install the engine.

4–150

CAUTION: *To remove perform this procedure the air conditioning system must be discharged. Mishandling of refrigerant gas can cause severe personal injury. If you are not completely familiar with the handling of refrigerant systems, have the system discharged by someone who is.*

1. Disconnect the battery ground.
2. Drain the cooling system.

CAUTION: *When draining the coolant, keep in mind that cats and dogs are attracted by the ethylene glycol antifreeze, and are quite likely to drink any that is left in an uncovered container or in puddles on the ground. This will prove fatal in sufficient quantity. Always drain the coolant into a sealable container. Coolant should be reused unless it is contaminated or several years old.*

3. Remove the radiator, discharge the refrigerant system (See Chapter 1) and remove the condenser.
4. Remove the fuel pump.

J-21884

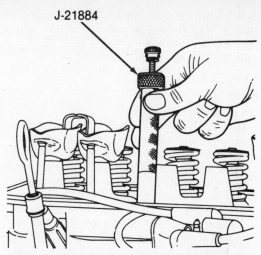

Using a special tool to remove the lifters from a 4-150

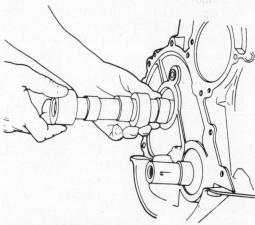

Removing the 4-150 camshaft

5. Matchmark the distributor and engine for installation. Note the rotor position by marking it on the distributor body. Unbolt and remove the distributor and wires.
6. Remove the rocker arm cover.
7. Remove the rocker arm assemblies.
8. Remove the pushrods.
NOTE: *Keep everything in order for installation.*

9. Using a tool J-21884, or equivalent, remove the hydraulic lifters.
10. Remove the pulley, vibration damper and timing case cover. Remove the crankshaft oil slinger.
NOTE: *If the camshaft sprocket appears to have been rubbing against the cover, check the oil pressure relief holes in the rear cam journal for debris.*
11. Remove the timing chain and sprockets.
12. Slide the camshaft from the engine.
13. Inspect all parts for wear and damage.

Lubricate all moving parts with engine oil supplement.
14. Slide the camshaft into the engine, carefully, to avoid damage to the bearing surfaces.
15. Install the timing chain and sprockets. Make sure that all camshaft timing marks align. Torque the camshaft sprocket bolt to 50 ft.lb. on 1984–86 models; 80 ft.lb. 0n 1987 models.
16. Install the timing case cover.
17. Using a tool J-21884, or equivalent, install the hydraulic lifters.
18. Install the pushrods.
19. Install the rocker arm assemblies.
20. Install the rocker arm cover.
21. Install the distributor and wires. When installing the distributor, make sure that all matchmarks align. It may be necessary to rotate the oil pump drive tang with a long-bladed screwdriver to facilitate installation of the distributor.
For 1987 engines: Position the engine at the number 1 cylinder TDC location. Rotate the gear slot on the oil pump shaft to a point slightly past the 3 o'clock position. Install the distributor with the rotor at the 5 o'clock position. When fully engaged, the rotor should be at the 6 o'clock position.
NOTE: *If the distributor is not installed correctly, or removed later, the complete installation procedure must be done again.*
22. Install the fuel pump.
23. Install the radiator.
24. Install the condenser and evacuate and charge the refrigerant system. (See Chapter 1).
25. Fill the cooling system.
26. Connect the battery ground.

4–151
1. Remove the air cleaner.
2. Drain the cooling system.
CAUTION: *When draining the coolant, keep in mind that cats and dogs are attracted by the ethylene glycol antifreeze, and are quite likely to drink any that is left in an uncovered container or in puddles on the ground. This will prove fatal in sufficient quantity. Always drain the coolant into a sealable container. Coolant should be reused unless it is contaminated or several years old.*
3. Remove the timing gear cover.
4. Disconnect the radiator hoses at the radiator. Remove the radiator.
5. Remove the two camshaft thrust plate screws through the holes in the camshaft gear.
6. Remove the tappets.
7. Remove the distributor, oil pump drive and fuel pump.
8. Remove the camshaft and gear assembly by pulling out through front of the block. Sup-

Removing 4-151 camshaft thrust plate screws

port the shaft carefully when removing it to prevent damaging the camshaft bearings.

9. Thoroughly coat the camshaft journals with a high quality engine oil supplement such as STP or its equivalent.

10. Install the camshaft assembly in engine block. Use care to prevent damaging the bearings or the camshaft.

11. Turn the crankshaft and camshaft so that the valve timing marks on the gear teeth are aligned. The engine is now in number four cylinder firing position. Install the camshaft thrust plate-to-block screws and tighten to 75 in.lb.

12. Install the timing gear cover and gasket.

13. Line up the keyway in the hub with the key on crankshaft and slide the hub onto the shaft. Install the center bolt and tighten to 160 ft.lb.

14. Install the valve tappets, pushrods, pushrod cover, oil pump shaft and gear assembly and the fuel pump. Install the distributor according to the following procedure:

   a. Turn the crankshaft 360 degrees to the firing position of the number one cylinder (number one exhaust and intake valve tappets both on base circle [heel] of the camshaft and the timing notch on the vibration damper is indexed with the top dead center mark [TDC] on the timing degree scale).

   b. Install the distributor and align the shaft so that the rotor arm points toward the number one cylinder spark plug contact.

15. Install the rocker arms and pivot balls over the pushrods. With the tappets on the base circle (heel) of camshaft, tighten the rocker arm capscrews to 20 ft.lb. Do not overtighten.

16. Install the cylinder head cover.

17. Install the intake manifold.

18. Install the radiator and lower radiator hose.

19. Install the belt, fan and shroud. Tighten the fan bolts to 18 ft.lb.

20. Install the upper radiator hose.

21. Tighten the belts.

6-225

1. Remove the engine.

CAUTION: *When draining the coolant, keep in mind that cats and dogs are attracted by the ethylene glycol antifreeze, and are quite likely to drink any that is left in an uncovered container or in puddles on the ground. This will prove fatal in sufficient quantity. Always drain the coolant into a sealable container. Coolant should be reused unless it is contaminated or several years old.*

2. Remove the intake manifold and carburetor assembly.

3. Remove the distributor.

4. Remove the fuel pump.

5. Remove the alternator, drive belts, cooling fan, fan pulley and water pump.

6. Remove the crankshaft pulley and the vibration damper.

7. Remove the oil pump.

8. Remove the timing chain cover.

9. Remove the timing chain and the camshaft sprocket, along with the distributor drive gear and the fuel pump eccentric.

10. Remove the rocker arm assemblies.

NOTE: *The pushrods need not be removed. But if they are, be sure that they are replaced in their original positions.*

11. Lift the tappets up so that they are not in contact with the camshaft. Use wire clips or clip type pins to hold the tappets up.

12. Carefully guide the camshaft forward out of the engine. Avoid marring the bearing surfaces.

13. Coat all moving parts with an engine oil supplement, such as STP or its equivalent.

14. Slide the camshaft, carefully, into position. Avoid marring the bearing surfaces.

15. Drop the tappets back onto the camshaft.

16. Install the rocker arm assemblies.

17. Install the timing chain and the camshaft sprocket, along with the distributor drive gear and the fuel pump eccentric.

18. Install the timing chain cover.

19. Install the oil pump.

20. Install the crankshaft pulley and the vibration damper.

21. Install the alternator, drive belts, cooling fan, fan pulley and water pump.

22. Install the fuel pump.

23. Install the distributor.

24. Install the intake manifold and carburetor assembly.

25. Install the engine.

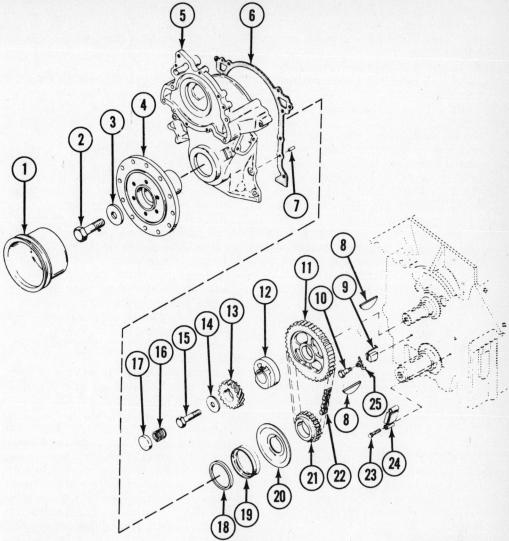

6-225 timing chain, sprockets and related parts

1. Crankshaft pulley
2. Crankshaft pulley bolt
3. Washer
4. Vibration damper
5. Timing gear cover
6. Gasket
7. Dowel pin
8. Woodruff key
9. Timing chain damper (right)
10. Damper bolt
11. Camshaft sprocket
12. Fuel pump eccentric
13. Distributor camshaft gear
14. Washer
15. Special bolt
16. Thrust spring
17. Thrust button
18. Oil shedder (crankshaft)
19. Crankshaft packing (front)
20. Crankshaft slinger
21. Crankshaft sprocket
22. Timing chain
23. Damper bolt
24. Timing chain damper (left)
25. Spring

6–226

1. Drain the cooling system and remove the radiator.

CAUTION: *When draining the coolant, keep in mind that cats and dogs are attracted by the ethylene glycol antifreeze, and are quite likely to drink any that is left in an uncovered container or in puddles on the ground. This will prove fatal in sufficient quantity. Always drain the coolant into a sealable container.*

Coolant should be reused unless it is contaminated or several years old.

2. Remove the timing chain and gears as described above.
3. Remove the fuel pump.
4. Remove the cylinder head.
5. Remove the oil pan.
6. Remove the oil pump.
7. Remove the tappet chamber cover.
8. Remove the valves and springs as described above.

9. Pull the tappets up and hold them in the up position with spring-type clothes pins.

10. Remove the camshaft thrust plate from the front of the block.

11. Pull the camshaft from the front of the block, being VERY careful to avoid damaging the journals and bearings.

12. Thoroughly clean the camshaft in a safe solvent.

13. Check the journals with a micrometer. If any journal is more than 0.001″ (0.0254mm) out of round, the camshaft should be replaced.

14. Cam faces should not show any wear or scoring. Total camshaft runout should not exceed 0.002″ (0.0508mm). Replace the camshaft if it is at all suspect.

15. With an inside micrometer, check the bearing diameter. If any bearing is more than 0.004″ (0.1016mm) oversize, it should be replaced. ALL BEARINGS MUST BE REPLACED AS A SET, IF ANY ONE IS WORN OR DAMAGED.

16. To remove the bearings, remove the core plug at the rear of the block and insert a bearing puller. Remove the bearings one at a time.

17. When installing new bearings, replace them one at a time, making sure that the oil holes are aligned. When installing the front bearing, the small groove from the oil hole must be toward the front of the engine. Coat the rim of the core plug with gasket sealer before installing it.

18. Coat the camshaft with clean engine oil and slide it into place. Install the thrust plate and torque the bolts to 15 ft.lb.

19. Drop the tappets onto the camshaft.

20. Install the valves and springs as described above.

21. Install the tappet chamber cover.

22. Install the oil pump.

23. Install the oil pan.

24. Install the cylinder head.

25. Install the fuel pump.

26. Install the timing chain and gears as described above.

27. Install the radiator.

28. Fill the cooling system and road test the car.

6–230

1. Remove the cylinder head.

2. Lift the rocker arm guide from the head.

3. Check the rocker arms to determine which ones do not have tension against them. Turn these parallel to the camshaft.

4. Remove tension on the remaining rocker arms by backing off on the adjusting nuts. Then, turn these parallel to the camshaft.

5. Unbolt the camshaft retainer from the cam bearing support deck. Remove the retainer. Some engines have a shim between the retainer and deck. Don't lose it!

6. Pull forward on the camshaft to remove it from the deck.

7. Unbolt and remove the cam bearing support deck from the head.

8. Inspect the camshaft for wear or damage. Camshaft runout should not exceed 0.0005″ (0.0127mm). Cam bearing clearance should not exceed 0.004″ (0.1016mm).

9. Coat all parts with engine oil supplement prior to installation. Don't forget the shim, if one was there to begin with. If a new cam bearing support deck is being installed, determine if a shim is needed. To do this, measure the distance between the centerline of the cam bearing deck front mounting holes and the retainer surface on the deck. If the dimension is 0.810″ (20.574mm), the retainer is to be installed without a shim. If the dimension is 0.780″ (19.812mm), a shim is required.

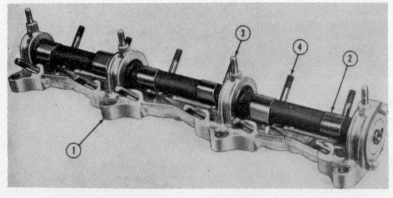

1. Cam bearing support deck
2. Camshaft
3. Rocker arm cover stud (1 of 4)
4. Rocker arm stud (1 of 12)

6-230 camshaft and cam bearing support deck

Checking bearing diameter of cam bearing support deck on the 6-230

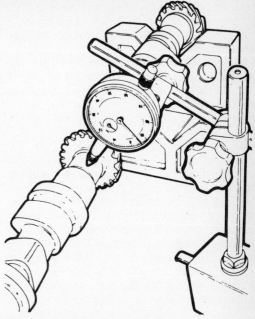

Check the camshaft for straightness

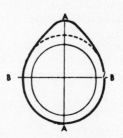

Camshaft lobe measurement

10. Install the cam bearing support deck on the head. Torque the nuts to 12–15 ft.lb.
11. Slide the camshaft into the deck.
12. Install the retainer. Some engines have a shim between the retainer and deck. Torque the nuts to 12–15 ft.lb.
13. Adjust the valves.
14. Install the rocker arm guide on the head.
15. Install the cylinder head.

6–232, 6–258

1. Drain the cooling system and remove the radiator. With air conditioning, remove the condenser and receiver assembly as a unit, without disconnecting any lines or discharging the system.
CAUTION: *When draining the coolant, keep in mind that cats and dogs are attracted by the ethylene glycol antifreeze, and are quite likely to drink any that is left in an uncovered container or in puddles on the ground. This will prove fatal in sufficient quantity. Always drain the coolant into a sealable container. Coolant should be reused unless it is contaminated or several years old.*
2. Remove the valve cover and gasket, the rocker assemblies, pushrods, cylinder head and gasket and the lifters.
NOTE: *The valve train components must be replaced in their original locations.*
3. Remove the drive belts, cooling fan, fan hub assembly, vibration damper and the timing chain cover.
4. Remove the fuel pump and distributor assembly, including the spark plug wires.
5. Rotate the crankshaft until the timing mark of the crankshaft sprocket is adjacent to, and on a center line with, the timing mark of the camshaft sprocket.
6. Remove the crankshaft sprocket, cam-

shaft sprocket, and the timing chain as an assembly.
7. Remove the front bumper or grille as required and carefully slide out the camshaft.
8. Coat all parts with engine oil supplement.
9. Slide the camshaft into place.
10. Install the front bumper and/or grille.
11. Install the crankshaft sprocket, camshaft sprocket, and the timing chain as an assembly.
12. Rotate the crankshaft until the timing mark of the crankshaft sprocket is adjacent to, and on a center line with, the timing mark of the camshaft sprocket.
13. Install the fuel pump and distributor assembly, including the spark plug wires.
14. Install the drive belts.
15. Install the cooling fan and fan hub assembly.
16. Install the vibration damper.
17. Install the cylinder head and gasket and the lifters.
18. Install the rocker assemblies and pushrods.

19. Install the valve cover and gasket.

20. Install the the timing chain cover.

21. With air conditioning, install the condenser and receiver.

NOTE: *The valve train components must be replaced in their original locations.*

22. Drain the cooling system and install the radiator.

8–304

1. Disconnect the battery cables.

2. Drain the radiator and both banks of the block. Remove the lower hose at the radiator, the by-pass hose at the pump, the thermostat housing and the radiator. With air conditioning, remove the condenser and receiver assembly as a unit, without disconnecting any lines or discharging the system.

CAUTION: *When draining the coolant, keep in mind that cats and dogs are attracted by the ethylene glycol antifreeze, and are quite likely to drink any that is left in an uncovered container or in puddles on the ground. This will prove fatal in sufficient quantity. Always drain the coolant into a sealable container. Coolant should be reused unless it is contaminated or several years old.*

3. Remove the distributor, all wires, and the coil from the manifold.

4. Remove the intake manifold as an assembly.

5. Remove the valve covers, rocker arms and pushrods.

6. Remove the lifters.

NOTE: *The valve train components must be replaced in their original locations.*

7. Remove the cooling fan and hub assembly, fuel pump, and heater hose at the water pump.

8. Remove the alternator and bracket as an assembly. Just move it aside, do not disconnect the wiring.

9. Remove the crankshaft pulley and the damper. Remove the lower radiator hose at the water pump.

10. Remove the timing chain cover.

11. Remove the distributor/oil pump drive gear, fuel pump eccentric, sprockets and the timing chain.

12. Remove the grille.

13. Remove the camshaft carefully by sliding it forward out of the engine.

14. Coat all parts with engine oil supplement.

15. Slide the camshaft, carefully, into the engine.

16. Install the grille.

17. Install the distributor/oil pump drive gear, fuel pump eccentric, sprockets and the timing chain.

18. Install the timing chain cover.

19. Install the crankshaft pulley and the damper.

20. Install the lower radiator hose at the water pump.

21. Install the alternator and bracket as an assembly.

22. Install the cooling fan and hub assembly.

23. Install the fuel pump.

24. Install the heater hose at the water pump.

25. Install the lifters.

NOTE: *The valve train components must be replaced in their original locations.*

26. Install the valve covers, rocker arms and pushrods.

27. Install the intake manifold as an assembly.

28. Install the distributor, all wires, and the coil on the manifold.

29 Install the radiator.

30. With air conditioning, install the condenser and receiver assembly.

31. Install the thermostat and housing.

32. Install the by-pass hose at the pump.

33. Install the lower hose at the radiator.

34. Fill the cooling system.

35. Connect the battery cables.

Pistons and Connecting Rods
REMOVAL

NOTE: *In most cases, this procedure is easier with the engine out of the vehicle.*

1. Remove the head(s).

2. Remove the oil pan.

3. Rotate the engine to bring each piston, in turn, to the bottom of its stroke. With the piston bottomed, use a ridge reamer to remove the ridge at the top of the cylinder. DO NOT CUT TOO DEEPLY!

4. Matchmark the rods and caps. If the pis-

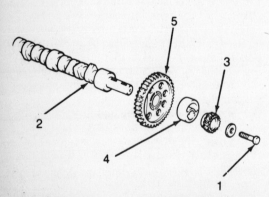

1. Retaining bolt
2. Camshaft
3. Distributor drive gear
4. Fuel pump eccentric
5. Sprocket

8-304 camshaft and related parts

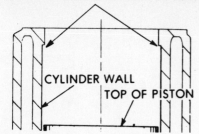

Cylinder bore ridge

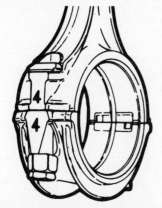

Number each rod and cap accordingly

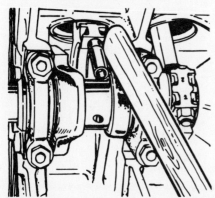

Push the piston out with a hammer handle

tons are to be removed from the connecting rod, mark the cylinder number on the piston with a silver pencil or quick drying paint for proper cylinder identification and cap-to-rod location. Remove the connecting rod capnuts and lift off the rod caps, keeping them in order. Install a guide hose over the threads of the rod bolts. This is to prevent damage to the bearing journal and rod bolt threads.

5. Using a hammer handle, push the piston and rod assemblies up out of the block.

PISTON PIN REMOVAL AND INSTALLATION

Use care at all times when handling and servicing connecting rods and pistons. To prevent possible damage to these units, do not clamp

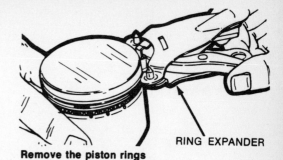

Remove the piston rings

Install the piston pin lock-rings (if used)

the rod or piston in a vise since they may become distorted. Do not allow the pistons to strike against one another, against hard objects or bench surfaces, since distortion of the piston contour or nicks in the soft aluminum material may result.

1. Remove the piston rings using a suitable piston ring remover.

2. Remove the piston pin lockring, if used. Install the guide bushing of the piston pin removing and installing tool.

3. Install the piston and connecting rod assembly on a support, and place the assembly in an arbor press. Press the pin out of the connecting rod, using the appropriate piston pin tool.

4. Assembly is the reverse of disassembly. Use new lockrings where needed.

INSPECTION

Cylinder Block

Check the cylinder walls for evidence of rust, which would indicate a cracked block. Check the block face for distortion with a straightedge. Maximum distortion variance is 0.005″ (0.127mm). The block cannot be planed, so it will have to be replaced if too distorted. Using a micrometer, check the cylinders for out-of-roundness.

Connecting Rods and Bearings

Wash connecting rods in cleaning solvent and dry with compressed air. Check for twisted or bent rods and inspect for nicks or cracks. Replace connecting rods that are damaged.

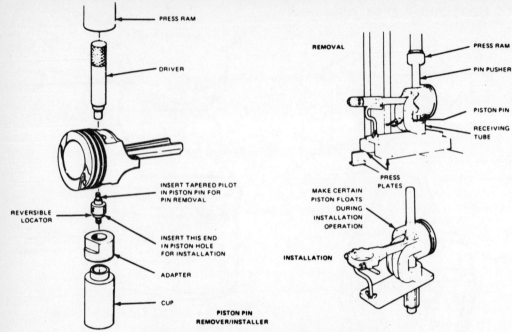

Piston pins must be pressed in with an arbor press

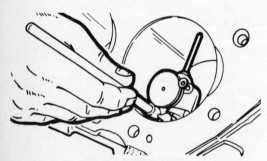

Measure the cylinder bore with a dial gauge

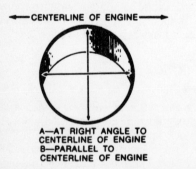

A—AT RIGHT ANGLE TO CENTERLINE OF ENGINE
B—PARALLEL TO CENTERLINE OF ENGINE

Cylinder bore measuring points. Take the top measurement ½ inch below the top; the bottom measurement ½ inch above the top of the piston at BDC

Inspect journals for roughness and wear. Slight roughness may be removed with a fine grit polishing cloth saturated with engine oil. Burrs may be removed with a fine oil stone by moving the stone on the journal circumference. Do not move the stone back and forth across

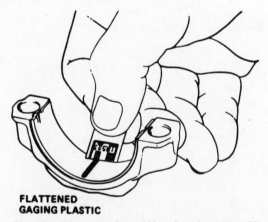

FLATTENED GAGING PLASTIC

Checking the connecting rod bearing clearance with Plastigage®

the journal. If the journals are scored or ridged, the crankshaft must be replaced.

The connecting rod journals should be checked for out-of-round and correct size with a micrometer.

NOTE: *Crankshaft rod journals will normally be standard size. If any undersized bearings are used, the size will be stamped on a counterweight.*

If plastic gauging material is to be used:

1. Clean oil from the journal bearing cap, connecting rod and outer and inner surfaces of the bearing inserts. Position the insert so that the tang is properly aligned with the notch in the rod and cap.

2. Place a piece of plastic gauging material in the center of lower bearing shell.

3. Remove the bearing cap and determine the bearing clearances by comparing the width of the flattened plastic gauging material at its widest point with the graduation on the container. The number within the graduation on the envelope indicates the clearance in thousandths of an inch or millimeters. If this clearance is excessive, replace the bearing and recheck the clearance with the plastic gauging material. Lubricate the bearing with engine oil before installation. Repeat the procedure on the remaining connecting rod bearings. All rods must be connected to their journals when rotating the crankshaft, to prevent engine damage.

Pistons

Clean varnish from piston skirts and pins with a cleaning solvent. DO NOT WIRE BRUSH ANY PART OF THE PISTON. Clean the ring grooves with a groove cleaner and make sure oil ring holes and slots are clean.

Inspect the piston for cracked ring lands, skirts or pin bosses, wavy or worn ring lands, scuffed or damaged skirts, eroded areas at the top of the piston. Replace pistons that are damaged or show signs of excessive wear. Inspect the grooves for nicks or burrs that might cause the rings to hang up.

Measure piston skirt (across center line of piston pin) and check piston clearance.

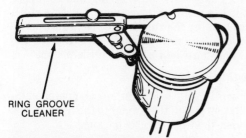

RING GROOVE
CLEANER

Clean the piston ring grooves

MEASURING THE OLD PISTONS

Check used piston-to-cylinder bore clearance as follows:

1. Measure the cylinder bore diameter with a telescope gauge.

2. Measure the piston diameter. When measuring the pistons for size or taper, measurements must be made with the piston pin removed.

3. Subtract the piston diameter from the cylinder bore diameter to determine piston-to-bore clearance.

4. Compare the piston-to-bore clearances obtained with those clearances recommended.

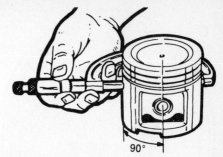

Measure the piston prior to fitting

Determine if the piston-to-bore clearance is in the acceptable range.

5. When measuring taper, the largest reading must be at the bottom of the skirt.

SELECTING NEW PISTONS

1. If the used piston is not acceptable, check the service piston size and determine if a new piston can be selected. (Service pistons are available in standard, high limit and standard oversize.

2. If the cylinder bore must be reconditioned, measure the new piston diameter, then hone the cylinder bore to obtain the preferred clearance.

3. Select a new piston and mark the piston to identify the cylinder for which it was fitted. (On some vehicles, oversize pistons may be found. These pistons will be 0.254mm (0.010″) oversize).

CYLINDER HONING

1. When cylinders are being honed, follow the manufacturer's recommendations for the use of the hone.

2. Occasionally, during the honing operation, the cylinder bore should be thoroughly cleaned and the selected piston checked for correct fit.

3. When finish-honing a cylinder bore, the hone should be moved up and down at a sufficient speed to obtain a very fine uniform surface finish in a cross-hatch pattern of approximately 45–65 degrees included angle. The finish marks should be clean but not sharp, free from imbedded particles and torn or folded metal.

4. Permanently mark the piston for the cylinder to which it has been fitted and proceed to hone the remaining cylinders.

NOTE: *Handle the pistons with care. Do not attempt to force the pistons through the cylinders until the cylinders have been honed to the correct size. Pistons can be distorted through careless handling.*

5. Thoroughly clean the bores with hot water and detergent. Scrub well with a stiff bris-

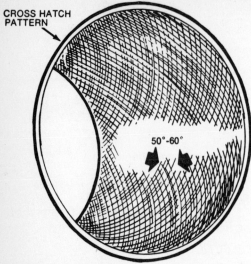

Cylinder bore after honing

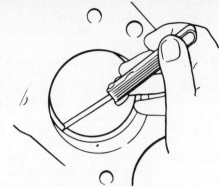

Check the piston ring end gap

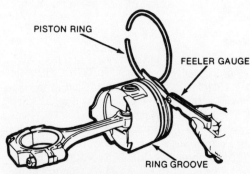

Check the piston ring side clearance

tle brush and rinse thoroughly with hot water. It is extremely essential that a good cleaning operation be performed. If any of the abrasive material is allowed to remain in the cylinder bores, it will rapidly wear the new rings and cylinder bores. The bores should be swabbed several times with light engine oil and a clean cloth and then wiped with a clean dry cloth. CYLINDERS SHOULD NOT BE CLEANED WITH KEROSENE OR GASOLINE. Clean the remainder of the cylinder block to remove the excess material spread during the honing operation.

CHECKING CYLINDER BORE

Cylinder bore size can be measured with inside micrometers or a cylinder gauge. The most wear will occur at the top of the ring travel.

Reconditioned cylinder bores should be held to not more than 0.025mm (0.001") taper.

If the cylinder bores are smooth, the cylinder walls should not be deglazed. If the cylinder walls are scored, the walls may have to be honed before installing new rings. It is important that reconditioned cylinder bores be thoroughly washed with a soap and water solution to remove all traces of abrasive material to eliminate premature wear.

RING TOLERANCES

When installing new rings, ring gap and side clearance should be checked as follows:

Piston Ring and Rail Gap

Each ring and rail gap must be measured with the ring or rail positioned squarely and at the bottom of the ring travel area of the bore.

Side Clearance

Each ring must be checked for side clearance in its respective piston groove by inserting a feeler gauge between the ring and its upper land. The piston grooves must be cleaned before checking the ring for side clearance specifications. To check oil ring side clearance, the oil rings must be installed on the piston.

RING INSTALLATION

For service ring specifications and detailed installation productions, refer to the instructions furnished with the parts package.

PISTON ASSEMBLY AND INSTALLATION

1. Using a ring expander, install new rings in the grooves, with their gaps staggered to be 270° apart.

2. Using a straightedge, check the rods for straightness. Check, also, for cracks. Before assembling the block, it's a good idea to have the block checked for cracks with Magnaflux® or its equivalent.

3. Install the pins and retainers.

4. Coat the pistons with clean engine oil and apply a ring compressor. Position the assembly over the cylinder bore and slide the piston into the cylinder slowly, taking care to avoid nicking the walls. The pistons will have a mark on the crown, such as a groove or notch

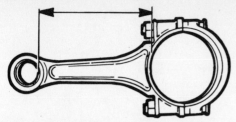

Check the connecting rod length (arrow)

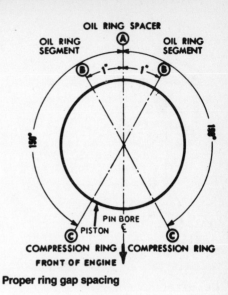

Proper ring gap spacing

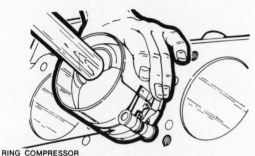

Install the piston using a ring compressor

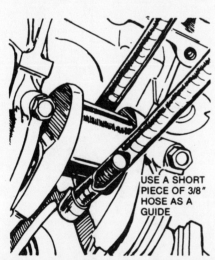

USE A SHORT PIECE OF 3/8" HOSE AS A GUIDE

Use lengths of vacuum hose or rubber tubing to protect the crankshaft journals and cylinder walls during piston installation

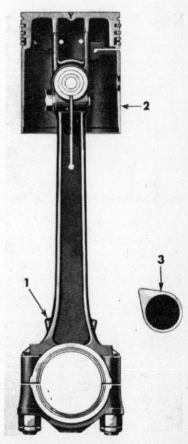

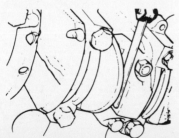

Check the connecting rod side clearance with a feeler gauge

1. Oil spray hole
2. Piston skirt T-slot
3. Relative position of camshaft

4-134 piston and rod assembly

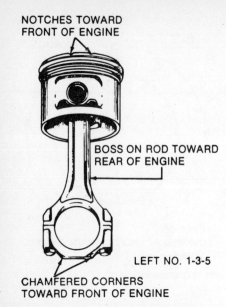

NOTCHES TOWARD FRONT OF ENGINE

BOSS ON ROD TOWARD REAR OF ENGINE

LEFT NO. 1-3-5

CHAMFERED CORNERS TOWARD FRONT OF ENGINE

V6-225 left bank piston and rod assembly

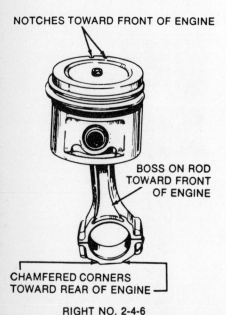

NOTCHES TOWARD FRONT OF ENGINE

BOSS ON ROD TOWARD FRONT OF ENGINE

CHAMFERED CORNERS TOWARD REAR OF ENGINE

RIGHT NO. 2-4-6

V6-225 right bank piston and rod assembly

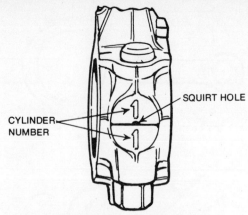

CYLINDER NUMBER

SQUIRT HOLE

6-232, 258 connecting rod numbering

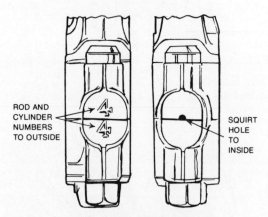

ROD AND CYLINDER NUMBERS TO OUTSIDE

SQUIRT HOLE TO INSIDE

4-151 rod number and squirt hole

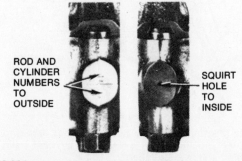

ROD AND CYLINDER NUMBERS TO OUTSIDE

SQUIRT HOLE TO INSIDE

8-304 connecting rod and cap mating

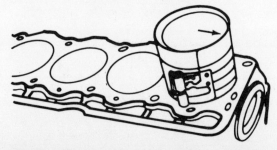

On the 4-150, the arrow on the piston crown faces front

or stamped symbol. This mark indicates the side of the piston which should face front. Lower the piston slowly, until it bottoms on the crankshaft. A good idea is to cover the rod studs with length of rubber hose to avoid nicking the crank journals. Assemble the rod caps at this time. Check the rod bearing clearances using Plastigage®, going by the instructions on the package.

5. Install the bearing caps with the stamped numbers matched. Torque the caps to the figure shown in the Torque Specifications Chart.

See the accompanying illustrations for proper piston and rod installation.

Rear Main Oil Seal

REPLACEMENT

L4–134, F4–134

NOTE: *On early L4–134 engines, the rear bearing is sealed by a wick packing. This packing is installed in a groove machined into the rear main bearing cap. On later L4–134 and all F4–134 engines, a steel-backed lip seal is used. This seal can be used to replace the older wick seal, and can be replaced without removing the crankshaft.*

The following steps apply to wick type seals:

1. Remove the engine from the vehicle.
2. Remove the timing chain cover and crankshaft timing gear.
3. Remove the oil pan and pickup unit.
4. Slide the thrust washers and adjusting shims off the front end of the crankshaft.
5. Move the two pieces of the rear main cap packing away from the sides of the cap.
6. Note the numbers of the main caps and block for position when installing.
7. Unbolt and remove the main bearing caps.

CAUTION: *Take great care in removing the caps. Lift them evenly and avoid binding on the dowels. If you suspect that any of the dowels were bent during removal, replace them.*

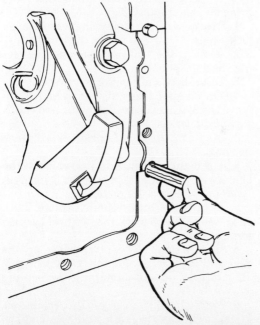

Late L-head and all F-head rear bearing cap packing

8. Unbolt and remove the connecting rod caps, taking care to note their position for installation.
9. Lift out the crankshaft.
10. Remove the rear main seal wicking from the grooves.
11. If a steel-backed lip type seal is being used to replace the older style wicking, go on to the next procedure for later L4–134 and all F4–134 engines. If a wick type seal is being used, clean the seal grooves, and insert the seal in the grooves with your fingers.
12. Using a round piece of wood, roll the seal tightly into the groove starting at one end and working toward the center, then the other end toward the center.
13. A small portion of the packing will protrude above the surface of the cap. This should be cut off flush with the cap at each end.

The following procedure should be used for later L4–134 and all F4–134 engines with steel-backed lip type seals:

1. Raise and support the vehicle on jackstands.
2. Remove the oil pan.
3. Remove the rear main bearing cap.
4. Using a center punch, drive the upper seal out of its groove just far enough to grasp it with a pliers, and pull it the rest of the way.
5. Apply a light film of chassis grease to the lower seal and install it in the cap.
6. Install the rubber packings in the upper crankcase half. The packings are of a predetermined length to allow about ¼" (6.35mm) protrusion. This protrusion is necessary for a positive seal. DO NOT TRIM THESE SEALS!
7. Apply a small amount of RTV sealant to both sides and face of the bearing cap and install it.
8. Torque the cap to the figure shown in the torque specifications chart.
9. Install the oil pan.

6–225

NOTE: *For removal of both upper and lower seals, the crankshaft must be removed from the engine. Crankshaft removal is easiest with the engine out of the vehicle.*

1. Remove engine.
2. Remove the timing case and gears, and any spacers and shims from the front of the crankshaft.
3. Remove the oil pan and oil pickup.
4. Note the mating of crankshaft and main caps. Match mark them with an indelible inker.
5. Unbolt the #1 main bearing cap. Using a pry bar, carefully lift the cap from the dowels. Take great care to avoid damaging the dowels. Any bent dowels must be replaced.

6. In the same manner, remove the next two caps.

7. To remove the rear cap, rear main bearing bolt remover, special tool W-323 or its equivalent must be used.

8. Match mark the connecting rod caps and remove them.

9. Lift out the crankshaft.

10. Remove the braided seal from the inner groove of the cap and the neoprene seals from the outer grooves.

11. Using a center punch, drive the block seal out just far enough to grasp with a pliers and pull out.

12. Dip a new block seal in engine oil and force it into place in the block.

13. Insert the new braided cap seal into the groove in the cap and coat it with engine oil.

14. Cut the ends of the braided seals flush with the cap and block surfaces.

15. The new neoprene seals are installed after the cap is torqued in place. These seals are supposed to project about $\frac{1}{16}''$ (1.5875mm) above the cap. DO NOT CUT THESE SEALS FLUSH WITH THE CAP! Before installation, dip the neoprene seals in kerosene for about 1–2 minutes. After installation squirt some more kerosene on the protruding ends of the seals. Then, peen the ends of the seals with a hammer to make sure of a tight seal at the upper parting line between the cap and block.

16. Installation of the crankshaft and remaining parts is the reverse of removal. Torque the main cap bolts evenly, one side then the other, a little at a time until the torque value is reached.

NOTE: *Whenever the second cap is removed, the thrust surfaces must be aligned. To do this, pry the crankshaft back and forth several times throughout its end travel with the*

cap bolts of the second main cap only finger tight.

4–150

1. Remove the transmission.

2. Remove the flywheel.

3. Pry out the seal from around the crankshaft flange.

4. Coat the inner lip of the new seal with clean engine oil.

5. Gently tap the new seal into place, flush with the block, using a rubber or plastic mallet.

6. Install the flywheel.

7. Install the transmission.

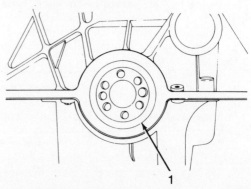

4-150 rear main seal. (1) indicates the actual seal around the crankshaft

4–151

NOTE: *The seal is a one piece unit that can be removed and installed without removing the oil pan or crankshaft.*

1. Raise and support the vehicle on jackstands.

2. Remove the transmission and transfer case as an assembly.

3. Disconnect and remove the starter.

4. On manual transmission vehicles, remove the flywheel inspection plate, and clutch slave cylinder.

5. Remove the flywheel or drive plate housing.

6. On manual transmission, remove the clutch assembly by backing out the bolts evenly around the pressure plate.

7. Remove the flywheel or drive plate. It is a good idea to match mark the flywheel location for assembly.

8. Using a small bladed screwdriver, pry the rear seal out from around the crankshaft hub. Be careful to avoid damaging the sealing groove or hub.

9. With a light hammer, tap the seal into position with the lip facing the front of the engine.

10. Install the flywheel or drive plate.

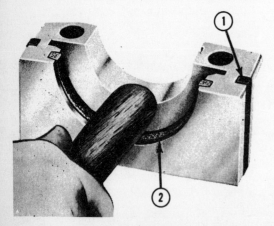

1. Neoprene seal
2. Fabric seal

Installing the V6-225 crankshaft rear oil seal

11. On manual transmission, install the clutch assembly by tightening the bolts evenly around the pressure plate.

12. Install the flywheel or drive plate housing.

13. On manual transmission vehicles, install the flywheel inspection plate, and clutch slave cylinder.

14. Install the starter.

15. Install the transmission and transfer case as an assembly.

6–232, 6–258, 8–304

This seal is a two piece neoprene type with a single lip.

1. Raise and support the vehicle on jackstands.

2. Remove the oil pan.

3. Remove the rear main bearing cap and discard the lower seal.

4. Loosen all remaining main bearing caps.

5. Using a center punch, carefully drive the upper half of the seal out of the block just far enough to graph with a pliers and pull out.

6. Remove the oil pan front and rear seals and the side gaskets.

7. Clean all gasket surfaces.

8. Wipe clean the sealing surface of the crankshaft and coat it lightly with engine oil.

9. Coat the lip of the upper seal with engine oil and install it in the block. The lip faces forward.

10. Coat both end tabs of the lower seal with RTV silicone sealer. Do not get any RTV sealer on the seal lip.

11. Coat the outer curved surface of the seal with liquid soap. Coat the seal lip with engine oil.

12. Install the seal into the cap, pressing firmly.

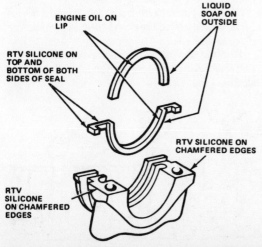

LIQUID SOAP ON OUTSIDE

ENGINE OIL ON LIP

RTV SILICONE ON TOP AND BOTTOM OF BOTH SIDES OF SEAL

RTV SILICONE ON CHAMFERED EDGES

RTV SILICONE ON CHAMFERED EDGES

Rear main seal installation for the 6-232, 6-258 and 8-304

13. Coat both chamferred edges of the cap with RTV sealer.

CAUTION: *Do not allow any RTV sealer to get on the mating surfaces of the cap or block as this will affect bearing clearance.*

14. Install the rear main cap.

15. Tighten all main bearing cap bolts gradually to 80 ft.lb.

16. Replace the oil pan.

Crankshaft

REMOVAL

L4–134, F4–134

1. Remove the engine from the vehicle.

2. Remove the fan, hub, timing cover, pulleys and timing gears from the engine.

3. Slide the thrust washers and adjusting shims from the front end of the crankshaft. Be careful to avoid losing or mismatching the washers and shims!

4. Remove the oil pan and pickup.

5. Pull the two pieces of the rear main cap packing out from the sides of the cap.

6. Note the match marks on the bearing caps and remove the nuts and washers from the cap dowels.

7. Using a pry bar under the ends of each main cap, carefully lift the caps off the dowels. Take great care to avoid damage to the caps or dowels, as bent dowels must be replaced.

8. Note the match marks on the connecting rod caps and remove the bearing caps from the rods.

9. Lift the crankshaft from the block.

4–151

1. Remove the engine and mount it on a work stand.

2. Remove the spark plugs.

3. Remove the fan and pulley.

4. Remove the vibration damper and hub.

5. Remove the oil pan and oil pump.

6. Remove the timing case cover.

7. Remove the crankshaft timing gear.

8. Remove the connecting rod bearing caps. Mark each for reassembly.

9. Remove the main bearing caps, marking each for reassembly.

10. Remove the crankshaft.

6–225

1. Remove the engine and mount it on a work stand.

2. Remove the flywheel.

3. Remove the fan and hub.

4. Remove the crankshaft pulley and vibration damper.

5. Remove the timing chain and sprocket.

6. Remove the oil pan, and pickup.

7. Remove the connecting rod caps, marking them for reassembly.

8. Mark the main bearing caps.

9. Remove the two bolts from the cap and carefully lift it off with the aid of a pry bar. Similarly remove the next two caps.

10. To remove the last cap, a special tool, main bearing bolt remover W-323 is necessary.

11. Lift the crankshaft from the block.

4–150, 6–232, 6–258 and 8–304

1. Remove the engine from the vehicle and mount it on a work stand.

2. Drain the oil.

3. Remove the flywheel or torque converter, match marking the pieces for installation.

4. Remove all drive belts.

5. Remove the fan and hub assembly.

6. Remove the crankshaft pulley and vibration damper.

7. Remove the timing case cover.

8. Remove the oil pan.

9. Remove the oil pump and pickup.

10. Remove the rod bearing caps, marking them for installation.

11. Remove the main bearing caps, marking them for installation.

12. Lift out the crankshaft.

NOTE: *A replacement oil pickup tube must be used. Do not attempt to install the original. Make sure the plastic button is inserted in the bottom of the pickup screen. Always use a new rear main seal. If new bearings are installed, check clearances with Plastigage®.*

INSPECTION

1. Check the crankshaft for wear or damage to the bearing surfaces of the journals. Crankshafts that are damaged can be reconditioned by a professional machine shop.

2. Using a dial indicator, check the crankshaft journal runout. Measure the crankshaft journals with a micrometer to determine the correct size rod and main bearings to be used. Whenever a new or reconditioned crankshaft is installed, new connecting rod bearings and main bearings should be installed.

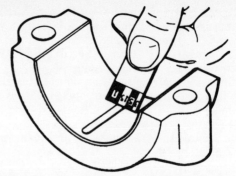

Checking main bearing oil clearance with Plastigage®

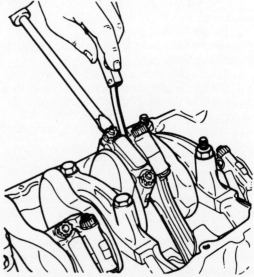

Checking rod side clearance with a flat feeler gauge. Use a small prybar to spread the rods

3. Clean all oil passages in the block (and crankshaft if it is being reused).

NOTE: *A new rear main seal should be installed any time the crankshaft is removed or replaced.*

4. Wipe the oil from the crankshaft journal and the outer and inner surfaces of the bearing shell.

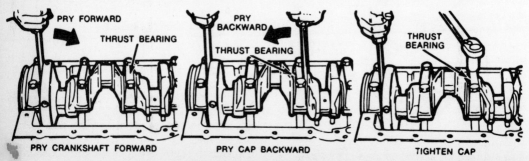

Crankshaft thrust bearing alignment

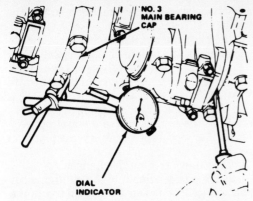

Checking crankshaft endplay with a dial indicator

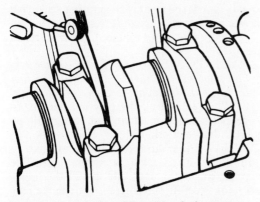

Checking crankshaft endplay with a feeler gauge

5. Place a piece of plastic gauging material in the center of the bearing.

6. Use a floor jack or other means to hold the crankshaft against the upper bearing shell. This is necessary to obtain accurate clearance readings when using plastic gauging material.

7. Install the bearing cap and bearing. Place engine oil on the cap bolts and install. Torque the bolts to specification.

8. Remove the bearing cap and determine the bearing clearance by comparing the width of the flattened plastic gauging material at its widest point with the graduations on the gauging material container. The number within the graduation on the envelope indicates the clearance in millimeters or thousandths of an inch. If the clearance is greater than allowed, REPLACE BOTH BEARING SHELLS AS A SET. Recheck the clearance after replacing the shells.

INSTALLATION

NOTE: *Main bearing clearances must be corrected by the use of selective upper and lower shells. UNDER NO CIRCUMSTANCES should the use of shims behind the shells to compensate for wear be attempted.*

1. Install new bearing upper halves in the block. If the crankshaft has been turned to resurface the journals, undersized bearing must be used to compensate. Lay the crankshaft in the block.

2. Install the lower bearing halves in the caps.

3. Use Plastigage® to check bearing fit.

4. When the bearings are properly fitted, install and torque the bearing caps.

5. Check crankshaft endplay to determine the need for thrust washers.

6. While you're at it, it's a good idea to replace the rear main seal at this time.

7. Install sufficient oil pan bolts in the block to align with the connecting rod bolts. Use rubber bands between the bolts to position the connecting rods as required. Connecting rod position can be adjusted by increasing the tension on the rubber bands with additional turns around the pan bolts or thread protectors.

8. Position the upper half of main bearings in the block and lubricate them with engine oil.

9. Position crankshaft keyway in the same position as removed and lower it into block. The connecting rods will follow the crank pins into the correct position as the crankshaft is lowered.

10. Lubricate the thrust flanges with clean engine oil or engine rebuilding oil. Install caps with the lower half of the bearings lubricated with engine oil. Lubricate the cap bolts with engine oil and install, but do not tighten.

11. With a block of wood, bump the shaft in each direction to align the thrust flanges of the main bearing. After bumping the shaft in each direction, wedge the shaft to the front and hold it while torquing the thrust bearing cap bolts.

NOTE: *In order to prevent the possibility of cylinder block and/or main bearing cap damage, the main bearing caps are to be tapped into their cylinder block cavity using a wood or rubber mallet before the bolts are installed. Do not use attaching bolts to pull the main bearing caps into their seats. Failure to observe this information may damage the cylinder block or a bearing cap.*

12. Torque all main bearing caps to specification. Check crankshaft endplay, using a flat feeler gauge.

13. Remove the connecting rod bolt thread protectors and lubricate the connecting rod bearings with engine oil.

14. Install the connecting rod bearing caps in their original position. Torque the nuts to specification.

15. Install all parts in reverse order of removal. See related procedures in this chapter for component installation.

Flywheel/Flex Plate and Ring Gear

NOTE: *Flex plate is the term for a flywheel mated with an automatic transmission.*

REMOVAL AND INSTALLATION

All Engines

NOTE: *The ring gear is replaceable only on engines mated with a manual transmission. Engine with automatic transmissions have ring gears which are welded to the flex plate.*

1. Remove the transmission and transfer case.

2. Remove the clutch, if equipped, or torque converter from the flywheel. The flywheel bolts should be loosened a little at a time in a cross pattern to avoid warping the flywheel. On Jeep vehicles with manual transmission, replace the pilot bearing in the end of the crankshaft if removing the flywheel.

3. The flywheel should be checked for cracks and glazing. It can be resurfaced by a machine shop.

4. If the ring gear is to be replaced, drill a hole in the gear between two teeth, being careful not to contact the flywheel surface. Using a cold chisel at this point, crack the ring gear and remove it.

6. Polish the inner surface of the new ring gear and heat it in an oven to about 600°F (316°C). Quickly place the ring gear on the flywheel and tap it into place, making sure that it is fully seated.

NOTE: *Never heat the ring gear past 800°F (426°C), or the tempering will be destroyed.*

7. Position the flywheel on the end of the crankshaft. Torque the bolts a little at a time, in a cross pattern, to the torque figure shown in the Torque Specifications Chart.

8. Install the clutch or torque converter.

9. Install the transmission and transfer case.

EXHAUST SYSTEM

CAUTION: *When working on exhaust systems, ALWAYS wear protective goggles! Avoid working on a hot exhaust system!*

Muffler

REMOVAL AND INSTALLATION

NOTE: *The following applies to exhaust systems using clamped joints. Most later model, original equipment systems use welded joints at the muffler. These joints will, of course, have to be cut.*

1. Raise and support the rear end on jackstands, placed under the frame, so that the axle hangs freely.

2. Remove the muffler clamps.

3. Remove the tailpipe hanger clamp.

4. Spray the joint liberally with a penetrant/rust dissolver compound such as Liquid Wrench®, WD-40®, or equivalent.

5. If the tailpipe cannot be pulled or twisted free from the muffler, drive a chisel between the muffler and tailpipe at several places to free it.

6. Disconnect the muffler hanger.

7. If the pipe leading into the muffler is not to be replaced, and cannot be pulled free of the muffler, heat the joint with an oxyacetylene torch until it is cherry red. Place a block of wood against the front of the muffler and drive it rearward to disengage it from the pipe.

If the pipe is being replaced, use a chisel to free it.

CAUTION: *When using a torch, make certain that no combustibles or brake or fuel lines are in the immediate area of the torch.*

8. When installing the new muffler, make sure that the locator slot and tab at the tailpipe joint index each other.

9. Drive the muffler onto the front pipe.

10. Position the system, without muffler clamps, under the Jeep and install the hangers. Make certain that there is sufficient clearance between the system components and the floor pan and axle. Then, install the muffler clamps and tighten the hangers.

NOTE: *Install the muffler clamps so that the shafts of the U-bolts covers the slots in the joint flanges.*

Front Exhaust Pipe (Head Pipe)

REMOVAL AND INSTALLATION

1. Raise and support the front end on jackstands.

2. Disconnect any oxygen sensor wires or air injection pipes.

3. Disconnect the front pipe at the manifold(s).

4. Disconnect the rear end of the pipe from the muffler or catalytic converter.

5. Installation is the reverse of removal. Torque the pipe-to-manifold nuts to 17 ft.lb. on 4-cylinder engines, or 20 ft.lb. on the 6- and 8-cylinder engines. Make sure the pipe is properly aligned.

Rear Exhaust Pipe or Tailpipe

REMOVAL AND INSTALLATION

NOTE: *Some vehicle use an intermediate pipe, also called a rear exhaust pipe. This pipe connects the front pipe with the muffler, or runs between the converter and muffler.*

1. Raise and support the rear end on jackstands.

2. If just the intermediate pipe is being replaced, cut it at the joints and collapse and remove the remainder from the front pipe and muffler or converter. If adjoining parts are also being replaced, the pipe may be chiseled off.

3. If just the tailpipe is being replaced, cut it just behind the muffler and collapse and remove the remainder from the muffler flange. Remove the tailpipe hanger.

4. When installing any pipe, position it in the system and make sure that it is properly aligned and has sufficient clearance at the floor pan. Position U-bolts so that the bolt shafts cover any slots in the pipe flanges. When the system is correctly aligned, tighten all U-bolts and hangers.

Catalytic Converter

REMOVAL AND INSTALLATION

1. Raise and support the rear end on jackstands.

2. Disconnect the downstream air injection tube at the converter.

3. On the 4-cylinder engine, the front pipe is bolted to the converter at a facing flange. On the 6- and 8-cylinder engines, the front pipe and converter are clamped together at a slip-fit joint. On all engines, the rear joint of the converter is a slip-fit.

4. To avoid damaging any components, it will probably be necessary to heat any slip-fit joint with an oxyacetylene torch, until the joint is cherry red. Then, place a block of wood against the converter and drive it off of the pipe.

CAUTION: *When using a torch, make certain that no combustibles or brake or fuel lines are in the immediate area of the torch.*

5. Position the replacement converter in the system and install the rear clamp. Hand tighten the nuts.

6. On 4-cylinder engines: bolt the flanges together at the front end. Tighten the bolts to 25 ft.lb. Tighten the rear clamp nuts to 45 ft.lb.

7. On 6- and 8-cylinder engines, install the front clamp, make sure that the converter is properly positioned and tighten the front and rear clamp nuts to 45 ft.lb.

8. Install the downstream air injection tube and tighten the clamps to 36–48 in.lb.

9. Lower the Jeep.

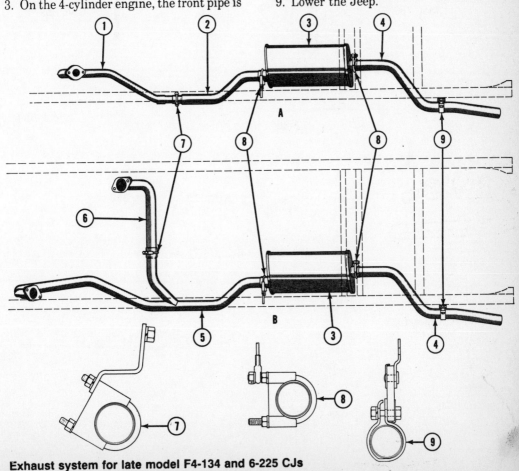

Exhaust system for late model F4-134 and 6-225 CJs

SPECIAL TOOLS

 B.Vi. 28-01

 Mot. 521-01

 J-22248

 Mot. 582

 Mot. 251-01

 J-9163

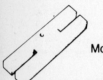 Mot. 252-01

 Mot. 788

 Mot. 853

 Mot. 789

 Mot. 851

 B.Vi. 859

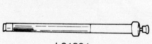 J-21884

 Mot. 854

 J-29114

 Mot. 852

Mot. 861

 Mot. LM

 Mot. 855

Emission Controls and Fuel System

4

EMISSION CONTROLS

There are three types of automotive pollutants: crankcase fumes, exhaust gases and gasoline evaporation. The equipment that is used to limit these pollutants is commonly called emission control equipment.

Crankcase Emission Controls

The crankcase emission control equipment consists of a positive crankcase ventilation valve (PCV), a closed or open oil filler cap and hoses to connect this equipment.

When the engine is running, a small portion of the gases which are formed in the combustion chamber during combustion, leak by the piston rings and enter the crankcase. Since these gases are under pressure, they tend to escape from the crankcase and enter the atmosphere. If these gases were allowed to remain in the the crankcase for any length of time, they would contaminate the engine oil and cause sludge to build up. If the gases were allowed to escape into the atmosphere, they would pollute the air, as they contain unburned hydrocarbons. The crankcase emission control equipment recycles these gases back into the engine combustion chamber where they are burned.

Emission Control Systems Usage

System	Application
Positive Crankcase Ventilation	1965 and later gasoline engines
Air injection	1965 and later gasoline engines
Thermostatically controlled air cleaner	All 1971 and later engines
Transmission controlled spark (TCS)	All AMC engines
Exhaust Gas Recirculation (EGR)	All 1971 and later engines
Evaporative emission control canister	All 1971 and later engines
Catalytic Converter	1979 and later gasoline engines
Vacuum throttle modulation	1979 and later gasoline engines

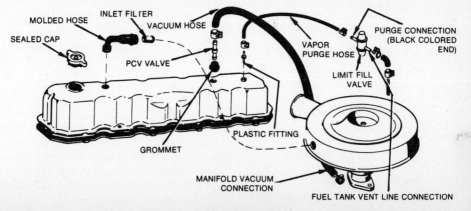

Typical PCV system

Crankcase gases are recycled in the following manner: while the engine is running, clean filtered air is drawn into the crankcase either directly through the oil filler cap, or through the carburetor air filter and then through a hose leading to the oil filler cap. As the air passes through the crankcase, it picks up the combustion gases and carries them out of the crankcase, up through the PCV valve and into the intake manifold. After they enter the intake manifold, they are drawn into the combustion chamber and burned.

The most critical component in the system is the PCV valve. This vacuum controlled valve regulates the amount of gases which are recycled into the combustion chamber. At low engine speeds, the valve is partially closed, limiting the flow of gases into the intake manifold. As engine speed increases, the valve opens to admit greater quantities of the gases into the intake manifold. If the valve should become blocked or plugged, the gases will be prevented from escaping from the crankcases by the normal route. Since these gases are under pressure, they will find their own way out of the crankcase. This alternate route is usually a weak oil seal or gasket in the engine. As the gas escapes by the gasket, it also creates an oil leak. Besides causing oil leaks, a clogged PCV valve also allows these gases to remain in the crankcase for an extended period of time, promoting the formation of sludge in the engine.

The above explanation and the troubleshooting procedure which follows applies to all engines with PCV systems.

TROUBLESHOOTING

With the engine running, pull the PCV valve and hose from the engine. Block off the end of the valve with your finger. The engine speed should drop at least 50 rpm when the end of the valve is blocked. If the engine speed does not drop at least 50 rpm, then the valve is defective and should be replaced.

REMOVAL AND INSTALLATION

1. Pull the PCV valve and hose from the engine.
2. Remove the PCV valve from the hose. Inspect the inside of the PCV valve from the hose. If it is dirty, disconnect if from the intake manifold and clean it.
3. If the PCV valve hose was removed, connect it to the intake manifold.
4. Connect the PCV valve to its hose.
5. Install the PCV valve on the engine.

Exhaust Emission Controls

All of the gasoline engines used in these Jeep vehicles, except the 6–226, have, at one time or another, incorporated the air injection system for controlling the emission of exhaust gases into the atmosphere. Since this type of emission control system is common to most of the engines, it will be explained here.

The exhaust emission air injection system consists of a belt driven air pump which directs compressed air through connecting hoses to a steel distribution manifold into stainless steel injection tubes in the exhaust port adjacent to each exhaust valve. The air, with its normal oxygen content, reacts with the hot, but incompletely burned exhaust gases and permits further combustion in the exhaust port or manifold.

AIR PUMP

The air injection pump is a positive displacement vane type which is permanently lubricated and requires little periodic maintenance. The only serviceable parts on the air pump are the filter, exhaust tube, and relief valve. The relief valve relieves the air flow when the pump pressure reaches a preset level. This occurs at high engine rpm. This serves to prevent damage to the pump and to limit maximum exhaust manifold temperatures.

Pump Air Filter

The air filter attached to the pump is a replaceable element type. The filter should be replaced every 12,000 miles under normal conditions and sooner under off-road use. Some models draw their air supply through the carburetor air filter.

Air Delivery Manifold

The air delivery manifold distributes the air from the pump to each of the air delivery tubes in a uniform manner. A check valve is integral with the air delivery manifold. Its function is to prevent the reverse flow of exhaust gases to the pump should the pump fail. This reverse flow would damage the air pump and connecting hose.

Air Injection Tubes

The air injection tubes are inserted into the exhaust ports. The tubes project into the exhaust ports, directing air into the vicinity of the exhaust valve.

Anti-Backfire Valve

The anti-backfire diverter valve prevents engine backfire by briefly interrupting the air being injected into the exhaust manifold during periods of deceleration or rapid throttle closure. On the 4–134 and all of the 1971 and later American Motors engines, the valve opens when a sudden increase in manifold vacuum

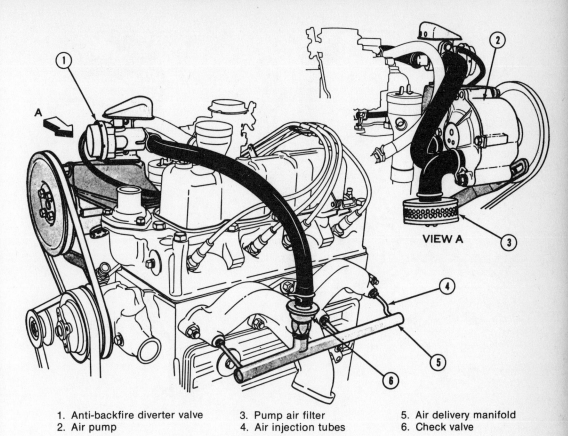

1. Anti-backfire diverter valve
2. Air pump
3. Pump air filter
4. Air injection tubes
5. Air delivery manifold
6. Check valve

F-head air pump system

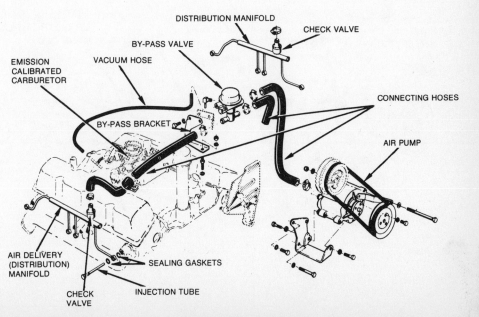

Typical V8 air pump system

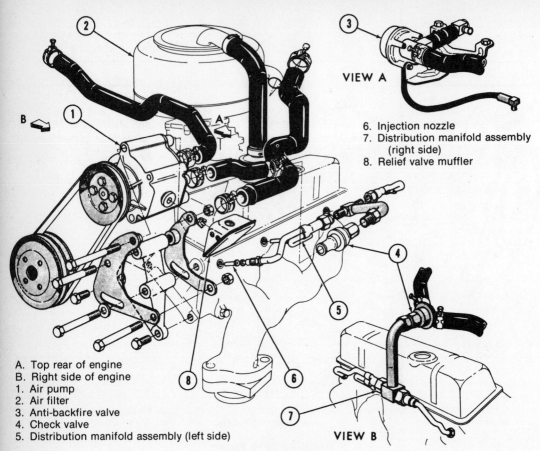

6. Injection nozzle
7. Distribution manifold assembly (right side)
8. Relief valve muffler

A. Top rear of engine
B. Right side of engine
1. Air pump
2. Air filter
3. Anti-backfire valve
4. Check valve
5. Distribution manifold assembly (left side)

VIEW A

VIEW B

V6 air pump system

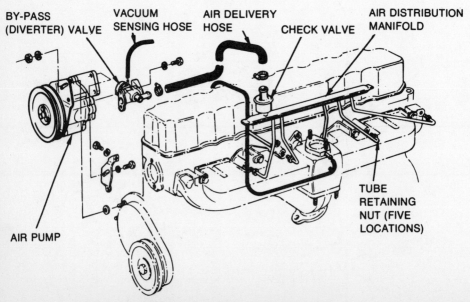

BY-PASS (DIVERTER) VALVE

VACUUM SENSING HOSE

AIR DELIVERY HOSE

CHECK VALVE

AIR DISTRIBUTION MANIFOLD

TUBE RETAINING NUT (FIVE LOCATIONS)

AIR PUMP

Air injection system, 1971 and later in-line six

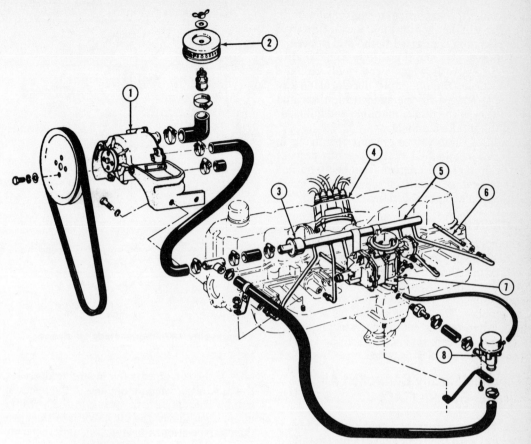

1. Air pump
2. Filter
3. Check valve
4. Distributor (special calibration)
5. Air delivery distribution manifold
6. Air injection tube(s)
7. Carburetor (special calibration)
8. Anti-backfire (gulp) valve

Air injection system: 1966–70 6-232

4-150 AIR diverter valve and manifold   **4-150 AIR pump mounting**

overcomes the diaphragm spring tension. With the valve in the open position, the air flow from the air pump is directed to the atmosphere.

On the 6–225 and the 1972 6–232, the anti-backfire valve is what is commonly called a gulp valve. During rapid deceleration the valve is opened by the sudden high vacuum condition in the intake manifold and gulps air into the intake manifold.

Both of these valves prevent backfiring in the exhaust manifold. Both valves also prevent an over right fuel mixture from being burned in the exhaust manifold, which would cause backfiring and possible damage to the engine.

Carburetor

The carburetors used on engines equipped with emission controls have specific flow characteristics that differ from the carburetors used on vehicles not equipped with emission control devices. The carburetors are identified by number. The correct carburetor should be used when replacement is necessary.

A carburetor dashpot is used on the 4–134 to control throttle closing speed.

Thermostatically Controlled Air Cleaner System (TAC)

This system consists of a heat shroud which is integral with the right side exhaust manifold, a hot air hose and a special air cleaner assembly equipped with a thermal sensor and a vacuum motor and air valve assembly.

The thermal sensor incorporates an air bleed valve which regulates the amount of vacuum applied to the vacuum motor, controlling the air valve position to supply either heated air from the exhaust manifold or air from the engine compartment.

During the warm-up period when underhood temperatures are low, the air bleed valve is closed and sufficient vacuum is applied to the vacuum motor to hold the air valve in the closed (heat on) position.

As the temperature of the air entering the air cleaner approaches approximately 115°F

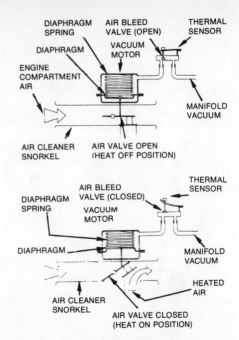

Vacuum controlled thermostatic air cleaner

(46°C), the air bleed valve opens to decrease the amount of vacuum applied to the vacuum motor. The diaphragm spring in the vacuum motor then moves the air valve into the open (heat off) position, allowing only underhood air to enter the air cleaner.

The air valve in the air cleaner will also open, regardless of air temperature, during heavy acceleration to obtain maximum air flow through the air cleaner.

Transmission Controlled Spark System

The purpose of this system is to reduce the emission of oxides of nitrogen by lowering the peak combustion pressure and temperature during the power stroke.

The system incorporates the following components:

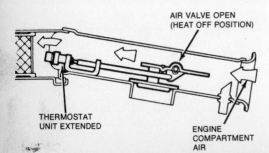
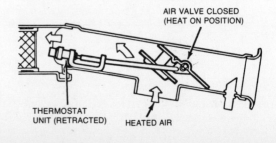

Non-vacuum thermostatically controlled air cleaner

Emission Controlled Distributor Vacuum Application Chart for Vehicles Equipped with TCS

Manual Transmission Gear		Automatic Transmission Vehicle Speed (mph)	Ambient Temperature Deg. F	Coolant Temperature Deg. F	Vacuum Applied to Distributor
3-sp	4-sp				
1–2	1–2–3	Under 25	Below 63	Below 160	Manifold
1–2	1–2–3	Under 25	Below 63	Above 160	Ported
1–2	1–2–3	Under 25	Above 63	Above 160	None
1–2	1–2–3	Under 25	Above 63	Below 160	Manifold
3	4	25–30	Below 63	Below 160	Manifold
3	4	25–30	Below 63	Above 160	Ported
3	4	25–30	Above 63	Above 160	Ported
3	4	25–30	Above 63	Below 160	Manifold

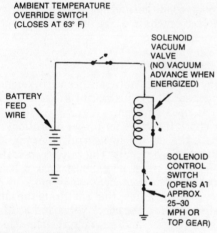

TCS electrical diagram

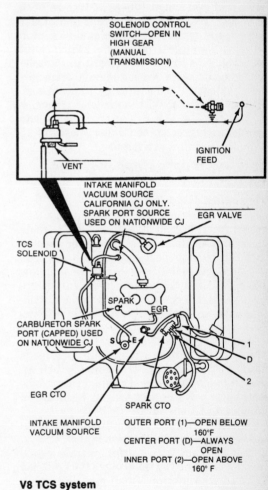

V8 TCS system

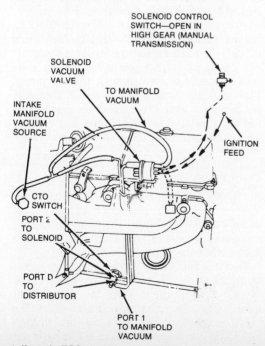

Inline six TCS system

AMBIENT TEMPERATURE OVERRIDE SWITCH

This switch, located at the firewall, senses ambient temperatures and completes the electrical circuit from the battery to the solenoid vacuum valve when the ambient temperatures are above 63°F (17°C).

SOLENOID VACUUM VALVE

This valve is attached to the ignition coil bracket at the right side of the engine (V8 engines) or to a bracket at the rear of the intake manifold (Sixes). When the valve is energized, carburetor vacuum is blocked off and the distributor vacuum line is vented to the atmosphere through a port in the valve, resulting in no vacuum advance. When the valve is deenergized, vacuum is applied to the distributor resulting in normal vacuum advance.

SOLENOID CONTROL SWITCH

This switch is located in the transmission valve body. It opens or closes in relation to car speed and gear range. When the transmission is in high gear, the switch opens and breaks the ground circuit to the solenoid vacuum valve. In lower gear ranges the switch closes and completes the ground circuit to the solenoid vacuum valve. With a manual transmission, the switch is operated by the transmission shifter shaft. With automatic transmissions, the switch is controlled by the speedometer gear speed. Under speeds of 25 mph, the switch is activated.

COOLANT TEMPERATURE OVERRIDE SWITCH

This switch is used only on the 8-304. It is threaded into the thermostat housing. The switch reacts to coolant temperatures to route either intake manifold or carburetor vacuum to the distributor vacuum advance diaphragm.

When the coolant temperature is below 160°F (71°C), intake manifold vacuum is applied through a hose connection to the distributor advance diaphragm, resulting in full vacuum advance.

When the coolant temperature is above 160°F (71°C), intake manifold vacuum is blocked off and carburetor vacuum is then applied through the solenoid vacuum valve to the distributor advance diaphragm, resulting in decreased vacuum advance.

The relationship between distributor vacuum advance and the operation of the TCS system and coolant temperature override switch can be determined by referring to the Emission Control Distributor Vacuum Application Charts.

MAINTENANCE AND SERVICE

Efficient performance of the exhaust emission control system is dependent upon precise maintenance.

Carburetor

Check the carburetor for the proper application. Check the dashpot for proper operation and adjust as required. When the throttle is released quickly, the arm of the dashpot should fully extend itself and should catch the throttle lever, letting it back to idle position gradually.

Proper idle mixture adjustment is imperative for best exhaust emission control. The idle adjustment should be made with the engine at normal operating temperature and the air cleaner in place. All lights and accessories must be turned off and the transmission must be in neutral. See the tune-up chapter for adjustment procedures.

Distributor

Check the distributor number for proper application. Check the distributor cam dwell angle and point condition and adjust to specifications or replace as required. See the tune-up chapter for procedures.

Anti-Backfire Diverter Valve

On the 4-134, the anti-backfire valve remains open except when the throttle is closed rapidly from an open position.

To check the valve for proper operation, accelerate the engine in neutral, allowing the throttle to close rapidly. The valve is operating satisfactorily when no exhaust system backfire occurs. A further check can be made by removing the large hose that runs from the anti-backfire valve to the check valve and accelerating the engine and allowing the throttle to close rapidly. If there is an audible momentary interruption of the flow of air, then it can be assumed that the valve is working correctly.

To check the valve on a 6-225 or 1972 6-232, listen for backfire when the throttle is released quickly. If none exists, the valve is doing its job. To check further, remove the large hose that connects the valve with the air pump. Place a finger over the open end of the hose, not the valve, and accelerate the engine, allowing the throttle to close rapidly. The valve is operating satisfactorily if there is a momentary audible rush of air.

Check Valve

The check valve in the air distribution manifold prevents the reverse flow of exhaust gases to the pump in the event the pump should become inoperative or should exhaust pressure ever exceed the pump pressure.

To check this valve for proper operation, remove the air supply hose from the pump at the distribution manifold. With the engine running, listen for exhaust leakage where the check valve is connected to the distribution manifold. If leakage is audible, the valve is not operating correctly.

Air Pump

Check for the proper drive belt tension and adjust as necessary. Do not pry on the die cast pump housing. Check to see if the pump is discharging air. Remove the air outlet hose at the pump. With the engine running, air should be felt at the pump outlet opening.

REMOVAL AND INSTALLATION

Air Pump

1. Loosen the air pump adjusting bracket bolts.
2. Remove the drive belt.
3. Remove the air pump intake and discharge hoses.
4. Remove the air pump from the engine.
5. To install, reverse the above procedure.

Anti-Backfire Valve

To remove the anti-backfire valve, disconnect the hoses and bracket-to-engine attaching screws. Install in the reverse order of removal.

Air Distribution Manifold and Air Injection Tubes

It is necessary to remove the exhaust manifold only on the 4–134 prior to removing the air distribution manifold and the air injection tubes. On all the other engines, these components can be removed with the manifolds on the engine.

1. Disconnect the air delivery hose from the air injection manifold. Remove the exhaust manifold on the 4–134.
2. Remove the air distribution manifold from the air injection tubes on the 4–134 only.
3. Unscrew the air injection tube from the exhaust manifold or the head. Some resistance may be encountered because of the normal buildup of carbon. The application of heat may be helpful in removing the air injection tubes.
4. Install in the reverse order of removal.
NOTE: *There are two lengths of tubes used with the 4–134. The shorter tubes are installed in number 1 and 4 cylinders. The air injection tubes must be installed on the exhaust manifold prior to installing the exhaust manifold on the engine.*

Exhaust Gas Recirculation (EGR) System

The EGR system consists of a diaphragm actuated flow control valve (EGR valve), coolant temperature override switch, low temperature vacuum signal modulator, high temperature vacuum signal modulator.

All 1977 and later California units have a back pressure sensor which modulates EGR signal vacuum according to the rise or fall of exhaust pressure in the manifold. A restrictor plate is not used in these applications.

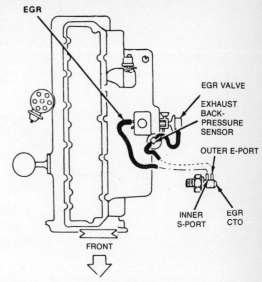

1974–79 six cylinder EGR system

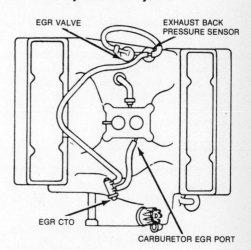

1974-79 8-304 EGR system

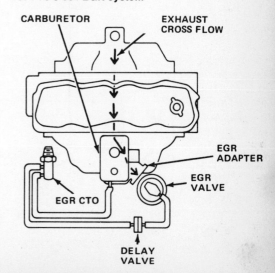

4-151 EGR system

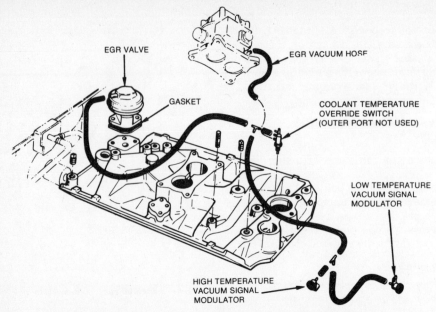

1973 V8 EGR system. The modulator isn't used on later models

The purpose of the EGR system is to limit the formation of nitrogen oxides by diluting the fresh air intake charge with a metered amount of exhaust gas, thereby reducing the peak temperatures of the burning gases in the combustion chambers.

EGR VALVE

The EGR valve is mounted on a machined surface at the rear of the intake manifold on the V8s and on the side of the intake manifold on the sixes.

The valve is held in a normally closed position by a coil spring located above the dia-phragm. A special fitting is provided at the carburetor to route ported (above the throttle plates) vacuum through hose connections to a fitting located above the diaphragm on the valve. A passage in the intake manifold directs exhaust gas from the exhaust crossover passage (V8) or from below the riser area (Sixes) to the EGR valve. When the diaphragm is actuated by vacuum, the valve opens and meters exhaust gas through another passage in the intake manifold to the floor of the intake manifold below the carburetor.

COOLANT TEMPERATURE OVERRIDE SWITCH

This switch is located in the intake manifold at the coolant passage adjacent to the oil filler tube on the V8s or at the left side of the engine

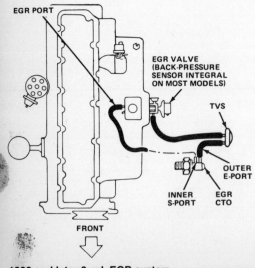

1980 and later 6-cyl. EGR system

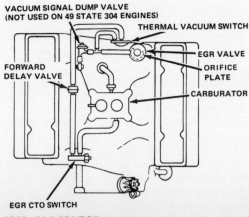

1980–81 8-304 EGR system

block (formerly the drain plug) on the Sixes. The outer port of the switch is open and not used. The inner port is connected by a host to the EGR fitting at the carburetor. The center port is connected to the EGR valve. When coolant temperature is below 115°F (46°C) (160°F [71°C] on the 8–304 with manual transmission), the center port of the switch is closed and no vacuum signal is applied to the EGR valve. Therefore, no exhaust gas will flow through the valve. When the coolant temperature reaches 115°F (46°C), both the center port and the inner port of the switch are open and a vacuum signal is applied to the EGR valve. This vacuum signal is, however, subject to regulation by the low and high temperature signal modulators.

LOW TEMPERATURE VACUUM SIGNAL MODULATOR

This unit is located just to the right of the radiator behind the grill opening. The low temperature vacuum signal modulator vacuum hose is connected by a plastic T-fitting to the EGR vacuum signal hose. The modulator is open when ambient temperatures are below 60°F (16°C). This causes a weakened vacuum signal to the EGR valve and a resultant decrease in the amount of exhaust gas being recirculated.

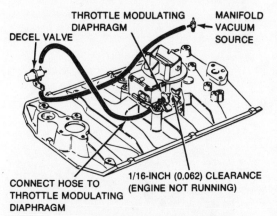

THROTTLE MODULATING DIAPHRAGM   MANIFOLD VACUUM SOURCE

DECEL VALVE

CONNECT HOSE TO THROTTLE MODULATING DIAPHRAGM

1/16-INCH (0.062) CLEARANCE (ENGINE NOT RUNNING)

Typical vacuum throttle modulating system

HIGH TEMPERATURE VACUUM SIGNAL MODULATOR

This unit is located at the right front fender inner panel. The high temperature vacuum signal modulator is connected to the EGR vacuum signal hose by a plastic T-fitting. The modulator opens when the underhood air temperatures reach 115°F (46°C) and it causes a weakened vacuum signal to the EGR valve, thus reducing the amount of exhaust gases being recirculated.

Electric Assist Choke

An electric assist choke is used to more accurately match the choke operation to engine requirements. It provides extra heat to the choke bimetal spring to speed up the choke valve opening after the underhood air temperature reaches 95°F ± 15°F (35°C). Its purpose is to reduce the emission of carbon monoxide (CO) during the engine's warmup period.

A special AC terminal is provided at the alternator to supply a 7 volt power source for the electric choke. A thermostatic switch within the choke cover closes when the underhood air temperature reaches 95°F ± 15°F (35°C) and allows current to flow to a ceramic heating element. The circuit is completed through the choke cover ground strap and choke housing to the engine. As the heating element warms up, heat is absorbed by an attached metal plate which in turn heats the coke bimetal spring.

After the engine is turned off, the thermostatic switch remains closed until the underhood temperature drops below approximately 65°F (18°C). Therefore, the heating element will immediately begin warming up when the engine is restarted, if the underhood temperature is above 65°F (18°C).

Fuel Tank Vapor Emission Control System

A closed fuel tank system is used on some models through 1974, some models 1975–78, and all 1979 models, to route raw fuel vapor from the fuel tank into the PCV system (sixes) or air cleaner snorkle (V8s), where it is burned along with the fuel-air mixture. The system prevents raw fuel vapors from entering the atmosphere.

The fuel vapor system consists of internal fuel tank venting, a vacuum-pressure fuel tank filler cap, an expansion tank or charcoal filled canister, liquid limit fill valve, and internal carburetor venting.

Fuel vapor pressure in the fuel tank forces the vapor through vent lines to the expansion tank or charcoal filled storage canister. The vapor then travels through a single vent line to the limit fill valve, which regulates the vapor flow to the valve cover or air cleaner.

The fuel tank vent line is routed through the limit fill valve to the valve cover on the left side on the 1972 V8s. On the 1973 Sixes, it travels to the intake manifold and on the V8s it is routed to the carburetor air cleaner.

LIMIT FILL VALVE

This valve is essentially a combination vapor flow regulator and pressure relief valve. It regulates vapor flow from the fuel tank vent line

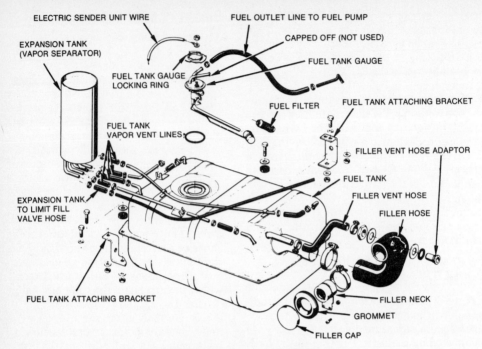

1972–73 fuel tank and vent lines

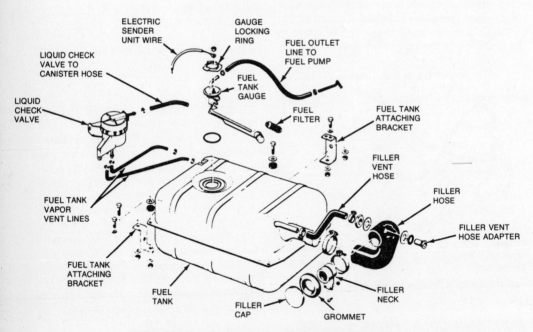

1974–78 fuel tank and vapor emission control system

into the valve cover. The valve consists of a housing, a spring loaded diaphragm and a diaphragm cover. As tank vent pressure increases, the diaphragm lifts, permitting vapor to flow through. The pressure at which this occurs is 4–6 in.H_2O column. This action regulates the flow of vapors under severe conditions, but generally prohibits the flow of vapor during normal temperature operation, thus minimizing driveability problems.

LIQUID CHECK VALVE

The liquid check valve prevents liquid fuel from entering the vapor lines leading to the storage canister. The check valve incorporates a float and needle valve assembly. If liquid fuel

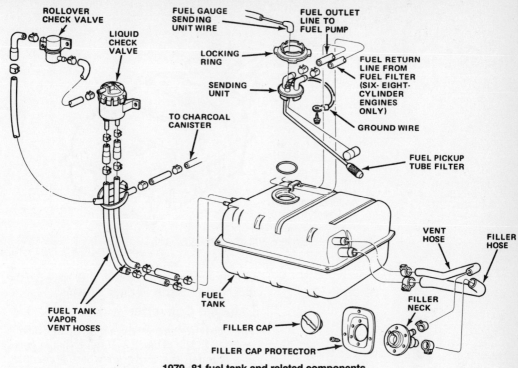

1979–81 fuel tank and related components

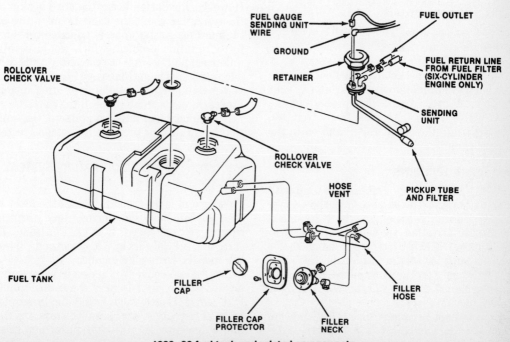

1982–86 fuel tank and related components

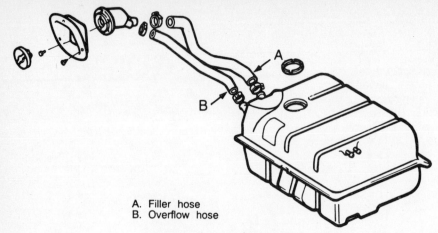

A. Filler hose
B. Overflow hose

1987 fuel tank and filler lines

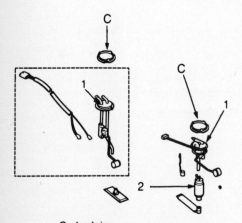

C. Lockring
1. Pick-up unit and float
2. Fuel pump

1987 fuel sending units. The 6-258 unit is in the dotted box

should enter the check valve, the float will rise and force the needle upward to close the vent passage. With no liquid fuel present in the check valve, fuel vapors pass freely from the tank, through the check valve, and on to the storage canister.

Feedback Systems

Two different feedback systems are used with 1981 and later Jeep vehicles. One, the C4 system is used with 4-151 engines built for sale in California. The other, the Computerized Emission Control (CEC) System is used on 6-258 engines built for sale in California. Each system is designed for the same purpose, to reduce exhaust emission using a Three-Way Catalytic Converter (TWC).

Each system is computerized, utilizing microprocessors, and each is highly complex, requiring professional service. Therefore, no ser-

vice procedures are given in this book for the diagnosis or repair of these systems.

Catalytic Converter

The catalytic converter is a muffler like device inserted in the exhaust system. Exhaust gases flow through the converter where a chemical change takes place, reducing carbon monoxide and hydrocarbons to carbon dioxide and water; the latter two elements being harmless. The catalysts promoting this reaction are platinum and palladium coated beads of alumina. Because of the chemical reaction which does take place in the converter, the temperature of the converter during operation is higher than the exhaust gases when they leave the engine. However, insulation keeps the outside skin of the converter about the same temperature as the muffler. An improperly adjusted carburetor or ignition problem which would permit unburned fuel to enter the converter could produce excessive heat. Excessive heat in the converter could result in bulging or other distortion of the converter's shape. If the converter is heat damaged and must be replaced, the ignition or carburetor problem must be corrected for.

Vacuum Throttle Modulating System (VTM)

This system is designed to reduce the level of hydrocarbon emission during rapid throttle closure at high speed. It is used on some 49 state and all California Wagoneer and Cherokee models, with a V8 engine.

The system consists of a deceleration valve located at the right front of the intake manifold, and a throttle modulating diaphragm located at the carburetor base. The valve and the diaphragm are connected by a vacuum hose and the valve is connected to direct manifold vacuum. During deceleration, manifold vacuum acts to delay, slightly, the closing of the throttle plate.

To adjust:

1. Run the engine to normal operating temperature and set the idle speed to specification. Shut off the engine.

2. Position the throttle lever against the curb idle adjusting screw.

3. Measure the clearance between the throttle modulating diaphragm plunger and the throttle lever. A clearance of $\frac{1}{16}''$ (1.5875mm) should exist.

4. Adjust the clearance, if necessary, by loosening the jam nut and turning the diaphragm assembly.

Choke Heat By-Pass Valve (CHBPV) 1976 and Later V8

When the engine is first started and begins to warm up, heated air from the exhaust crossover passage in the intake manifold is routed through a heat tube to the choke housing containing the thermostatic spring for regulating the choke flap. A thermostatic by-pass valve, which is integral with the choke heat tube, helps prevent premature choke valve opening during the early part of the warmup period. This is important when ambient temperatures are relatively low and adverse driveability could occur if the choke was opened too soon.

The thermostatic by-pass valve regulates the temperature of the hot airflow to the choke housing by allowing outside unheated air to enter the heat tube. A thermostatic disc in the valve is calibrated to close the valve at 75°F (24°C) and open it at 55°F (13°C).

Fuel Return System

The purpose of the fuel return system is to reduce high temperature fuel vapor problems. The system consists of a fuel return line to the fuel tank and special fuel filter with an extra outlet nipple to which the return line is connected. During normal operation, a small amount of fuel is returned to the fuel tank. During periods of high underhood temperatures, vaporized fuel in the fuel line is returned to the fuel tank and not passed through the carburetor.

NOTE: *The extra nipple on the special fuel filter should be positioned upward to ensure proper operation of the system.*

Emission Control Checks

ANTI-BACKFIRE DIVERTER VALVE

On the F4–134, the anti-backfire valve remains open except when the throttle is closed rapidly from an open position.

To check the valve for proper operation, accelerate the engine in neutral, allowing the throttle to close rapidly. The valve is operating satisfactorily when no exhaust system backfire occurs. A further check can be made by removing the large hose that runs from the anti-backfire valve to the check valve and accelerating the engine and allowing the throttle to close rapidly. If there is an audible momentary interruption of the flow of air then it can be assumed that the valve is working correctly.

To check the valve on a V6, listen for backfire when the throttle is released quickly. If none exists, the valve is doing its job. To check further, remove the large hose that connects the valve with the air pump. Place a finger over the open end of the hose, not the valve, and accelerate the engine, allowing the throttle to close rapidly. The valve is operating satisfactorily if there is a momentary audible rush of air.

To check the diverter valve on American Motors engines, start the engine and let it idle. With the engine idling, there should be little or no air coming out the vents. When the engine is accelerated to 2,000–3,000 rpm, a strong flow of air should be felt at the vents. If the flow of air from the air pump is not diverted through the diverter valve vents when the engine is accelerated to the above mentioned rpm, check and make sure that the vacuum sensing line leading to the valve has vacuum and is not leaking or disconnected. The diverter valve should bleed air when 20 in.Hg or more vacuum is applied to the vacuum sensing line or when the output of the air pump exceeds 5 psi. When the engine is slowly accelerated, the diverter valve should begin to bleed off air between 2,500 and 3,500 rpm.

CHECK VALVE

The check valve in the air distribution manifold prevents the reverse flow of exhaust gases to the pump in the event the pump should become inoperative or should exhaust pressure ever exceed the pump pressure.

To check this valve for proper operation, remove the air supply hose from the pump at the distribution manifold. With the engine running, listen for exhaust leakage where the check valve is connected to the distribution manifold. If leakage is audible, the valve is not operating correctly. A small amount of leakage is normal.

AIR PUMP

Check for the proper drive belt tension and adjust as necessary. Do not pry on the die cast pump housing. Check to see if the pump is discharging air. Remove the air outlet hose at the pump. With the engine running, air should be felt at the pump outlet opening.

EGR VALVE

With the engine idling and at normal operating temperature, manually depress the EGR valve diaphragm. This should cause engine speed to drop about 200 rpm. This indicates that the EGR valve had been properly cutting off the flow of exhaust gas at idle and is operating properly.

If the engine speed did not change and the idle is smooth, exhaust gases are not reaching the combustion chambers. The probable cause of this is a plugged passage between the EGR valve and the intake manifold.

If the engine idle is rough and rpm is not affected by depressing the EGR valve diaphragm, the EGR valve is not closing off the flow of exhaust at idle like it's supposed to and there is most likely a fault in the hoses, hose routing, or the EGR valve itself.

NOTE: *The EGR valve can be removed and cleaned with a wire brush and a* $^9/_{16}$*" (14.2875mm) drill bit coated with grease (to hold dirt particles) inserted in discharge passage. The drill should be held with a pair of pliers only.*

EGR CTO SWITCH

Before checking the operating of the EGR CTO switch, make sure that the engine coolant is below 100°F (38°C).

1. Check the vacuum lines for leaks and proper routing.
2. Disconnect the vacuum lines at the backpressure sensor, if so equipped, or at the EGR valve, and connect the line to a vacuum gauge.
3. Operate the engine at 1,500 rpm. No vacuum should be indicated at the gauge. If vacuum is indicated, replace the EGR CTO switch.
4. Allow the engine to idle until the coolant temperature exceeds 115°F (46°C).
5. Accelerate the engine to 1,500 rpm. Vacuum should be present at the gauge. If not, replace the EGR CTO switch.

EXHAUST BPS UNIT

1. Make sure that all the EGR vacuum lines are routed correctly and are not leaking.
2. Install a "T" in the vacuum line between the EGR valve and BPS, and attach a vacuum gauge to the "T".
3. Start the engine and allow it to idle. No vacuum should be present. If vacuum is indicated at idle speed, make sure of correct line connections. Also, be sure that manifold vacuum is not the source. If the carburetor is providing the vacuum, look for a partially open

throttle plate which could cause premature ported vacuum to the BPS unit.

4. Accelerate the engine to 2,000 rpm and observe the vacuum gauge for the following:
   a. If the coolant is below 115°F (46°C), no vacuum should be present.
   b. With coolant temperature above 115°F (46°C), ported vacuum should be indicated.
   c. If no vacuum is indicated at any time, make sure that vacuum is being applied to the inlet side of the BPS. If correct, remove the BPS and either clean it with a wire brush (if blocked) or replace it.

SPARK CTO SWITCH

Before testing the spark CTO switch, make sure that the engine coolant temperature is below 160°F (71°C).

1. Remove all the hoses from the CTO switch and plug those which will create a vacuum leak.
2. Connect a vacuum line from a manifold vacuum source to the top port of the CTO switch.
3. Connect a vacuum gauge to the center port.
4. Start the engine. Manifold vacuum should be indicated on the gauge. If not, replace the switch.
5. With the engine still running and the coolant temperature still below 160°F (71°C), disconnect the vacuum line from the top port and connect it to the bottom port.
6. No vacuum should be indicated. Replace the switch if there is vacuum.
7. Allow the engine to run until the coolant temperature exceeds 160°F (71°C). Manifold vacuum should be indicated. If not, replace the CTO switch.
8. Disconnect the hose from the bottom port and connect it to the top port again. With the coolant temperature above 160°F (71°C), no vacuum should be indicated. If there is, replace the CTO switch.

TVS FUNCTIONAL TEST

1. Allow the air cleaner to cool to between 40 and 50°F (4½–10°C).
2. Disconnect the vacuum hoses from the TVS and connect an external vacuum source to one nipple and a vacuum gauge to the other.
3. Apply vacuum to the TVS. Vacuum should not be present when the air temperature is 40–50°F (4½–10°C). If vacuum is present, replace the switch.
4. Start the engine and allow the air cleaner to warm above 50°F (10°C). Vacuum should be present.

CARBURETED FUEL SYSTEM

Fuel Pump

REMOVAL AND INSTALLATION

All Engines

1. Disconnect the inlet and outlet fuel lines, and any vacuum lines.
2. Remove the two fuel pump body attaching nuts and lockwashers.
3. Pull the pump and gasket, or O-ring, free of the engine. Make sure that the mating surfaces of the fuel pump and the engine are clean.
4. Cement a new gasket to the mounting flange of the fuel pump.
5. Position the fuel pump on the engine block so that the lever of the fuel pump rests on the fuel pump cam of the camshaft.
6. Secure the fuel pump to the block with the two cap screws and lock washers.
7. Connect the intake and outlet fuel lines to the fuel pump, and any vacuum lines.

FUEL PUMP TESTING

Volume Check

Disconnect the fuel line from the carburetor. Place the open end in a suitable container.

Start the engine and operate it at normal idle speed. The pump should deliver at least one pint in 30 seconds.

Pressure Check

Disconnect the fuel line at the carburetor. Disconnect the fuel return line from the fuel filter if so equipped, and plug the nipple on the filter. Install a T-fitting on the open end of the fuel line and refit the line to the carburetor. Plug a pressure gauge into the remaining opening of the T-fitting. The hose leading to the pressure gauge should not be any longer than 6 inches. Start the engine and let it run at idle speed. Bleed any air out of the hose between the gauge and the T-fitting. On pumps with a fuel return line, the line must be plugged. Start the engine. Fuel pressures are as follows:

4–134: 2.50–3.75psi @ 1,800 rpm
4–150: 4.00–5.00psi @ idle
4–151: 6.5–8.0psi @ idle
6–225: 3.75psi minimum @ 600 rpm
6–226: 3.50–5.50psi @ 1,800 rpm
6–230: 3.50–5.50psi @ 600 rpm
6–232: 3.00–5.00psi @ idle
6–258: 3.00–5.00psi @ idle
8–304: 4.00–6.00psi @ idle

Troubleshooting Basic Fuel System Problems

Problem	Cause	Solution
Engine cranks, but won't start (or is hard to start) when cold	• Empty fuel tank • Incorrect starting procedure • Defective fuel pump • No fuel in carburetor • Clogged fuel filter • Engine flooded • Defective choke	• Check for fuel in tank • Follow correct procedure • Check pump output • Check for fuel in the carburetor • Replace fuel filter • Wait 15 minutes; try again • Check choke plate
Engine cranks, but is hard to start (or does not start) when hot— (presence of fuel is assumed)	• Defective choke	• Check choke plate
Rough idle or engine runs rough	• Dirt or moisture in fuel • Clogged air filter • Faulty fuel pump	• Replace fuel filter • Replace air filter • Check fuel pump output
Engine stalls or hesitates on acceleration	• Dirt or moisture in the fuel • Dirty carburetor • Defective fuel pump • Incorrect float level, defective accelerator pump	• Replace fuel filter • Clean the carburetor • Check fuel pump output • Check carburetor
Poor gas mileage	• Clogged air filter • Dirty carburetor • Defective choke, faulty carburetor adjustment	• Replace air filter • Clean carburetor • Check carburetor
Engine is flooded (won't start accompanied by smell of raw fuel)	• Improperly adjusted choke or carburetor	• Wait 15 minutes and try again, without pumping gas pedal • If it won't start, check carburetor

Carburetor Specification Charts

Carter BBD

Engine	Years	Float Level Dry (in.)	Step-Up Piston Gap (in.)	Fast Idle Cam Setting (in.)	Fast Idle rpm	Choke Unloader (in.)	Initial Choke Valve Clearance (in.)	Automatic Choke Setting
6-258	1977–78	1/4	3/64	3/32	1,700	9/64	1/8	2 rich
	1979	1/4	1/32	①	②	9/32	③	1 rich
	1980	1/4	1/32	④	⑤	9/32	⑥	⑦
	1981	1/4	1/32	3/32	⑤	9/32	9/64	1 rich
	1982	1/4	1/32	⑧	1,700	9/32	5/32	1 rich
	1983–84	1/4	1/32	3/32	⑤	9/32	5/32	1 rich
	1985–87	1/4	1/32	3/32	⑤	9/32	9/64	TR

TR: Tamper Resistant
① Except High Altitude: 7/64
  High Altitude: 3/64
② Man. Trans.: 1,500
  Auto. Trans.: 1,600
③ Man. Trans., except High Altitude: 0.140
  Man. Trans., High Altitude: 0.128
  Auto. Trans.: 0.150
④ Except High Altitude: 3/32
  High Altitude: 5/64

⑤ Man. Trans.: 1,700
  Auto. Trans.: 1,850
⑥ Except High Altitude: 0.140
  High Altitude: 0.116
⑦ Except High Altitude: 2 rich
  High Altitude: 1 rich
⑧ Auto. Trans.: 7/64
  Man. Trans.: 5/32

Carter WCD

Engine	Years	Float Level (in.)	Float Drop (in.)	Dashpot Setting (in.)	Fast Idle (in.)	Choke Unloader (in.)	Initial Choke Clearance (in.)	Automatic Choke Setting
6-226	All	3/16	—	—	0.04	1/8	—	Index

Carter YF

Engine	Years	Float Level (in.)	Float Drop (in.)	Dashpot Setting (in.)	Fast Idle (in.)	Choke Unloader (in.)	Initial Choke Clearance (in.)	Automatic Choke Setting
-134	1945–64	5/16	—	—	1,500	—	—	—
	1966–71	29/64	1 1/4	3/32	1,600	19/64	15/64	Notch
6-232, 6-258	1972–73	19/64	1 1/4	3/32	1,800	9/32	7/32	1 rich
6-258	1974	31/64	1 25/64	3/32	1,600	9/32	7/32	1 rich
	1975	31/64	1 25/64	5/64	1,600	9/32	7/32	1 rich
	1976	31/64	1 3/8	5/64	1,600	9/32	7/32	1 rich

Carter YFA

Engine	Years	Float Level (in.)	Choke Valve Clearance (in.)	Fast Idle Cam Setting (in.)	Choke Unloader (in.)	Fast Idle Speed rpm	Automatic Choke Setting
4-150	1984	39/64	15/64	11/64	15/64	2,000 MT 2,300 AT	TR
	1985	39/64	9/32	11/64	15/64	2,000 MT 2,300 AT	TR

MT: Manual Transmission
AT: Automatic Transmission
TR: Tamper Resistant

Rochester 2G

Engine	Years	Float Level (in.)	Fast Float Drop (in.)	Idle Speed rpm	Choke Unloader (in.)	Initial Choke Valve Clearance (in.)
6-225	1966–68	1 5/32	1 7/8	1,800	1/32	1/4
	1969–71	1 5/32	1 7/8	1,800	3/64	1/4

Rochester 2GV

Engine	Years	Float Level (in.)	Fast Float Drop (in.)	Idle Speed rpm	Choke Unloader (in.)	Initial Choke Valve Clearance (in.)
6-225	1966–68	1 5/32	1 7/8	1,800	1/32	1/4

Rochester 2SE/E2SE

Engine	Years	Float Level (in.)	Choke Coil Lever (in.(	Fast Idle Cam Clearance (in.)	Choke Vacuum Break (in.) Primary	Secondary	Choke Unloader (in.)	Air Valve Valve Rod (deg.)
4-151	1980–83	①	5/64	1/8	9/64	②	17/64	2

① 2SE/E2SE Man. Trans. and Calif.: 13/64
2SE Auto. Trans.: 1/4 E2SE Auto. Trans.: 13/64
② Man. Trans.: 3/64–5/64
  Auto Trans.: 5/64

Autolite/Motorcraft 2100

Engine	Years	Float Level Dry (in.)	Float Level Wet (in.)	Dashpot Setting (in.)	Fast Idle rpm	Choke Unloader (in.)	Initial Choke Valve Clearance (in.)	Automatic Choke Setting
8-304	1972–75	2/5	25/32	9/64	2,200	①	0.013	2 rich

① 1972–73: 1/4
   1974–75: 9/32

Motorcraft 2150

Engine	Years	Float Level Dry (in.)	Float Level Wet (in.)	Fast Idle Cam Setting (in.)	Fast Idle rpm	Choke Unloader (in.)	Initial Choke Valve Clearance (in.)	Automatic Choke Setting
8-304	1976–79	17/39	59/64	①	②	9/32	7/64	②
	1980–81	11/32	59/64	5/64	②	1/3	7/64	②

① Man. Trans.: 0.086
   Auto. Trans.: 0.093
② Man. Trans., except Calif.: 2 rich
   Calif. and Auto. Trans.: 1 rich

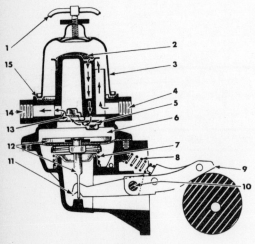

1. Strainer bail and seat
2. Filtering screen
3. Bowl
4. Fuel inlet
5. Inlet valve
6. Pump chamber
7. Diaphragm spring
8. Rocker arm spring
9. Rocker arm
10. Rocker arm pin
11. Rocker arm link
12. Diaphragm and pull rod
13. Outlet valve
14. Fuel outlet
15. Body screw

L4-134 fuel pump

1. Fuel outlet   2. Vapor return   3. Fuel inlet

Non-serviceable V6 fuel pump

Carburetors

REMOVAL AND INSTALLATION

All Engines

To remove the carburetor from any engine, first remove the air cleaner from the top of the carburetor. Remove all lines and hoses, noting their positions to facilitate installation. Remove all throttle and choke linkage at the carburetor. Remove the carburetor attaching nuts

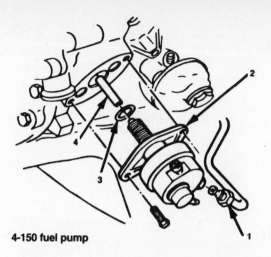

4-150 fuel pump

which hold it to the intake manifold. Lift the carburetor from the engine along with the carburetor base gasket. Discard the gasket. Install the carburetor in the reverse order of removal, using a new base gasket. To avoid any distortion of the carburetor body, always tighten the nuts alternately, in a criss-cross pattern to about 15 ft.lb.

OVERHAUL

Efficient carburetion depends greatly on careful cleaning and inspection during overhaul, since dirt, gum, water, or varnish in or on the carburetor parts are often responsible for poor performance.

Overhaul your carburetor in a clean, dust-free area. Carefully disassemble the carburetor, referring often to the exploded views. Keep all similar and look-alike parts segregated during disassembly and cleaning to avoid accidental interchange during assembly. Make a note of all jet sizes.

When the carburetor is disassemble, wash all parts (except diaphragms, electric choke units, pump plunger, and any other plastic, leather, fiber or rubber parts) in clean carburetor solvent. Do not leave parts in the solvent any longer than is necessary to sufficiently loosen the deposits. Excessive cleaning may remove the special finish from the float bowl and choke valve bodies, leaving these parts unfit for service. Rinse all parts in clean solvent and blow them dry with compressed air or allow them to air dry. Wipe clean all cork, plastic, leather and fiber parts with a clean, lint-free cloth.

Blow out all passages and jets with compressed air and be sure that there are not restrictions or blockages. Never use wire or similar tools to clean jets, fuel passages, or air

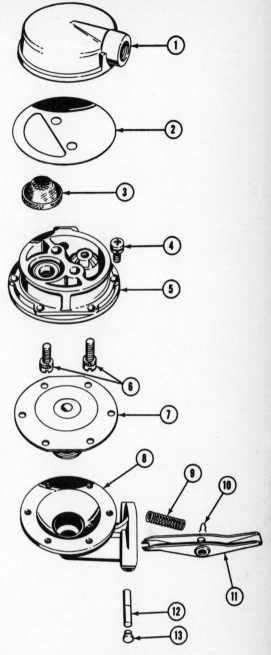

1. Housing cover
2. Air dome diaphragm
3. Strainer
4. Screw and washer
5. Housing
6. Cover screw and lockwashers
7. Main diaphragm
8. Pump body
9. Cam lever return spring
10. Pin retainer
11. Cam lever
12. Cam lever pin
13. Lever seal shaft plug

F-head fuel pump used with electric wipers

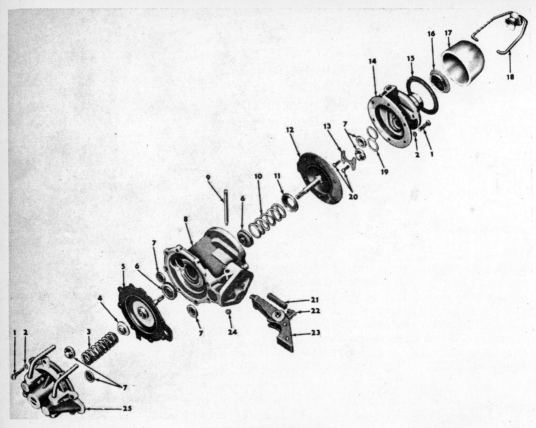

1. Cover screw	10. Fuel diaphragm	19. Gasket
2. Lockwasher	11. Oil seal retainer	20. Screw
3. Diaphragm spring	12. Diaphragm and rod	21. Rocker arm spring
4. Spring seat	13. Valve retainer	22. Link spacer
5. Diaphragm and rod	14. Cover	23. Rocker arm
6. Oil seal	15. Gasket	24. Washer
7. Valve assembly	16. Screen	25. Body
8. Body	17. Bowl	
9. Rocker arm pin spring	18. Bail	

4-134 combined fuel and vacuum pump

bleeds. Clean all jets and valves separately to avoid accidental interchange.

Check all parts for wear or damage. If wear or damage is found, replace the defective parts. Especially check the following:

1. Check the float needle and seat for wear. If wear is found, replace the complete assembly.

2. Check the float hinge pin for wear and the float(s) for dents or distortion. Replace the float if fuel has leaked into it.

3. Check the throttle and choke shaft bores for wear or an out-of-round condition. Damage or wear to the throttle arm, shaft, or shaft bore will often require replacement of the throttle body. These parts require a close tolerance of fit. Wear may allow air leakage, which could affect starting and idling.

NOTE: *Throttle shafts and bushings are not included in overhaul kits. They can be purchased separately.*

4. Inspect the idle mixture adjusting needles for burrs or grooves. Any such condition requires replacement of the needle, since you will not be able to obtain a satisfactory idle.

5. Test the accelerator pump check valves. They should pass air one way but not the other. Test for proper seating by blowing and sucking on the valve. Replace the valve if necessary. If the valve is satisfactory, wash the valve again to remove breath moisture.

6. Check the bowl cover for warped surfaces with a straightedge.

7. Closely inspect the valves and seats for wear and damage, replacing as necessary.

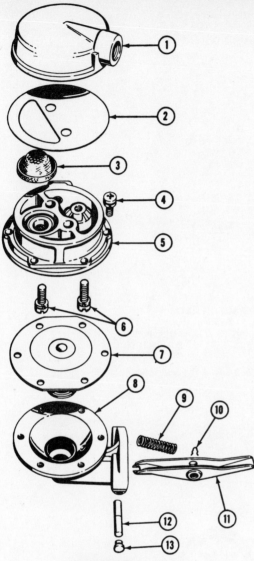

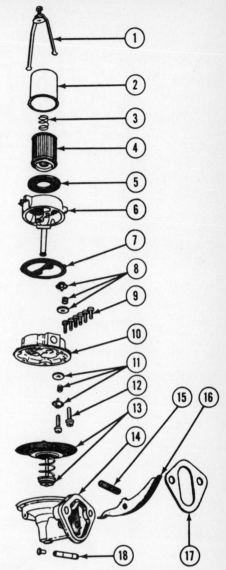

1. Housing cover
2. Air dome diaphragm
3. Strainer
4. Screw and washer
5. Housing
6. Cover screw and lockwasher
7. Main diaphragm
8. Pump body
9. Cam lever return spring
10. Pin retainer
11. Cam lever
12. Cam lever pin
13. Lever seal shaft plug

6-230 fuel pump

1. Ball	10. Valve housing
2. Bowl	11. Valve assembly
3. Spring	12. Screws
4. Filter	13. Diaphragm and oil seal
5. Gasket	14. Pump body
6. Pump body	15. Cam lever spring
7. Gasket	16. Cam lever
8. Valve assembly	17. Gasket
9. Screws	18. Cam lever pin and plug

1966–70 6-232 fuel pump, used on some 4-134 engines

8. After the carburetor is assembled, check the choke valve for freedom of operation.

Carburetor overhaul kits are recommended for each overhaul. These kits contain all gaskets and new parts to replace those that deteriorate most rapidly. Failure to replace all parts

supplied with the kit (especially gaskets) can result in poor performance later.

Carburetor manufacturers supply overhaul kits of three basic types: minor repair, major repair, and gasket kits. Basically, they contain the following:

Minor Repair Kits
• All gaskets

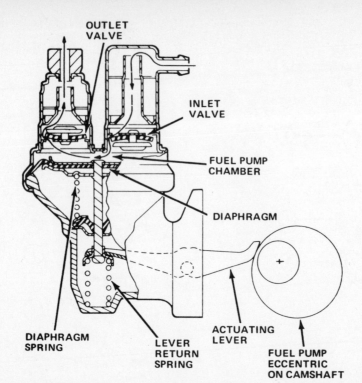

OUTLET
VALVE

INLET
VALVE

FUEL PUMP
CHAMBER

DIAPHRAGM

DIAPHRAGM
SPRING

LEVER
RETURN
SPRING

ACTUATING
LEVER

FUEL PUMP
ECCENTRIC
ON CAMSHAFT

Fuel pump used on late model 6-232 and all 6-258, 8-304, 4-151 and 1984–86 4-150 engines

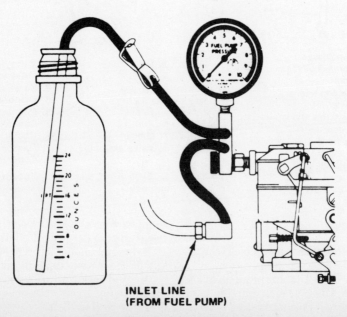

INLET LINE
(FROM FUEL PUMP)

Fuel pump pressure and volume test

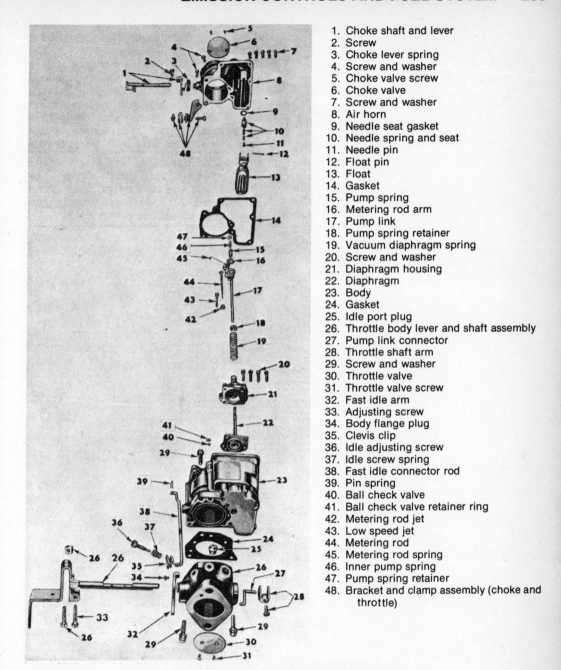

1. Choke shaft and lever
2. Screw
3. Choke lever spring
4. Screw and washer
5. Choke valve screw
6. Choke valve
7. Screw and washer
8. Air horn
9. Needle seat gasket
10. Needle spring and seat
11. Needle pin
12. Float pin
13. Float
14. Gasket
15. Pump spring
16. Metering rod arm
17. Pump link
18. Pump spring retainer
19. Vacuum diaphragm spring
20. Screw and washer
21. Diaphragm housing
22. Diaphragm
23. Body
24. Gasket
25. Idle port plug
26. Throttle body lever and shaft assembly
27. Pump link connector
28. Throttle shaft arm
29. Screw and washer
30. Throttle valve
31. Throttle valve screw
32. Fast idle arm
33. Adjusting screw
34. Body flange plug
35. Clevis clip
36. Idle adjusting screw
37. Idle screw spring
38. Fast idle connector rod
39. Pin spring
40. Ball check valve
41. Ball check valve retainer ring
42. Metering rod jet
43. Low speed jet
44. Metering rod
45. Metering rod spring
46. Inner pump spring
47. Pump spring retainer
48. Bracket and clamp assembly (choke and throttle)

Carter YF carburetor used on the 4-134 engine

- Float needle valve
- Volume control screw
- All diaphragms
- Spring for the pump diaphragm
Major Repair Kits
- All jets and gaskets
- All diaphragms
- Float needle valve
- Volume control screw
- Pump ball valve
- Main jet carrier

- Float
- Complete intermediate rod
- Intermediate pump lever
- Complete injector tube
- Some cover holddown screws and washers
Gasket Kits
- All gaskets

After cleaning and checking all components, reassemble the carburetor, using new parts and referring to the exploded view. When reassembling, make sure that all screws and jets

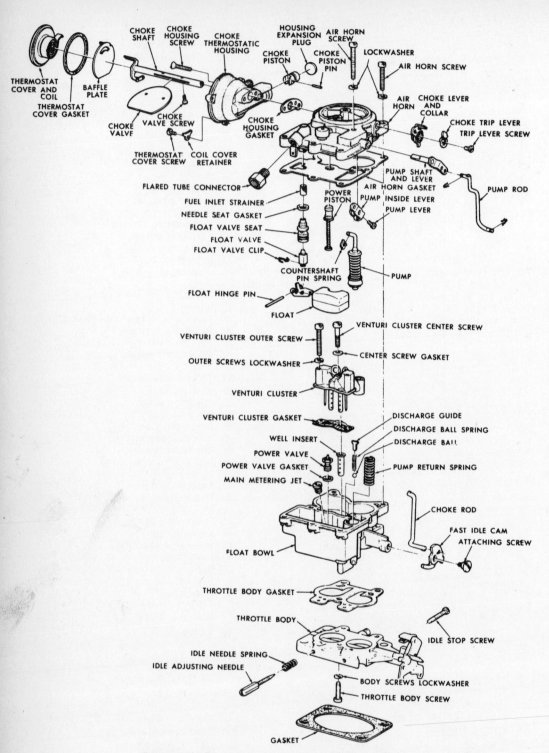

Rochester 2GC carburetor used on V6-225 engines

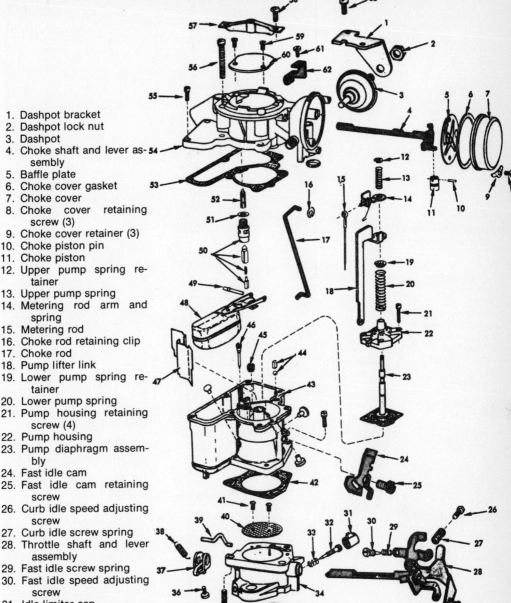

1. Dashpot bracket
2. Dashpot lock nut
3. Dashpot
4. Choke shaft and lever assembly
5. Baffle plate
6. Choke cover gasket
7. Choke cover
8. Choke cover retaining screw (3)
9. Choke cover retainer (3)
10. Choke piston pin
11. Choke piston
12. Upper pump spring retainer
13. Upper pump spring
14. Metering rod arm and spring
15. Metering rod
16. Choke rod retaining clip
17. Choke rod
18. Pump lifter link
19. Lower pump spring retainer
20. Lower pump spring
21. Pump housing retaining screw (4)
22. Pump housing
23. Pump diaphragm assembly
24. Fast idle cam
25. Fast idle cam retaining screw
26. Curb idle speed adjusting screw
27. Curb idle screw spring
28. Throttle shaft and lever assembly
29. Fast idle screw spring
30. Fast idle speed adjusting screw
31. Idle limiter cap
32. Idle mixture screw
33. Idle mixture screw spring
34. Throttle body
35. Throttle body retaining screw (3)
36. Throttle shaft arm set screw
37. Throttle shaft arm
38. Throttle shaft return spring
39. Pump connector link
40. Throttle valve
41. Throttle valve retaining screw (2)
42. Throttle body gasket
43. Main body

44. Pump discharge check ball and weight
45. Metering rod jet
46. Low speed jet
47. Fuel bowl baffle
48. Float and lever assembly
49. Float pin
50. Needle and seat assembly
51. Needle seat gasket
52. Screen
53. Air horn gasket
54. Air horn
55. Short air horn retaining screw (3)

56. Long air horn retaining screw (3)
57. Air cleaner bracket
58. Air cleaner bracket retaining screw (2)
59. Choke valve retaining screw (2)
60. Choke valve
61. Choke lever retaining screw
62. Choke lever
63. Dashpot bracket retaining screw

Carter YF carburetor used on 6-232, 258 engines

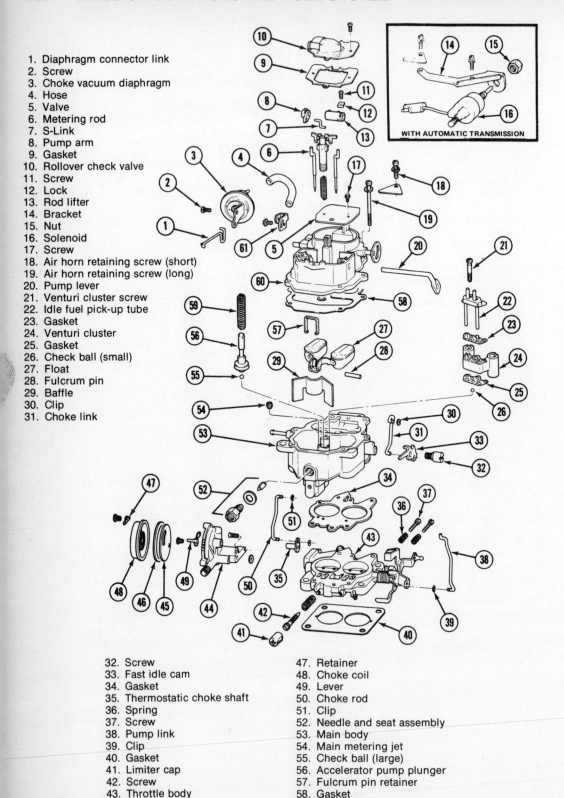

1. Diaphragm connector link
2. Screw
3. Choke vacuum diaphragm
4. Hose
5. Valve
6. Metering rod
7. S-Link
8. Pump arm
9. Gasket
10. Rollover check valve
11. Screw
12. Lock
13. Rod lifter
14. Bracket
15. Nut
16. Solenoid
17. Screw
18. Air horn retaining screw (short)
19. Air horn retaining screw (long)
20. Pump lever
21. Venturi cluster screw
22. Idle fuel pick-up tube
23. Gasket
24. Venturi cluster
25. Gasket
26. Check ball (small)
27. Float
28. Fulcrum pin
29. Baffle
30. Clip
31. Choke link

WITH AUTOMATIC TRANSMISSION

32. Screw
33. Fast idle cam
34. Gasket
35. Thermostatic choke shaft
36. Spring
37. Screw
38. Pump link
39. Clip
40. Gasket
41. Limiter cap
42. Screw
43. Throttle body
44. Choke housing
45. Baffle
46. Gasket

47. Retainer
48. Choke coil
49. Lever
50. Choke rod
51. Clip
52. Needle and seat assembly
53. Main body
54. Main metering jet
55. Check ball (large)
56. Accelerator pump plunger
57. Fulcrum pin retainer
58. Gasket
59. Spring
60. Air horn
61. Lever

Carter BBD used on the 6-258 through 1983

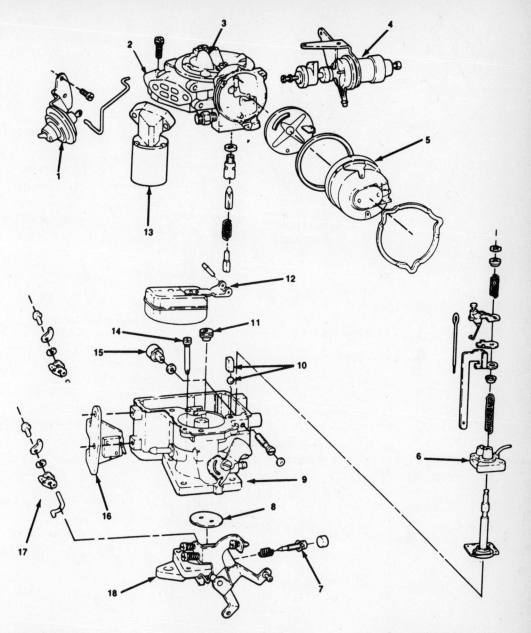

1. Vacuum break
2. Air horn
3. Choke plate
4. Sole-vac throttle positioner
5. Choke assembly
6. Accelerator pump assembly
7. Idle mixture screw with O-ring
8. Throttle plate
9. Main body
10. Accelerator pump check ball and weight
11. Main metering jet
12. Float assembly
13. Mixture control solenoid
14. Low speed jet
15. Accelerator pump vent valve
16. Wide open throttle (WOT) switch
17. Throttle shaft and lever
18. Throttle body

Carter YFA

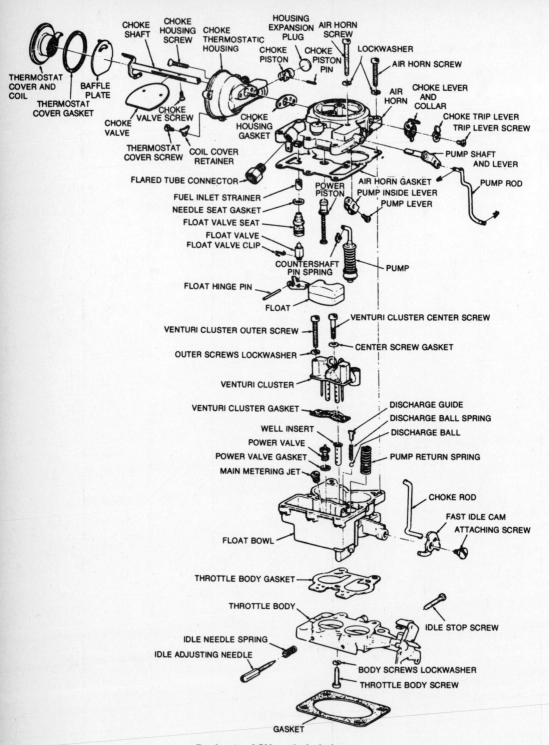

Rochester 2GV exploded view

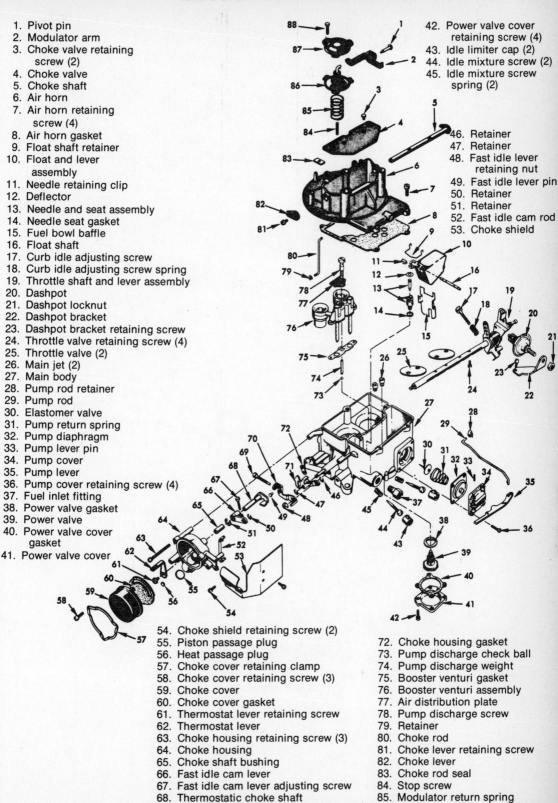

1. Pivot pin
2. Modulator arm
3. Choke valve retaining screw (2)
4. Choke valve
5. Choke shaft
6. Air horn
7. Air horn retaining screw (4)
8. Air horn gasket
9. Float shaft retainer
10. Float and lever assembly
11. Needle retaining clip
12. Deflector
13. Needle and seat assembly
14. Needle seat gasket
15. Fuel bowl baffle
16. Float shaft
17. Curb idle adjusting screw
18. Curb idle adjusting screw spring
19. Throttle shaft and lever assembly
20. Dashpot
21. Dashpot locknut
22. Dashpot bracket
23. Dashpot bracket retaining screw
24. Throttle valve retaining screw (4)
25. Throttle valve (2)
26. Main jet (2)
27. Main body
28. Pump rod retainer
29. Pump rod
30. Elastomer valve
31. Pump return spring
32. Pump diaphragm
33. Pump lever pin
34. Pump cover
35. Pump lever
36. Pump cover retaining screw (4)
37. Fuel inlet fitting
38. Power valve gasket
39. Power valve
40. Power valve cover gasket
41. Power valve cover

42. Power valve cover retaining screw (4)
43. Idle limiter cap (2)
44. Idle mixture screw (2)
45. Idle mixture screw spring (2)
46. Retainer
47. Retainer
48. Fast idle lever retaining nut
49. Fast idle lever pin
50. Retainer
51. Retainer
52. Fast idle cam rod
53. Choke shield

54. Choke shield retaining screw (2)
55. Piston passage plug
56. Heat passage plug
57. Choke cover retaining clamp
58. Choke cover retaining screw (3)
59. Choke cover
60. Choke cover gasket
61. Thermostat lever retaining screw
62. Thermostat lever
63. Choke housing retaining screw (3)
64. Choke housing
65. Choke shaft bushing
66. Fast idle cam lever
67. Fast idle cam lever adjusting screw
68. Thermostatic choke shaft
69. Fast idle speed adjusting screw
70. Fast idle lever
71. Fast idle cam

72. Choke housing gasket
73. Pump discharge check ball
74. Pump discharge weight
75. Booster venturi gasket
76. Booster venturi assembly
77. Air distribution plate
78. Pump discharge screw
79. Retainer
80. Choke rod
81. Choke lever retaining screw
82. Choke lever
83. Choke rod seal
84. Stop screw
85. Modulator return spring
86. Modulator diaphragm assembly
87. Modulator cover
88. Modulator retaining screw (3)

Autolite 2100 carburetor used on 8-304 engines

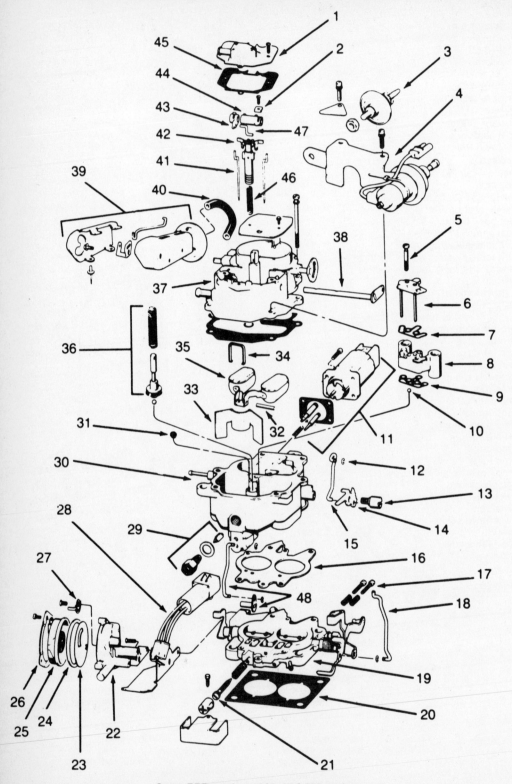

Carter BBD used on 1984–87 6-258 engines

are tight in their seats, but do not overtighten, as the tips will be distorted. Tighten all screws gradually, in rotation. Do not tighten needle valves into their seats; uneven jetting will result. Always use new gaskets. Be sure to adjust the float level when reassembling.

FLOAT AND FUEL LEVEL ADJUSTMENT

4-134 Carter YF

1. Remove and invert the bowl cover.
2. Remove the bowl cover gasket.
3. Allow the weight of the float to rest on the needle and spring. Be sure that there is no compression of the spring other than by the weight of the float.
4. Adjust the level by bending the float arm lip that contacts the needle (not the arm) to provide:
- CJ-2A, CJ-3A.....................⅜" (9.525mm)
- CJ-3B, CJ-5, CJ-6 prior to 1968..$\frac{5}{16}$" (7.9375mm)
- CJ-5, CJ-6 1968 and later........$\frac{17}{64}$" (6.75mm)

4-150 Carter YFA

1. Remove the top of the carburetor and the gasket.
2. Invert the carburetor top and check the clearance from the top of the float to the bottom edge of the air horn with a float level gauge. Hold the carburetor top at eye level when making the check. The float arm should be resting on the inlet needle pin. To adjust, bend the float arm. DO NOT BEND THE TAB AT THE END OF THE ARM! See the Carburetor Specifications chart for the correct clearance.

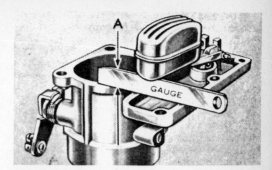

Float level adjustment for the Carter YF on the 4-134 or 6-226

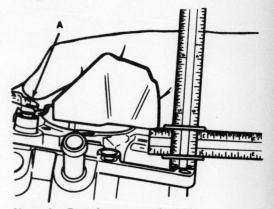

Measuring float clearance on the 4-150

4-151 2SE, E2SE

NOTE: *Special tools are needed for this job.*
1. Start the engine and run it to normal operating temperature.
2. Remove the vent stack screws and the vent stack.
3. Remove the air horn screw adjacent to the vent stack.

1. Rollover check valve and bowl vent
2. Lock
3. Dashpot
4. Solenoid and bracket
5. Cluster screw
6. Idle fuel pickup tube
7. Gasket
8. Venturi cluster
9. Gasket
10. Check ball (small)
11. Stepper motor (actuator)
12. Clip
13. Screw
14. Fast idle cam
15. Choke link
16. Gasket
17. Screw
18. Pump link
19. Throttle body
20. Flange gasket
21. Idle mixture screw
22. Choke housing
23. Baffle
24. Gasket

25. Choke coil
26. Retainer
27. Lever
28. Wide open throttle switch and bracket
29. Needle and seat assembly
30. Main body
31. Main metering jet
32. Pin
33. Baffle
34. Fulcrum retainer
35. Float
36. Spring and accelerator pump plunger
37. Air horn
38. Accelerator pump lever
39. Choke vacuum diaphragm and housing
40. Hose
41. Metering rod
42. Vacuum piston
43. Pump arm
44. Rod lifter
45. Gasket
46. Spring
47. S-Link
48. Choke rod and shaft

Carter BBD used on 1984–87 6-258 engines

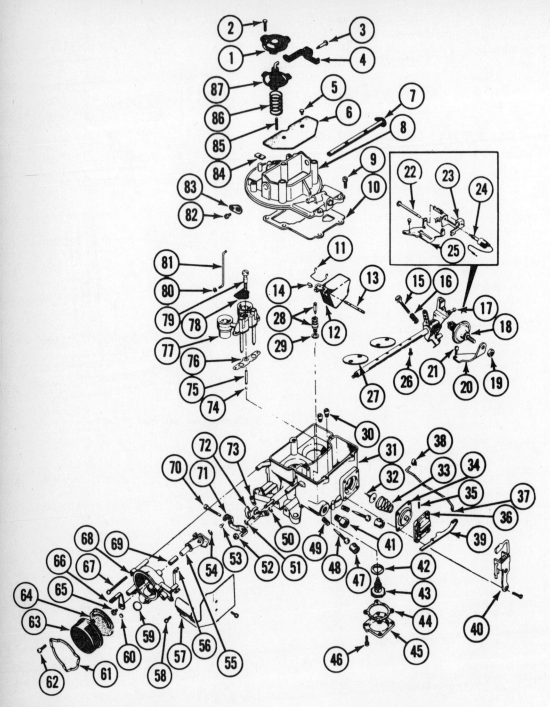

1. Modulator cover (if equipped)
2. Modulator retaining screw (3) (if equipped)
3. Pivot pin
4. Modulator arm
5. Choke valve retaining screw (2)
6. Choke valve
7. Choke shaft
8. Air horn
9. Air horn retaining screw (4)
10. Air horn gasket

11. Float and lever assembly
12. Float shaft retainer
13. Float shaft
14. Needle retaining clip
15. Curb idle adjusting screw
16. Curb idle adjusting screw spring
17. Throttle shaft and lever assembly
18. Dashpot
19. Dashpot locknut
20. Dashpot bracket

Motorcraft 2150 carburetor used on 8-304 engines

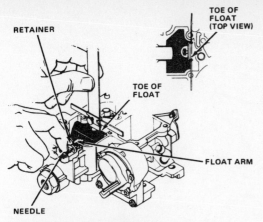

RETAINER

TOE OF
FLOAT
(TOP VIEW)

TOE OF
FLOAT

FLOAT ARM

NEEDLE

2SE and E2SE float adjustment

4. With the engine idling and the choke fully opened, carefully insert float gauge J-9789-136 for E2SE carbs and tool J-9789-138 for 2SE carbs, into the air horn screw hole and vent hole. Allow the gauge to rest freely on the float. DO NOT PRESS DOWN ON THE FLOAT!

5. With the gauge at eye level, observe the mark that aligns with the top of the casting at the vent hole. The float level should be within $\frac{1}{16}''$ (0.1524mm) of the figure in the Carbure-

tor Specifications Charts. If not, remove the air horn and adjust the float as follows:

a. Hold the retainer pin firmly in place and push the float down, lightly, against the inlet needle.

b. Using an adjustable T-scale, at a point $\frac{3}{16}''$ (4.7625mm) from the end of the float, at the toe, measure the distance from the float bowl top surface (gasket removed) to the top of the float at the toe. The distance should be that shown in the Carburetor Specifications Charts. If not, remove the float and bend the arm.

6–225 Rochester 2G

The procedure for adjusting the float level of the two barrel carburetor installed on the V6 is the same as the procedure for the 4–134 up to step 4.

The actual measurement is taken from the air horn gasket to the lip at the toe of the float. This distance should be $\frac{5}{32}''$ (3.96875mm). To adjust the float level, bend the float arm as required.

The float drop adjustment is accomplished in the following manner: With the bowl cover turned in the upright position, measure the distance from the gasket to the notch at the toe

21. Dashpot bracket retaining screw
22. Adjusting screw
23. Carriage
24. Electric solenoid
25. Mounting bracket
26. Throttle valve retaining screw (4)
27. Throttle valve (2)
28. Needle and seat assembly
29. Needle seat gasket
30. Main jet (2)
31. Main body
32. Elastomer valve
33. Pump return spring
34. Pump diaphragm
35. Pump lever pin
36. Pump cover
37. Pump rod
38. Pump rod retainer
39. Pump lever
40. Bowl vent bellcrank
41. Fuel inlet fitting
42. Power valve gasket
43. Power valve
44. Power valve cover gasket
45. Power valve cover
46. Power valve cover retaining screw (4)
47. Idle limiter cap (2)
48. Idle mixture screw (2)
49. Idle mixture screw spring (2)
50. Retainer
52. Fast idle lever retaining nut
53. Fast idle lever pin
54. Retainer

55. Lever and shaft
56. Fast idle cam rod
57. Choke shield
58. Choke shield retaining screw (2)
59. Piston passage plug
60. Heat passage plug
61. Choke cover retaining clamp
62. Choke cover retaining screw (3)
63. Choke cover and coil
64. Choke cover gasket
65. Coil lever retaining screw
66. Coil lever
67. Choke housing retaining screw (3)
68. Choke housing
69. Choke shaft bushing
70. Fast idle speed adjusting screw
71. Fast idle lever
72. Fast idle cam
73. Choke housing gasket
74. Pump discharge check ball
75. Pump discharge weight
76. Booster venturi gasket
77. Booster venturi assembly
78. Air distribution plate
79. Pump discharge screw
80. Retainer
81. Choke rod
82. Choke lever retaining screw
83. Choke plate lever
84. Choke rod seal
85. Stop screw
86. Modulator return spring (if equipped)
87. Modulator diaphragm assembly (if equipped)

Motorcraft 2150 carburetor used on 8-304 engines

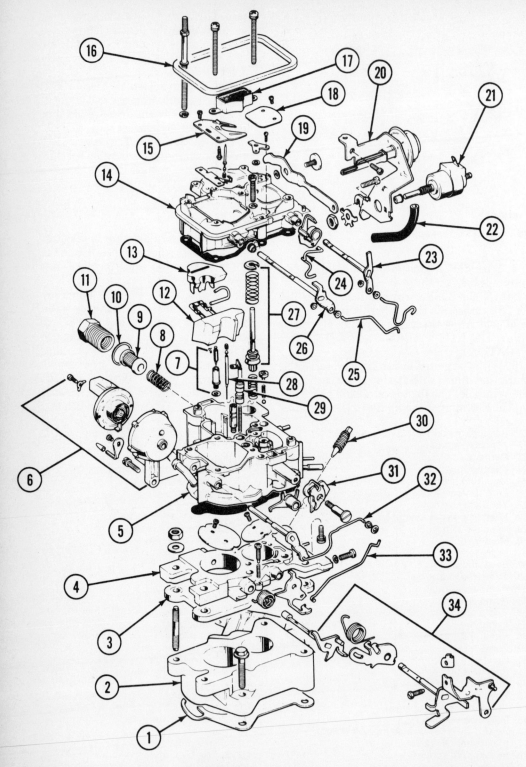

1. Gasket
2. Intake adapter
3. Insulator
4. Throttle body
5. Main body
6. Electric stat cover and coil
7. Needle seat assembly
8. Spring
9. Fuel inlet filter
10. Gasket
11. Fuel inlet fitting
12. Float assembly

Rochester 2SE carburetor used on 49 states 4-151 engines; the E2SE used on California engines is similar

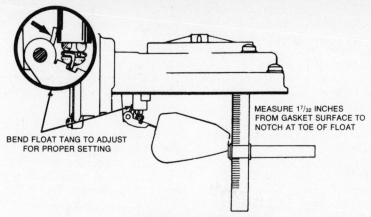

MEASURE 1⁷⁄₃₂ INCHES
FROM GASKET SURFACE TO
NOTCH AT TOE OF FLOAT

BEND FLOAT TANG TO ADJUST
FOR PROPER SETTING

V6 float drop adjustment

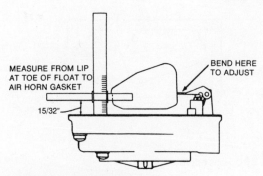

MEASURE FROM LIP
AT TOE OF FLOAT TO
AIR HORN GASKET

BEND HERE
TO ADJUST

15/32"

V6 float level adjustment

of the float. Bend the tang as required to obtain a measurement of $1\frac{7}{32}''$ (30.96mm).

6–226 – Carter Model YF

1. Remove and invert the bowl cover.
2. Remove the bowl cover gasket.
3. Allow the weight of the float to rest on the needle and spring. Be sure that there is no compression of the spring other than by the weight of the float.
4. Adjust the level by bending the float arm lip that contacts the needle (not the arm) to provide $\frac{9}{32}''$ of clearance.

6–226 – Carter WCD

1. Remove the bowl cover and turn it upside down.
2. Remove the gasket.
3. With the tip of the float resting on the needle, measure the distance between the top of the float and the machined surface of the bowl casting. The gap should be $\frac{3}{16}''$.
4. If not, adjust it by bending the float arms.

6–226 – Carter WGD

1. Remove the bowl cover and turn it upside down.
2. Remove the gasket.
3. With the tip of the float resting on the needle, measure the distance between the top of the float and the machined surface of the bowl casting. The gap should be $\frac{9}{32}''$.
4. If not, adjust it by bending the float arms.

6–230 – Holley 1920

1. Remove the carburetor.
2. Slide float gauge J-10238 into position at the economizer body baffle and check the setting. The float should just touch the gauge.
3. If necessary, bend the float tab with needle nosed pliers. Do not allow the float tab to contact the float needle during this operation. Recheck the setting.
4. Slide the economizer diaphragm into position, making sure that the vacuum holes are aligned and that the stem is on the power valve.
5. Install and tighten the cover screws.

6–230 – Holley 2415

1. Park the vehicle on level ground and run the engine until it is idling at normal operating temperature.

13. Float baffle	21. Idle stop solenoid	29. Power piston
14. Air horn	22. Vacuum hose	30. Idle needle and spring
15. Air valve	23. Vacuum break lever	31. Fast idle cam
16. Air horn gasket	24. Choke link	32. Intermediate choke rod
17. Vent screen	25. Air valve rod	33. Pump rod
18. Choke valve	26. Air valve lever	34. Throttle lever assembly
19. Pump lever	27. Accelerator pump	
20. Vacuum break and bracket	28. Metering rod	

Rochester 2SE carburetor used on 49 states 4-151 engines; the E2SE used on California engines is similar

2. With the engine idling, remove the fuel level check plug. The fuel level should be within $\frac{1}{16}$" of the bottom of the check plug port.

3. To adjust the level, loosen the fuel valve seat lock screw slightly with a screwdriver and turn the adjusting nut with a $\frac{5}{8}$" wrench. Turn the nut clockwise to lower, and counterclockwise to raise, the fuel level. A $\frac{1}{6}$ turn equals a $\frac{1}{16}$" change in the level.

4. After adjustment, tighten the lock screw and recheck the level.

6–232, 6–258 Carter YF

Remove and invert the air horn assembly and remove the gasket. Measure the distance between the top of the float at the free end, and the air horn casting. The measurement should be $\frac{29}{64}$–$\frac{31}{64}$" (11.51–12.30mm). Adjust by bending the float lever.

NOTE: *The fuel inlet needle must be held off its seat while bending the float lever in order to prevent damage to the needle and seat.*

To adjust the float drop, hold the air horn in the upright position and measure the distance between the top of the float, at the extreme outer end, and the air horn casting. The measurement should be 1¼" (31.75mm) to 1973,

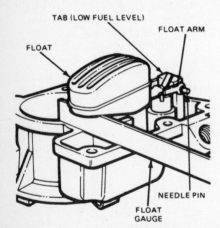

6-232, 258 Carter YF float adjustment

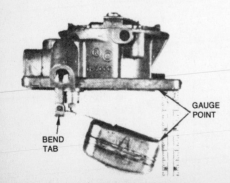

6-232, 258 Carter YF float drop adjustment

1⅜" (34.92mm) 1974–78. Adjust by bending the tab at the rear of the float lever.

6–258 Carter BBD 2–bbl

1. Remove the air horn.

2. Apply light finger pressure to the vertical float tab to exert GENTLE pressure against the inlet needle.

3. Lay a straight edge across the float bowl and measure the gap between the straight edge and the top of the float at its highest point. The gap should be ¼" (6.35mm).

4. To adjust, remove the float and bend the lower tab. Replace the float and check the gap.

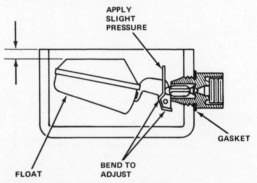

BBD float adjustment

8–304 Autolite 2100, Motorcraft 2150 Dry Adjustment

With the air horn assembly and the gasket removed raise the float by pressing down on the float tab until the fuel inlet needle is lightly seated. Using a T-scale, measure the distance from the fuel bowl machined surface to either corner of the float ⅛" (3.175mm) from the free end. The measurement should be ¾" (19.05mm) through 1975, $\frac{3}{16}$–$\frac{15}{32}$" (4.7625–11.90625mm) 1976–81. To adjust bend the float tab and hold the fuel inlet needle off its eat in order to prevent damage to the seat and the tip of the needle.

8–304 Motorcraft 2150 Wet Adjustment

CAUTION: *Exercise extreme care when performing this adjustment as fuel vapors and liquid fuel are present!*

1. Place the vehicle on a flat, level surface and run the engine to normal operating temperature. Turn off the engine and remove the air cleaner.

2. Remove the air horn attaching screws, but leave the air horn in place.

3. Start the engine and let it idle for one minute. Shut off the engine and remove the air horn and gasket.

4. Use a T-scale to measure the vertical distance between the machined surface of the car-

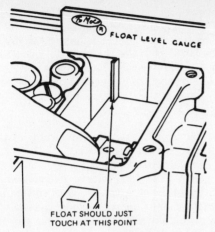

Autolite 2100 and Motorcraft 2150 dry float adjustment

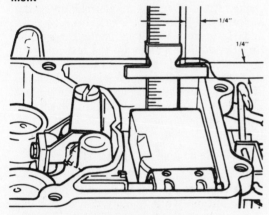

Motorcraft 2150 wet float adjustment

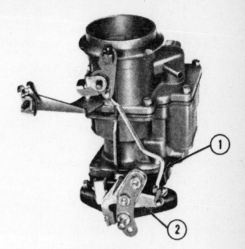

1. Fast idle connector rod
2. Fast idle link

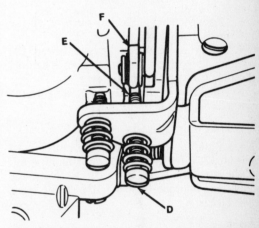

Carter YFA fast idle adjustment. (D) is the fast idle cam screw; (E) is the second step; (F) is the cam

buretor body and the fuel level in the bowl. Make this measurement as near the center of the bowl as possible. The proper distance is $^{59}/_{64}$" (23.42mm). To adjust, bend the float tab.

NOTE: *Every time an adjustment is made, the air horn must be replaced, and the engine started and idled for one minute to stabilize the fuel level.*

5. Install the air horn and gasket when adjustment is completed.

FAST IDLE LINKAGE ADJUSTMENT

NOTE: *This adjustment is performed with the air cleaner removed.*

4–134 Carter YF

With the choke held in the wide open position, the lip on the fast idle rod should contact the boss on the body casting. Adjust it by bending the fast idle link at the offset in the link.

4–150

1. Run the engine to normal operating temperature. Connect a tachometer according to the maker's instructions.

2. Disconnect and plug the EGR valve vacuum hose.

3. Position the fast idle adjustment screw on the second stop of the fast idle cam with the transmission in neutral.

4. Adjust the fast idle speed to 2300 rpm for auto. trans. and 2000 rpm for man. trans.

5. Idle the engine and reconnect the EGR hose.

4–151 Rochester 2SE, E2SE

1. Make sure the choke coil adjustment is correct and that the fast idle speed is correct.

2. Obtain a Choke Angle Gauge, tool #J-26701-A. Rotate the degree scale to the zero degree mark opposite the pointer.

3. With the choke valve completely closed, place the magnet on the tool squarely on the

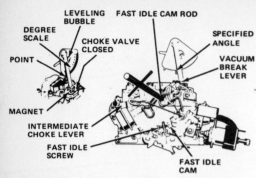

2SE, E2SE fast idle cam position adjustment

choke plate. Rotate the bubble unit until it is centered.

4. Rotate the degree scale until the 25 degree mark is opposite the pointer. On carburetors with choke cover sticker number 70172, the angle is 18 degrees.

5. Place the fast idle screw on the second step of the cam.

6. Close the choke plate by pushing on the intermediate choke lever.

7. Push the vacuum brake lever toward the open choke position until the lever is against the rear tank on the choke lever.

8. Adjust by bending the fast idle cam rod until the bubble is centered.

6–225 Rochester 2G

No fast idle speed adjustment is required. Fast idle is controlled by the curb adjustment screw. If the curb idle speed is set correctly and the choke rod is properly adjusted, fast idle speed will be correct.

6–226

WCD

1. Loosen the choke lever clamp screw on the choke shaft.

2. Insert a 0.04″ (1.01mm) feeler gauge between the lip of the fast idle cam and the boss of the flange.

3. Hold the choke valve closed tightly and take the slack out of the linkage by pressing the choke lever toward the closed position.

4. Hold it in this position and tighten the clamp screw.

5. With the choke valve tightly closed, tighten the fast idle adjusting screw until there is a gap of 0.016″ (0.406mm) between the throttle valve and the air horn wall. Make sure that the fast idle screw is on the high step of the cam during this adjustment.

WGD

1. Remove the choke coil houisng, gasket and baffle plate.

2. Crack the throttle and hold the choke plate closed. Then, close the throttle.

3. At this point, there should be a gap of 0.018–0.023″ between the throttle valve and air horn wall, opposite the idle port.

4. Adjust the gap by bending the choke connecting rod at the lower angle.

6–230

1. Connect a tachometer according to the manufacturer's instructions.

2. On vehicles equipped with a manual choke, adjust the choke wire to give maximum operation of the choke valve. With the engine off the the choke fully open, adjust the fast idle screw to obtain a 0.030″ (0.762mm) gap between the end of the screw and the cam.

3. On vehicles equipped with an automatic choke, run the engine to normal operating temperature. With the choke valve fully open and the engine idling in neutral, open the throttle slightly and rotate the fast idle cam until the fast idle screw contacts the second step of the fast idle cam. Release the throttle. The linkage pullback spring will cause the fast idle adjusting screw to hold the cam in this position. The tachometer should read 2,100 rpm. If not, turn the adjusting screw until it does.

6–232, 6–258 through 1973 Carter YF

Partially open the throttle and close the choke valve to rotate the fast idle cam into the cold start position. While holding the choke valve closed, release the throttle. With the fast idle cam in this position, the fast idle adjusting screw must be aligned with the index mark at the back side of the cam. Adjust by bending the choke rod at its upper angle.

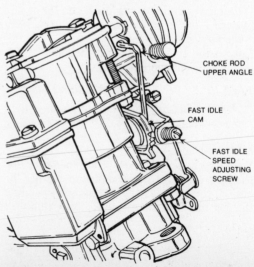

Carter YF fast idle adjustment on the 6-232, 6-258

6–232, 6–258 1974–78 Carter YF

Position the fast idle screw on the second stop of the fast idle cam, against the shoulder of the high step on the cam. Adjust by bending the choke plate connecting rod to obtain $\frac{13}{64}$" (5.16mm) clearance between the lower edge of the choke plate and the air horn wall.

6–258 Carter BBD 2-bbl

1. Loosen the choke housing cover and turn it ¼ turn right. Tighten one screw.
2. Slightly open the throttle and place the fast idle screw on the second cam step.
3. Measure the distance between the choke plate and the air horn wall. The distance should be $\frac{7}{64}$" (2.778mm).
4. If adjustment is necessary, bend the fast idle cam link down to increase and up to decrease the gap.
5. Return the choke cover cap to the original setting.

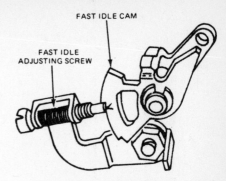

CONVENTIONAL ONE-PIECE FAST IDLE LEVER

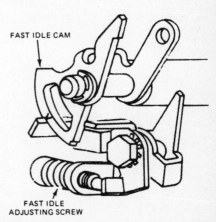

Fast idle cam index setting—Autolite (Motorcraft) 2100

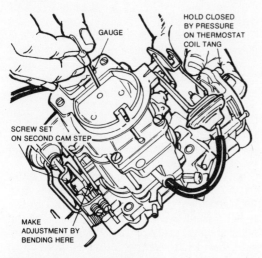

BBD fast idle cam adjustment

8–304 Autolite 2100, Motorcraft 2150

Push down on the fast idle cam lever until the fast idle speed adjusting screw is contacting the second step (index), and against the shoulder of the high step. Measure the clearance between the lower edge of the choke valve and air horn wall. Adjust by turning the fast idle cam lever screw to obtain $\frac{19}{64}$" (7.54mm) through 1975 and ⅛" (3.175mm) 1976–79. Adjust the automatic choke.

INITIAL CHOKE VALVE CLEARANCE

1. Position the fast idle screw on the top step of the fast idle cam.
2. Using a vacuum pump, seat the choke vacuum break.
3. Apply light closing pressure in the choke

plate to position the plate as far closed as possible without forcing it.
4. Measure the distance between the air horn wall and the choke plate. If it is not that specified in the Carburetor Specifications Chart, bend the choke vacuum break link until it is.

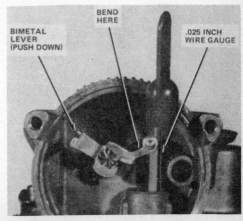

YF initial choke valve clearance adjustment

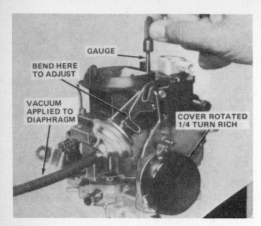

BBD initial choke valve clearance adjustment

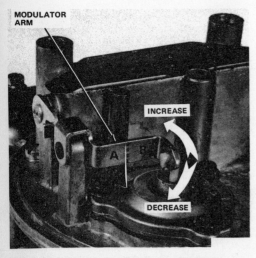

2100 initial choke valve clearance adjustment

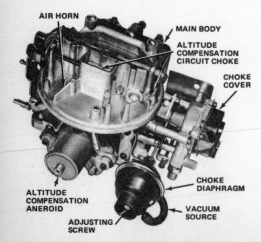

2150 initial choke valve clearance adjustment

CHOKE SETTING ADJUSTMENT

4–134 and V6–225

The choke is manually operated by a cable that runs from the dash mounted control pull knob to the set screw on the choke actuating arm. To adjust the choke, loosen the set screw at the choke actuating lever and push in the dash knob as far as it will go. Open the choke plate as far as it will go and hold it with your finger while the set screw is tightened.

6–232, 258 and 8–304

The automatic choke setting is made by loosening the choke cover in the desired direction as indicated by an arrow on the face of the cover. the original setting will be satisfactory for most driving conditions. However, if the engine stumbles or stalls on acceleration during warmup, the choke may be set richer or leaner no more than two graduations from the original setting.

4–150, 4–151

NOTE: *Once the rivets and choke cover are removed, a choke cover retainer kit is necessary for assembly.*

1. Remove the rivets, retainers, choke cover and coil following the instructions found in the cover retainer kit.

2. Position the fast idle adjustment screw on the highest stop of the fast idle cam.

3. Push on the intermediate choke lever and close the choke plate.

4. Insert the proper plug gauge, 0.050–0.080″ (1.27–2.032mm) for manual trans. and 0.85″ (21.59mm) for automatic trans., in the hole adjacent to the coil lever. The edge of the lever should barely contact the plug gauge.

5. Bend the intermediate choke rod to adjust.

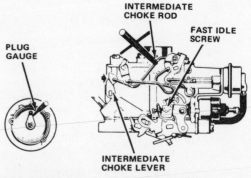

2SE, E2SE choke coil lever adjustment

6–226

Loosen the choke cover screws and turn the cover, clockwise, until the indictaor on the houisng aligns with the notch on the casting. Tighten the screws.

UNLOADER ADJUSTMENT

6–232, 258

With the throttle held fully open, apply pressure on the choke valve toward the closed position and measure the clearance between the lower edge of the choke valve and the air horn wall. The measurement should be ¼″ (6.35mm) 1972–73, $\frac{9}{32}$″ (7.14375mm) 1974–87. Adjust by bending the tang on the throttle lever which contacts the fast idle cam. Bend toward the cam to increase the clearance.

NOTE: *Do not bend the unloader down from a horizontal plane. After making the adjustment, make sure the unloader tang does not contact the main body flange when the throttle is fully open. A clearance of 0.070″ (1.778mm) must be present. Final unloader adjustment must always be done on the vehicle. The throttle should be fully opened by depressing the accelerator pedal to the floor. This is to assure that full throttle is obtained.*

4–150, 4–151

1. Obtain a Carburetor Choke Angle Gauge, tool #J-26701-A. Rotate the scale on the gauge until the 0 mark is opposite the pointer.

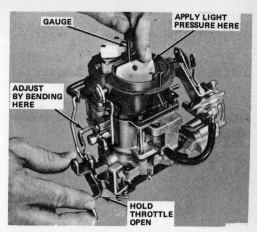

BBD choke unloader adjustment

2. Close the choke plate completely and set the magnet squarely on top of it.
3. Rotate the bubble until it is centered.
4. Rotate the degree scale until the 32° mark is opposite the pointer. On carburetors with choke cover sticker number 70172 the setting is 19°.
5. Hold the primary throttle valve wide open.
6. Bend the throttle lever tang until the bubble is centered.

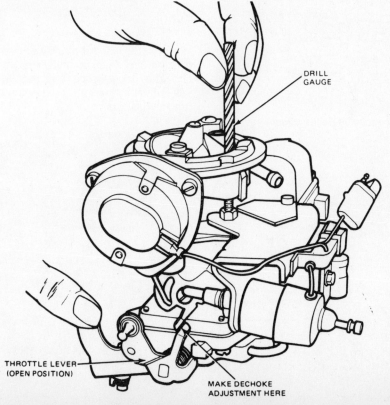

Carter YF choke unloader adjustment

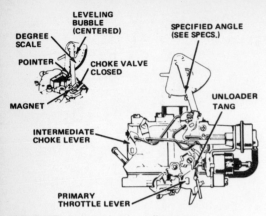

2SE, E2SE choke unloader adjustment

6–225, 8–304

With the throttle held fully open, apply pressure on the choke valve toward the closed position and measure the clearance between the lower edge of the choke valve and the air horn wall. The setting should be ¼" (6.35mm); $\frac{5}{16}$" (7.9375mm) for 1979. Adjust by bending the tang on the fast idle lever, which is located on the throttle linkage. Refer to the "Note" under

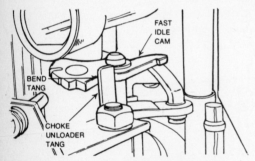

Motorcraft 2150 choke unloader adjustment

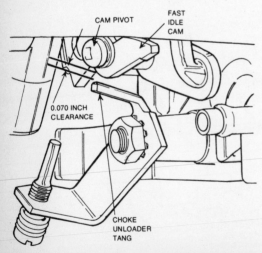

Motorcraft 2150 choke unloader/fast idle cam clearance

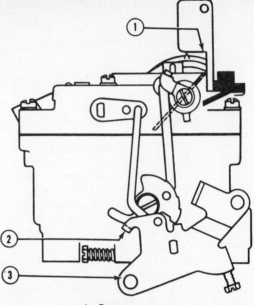

1. Gauge
2. Unloader tang
3. Throttle lever

Choke unloader adjustment: Rochester 2GV, 6-225 and 8-350

the procedure for adjusting the unloader on the Sixes.

DASHPOT ADJUSTMENT

Inline Sixes and V8

With the throttle set at curb idle position fully depress the dashpot stem and measure the clearance between the stem and the throttle lever. Adjust by loosening the lock nut and turning the dashpot.

Dashpot adjustment: Carter YF

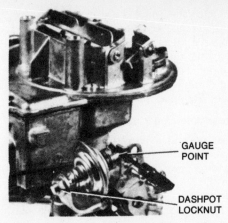

GAUGE POINT

DASHPOT LOCKNUT

Dashpot adjustment: Autolite 2100

F4–134 and V6

The adjustment is made with the engine idling. Loosen the dashpot locknut and turn the assembly until the plunger contacts the throttle lever without being depressed. Then, turn the assembly 2½ turns against the lever, depressing the plunger. Tighten the locknut.

1. Throttle lever   3. Dashpot
2. Plunger   4. Locknut

Dashpot adjustment: Carter YF, 4-134

VACUUM (STEP UP) PISTON GAP

Carter BBD

1. Turn the adjusting screw, mounted on top of the unit, so that the gap between the metering rod lifter lower edge, and the top of the vacuum piston, is as specified in the Carburetor Specifications Charts.

2. Counting the number of turns involved, turn the curb idle adjustment screw counterclockwise, until the throttle valves are completely closed.

3. Fully depress the vacuum piston, while exerting moderate pressure on the metering

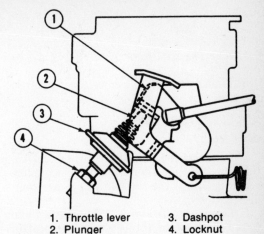

1. Throttle lever   3. Dashpot
2. Plunger   4. Locknut

Dashpot adjustment: Rochester 2GV

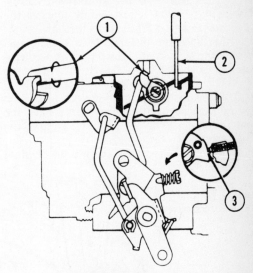

1. Choke lever tang
2. Wire gauge
3. Idle speed adjustment screw

2GV choke rod adjustment

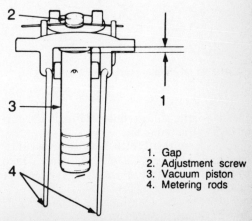

1. Gap
2. Adjustment screw
3. Vacuum piston
4. Metering rods

Carter BBD vacuum piston gap adjustment

rod lifter tab. In this position, tighten the rod lifter lock screw.

4. Release the piston and rod lifter.

NOTE: *The accelerator pump should now be adjusted.*

5. Return the curb idle adjustment screw to its original position.

ACCELERATOR PUMP

Carter BBD

1. Counting the number of turns involved, turn the curb idle adjustment screw counterclockwise, until the throttle valves are completely closed.

2. Open the choke valve so that the fast idle cam will allow the throttle valves to seat in their bores.

3. Turn the curb idle adjustment screw clockwise, so that it just barely touches the stop, then, turn it 2 full turns further.

4. Measure the distance between the surface of the air horn and the top of the accelerator pump shaft with a T-scale. The distance should be 13.1mm (0.516″ or $^{33}/_{64}$″).

5. If the dimension is not correct, loosen the pump arm adjusting screw and rotate the sleeve to adjust the pump travel. Tighten the lock screw.

6. Return the curb idle screw to its original position.

D. Flange
E. Gauge
F. Adjusting screw

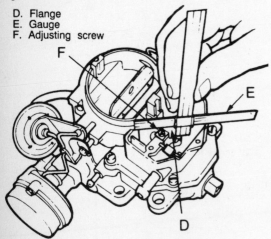

Carter BBD accelerator pump adjustment

Carter WCD

1. Place the pump connector link in the outer hole of the pump arm.

2. Back out the throttle lever setscrew until the throttle plates seat in their bores. Make certain that the fast idle adjusting screw isn't holding the throttle open.

3. Place pump travel gauge, T109-117S, or its equivalent, inverted on the edge of the dust cover boss on the bowl cover.

4. Turn the knurled nut of the gauge until the finger just touches the upper end of the plunger shaft. The measured distance should be ½″ from the dust cover boss to the top of the plunger. This corresponds to an indicated gauge number of 33. Adjust by bending the link at the upper bend.

Autolite/Motorcraft 2100 and 2150

Under normal driving conditions, the pump rod should be in the inboard hole of the pump actuating lever and the third hole (counting from the bottom up) of the overtravel lever.

Under extremely hot conditions, the rod should be placed in the second hole of the overtravel lever.

Under extremely cold conditions, the rod should be placed in the fourth hole of the overtravel lever.

METERING ROD

Carter YFA

1. Remove the air horn and gasket.

2. Make sure that the idle speed adjustment screw allows the throttle plate to close tightly in the bore.

3. Press down on the top of the pump diaphragm shaft until it bottoms.

4. In this position, adjust the metering rod by turning the adjusting screw counterclockwise, until the metering rod lightly bottoms in the main metering jet.

5. Turn the adjusting screw 1 full turn more.

6. Install the air horn and gasket, and adjust the curb idle speed.

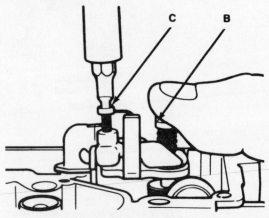

B. Diaphragm shaft
C. Adjustment screw

Metering rod adjustment

Carter WCD

1. Perform a pump adjustment.

2. Counting the number of threads in-

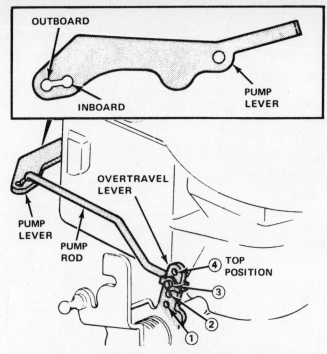

2100, 2150 accelerator pump adjustment points

volved, back out the throttle lever screw until the throttle plates are seated in their bores.

3. Press down on the vacumeter link until the metering rods bottom.

4. In this position, move the metering rod arm until the lip contacts the vacumeter link.

5. Hold it in place and tighten the metering rod setscrew.

Carter WGD

1. Perform a pump adjustment.

2. Counting the number of threads involved, back out the throttle lever screw until the throttle plates are seated in their bores.

3. Press down on the vacumeter link until the metering rods bottom.

4. In this position, move the metering rod arm until the lip contacts the vacumeter link.

5. Hold it in place and tighten the metering rod setscrew.

Governor

ADJUSTMENT

1. Connect a tachometer to the engine. Adjust the carburetor to obtain a smooth idle at 600 rpm. Shut off the engine.

2. Check the throttle linkage to be sure that the throttle plate can be set at the wide open position. Make sure that the throttle and governor linkage are operating freely.

3. Place the carburetor in the wide open throttle position and pull the governor handle all the way out.

4. Adjust the governor-to-bell crank rod so that the linkage will hold the carburetor in the wide open throttle position.

5. Close the governor control and start the engine.

6. Pull the governor control out to the last notch and adjust the cable length at the adjusting yoke so that the engine will run at 2,600 rpm.

7. Close the governor control and make sure that the engine returns to the 600 rpm idle speed. Check that the linkage operates freely. If the engine does not return to the 600 rpm figure, loosen the locknut, at the dashpanel, which retains the governor hand control to the rod, and back off the handle until the idle speed adjusting screw rests on the stop. Tighten the locknut.

THROTTLE BODY INJECTION FUEL SYSTEM

NOTE: *This book contains simple testing and service procedures for for your Jeep fuel injection system. More comprehensive testing and diagnosis procedures may be found in CHILTON'S GUIDE TO FUEL INJECTION AND FEEDBACK CARBURETORS,*

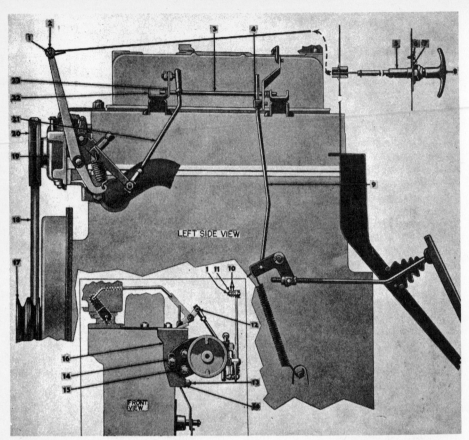

1. Pivot bolt
2. Cotter pin
3. Governor bellcrank
4. Adjusting block
5. Governor control
6. Screw
7. Control bezel
8. Handle
9. Vertical rod
10. Washer
11. Nut
12. Nut and lockwasher
13. Stud
14. Washer
15. Screw
16. Support bracket
17. Fan drive pulley
18. Governor drive belt
19. Governor (Novi)
20. Governor drive pulley
21. Horizontal rod
22. Bellcrank bracket
23. Washer

Governor on a 4F-134 engine

book part number 7488, available at your local retailer.

Fuel Pump

REMOVAL AND INSTALLATION

1. Disconnect the negative battery cable. Remove all necessary components in order to gain access to the fuel tank sending unit.

2. Drain the fuel from the fuel tank. Raise and support the vehicle safely.

3. Remove the fuel inlet and outlet hoses from the sending unit. Remove the sending unit wires.

4. Remove the sending unit retaining lock ring. Remove the sending unit, which incorporates the electric fuel pump, along with the O-ring seal from the fuel tank.

4. Installation is the reverse of removal. Be sure to use a new O-ring seal.

Throttle Body

REMOVAL AND INSTALLATION

1. Disconnect the negative battery cable. Remove the upper air cleaner assembly.

2. Remove the lower air cleaner assembly retaining bolts. Remove the lower air cleaner assembly.

3. Remove the throttle cable and the return spring. Disconnect the wire harness connector from the injector.

4. Disconnect the wire harness connector from the wide open throttle switch. Disconnect the wire harness connector from the ISC motor.

5. Disconnect the fuel supply pipe from the throttle body. Disconnect the fuel return pipe from the throttle body.

6. Disconnect the vacuum hoses from the

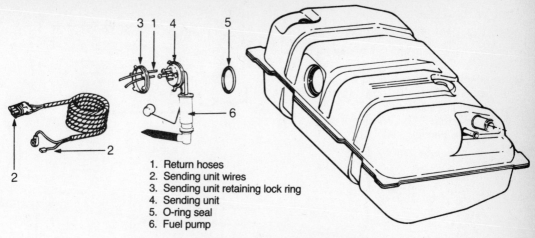

1. Return hoses
2. Sending unit wires
3. Sending unit retaining lock ring
4. Sending unit
5. O-ring seal
6. Fuel pump

Fuel pump used on the fuel injected 4-150

throttle body assembly. Disconnect the potentiometer wire connector.

7. Remove the throttle body to manifold retaining bolts. Remove the throttle body assembly from the intake manifold.

8. Clean the manifold and throttle body mating surfaces. Be sure to use a new gasket between the throttle body assembly and the intake manifold.

9. Install the throttle body assembly from the intake manifold. Torque the nuts to 15 ft.lb.

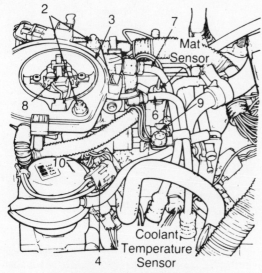

2. Lower air cleaner retaining bolts
3. Lower air cleaner assembly
4. Wide open throttle switch
6. Fuel inlet line
7. Fuel return line
8. Injector wiring connector
9. Potentiometer wire
10. Throttle body retaining bolts

Points of disconnection when removing the throttle body

5. ISC motor

ISC motor location

10. Connect the vacuum hoses to the throttle body assembly. Connect the potentiometer wire connector.

11. Connect the fuel supply pipe to the throttle body. Connect the fuel return pipe to the throttle body.

12. Connect the wire harness connector to the wide open throttle switch. Connect the wire harness connector to the ISC motor.

13. Install the throttle cable and the return spring. Connect the wire harness connector to the injector.

14. Install the lower air cleaner assembly. Install the lower air cleaner assembly retaining bolts.

15. Install the upper air cleaner assembly.

16. Connect the negative battery cable.

Fuel Body Assembly

REMOVAL AND INSTALLATION

1. Remove the throttle body assembly from the vehicle.

2. Remove the Torx® head screws that retain the fuel body to the throttle body. Remove and discard the gasket.

3. Installation is the reverse of removal. Be sure to use a new gasket.

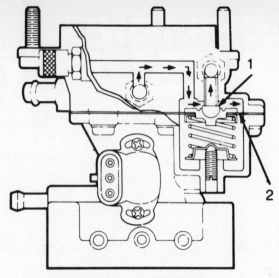

1. Relief valve   2. Diaphragm

Fuel pressure regulator

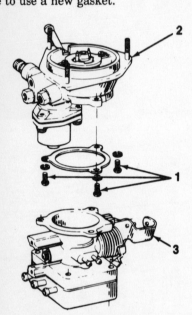

1. Fuel body retaining screws
2. Fuel body
3. Throttly body

Fuel body assembly removal

Fuel Pressure Regulator

REMOVAL AND INSTALLATION

1. Remove the throttle body assembly from the vehicle.

2. Remove the three retaining screws that hold the pressure regulator to the fuel body.

3. Remove the pressure regulator assembly. Note the location of the components for reassembly. Discard the gasket.

4. Installation is the reverse of the removal procedure. Be sure to use a new gasket.

Fuel Injector

REMOVAL AND INSTALLATION

1. Remove the air cleaner and hose assembly.

2. Remove the fuel injector wire. Remove the fuel injector retainer clip screws. Remove the fuel injector retainer clip.

3. Using a small pair of pliers, gently grasp the center collar of the injector, between the

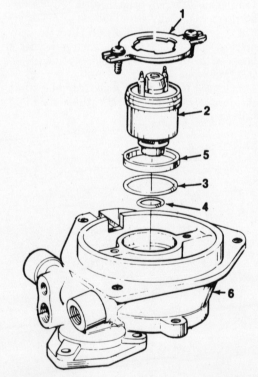

1. Retainer clip
2. Injector
3. Upper O-ring
4. Lower O-ring
5. Backup ring
6. Fuel body

Injector removal

electrical terminals, and carefully remove the injector using a lifting-twisting motion.

4. Discard the upper and lower O-rings. Note that the back up ring fits over the upper O-ring.

5. Installation is the reverse of the removal

CHILTON'S
FUEL ECONOMY
& TUNE-UP TIPS

55 WAYS TO IMPROVE FUEL ECONOMY

Tune-up • Spark Plug Diagnosis • Emission Controls

Fuel System • Cooling System • Tires and Wheels

General Maintenance

CHILTON'S FUEL ECONOMY & TUNE-UP TIPS

Fuel economy is important to everyone, no matter what kind of vehicle you drive. The maintenance-minded motorist can save both money and fuel using these tips and the periodic maintenance and tune-up procedures in this Repair and Tune-Up Guide.

There are more than 130,000,000 cars and trucks registered for private use in the United States. Each travels an average of 10-12,000 miles per year, and, and in total they consume close to 70 billion gallons of fuel each year. This represents nearly ⅔ of the oil imported by the United States each year. The Federal government's goal is to reduce consumption 10% by 1985. A variety of methods are either already in use or under serious consideration, and they all affect you driving and the cars you will drive. In addition to "down-sizing", the auto industry is using or investigating the use of electronic fuel delivery, electronic engine controls and alternative engines for use in smaller and lighter vehicles, among other alternatives to meet the federally mandated Corporate Average Fuel Economy (CAFE) of 27.5 mpg by 1985. The government, for its part, is considering rationing, mandatory driving curtailments and tax increases on motor vehicle fuel in an effort to reduce consumption. The government's goal of a 10% reduction could be realized — and further government regulation avoided — if every private vehicle could use just 1 less gallon of fuel per week.

How Much Can You Save?

Tests have proven that almost anyone can make at least a 10% reduction in fuel consumption through regular maintenance and tune-ups. When a major manufacturer of spark plugs sur-

TUNE-UP

1. Check the cylinder compression to be sure the engine will really benefit from a tune-up and that it is capable of producing good fuel economy. A tune-up will be wasted on an engine in poor mechanical condition.

2. Replace spark plugs regularly. New spark plugs alone can increase fuel economy 3%.

3. Be sure the spark plugs are the correct type (heat range) for your vehicle. See the Tune-Up Specifications.

Heat range refers to the spark plug's ability to conduct heat away from the firing end. It must conduct the heat away in an even pattern to avoid becoming a source of pre-ignition, yet it must also operate hot enough to burn off conductive deposits that could cause misfiring.

The heat range is usually indicated by a number on the spark plug, part of the manufacturer's designation for each individual spark plug. The numbers in bold-face indicate the heat range in each manufacturer's identification system.

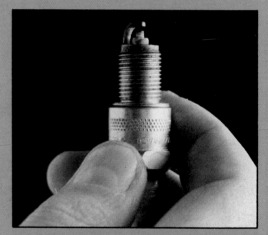

Periodically, check the spark plugs to be sure they are firing efficiently. They are excellent indicators of the internal condition of your engine.

Manufacturer	Typical Designation
AC	R **45** TS
Bosch (old)	WA **145** T30
Bosch (new)	HR **8** Y
Champion	RBL **15** Y
Fram/Autolite	4**15**
Mopar	P-**62** PR
Motorcraft	BRF-**42**
NGK	BP **5** ES-15
Nippondenso	W **16** EP
Prestolite	14GR **5** 2A

On AC, Bosch (new), Champion, Fram/Autolite, Mopar, Motorcraft and Prestolite, a higher number indicates a hotter plug. On Bosch (old), NGK and Nippondenso, a higher number indicates a colder plug.

4. Make sure the spark plugs are properly gapped. See the Tune-Up Specifications in this book.

5. Be sure the spark plugs are firing efficiently. The illustrations on the next 2 pages show you how to "read" the firing end of the spark plug.

6. Check the ignition timing and set it to specifications. Tests show that almost all cars have incorrect ignition timing by more than 2°.

veyed over 6,000 cars nationwide, they found that a tune-up, on cars that needed one, increased fuel economy over 11%. Replacing worn plugs alone, accounted for a 3% increase. The same test also revealed that 8 out of every 10 vehicles will have some maintenance deficiency that will directly affect fuel economy, emissions or performance. Most of this mileage-robbing neglect could be prevented with regular maintenance.

Modern engines require that all of the functioning systems operate properly for maximum efficiency. A malfunction anywhere wastes fuel. You can keep your vehicle running as efficiently and economically as possible, by being aware of your vehicle's operating and performance characteristics. If your vehicle suddenly develops performance or fuel economy problems it could be due to one or more of the following:

PROBLEM	POSSIBLE CAUSE
Engine Idles Rough	Ignition timing, idle mixture, vacuum leak or something amiss in the emission control system.
Hesitates on Acceleration	Dirty carburetor or fuel filter, improper accelerator pump setting, ignition timing or fouled spark plugs.
Starts Hard or Fails to Start	Worn spark plugs, improperly set automatic choke, ice (or water) in fuel system.
Stalls Frequently	Automatic choke improperly adjusted and possible dirty air filter or fuel filter.
Performs Sluggishly	Worn spark plugs, dirty fuel or air filter, ignition timing or automatic choke out of adjustment.

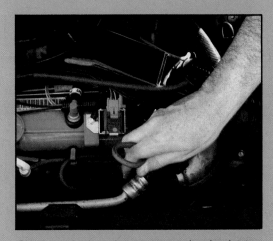

Check spark plug wires on conventional point type ignition for cracks by bending them in a loop around your finger.

Be sure that spark plug wires leading to adjacent cylinders do not run too close together. (Photo courtesy Champion Spark Plug Co.)

7. If your vehicle does not have electronic ignition, check the points, rotor and cap as specified.

8. Check the spark plug wires (used with conventional point-type ignitions) for cracks and burned or broken insulation by bending them in a loop around your finger. Cracked wires decrease fuel efficiency by failing to deliver full voltage to the spark plugs. One misfiring spark plug can cost you as much as 2 mpg.

9. Check the routing of the plug wires. Misfiring can be the result of spark plug leads to adjacent cylinders running parallel to each other and too close together. One wire tends to pick up voltage from the other causing it to fire "out of time".

10. Check all electrical and ignition circuits for voltage drop and resistance.

11. Check the distributor mechanical and/or vacuum advance mechanisms for proper functioning. The vacuum advance can be checked by twisting the distributor plate in the opposite direction of rotation. It should spring back when released.

12. Check and adjust the valve clearance on engines with mechanical lifters. The clearance should be slightly loose rather than too tight.

SPARK PLUG DIAGNOSIS

Normal

APPEARANCE: This plug is typical of one operating normally. The insulator nose varies from a light tan to grayish color with slight electrode wear. The presence of slight deposits is normal on used plugs and will have no adverse effect on engine performance. The spark plug heat range is correct for the engine and the engine is running normally.

CAUSE: Properly running engine.

RECOMMENDATION: Before reinstalling this plug, the electrodes should be cleaned and filed square. Set the gap to specifications. If the plug has been in service for more than 10-12,000 miles, the entire set should probably be replaced with a fresh set of the same heat range.

Oil Deposits

APPEARANCE: The firing end of the plug is covered with a wet, oily coating.

CAUSE: The problem is poor oil control. On high mileage engines, oil is leaking past the rings or valve guides into the combustion chamber. A common cause is also a plugged PCV valve, and a ruptured fuel pump diaphragm can also cause this condition. Oil fouled plugs such as these are often found in new or recently overhauled engines, before normal oil control is achieved, and can be cleaned and reinstalled.

RECOMMENDATION: A hotter spark plug may temporarily relieve the problem, but the engine is probably in need of work.

Incorrect Heat Range

APPEARANCE: The effects of high temperature on a spark plug are indicated by clean white, often blistered insulator. This can also be accompanied by excessive wear of the electrode, and the absence of deposits.

CAUSE: Check for the correct spark plug heat range. A plug which is too hot for the engine can result in overheating. A car operated mostly at high speeds can require a colder plug. Also check ignition timing, cooling system level, fuel mixture and leaking intake manifold.

RECOMMENDATION: If all ignition and engine adjustments are known to be correct, and no other malfunction exists, install spark plugs one heat range colder.

Photos Courtesy Fram Corporation

Carbon Deposits

APPEARANCE: Carbon fouling is easily identified by the presence of dry, soft, black, sooty deposits.

CAUSE: Changing the heat range can often lead to carbon fouling, as can prolonged slow, stop-and-start driving. If the heat range is correct, carbon fouling can be attributed to a rich fuel mixture, sticking choke, clogged air cleaner, worn breaker points, retarded timing or low compression. If only one or two plugs are carbon fouled, check for corroded or cracked wires on the affected plugs. Also look for cracks in the distributor cap between the towers of affected cylinders.

RECOMMENDATION: After the problem is corrected, these plugs can be cleaned and reinstalled if not worn severely.

MMT Fouled

APPEARANCE: Spark plugs fouled by MMT (Methycyclopentadienyl Maganese Tricarbonyl) have reddish, rusty appearance on the insulator and side electrode.

CAUSE: MMT is an anti-knock additive in gasoline used to replace lead. During the combustion process, the MMT leaves a reddish deposit on the insulator and side electrode.

RECOMMENDATION: No engine malfunction is indicated and the deposits will not affect plug performance any more than lead deposits (see Ash Deposits). MMT fouled plugs can be cleaned, regapped and reinstalled.

High Speed Glazing

APPEARANCE: Glazing appears as shiny coating on the plug, either yellow or tan in color.

CAUSE: During hard, fast acceleration, plug temperatures rise suddenly. Deposits from normal combustion have no chance to fluff-off; instead, they melt on the insulator forming an electrically conductive coating which causes misfiring.

RECOMMENDATION: Glazed plugs are not easily cleaned. They should be replaced with a fresh set of plugs of the correct heat range. If the condition recurs, using plugs with a heat range one step colder may cure the problem.

Ash (Lead) Deposits

APPEARANCE: Ash deposits are characterized by light brown or white colored deposits crusted on the side or center electrodes. In some cases it may give the plug a rusty appearance.

CAUSE: Ash deposits are normally derived from oil or fuel additives burned during normal combustion. Normally they are harmless, though excessive amounts can cause misfiring. If deposits are excessive in short mileage, the valve guides may be worn.

RECOMMENDATION: Ash-fouled plugs can be cleaned, gapped and reinstalled.

Detonation

APPEARANCE: Detonation is usually characterized by a broken plug insulator.

CAUSE: A portion of the fuel charge will begin to burn spontaneously, from the increased heat following ignition. The explosion that results applies extreme pressure to engine components, frequently damaging spark plugs and pistons.

Detonation can result by over-advanced ignition timing, inferior gasoline (low octane) lean air/fuel mixture, poor carburetion, engine lugging or an increase in compression ratio due to combustion chamber deposits or engine modification.

RECOMMENDATION: Replace the plugs after correcting the problem.

Photos Courtesy Champion Spark Plug Co.

EMISSION CONTROLS

13. Be aware of the general condition of the emission control system. It contributes to reduced pollution and should be serviced regularly to maintain efficient engine operation.

14. Check all vacuum lines for dried, cracked or brittle conditions. Something as simple as a leaking vacuum hose can cause poor performance and loss of economy.

15. Avoid tampering with the emission control system. Attempting to improve fuel econ-

FUEL SYSTEM

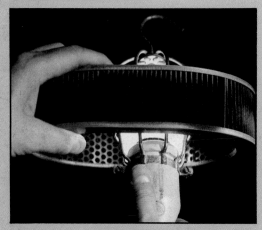

Check the air filter with a light behind it. If you can see light through the filter it can be reused.

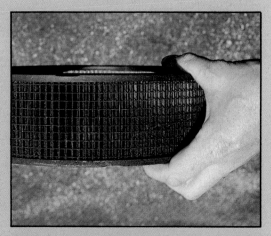

Extremely clogged filters should be discarded and replaced with a new one.

18. Replace the air filter regularly. A dirty air filter richens the air/fuel mixture and can increase fuel consumption as much as 10%. Tests show that ⅓ of all vehicles have air filters in need of replacement.

19. Replace the fuel filter at least as often as recommended.

20. Set the idle speed and carburetor mixture to specifications.

21. Check the automatic choke. A sticking or malfunctioning choke wastes gas.

22. During the summer months, adjust the automatic choke for a leaner mixture which will produce faster engine warm-ups.

COOLING SYSTEM

29. Be sure all accessory drive belts are in good condition. Check for cracks or wear.

30. Adjust all accessory drive belts to proper tension.

31. Check all hoses for swollen areas, worn spots, or loose clamps.

32. Check coolant level in the radiator or expansion tank.

33. Be sure the thermostat is operating properly. A stuck thermostat delays engine warm-up and a cold engine uses nearly twice as much fuel as a warm engine.

34. Drain and replace the engine coolant at least as often as recommended. Rust and scale

TIRES & WHEELS

38. Check the tire pressure often with a pencil type gauge. Tests by a major tire manufacturer show that 90% of all vehicles have at least 1 tire improperly inflated. Better mileage can be achieved by over-inflating tires, but never exceed the maximum inflation pressure on the side of the tire.

39. If possible, install radial tires. Radial tires deliver as much as ½ mpg more than bias belted tires.

40. Avoid installing super-wide tires. They only create extra rolling resistance and decrease fuel mileage. Stick to the manufacturer's recommendations.

41. Have the wheels properly balanced.

omy by tampering with emission controls is more likely to worsen fuel economy than improve it. Emission control changes on modern engines are not readily reversible.

16. Clean (or replace) the EGR valve and lines as recommended.

17. Be sure that all vacuum lines and hoses are reconnected properly after working under the hood. An unconnected or misrouted vacuum line can wreak havoc with engine performance.

23. Check for fuel leaks at the carburetor, fuel pump, fuel lines and fuel tank. Be sure all lines and connections are tight.

24. Periodically check the tightness of the carburetor and intake manifold attaching nuts and bolts. These are a common place for vacuum leaks to occur.

25. Clean the carburetor periodically and lubricate the linkage.

26. The condition of the tailpipe can be an excellent indicator of proper engine combustion. After a long drive at highway speeds, the inside of the tailpipe should be a light grey in color. Black or soot on the insides indicates an overly rich mixture.

27. Check the fuel pump pressure. The fuel pump may be supplying more fuel than the engine needs.

28. Use the proper grade of gasoline for your engine. Don't try to compensate for knocking or "pinging" by advancing the ignition timing. This practice will only increase plug temperature and the chances of detonation or pre-ignition with relatively little performance gain.

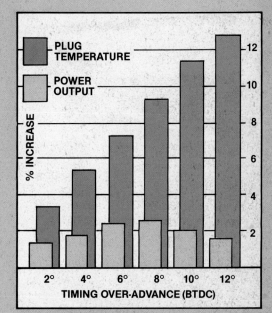

Increasing ignition timing past the specified setting results in a drastic increase in spark plug temperature with increased chance of detonation or preignition. Performance increase is considerably less. (Photo courtesy Champion Spark Plug Co.)

that form in the engine should be flushed out to allow the engine to operate at peak efficiency.

35. Clean the radiator of debris that can decrease cooling efficiency.

36. Install a flex-type or electric cooling fan, if you don't have a clutch type fan. Flex fans use curved plastic blades to push more air at low speeds when more cooling is needed; at high speeds the blades flatten out for less resistance. Electric fans only run when the engine temperature reaches a predetermined level.

37. Check the radiator cap for a worn or cracked gasket. If the cap does not seal properly, the cooling system will not function properly.

42. Be sure the front end is correctly aligned. A misaligned front end actually has wheels going in differed directions. The increased drag can reduce fuel economy by .3 mpg.

43. Correctly adjust the wheel bearings. Wheel bearings that are adjusted too tight increase rolling resistance.

Check tire pressures regularly with a reliable pocket type gauge. Be sure to check the pressure on a cold tire.

GENERAL MAINTENANCE

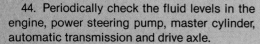

Check the fluid levels (particularly engine oil) on a regular basis. Be sure to check the oil for grit, water or other contamination.

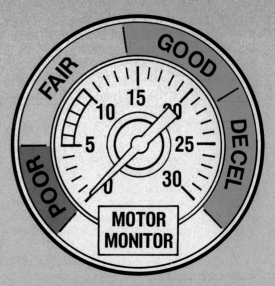

A vacuum gauge is another excellent indicator of internal engine condition and can also be installed in the dash as a mileage indicator.

44. Periodically check the fluid levels in the engine, power steering pump, master cylinder, automatic transmission and drive axle.

45. Change the oil at the recommended interval and change the filter at every oil change. Dirty oil is thick and causes extra friction between moving parts, cutting efficiency and increasing wear. A worn engine requires more frequent tune-ups and gets progressively worse fuel economy. In general, use the lightest viscosity oil for the driving conditions you will encounter.

46. Use the recommended viscosity fluids in the transmission and axle.

47. Be sure the battery is fully charged for fast starts. A slow starting engine wastes fuel.

48. Be sure battery terminals are clean and tight.

49. Check the battery electrolyte level and add distilled water if necessary.

50. Check the exhaust system for crushed pipes, blockages and leaks.

51. Adjust the brakes. Dragging brakes or brakes that are not releasing create increased drag on the engine.

52. Install a vacuum gauge or miles-per-gallon gauge. These gauges visually indicate engine vacuum in the intake manifold. High vacuum = good mileage and low vacuum = poorer mileage. The gauge can also be an excellent indicator of internal engine conditions.

53. Be sure the clutch is properly adjusted. A slipping clutch wastes fuel.

54. Check and periodically lubricate the heat control valve in the exhaust manifold. A sticking or inoperative valve prevents engine warm-up and wastes gas.

55. Keep accurate records to check fuel economy over a period of time. A sudden drop in fuel economy may signal a need for tune-up or other maintenance.

© 1980 Chilton Book Company, Radnor, PA 19089

procedure. Lubricate both O-rings with light oil before installation.

Throttle Position Sensor
REMOVAL AND INSTALLATION

1. Remove the upper and lower air cleaner assemblies.
2. Remove the throttle body assembly from the vehicle.
3. Remove the two Torx® head retaining screws holding the TPS assembly to the throttle body.
4. Remove the throttle position sensor from the throttle shaft lever.
5. Installation is the reverse of removal.

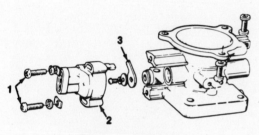

1. Retaining screws
2. TPS
3. Throttle shaft lever

Throttle position sensor mounting

Idle Speed Actuator Motor
REMOVAL AND INSTALLATION

NOTE: *The closed throttle switch is integral with the motor.*
1. Disconnect the throttle return spring.

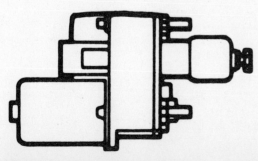

Idle speed actuator motor

Disconnect the wire harness connector from the motor.
2. Remove the motor to bracket retaining nuts. Be sure to use a back up wrench as not to remove the motor studs which hold the motor together.
3. Remove the motor from the bracket.
4. Installation is the reverse of removal.

FUEL TANK

REMOVAL AND INSTALLATION
Through 1969

1. Make sure that the tank is either completely drained or that the level is at least below any of the vent lines or filler openings so that when these lines are disconnected fuel will not run out.
2. Remove the driver's seat from the vehicle.
3. Disconnect all of the vent line hoses, the fuel gauge electrical lead, the fill hose and the fuel outlet line at the tank.
4. Remove the tank holddown screws from the mounting brackets, or the holddown strap, and lift the tank from the vehicle.
5. If there is still gas in the tank, be careful not to spill any fuel when lifting it out of the vehicle. Also, empty the tank of all fuel and flush it with water before soldering or welding the tank.
6. Install the tank in the reverse order of removal.

1970–87

The fuel tank is attached to the frame by brackets and bolts. The brackets are attached to the tank at the seam flange or the skid plate.

Before removing the fuel tank, make sure that the level of the fuel inside the tank is at least below any of the various hoses connected. It is best to either drain or siphon the majority of fuel out of the tank to make it easier to handle while removing it.

SPECIAL TOOLS

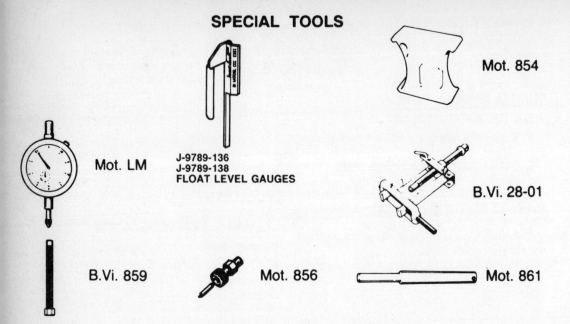

Mot. LM

J-9789-136
J-9789-138
FLOAT LEVEL GAUGES

Mot. 854

B.Vi. 28-01

B.Vi. 859

Mot. 856

Mot. 861

Chassis Electrical

5

UNDERSTANDING AND TROUBLESHOOTING ELECTRICAL SYSTEMS

Electrical problems generally fall into one of three areas:

1. The component that is not functioning is not receiving current.
2. The component itself is not functioning.
3. The component is not properly grounded.

Problems that fall into the first category are by far the most complicated. It is the current supply system to the component which contains all the switches, relays, fuses, etc.

The electrical system can be checked with a test light and a jumper wire. A test light is a device that looks like a pointed screwdriver with a wire attached to it. It has a light bulb in its handle. A jumper wire is a piece of insulated wire with an alligator clip attached to each end. To check the system you must follow the wiring diagram of the vehicle being worked on. A wiring diagram is a road map of the car's electrical system.

If a light bulb is not working, you must follow a systematic plan to determine which of the three causes is the problem.

1. Turn on the switch that controls the inoperable bulb.
2. Disconnect the power supply wire from the bulb.
3. Attach the ground wire on the test light to a good metal ground.
4. Touch the probe end of the test light to the end of the power supply wire that was disconnected from the bulb. If the bulb is receiving current, the test light will glow.

NOTE: *If the bulb is one which works only when the ignition key is turned on (turn signal), make sure the key is turned on.*

5. If the test light does not go on, then the problem is in the circuit between the battery and the bulb. As mentioned before, this in-

cludes all the switches, fuses, and relays in the system. Turn to the wiring diagram and find the bulb on the diagram. Follow the wire that runs back to the battery. The problem is an open circuit between the battery and the bulb. If the fuse is blown and, when replaced, immediately blows again, there is a short circuit in the system which must be located and repaired. If there is a switch in the system, bypass it with a jumper wire. This is done by connecting one end of the jumper wire to the power supply wire into the switch and the other

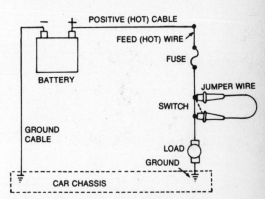

Bypassing a switch with a jumper wire

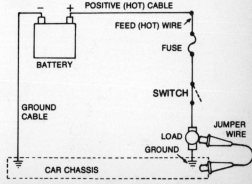

Checking for a bad ground with a jumper wire

Troubleshooting Basic Turn Signal and Flasher Problems

Most problems in the turn signals or flasher system, can be reduced to defective flashers or bulbs, which are easily replaced. Occasionally, problems in the turn signals are traced to the switch in the steering column, which will require professional service.

F = Front   R = Rear   • = Lights off   o = Lights on

Problem		Solution
Turn signals light, but do not flash		• Replace the flasher
No turn signals light on either side		• Check the fuse. Replace if defective. • Check the flasher by substitution • Check for open circuit, short circuit or poor ground
Both turn signals on one side don't work		• Check for bad bulbs • Check for bad ground in both housings
One turn signal light on one side doesn't work		• Check and/or replace bulb • Check for corrosion in socket. Clean contacts. • Check for poor ground at socket
Turn signal flashes too fast or too slow		• Check any bulb on the side flashing too fast. A heavy-duty bulb is probably installed in place of a regular bulb. • Check the bulb flashing too slow. A standard bulb was probably installed in place of a heavy-duty bulb. • Check for loose connections or corrosion at the bulb socket
Indicator lights don't work in either direction		• Check if the turn signals are working • Check the dash indicator lights • Check the flasher by substitution
One indicator light doesn't light		• On systems with 1 dash indicator: See if the lights work on the same side. Often the filaments have been reversed in systems combining stoplights with taillights and turn signals. Check the flasher by substitution • On systems with 2 indicators: Check the bulbs on the same side Check the indicator light bulb Check the flasher by substitution

end of the jumper wire to the wire coming out of the switch. Again, consult the wiring diagram. If the test light lights with the jumper wire installed, the switch or whatever was bypassed is defective.

NOTE: *Never substitute the jumper wire for the bulb, as the bulb is the component required to use the power from the source.*

6. If the bulb in the test light goes on, then the current is getting to the bulb that is not working in the car. This eliminates the first of the three possible causes. Connect the power supply wire and connect a jumper wire from the bulb to a good metal ground. Do this with the switch which controls the bulb turned on, and also the ignition switch turned on if it is required for the light to work. If the bulb works with the jumper wire installed, then it has a bad ground. This is usually caused by the metal area on which the bulb mounts to the car being coated with some type of foreign matter.

7. If neither test located the source of the trouble, then the light bulb itself is defective. The above test procedure can be applied to any

Troubleshooting Basic Lighting Problems

Problem	Cause	Solution
Lights		
One or more lights don't work, but others do	• Defective bulb(s) • Blown fuse(s) • Dirty fuse clips or light sockets • Poor ground circuit	• Replace bulb(s) • Replace fuse(s) • Clean connections • Run ground wire from light socket housing to car frame
Lights burn out quickly	• Incorrect voltage regulator setting or defective regulator • Poor battery/alternator connections	• Replace voltage regulator • Check battery/alternator connections
Lights go dim	• Low/discharged battery • Alternator not charging • Corroded sockets or connections • Low voltage output	• Check battery • Check drive belt tension; repair or replace alternator • Clean bulb and socket contacts and connections • Replace voltage regulator
Lights flicker	• Loose connection • Poor ground • Circuit breaker operating (short circuit)	• Tighten all connections • Run ground wire from light housing to car frame • Check connections and look for bare wires
Lights "flare"—Some flare is normal on acceleration—if excessive, see "Lights Burn Out Quickly"	• High voltage setting	• Replace voltage regulator
Lights glare—approaching drivers are blinded	• Lights adjusted too high • Rear springs or shocks sagging • Rear tires soft	• Have headlights aimed • Check rear springs/shocks • Check/correct rear tire pressure
Turn Signals		
Turn signals don't work in either direction	• Blown fuse • Defective flasher • Loose connection	• Replace fuse • Replace flasher • Check/tighten all connections
Right (or left) turn signal only won't work	• Bulb burned out • Right (or left) indicator bulb burned out • Short circuit	• Replace bulb • Check/replace indicator bulb • Check/repair wiring
Flasher rate too slow or too fast	• Incorrect wattage bulb • Incorrect flasher	• Flasher bulb • Replace flasher (use a variable load flasher if you pull a trailer)
Indicator lights do not flash (burn steadily)	• Burned out bulb • Defective flasher	• Replace bulb • Replace flasher
Indicator lights do not light at all	• Burned out indicator bulb • Defective flasher	• Replace indicator bulb • Replace flasher

Troubleshooting Basic Dash Gauge Problems

Problem	Cause	Solution
Coolant Temperature Gauge		
Gauge reads erratically or not at all	• Loose or dirty connections • Defective sending unit • Defective gauge	• Clean/tighten connections • Bi-metal gauge: remove the wire from the sending unit. Ground the wire for an instant. If the gauge registers, replace the sending unit. • Magnetic gauge: Disconnect the wire at the sending unit. With ignition ON gauge should register COLD. Ground the wire; gauge should register HOT.
Ammeter Gauge—Turn Headlights ON (do not start engine). Note reaction		
Ammeter shows charge Ammeter shows discharge Ammeter does not move	• Connections reversed on gauge • Ammeter is OK • Loose connections or faulty wiring • Defective gauge	• Reinstall connections • Nothing • Check/correct wiring • Replace gauge
Oil Pressure Gauge		
Gauge does not register or is inaccurate	• On mechanical gauge, Bourdon tube may be bent or kinked • Low oil pressure • Defective gauge • Defective wiring • Defective sending unit	• Check tube for kinks or bends preventing oil from reaching the gauge • Remove sending unit. Idle the engine briefly. If no oil flows from sending unit hole, problem is in engine. • Remove the wire from the sending unit and ground it for an instant with the ignition ON. A good gauge will go to the top of the scale. • Check the wiring to the gauge. If it's OK and the gauge doesn't register when grounded, replace the gauge. • If the wiring is OK and the gauge functions when grounded, replace the sending unit
All Gauges		
All gauges do not operate All gauges read low or erratically All gauges pegged	• Blown fuse • Defective instrument regulator • Defective or dirty instrument voltage regulator • Loss of ground between instrument voltage regulator and car • Defective instrument regulator	• Replace fuse • Replace instrument voltage regulator • Clean contacts or replace • Check ground • Replace regulator
Warning Lights		
Light(s) do not come on when ignition is ON, but engine is not started Light comes on with engine running	• Defective bulb • Defective wire • Defective sending unit • Problem in individual system • Defective sending unit	• Replace bulb • Check wire from light to sending unit • Disconnect the wire from the sending unit and ground it. Replace the sending unit if the light comes on with the ignition ON. • Check system • Check sending unit (see above)

Troubleshooting the Heater

Problem	Cause	Solution
Blower motor will not turn at any speed	• Blown fuse • Loose connection • Defective ground • Faulty switch • Faulty motor • Faulty resistor	• Replace fuse • Inspect and tighten • Clean and tighten • Replace switch • Replace motor • Replace resistor
Blower motor turns at one speed only	• Faulty switch • Faulty resistor	• Replace switch • Replace resistor
Blower motor turns but does not circulate air	• Intake blocked • Fan not secured to the motor shaft	• Clean intake • Tighten security
Heater will not heat	• Coolant does not reach proper temperature • Heater core blocked internally • Heater core air-bound • Blend-air door not in proper position	• Check and replace thermostat if necessary • Flush or replace core if necessary • Purge air from core • Adjust cable
Heater will not defrost	• Control cable adjustment incorrect • Defroster hose damaged	• Adjust control cable • Replace defroster hose

Troubleshooting Basic Windshield Wiper Problems

Problem	Cause	Solution
Electric Wipers		
Wipers do not operate— Wiper motor heats up or hums	• Internal motor defect • Bent or damaged linkage • Arms improperly installed on linking pivots	• Replace motor • Repair or replace linkage • Position linkage in park and reinstall wiper arms
Wipers do not operate— No current to motor	• Fuse or circuit breaker blown • Loose, open or broken wiring • Defective switch • Defective or corroded terminals • No ground circuit for motor or switch	• Replace fuse or circuit breaker • Repair wiring and connections • Replace switch • Replace or clean terminals • Repair ground circuits
Wipers do not operate— Motor runs	• Linkage disconnected or broken	• Connect wiper linkage or replace broken linkage
Vacuum Wipers		
Wipers do not operate	• Control switch or cable inoperative • Loss of engine vacuum to wiper motor (broken hoses, low engine vacuum, defective vacuum/fuel pump) • Linkage broken or disconnected • Defective wiper motor	• Repair or replace switch or cable • Check vacuum lines, engine vacuum and fuel pump • Repair linkage • Replace wiper motor
Wipers stop on engine acceleration	• Leaking vacuum hoses • Dry windshield • Oversize wiper blades • Defective vacuum/fuel pump	• Repair or replace hoses • Wet windshield with washers • Replace with proper size wiper blades • Replace pump

of the components of the chassis electrical system by substituting the component that is not working for the light bulb. Remember that for any electrical system to work, all connections must be clean and tight.

HEATER AND AIR CONDITIONING

Blower Motor

REMOVAL AND INSTALLATION

Through 1977

1. Disconnect the battery ground cable. Detach any interfering control cables.
2. Disconnect the electrical connections:
   a. Heater switch
   b. Ground wire
   c. Battery connector
3. Remove the screws that hold the motor to the heater assembly and remove the blower motor housing and motor.
4. Remove fan and blower motor from blower motor housing.

1978–87

The heater housing assembly has to be removed to get out the blower motor.
1. Drain about two quarts of coolant.
CAUTION: *When draining the coolant, keep in mind that cats and dogs are attracted by the ethylene glycol antifreeze, and are quite likely to drink any that is left in an uncovered container or in puddles on the ground. This will prove fatal in sufficient quantity. Always drain the coolant into a sealable container. Coolant should be reused unless it is contaminated or several years old.*
2. Disconnect the heater hoses at the engine side of the firewall.

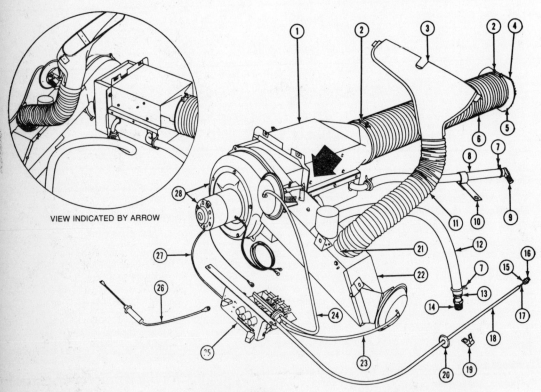

VIEW INDICATED BY ARROW

1. Heater assembly	11. Defroster hose	21. Defroster bushing
2. Hose clamp	12. Hot water hose	22. Heat distributor assembly
3. Defroster nozzle	13. Heater nipple	23. Heater control tube
4. Air duct screen	14. Reducing bushing	24. Heater control tube
5. Air duct and heater collar	15. Inverted flared tube nut	25. Heater control assembly
6. Air duct intake tube	16. Inverted flared tube connector	26. Fuse holder assembly
7. Hose clamp	17. Heater vacuum to engine tube	27. Bowden wire (control panel to
8. Straight hot water hose	18. Heater control tube	heater)
9. Heater tube elbow	19. Clip	28. Blower and air inlet assembly
10. Heater hose support bracket	20. Grommet	

Heater assembly through 1971. Earlier heaters are less complicated

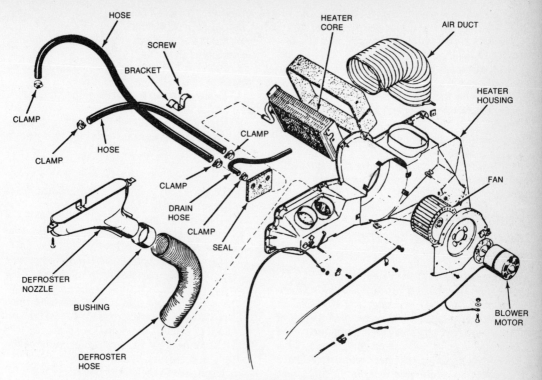

1972–77 heater assembly

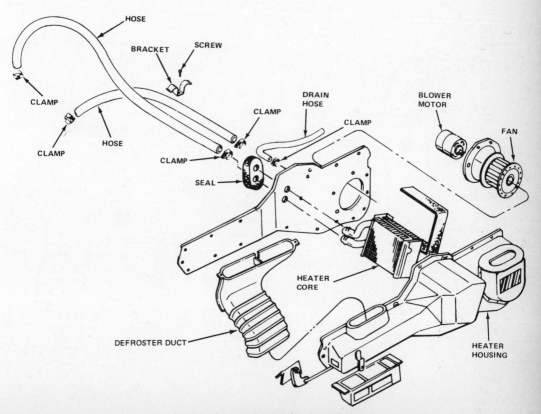

1979–83 heater/defroster components

3. Detach the heater control cables.

4. Disconnect the motor wiring.

5. Detach the water drain hose and the defroster hose.

6. Remove the nuts from the studs in the engine compartment.

7. Tilt the heater housing assembly down and pull it back toward the inside of the vehicle.

8. Remove the attaching screws and the blower motor.

9. On installation, make sure that the seals around the core tubes and blower motor are in place.

Heater Core

REMOVAL AND INSTALLATION

Through 1974

1. Drain the cooling system.

CAUTION: *When draining the coolant, keep in mind that cats and dogs are attracted by the ethylene glycol antifreeze, and are quite likely to drink any that is left in an uncovered container or in puddles on the ground. This will prove fatal in sufficient quantity. Always drain the coolant into a sealable container.*

Coolant should be reused unless it is contaminated or several years old.

2. Mark the duct halves to be sure they are reassembled properly.

3. Remove the screws that fasten the two halves of the duct together.

4. Remove the screws that secure the heater core to the duct.

5. Remove the heater core from the vehicle.

6. Install in reverse order of the above procedure.

1975–76

1. Drain about two quarts of coolant from the radiator.

CAUTION: *When draining the coolant, keep in mind that cats and dogs are attracted by the ethylene glycol antifreeze, and are quite likely to drink any that is left in an uncovered container or in puddles on the ground. This will prove fatal in sufficient quantity. Always drain the coolant into a sealable container. Coolant should be reused unless it is contaminated or several years old.*

2. Disconnect the battery cables, remove the battery and battery box.

3. Disconnect the heater hoses.

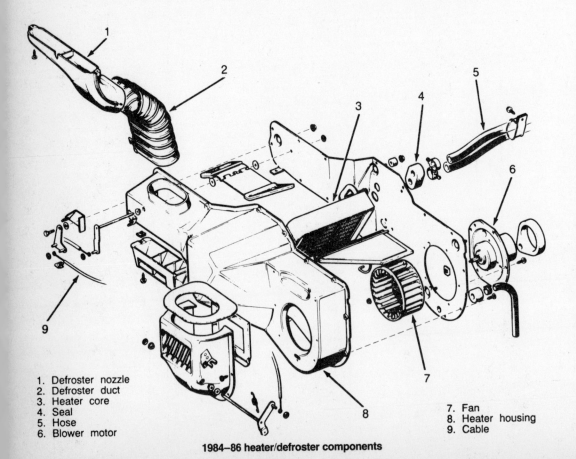

1. Defroster nozzle
2. Defroster duct
3. Heater core
4. Seal
5. Hose
6. Blower motor
7. Fan
8. Heater housing
9. Cable

1984–86 heater/defroster components

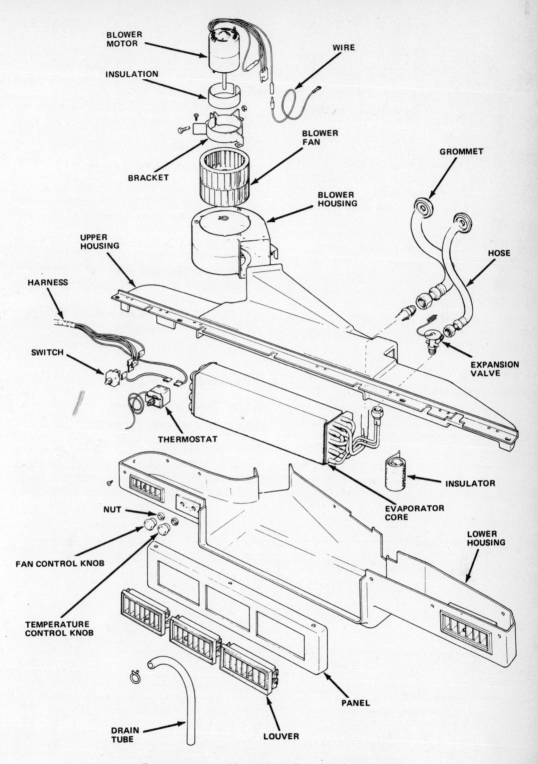

BLOWER MOTOR

INSULATION

BRACKET

WIRE

BLOWER FAN

BLOWER HOUSING

GROMMET

HOSE

UPPER HOUSING

HARNESS

SWITCH

THERMOSTAT

EXPANSION VALVE

INSULATOR

EVAPORATOR CORE

NUT

FAN CONTROL KNOB

LOWER HOUSING

TEMPERATURE CONTROL KNOB

PANEL

DRAIN TUBE

LOUVER

Evaporator assembly used on all models through 1987

4. Disconnect the damper door control cables.

5. Disconnect the blower motor wiring harness at the switch and ground wire at the instrument panel.

6. Remove the glove box.

7. Disconnect the water drain hose and defroster hose.

8. Disconnect the heater-to-air deflector duct at the heater housing.

9. Remove the nuts from the heater housing studs in the engine compartment and remove the heater housing assembly.

10. Remove the heater core from the heater housing.

11. Install the heater core in the reverse order of removal, refill the radiator, run the engine and check for leaks.

1978–87

The heater housing assembly has to be removed to get out the heater core. The procedure is the same as for blower motor removal and installation.

Evaporator

REMOVAL AND INSTALLATION

1. Discharge the system. See Chapter 1.

2. Disconnect the inlet (suction) and outlet hoses at the evaporator. Cap the openings at once.

3. Remove the hose clamps and dash grommet screws.

4. Remove the evaporator housing-to-dash panel screws and the housing mounting bracket screw.

5. Lower the housing and pull the hoses and hose grommets through the dash opening.

6. The blower motor and evaporator core can now be removed for service.

7. After installing all the parts, evacuate, charge and leak test the system.

Control Panel

REMOVAL AND INSTALLATION

NOTE: *Through 1986, there was no control panel as such. The fan switch was removable. The following applies, therefore, to 1987 models only.*

1. Remove the instrument cluster bezel screws.

2. Remove the bezel.

3. Remove the control panel attaching screws.

4. Pull the panel toward you and disconnect the cables, hoses and wires.

5. Installation is the reverse of removal.

WINDSHIELD WIPERS

Wiper Blades and Arms

REMOVAL AND INSTALLATION

To remove the blade, pull it away from the windshield. Push against the tip of the wiper arm to compress the locking spring and disengage the retaining pin. Pivot the blade clock-

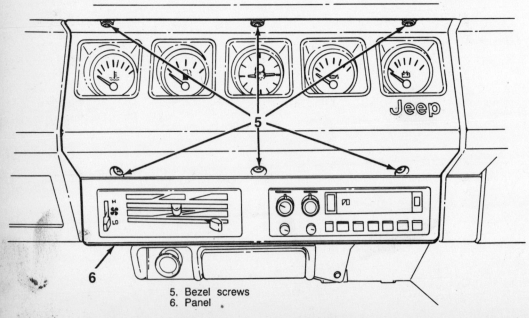

5. Bezel screws
6. Panel

1987 heater/air conditioning control panel

wise to unhook it from the arm. To install the blade, just snap it into position.

To remove the arm, simply pry it straight off carefully. When you reinstall it, make sure that it doesn't hit the rubber molding at either edge of the windshield while running.

Motor

REMOVAL AND INSTALLATION

Through 1971

ALL EXCEPT UTILITY MODELS

1. Remove the windshield wiper assembly from the pivot shaft.
2. Remove the vacuum hose or wire from the motor.
3. Remove all attaching screws that hold the motor to the windshield assembly and remove the motor from the vehicle.
4. Install in the reverse order.

UTILITY MODELS

A vacuum type wiper motor is used and is located on the firewall in the engine compartment, directly behind the engine. Release the tension on the cables by loosening the nut attaching the tensioner to the mounting bracket. Then, unbolt and remove the motor.

After installing the motor, adjust the cable tension as described below.

1972–75

1. Remove the crash pad, if any. Remove the extreme left plastic hole plug from the bottom of the windshield frame air duct and disconnect the drive link from the motor crank.
2. Loosen the wiper control knob setscrew.

3. Remove the control switch and mark the location of the wires on the switch prior to removing them from the switch.
4. Remove the motor cover and the motor.
5. Install in the reverse order of the above procedure.

NOTE: *The motor cover must be sealed when installing.*

1976–87

1. If your Jeep has crash padding, you have to fold the windshield down for access. Even if you don't have the padding, you can't get the

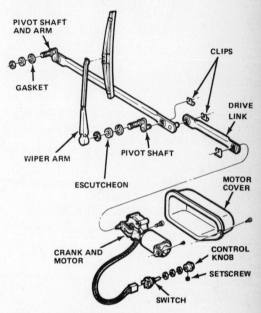

1976–78 windshield wiper components

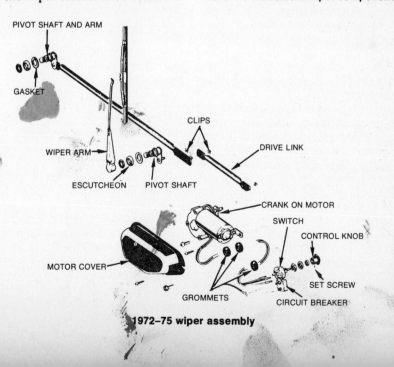

1972–75 wiper assembly

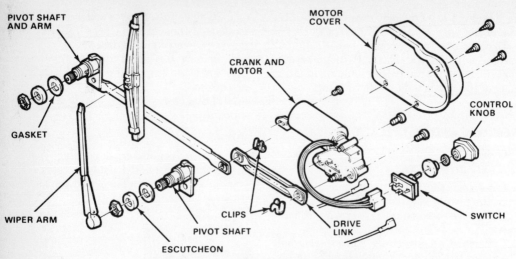

PIVOT SHAFT AND ARM

MOTOR COVER

CRANK AND MOTOR

CONTROL KNOB

GASKET

WIPER ARM

CLIPS

PIVOT SHAFT

ESCUTCHEON

DRIVE LINK

SWITCH

1979 and later windshield wiper components

wires out to remove the motor from the vehicle, unless the windshield is down.

2. Remove the wiper motor cover.

3. Remove the left access plug from the bottom of the windshield.

4. Disconnect the drive link from the left wiper pivot by sliding the clip off.

5. Detach the wiring from the switch.

6. Remove the mounting screws and the wiper motor.

7. Reverse the procedure for installation.

Linkage

REMOVAL AND INSTALLATION

1945–71

NOTE: *Jeep vehicles through 1971, except for Utility Models, have no windshield wiper linkage.*

UTILITY MODELS

These vehicles employ a cable system to actuate the wiper arms.

1. Release the tension on the cable by loosening the tension attaching nut.

2. Disengage the ferrule at the end of the cable from the wiper arm and remove the cable.

3. The cable is installed by engaging the the ferrule in the slot in the wiper arm and passing the cable through the slot.

4. Once the cable is installed, it must be adjusted as follows:

a. Be sure that the tensioner attaching bolts are tight. The left and right tensioners are not interchangeable.

b. Loosen, but don't remove, the tensioner locknut on the bracket.

c. When the locknuts are loosened, the tensioners should automatically take up

the cable slack. It may be necessary to tap the stud to free the tensioner locknut. In some cases, it may help to pry the bracket outwards to get the tensioners to take up the slack.

d. Tighten the locknuts firmly. If there is still slack, proceed to Step e.

e. Using a file, elongate the holes in the tensioner bracket, toward the center of the vehicle an additonal $\frac{1}{16}$". This should provide enough tensioner movement.

f. If slack is still present, replace the cables.

1972–75

1. Remove the wiper arms and pivot shaft nuts, washers, escutcheons and gaskets.

2. Disconnect the drive arm from the motor crank.

3. Remove the individual links where necessary, to remove the pivot shaft bodies without excessive interference.

4. Reverse the procedure for installation.

1976–87

1. Remove the wiper arms.

2. Remove the nuts attaching the pivots to the windshield frame.

3. Remove the necessary components from the top of the windshield frame.

4. Remove the windshield holddown knobs and fold the windshield forward.

5. Remove the access hole covers on both sides of the windshield.

6. Disconnect the wiper motor drive link from the left wiper pivot.

7. Remove the wiper pivot shafts and linkage from the access hole.

8. Install the linkage in the reverse order.

INSTRUMENT PANEL

Instrument Cluster

REMOVAL AND INSTALLATION

Through 1975

1. Disconnect one battery cable.
2. Separate the speedometer cable from the speedometer head.
3. Remove the screws that hold up the heater control bracket (1972 and later only).
4. Remove the attaching nuts that hold the cluster to the dash.
5. Remove the gauge wires and remove the cluster assembly.

6. Install in the reverse order. After installing the cluster, connect the battery and check all of the lights and gauges for proper operation.

1976–86

1. Disconnect the negative battery cable.
2. Disconnect the speedometer cable from the back of the speedometer.
3. Remove the instrument cluster attaching nuts and remove the cluster.
4. Disconnect the instrument cluster electrical connectors and remove the cluster from the vehicle.
5. Install in the reverse order.

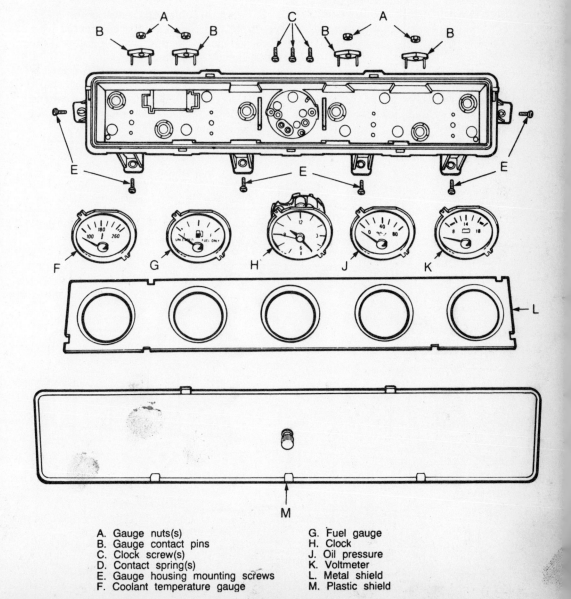

A. Gauge nuts(s)
B. Gauge contact pins
C. Clock screw(s)
D. Contact spring(s)
E. Gauge housing mounting screws
F. Coolant temperature gauge
G. Fuel gauge
H. Clock
J. Oil pressure
K. Voltmeter
L. Metal shield
M. Plastic shield

1987 gauge cluster

1987

GAUGE CLUSTER

1. Disconnect the battery ground.
2. Remove the six bezel screws.
3. Remove the six cluster attaching screws.
4. Pull the cluster, gently, towards you and disconnect the wiring connector.
5. Lift out the cluster.
6. Release the seven locking tabs and remove the plastic lens shield.
7. Remove the metal shield.
8. Remove the gauge nuts to free the gauges.
9. When installing the gauges, the gauge contact pins will be driven into place as you tighten the gauge nuts, so be careful to align them properly. When installing the cluster, be careful to avoid overtorquing the fasteners!

SPEEDOMETER

1. Remove the five shroud attaching screws.
2. Exert downward pressure on the top of the shroud and upward pressure on the bottom of the shroud while pulling the shroud towards you. This will release the retaining tabs.

3. Remove the two speedometer attaching screws and pull the speedometer towards you. Disconnect the cable.
4. Installation is the reverse of removal.

TACHOMETER

1. Remove the five shroud attaching screws.
2. Exert downward pressure on the top of the shroud and upward pressure on the bottom of the shroud while pulling the shroud towards you. This will release the retaining tabs.
3. Remove the two tachometer attaching screws and pull the tachometer towards you. Disconnect the wiring.
4. Installation is the reverse of removal.

SPEEDOMETER CABLE REPLACEMENT

1. Reach up behind the center of the speedometer head. The cable is connected by a threaded ring. Unscrew the ring and pull the cable sheath from the head.
2. The cable core can be pulled from the sheath.
3. If the core is broken, detach the other end of the sheath from the transmission. Pull out the broken end.

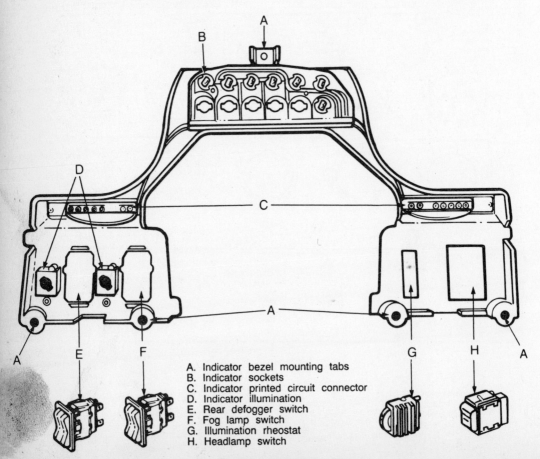

A. Indicator bezel mounting tabs
B. Indicator sockets
C. Indicator printed circuit connector
D. Indicator illumination
E. Rear defogger switch
F. Fog lamp switch
G. Illumination rheostat
H. Headlamp switch

1987 Indicator bezel

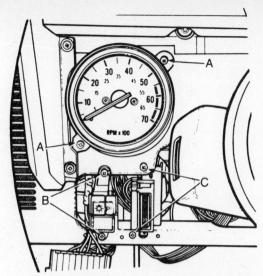

Tachometer removal. A, B, and C are attaching screws

4. When installing the cable, apply a very small amount of speedometer cable graphite lubricant.

Radio

REMOVAL AND INSTALLATION

Through 1975

The only factory installed radio available on these models was offered in 1975. It is a simple underdash unit, similar to those dealer in-

stalled in earlier models. Removal and installation are obvious.

1976-87

1. Disconnect the battery ground cable.
2. Remove the control knobs, nuts, and bezel.
3. On 1976 and early 1977 models, you may have to detach the defroster hose. With air conditioning, remove the screws and lower the assembly.
4. Disconnect the radio bracket from the instrument panel.
5. Tilt the radio down and remove it toward the steering wheel.
6. Detach the antenna, speaker, and power wires.
7. Reverse the procedure for installation.

LIGHTING

Headlight

REMOVAL AND INSTALLATION

Through 1986

1. Remove the one lower attaching screw from the headlight trim ring. Pull out slightly at the bottom and push up to disengage the upper retaining tab.
2. Remove the trim ring.
3. Remove the three retaining screws from the retaining ring.

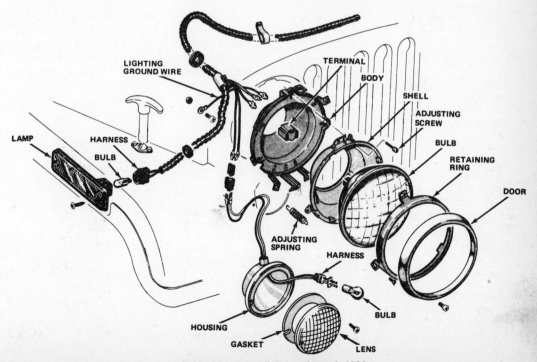

Typical front end lighting through 1986

VERTICAL ADJUSTMENT   HORIZONTAL ADJUSTMENT

1972–86 headlight adjustment

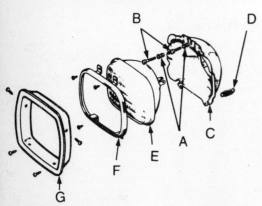

A. Plastic adjuster nut(s)
B. Adjusting screw(s)
C. Headlamp bucket
D. Adjusting spring
E. Headlamp
F. Retaining ring
G. Trim ring

1987 headlight assembly

4. Pull the headlamp out and disconnect the wire harness.

NOTE: *When installing the headlamp, the number 2 is placed at the top of the lamp.*

Removing the headlight bezel on a 1987 Wrangler

5. Install in reverse order of the above procedure. Check for proper seating of the lamp in its mounting ring and check for proper alignment.

1987

1. Remove the four trim ring screws and the trim ring.
2. Remove the four retaining ring screws.
3. Pull out on the lamp and disconnect the wiring plug.
4. Installation is the reverse of removal.

FUSIBLE LINKS

Fusible links are sections of wire, with special insulation, designed to melt under electrical overload. There is usually one in the main wire from the battery, and near the alternator output side. If one melts, it must be replaced with a new link of the correct amperage rating. Never replace a melted link with ordinary wire; you run the risk of melting your entire wiring harness.

Removing the headlight retaining ring and headlight on a 1987 Wrangler

REMOVE EXISTING VINYL TUBE SHIELDING
REINSTALL OVER FUSE LINK BEFORE CRIMPING
FUSE LINK TO WIRE ENDS

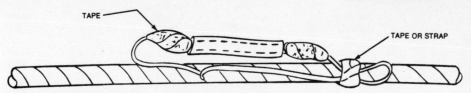

TAPE

TAPE OR STRAP

TYPICAL REPAIR USING THE SPECIAL #17 GA. (9.00″ LONG-YELLOW) FUSE LINK REQUIRED FOR THE AIR/COND.
CIRCUITS (2) #687E and #261A LOCATED IN THE ENGINE COMPARTMENT

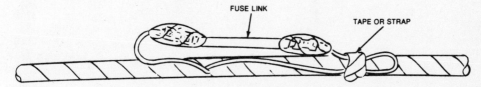

FUSE LINK

TAPE OR STRAP

TYPICAL REPAIR FOR ANY IN-LINE FUSE LINK USING THE SPECIFIED GAUGE FUSE LINK FOR THE SPECIFIC CIRCUIT

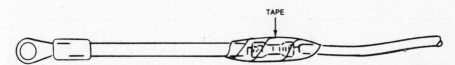

TAPE

TYPICAL REPAIR USING THE EYELET TERMINAL FUSE LINK OF THE SPECIFIED GAUGE FOR ATTACHMENT TO A CIRCUIT WIRE END

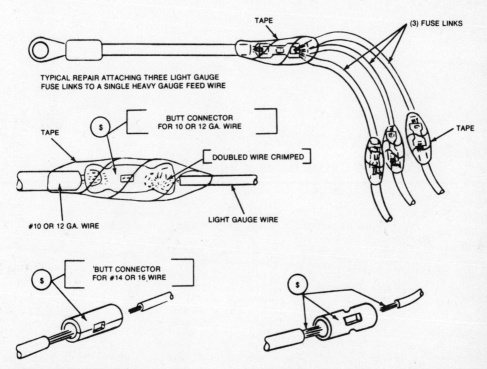

TAPE

(3) FUSE LINKS

TYPICAL REPAIR ATTACHING THREE LIGHT GAUGE
FUSE LINKS TO A SINGLE HEAVY GAUGE FEED WIRE

TAPE

BUTT CONNECTOR
FOR 10 OR 12 GA. WIRE

$

DOUBLED WIRE CRIMPED

TAPE

#10 OR 12 GA. WIRE

LIGHT GAUGE WIRE

'BUTT CONNECTOR
FOR #14 OR 16 WIRE

$

$

FUSIBLE LINK REPAIR PROCEDURE

General fuse link repair procedure

Light Bulb Specification Chart

Item	6-volt models	Early F-Head 12-volt	Late F-Head and 6-225	1972–83	1984–87
Headlights	5040S/6006	5400S/6012	6012	①	⑤
Front parking	63	67	1157	194	④
Front Signal	1158	1176/1034	1157	1157A	1157NA
Stop/tail/signal	1158	1034	1157	1157	1157
License plate	—	—	1155	1155	1155
High beam	51	53/57	53/57	②	53
Signals	51	53	53	②	53
Charge indicator	51	53/57	53/57	②	53
Oil presure	51	57	57	②	53
Instrument cluster	55	57	57	②	53
Dome lamp	—	—	—	—	212
Heater controls	—	—	57	1816	53
Clock	—	—	—	③	1816
Ignition switch	—	—	—	②	53
Shift selector	—	—	—	③	1892
4WD indicator	—	—	—	57	47
Parking brake warning	—	—	57	158	158
Radio	—	—	—	1893	1893
Courtesy lights	—	—	—	89	89
Glove box	—	—	—	1891	—
Back-up	—	—	1156	1156	1156
4-way flasher	—	—	1157	552	552
Side marker	63	67	1157	194	194

① 1972–73: 6012
   1974–83: 6014
② 1972: 57
   1973–83: 53
③ 1972–76: 1816
   1977–83: 1892
④ 1984–86: 1157NA
   1987: 2057NA
⑤ 1984–86: 6014 or W6014
   1987: H6054

Fuse and Circuit Breaker Specification Chart

Item	1945–71	1972–75	1976–77	1978–83	1984–86	1987
Air conditioner	—	—	25 amp	2 amp		
Back-up lights	—	9 amp	9 amp	15amp		
Lighter	—	14 amp	15 amp	10 amp		
Clock	—	—				
Cluster feed	—	—	3 amp	3 amp		
Control panel	—	—	3 amp	3 amp		
Turn signal	①	9 amp	10 amp	10 amp		
Tail and stop	20 amp	20 amp	20 amp	②		
4-way flasher	14 amp	14 amp	15 amp	②		
Headlights	—	25 amp CB	25 amp CB	20 amp CB		
Heater	14 amp	15 amp	25 amp	25 amp		
Brake warning light	—	9 amp	3 amp	3 amp		
Radio	—	—	③	③		
Windshield wipers	14 amp	6 amp CB	4.5 amp CB	4.5 amp CB	4.5 amp CB	6.7 amp CB

① 6-volt: 14 amp
   Early 12-volt: 9 amp
   Later 12-volt: 14 amp
② Check marking on fuse box; 10, and 15 and 20 amp fuses have been used
③ 10 amp in panel; 5 amp in line

Drive Train

6

UNDERSTANDING THE MANUAL TRANSMISSION AND CLUTCH

Because of the way an internal combustion engine breathes, it can produce torque, or twisting force, only within a narrow speed range. Most modern, overhead valve engines must turn at about 2,500 rpm to produce their peak torque. By 4,500 rpm they are producing so little torque that continued increases in engine speed produce no power increases.

The manual transmission and clutch are employed to vary the relationship between engine speed and the speed of the wheels so that adequate engine power can be produced under all circumstances. The clutch allows engine torque to be applied to the transmission input shaft gradually, due to mechanical slippage. The car can, consequently, be started smoothly from a full stop.

The transmission changes the ratio between the rotating speeds of the engine and the wheels by the use of gears. On Jeep vehicles, 3-speed or 4-speed transmissions are most common. The lower gears allow full engine power to be applied to the rear wheels during acceleration at low speeds.

The clutch drive plate is a thin disc, the center of which is splined to the transmission input shaft. Both sides of the disc are covered with a layer of material which is similar to brake lining and which is capable of allowing slippage without roughness or excessive noise.

The clutch cover is bolted to the engine flywheel and incorporates a diaphragm spring which provides the pressure to engage the clutch. The cover also houses the pressure plate. The driven disc is sandwiched between the pressure plate and the smooth surface of the flywheel when the clutch pedal is released, thus forcing it to turn at the same speed as the engine crankshaft.

The transmission contains a mainshaft which passes all the way through the transmission, from the clutch to the driveshaft. This shaft is separated at one point, so that front and rear portions can turn at different speeds.

Power is transmitted by a countershaft in the lower gears and reverse. The gears of the countershaft mesh with gears on the mainshaft, allowing power to be carried from one to the other. All the countershaft gears are integral with that shaft, while several of the mainshaft gears can either rotate independently of the shaft or be locked to it. Shifting from one gear to the next causes one of the gears to be freed from rotating with the shaft and locks another to it. Gears are locked and unlocked by internal dog clutches which slide between the center of the gear and the shaft. The forward gears usually employ synchronizers; friction members which smoothly bring gear and shaft to the same speed before the toothed dog clutches are engaged.

The clutch is operating properly if:

1. It will stall the engine when released with the vehicle held stationary.

2. The shift lever can be moved freely between first and reverse gears when the vehicle is stationary and the clutch disengaged.

A clutch pedal free-play adjustment is incorporated in the linkage. If there is about 1–2″ of motion before the pedal begins to release the clutch, it is adjusted properly. Inadequate free-play wears all parts of the clutch releasing mechanisms and may cause slippage. Excessive free-play may cause inadequate release and hard shifting of gears.

Some clutches use a hydraulic system in place of mechanical linkage. If the clutch fails to release, fill the clutch master cylinder with fluid to the proper level and pump the clutch pedal to fill the system with fluid. Bleed the system in the same way as a brake system. If leaks are located, tighten loose connections or overhaul the master or slave cylinder as necessary.

MANUAL TRANSMISSION

REMOVAL AND INSTALLATION

1945–71

ALL CJ MODELS

CAUTION: *The clutch driven disc contains asbestos, which has been determined to be a cancer causing agent. Never clean clutch* *surfaces with compressed air! Avoid inhaling any dust from any clutch surface! When cleaning clutch surfaces, use a commercially available brake cleaning fluid.*

1. Raise and support the vehicle on jackstands.

2. Drain the transmission and transfer case.

3. Remove the shift lever and shift housing. On CJ-2A models up to serial #38221 remove the remote linkage as follows:

a. Remove the shift rods from the transmission and from the steering remote control clutch levers.

Troubleshooting the Manual Transmission and Transfer Case

Problem	Cause	Solution
Transmission shift hard	• Clutch adjustment incorrect • Clutch linkage or cable binding • Shift rail binding	• Adjust clutch • Lubricate or repair as necessary • Check for mispositioned selector arm roll pin, loose cover bolts, worn shift rail bores, worn shift rail, distorted oil seal, or extension housing not aligned with case. Repair as necessary.
	• Internal bind in transmission caused by shift forks, selector plates, or synchronizer assemblies • Clutch housing misalignment • Incorrect lubricant • Block rings and/or cone seats worn	• Remove, dissemble and inspect transmission. Replace worn or damaged components as necessary. • Check runout at rear face of clutch housing • Drain and refill transmission • Blocking ring to gear clutch tooth face clearance must be 0.030 inch or greater. If clearance is correct it may still be necessary to inspect blocking rings and cone seats for excessive wear. Repair as necessary.
Gear clash when shifting from one gear to another	• Clutch adjustment incorrect • Clutch linkage or cable binding • Clutch housing misalignment • Lubricant level low or incorrect lubricant • Gearshift components, or synchronizer assemblies worn or damaged	• Adjust clutch • Lubricate or repair as necessary • Check runout at rear of clutch housing • Drain and refill transmission and check for lubricant leaks if level was low. Repair as necessary. • Remove, disassemble and inspect transmission. Replace worn or damaged components as necessary.
Transmission noisy	• Lubricant level low or incorrect lubricant • Clutch housing-to-engine, or transmission-to-clutch housing bolts loose • Dirt, chips, foreign material in transmission • Gearshift mechanism, transmission gears, or bearing components worn or damaged • Clutch housing misalignment	• Drain and refill transmission. If lubricant level was low, check for leaks and repair as necessary. • Check and correct bolt torque as necessary • Drain, flush, and refill transmission • Remove, disassemble and inspect transmission. Replace worn or damaged components as necessary. • Check runout at rear face of clutch housing

Troubleshooting the Manual Transmission and Transfer Case (cont.)

Problem	Cause	Solution
Jumps out of gear	• Clutch housing misalignment	• Check runout at rear face of clutch housing
	• Gearshift lever loose	• Check lever for worn fork. Tighten loose attaching bolts.
	• Offset lever nylon insert worn or lever attaching nut loose	• Remove gearshift lever and check for loose offset lever nut or worn insert. Repair or replace as necessary.
	• Gearshift mechanism, shift forks, selector plates, interlock plate, selector arm, shift rail, detent plugs, springs or shift cover worn or damaged	• Remove, disassemble and inspect transmission cover assembly. Replace worn or damaged components as necessary.
	• Clutch shaft or roller bearings worn or damaged	• Replace clutch shaft or roller bearings as necessary
	• Gear teeth worn or tapered, synchronizer assemblies worn or damaged, excessive end play caused by worn thrust washers or output shaft gears	• Remove, disassemble, and inspect transmission. Replace worn or damaged components as necessary.
	• Pilot bushing worn	• Replace pilot bushing
Will not shift into one gear	• Gearshift selector plates, interlock plate, or selector arm, worn, damaged, or incorrectly assembled	• Remove, disassemble, and inspect transmission cover assembly. Repair or replace components as necessary.
	• Shift rail detent plunger worn, spring broken, or plug loose	• Tighten plug or replace worn or damaged components as necessary
	• Gearshift lever worn or damaged	• Replace gearshift lever
	• Synchronizer sleeves or hubs, damaged or worn	• Remove, disassemble and inspect transmission. Replace worn or damaged components.
Locked in one gear—cannot be shift out	• Shift rail(s) worn or broken, shifter fork bent, setscrew loose, center detent plug missing or worn	• Inspect and replace worn or damaged parts
	• Broken gear teeth on countershaft gear, clutch shaft, or reverse idler gear	• Inspect and replace damaged part
	Gearshift lever broken or worn, shift mechanism in cover incorrectly assembled or broken, worn damaged gear train components	• Disassemble transmission. Replace damaged parts or assemble correctly.
Transfer case difficult to shift or will not shift into desired range	• Vehicle speed too great to permit shifting	• Stop vehicle and shift into desired range. Or reduce speed to 3–4 km/h (2–3 mph) before attempting to shift.
	• If vehicle was operated for extended period in 4H mode on dry paved surface, driveline torque load may cause difficult shifting	• Stop vehicle, shift transmission to neutral, shift transfer case to 2H mode and operate vehicle in 2H on dry paved surfaces
	• Transfer case external shift linkage binding	• Lubricate or repair or replace linkage, or tighten loose components as necessary
	• Insufficient or incorrect lubricant	• Drain and refill to edge of fill hole with SAE 85W-90 gear lubricant only
	• Internal components binding, worn, or damaged	• Disassemble unit and replace worn or damaged components as necessary
Transfer case noisy in all drive modes	• Insufficient or incorrect lubricant	• Drain and refill to edge of fill hole with SAE 85W-90 gear lubricant only. Check for leaks and repair if necessary.

Troubleshooting the Manual Transmission and Transfer Case (cont.)

Problem	Cause	Solution
		Note: If unit is still noisy after drain and refill, disassembly and inspection may be required to locate source of noise.
Noisy in—or jumps out of four wheel drive low range	• Transfer case not completely engaged in 4L position	• Stop vehicle, shift transfer case in Neutral, then shift back into 4L position
	• Shift linkage loose or binding	• Tighten, lubricate, or repair linkage as necessary
	• Shift fork cracked, inserts worn, or fork is binding on shift rail	• Disassemble unit and repair as necessary
Lubricant leaking from output shaft seals or from vent	• Transfer case overfilled	• Drain to correct level
	• Vent closed or restricted	• Clear or replace vent if necessary
	• Output shaft seals damaged or installed incorrectly	• Replace seals. Be sure seal lip faces interior of case when installed. Also be sure yoke seal surfaces are not scored or nicked. Remove scores, nicks with fine sandpaper or replace yoke(s) if necessary.
Abnormal tire wear	• Extended operation on dry hard surface (paved) roads in 4H range	• Operate in 2H on hard surface (paved) roads

Manual Transmission Application Chart

Transmission Types	Years	Models
AISIN AX5 5-sp**	1987	Standard on some models
Peugeot BA 10/5 5-sp**	1987	Standard on some models
Tremec T-150 3-sp	1976–79	Standard on all models
Tremec T-176 4-sp	1980	All CJ-5 and CJ-7 w/8-304
	1981	Some CJ-5, CJ-7 w/6-258
		All models w/8-304
	1982–83	All models w/6/258
	1984–86	Standard on some models with 6-258
Warner SR-4 4-sp	1980	CJ-7 w/258
	1981	All CJ-5, CJ-7 w/4-151
		Some CJ-5 and CJ-7 w/6-258
Warner T-4 4-sp	1982–83	Standard on all models w/4-151
	1984–86	Standard on all models w/4-150
		Standard on some models w/6-258
Warner T-5 5-sp	1982–82	Optional on CJ-5 w/4-151
		Optional on CJ-7 and Scrambler w/6-258
	1984–86	Optional on all models
Warner T-14A 3-sp	1972–75	Standard on all models
Warner T-18 4-sp	1971–75	Optional on all models
Warner T-18A 4-sp	1976–	Optional on all models
Warner T-86 4-sp OD	1947–58	Optional on 2-WD Utility models w/6-226 engine
Warner T-86AA 3-sp	1955–71	Standard on all V6 models
Warner T-90 3-sp	1947–58	Standard on 4-WD models w/4-1-134 engine
Warner T-90C* 3-sp	1945–71	Standard on all models
Warner T-90J 3-sp	1947–58	Standard on 4-WD Utility models w/6-226 engines
Warner T-96 4-sp OD	1947–58	Optional on 2WD Utility models w/4-134 engine
Warner T-98A 4-sp	1955–71	Optional on all models

*On CJ-2A models up to serial #38221, the transmission has external linkage.
**Which transmission is in your vehicle is determined by availability at the time of production.
OD: Equipped with a Warner R-10B overdrive

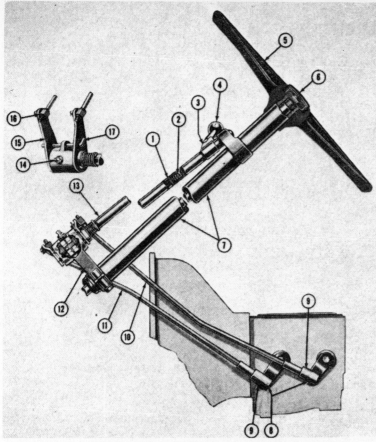

1. Stop screw
2. Bias spring
3. Gearshift lever
4. Lever ball
5. Steering sheel
6. Horn button
7. Column and bearing
8. End nuts
9. Shift rod ends
10. Shift rod
11. Shift rod
12. Cross-shift bracket
13. Control shaft
14. Lubrication fitting
15. Lever and clutch
16. Adjusting yoke
17. Aligning rod

Remote linkage used on CJ-2A models prior to serial number 38221

b. Remove the shift lever fulcrum pin and remove the shift lever.

c. Remove the toe plates from the floor pan at the steering column.

d. Remove the two screws holding the linkage housing to the steering column, and lift the housing from the positioning pin.

e. Remove the shift assembly down through the floor pan.

f. Remove the lower clutch and shift lever from the housing by turning counterclockwise.

g. Remove the upper clutch and shift lever in the same manner.

4. Remove the set screw from the transfer case shift lever pivot pin. Remove the pivot pin, shift levers, and shift lever springs.

5. If the vehicle is equipped with a power take-off, remove the shift lever plate screws and lift out the lever.

6. Disconnect the front and rear driveshafts from the transfer case. If the vehicle is equipped with a power take-off, disconnect the transfer case end of the PTO driveshaft.

7. Disconnect the speedometer cable at the transfer case.

8. Disconnect the hand brake cable.

9. Disconnect the clutch cable at the bellcrank.

10. Place jacks under the transmission and engine. Protect the oil pan with a wood block.

11. Remove the nuts holding the rear mount to the crossmember.

12. Remove the transfer case-to-crossmember bolt.

13. Remove the frame center crossmember-to-frame side rail bolts and remove the crossmember. Remove the transmission-to-bellhousing bolts.

14. Force the transmission to the right to disengage the clutch control lever tube ball joint.

15. Lower the engine and transmission. Slide the transmission and transfer case assemblies toward the rear until they clear the clutch.

16. Remove the six screws and lockwashers attaching the transfer case rear cover and remove the cover. If the vehicle is equipped with a power take-off, remove the PTO shift unit.

17. Remove the cotter pin, nut, and washer holding the transfer case main drive gear on the rear end of the transmission mainshaft. If

possible, remove the main drive gear. If that's not possible, see step 19.

18. Remove the transmission-to-transfer case bolts.

19. Install a transmission mainshaft retaining plate tool #W-194 to prevent the mainshaft from pulling out of the case. If this tool is not available, loop a piece of wire around the mainshaft directly in back of the second speed gear. Install the shift housing right and left bolts part way into the case. Attach each end of the wire to the bolts. Support the transfer case, and with a soft mallet, tap lightly on the end of the mainshaft to loosen the gear and separate the two units.

20. Join the transfer case and transmission. Remove the wire or special holding tool. Remove the shift housing right and left bolts.

21. Install the transmission-to-transfer case bolts. Torque them to 35 ft.lb.

22. Install the main drive gear. Install the cotter pin, nut, and washer holding the transfer case main drive gear on the rear end of the transmission mainshaft.

23. Install the transfer case rear cover and Install the cover. If the vehicle is equipped with a power take-off, Install the PTO shift unit.

24. Slide the transmission and transfer case assemblies forward until they engage the clutch.

25. Force the transmission to the right to engage the clutch control lever tube ball joint.

26. Install the transmission-to-bellhousing bolts. Torque them to 30 ft.lb.

27. Install the frame center crossmember. Torque the bolts to 50 ft.lb.

28. Install the transfer case-to-crossmember bolt. Torque it to 45 ft.lb.

29. Install the nuts holding the rear mount to the crossmember. Torque them to 40 ft.lb.

30. Connect the clutch cable at the bellcrank.

31. Connect the hand brake cable.

32. Connect the speedometer cable at the transfer case.

33. Connect the front and rear driveshafts to the transfer case. If the vehicle is equipped with a power take-off, connect the transfer case end of the pto driveshaft.

34. If the vehicle is equipped with a power take-off, install the shift lever.

35. Install the set screw in the transfer case shift lever pivot pin. Install the pivot pin, shift levers, and shift lever springs.

36. Install the shift lever and shift housing. On CJ-2A models up to serial #38221, install the remote linkage as follows:

a. Install the upper clutch and shift lever on the housing by turning counterclockwise.

b. Install the lower clutch and shift lever on the housing by turning counterclockwise.

c. Install the shift assembly down through the floor pan.

d. Install the two screws holding the linkage housing to the steering column, and lower the housing onto the positioning pin.

d. Install the toe plates on the floor pan at the steering column.

e. Install the shift lever. Install the shift lever fulcrum pin.

f. Install the shift rods at the transmission and the steering remote control clutch levers.

37. Fill the transmission and transfer case.

2-WD UTILITY MODELS

NOTE: *The following applies to models both with and without overdrive.*

CAUTION: *The clutch driven disc contains asbestos, which has been determined to be a cancer causing agent. Never clean clutch surfaces with compressed air! Avoid inhaling any dust from any clutch surface! When cleaning clutch surfaces, use a commercially available brake cleaning fluid.*

1. Raise and support the front end on jackstands.

2. Disconnect the battery ground.

3. Remove the remote linkage as follows:

a. Remove the shift rods from the transmission and from the steering remote control clutch levers.

b. Remove the shift lever fulcrum pin and remove the shift lever.

c. Remove the toe plates from the floor pan at the steering column.

d. Remove the two screws holding the linkage housing to the steering column, and lift the housing from the positioning pin.

e. Remove the shift assembly down through the floor pan.

f. Remove the lower clutch and shift lever from the housing by turning counterclockwise.

g. Remove the upper clutch and shift lever in the same manner.

3. Disconnect and tag the wires at the overdrive solenoid.

4. Disconnect and tag the wires at the overdrive rail switch.

5. Matchmark and disconnect the driveshaft at the transmission or overdrive.

6. Disconnect the speedometer cable at the transmission or overdrive. Plug the hole.

7. Disconnect the overdrive control cable.

8. Remove the support at the rear of the overdrive. Keep the spacers together.

9. Remove the overdrive governor.

10. Place a jack under the bellhousing and

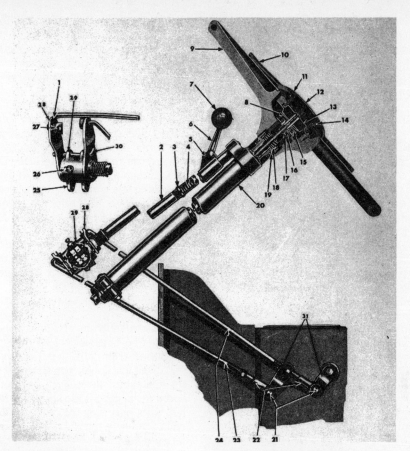

1. Low and reverse lever and clutch
2. Shaft assembly
3. Screw
4. Cross shift bias spring
5. Lever fulcrum pin
6. Shift lever
7. Shift lever ball
8. Horn button ground spring
9. Steering wheel
10. Horn ring
11. Horn button
12. Horn button emblem
13. Horn button contact cup
14. Horn button snapring
15. Steering wheel nut
16. Horn button spring
17. Horn button spring cup
18. Steering column bearing spring
19. Steering column bearing assembly
20. Steering column bearing and bracket
21. Clevis pin
22. Adjusting yoke
23. Second and high control rod
24. Low and reverse control rod
25. Cross shift bracket assembly
26. Lubricating fitting
27. Shift rod anti-rattle spring
28. Gearshift lever
29. Housing
30. Rod
31. Control lever

Column mounted transmission linkage for Utility vehicles

take up the weight of the engine. Protect the oil pan with a block of wood.

11. Place a floor jack under the transmission and support it without lifting the engine.

12. Remove the transmission-to-bellhousing bolts.

13. Pull the transmission back about ¾".

14. Insert a thin prybar through the opening in the side of the bellhousing and pry the clutch release fork from engagement with the clutch release bearing carrier.

15. Pull the transmission back until it clears the bellhousing and remove it with the clutch release bearing carrier mounted in the main drive gear bearing retainer.

16. Raise the transmission and slide it into place in the bellhousing. Make sure that the clutch release bearing engages the release fork.

17. Install the transmission-to-bellhousing bolts. Torque the bolts to 30 ft.lb.

18. Install the overdrive governor.

19. Install the support at the rear of the overdrive. Keep the spacers together.

20. Connect the overdrive control cable.
21. Connect the speedometer cable at the transmission or overdrive.
22. Connect the driveshaft at the transmission or overdrive.
23. Connect the wires at the overdrive rail switch.
24. Connect tag the wires at the overdrive solenoid.
25. Install the remote linkage as follows:

   a. Install the upper clutch and shift lever on the housing by turning counterclockwise.

   b. Install the lower clutch and shift lever on the housing by turning counterclockwise.

   c. Install the shift assembly down through the floor pan.

   d. Install the two screws holding the linkage housing to the steering column, and lower the housing onto the positioning pin.

   d. Install the toe plates on the floor pan at the steering column.

   e. Install the shift lever. Install the shift lever fulcrum pin.

   f. Install the shift rods at the transmission and the steering remote control clutch levers.

26. Connect the battery.

4-WD UTILITY MODELS

CAUTION: *The clutch driven disc contains asbestos, which has been determined to be a cancer causing agent. Never clean clutch surfaces with compressed air! Avoid inhaling any dust from any clutch surface! When cleaning clutch surfaces, use a commercially available brake cleaning fluid.*

1. Raise and support the vehicle on jackstands.
2. Drain the transmission and transfer case.
3. Remove the shift lever and shift housing.
4. Remove the set screw from the transfer case shift lever pivot pin. Remove the pivot pin, shift levers, and shift lever springs.
5. If the vehicle is equipped with a power take-off, remove the shift lever plate screws and lift out the lever.
6. Disconnect the front and rear driveshafts from the transfer case. If the vehicle is equipped with a power take-off, disconnect the transfer case end of the PTO driveshaft.
7. Disconnect the speedometer cable at the transfer case.
8. Disconnect the hand brake cable.
9. Disconnect the clutch cable at the bellcrank.
10. Place jacks under the transmission and engine. Protect the oil pan with a wood block.
11. Remove the nuts holding the rear mount to the crossmember.

12. Remove the transfer case-to-crossmember bolt.
13. Remove the frame center crossmember-to-frame side rail bolts and remove the crossmember. Remove the transmission-to-bellhousing bolts.
14. Force the transmission to the right to disengage the clutch control lever tube ball joint.
15. Lower the engine and transmission. Slide the transmission and transfer case assemblies toward the rear until they clear the clutch.
16. Remove the six screws and lockwashers attaching the transfer case rear cover and remove the cover. If the vehicle is equipped with a power take-off, remove the PTO shift unit.
17. Remove the cotter pin, nut, and washer holding the transfer case main drive gear on the rear end of the transmission mainshaft. If possible, remove the main drive gear. If that's not possible, see step 19.
18. Remove the transmission-to-transfer case bolts.
19. Install a transmission mainshaft retaining plate tool #W-194 to prevent the mainshaft from pulling out of the case. If this tool is not available, loop a piece of wire around the mainshaft directly in back of the second speed gear. Install the shift housing right and left bolts part way into the case. Attach each end of the wire to the bolts. Support the transfer case, and with a soft mallet, tap lightly on the end of the mainshaft to loosen the gear and separate the two units.
20. Join the transfer case and transmission. Remove the wire or special holding tool. Remove the shift housing right and left bolts.
21. Install the transmission-to-transfer case bolts. Torque them to 35 ft.lb.
22. Install the main drive gear. Install the cotter pin, nut, and washer holding the transfer case main drive gear on the rear end of the transmission mainshaft.
23. Install the transfer case rear cover and Install the cover. If the vehicle is equipped with a power take-off, Install the PTO shift unit.
24. Slide the transmission and transfer case assemblies forward until they engage the clutch.
25. Force the transmission to the right to engage the clutch control lever tube ball joint.
26. Install the transmission-to-bellhousing bolts. Torque them to 30 ft.lb.
27. Install the frame center crossmember. Torque the bolts to 50 ft.lb.
28. Install the transfer case-to-crossmember bolt. Torque it to 45 ft.lb.
29. Install the nuts holding the rear mount to the crossmember. Torque them to 40 ft.lb.
30. Connect the clutch cable at the bellcrank.

31. Connect the hand brake cable.

32. Connect the speedometer cable at the transfer case.

33. Connect the front and rear driveshafts to the transfer case. If the vehicle is equipped with a power take-off, connect the transfer case end of the PTO driveshaft.

34. If the vehicle is equipped with a power take-off, install the shift lever.

35. Install the set screw in the transfer case shift lever pivot pin. Install the pivot pin, shift levers, and shift lever springs.

36. Install the shift lever and shift housing.

37. Fill the transmission and transfer case.

1972–86

CAUTION: *The clutch driven disc contains asbestos, which has been determined to be a cancer causing agent. Never clean clutch surfaces with compressed air! Avoid*

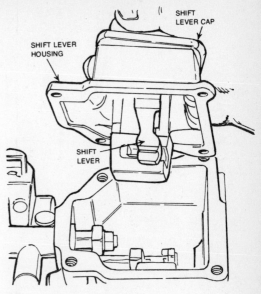

SR-4 shift lever removal

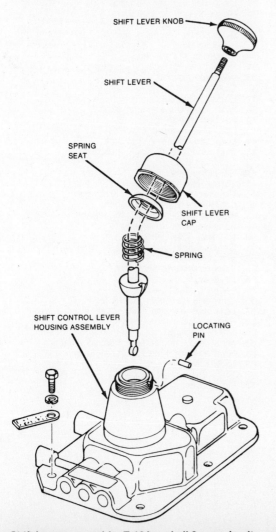

Shift lever removal for T-18A and all 3-speed units starting in 1974

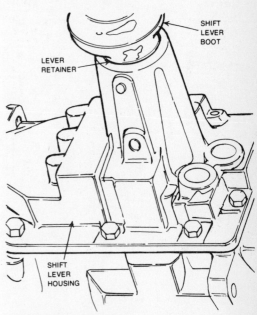

T-176 shift lever removal

inhaling any dust from any clutch surface! When cleaning clutch surfaces, use a commercially available brake cleaning fluid.

1. Remove all floor lever knobs, trim rings and boots.

2. Remove the floor pan section from above the transmission shift control and unbolt the lever assembly from the transmission (early 3-speed models). On the 4-speed models exc. SR-4 and T-176, and 3-speeds starting 1976, unscrew the shift control housing cap, remove the washer, spring, shift lever and pin. On SR-4 models, remove the shift lever housing bolts

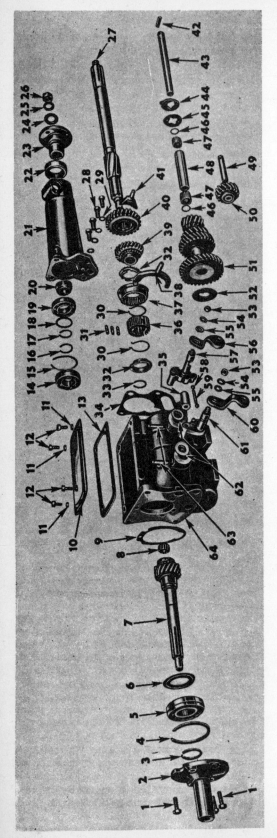

1. Main bearing retainer bolt
2. Main bearing retainer
3. Main drive gear snapring
4. Bearing snapring
5. Main drive gear bearing
6. Oil baffle
7. Main drive gear
8. Pilot bearing rollers
9. Bearing retainer gasket
10. Case cover
11. Case cover bolt gasket
12. Case cover bolt
13. Case cover gasket
14. Rear main shaft bearing
14. Rear bearing snapring
16. Mainshaft snapring
17. Rear bearing snapring
18. Rear bearing washer
29. Rear mainshaft bearing
20. Speedometer drive gear
21. Rear bearing retainer
22. Mainshaft oil seal
23. Coupling flange
24. Mainshaft washer
25. Mainshaft nut lockwasher
26. Mainshaft nut
27. Mainshaft
28. Rear bearing retainer bolt
29. Retainer bolt lockwasher
30. Synchronizer spring
31. Synchronizer shifting plate
32. Blocking ring
33. Clutch hub snapring
34. Rear bearing retainer gasket
35. Interlock sleeve
36. Clutch hub
37. Clutch sleeve
38. High intermediate shift fork
39. Second speed gear
40. Low and reverse gear
41. Low and reverse shift fork
42. Idler and countershaft lockplate
43. Countershaft
44. Thrust washer
45. Thrust washer
46. Countershaft bearing shift spacer
47. Countershaft bearing rollers
48. Countershaft bearing long spacer
49. Reverse idler gear shaft
50. Reverse idler gear
51. Countershaft gear
52. Thrust washer
53. Control lever-to-shaft nut
54. Lever-to-shaft lockwasher
55. Lever-to-shaft washer
56. Low and reverse control lever
57. Low and reverse shift lever
58. Poppet ball
59. Poppet spring
60. High and intermediate control lever
61. High and intermediate shift lever
62. Shift shaft oil seal
63. Shift lever shaft pin
64. Transmission case

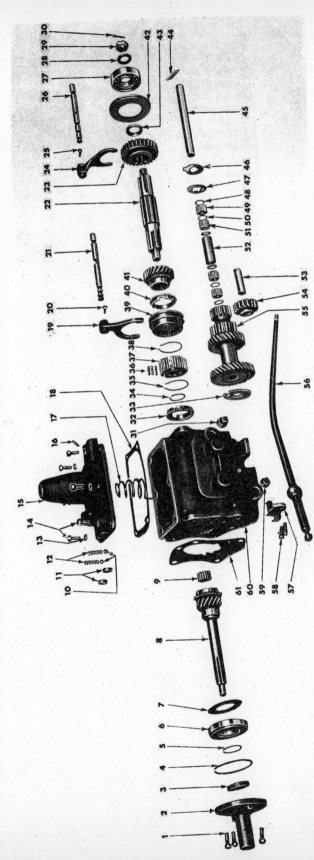

1. Bearing retainer bolt
2. Bearing retainer
3. Bearing retainer oil seal
4. Bearing snapring
5. Main drive gear snapring
6. Main drive gear bearing
7. Front bearing washer
8. Main drive gear
9. Pilot roller bearing
10. Poppet ball
11. Shift rail cap
12. Poppet spring
13. Lockwasher
14. Shift housing bolt
15. Shift housing
16. Interlock plunger
17. Shift lever spring
18. Shift housing gasket
19. High and intermediate shift fork
20. Shift fork pin
21. High and intermediate shift rail
22. Mainshaft
23. Sliding gear
24. Low and reverse shift fork
25. Shift fork pin
26. Low and reverse shift rail
27. Rear bearing
28. Mainshaft washer
29. Mainshaft nut
30. Cotter pin
31. Filler plug
32. Blocking ring
33. Front countershaft thrust washer
34. Clutch hub snapring
35. Synchronizer spring
36. Synchronizer plate
37. Clutch hub
38. Synchronizer spring
39. Clutch sleeve
40. Blocking ring
41. Second speed gear
42. Rear bearing adapter
43. Bearing spacer
44. Lockplate
45. Countershaft
46. Rear countershaft thrust washer
47. Rear countershaft thrust washer
48. Countershaft bearing washer
49. Countershaft bearing rollers
50. Countershaft bearing washer
51. Countershaft bearing rollers
52. Countershaft bearing spacer
53. Reverse gear shaft
54. Reverse idler gear
55. Countershaft gear set
56. Shift lever
57. Oil collector
58. Oil collector screw
59. Drain plug
60. Transmission case
61. Bearing retainer gasket

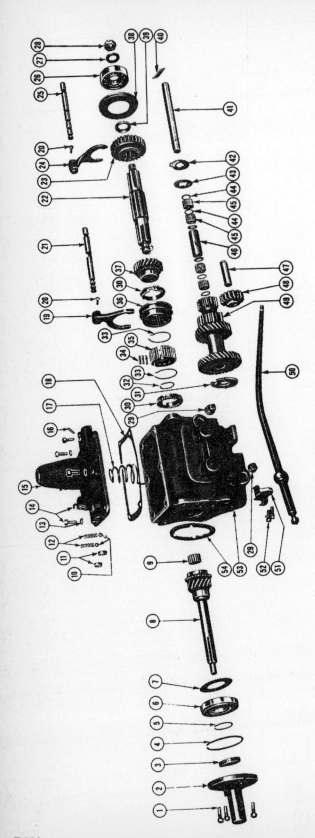

1. Bearing retainer bolt
2. Bearing retainer
3. Bearing retainer oil seal
4. Bearing snapring
5. Main drive gear snapring
6. Main drive gear bearing
7. Front bearing washer
8. Main drive gear
9. Pilot roller bearing
10. Poppet ball
11. Shift rail cap
12. Poppet spring
13. Lockwasher
14. Shift housing bolt
15. Control housing
16. Interlock plunger
17. Shift lever spring
18. Shift tower gasket
19. High and intermediate shift fork
20. Shift fork pin
21. High and intermediate shift rail
22. Mainshaft
23. Sliding gear
24. Low and reverse shift fork
25. Low and reverse shift rail
26. Rear bearing
27. Mainshaft washer
28. Mainshaft nut
29. Filler plug
30. Blocking ring
31. Front countershaft thrust washer
32. Clutch hub snapring
33. Synchronizer spring
34. Synchronizer plate
35. Clutch hub
36. Clutch sleeve
37. Second speed gear
38. Rear bearing adapter
39. Bearing spacer
40. Lockplate
41. Countershaft
42. Rear countershaft thrust washer
43. Rear countershaft thrust washer
44. Countershaft bearing washer
45. Countershaft bearing
46. Countershaft bearing spacer
47. Reverse gear shaft
48. Reverse idler gear
49. Countershaft gear set
50. Shift lever
51. Oil collector
52. Oil collector screw
53. Transmission case
54. Bearing retainer gasket

T-98A

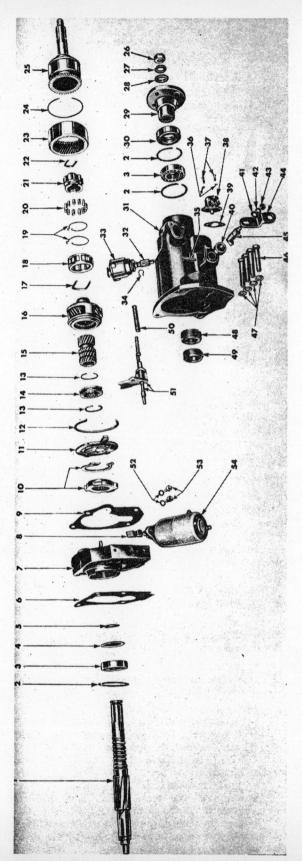

1. Transmission mainshaft
2. Mainshaft bearing snapring
3. Mainshaft bearing
4. Mainshaft oil baffle
5. Mainshaft snapring
6. Adapter to transmission gasket
7. Overdrive housing adapter
8. Sun gear pawl
9. Housing to adapter gasket
10. Balk ring and gear plate
11. Overdrive cover plate
12. Cover plate snapring
13. Sun gear snapring
14. Sun gear shifting collar
15. Sun gear
16. Planetary gear cage
17. Roller retainer clip
18. Freewheel roller retainer
19. Roller retainer spring
20. Freewheel roller
21. Freewheel cam
22. Cam retainer clip
23. Overdrive ring gear
24. Ring gear snapring
25. Mainshaft
26. Mainshaft nut
27. Mainshaft lockwasher
28. Mainshaft washer
29. Coupling flange
30. Mainshaft oil seal
31. Housing
32. Governor driven gear
33. Governor
34. Driven gear retaining ring
35. Control shaft pin
36. Rail switch lockwasher
37. Rail switch screw
38. Rail switch
39. Rail switch gasket
40. Control shaft oil seal
41. Control lever washer
42. Control lever lockwasher
43. Control lever nut
44. Control lever
45. Control shaft
46. Housing to transmission bolt
47. Housing to transmission lockwasher
48. Speedometer drive gear
49. Governor drive gear
50. Shift retractor spring
51. Shift rail and fork
52. Solenoid lockwasher
53. Solenoid bolt
54. Solenoid

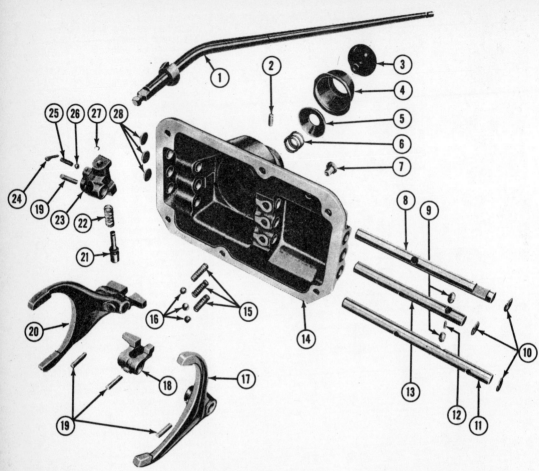

1. Shift lever
2. Control housing pin
3. Shift handle
4. Control housing cap
5. Washer
6. Control lever spring
7. Breather assembly
8. Reverse shift rail
9. Shift rail interlock plunger
10. Expansion plug

11. Low and second shift rail
12. Shift rail interlock pin
13. Direct and third shift rail
14. Control housing
15. Shift rail poppet spring
16. Shift rail poppet ball
17. Lockwire
18. Low and second shift fork
19. Lock pin
20. Shift rail end

21. Direct and third shift fork
22. Reverse plunger
23. Reverse plunger spring
24. Reverse rail end
25. Cotter pin
26. Reverse plunger poppet spring
27. Reverse plunger poppet ball
28. C-washer

T-18 control tower

and remove the shift lever and housing assembly.

3. On T-18A, remove the transfer case shift lever and bracket assembly. On T-176 models, press and turn the lever retainer and remove the shift lever assembly.

4. Raise the vehicle.

5. Index mark the driveshafts for proper alignment at installation.

6. Remove the front driveshaft.

7. Disconnect the front end of the rear driveshaft from the transfer case.

8. Disconnect the clutch cable and remove the cable mounting bracket from the transfer case on 1972 models only.

9. Disconnect the speedometer cable, backup light switch wires, transmission controlled spark advance, and parking brake cable if connected to the crossmember.

10. If equipped with a V8 engine, disconnect the exhaust pipe at the manifolds and lower them. Support the engine with a jack. Disconnect the support support crossmember from the frame side rail.

11. Remove the bolts that attach the transmission to the clutch housing.

12. Lower the transmission slightly.

13. Move the transmission and transfer case assembly and crossmember backward far enough for the transmission clutch shaft to clear the clutch housing.

14. Remove the assembly from under the vehicle.

15. If the transmission and transfer case

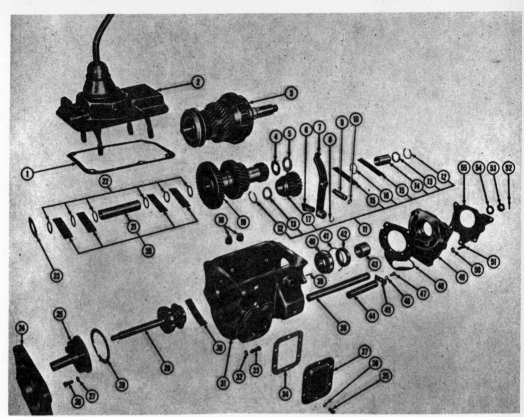

1. Control housing
2. Control housing assembly
3. Mainshaft assembly
4. Thrust washer
5. Thrust washer
6. Reverse shifting shoe
7. Reverse shifting arm
8. C-washer
9. Reverse shifting arm pivot
10. O-ring
11. Reverse idler gear assembly
12. Snapring
13. Thrust washer
14. Sleeve
15. Bearing rollers
16. Spacer
17. Reverse idler gear
18. Pipe plug
19. Countershaft gears
20. Bearing rollers
21. Spacer
22. Spacer
23. Thrust washer
24. Bellhousing-to-transmission adapter plate
25. Bearing retainer
26. Bearing retainer bolt
27. Bearing retainer lockwasher
28. Bearing retainer gasket

29. Main drive gear
30. Bearing rollers
31. Transmission case
32. Adapter plate lockwasher
33. Adapter plate capscrew
34. Slide opening cover gasket
35. Slide opening cover bolt
36. Slide opening cover lockwasher
37. Slide opening cover
38. Countershaft
39. Shifting arm pivot taper pin
40. Bearing
41. Snapring
42. Oil seal
43. Spacer
44. Reverse-idler gear shaft
45. Lockplate
46. Lockplate lockwasher
47. Lockplate bolt
48. Gasket
49. Adapter plate
50. Adapter plate lockwasher
51. Adapter plate bolt
52. Cotter key
53. Nut
54. Washer
55. Gasket

T-18

were separated, join them and torque the bolts to 30 ft.lb.

16. Position the wave washer and the throwout bearing and sleeve assembly in the throwout fork. Center the bearing over the pressure plate release levers.

17. Protect the splines and throwout bearing alignment and slowly slide the transmission into position. Some maneuvering may be necessary in order to match the transmission input shaft splines and the clutch driven plate splines.

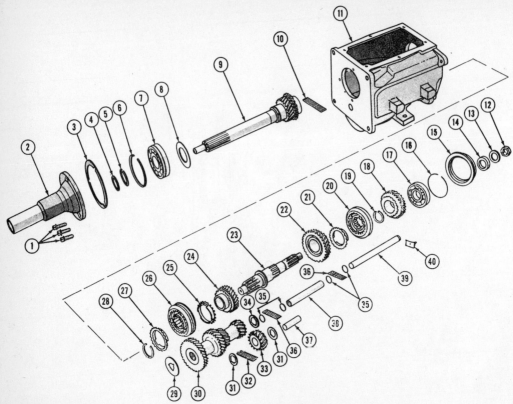

1. Retainer screws
2. Main drive gear bearing retainer
3. Retainer gasket
4. Oil seal
5. Snapring (small)
6. Snapring (large)
7. Main drive gear bearing
8. Oil retaining washer (slinger)
9. Main drive gear
10. Mainshaft plot bearing rollers
11. Case
12. Nut
13. Flatwasher
14. Spacer
15. Bearing adapter
16. Snapring
17. Mainshaft bearing
18. Reverse gear
19. Snapring
20. Low synchronizer assembly

21. Synchronizer blocking ring
22. Low gear
23. Mainshaft
24. Second gear
25. Synchronizer blocking ring
26. Second-third synchronizer assembly
27. Synchronizer blocking ring
28. Snapring
29. Countershaft front thrust washer (large)
30. Countershaft gear
31. Reverse idler gear bearing washer
32. Reverse idler gear roller bearings
33. Reverse idler gear
34. Countershaft rear thrust washer (small)
35. Countershaft bearing spacer washer
36. Reverse idler shaft
37. Countershaft roller bearings
38. Spacer washer
39. Countershaft
40. Lockplate

T-14A

18. Install the bolts that attach the transmission to the clutch housing. Torque them to 54 ft.lb.

19. If equipped with a V8 engine, Connect the exhaust pipe at the manifolds and lower them. Support the engine with a jack. Connect the support crossmember to the frame side rail. Torque the bolts to 30 ft.lb.

20. Connect the speedometer cable, back-up light switch wires, transmission controlled spark advance, and parking brake cable if connected to the crossmember.

21. Install the clutch cable mounting bracket on the transfer case on 1972 models only. Connect the clutch cable.

22. Connect the front end of the rear driveshaft to the transfer case.

23. Install the front driveshaft.

24. Lower the vehicle.

25. On T-18A, install the transfer case shift lever and bracket assembly. On T-176 models, press and turn the lever retainer and install the shift lever assembly.

26. Install the floor pan section from above

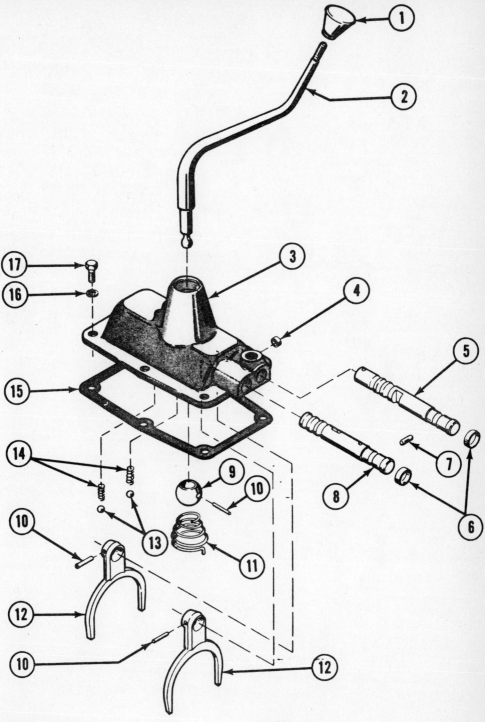

1. Shift lever knob
2. Shift lever
3. Control housing
4. Plug
5. Shift rail (second-third)
6. Shift rail cap
7. Interlock plunger
8. Shift rail (low-reverse)
9. Shift lever fulcrum ball
10. Pin
11. Shift lever support spring
12. Shift fork
13. Poppet ball
14. Poppet spring
15. Gasket
16. Lockwasher
17. Bolt

T-14A control tower

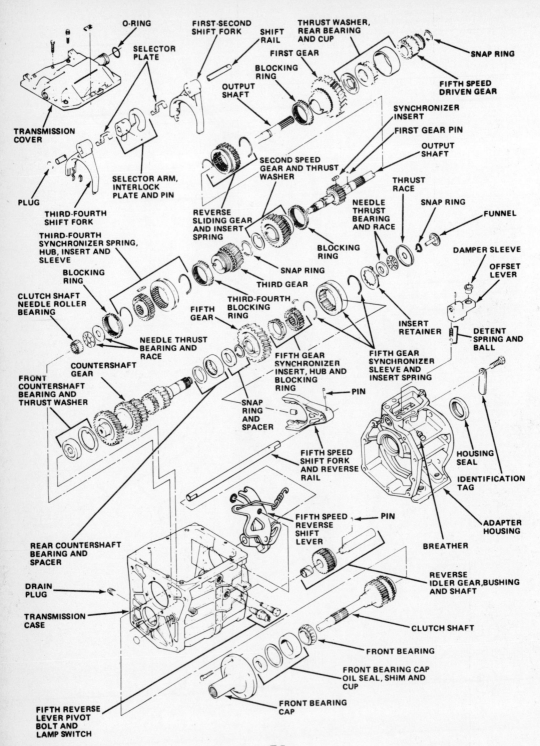

O-RING

SELECTOR PLATE

FIRST-SECOND SHIFT FORK

SHIFT RAIL

THRUST WASHER, REAR BEARING AND CUP

FIRST GEAR

SNAP RING

BLOCKING RING

FIFTH SPEED DRIVEN GEAR

OUTPUT SHAFT

TRANSMISSION COVER

SYNCHRONIZER INSERT

FIRST GEAR PIN

OUTPUT SHAFT

PLUG

SELECTOR ARM, INTERLOCK PLATE AND PIN

SECOND SPEED GEAR AND THRUST WASHER

THRUST RACE

THIRD-FOURTH SHIFT FORK

REVERSE SLIDING GEAR AND INSERT SPRING

NEEDLE THRUST BEARING AND RACE

SNAP RING

FUNNEL

THIRD-FOURTH SYNCHRONIZER SPRING, HUB, INSERT AND SLEEVE

BLOCKING RING

DAMPER SLEEVE

BLOCKING RING

SNAP RING

OFFSET LEVER

CLUTCH SHAFT NEEDLE ROLLER BEARING

THIRD GEAR

FIFTH GEAR

THIRD-FOURTH BLOCKING RING

INSERT RETAINER

DETENT SPRING AND BALL

NEEDLE THRUST BEARING AND RACE

FIFTH GEAR SYNCHRONIZER INSERT, HUB AND BLOCKING RING

FIFTH GEAR SYNCHRONIZER SLEEVE AND INSERT SPRING

COUNTERSHAFT GEAR

FRONT COUNTERSHAFT BEARING AND THRUST WASHER

SNAP RING AND SPACER

PIN

FIFTH SPEED SHIFT FORK AND REVERSE RAIL

HOUSING SEAL

IDENTIFICATION TAG

REAR COUNTERSHAFT BEARING AND SPACER

FIFTH SPEED REVERSE SHIFT LEVER

PIN

ADAPTER HOUSING

DRAIN PLUG

BREATHER

REVERSE IDLER GEAR, BUSHING AND SHAFT

TRANSMISSION CASE

CLUTCH SHAFT

FRONT BEARING

FRONT BEARING CAP OIL SEAL, SHIM AND CUP

FIFTH REVERSE LEVER PIVOT BOLT AND LAMP SWITCH

FRONT BEARING CAP

T-5

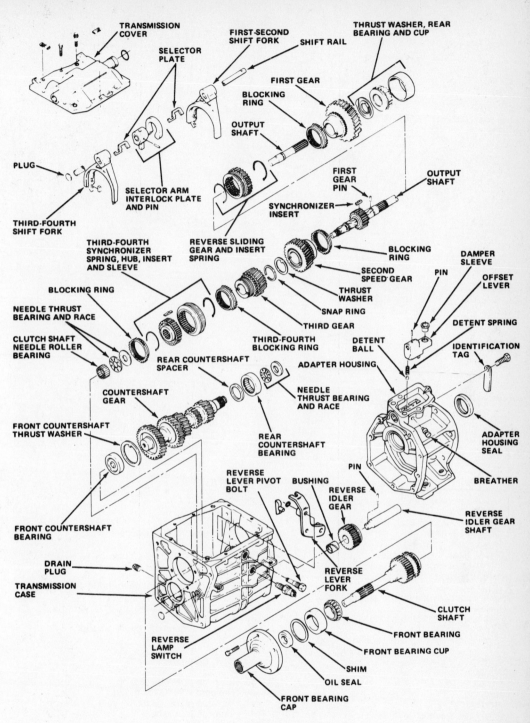

TRANSMISSION COVER

SELECTOR PLATE

FIRST-SECOND SHIFT FORK

SHIFT RAIL

THRUST WASHER, REAR BEARING AND CUP

FIRST GEAR

BLOCKING RING

OUTPUT SHAFT

PLUG

SELECTOR ARM INTERLOCK PLATE AND PIN

FIRST GEAR PIN

OUTPUT SHAFT

SYNCHRONIZER INSERT

THIRD-FOURTH SHIFT FORK

THIRD-FOURTH SYNCHRONIZER SPRING, HUB, INSERT AND SLEEVE

REVERSE SLIDING GEAR AND INSERT SPRING

BLOCKING RING

DAMPER SLEEVE

PIN

OFFSET LEVER

SECOND SPEED GEAR

BLOCKING RING

THRUST WASHER

NEEDLE THRUST BEARING AND RACE

SNAP RING

THIRD GEAR

DETENT SPRING

CLUTCH SHAFT NEEDLE ROLLER BEARING

THIRD-FOURTH BLOCKING RING

DETENT BALL

IDENTIFICATION TAG

REAR COUNTERSHAFT SPACER

ADAPTER HOUSING

COUNTERSHAFT GEAR

NEEDLE THRUST BEARING AND RACE

ADAPTER HOUSING SEAL

FRONT COUNTERSHAFT THRUST WASHER

REAR COUNTERSHAFT BEARING

PIN

BREATHER

FRONT COUNTERSHAFT BEARING

REVERSE LEVER PIVOT BOLT

BUSHING

REVERSE IDLER GEAR

REVERSE IDLER GEAR SHAFT

DRAIN PLUG

TRANSMISSION CASE

REVERSE LEVER FORK

CLUTCH SHAFT

FRONT BEARING

REVERSE LAMP SWITCH

FRONT BEARING CUP

SHIM

OIL SEAL

FRONT BEARING CAP

T-4

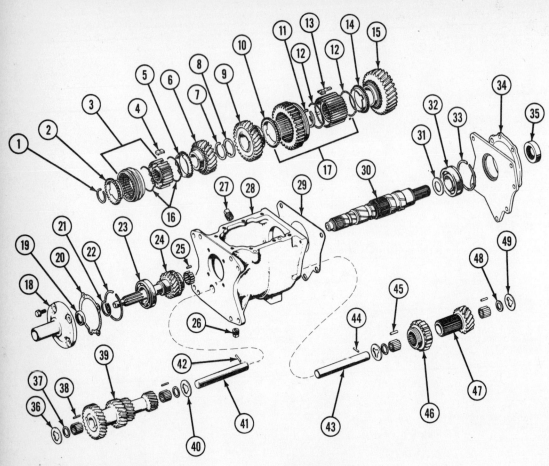

1. Third-fourth gear snapring
2. Fourth gear synchronizer ring
3. Third-fourth gear clutch assembly
4. Third-fourth gear plate
5. Third gear synchronizer ring
6. Third speed gear
7. Second gear snapring
8. Second gear thrust washer
9. Second speed gear
10. Second gear synchronizer ring
11. Mainshaft snapring
12. First-second synchronizer spring
13. Low-second plate
14. First gear synchronizer ring
15. First gear
16. Third-fourth synchronizer spring
17. First-second gear clutch assembly
18. Front bearing cap
19. Oil seal
20. Gasket
21. Snapring
22. Lockring
23. Front ball bearing
24. Clutch shaft
25. Roller bearing

26. Drain plug
27. Fill plug
28. Case
29. Gasket
30. Spline shaft
31. First gear thrust washer
32. Rear ball bearing
33. Snapring
34. Adapter plate
35. Adapter seal
36. Front countershaft gear thrust washer
37. Roller washer
38. Rear roller bearing
39. Countershaft gear
40. Rear countershaft thrust washer
41. Countershaft
42. Pin
43. Idler gear shaft
44. Pin
45. Idler gear roller bearing
46. Reverse idler sliding gear
47. Reverse idler gear
48. Idler gear washer
49. Idler gear thrust washer

T-176

1. Third-fourth shift insert
2. Third-fourth shift fork
3. Selector interlock plate
4. Selector arm plate (2)
5. Selector arm
6. Selector arm roll pin
7. First-second shift fork insert
8. First-second shift fork

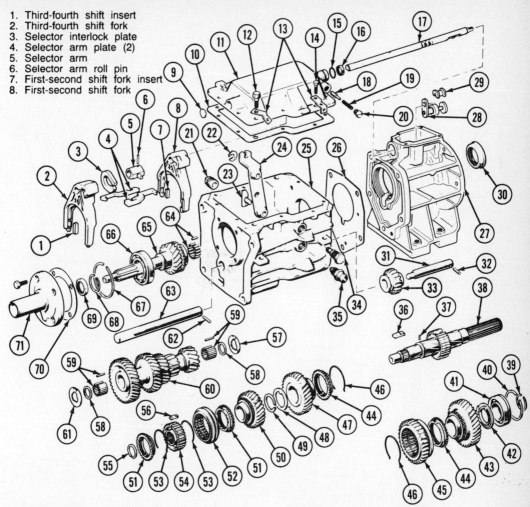

9. Shift rail plug
10. Transmission cover gasket
11. Transmission cover
12. Transmission cover dowel bolt (2)
13. Clip
14. Transmission cover bolt (8)
15. Shift rail O-ring seal
16. Shift rail Oil seal
17. Shift rail
18. Detent spring
20. Detent plug
21. Fill plug
22. Reverse lever pivot bolt C-clip
23. Reverse lever fork
24. Reverse lever
25. Transmission case
26. Gasket
27. Adapter housing
28. Offset lever
29. Offset lever insert
30. Extension housing oil seal
31. Reverse idler shaft
32. Reverse idler shaft roll pin
33. Reverse idler gear
34. Reverse lever pivot bolt
35. Backup lamp switch
36. First-second synchronizer insert (3)
37. First gear roll pin
38. Output shaft and hub assembly
39. Rear bearing retaining snapring
40. Rear bearing locating snapring

41. Rear bearing
42. First gear thrust washer
43. First gear
44. First-second synchronizer blocking ring (2)
45. First-reverse sleeve and gear
46. First-second synchronizer insert spring (2)
47. Second gear
48. Second gear thrust washer (tabbed)
49. Second gear snapring
50. Third gear
51. Third-fourth synchronizer blocking ring (2)
52. Third-fourth synchronizer sleeve
53. Third-fourth synchronizer insert spring (2)
54. Third-fourth synchronizer hub
55. Hub shaft snapring
56. Third-fourth synchronizer insert (3)
57. Countershaft gear rear thrust washer (metal)
58. Countershaft needle bearing retainer (2)
59. Countershaft needle bearing (50)
60. Countershaft gear
61. Countershaft gear front thrust washer (plastic)
62. Countershaft roll pin
63. Countershaft
64. Clutch shaft roller bearings (15)
65. Clutch shaft
66. Front bearing
67. Front bearing locating snapring
68. Front bearing retaining snapring
69. Front bearing cap oil seal
70. Front bearing cap gasket
71. Front bearing cap

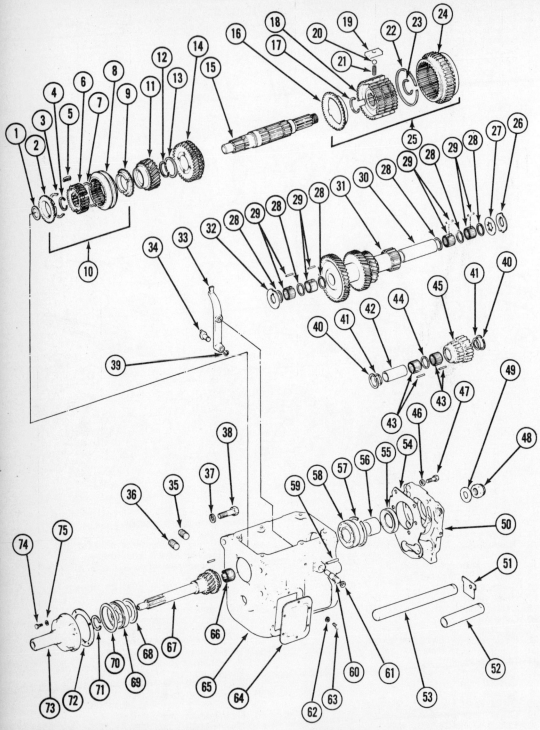

1. Mainshaft pilot bearing roller spacer
2. Third-fourth blocking ring
3. Third-fourth retaining ring
4. Third-fourth synchronizer snapring
5. Third-fourth shifting plate (3)
6. Third-fourth clutch hub
7. Third-fourth retaining ring
8. Third-fourth clutch sleeve
9. Third-fourth blocking ring
10. Third-fourth gear synchronizer assembly
11. Third gear
12. Mainshaft snapring
13. Second gear thrust washer
14. Second gear
15. Mainshaft
16. Second gear blocking ring
17. Mainshaft snapring
18. First-second clutch hub
19. First-second shifting plate (3)
20. Poppet spring (3)
22. First-second insert spring
23. Mainshaft snapring

T-18A

24. First-second clutch sleeve
25. Second gear synchronizer assembly
26. Countershaft gear thrust washer (steel) (rear)
27. Countershaft gear thrust washer (steel backed bronze) (rear)
28. Countershaft gear bearing washer
29. Countershaft gear bearing rollers (88)
30. Countershaft gear bearing spacer
31. Countershaft gear
32. Countershaft gear thrust washer (front)
33. Reverse shifting arm
34. Reverse shifting arm shoe
35. Filler plug
36. Drain plug
37. Lockwasher
38. Bolt (transmission-to-clutch Housing)
39. C-washer
40. Reverse idler gear snapring
41. Reverse idler gear thrust washer
42. Reverse idler shaft sleeve
43. Reverse idler gear bearing rollers (74)
44. Reverse idler gear bearing washer
45. Reverse idler gear
46. Lockwasher (6)
47. Adapter plate bolts (6)
48. Drive gear locknut
49. Washer

50. Adapter plate
51. Countershaft-reverse idler shaft lockplate
52. Reverse idler gear shaft
53. Countershaft
54. Adapter plate gasket
55. Adapter plate seal
56. Speedometer gear spacer
57. Rear bearing locating snapring
58. Rear bearing
59. Reverse shifting arm pivot pin
60. Reverse shifting arm pivot
61. Reverse shifting arm pivot O-ring
62. Washer (6)
63. Side cover bolt (6)
64. Side cover
65. Transmission case
66. Mainshaft pilot bearing rollers (22)
67. Clutch shaft
68. Front bearing retainer washer
69. Front bearing
70. Front bearing locating snapring
71. Front bearing lockring
72. Front bearing cap gasket
73. Front bearing cap
74. Front bearing cap bolts (4)
75. Lockwashers (4)

T-18A

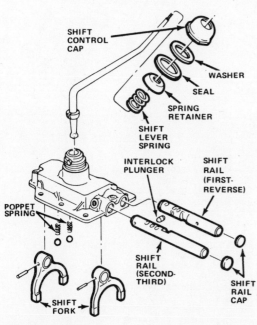

T-150 control tower

the transmission shift control and install the shift lever assembly from the transmission (early 3-speed models). On the 4-speed models exc. SR-4 and T-176, and 3-speeds starting 1976, unscrew the shift control housing cap, install the washer, spring, shift lever and pin. On SR-4 models, install the shift lever housing bolts and install the shift lever and housing assembly.

27. Install all floor lever knobs, trim rings and boots.

1987

AX-5

CAUTION: *The clutch driven disc contains asbestos, which has been determined to be a cancer causing agent. Never clean clutch surfaces with compressed air! Avoid inhaling any dust from any clutch surface! When cleaning clutch surfaces, use a commercially available brake cleaning fluid.*

1. Raise the outer gearshift lever boot and remove the upper part of the console.
2. Remove the lower part of the console.
3. Remove the inner boot.
4. Remove the gearshift lever and stub shaft by pressing down on the stub shaft retainer and rotating the retainer counterclockwise to release it from the lugs in the shift tower. Then, lift the retainer, stub shaft and shift lever up and out of the tower Don't remove the shift lever from the stub shaft.
5. Raise and support the truck on jackstands.
6. Drain the transmission and transfer case.
7. Matchmark the rear driveshaft and yoke for installation alignment.
8. Unbolt and remove the rear driveshaft.
9. Position a floor jack under the transmission and take up the weight slightly.
10. Unbolt and remove the rear crossmember.
11. Disconnect the hydraulic line from the

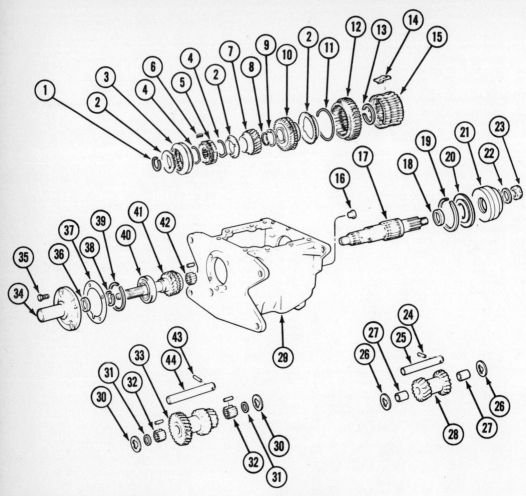

1. Mainshaft retaining snapring
2. Synchronizer blocking rings (3)
3. Second-third synchronizer sleeve
4. Second-third synchronizer insert spring (2)
5. Second-third hub
6. Second-third synchronizer insert (3)
7. Second gear
8. First gear retaining snapring
9. First gear tabbed thrust washer
10. First gear
11. First-reverse synchronizer insert spring
12. First-reverse sleeve and gear
13. First-reverse hub retaining snapring
14. First-reverse synchronizer insert (3)
15. First-reverse hub
16. Countershaft access plug
17. Mainshaft
18. Mainshaft spacer
19. Rear bearing adapter lockring
20. Oil slinger/spacer
21. Rear bearing and adapter assembly
22. Washer

23. Locknut
24. Roll pin
25. Reverse idler gear shaft
26. Thrust washer
27. Bushing (part of idler gear)
28. Reverse idler gear
29. Transmission case
30. Thrust washer (2)
31. Bearing retainer (2)
32. Countershaft needle bearings (50)
33. Countershaft gear
34. Front bearing cap
35. Bolt (4)
36. Front bearing cap oil seal
37. Gasket
38. Front bearing retainer snapring
39. Front bearing lockring
40. Front bearing
41. Clutch shaft
42. Mainshaft pilot roller bearings
43. Roll pin
44. Countershaft

T-150

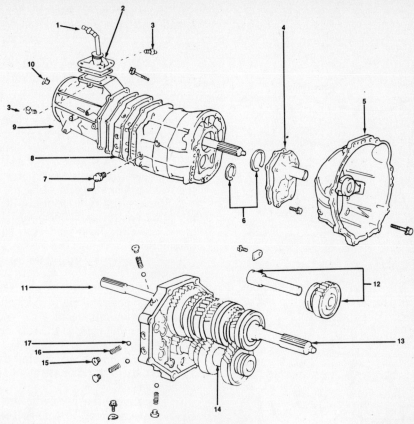

1. Shift lever
2. Shift lever retainer
3. Restrict pins
4. Front bearing retainer
5. Clutch housing
6. Snapring
7. Back-up light switch
8. Intermediate plate
9. Adapter housing
10. Adapter screw plug
11. Output shaft
12. Reverse idler gear
13. Input shaft
14. Counter gear
15. Straight screw plug
16. Spring
17. Locking ball

AX-5

A. Dust boot
B. Stub shaft

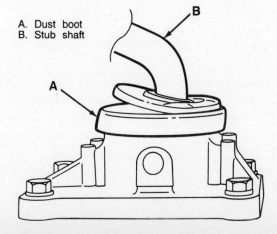

Dust boot removal from the AX-5 shifter

clutch slave cylinder. Disconnect the speedometer cable.

12. Disconnect the back-up light switch.

13. Disconnect the transfer case vent hose at the case.

14. Disconnect all linkage and hoses from the transfer case and transmission.

15. Matchmark the front driveshaft and yoke.

16. Remove the front driveshaft.

17. Chain the transmission to the jack.

18. Unbolt the transmission from the engine and lower the jack while pulling back.

19. Install the transmission to the engine. Transmission-to-transfer case adapter nut: 26 ft.lb.

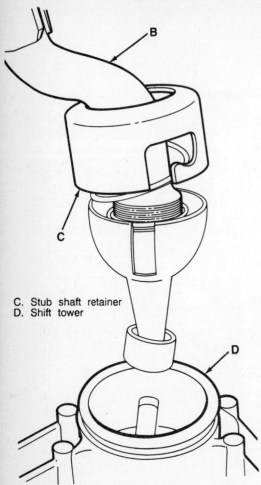

C. Stub shaft retainer
D. Shift tower

Stub shaft removal from the AX-5 shifter

33. Raise the outer gearshift lever boot and install the upper part of the console.

BA10/5

CAUTION: *The clutch driven disc contains asbestos, which has been determined to be a cancer causing agent. Never clean clutch surfaces with compressed air! Avoid inhaling any dust from any clutch surface! When cleaning clutch surfaces, use a commercially available brake cleaning fluid.*

1. Remove the shift lever knob.
2. Remove the shift lever outer boots and the transmission tower dust boot.
3. Remove the shift lever stub shaft retaining plate (snapring on some models) and remove the shift lever and stub shaft as an assembly.
4. Raise and support the truck on jackstands.
5. Drain the transmission and transfer case.
6. Matchmark the rear driveshaft and yoke for installation alignment.
7. Unbolt and remove the rear driveshaft.
8. Position a floor jack under the transmission and take up the weight slightly.
9. Unbolt and remove the rear crossmember.
10. Disconnect the hydraulic line from the clutch slave cylinder. Disconnect the speedometer cable.
11. Disconnect the back-up light switch.
12. Disconnect the transfer case vent hose at the case.
13. Disconnect all linkage and hoses from the transfer case and transmission.
14. Matchmark the front driveshaft and yoke.
15. Remove the front driveshaft.
16. Chain the transmission to the jack.
17. Unbolt the transmission from the engine and lower the jack while pulling back.
18. Slide the transmission and transfer case assembly into place, engaging the clutch assembly. Transmission-to-transfer case adapter nut: 26 ft.lb. Transmission case-to-engine: 28 ft.lb.
19. Install the front driveshaft. U-joint strap bolts: 15 ft.lb.
20. Connect all linkage and hoses at the transfer case and transmission.
21. Connect the transfer case vent hose at the case.
22. Connect the back-up light switch.
23. Connect the hydraulic line to the clutch slave cylinder.
24. Connect the speedometer cable.
25. Install the rear crossmember. Rear cross-member-to-side sill: 30 ft.lb. Rear support isolator-to-transmission: 33 ft.lb.

20. Install the front driveshaft. U-joint flange nut-to-transfer case: 35 ft.lb.
21. Connect all linkage and hoses at the transfer case and transmission.
22. Connect the transfer case vent hose at the case.
23. Connect the back-up light switch.
24. Connect the hydraulic line from the clutch slave cylinder.
25. Connect the speedometer cable.
26. Install the rear crossmember. Rear cross-member-to-side sill: 30 ft.lb. Rear support isolator-to-transmission: 33 ft.lb.
27. Install the rear driveshaft. U-joint flange nut-to-transfer case: 35 ft.lb.
28. Fill the transmission and transfer case.
29. Lower the truck.
30. Install the gearshift lever and stub shaft by pressing down on the stub shaft retainer and rotating the retainer clockwise.
31. Install the inner boot.
32. Install the lower part of the console.

26. Position a floor jack under the transmission and take up the weight slightly.

27. Install the rear driveshaft. U-joint strap bolts: 15 ft.lb.

28. Matchmark the rear driveshaft and yoke for installation alignment.

29. Drain the transmission and transfer case.

30. Raise and support the truck on jackstands.

31. Install the shift lever stub shaft retaining plate (snapring on some models) and install the shift lever and stub shaft as an assembly.

32. Install the shift lever outer boots and the transmission tower dust boot.

33. Install the shift lever knob.

Shift Linkage Adjustment

CJ-2A and 2-WD Utility Models

First disconnect the shift rods from the remote control levers. Check for binding of the remote control shaft on the steering column and make the necessary adjustments to eliminate any binding condition.

If the shift is not smooth and positive, first make sure that the transmission is in Neutral and then remove the shift rods at the transmission by removing the clevis pins. Slip a short piece of snug fitting ¼" (6.35mm) aligning rod through the gearshift levers and housing.

This places the shift lever and clutch assemblies in the Neutral position. Adjust the shift rod yokes at the transmission end so that the clevis pins can be installed freely without moving the shift levers on the transmission. Remove the alignment pin.

If shifting from First to Second is difficult or the transmission hangs up in First gear, shorten the Low and Reverse rod one turn at a time and until the condition is corrected. Usually three turns are required. Should the fault continue after completing the above adjustment, check further as follows. First, remove the lubricating fitting from the shifter housing.

Use a narrow feeler gauge which will enter the opening for the lubricator and check the clearance between the faces of the shifting clutches. The clearance should be 0.015" (0.381mm) to 0.031" (0.787mm). If the clearance is greater, the assembly must be removed for adjustment. The shift dog which engages the clutch slots should not have more than 0.009" (0.2286mm) clearance in the slots. If the clearance between the clutch grooves and cross pins is too great, these parts must be replaced.

To remove the remote control housing from the steering column for repairs, the following procedure is suggested:

1. Remove the shifting rods from the transmission and also from the steering column remove control clutch levers.

2. Remove the gearshift lever fulcrum pin and the gearshift lever.

3. Remove the plates on the toe board of the steering post.

4. Remove the two screws that hold the remote control housing to the steering post and lift the housing from the positioning pin.

5. Remove the assembly down through the floor pan.

6. Remove the lower clutch and shift lever from the housing by turning counterclockwise.

7. Remove the upper clutch and shift lever in the same manner.

8. Wash all of the parts in a suitable cleaning solution and replace all worn parts before reassembling.

9. Assemble the upper clutch assembly in the housing making sure that the alignment hole in the housing faces the engine. Turn the upper lever assembly in as far as it will go and then back off one full turn until the hole in the clutch lever aligns with the hole in the housing.

10. Assemble the lower clutch lever assembly in the housing until the faces of the clutches contact, then back off not more than ½ of a turn which should bring the aligning hole in the lever in line with the hole in the housing. If the ½ turn does not bring the alignment hole into the proper position, it will be necessary to grind off the face of the lower clutch so that it can be backed off ½ turn from contact with the upper clutch. The proper clearance of 0.015" (0.381mm) is obtained when the lower clutch is backed off ½ turn.

11. Assemble the unit to the steering post in the reverse order of removal and adjust the remote control rods.

12. If, after assembly, the shifter dog catches on the edge of the slot in the clutch when moving the lever up and down, disconnect the shift rod at the transmission end and either lengthen or shorten it slightly to correct this condition.

Back-Up Light Switch

REMOVAL AND INSTALLATION

The switch is threaded into the transmission and is replaced by unscrewing. No adjustments are possible. Switch locations are as follows:

- AX-5 and BA 10/5: right side of the case
- SR-4, T4 and T5: left side of the case
- T-176: on the top cover behind the shifter
- T-14A, T-18, T-18A and T-150: in the top cover

Troubleshooting Basic Clutch Problems

Problem	Cause
Excessive clutch noise	Throwout bearing noises are more audible at the lower end of pedal travel. The usual causes are: • Riding the clutch • Too little pedal free-play • Lack of bearing lubrication A bad clutch shaft pilot bearing will make a high pitched squeal, when the clutch is disengaged and the transmission is in gear or within the first 2″ of pedal travel. The bearing must be replaced. Noise from the clutch linkage is a clicking or snapping that can be heard or felt as the pedal is moved completely up or down. This usually requires lubrication. Transmitted engine noises are amplified by the clutch housing and heard in the passenger compartment. They are usually the result of insufficient pedal free-play and can be changed by manipulating the clutch pedal.
Clutch slips (the car does not move as it should when the clutch is engaged)	This is usually most noticeable when pulling away from a standing start. A severe test is to start the engine, apply the brakes, shift into high gear and SLOWLY release the clutch pedal. A healthy clutch will stall the engine. If it slips it may be due to: • A worn pressure plate or clutch plate • Oil soaked clutch plate • Insufficient pedal free-play
Clutch drags or fails to release	The clutch disc and some transmission gears spin briefly after clutch disengagement. Under normal conditions in average temperatures, 3 seconds is maximum spin-time. Failure to release properly can be caused by: • Too light transmission lubricant or low lubricant level • Improperly adjusted clutch linkage
Low clutch life	Low clutch life is usually a result of poor driving habits or heavy duty use. Riding the clutch, pulling heavy loads, holding the car on a grade with the clutch instead of the brakes and rapid clutch engagement all contribute to low clutch life.

CLUTCH

REMOVAL AND INSTALLATION

4–134

CAUTION: *The clutch driven disc contains asbestos, which has been determined to be a cancer causing agent. Never clean clutch surfaces with compressed air! Avoid inhaling any dust from any clutch surface! When cleaning clutch surfaces, use a commercially available brake cleaning fluid.*

1. Remove the transmission and transfer case from the vehicle.
2. Remove the flywheel housing.
3. Mark the clutch pressure plate and engine flywheel with a center punch so the clutch assembly may be installed in the same position after adjustments or replacement are complete.
4. Loosen the clutch pressure plate bracket bolts equally, a little at a time, to prevent distortion and relieve the clutch springs evenly. Remove the bolts.
5. Remove the pressure plate assembly

(bracket and pressure plate) and driven plate from the flywheel. The driven plate will just be resting on the pressure plate housing since it usually is mounted on the input shaft of the transmission, which has been removed. Be

1. Driven plate and hub	7. Release lever
2. Pressure plate	8. Return spring
3. Pivot pin	9. Adjusting screw
4. Bracket	10. Jam nut
5. Spring cup	11. Washer
6. Pressure spring	

4-134 Auburn clutch

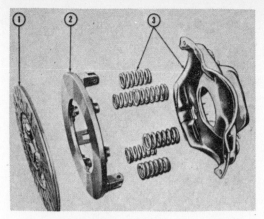

1. Driven plate and hub
2. Pressure plate
3. Backing plate and pressure spring

4-134 Rockford clutch

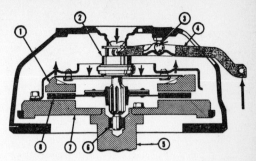

1. Pressure plate
2. Throwout bearing
3. Pivot point
4. Clutch fork

5. Engine crankshaft
6. Pilot bearing
7. Flywheel
8. Driven plate

V6 clutch cutaway

careful that it does not fall down and cause injury.

6. The clutch release bearing (throwout bearing) is lubricated at time of assembly and no attempt should be made to lubricate it. Put a small amount of grease in the pilot bushing.

7. Install the driven plate with the short end of the hub toward the flywheel. Use a spare transmission mainshaft or an aligning arbor to align the pressure plate assembly and the driven plate.

8. Leave the arbor in place while tightening the pressure plate screws evenly a turn or two at a time. Torque the bolts to 25 ft.lb.

9. Install the flywheel housing. Torque the bolts to 40–50 ft.lb.

10. Install the transmission and transfer case.

6–225

CAUTION: *The clutch driven disc contains asbestos, which has been determined to be a cancer causing agent. Never clean clutch surfaces with compressed air! Avoid inhaling any dust from any clutch surface! When cleaning clutch surfaces, use a commercially available brake cleaning fluid.*

1. Remove the transmission and transfer case.

2. Remove the clutch throwout bearing and pedal return spring from the clutch fork.

3. Remove the flywheel housing from the engine.

4. Disconnect the clutch form from the ball stud by forcing it toward the center of the vehicle.

5. Mark the clutch cover and flywheel with a center punch so that the cover an later be installed in the same position on the flywheel. This is necessary to maintain engine balance.

6. Loosen the clutch attaching bolts alternately, one turn at a time to avoid distorting the clutch cover flange, until the diaphragm spring is released.

7. Support the pressure plate and cover assembly while removing the last of the bolts; remove the pressure plate and driven plate from the flywheel.

8. If it is necessary to disassemble the pressure plate assembly, note the position of the grooves on the edge of the pressure plate and cover. These marks must be aligned during assembly to maintain balance. The clutch diaphragm spring and two pivot rings are riveted to the clutch cover. Inspect the spring, rings and cover for excessive wear or damage. If there is a defect, replace the complete cover assembly.

9. Replace the clutch assembly in reverse order of the removal procedure, taking note of the following:

   a. Use extreme care at all times not to get the clutch driven plate dirty in any way.

   b. Lightly lubricate the inside of the clutch driven plate's spline with a coat of wheel bearing grease. Do the same to the input shaft of the transmission. Wipe off all excess grease so that none will fly off and get onto the driven plate.

   c. Lubricate the throwout bearing collar, the ball stud and the clutch fork with wheel bearing grease.

   d. Use a pilot shaft or a spare transmission main shaft to align the driven shaft and the clutch pressure plate when attaching the assembly to the flywheel.

   e. Tighten down on the clutch-to-flywheel attaching bolts alternately so that the clutch is drawn squarely into position on the flywheel. Each bolt must be tightened one turn at a time to avoid bending the clutch cover flange. Torque the bolts to 30–40 ft.lb.

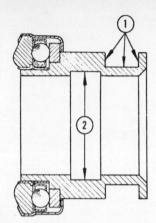

1. Coat this groove
2. Pack this recess

Lubrication points on the 6-225 throwout bearing collar

1972–87 except 4–151

CAUTION: *The clutch driven disc contains asbestos, which has been determined to be a cancer causing agent. Never clean clutch surfaces with compressed air! Avoid inhaling any dust from any clutch surface! When cleaning clutch surfaces, use a commercially available brake cleaning fluid.*

1. Remove the transmission.
2. Remove the starter.
3. Remove the throwout bearing and sleeve assembly.
4. Remove the bell housing.
5. Mark the clutch cover, pressure plate and the flywheel with a center punch so that these parts can be later installed in the same position.
6. Remove the clutch cover-to-flywheel attaching bolts. When removing these bolts, loosen them in rotation, one or two turns at a time, until the spring tension is released. The clutch cover is a steel stamping which could be warped by improper removal procedures, resulting in clutch chatter when reused.
7. Remove the clutch assembly from the flywheel.

8. The clutch release bearing (throwout bearing) is lubricated at time of assembly and no attempt should be made to lubricate it. Put a small amount of grease in the pilot bushing.
9. Install the driven plate with the short end of the hub toward the flywheel. Use a spare transmission mainshaft or an aligning arbor to align the pressure plate assembly and the driven plate.
10. Leave the arbor in place while tightening the pressure plate screws evenly a turn or two at a time. Torque the bolts to 40 ft.lb.
11. Install the bellhousing. Torque the bolts to 40 ft.lb.
12. Install the throwout bearing and sleeve assembly.
13. Install the starter.
14. Install the transmission.

4–151

CAUTION: *The clutch driven disc contains asbestos, which has been determined to be a cancer causing agent. Never clean clutch surfaces with compressed air! Avoid inhaling any dust from any clutch surface! When cleaning clutch surfaces, use a commercially available brake cleaning fluid.*

1. Remove the shift lever boot.
2. Remove the shift lever assembly.
3. Raise the vehicle and support it on jackstands.
4. Remove the transmission and transfer case.
5. Remove the slave cylinder-to-clutch housing bolts.
6. Disengage the slave cylinder pushrod from the throwout lever and move the cylinder out of the way.
7. Remove the starter.
8. Remove the throwout bearing.
9. Unbolt and remove the clutch housing.
10. Mark the position of the clutch pressure plate and remove the pressure plate bolts evenly, a little at a time in rotation.
11. Remove the pilot bushing lubricating

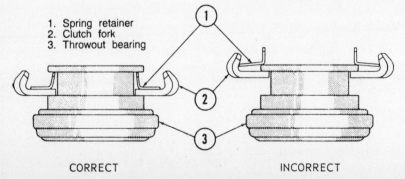

1. Spring retainer
2. Clutch fork
3. Throwout bearing

CORRECT   INCORRECT

6-225 throwout bearing installation

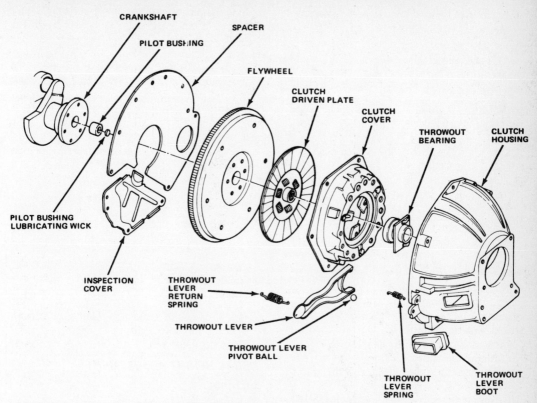

6-232, 258 and 8-304 clutch assembly

wick from its bore in the crankshaft and soak the wick in clean engine oil.

12. The clutch release bearing (throwout bearing) is lubricated at time of assembly and no attempt should be made to lubricate it.

13. Install the driven plate with the short end of the hub toward the flywheel. Use a spare transmission mainshaft or an aligning arbor to align the pressure plate assembly and the driven plate.

14. Leave the arbor in place while tightening the pressure plate screws evenly a turn or two at a time. Torque the pressure plate bolts to 23 ft.lb.

15. Install the pilot bushing lubricating wick in its bore in the crankshaft.

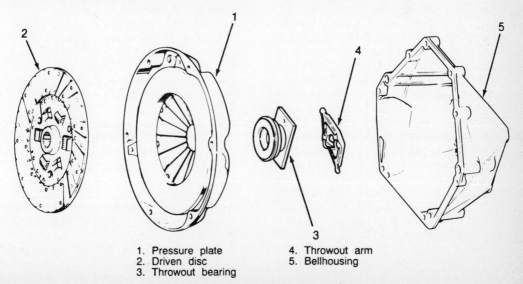

1. Pressure plate
2. Driven disc
3. Throwout bearing
4. Throwout arm
5. Bellhousing

4-150 clutch assembly

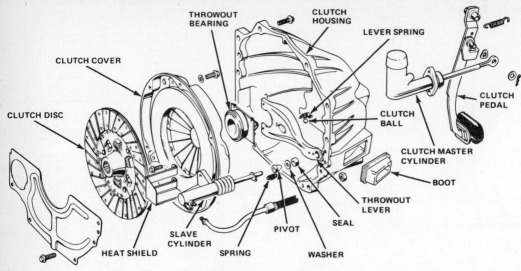

4-151 clutch assembly

16. Install the clutch housing. Torque the clutch housing to 54 ft.lb.

17. Install the throwout bearing.

18. Install the starter.

19. Engage the slave cylinder pushrod in the throwout lever.

20. Install the slave cylinder-to-clutch housing bolts.

21. Install the transmission and transfer case. Torque the transmission-to-clutch housing bolts to 54 ft.lb.; the transfer case-to-transmission bolts to 30 ft.lb.

22. Lower the vehicle.

23. Install the shift lever assembly.

24. Install the shift lever boot.

CLUTCH LINKAGE ADJUSTMENT

Through 1971

As the clutch facings wear out the free travel of the clutch pedal diminishes. When sufficient wear occurs, the pedal clearance must be adjusted to 1–1½" (25.4–38.1mm) on CJ models; 1" (25.4mm) on Utility models. The free pedal clearance is adjusted by lengthening or shortening the clutch fork cable.

To make this adjustment on all but the 6–226, loosen the jam nut on the cable clevis and lengthen or shorten the cable to obtain the proper clearance at the pedal pad, then tighten the jam nut.

To make this adjustment on the 6–226, loosen the two locknuts on he pedal adjusting rod. Turn the nuts forward to increase, or backwards to decrease the free travel. Tighten the locknuts.

NOTE: *On some older Jeep vehicles, a side movement of the clutch and brake pedals may develop. This is the result of wear on the ped-*

als, shafts, and bushings. One way to compensate for this wear is to install a pedal slack adjuster kit.

PEDAL HEIGHT ADJUSTMENT

1972 Only

The clutch pedal has an adjustable stop located on the pedal support bracket directly behind the instrument cluster.

Adjust the stop to provide the specified clearance between the top of the pedal pad and the closest point on the bar floor pan. The distance must be 8".

CONTROL CABLE ADJUSTMENT

1972

1. Lift up the clutch pedal against the pedal support bracket stop.

2. Unhook the clutch fork return spring.

3. Loosen the ball adjusting nut until some cable slack exists.

4. Adjust the ball adjusting nut until the slack is removed from the cable and the clutch throwout bearing contacts the pressure plate fingers.

5. Back off the ball adjusting nut ¾ of a turn to provide the proper amount of free play. Tighten the jam nut.

6. Hook the clutch fork return spring.

1973–75

1. Adjust the bellcrank outer support bracket to provide approximately ⅛" (3.175mm) of bellcrank end play.

2. Lift up the clutch pedal against the pedal stop.

3. On the clutch push rod (pedal to bellcrank) adjust the lower ball pivot assembly

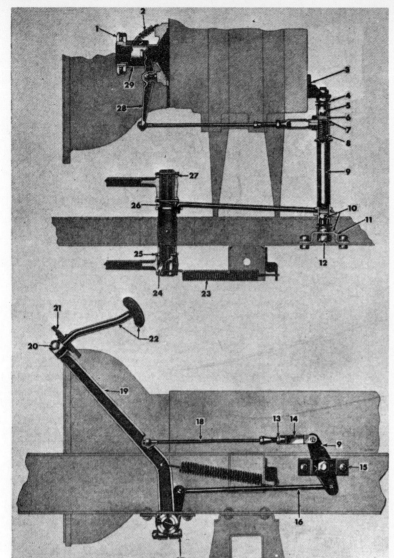

1. Clutch release bearing
2. Carrier spring
3. Bracket
4. Dust seal
5. Ball stud
6. Pad
7. Retainer
8. Control tube spring
9. Control lever and tube
10. Ball stud and bracket
11. Frame bracket
12. Ball stud nut
13. Yoke lock nut
14. Adjusting yoke
15. Bolt
16. Pedal release rod
17. Pedal clamp bolt
18. Control cable
19. Clutch pedal
20. Screw and lockwasher
21. Draft pad
22. Pedal pad and shank
23. Retracting spring
24. Pedal to shaft key
25. Washer
26. Pedal shaft
27. Master cylinder tie bar
28. Control lever
29. Bearing carrier

Clutch linkage used on CJ-3B, CJ-5 and CJ-6 through 1971

onto or off the rod (as required) to position the bellcrank inner lever parallel to the front face of the clutch housing (slightly forward from vertical).

4. Adjust the clutch fork release rod (bellcrank to release fork) to obtain the maximum specified clutch pedal free play of ¾" (19.05mm) on 1973–74 models and 1" (25.4mm) on 1975 models.

1976–83

NOTE: *4–151 and all 1984 and later models have a non-adjustable hydraulic clutch.*

1. Lift the pedal up against the stop.
2. Loosen the release rod adjuster jam nut, under the vehicle.

3. Adjust the pedal free-play to about one inch.
4. Tighten the jam nut.

Clutch Master Cylinder
REMOVAL AND INSTALLATION

1. Raise and support the truck on jackstands.
2. Disconnect the hydraulic line at the cylinder. Cap the line.
3. Unbolt and remove the slave cylinder from the clutch housing.
4. Installation is the reverse of removal. Torque the mounting bolts to 16 ft.lb. Refill and bleed the system.

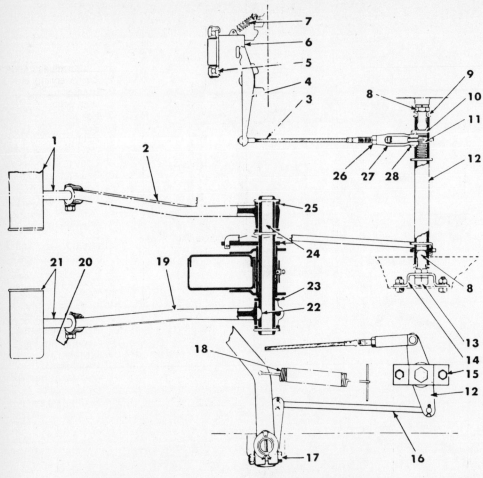

1. Brake pedal pad	15. Bracket to frame bolt
2. Brake pedal	16. Pedal rod
3. Control cable	17. Pedal clamp bolt
4. Control lever	18. Pedal retracting spring
5. Release bearing	19. Clutch pedal
6. Release bearing carrier	20. Pedal pad clamp bolt
7. Bearing carrier spring	21. Clutch pedal pad
8. Ball stud	22. Pedal to shaft key
9. Dust seal	23. Pedal shaft washer
10. Control tube retainer	24. Pedal shaft
11. Control tube spring	25. Brake master cylinder tee bar
12. Control tube and lever	26. Adjusting yoke lock nut
13. Ball stud nut	27. Adjusting yoke
14. Frame bracket	28. Adjusting yoke clevis pin

CJ-2A, CJ-3A clutch linkage

OVERHAUL

Through 1986

1. Remove the cover and reservoir cap.

2. Remove and discard the dust boot from the pusrod.

3. Remove the pushrod seal.

4. Remove and discard the pushrod retaining snapring.

5. Remove the pushrod, washer and seal. Discard the seal.

6. Remove the plunger, valve spring and stem. It may be necessary to tap the assembly out of the bore with a rubber mallet.

7. Compress the valve spring enough to pry off the retainer and remove the spring and stem assembly from the plunger. The retainer

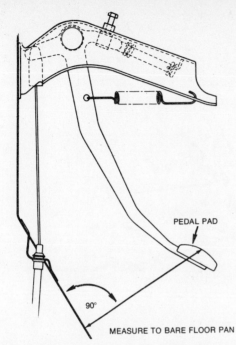

Clutch pedal height adjustment—1972 only

PEDAL PAD

90°

MEASURE TO BARE FLOOR PAN

tab should be pried upward with a thin screwdriver.

8. Remove the seal from the plunger and discard it.

9. Remove the spring retainer and valve stem from the spring.

10. Remove the valve stem from the retainer and remove the spring washer and stem tip seal from the end of the valve stem. Discard the stem tip seal and the spring washer.

11. Clean all parts thoroughly in a safe brake cleaning solvent. Discard any parts that show signs of wear, pitting or damage. If the core shows signs of excessive wear, deep pitting, severe corrosion or scoring, replace the entire master cylinder. Minor bore imperfections can be corrected by honing.

12. Lubricate the bore with clean brake fluid.

13. Position the new seals on the plunger and valve stem. Make sure that the lip of the plunger seal faces the stem end of the plunger. The should of the stem tip seal should fit into the undercut at the end of the valve stem.

14. Install the new spring washer on the stem.

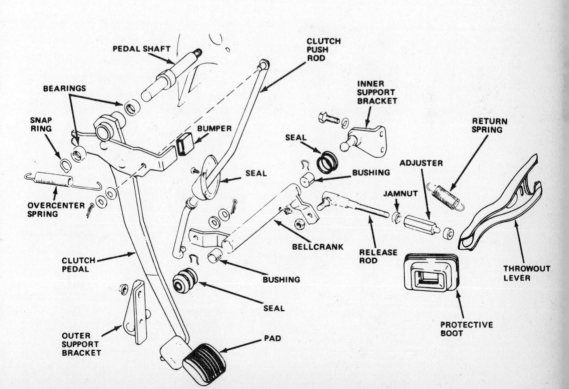

1976—83 clutch linkage for all except the 4-151

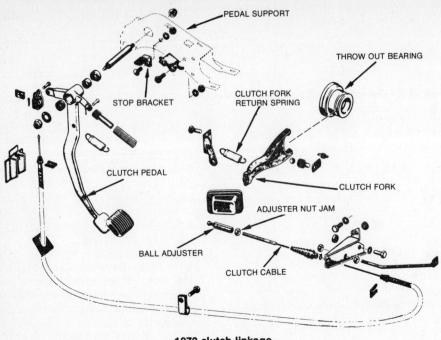

PEDAL SUPPORT

THROW OUT BEARING

STOP BRACKET

CLUTCH FORK
RETURN SPRING

CLUTCH PEDAL

CLUTCH FORK

ADJUSTER NUT JAM

BALL ADJUSTER

CLUTCH CABLE

1972 clutch linkage

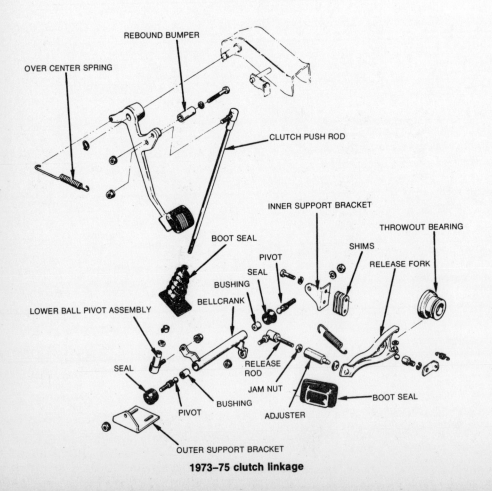

REBOUND BUMPER

OVER CENTER SPRING

CLUTCH PUSH ROD

INNER SUPPORT BRACKET

THROWOUT BEARING

BOOT SEAL

SHIMS

PIVOT

RELEASE FORK

SEAL

BUSHING

LOWER BALL PIVOT ASSEMBLY

BELLCRANK

RELEASE
ROD

SEAL

JAM NUT

BOOT SEAL

PIVOT

BUSHING

ADJUSTER

OUTER SUPPORT BRACKET

1973–75 clutch linkage

1. Rubber outer cover
2. Reservoir cap
3. Dust boot
4. Push rod
5. Clutch master cylinder
6. Push rod seal
7. Retaining snap ring
8. Retaining washer
9. Plunger
10. Valve spring
11. Valve stem retainer
12. Plunger seal
13. Spring retainer
14. Valve stem
15. Spring washer
16. Stem tip seal
17. Cap seal
   A. Valve stem assembly

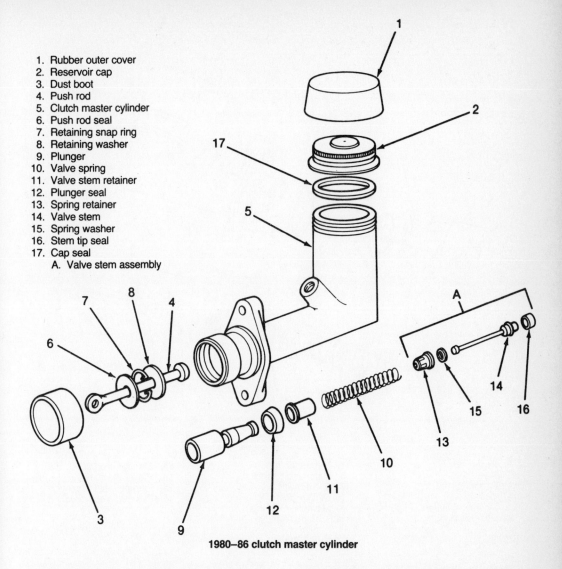

1980–86 clutch master cylinder

15. Install the new plastic spring retainer on the stem and over the spring washer. The large end of the retainer faces the end of the stem.

16. Install the valve spring over the stem and the seat spring on the valve stem retainer.

17. Install the assembled valves spring, the retainer and the stem assembly on the plunger.

18. Compress the spring against the plunger. When the end of the stem passes through the valve stem retainer and seats in the small bore in the end of the plunger, bend the retainer tab on the valve stem retainer downward to lock the stem and retainer on the plunger.

19. Lubricate the spring and plunger assembly with clean brake fluid and insert the assembly, spring end first, into the bore.

20. Install the new seal and dust boot on the pushrod.

21. Lubricate the ball end of the pushrod and the lip of the seal and dust boot with clean brake fluid, or the lubricant supplied in the overhaul kit.

22. Insert the pushrod and retaining washer into the bore.

23. Install the new snapring. Properly position the seal and dust boot.

1987

1. Remove the cover and reservoir cap.

2. Remove and discard the dust boot from the pusrod.

3. Remove and discard the pushrod retaining snapring.

4. Remove the pushrod and washer.

5. Remove the plunger, valve spring and stem. It may be necessary to tap the assembly out of the bore with a rubber mallet.

6. Compress the valve spring enough to pry off the retainer and remove the spring and

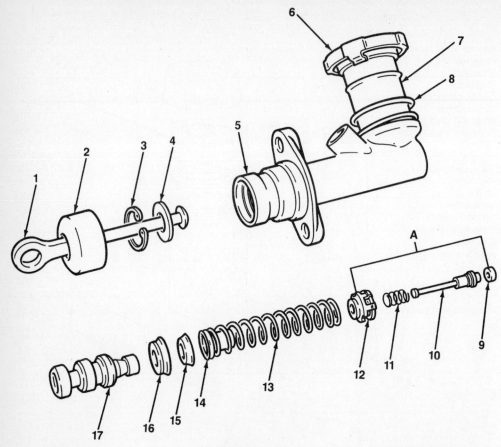

1. Push rod
2. Dust boot
3. Snapring
4. Washer
5. Master cylinder
6. Reservoir cap
7. Reservoir
8. Retaining clamp
9. Stem tip seal
10. Valve stem
11. Retainer spring
12. Spring retainer
13. Plunger spring
14. Valve stem retainer
15. Plunger rear seal
16. Plunger front seal
17. Plunger

1987 clutch master cylinder

stem assembly from the plunger. The retainer tab should be pried upward with a thin screwdriver.

7. Remove the seals from the plunger and discard them.

8. Remove the spring retainer and valve stem from the spring.

9. Remove the valve stem from the retainer and remove the spring washer and stem tip seal from the end of the valve stem. Discard the stem tip seal and the spring washer.

10. Clean all parts thoroughly in a safe brake cleaning solvent. Discard any parts that show signs of wear, pitting or damage. If the core shows signs of excessive wear, deep pitting, severe corrosion or scoring, replace the entire master cylinder. Minor bore imperfections can be corrected by honing.

11. Lubricate the bore with clean brake fluid.

12. Position the new seal on the valve stem.

The shoulder of the stem tip seal should fit into the undercut at the end of the valve stem.

13. Install the new seals on the plunger. The seal lips face the valve stem end of the plunger.

14. Install the new spring and retainer on the stem.

15. Install the plunger retainer in the spring.

16. Insert the plunger into the retainer.

17. Compress the spring against the plunger. When the end of the stem passes through the valve stem retainer and seats in the small bore in the end of the plunger, bend the retainer tab on the valve stem retainer downward to lock the stem and retainer on the plunger.

18. Lubricate the spring and plunger assembly with clean brake fluid and insert the assembly, spring end first, into the bore.

19. Install the new dust boot on the pushrod.

20. Lubricate the ball end of the pushrod and the lip of the dust boot with clean brake fluid,

or the lubricant supplied in the overhaul kit.

21. Insert the pushrod and retaining washer into the bore.

22. Install the new snapring. Properly position the dust boot.

Clutch Slave Cylinder

REMOVAL AND INSTALLATION

1980–86

1. Raise and support the truck on jackstands.

2. Disconnect the hydraulic line at the cylinder. Cap the line.

3. Unbolt and remove the slave cylinder from the clutch housing.

4. Installation is the reverse of removal. Torque the mounting bolts to 16 ft.lb. Refill and bleed the system.

1987

1. Disconnect the master cylinder line at the slave cylinder inlet line.

2. Remove the transmission and transfer case.

3. Slide the rubber insulator out of the insulator bracket and off of the hydraulic lines.

4. Unbolt the insulator bracket from the bellhousing and slide it off of the lines.

5. Remove the cylinder and bearing retaining nut. Pry the nut up and off of the mounting pin on the transmission front case.

6. Being careful to avoid kinking the lines, slide the cylinder and bearing assembly off of the input shaft.

NOTE: *Don't remove the lines from the slave cylinder. They are not meant to be removed and will be damaged if removal is attempted.*

Also, some replacement cylinder/bearing assemblies will come with nylon retaining straps. These straps are meant to hold the assembly together during shipment. DO NOT REMOVE THEM! They are designed to break off the first time piston movement takes place.

7. Install the assembly on the input shaft.

8. Guide the lines through the opening in the bellhousing.

9. Position the cylinder mounting boss over the pin on the transmission front face.

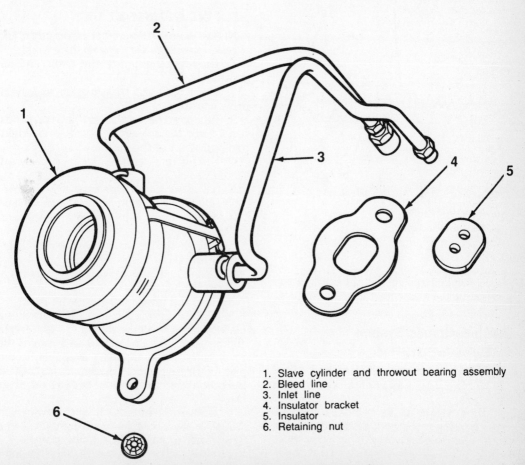

1. Slave cylinder and throwout bearing assembly
2. Bleed line
3. Inlet line
4. Insulator bracket
5. Insulator
6. Retaining nut

1987 clutch slave cylinder and throwout bearing

10. Secure the assembly to the mounting pin with the nut.

11. Install the insulator and bracket.

12. Install the transmission and transfer case.

13. Fill and bleed the system.

OVERHAUL

1980–86

1. Clean the outside of the cylinder.

2. Remove the dust boot.

3. Remove the pushrod, boot, plunger and spring as an assembly.

4. Remove the spring and seal from the plunger.

5. Remove the snapring and separate the pushrod and boot from the plunger.

6. Clean all parts and replace the cylinder if the bore is excessively worn, pitted, knicked or corroded. Minor imperfections in the bore can be removed through honing.

7. Rebuild the cylinder using a rebuilding kit. Lubricate all parts with clean brake fluid, including the cylinder bore.

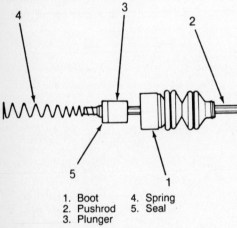

1. Boot	4. Spring
2. Pushrod	5. Seal
3. Plunger	

1980–86 slave cylinder

1987

The slave cylinder is not rebuildable and must be replaced as an assembly if defective.

Clutch Hydraulic System

BLEEDING THE SYSTEM

1. Fill the reservoir with clean brake fluid.

2. Raise and support the truck on jackstands.

3. Remove the slave cylinder from the clutch housing, but do not disconnect the hydraulic line. There is enough play in the line to do this.

4. Remove the slave cylinder pushrod.

5. Using a wood dowel, compress the slave cylinder plunger.

6. Attach one end of a rubber hose to the slave cylinder bleeder screw and place the other end in a glass jar, filled halfway with clean brake fluid. Make sure that the hose will stay submerged.

7. Loosen the bleeder screw.

8. Have an assistant press and hold the clutch pedal to the floor. Tighten the bleeder screw with the pedal at the floor. Bubbles will have appeared in the jar when the pedal was depressed.

9. Have your assistant release the pedal, then perform the sequence again, until bubbles no longer appear in the jar.

10. Install the slave cylinder and lower the truck. Test the clutch.

Overdrive

2-WD Utility models were offered with an optional Warner R10B planetary overdrive unit. The unit is electrically engaged at the discretion of the driver. It provides a reduction of about 30%.

REMOVAL AND INSTALLATION

NOTE: *Because the unit is essentially a 4th gear, removal is the same as disassembly.*

1. Raise and support the front end on jackstands.

2. Drain both the transmission and overdrive housings.

3. Remove the two solenoid attachings bolts. Turn the solenoid ¼ turn to the right and pull it out of the unit.

4. Unbolt and remove the overdrive rail switch.

NOTE: *This switch was used only on vehicles with the 4–134 engine up to ands including vehicle serial numbers 54747-10084 and 54874-10096.*

5. Remove the governor from the right side.

6. Disconnect the speedometer cable.

7. Unbolt and remove the transmission cover from the housing.

8. Shift the transmission into 1st gear.

9. Place transmission mainshaft retaining plate tool W-194 on the rear of the 1st/reverse sliding gear. Attach the tool with two of the cover bolts. If the tool isn't available, loop a piece of wire around the mainshaft, just behind the gear and secure the wire to two front cover bolts.

10. Remove the nut attaching the companion flange to the overdrive mainshaft. Hold the flange with a holding tool, if necessary.

11. Remove the companion flange, using a puller, if necessary.

12. Using a punch, drive the overdrive control shaft tapered pin out, from the bottom.

13. Pull out the control shaft to disengage the shaft rail.

14. Remove the bolts attaching the overdrive housing and adapter to the transmission.

15. Pull the overdrive housing rearward, while, at the same time, pushing forward on the overdrive mainshaft to prevent the mainshaft from coming off with the housing.

16. Slide the overdrive housing into place, while holding the mainshaft.

17. nstall the bolts attaching the overdrive housing and adapter to the transmission. Torque them to 30 ft.lb.

18. Push in the control shaft to engage the shaft rail.

19. Drive the overdrive control shaft tapered pin into place from the top.

20. Install the companion flange.

21. Install the nut attaching the companion flange to the overdrive mainshaft. Hold the flange with a holding tool, if necessary. Torque the nut to 75 ft.lb.

22. Remove transmission mainshaft retaining plate tool W-194 or the wire.

23. Install the transmission cover.

24. Connect the speedometer cable.

25. Install the governor.

26. Install the overdrive rail switch.

NOTE: *This switch was used only on vehicles with the 4–134 engine up to ands including vehicle serial numbers 54747-10084 and 54874-10096.*

27. Push the solenoid into the unit and turn it ¼ turn to the left. Install the two solenoid attachings bolts.

28. Fill both the transmission and overdrive housings.

29. Lower the front end.

AUTOMATIC TRANSMISSION

Understanding Automatic Transmissions

The automatic transmission allows engine torque and power to be transmitted to the rear wheels within a narrow range of engine operating speeds. The transmission will allow the engine to turn fast enough to produce plenty of power and torque at very low speeds, while keeping it at a sensible rpm at high vehicle speeds. The transmission performs this job entirely without driver assistance. The transmission uses a light fluid as the medium for the transmission of power. This fluid also works in the operation of various hydraulic control circuits and as a lubricant. Because the transmission fluid performs all of these three functions, trouble within the unit can easily travel from one part to another. For this reason, and because of the complexity and unusual operating principles of the transmission, a very sound understanding of the basic principles of operation will simplify troubleshooting.

THE TORQUE CONVERTER

The torque converter replaces the conventional clutch. It has three functions:

1. It allows the engine to idle with the vehicle at a standstill, even with the transmission in gear.

2. It allows the transmission to shift from range to range smoothly, without requiring that the driver close the throttle during the shift.

3. It multiplies engine torque to an increasing extent as vehicle speed drops and throttle opening is increased. This has the effect of making the transmission more responsive and reduces the amount of shifting required.

The torque converter is a metal case which is shaped like a sphere that has been flattened on opposite sides. It is bolted to the rear end of the engine's crankshaft. Generally, the entire metal case rotates at engine speed and serves as the engine's flywheel.

The case contains three sets of blades. One set is attached directly to the case. This set forms the torus or pump. Another set is directly connected to the output shaft, and forms the turbine. The third set is mounted on a hub which, in turn, is mounted on a stationary shaft through a one-way clutch. This third set is known as the stator.

A pump, which is driven by the covnerter hub at engine speed, keeps the torque converter full of transmission fluid at all times. Fluid flows continuously through the unit to provide cooling.

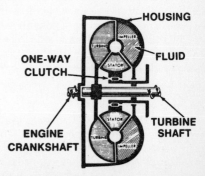

The torque converter housing is roated by the engine's crankshaft, and turns the impeller. The impeller spins the turbine, which gives motion to the turbine shaft, driving the gears

Under low-speed acceleration, the torque converter functions as follows:

The torus is turning faster than the turbine. It picks up fluid at the center of the converter and, through centrifugal force, slings it outward. Since the outer edge of the converter moves faster than the portions at the center, the fluid picks up speed.

The fluid then enters the outer edge of the turbine blades. It then travels back toward the center of the converter case along the turbine blades. In impinging upon the turbine blades, the fluid loses the energy picked up in the torus.

If the fluid were now to immediately be returned directly into the torus, both halves of the converter would have to turn at approximately the same speed at all times, and torque input and output would both be the same.

In flowing through the torus and turbine, the fluid picks up two types of flow, or flow in two spearate directions. It flows through the turbine blades, and it spins with the engine. The stator, whose blades are stationary when the vehicle is being accelerated at low speeds, converts one type of flow into another. Instead of allowing the fluid to flow straight back into the torus, the stator's curved blades turn the fluid almost 90 degrees toward the direction of rotation of the engine. Thus the fluid does not flow as fast toward the torus, but is already spinning when the torus picks it up. This has the effect of allowing the torus to turn much faster than the turbine. This difference in speed may be compared to the difference in speed between the smaller and larger gears in any gear train. The result is that engine power output is higher, and engine torque is multiplied.

As the speed of the turbine increases, the fluid spins faster and faster in the direction of engine rotation. As a result, the ability of the stator to redirect the fluid flow is reduced. Under cruising conditions, the stator is eventually forced to rotate on its one-way clutch in the direction of engine rotation. Under these conditions, the torque converter begins to behave almost like a solid shaft, with the torus and turbine speeds being almost equal.

THE PLANETARY GEARBOX

The ability of the torque converter to multiply engine torque is limited. Also, the unit tends to be more efficient when the turine is rotating at relatively high speeds. Therefore, a planetary gearbox is used to carry the power output of the turbine to the driveshaft.

Planetary gears function very similarly to conventional transmission gears. However,

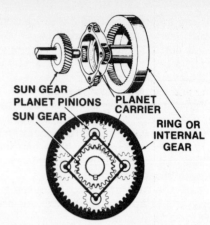

Planetary gears are similar to manual transmission gears but are composed of three parts

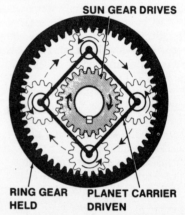

Planetary gears in the maximum reduction (low) range. The ring gear is held and a lower gear ration is obtained

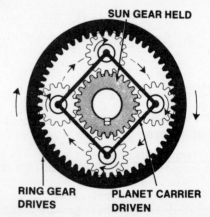

Planetary gears in the minimum reduction (drive) range. The ring gear is allowed to revolve, providing a higher gear ratio

their construction is different in that three elements make up one gear system, and, in that all three elements are different from one another. The three elements are: an outer gear that is shaped like a hoop, with teeth cut into the inner surface; a sun gear, mounted on a shaft and located at the very center of the outer gear; and a set of three planet gears, held by pins in a ring-like planet carrier, meshing with both the sun gear and the outer gear. Either the outer gear or the sun gear may be held stationary, providing more than one possible torque multiplication factor for each set of gears. Also, if all three gears are forced to rotate at the same speed, the gearset forms, in effect, a solid shaft.

Most modern automatics use the planetary gears to provide either a single reduction ratio of about 1.8:1, or two reduction gears: a low of about 2.5:1, and an intermediate of about 1.5:1. Bands and clutches are used to hold various portions of the gearsets to the transmission case or to the shaft on which they are mounted. Shifting is accomplished, then, by changing the portion of each planetary gearset which is held to the tranmission case or to the shaft.

THE SERVOS AND ACCUMULATORS

The servos are hydraulic pistons and cylinders. They resemble the hydraulic actuators used on many familiar machines, such as bulldozers. Hydraulic fluid enters the cylinder, under pressure, and forces the piston to move to engage the band or clutches.

The accumulators are used to cushion the engagement of the servos. The transmission fluid must pass through the accumulator on the way to the servo. The accumulator housing contains a thin piston which is sprung away from the discharge passage of the accumulator. When fluid passes through the accumulator on the way to the servo, it must move the piston against spring pressure, and this action smooths out the action of the servo.

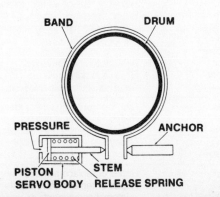

Servos, operated by pressure, are used to apply or release the bands, to either hold the ring gear or allow it to rotate

THE HYDRAULIC CONTROL SYSTEM

The hydraulic pressure used to operate the servos comes from the main transmission oil pump. This fluid is channeled to the various servos through the shift valves. There is generally a manual shift valve which is operated by the tranmission selector lever and an automatic shift valvee for each automatic upshift the transmission provides: i.e., 2-speed automatics have a low-high shift valve, while 3-speeds have a 1–2 valve, and a 2–3 vavle.

There are two pressures which effect the operation of these valves. One is the governor pressure which is affected by vehicle speed. The other is the modulator pressure which is affected by intake manifold vacuum or throttle position. Governor pressure rises with an increase in vehicle speed, and modulator pressure rises as the throttle is opened wider. By responding to these two pressures, the shift valves cause the upshift points to be delayed with increased throttle opening to make the best use of the engine's power output.

Most transmissions also make use of an auxiliary circuit for downshifting. This circuit may be actuated by the throttle linkage or the vacuum line which actuates the modulator, or by a cable or solenoid. It applies pressure to a special downshift surface on the shift valve or valves.

The transmission modulator also governs the line pressure, used to actuate the servos. In this way, the clutches and bands will be actuated with a force matching the torque output of the engine.

Pan Removal and Fluid Change

Chrysler 904 and 999

1. Raise and support the truck on jackstands.

2. The pan has no drain plug, so remove the bolts at one corner and loosen the other pan bolts so that the fluid drains neatly from the one, low hanging corner.

3. Remove the remaining bolts and remove the pan. Discard the gasket.

4. Unbolt and remove the filter from the valve body.

5. Install the new filter and torque the bolts to 35 in.lb.

6. Coat a new pan gasket with sealer and install the pan. Torque the bolts to 150 in.lb. (12 ft.lb.). Fill the transmission.

Turbo Hydra-Matic 400

Since the Turbo Hydra-Matic transmission doesn't have a drain plug, the fluid is drained

Troubleshooting Basic Automatic Transmission Problems

Problem	Cause	Solution
Fluid leakage	• Defective pan gasket	• Replace gasket or tighten pan bolts
	• Loose filler tube	• Tighten tube nut
	• Loose extension housing to transmission case	• Tighten bolts
	• Converter housing area leakage	• Have transmission checked professionally
Fluid flows out the oil filler tube	• High fluid level	• Check and correct fluid level
	• Breather vent clogged	• Open breather vent
	• Clogged oil filter or screen	• Replace filter or clean screen (change fluid also)
	• Internal fluid leakage	• Have transmission checked professionally
Transmission overheats (this is usually accompanied by a strong burned odor to the fluid)	• Low fluid level	• Check and correct fluid level
	• Fluid cooler lines clogged	• Drain and refill transmission. If this doesn't cure the problem, have cooler lines cleared or replaced.
	• Heavy pulling or hauling with insufficient cooling	• Install a transmission oil cooler
	• Faulty oil pump, internal slippage	• Have transmission checked professionally
Buzzing or whining noise	• Low fluid level	• Check and correct fluid level
	• Defective torque converter, scored gears	• Have transmission checked professionally
No forward or reverse gears or slippage in one or more gears	• Low fluid level	• Check and correct fluid level
	• Defective vacuum or linkage controls, internal clutch or band failure	• Have unit checked professionally
Delayed or erratic shift	• Low fluid level	• Check and correct fluid level
	• Broken vacuum lines	• Repair or replace lines
	• Internal malfunction	• Have transmission checked professionally

Lockup Torque Converter Service Diagnosis

Problem	Cause	Solution
No lockup	• Faulty oil pump	• Replace oil pump
	• Sticking governor valve	• Repair or replace as necessary
	• Valve body malfunction (a) Stuck switch valve (b) Stuck lockup valve (c) Stuck fail-safe valve	• Repair or replace valve body or its internal components as necessary
	• Failed locking clutch	• Replace torque converter
	• Leaking turbine hub seal	• Replace torque converter
	• Faulty input shaft or seal ring	• Repair or replace as necessary
Will not unlock	• Sticking governor valve	• Repair or replace as necessary
	• Valve body malfunction (a) Stuck switch valve (b) Stuck lockup valve (c) Stuck fail-safe valve	• Repair or replace valve body or its internal components as necessary
Stays locked up at too low a speed in direct	• Sticking governor valve	• Repair or replace as necessary
	• Valve body malfunction (a) Stuck switch valve (b) Stuck lockup valve (c) Stuck fail-safe valve	• Repair or replace valve body or its internal components as necessary

Lockup Torque Converter Service Diagnosis (cont.)

Problem	Cause	Solution

Locks up or drags in low or second	• Faulty oil pump
	• Valve body malfunction
	  (a) Stuck switch valve
	  (b) Stuck fail-safe valve
		• Replace oil pump
		• Repair or replace valve body or its internal components as necessary

Sluggish or stalls in reverse	• Faulty oil pump
	• Plugged cooler, cooler lines or fittings
	• Valve body malfunction
	  (a) Stuck switch valve
	  (b) Faulty input shaft or seal ring
		• Replace oil pump as necessary
		• Flush or replace cooler and flush lines and fittings
		• Repair or replace valve body or its internal components as necessary

Loud chatter during lockup engagement (cold)	• Faulty torque converter • Failed locking clutch • Leaking turbine hub seal	• Replace torque converter • Replace torque converter • Replace torque converter
Vibration or shudder during lockup engagement	• Faulty oil pump • Valve body malfunction • Faulty torque converter • Engine needs tune-up	• Repair or replace oil pump as necessary • Repair or replace valve body or its internal components as necessary • Replace torque converter • Tune engine
Vibration after lockup engagement	• Faulty torque converter • Exhaust system strikes underbody • Engine needs tune-up • Throttle linkage misadjusted	• Replace torque converter • Align exhaust system • Tune engine • Adjust throttle linkage
Vibration when revved in neutral Overheating: oil blows out of dip stick tube or pump seal	• Torque converter out of balance • Plugged cooler, cooler lines or fittings • Stuck switch valve	• Replace torque converter • Flush or replace cooler and flush lines and fittings • Repair switch valve in valve body or replace valve body
Shudder after lockup engagement	• Faulty oil pump • Plugged cooler, cooler lines or fittings • Valve body malfunction • Faulty torque converter • Fail locking clutch • Exhaust system strikes underbody • Engine needs tune-up • Throttle linkage misadjusted	• Replace oil pump • Flush or replace cooler and flush lines and fittings • Repair or replace valve body or its internal components as necessary • Replace torque converter • Replace torque converter • Align exhaust system • Tune engine • Adjust throttle linkage

Automatic Transmission Application Chart

Transmission Type	Years	Models
Turbo Hydra-Matic 400	1976–79	CJ-7
Chrysler 904	1981	CJ-7 w/4-151
Chrysler 999	1980–81	CJ-7 w/6-258 and 8-304
	1982-86	CJ-7 and Scrambler w/6-258
	1987	Wrangler w/6-258

Transmission Fluid Indications

The appearance and odor of the transmission fluid can give valuable clues to the overall condition of the transmission. Always note the appearance of the fluid when you check the fluid level or change the fluid. Rub a small amount of fluid between your fingers to feel for grit and smell the fluid on the dipstick.

If the fluid appears:	It indicates:
Clear and red colored	• Normal operation
Discolored (extremely dark red or brownish) or smells burned	• Band or clutch pack failure, usually caused by an overheated transmission. Hauling very heavy loads with insufficient power or failure to change the fluid, often result in overheating. Do not confuse this appearance with newer fluids that have a darker red color and a strong odor (though not a burned odor).
Foamy or aerated (light in color and full of bubbles)	• The level is too high (gear train is churning oil) • An internal air leak (air is mixing with the fluid). Have the transmission checked professionally.
Solid residue in the fluid	• Defective bands, clutch pack or bearings. Bits of band material or metal abrasives are clinging to the dipstick. Have the transmission checked professionally.
Varnish coating on the dipstick	• The transmission fluid is overheating

by loosening the pan and allowing the fluid to run out over the top of the pan.

To avoid making a really big mess, place a drain pan under one corner of the transmission pan and remove the two attaching screws nearest to either side of that particular corner. One by one, and in a progressive manner, loosen all of the other attaching screws holding the transmission pan, leaving the ones farthest away from the drain corner tighter than the rest. When the majority of the fluid has drained, hold the pan up with one hand, remove the remaining attaching screws and carefully lower the pan. There will be some automatic transmission fluid left in the pan, so be careful not to spill any. The filter is located directly under the oil pan.

There are filter replacement kits available for changing the transmission fluid filter. The kit includes a new filter, pan gasket and, in most cases, a new rubber O-ring to seal the intake pipe. If a new O-ring is not provided, leave the old one in place. If you can see that the old O-ring is cracked or damaged in any way, it is necessary to replace it with a new one, which can be obtained at a Jeep or GM dealer.

1. Remove the oil filter retainer bolt and remove the oil filter assembly from the transmission.
2. Remove the intake pipe from the filter and the intake pipe-to-case O-ring, if it is to be replaced.
3. Coat the new rubber O-ring with transmission fluid and position it in the groove at the inlet opening.
4. Slide the inlet pipe onto the new filter and position the filter on the transmission, guiding the inlet pipe in place.
5. Install the filter retaining bolt and tighten securely.
6. Clean the pan in a suitable solvent and wipe it dry with a clean, lint-free cloth.
7. Install the pan in the reverse order of removal using a new pan-to-transmission gasket and torquing the bolts in an alternating pattern to 10–13 ft.lb.

Auxiliary Oil Cooler

REMOVAL AND INSTALLATION

1. Remove the attaching screws and lift off the grille panel.
2. Using masking tape, mark the cooler lines for installation.
3. Place a drain pan on the ground, under the cooler.
4. Loosen the clamps securing the hoses to the cooler and slide them out of the way.
5. Twist the hoses to free them from the cooler pipes and slide the off. Cap the hose ends and cooler outlets to prevent dirt from entering.
6. Unbolt and remove the cooler.
7. Installation is the reverse of removal. Add sufficient fluid to refill the system.

SHIFT LINKAGE ADJUSTMENT

1976–79

1. Place the column shift lever in Neutral.
2. Loosen the gearshift rod clamp adjustment locknut under the vehicle. Make sure

that the lever on the transmission is fully in the Neutral position.

3. Tighten the locknut.

4. Check that the engine can be started only in Park and Neutral and that each gear position is fully engaged.

1980–87

1. Raise and support the vehicle on jackstands.

2. Loosen the shift rod trunnion jamnuts.

3. Remove the lockpin retaining the trunnion to the bell crank and disengage the trunnion at the bell crank.

4. Place the shift lever in Park and lock the column.

5. Move the transmission case lever as far into the Park (rearward) position as possible. Check that the driveshaft will not rotate in this position.

6. Adjust the shift rod trunnion to obtain free pin fit in the bell crank arm and tighten the trunnion jamnuts.

NOTE: *All play must be eliminated for proper adjustment. Eliminate play by pulling downward on the shift rod and pressing on the outer bell crank.*

7. Move the gearshift lever to Park and Neutral and check to see if the engine starts.

8. Road test the vehicle.

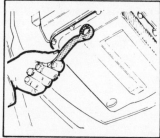

1. Position a catch pan under the transmission. If equipped, remove the drain plug. Be careful; the fluid may be hot.

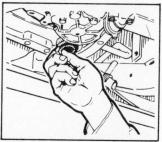

4. Remove the old O-ring from the filter neck and replace with new O-Ring supplied with filter kit.

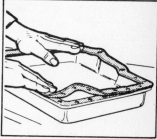

7. Install a new gasket on the pan.

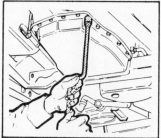

2. Many late-model vehicles have no drain plug. Loosen the pan bolts and allow one corner of the pan to tilt slightly to drain the fluid.

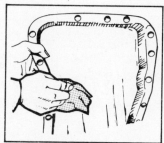

5. Clean the pan thoroughly with gasoline and allow to air dry completely.

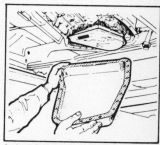

8. Install the new pan and gasket. Do not overtighten the screws.

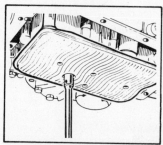

3. The filter or screen is held on by bolts or screws. Remove the filter or screen straight down.

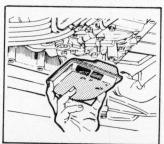

6. Install the new filter. Be sure the intake pipe is seated in the O-ring. Some transmissions use a screen which can be cleaned in gasoline and air dried.

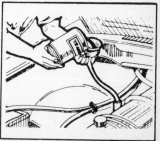

9. Fill the transmission with the required amount of fluid. Do not overfill. Start the engine and shift through all the gears. Check the fluid level and add fluid if necessary.

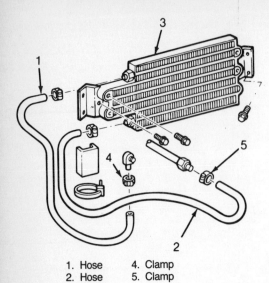

1. Hose
2. Hose
3. Cooler
4. Clamp
5. Clamp

Auxiliary oil cooler

BAND ADJUSTMENTS

NOTE: *The GM Turbo Hydra-Matic 400 used in 1976–79 models, does not have any band adjustments. The following apply only to the Chrysler built 904 and 999 used in 1980 and later models.*

Front Band

1980–81

1. Raise and support the vehicle on jackstands.

2. Loosen the adjusting screw locknut and back the locknut off five turns.

3. Mark the adjusting screw location. Check that it turns freely. If not, squirt some Liquid Wrench®, WD-40®, or similar substance on it.

4. Tighten the adjusting screw to 36 in.lb. using, if necessary, an adapter such as the one pictured, and a $\frac{5}{16}$" (7.9375mm) square socket.

NOTE: *If the adapter is not used, and the*

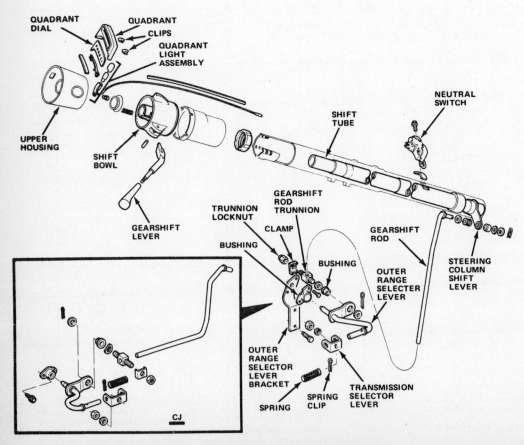

1976–79 automatic transmission shift linkage

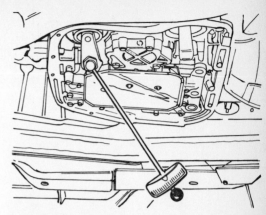

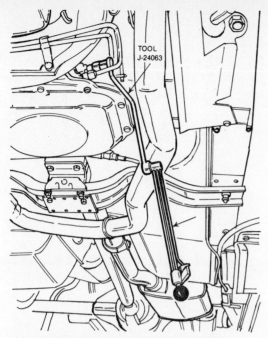

Chrysler 904 and 999 front band adjustment

Chrysler 904 and 999 rear band adjustment

torque wrench is applied directly to the adjuster, tighten the adjuster to 72 in.lb.

5. Back off the adjuster two full turns.

6. Hold the adjuster firmly and tighten the locknut to 35 ft.lb.

7. Lower the vehicle.

1983–87

1. Raise and support the truck on jackstands. The front band adjusting screw is located on the left side of the case, just above the control levers.

2. Loosen the locknut and back it off about five turns.

3. Make sure that the screw turns freely. Use penetrating oil if it binds.

4. Tighten the screw to 72 in.lb.

5. Back off the screw 2½ turns.

6. Tighten the locknut to 35 ft.lb. Hold the screw still while tightening the locknut.

7. Lower the truck.

Rear Band

1980–86

NOTE: *The transmission oil pan must be removed to gain access to the adjusting screw.*

1. Raise and support the vehicle on jackstands.

2. Remove the pan.

3. Remove the adjusting screw locknut.

4. Tighten the adjusting screw to 41 in.lb. using a torque wrench and a ¼" (6.35mm) hex head socket.

5. Back off the adjusting screw four full turns.

6. Hold the adjusting screw firmly, install the locknut and tighten it to 35 ft.lb.

7. Install the oil pan and new gasket. Torque the bolts to 12 ft.lb.

8. Lower the vehicle. Fill the transmission with Dexron®II fluid.

1987

1. Raise and support the truck on jackstands.

2. Drain the fluid and remove the pan.

3. Remove the adjusting screw locknut.

4. Tighten the adjusting screw to 72 in.lb. using a torque wrench and a ¼" (6.35mm) hex head socket.

5. Back off the adjusting screw 7 full turns.

6. Hold the adjusting screw still and tighten the locknut to 35 ft.lb.

7. Replace the pan and fill the unit with Dexron®II fluid.

THROTTLE LINKAGE ADJUSTMENT

4–151

1. Remove the air cleaner.

2. Remove the spark plug wire holder from the throttle cable bracket and move the holder and wires aside.

3. Raise and support the vehicle on jackstands.

4. Hold the throttle control lever rearward against its stop. Hook one end of a spare spring to the lever and hook the opposite end to any convenient point. This will hold the lever in position.

5. Lower the vehicle.

6. Block the choke open and move the carburetor linkage completely off the fast idle cam.

7. On vehicles without air conditioning, turn the ignition to ON to energize the solenoid.

8. Unlock the throttle control cable by re-

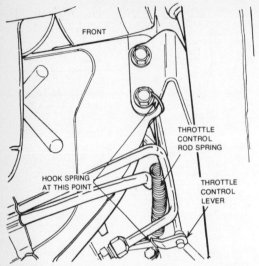

Installing the throttle control lever spring on the 4-151

leasing the T shaped adjuster clamp on the cable by lifting it upward with a small screwdriver.

9. Grasp the outer sheath of the cable and move the cable and sheath forward to remove any load on the cable bell crank.

10. Adjust the cable by moving the cable and sheath rearward until there is no play at all between the plastic cable and the bell crank ball.

11. When play has been eliminated, lock the cable by pressing the T shaped clamp downward until it snaps into place.

12. Turn the ignition off. Install all parts and remove the spare spring.

6–258

1. Disconnect the throttle control rod spring at the carburetor.

2. Raise and support the vehicle on jackstands.

3. Use the throttle control rod spring to hold the throttle control lever forward against its stop, by hooking one end of the spring on the throttle control lever and the other end on the throttle linkage bell crank bracket which is attached to the transmission housing.

4. Block the choke plate open and move the throttle linkage off the fast idle cam.

5. On carburetors equipped with a throttle operated solenoid valve, turn the ignition ON to energize the solenoid, then open the throttle halfway to allow the solenoid to lock and return the carburetor to the idle position.

6. Loosen the retaining bolt on the throttle control adjusting link. DO NOT REMOVE THE SPRING CLIP AND NYLON WASHER!

7. Pull on the end of the link to eliminate play and tighten the retaining bolt.

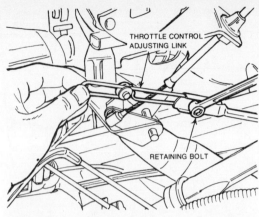

Tightening the link retaining bolt on the 1980 and later 6-258

8. Remove the throttle control rod spring and install it on the control rod from where it cam.

9. Lower the vehicle.

8–304

1. Disconnect the throttle control rod spring at the carburetor.

2. Raise and support the vehicle on jackstands.

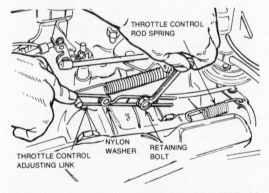

Tightening the link retaining bolt on 1980–81 8-304

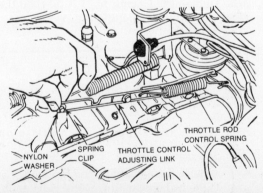

Installing the nylon washer and spring clip on the 1980 and later 8-304

3. Use the throttle control rod spring to hold the transmission throttle valve control lever against its stop.

4. Block the choke plate open and make sure the throttle linkage is off the fast idle cam.

NOTE: *On carburetors equipped with a throttle operated solenoid valve, turn the ignition to ON to energize the solenoid. Then turn the throttle half way to allow the solenoid to lock and return the carburetor to idle.*

5. Loosen the retaining bolt on the throttle control rod adjuster link. Remove the spring clip and move the nylon washer to the rear of the link.

6. Push on the end of the link to eliminate play and tighten the link retaining bolt.

7. Install the nylon washer and spring clip.

8. Remove the throttle control rod spring and install it in its intended position.

9. Lower the vehicle.

Neutral Safety/Back-up Light Switch
ADJUSTMENT/REPLACEMENT

GM Turbo Hydra-Matic

This switch prevents the engine from being started in any position other than Park or Neutral. It also controls the backup lights.

1. Set the parking brake.

2. Make sure the shift linkage is adjusted correctly.

3. Remove the switch from the base of the steering column, inside the vehicle.

4. Shift into Park and lock the column by removing the key.

5. Move the switch lever until it aligns with the letter P on the back of the switch. Insert a $\frac{3}{32}$″ (2.38mm) drill bit in the hole below the letter N on the switch. Move the switch lever till it stops against the drill bit.

6. Install the switch on the column, tighten the screws, and remove the drill bit.

7. Check that the engine will start only in Park and Neutral, and that the backup lights come on only in Reverse.

Chrysler 904, 999

The switch is mounted in the transmission and has no direct adjustment. Proper operation is determined by correct shift linkage adjustment.

To replace the switch:

1. Raise and support the front end on jackstands.

2. Place a drain pan under the switch.

3. Unscrew the switch from the transmission.

4. Replace the switch, using a new seal. Tighten the switch to 24 ft.lb.

5. Refill the transmission.

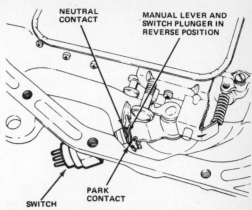

Chrysler 904 or 999 neutral start and backup light switch

Transmission
REMOVAL AND INSTALLATION

1976–79

1. Remove the dipstick.

2. Detach the radiator shroud.

3. Mark the driveshafts for reinstallation.

4. If the vehicle has low range, disconnect the shift linkage and remove the unit.

5. Detach the speedometer cable.

6. Mark and remove the Emergency Drive hoses and wire.

7. Unbolt the vacuum line bracket at the rear of the transfer case.

8. Detach the downshift solenoid wire at the transmission.

9. Remove the starter.

10. Remove the torque converter housing inspection cover.

11. Matchmark the torque converter and drive plate for reassembly. Remove the bolts.

12. Remove the rear support cushion to crossmember nuts.

13. Support the transmission with a transmission jack, using a safety chain.

14. Remove the rear crossmember.

15. Detach the transmission shift linkage. Detach the linkage bracket, bushing, and lever from the frame.

16. Detach and wire up the front driveshaft.

17. Detach the cooler lines from the transmission.

18. Disconnect the vacuum hose at the modulator.

19. Support the engine.

20. Remove the converter housing to engine bolts.

21. Remove the dipstick tube.

22. Move the transmission back till it clears the engine. Hold the converter in place and lower the transmission.

23. On installation, align the torque convert-

er and drive plate matchmarks. Dowels on the engine must line up with holes in the converter housing. Torque the transmission-to-engine bolts 42 ft.lb.

24. Move the transmission back till it clears the engine. Hold the converter in place and lower the transmission.

25. Install the dipstick tube.

26. Connect the vacuum hose at the modulator.

27. Attach the cooler lines from the transmission.

28. Attach the front driveshaft.

29. Attach the transmission shift linkage.

30. Attach the linkage bracket, bushing, and lever to the frame.

31. Install the rear crossmember. Torque the bolts to 30 ft.lb.

32. Install the rear support cushion to crossmember nuts.

33. Matchmark the torque converter and drive plate for reassembly. Install the bolts. Torque them to 33 ft.lb.

34. Install the torque converter housing inspection cover.

35. Install the starter.

36. Attach the downshift solenoid wire at the transmission.

37. Bolt the vacuum line bracket to the rear of the transfer case.

38. Install the Emergency Drive hoses and wire.

39. Attach the speedometer cable.

40. If the vehicle has low range, connect the shift linkage and install the unit.

41. Install the radiator shroud.

42. Install the dipstick.

1980–87

1. Remove the fan shroud.

2. Disconnect the transmission fill tube upper bracket.

3. Raise and support the vehicle on jackstands.

4. Remove the converter housing inspection cover.

5. Remove the fill tube.

6. Remove the starter.

7. Mark the driveshafts for installation.

8. Remove the driveshafts.

9. On 8–304 models, disconnect the exhaust pipes at the manifolds.

10. Disconnect the gearshift and throttle linkages.

11. Disconnect the neutral start switch.

12. Mark the driveplate and converter for realignment.

13. Remove the converter-to-driveplate bolts.

14. Take up the transmission weight with a floor jack. It's a good idea to chain the transmission to the jack.

15. Remove the rear crossmember-to-transmission bolts.

16. Remove the rear crossmember.

17. Lower the transmission slightly and disconnect the fluid cooler lines.

18. Remove the transmission-to-engine bolts.

19. Roll the transmission rearward to clear the crankshaft, lower the jack and remove the unit.

20. Position the transmission against the engine.

21. Install the transmission-to-engine bolts. Torque the bolts to 28 ft.lb.

22. Connect the fluid cooler lines.

23. Install the rear crossmember. Torque the bolts to 30 ft.lb.

24. Install the rear crossmember-to-transmission bolts. Torque the bolts to 33 ft.lb.

25. Install the converter-to-driveplate bolts. Torque the bolts to 40 ft.lb. on the 4–151; 26 ft.lb. on the 6–258 and 8–304.

26. Connect the neutral start switch.

27. Connect the gearshift and throttle linkages.

28. On 8–304 models, connect the exhaust pipes at the manifolds.

29. Install the driveshafts.

30. Install the starter.

31. Install the fill tube.

32. Install the converter housing inspection cover.

33. Lower the vehicle.

34. Connect the transmission fill tube upper bracket.

35. Install the fan shroud.

MANUAL TRANSFER CASE

REMOVAL AND INSTALLATION

Through 1971

The transfer case can be removed without removing the transmission.

1. Drain the transfer case and transmission and replace the drain plugs.

2. Disconnect the brake cable.

3. Disconnect the front and rear driveshafts at the transfer case.

4. Disconnect the speedometer cable at the transfer case.

5. Disconnect the transfer case shift levers. On vehicles equipped with two shift levers loosen the set screw and remove the pivot pin. Use a prying tool to pry the shift lever springs away from the shift levers. On models

Transfer Case Application Chart

Transfer Case Type	Years	Models
Dana 300	1980–86	All models
New Process NP-207	1987	All models
Spicer 18	1945–71	All models
Spicer 20	1972–79	All models
Warner Quadra-Trac®	1976–79	Standard on CJ-7 w/automatic trans.

equipped with a single shift lever remove the pivot pin cotter key and the adjusting rod attaching nut to remove the shift lever.

6. Remove the cover plate on the rear face of the transfer case or power take-off shift unit. Remove the cotter key, nut and washer from the transmission main shaft.

7. If possible, remove the transfer case main drive gear from the transmission main shaft. If it is not possible, continue on.

8. Remove the transmission-to-transfer case mounting bracket bolt and nut.

9. Remove the transmission-to-transfer case attaching bolts.

10. Remove the transfer case. If the transfer case main drive gear has not been removed in step 7, proceed as follows: Brace the end of the transmission main shaft so that it cannot be moved in the transmission, then pull the transfer case to the rear to loosen the gear. Remove the gear. When separating the two housing, be careful that the transmission main shaft bearing, which bears in both housings, remains in the transmission case.

NOTE: *f the transfer case is being removed from the transmission with the two units out of the vehicle, use the above procedure starting from step 6 and replacing step 10 with the following procedure:*

11. Remove the transmission shift housing. Install a transmission mainshaft retaining plate, tool W-194, to prevent the mainshaft from pulling out of the transmission case. Should this tool be unavailable, loop a piece of wire around the mainshaft directly in back of the mainshaft second speed gear. Install the transmission shift housing right and left front attaching bolts part way into the transmission case. Twist the wire and attach each end to one of the screws. Tighten the wire. With the mainshaft securely in place, support the transfer case and with a rawhide mallet or brass drift and hammer, then tap lightly on the end of the mainshaft to loosen the gear and separate the two units.

12. Install the transfer case. If the transfer case main drive gear was not removed in step 7, proceed as follows:

    a. Install the gear.

    b. When separating the two housings, be careful that the transmission mainshaft bearing, which bears in both housings, remains in the transmission case. When installing the transfer case gear on the transmission rear splined driveshaft, tighten the large gear nut securely and insert the cotter pin. Sink the cotter pin well into the nut slots so it will clear the power take-off drive (if so equipped).

    c. Brace the end of the transmission main shaft so that it cannot be moved in the transmission, then pull the transfer case to the rear to loosen the gear.

13. Remove transmission mainshaft retaining plate, tool W-194, or the wire.

14. Install the transmission shift housing. When installing the rear adapter plate on a 4-speed transmission, be sure that the cap screw heads do not protrude beyond the adapter plate face and that they do not interfere with the transfer case fitting tightly against the rear adapter plate.

15. Install the transmission-to-transfer case attaching bolts.

16. Install the transmission-to-transfer case mounting bracket bolt and nut.

17. Install the transfer case main drive gear on the transmission main shaft.

18. Install the cotter key, nut and washer from the transmission main shaft.

19. Install the cover plate on the rear face of the transfer case or power take-off shift unit.

20. Connect the transfer case shift levers. On vehicles equipped with two shift levers loosen the set screw and Install the pivot pin. On models equipped with a single shift lever install the pivot pin cotter key and the adjusting rod attaching nut to install the shift lever.

21. Connect the speedometer cable at the transfer case.

22. Connect the front and rear driveshafts at the transfer case.

23. Connect the brake cable.

24. Fill the transfer case and transmission.

1972–75

1. Remove the transfer case shift lever knob and trim ring and boot.

2. Remove the transfer case shift lever.

3. Lift and support the vehicle.

1. Companion flange
2. Brake drum
3. Emergency brake
4. Operating lever
5. Oil seal
6. Lever stud
7. Rear cap
8. Shims
9. Screw
10. Lockwasher

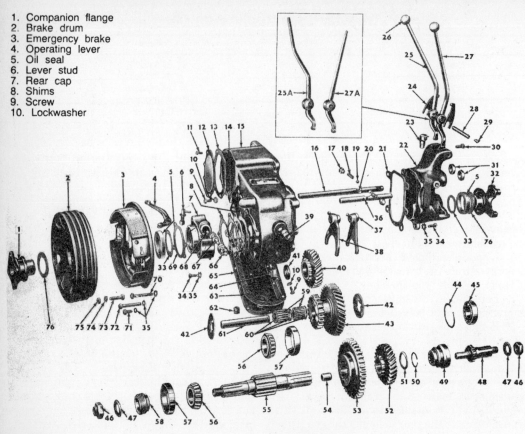

11. Bolt
12. Rear cover
13. Gasket
14. Lockplate
15. Transfer case
16. Shift rod
17. Poppet plug
18. Poppet ring
19. Poppet ball
20. Interlock
21. Gasket
22. Front cap
23. Breather
24. Shift lever spring
25. Shift lever
25a. Shift lever (used with 4-speed transmission)
26. Shift lever knob
27. Shift lever
27a. Shift lever (used with 4-speed transmission)
28. Pivot pin
29. Lubrication fitting
30. Set screw
31. Oil seal
32. Front yoke
33. Gasket
34. Bolt
35. Lockwasher
36. Shift rod
37. Shift fork
38. Shift fork
39. Filler pipe plug
40. Mainshaft gear
41. Plain washer
42. Thrust washer
43. Intermediate gear

44. Snapring
45. Bearing
46. Nut
47. Washer
48. Output clutch shaft
49. Output clutch gear
50. Snapring
51. Thrust washer
52. Output shaft gear
53. Sliding gear
54. Bushing
55. Output shaft
56. Cone and rollers
57. Bearing cup
58. Speedometer gear
59. Needle bearings
60. Bearing spacer
61. Intermediate shaft
62. Drain plug
63. Gasket
64. Nut
65. Bottom cover
66. Sleeve
67. Speedometer gear
68. Bushing
69. Gasket
70. Bolt
71. Bolt
72. Hex nut
72. Bolt
73. Bolt
74. Lockwasher
75. Nut
76. Output shaft seal

Spicer 18 dual lever transfer case

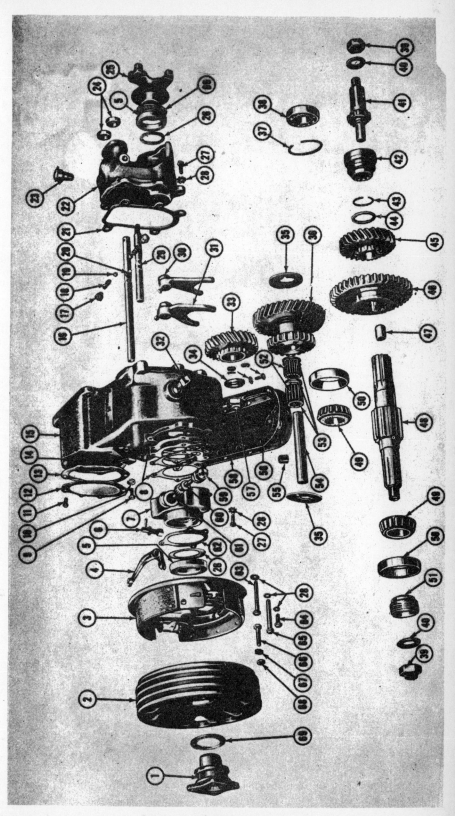

Spicer 18 single lever transfer case

1. Companion flange and oil seal guard
2. Emergency brake drum
3. Emergency brake
4. Brake operating lever
5. Bearing cap oil seal
6. Brake operating lever stud
7. Rear bearing cap
8. Rear bearing cap shim set
9. Bolt
10. Lockwasher
11. Bolt
12. Transfer case rear cover
13. Rear gasket cover
14. Intermediate shaft lockplate
15. Transfer case
16. Shift rod
17. Poppet plug
18. Poppet spring
19. Poppet ball
20. Shift rod interlock
21. Bearing cap gasket
22. Front bearing shaft cap
23. Breather
24. Shift rod oil seal
25. End yoke
26. Oil seal gasket
27. Bolt
28. Lockwasher
29. Shift rod
30. Front wheel drive shift fork
31. Underdrive and direct shift fork
32. Filler plug
33. Mainshaft gear
34. Mainshaft washer
35. Thrust washer
36. Intermediate gear
37. Bearing shaft snapring
38. Output clutch shaft bearing
39. Companion flange nut
40. Plain washer
41. Output clutch shaft
42. Output clutch shaft gear
43. Output shaft gear snapring
44. Thrust washer
45. Output shaft gear
46. Output shaft sliding gear
47. Pilot bushing
48. Output shaft
49. Cone and rollers
50. Output shaft bearing cup.
51. Speedometer drive gear (6-t)
52. Needle bearing
53. Bearing spacer
54. Intermediate shaft
55. Drain plug
56. Bottom cover gasket
57. Mainshaft nut
58. Transfer case bottom cover
59. Speedometer driven gear sleeve
60. Speedometer driven gear (15-t)
61. Speedometer driven gear bushing
62. Backing plate gasket
63. Bolt
64. Bolt
65. Bolt
66. Bolt
67. Lockwasher
68. Nut
69. Output shaft felt seal

Spicer 18 single lever transfer case

4. Drain the transfer case lubricant.

5. Mark the yokes for reference during assembly and disconnect the front and rear driveshafts from the transfer case.

6. Install the transfer case drain plug.

7. Disconnect the parking brake cable at the equalizer and mounting bracket.

8. Disconnect the speedometer cable.

9. Remove the screws which attach the transfer case to the transmission. Install two ⅜" x 4" (9.525mm x 101.6mm) threaded dowel pins, one on each side of the case.

10. Remove the transfer case.

11. Remove the gasket between the transmission and the transfer case.

12. Place a new gasket on the dowel pins in the transmission case before installing the transfer case back onto the transmission.

13. Shift the transfer case to 4WD Low position.

14. Position the transfer case on the dowel pins.

15. Rotate the transfer case output shaft until the gears engage with the output gear on the transmission. Slide the transfer case forward to the transmission.

NOTE: *Be sure that the transfer case fits flush against the transmission. Severe damage will result if the transfer case bolts are tightened while the transfer case is binding.*

16. Install one attaching screw. Remove the dowel pins and install all of the remaining attaching screws.

17. Connect the driveshafts in the same positions from which they were removed.

18. Connect the speedometer cable and parking brake cable.

19. Fill the transfer case with the proper amount of lubricant. See Chapter 1.

20. Lower the vehicle.

21. Install the transfer case lever, trim boot and lever knob.

1976–79

1. Remove the shift lever knob, trim ring, and boot.

2. Remove the transmission access cover from the floorpan.

3. Drain the lubricant from the transfer case and transmission.

4. Disconnect the torque reaction bracket from the frame crossmember, if so equipped.

5. Support the engine and transmission by placing a jackstand under the clutch housing.

6. Remove the rear frame crossmember.

7. mark the driveshaft yokes for reference during assembly and disconnect the front and rear driveshafts from the transfer case.

8. Disconnect the speedometer cable from the transfer case.

1. Output shaft yoke end
2. Output shaft oil seal
3. Rear bearing cap
4. Rear bearing adjusting shims
5. Rear cover
6. Rear cover gasket
7. Lockplate
8. Transfer case housing
9. Underdrive and direct shift rod
10. Poppet plug
11. Poppet spring
12. Poppet ball
13. Shift rod interlock
14. Front bearing cap gasket
15. Front bearing cap
16. Breather
17. Shift lever spring
18. Under drive shift lever
19. Shift lever ball
20. Front wheel drive shift lever
21. Shift lever pivot pin
22. Hydraulic fitting
23. Oil seal
24. Dust shield
25. Oil seal gasket
26. Front wheel drive shift rod
27. Set screw
28. Front wheel drive shift fork
29. Underdrive shift fork
30. Filler plug

31. Main drive gear
32. Main shift washer
33. Thrust washer
34. Intermediate gear
35. Snapring
36. Clutch shaft bearing
37. Output yoke nut
38. Output yoke washer
39. Output clutch shaft
40. Clutch gear
41. Output shaft snapring
42. Thrust washer
43. Output shaft gear
44. Output shaft sliding gear
45. Output shaft pilot bushing
46. Output shaft
47. Output shaft bearing cone and rollers
48. Output shaft bearing cup
49. Speedometer drive gear
50. Intermediate gear bearing spacers
51. Intermediate gear bearing
52. Intermediate shaft
53. Drain plug
54. Bottom cover gasket
55. Output shaft nut
56. Cotter pin
57. Bottom cover
58. Speedometer gear sleeve
59. Speedometer driven gear
60. Speedometer driven gear bushing

Spicer 18 transfer case used in Utility models

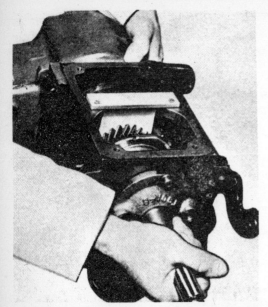

Transmission mainshaft retaining plate installed for removing the Spicer 18 transfer case from the transmission

9. Remove the bolts attaching the transfer case to the transmission and remove the transfer case. Remove the gasket which goes between the the transmission and transmission case.

NOTE: *here is one transfer case attaching bolt located at the bottom right corner of the transmission that must be removed from the front end of the case.*

10. Install the transmission-to-transfer case gasket on the transmission.

11. Shift the transfer case into the 4WD low position.

12. Install a ⅜–16 x 4" (9.525mm–16 x 101.6mm)dowel pin on each side of the transmission to assist in guiding the transfer case into place during installation.

13. Position the transfer case on the dowel pins and slide the case forward until it seats against the transmission. It may be necessary to rotate the transfer case output shaft until the mainshaft gear on the transmission engages the rear output shaft gear in the transfer case.

NOTE: *Make sure that the transfer case is flush against the transmission. The case could be cracked if the attaching bolts are tightened while the transfer case is cocked or binding.*

14. Install two transfer case attaching bolts, but do not tighten them completely.

15. Remove the dowel pins and install the remaining attaching bolts, retightening them all to 30 ft.lb.

16. Fill the transfer case with SAE 80W-90 gear lubricant (API GL-4).

17. Assemble the remaining components in the reverse order of removal.

1980–86

1. On models with automatic transmission, remove the shift lever knob, trim ring, and boot from the transfer case shift lever.

2. On models with manual transmission, remove the shift lever knob, trim ring, and boot from the transmission and transfer case levers.

3. Remove the transmission access plate from the floor pan.

4. Raise and support the vehicle on jackstands.

5. Support the engine at the clutch housing and remove the rear crossmember.

6. Mark the front and rear driveshaft-to-transfer case position and disconnect them at the transfer case.

7. Disconnect the speedometer cable at the transfer case.

8. Disconnect the parking brake cable at the equalizer.

9. Disconnect the exhaust pipe bracket at the transfer case.

10. Unbolt the transfer case from the transmission and remove it.

11. Attach the transfer case to the transmission Torque the bolts to 30 ft.lb..

12. Connect the exhaust pipe bracket at the transfer case.

13. Connect the parking brake cable at the equalizer.

14. Connect the speedometer cable at the transfer case.

15. Connect the front and rear driveshafts at the transfer case.

16. Install the rear crossmember. Torque the bolts to 30 ft.lb.

17. Lower the vehicle.

18. Install the transmission access plate.

19. On models with manual transmission, install the shift lever knob, trim ring, and boot on the transmission and transfer case levers.

20. On models with automatic transmission, install the shift lever knob, trim ring, and boot on the transfer case shift lever.

NOTE: *Some 1980–81 vehicles have experienced difficult transfer case shifting. This may be the result of the transfer case shift lever shaft being bent at the threaded end. To correct this condition, the shift lever shaft and, if necessary, the lever must be replaced. The part numbers are:*
• Shaft: 5360045
• Lever w/4-cyl & SR-4, CJ-5 and CJ-7: 5360044
• Lever w/6 or 8 & T-176, CJ-7: 5360044

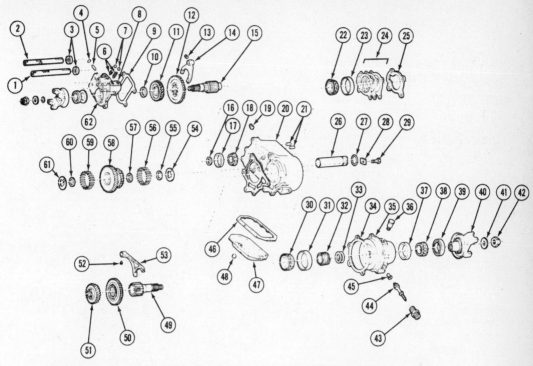

1. Shift rod—rear output shaft shift fork
2. Shift rod—front output shaft shift fork
3. Shift rod oil seal
4. Interlock plug
5. Interlock
6. Poppet ball spring
7. Poppet ball
8. Front bearing cap
9. Front bearing cap gasket
10. Front output shaft thrust washer
11. Front output shaft gear
12. Front output shaft sliding gear
13. Setscrew
14. Front output shaft shift fork
15. Front output shaft
16. Front output shaft spacer
17. Front output shaft front bearing cup
18. Front output shaft front bearing
19. Filler plug
20. Transfer case
21. Thimble cover
22. Front output shaft rear bearing
23. Front output shaft rear bearing cup
24. Front output shaft rear bearing cup shims
25. Cover plate
26. Intermediate shaft
27. Intermediate shaft O-ring
28. Lock plate
29. Lock plate bolt
30. Rear output shaft front bearing
31. Rear output shaft front bearing cup
32. Speedometer drive gear
33. Rear output shaft bearing shim
34. Rear bearing cap gasket
35. Rear bearing cap
36. Breather
37. Rear bearing cap cup
38. Rear bearing cap bearing
39. Rear bearing cap oil seal
40. Rear yoke
41. Rear yoke washer
42. Rear yoke nut
43. Speedometer sleeve
44. Speedometer driven gear
45. Speedometer bushing
46. Bottom cover gasket
47. Bottom cover
48. Drain plug
49. Rear output shaft
50. Rear output shaft sliding gear
51. Mainshaft gear
52. Setscrew
53. Rear output shaft shift fork
54. Intermediate gear thrust washer
55. Intermediate gear bearing spacer
56. Intermediate gear shaft needle bearings
57. Intermediate gear bearing spacer
58. Intermediate gear
59. Intermediate gear shaft needle bearings
60. Intermediate gear bearing spacer
61. Intermediate gear thrust washer
62. Front bearing cap

Dana 20 transfer case components

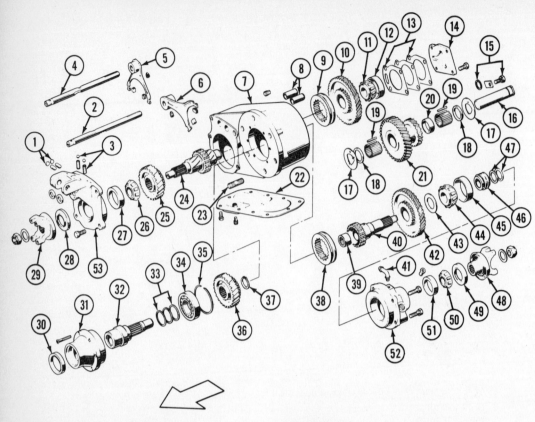

1. Interlock plugs and interlocks
2. Shift rod—rear output shaft fork
3. Poppet balls and springs
4. Shift rod—front output shaft fork
5. Front output shaft shift fork
6. Rear output shaft shift fork
7. Transfer case
8. Thimble covers
9. Clutch sleeve—front output shaft
10. Clutch gear—front output shaft
11. Bearing—front output shaft rear
12. Race—front output shaft bearing
13. End play shims—front output shaft
14. Cover plate
15. Lock plate, bolt and washer
16. Intermediate gear shaft
17. Thrust washer
18. Bearing spacer (thin)
19. Intermediate gear shaft needle bearings
20. Bearing spacer (thick)
21. Intermediate gear
22. Bottom cover
23. Stud (case-to-trans.)
24. Front output shaft
25. Front output shaft gear
26. Front ouput shaft bearing (front)
27. Front output shaft bearing race

28. Oil seal
29. Front yoke
30. Seal
31. Support—input shaft
32. Input shaft
33. Shims
34. Input shaft bearing
35. Input shaft bearing snap ring
36. Rear output shaft gear
37. Snap ring
38. Clutch sleeve—rear output shaft
39. Input shaft rear bearing (needle) (or pilot bear-
    ing)
40. Rear output shaft
41. Vent
42. Clutch gear—rear output shaft
43. Thrust washer
44. Bearing—rear output shaft front
45. Race—rear output shaft bearing
46. Speedometer drive gear
47. End play shims
48. Rear yoke
49. Rear output shaft oil seal
50. Bearing—rear output shaft rear
51. Bearing race
52. Rear bearing cap
53. Front bearing cap

Dana 300 transfer case components

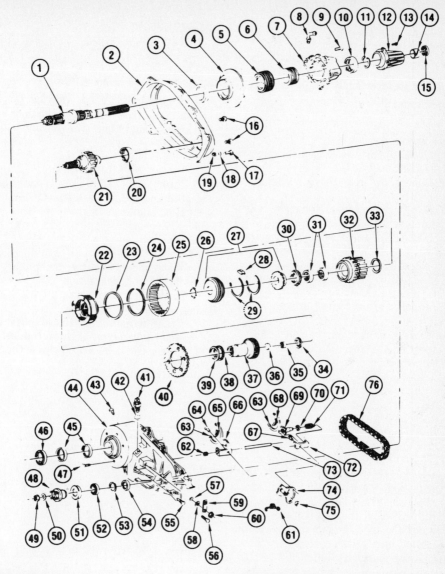

1. Main driveshaft
2. Case housing
3. Oil pump housing seal
4. Oil pump housing
5. Oil pump
6. Speed drive gear
7. Mainshaft rear bearing retaining ring
8. Case vent connector
9. Bolt
10. Mainshaft rear bearing
11. Mainshaft rear bearing retaining ring
12. Mainshaft extension
13. Hex bolt
14. Case mainshaft extension bushing
15. Main shaft extension seal
16. Case oil plug
17. Hex (m10 x 1.5mm x 35mm) (2 req'd) bolt
18. Alignment dowel washer housing; alignment

19. Housing alignment dowel
20. Front output shaft pilot bearing
21. Front output shaft
22. Planet gear assembly carrier

23. Planet gear carrier retaining ring thrust washer
24. Planet gear carrier retaining ring
25. Planet gear carrier annulus gear
26. Main driveshaft synchronizer retaining ring
27. Main driveshaft assembly synchronizer
28. Synchronizer strut
29. Synchronizer strut spring
30. Synchronizer stop ring
31. Drive chain sprocket bearing
32. Drive chain sprocket
33. Drive chain sprocket thrust washer
34. Input main drive gear thrust washer
35. Input drive gear pilot bearing
36. Cup plug
37. Input main drive assembly gear
38. Input drive gear thrust bearing
39. Input drive gear thrust bearing washer
40. Low range lockplate
41. Vacuum four wheel switch
42. Four wheel drive indicator light switch seal
43. Oil access hole plug
44. Case (front half) housing
45. Input drive bearing

NP-207 transfer case used in 1987 models

• Lever w/6-cyl & SR-4, CJ-7: 5360129
To correct the condition:

1. Remove the transfer case.
2. Remove the defective lever shaft, and lever.
3. Install new lever shaft and lever.
4. Install the transfer case.

1987

1. Shift the case into 4H.
2. Raise and support the Jeep on jackstands.
3. Drain the case.
4. Matchmark the rear driveshaft and remove it.
5. Disconnect the speedometer cable, vacuum hoses and vent hose from the case.
6. Support the transmission with a floor jack.
7. Remove the crossmember.
8. Matchmark the front driveshaft and remove it.
9. Disconnect the shift lever linkage rod at the case.
10. Remove the shift lever bracket bolts.
11. Support the transfer case with a floor jack or transmission jack and remove the attaching bolts.
12. Pull the case out of the Jeep.
13. Install the case.
14. Install the attaching bolts. Torque them to 26 ft.lb.
15. Install the shift lever bracket bolts.
16. Connect the shift lever linkage rod at the case.
17. Install the front driveshaft.
18. Install the crossmember. Torque the frame bolts to 30 ft.lb.; the case bolts to 33 ft.lb.
19. Connect the speedometer cable, vacuum hoses and vent hose at the case.
20. Install the rear driveshaft.
21. Fill the case.
22. Lower the Jeep.

TRANSFER CASE SHIFT LINKAGE ADJUSTMENT

NOTE: *Only the Spicer 18 and New Process 207 have adjustable linkage.*

Spicer 18 models through 1971

This linkage should be adjusted to give ½" (12.7mm) clearance between the floor pan and the lever when in four wheel drive, low range.

NP-207

1. Place the shift lever in the 2WD position.
2. Insert a ⅛" (3.175mm) spacer between the gate and the forward edge of the lever.
3. Hold the lever in this position.
4. Raise and support the front end on jackstands.
5. loosen the lockbolt on the adjusting trunnion just enough to allow the linkage rod to slide freely in the trunnion.
6. Move the range lever all the way rearward, to the 2WD position.
7. Position the linkage rod so that it is a free fit in the range lever. Tighten the locknut.
8. Lower the vehicle and check the linkage operation.

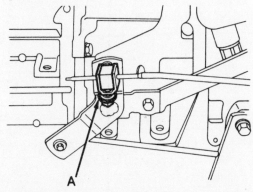

NP-207 range control adjustment; A is the adjustment point.

46. Input drive gear seal
47. Hex bolt
48. Front output driveshaft flange yoke
49. Front output driveshaft yoke nut
50. Front output driveshaft yoke (rubber)
51. Front output driveshaft yoke deflector
52. Front output driveshaft seal
53. Front output driveshaft retaining ring
54. Front output driveshaft bearing
55. Shift sector spring screw
56. Screw
57. Shift sector & shaft oil seal
58. Shift sector & shaft retainer
59. Shifter shaft lever
60. Shift shaft lever nut
61. Shift sector assembly spring

62. Range fork bushing
63. Fork end pad
64. Range shift fork pin
65. Range shift fork center
66. Range shift assembly fork
67. Mode shft fork bracket pin
68. Mode shift fork center pad
69. Mode shift assembly fork
70. Mode shift fork spring cup
71. Mode shift fork spring
72. Mode shift fork assembly bracket
73. Shift fork shaft
74. W/shf, shift sector
75. Shift sector shaft spacer
76. Drive chain

NP-207 transfer case used in 1987 models

AUTOMATIC TRANSFER CASE

Quadra-Trac®

The Warner Quadra-Trac® full-time, automatic transfer case was offered as optional equipment on CJ-7 models from 1976–79. The option was dropped after the 1979 model year.

NOTE: *Complete assembly removal is normally not required except when the front output shaft, front annular bearing, transmission output shaft seals or the transfer case (front housing) require service. To service the chain, drive sprocket, differential unit, diaphragm control system, needle bearing, thrust washer or rear output shaft, the rear half of the Quadra-Trac® transfer case can be removed, giving access to these components without removing the unit from the vehicle.*

REMOVAL AND INSTALLATION

1. Raise and support the vehicle.
2. Mark the front and rear output shaft yokes and universal joints to provide alignment references to be used during assembly.
3. Disconnect the front driveshaft rear universal joint from the transfer case front yoke.
4. Disconnect the rear driveshaft front universal joint from the transfer case rear yoke.
5. Remove the bolts that attach the exhaust pipe support bracket to the transfer case. Support the transmission and remove the rear crossmember.
6. Mark and remove the diaphragm control vacuum hoses, lockout indicator switch wire and speedometer cable.
7. Disconnect the parking brake cable guide from the pivot on the right frame side.

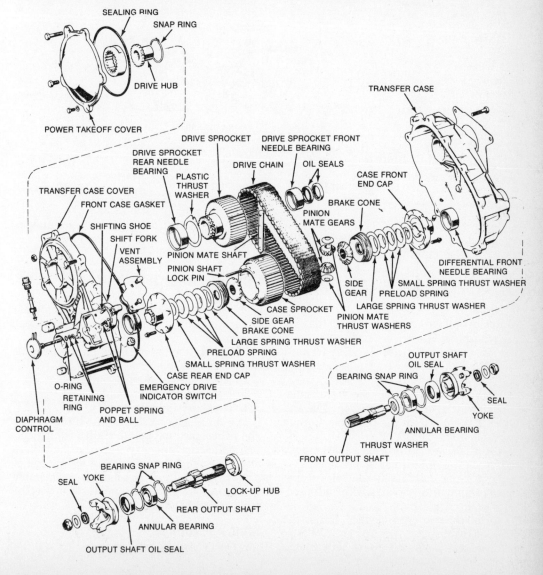

Warner Quadra-Trac® transfer case without low range

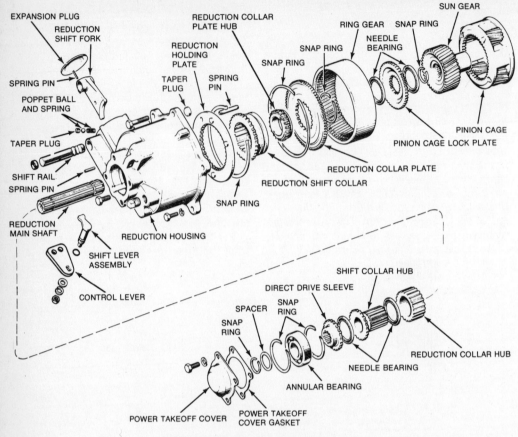

EXPANSION PLUG
REDUCTION SHIFT FORK
SPRING PIN
POPPET BALL AND SPRING
TAPER PLUG
SHIFT RAIL SPRING PIN
REDUCTION MAIN SHAFT
SHIFT LEVER ASSEMBLY
CONTROL LEVER
REDUCTION HOUSING
REDUCTION HOLDING PLATE
TAPER PLUG
SPRING PIN
SNAP RING
REDUCTION COLLAR PLATE HUB
SNAP RING
SNAP RING
RING GEAR
NEEDLE BEARING
SNAP RING
SUN GEAR
PINION CAGE
PINION CAGE LOCK PLATE
REDUCTION COLLAR PLATE
REDUCTION SHIFT COLLAR

POWER TAKEOFF COVER
POWER TAKEOFF COVER GASKET
SNAP RING
SPACER
SNAP RING
DIRECT DRIVE SLEEVE
SHIFT COLLAR HUB
REDUCTION COLLAR HUB
NEEDLE BEARING
ANNULAR BEARING

Warner Quadra-Trac® low range unit

8. Remove the two transfer case-to-transmission bolts which enter from the front side and the two that enter from the rear side.

9. Move the transfer case assembly backward until the unit is free of the transmission output shaft and lower the assembly from the vehicle.

10. Remove all gasket material from the rear of the transmission.

11. Slide the transfer case assembly forward until the unit engages the transmission output shaft.

12. Install the two transfer case-to-transmission bolts which enter from the front side and the two that enter from the rear side. Torque the bolts to 40 ft.lb.

13. Connect the parking brake cable guide to the pivot on the right frame side.

14. Install the diaphragm control vacuum hoses, lockout indicator switch wire and speedometer cable.

15. Install the rear crossmember. Torque the bolts to 35 ft.lb.

16. Install the bolts that attach the exhaust pipe support bracket to the transfer case.

17. Connect the rear driveshaft front universal joint to the transfer case rear yoke.

18. Connect the front driveshaft rear universal joint to the transfer case front yoke.

19. Lower the vehicle.

POWER TAKE-OFF

Jeep vehicles were available with an optional power take-off unit. The PTO consists of four assemblies:

1. The shift unit, mounted on the transfer case.

2. The driveshaft and U-joints.

3. The shaft drive assembly.

4. The pulley drive assembly.

The shaft drive exits the rear of the vehicle and is designed to operate trailed equipment. The pulley drive is driven by the shaft drive and is designed to operate stationary equipment by a belt drive. The shaft drive assembly was installed far more frequently than was the pulley drive assembly.

Shift Assembly
REMOVAL AND INSTALLATION

Drive for the PTO is taken from the transfer case main drive gear through an internal slid-

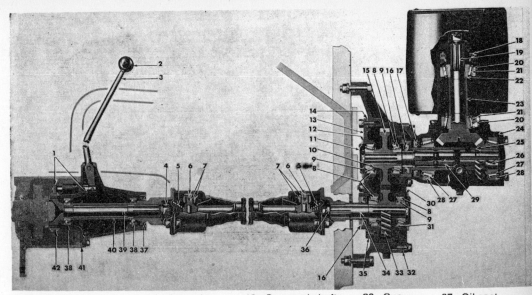

1. Fork and rod	10. Snap ring	19. Gear and shaft	28. Cup	37. Oil seal
2. Ball	11. Plate	20. Cup	29. Shaft	38. Ball bearing
3. Lever	12. Gasket	21. Cone and roller	30. Gasket	39. Gear and shaft
4. Nut	13. Retainer	22. Shims	31. Shims	40. Spacer
5. Button and spring	14. Gasket	23. Spacer	32. Gasket	41. Gasket
6. Spring	15. Gear	24. Shims	33. Gear	42. Sleeve
7. Trunnion and ball	16. Oil seal	25. Shims	34. Shaft	
8. Cup	17. Oil seal	26. Pinion	35. Gasket	
9. Bearing	18. Oil seal	27. Cone and roller	36. Washer	

Power Take-Off assembly

ing gear. The sliding gear is mounted in the shift housing.

1. Remove the bolts in the driveshaft companion flange at the PTO front U-joint.
2. Unbolt and remove the shift lever.
3. Remove the five bolts securing the shift unit to the transfer case and pull it rearward from the case.
4. Installation is the reverse of removal.

DISASSEMBLY AND ASSEMBLY

1. Carefully pry the shift rail and fork froward to clear the poppet ball and spring. Be careful to avoid damaging or losing the ball and spring. Remove the shifting sleeve.
2. Remove the attaching nut and the companion flange.
3. Drive the shaft forward out of the housing.
4. Remove the spacer and bearing from the shaft.
5. Remove the bearing from the housing.
6. Clean and inspect all parts and assemble in reverse of disassembly.

Shaft Drive Unit
REMOVAL AND INSTALLATION

The standard 6 splined 1⅜" (34.925mm) diameter output shaft is driven through two helical cut gears mounted in a housing attached to the

vehicle at the center of the frame rear crossmember.

1. Disconnect the rear U-joint at the companion flange.
2. Remove the retaining screw and the flange.
3. Unbolt and remove the assembly from the vehicle.
4. Installation is the reverse of removal.

DISASSEMBLY AND ASSEMBLY

1. Drain the oil from the unit.
2. Remove the rear bearing cover.
3. Remove the nut and lockwasher from the input shaft.
4. Unbolt and remove the input shaft bearing retainer and remove the bearing. Take care not to lose the shims between the gear and the bearing case.
5. Remove the bearing cone, cup and snapring.
6. Remove the oil seal retainer and pilot assembly.
7. Press the shaft through the housing, removing the bearing cone, oil seal and retainer as an assembly.
8. Remove the input shaft gear through the rear opening. Push out the bearing cup and remove the snapring. Remove the bearing cone and oil seal from the shaft.

Troubleshooting Basic Driveshaft and Rear Axle Problems

When abnormal vibrations or noises are detected in the driveshaft area, this chart can be used to help diagnose possible causes. Remember that other components such as wheels, tires, rear axle and suspension can also produce similar conditions.

BASIC DRIVESHAFT PROBLEMS

Problem	Cause	Solution
Shudder as car accelerates from stop or low speed	• Loose U-joint • Defective center bearing	• Replace U-joint • Replace center bearing
Loud clunk in driveshaft when shifting gears	• Worn U-joints	• Replace U-joints
Roughness or vibration at any speed	• Out-of-balance, bent or dented driveshaft • Worn U-joints • U-joint clamp bolts loose	• Balance or replace driveshaft • Replace U-joints • Tighten U-joint clamp bolts
Squeaking noise at low speeds	• Lack of U-joint lubrication	• Lubricate U-joint; if problem persists, replace U-joint
Knock or clicking noise	• U-joint or driveshaft hitting frame tunnel • Worn CV joint	• Correct overloaded condition • Replace CV joint

BASIC REAR AXLE PROBLEMS

First, determine when the noise is most noticeable.

Drive Noise: Produced under vehicle acceleration.

Coast Noise: Produced while the car coasts with a closed throttle.

Float Noise: Occurs while maintaining constant car speed (just enough to keep speed constant) on a level road.

Road Noise

Brick or rough surfaced concrete roads produce noises that seem to come from the rear axle. Road noise is usually identical in Drive or Coast and driving on a different type of road will tell whether the road is the problem.

Tire Noise

Tire noises are often mistaken for rear axle problems. Snow treads or unevenly worn tires produce vibrations seeming to originate elsewhere. **Temporarily** inflating the tires to 40 lbs will significantly alter tire noise, but will have no effect on rear axle noises (which normally cease below about 30 mph).

Engine/Transmission Noise

Determine at what speed the noise is most pronounced, then stop the car in a quiet place. With the transmission in Neutral, run the engine through speeds corresponding to road speeds where the noise was noticed. Noises produced with the car standing still are coming from the engine or transmission.

Front Wheel Bearings

While holding the car speed steady, lightly apply the footbrake; this will often decease bearing noise, as some of the load is taken from the bearing.

Rear Axle Noises

Eliminating other possible sources can narrow the cause to the rear axle, which normally produces noise from worn gears or bearings. Gear noises tend to peak in a narrow speed range, while bearing noises will usually vary in pitch with engine speeds.

9. Remove the output shaft in the same manner as the input shaft.

10. Adjustment of the tapered roller bearings on both shafts is accomplished by shim packs placed between the gear hubs and bearing cones.

11. Assembly is the reverse of disassembly. Fill the unit with 90W gear oil.

Pulley Drive Unit

REMOVAL AND INSTALLATION

This procedure is accomplished simply by unbolting and removing the unit.

DISASSEMBLY AND ASSEMBLY

1. Remove the unit from the vehicle.
2. Drain the oil and clean the unit.

NOISE DIAGNOSIS

The Noise Is	Most Probably Produced By
• Identical under Drive or Coast	• Road surface, tires or front wheel bearings
• Different depending on road surface	• Road surface or tires
• Lower as the car speed is lowered	• Tires
• Similar with car standing or moving	• Engine or transmission
• A vibration	• Unbalanced tires, rear wheel bearing, unbalanced driveshaft or worn U-joint
• A knock or click about every 2 tire revolutions	• Rear wheel bearing
• Most pronounced on turns	• Damaged differential gears
• A steady low-pitched whirring or scraping, starting at low speeds	• Damaged or worn pinion bearing
• A chattering vibration on turns	• Wrong differential lubricant or worn clutch plates (limited slip rear axle)
• Noticed only in Drive, Coast or Float conditions	• Worn ring gear and/or pinion gear

Power Take-Off Chart and Vehicle Ground Speeds
All Gearshift Positions
Miles Per Hour

Governor Control Position	Transfer In	PTO 1 to 1 Gear Ratio						Engine Speed rpm
		Transmission Gear In						
		Low		Intermediate		High		
		PTO Shaft rpm	Jeep Speed mph	PTO Shaft rpm	Jeep Speed mph	PTO Shaft rpm	Jeep Speed mph	
1	Low	358	2.22	644	4.01	1,000	6.22	1,000
	High	358	5.40	644	9.75	1,000	15.13	
2	Low	428	2.67	773	4.81	1,200	7.47	1,200
	High	428	6.48	773	11.71	1,200	18.15	
3	Low	500	3.11	902	5.62	1,400	8.72	1,400
	High	500	7.56	902	13.66	1,400	21.17	
4	Low	571	3.56	1.301	6.42	1,600	9.96	1,600
	High	571	8.65	1,301	15.61	1,600	24.20	
5	Low	643	4.00	1,160	7.22	1,800	12.08	1,800
	High	643	9.73	1,160	17.56	1,800	27.22	
6	Low	714	4.44	1,289	8.02	2,000	12.45	2,000
	High	714	11.89	1,289	19.51	2,000	30.25	
7	Low	786	4.89	1,418	8.83	2,200	13.70	2,200
	High	786	11.89	1,418	21.46	2,200	33.27	
8	Low	857	5.34	1,547	9.63	2,400	14.84	2,400
	High	857	12.97	1,547	23.41	2,400	36.31	
9	Low	929	5.78	1,657	10.43	2,600	16.19	2,600
	High	929	14.05	1,657	25.36	2,600	39.33	

3. Remove the retaining nut and remove the pulley.

4. Unbolt and remove the pulley shaft housing from the gear housing. Don't lose the shims.

5. Press the pulley shaft through the housing, removing the inner bearing cone, spacer and shim pack.

6. Remove the oil seal and outer bearing cone.

7. Remove the bearing retaining cover from the gear housing, then remove the shim pack.

8. Using a brass drift, tap the shaft through the housing; the bearing and gear will come out with it. Be careful not to lose the shim pack.

9. Clean and inspect all parts. Assembly is the reverse of disassembly. Fill the unit with 90W gear oil.

DRIVELINE

Front and Rear Driveshafts

REMOVAL AND INSTALLATION

In order to remove the front and rear driveshafts, unscrew the holding nuts from the universal joint's U-bolts, remove the U-bolts and slide the shaft forward or backward toward the slip joint. The shaft can then be removed from the end yokes and removed from under the vehicle.

Each shaft is equipped with a splined slip joint at one end to allow for variations in length caused by vehicle spring action. Some slip joints are marked with arrows at the spline and sleeve yoke. When installing, align the arrows. If the slip joint is not marked with arrows, align the yokes at the front and rear of the shaft in the same horizontal plane. This is necessary in order to avoid vibration in the drive train. Torque the U-bolt nuts to 15 ft.lb.

U-Joints

Most Jeep vehicles use a conventional universal joint at both ends of both driveshafts. The CJ-7 and Scrambler with automatic transmission use a double, or constant velocity, joint at the transfer case end of the front driveshaft. Universal joints through 1971 are held together by snaprings on the outside of the bearing caps; 1972–87 models have C-type retainer rings on the inside of the bearing caps. The constant velocity joint is also assembled with snaprings on the outside.

On 1945–71 vehicles, three types of front axle U-joints were used; the Bendix type and the Rzeppa type, used on Axle models 25 and 27, and the more familiar single cross cardan type used on axle model 27AF. All axles after 1972 use the single cross cardan type.

OVERHAUL

Through 1971

1. Remove the snaprings by pinching the ends together with a pair of pliers. If the rings do not readily snap out of the groove, tap the end of the bearing lightly to relieve pressure against the rings.

2. After removing the snaprings, press on the end of one bearing until the opposite bearing is pushed from the yoke arm. Turn the joint over and press the first bearing back out of that arm by pressing on the exposed end of the journal shaft. To drive it out, use a soft drift with a flat face, about $1/32''$ (0.79375mm) smaller in diameter than the hole in the yoke; otherwise there is danger of damaging the bearing.

3. Repeat the procedure for the other two bearings, then lift out the journal assembly by sliding it to one side.

4. Wash all parts in cleaning solvent and inspect the parts after cleaning. Replace the journal assembly if it is worn extensively. Make sure that the grease channel in each journal trunnion is open.

5. Pack all of the bearing caps $1/3$ full of grease and install the rollers (bearings).

6. Press one of the cap/bearing assemblies into one of the yoke arms just far enough so that the cap will remain in position.

7. Place the journal in position in the installed cap, with a cap/bearing assembly placed on the opposite end.

8. Position the free cap so that when it is driven from the opposite end it will be inserted into the opening of the yoke. Repeat this operation for the other two bearings.

9. Install the retaining clips. If the U-joint binds when it is assembled, tap the arms of the yoke slightly to relieve any pressure on the bearings at the end of the journal.

Bendix Joint

With ordinary shop equipment it is nearly impossible to satisfactorily rebuild this unit. For

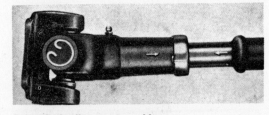

Driveshaft alignment markings

1. U-bolt nut
2. U-bolt washer
3. U-bolt
4. Universal joint journal
5. Lubrication fitting
6. Snap ring
7. Universal joint sleeve yoke
8. Rubber washer
9. Dust cap
10. Propeller shaft tube

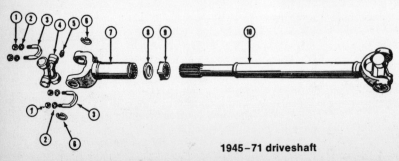

1945–71 driveshaft

1. Outer shaft
2. Lock pin
3. Center ball pin
4. Universal joint ball
5. Center ball
6. Inner shaft

Bendix front axle U-joint

this reason, the factory no longer supplies parts. After considerable mileage, a joint may pull apart upon removal from the vehicle. This does not mean that the joint is no longer usable. To assemble the axle shaft and universal:

1. Place the differential half of the shaft in a vise with the ground portion above the jaws.

2. Install the center ball (the one with the drilled hole) in the socket in the shaft, with the hole and groove visible.

3. Drop the center ball pin into the drilled hole in the wheel half of the shaft.

4. Place the wheel half of the shaft on the center ball. Slip the three balls into the races.

5. Turn the center ball until the groove lines up with the race for the remaining ball. Slip the ball into the race and straighten the wheel end of the shaft.

6. Turn the center ball until the pin drops into the hole in the ball.

7. Install the lock pin and center punch both ends to secure it.

Rzeppa Joint

With the joint removed, determine the method of attachment of the axle to the joint. If three bolts are used, use step 1; if there are no screws, skip 1 and proceed to step 2.

1. Remove the three screws securing the front axle to the joint. Pull the shaft free of the

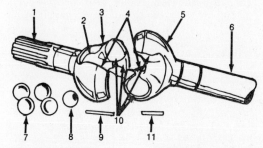

1. Outer shaft	7. Ball
2. Ground faces	8. Center ball
3. Outer yoke	9. Center ball pin
4. Flanges	10. Races
5. Inner yoke	11. Lock pin
6. Inner shaft	

Component view of the Bendix joint

splined inner race. Remove the retaining ring and remove the axle shaft retainer.

2. To remove the axle shaft from the joint, use a wooden pry, and exert force in the direction of the axis of the axle shaft. Use a mallet, if necessary, to exert enough force to drive the retaining ring, installed on the end of the shaft, into its groove in the spline, permitting the joint to be slipped off the shaft.

3. Push down on various points of the inner race and cage until the balls can be removed with the help of a small screwdriver.

4. There are two large rectangular holes in the cage as well as four small holes. Turn the cage so that the two bosses in the spindle shaft will drop onto the rectangular holes and lift out the cage.

5. To remove the inner race, turn it so that one of the bosses will drop into a rectangular

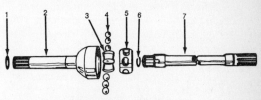

1. Outer axle shaft snap ring
2. Outer shaft
3. Universal joint inner race
4. Ball
5. Cage
6. Axle shaft retainer snap ring
7. Inner shaft

Rzeppa front axle U-joint

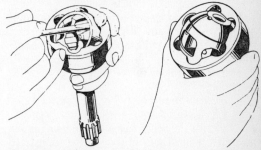

Removing the balls from the Rzeppa joint using a small screwdriver

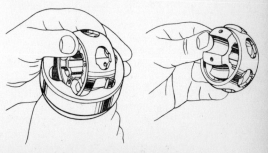

Removing the Rzeppa joint ball cage

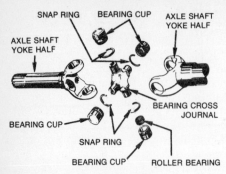

1972–87 single cross Cardan U-joint

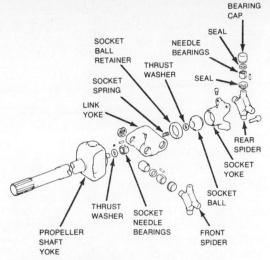

Constant velocity joint

hole in its cage and shift the race to one side. Lift it out.

6. Assembly is the reverse of disassembly. Take care to keep all parts as clean as possible.

1972–87 Single Cross Cardan Joint

1. Clamp the yoke, not the tube, in a vise.
2. Remove the bearing cap C-retainers. Tap on the bearing caps to relieve pressure as necessary.
3. Support the yoke on the vise jaws.
4. Tap one bearing cap in until the opposite one comes out.
5. Turn the yoke around and tap the exposed end of the spider to drive the remaining bearing cap out.
6. Clean all parts in solvent and dry. Use all the parts in the repair kit, even if some of the old ones seem usable.
7. Lubricate all needle bearings, bearing caps, and bearing surfaces with chassis grease.
8. Place the seals on the spider.
9. Install one cap and needle bearing assembly partway into the shaft yoke.
10. Install the spider and the opposite bearings and cap.
11. Support the yoke and seat both caps with a hammer.
12. Install the retainer C-clips. Tap the bearing caps as necessary.
13. Install the other two cap and bearing assemblies. Hold them in place with tape until the shaft is reinstalled.

1976–86 Constant Velocity (Double Cardan) Joint

1. Remove the bearing cap retainer snaprings.
2. Mark all components for reassembly.
3. Use a ⅝″ (15.875mm) socket as a bearing cap driver and a 1¹⁄₁₆″ (26.9875mm) socket as a bearing cap receiver. Squeeze the assembly in a vise to force out the bearing caps.
4. Repeat the operation of step 3 to remove the bearing caps at the other end of the joint.
5. Clean all parts in solvent and dry.
NOTE: *Do not disassemble the socket yoke, centering ball, spring, needle bearings, re-*

tainer, and thrust washers. These parts are sold as an assembly only.
6. Lubricate all bearings and contact surfaces with chassis grease.
7. Install the bearing caps on the transfer case yoke ends of the rear spider. Tape them in place.
8. Assemble the socket yoke and the rear spider.
9. Place the rear spider in the link yoke and install the bearing caps. Press them into place with the ⅝″ (15.875mm) socket. Install the snaprings.
10. Install the front spider, bearing caps, and snaprings in the driveshaft yoke.
11. Install the thrust washer and socket spring in the ball socket bearing bore. Install the thrust washer on the ball socket bearing boss on the driveshaft yoke. Align the ball socket bearing boss with the ball socket bearing bore and insert the boss into the bore.
12. Align the front spider with the link yoke and install the bearing caps and snaprings.

DRIVE AXLE

Understanding Drive Axles

The drive axle is a special type of transmission that reduces the speed of the drive from the engine and transmission and divides the power to the wheels. Power enters the axle from the driveshaft via the companion flange. The flange is mounted on the drive pinion shaft. The drive pinion shaft and gear which carry the power into the differential turn at engine speed. The gear on the end of the pinion shaft drives a large ring gear the axis of rotation of which is 90 degrees away from the of the pinion. The pinion and gear reduce the gear ratio of the axle, and change the direction of rotation to turn the axle shafts which drive both wheels. The axle gear ratio is found by dividing the number of pinion gear teeth into the number of ring gear teeth.

The ring gear drives the differential case. The case provides the two mounting points for the ends of a pinion shaft on which are mounted two pinion gears. The pinion gears drive the two side gears, one of which is located on the inner end of each axle shaft.

By driving the axle shafts through the arrangement, the differential allows the outer drive wheel to turn faster than the inner drive wheel in a turn.

The main drive pinion and the side bearings, which bear the weight of the differential case, are shimmed to provide proper bearing preload, and to position the pinion and ring gears properly.

NOTE: *The proper adjustment of the relationship of the ring and pinion gears is critical. It should be attempted only by those with extensive equipment and/or experience.*

Limited-slip differentials include clutches which tend to link each axle shaft to the differential case. Clutches may be engaged either by spring action or by pressure produced by the torque on the axles during a turn. During turning on a dry pavement, the effects of the clutches are overcome, and each wheel turns at the required speed. When slippage occurs at either wheel, however, the clutches will transmit some of the power to the wheel which has the greater amount of traction. Because of the presence of clutches, limited-slip units require a special lubricant.

Determining Axle Ratio

The drive axle is said to have a certain axle ratio. This number (usually a whole number and a decimal fraction) is actually a comparison of the number of gear teeth on the ring gear and the pinion gear. For example, a 4.11 rear means that theoretically, there are 4.11 teeth on the ring gear and one tooth on the pinion gear or, put another way, the driveshaft must turn 4.11 times to turn the wheels once. Actu-

ally, on a 4.11 rear, there might be 37 teeth on the ring gear and 9 teeth on the pinion gear. By dividing the number of teeth on the pinion gear into the number of teeth on the ring gear, the numerical axle ratio (4.11) is obtained. This also provides a good method of ascertaining exactly what axle ratio one is dealing with.

Another method of determining gear ratio is to jack up and support the car so that both rear wheels are off the ground. Make a chalk mark on the rear wheel and the driveshaft. Put the transmission in neutral. Turn the rear wheel one complete turn and count the number of turns that the driveshaft makes. The number of turns that the driveshaft makes in one complete revolution of the rear wheel is an approximation of the rear axle ratio.

REAR AXLE

NOTE: *Two different types of shafts have been used: the tapered shaft and the the flanged shaft. The differences are obvious. The terms, tapered and flanged, refer to the outer end of the shaft. The tapered shaft has a single retaining nut on the outer end of the axle shaft. The flanged shaft has a mounting flange for the brake drum on the outer end of the shaft and the shaft is held in place by a retaining plate. One other important point, some tapered and flanged axles have an inner oil seal fitted in the axle shaft housing, inboard of the bearing; some do not. If your axle does not have one, don't install one when replacing the bearing! Axles with an inner seal rely on chassis lube for bearing lubrication and must be prelubed prior to installation. Axles without an inner seal rely on differential oil to lubricate the bearing.*

Pinion Oil Seal
REMOVAL AND INSTALLATION
Semi-Floating Axle w/Tapered Shaft

NOTE: *Special tools are needed for this job.*

1. Raise and support the vehicle and remove the rear wheels and brake drums.

Rear Axle Application Chart

Axle Type	Years	Models
AMC 7⁹⁄₁₆″ ring gear	1984–86	All models
AMC 8⅞″ ring gear	1973–83	All models
DanaSpicer 23-2	1945–49	CJ-2A before serial #13453
Dana/Spicer 27	1955–64	DJ-3A
Dana 35C	1987	All models
Dana/Spicer 41-2	1945–49	CJ-2A after serial #13453
Dana/Spicer 44	1947–64	Utility Models w/3700 lb GVW
	1948–72	CJ-3A, CJ-3B, CJ-5, CJ-6
Dana/Spicer 53	1947–64	Utility Models w/4500 lb GVW

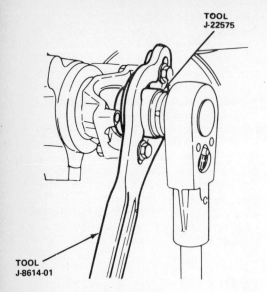

Pinion nut removal on all axles

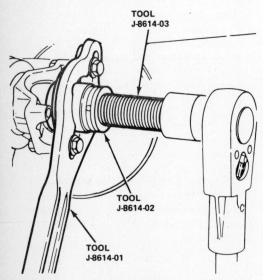

Pinion yoke removal on all axles

2. Mark the driveshaft and yoke for reassembly and disconnect the driveshaft from the rear yoke.

3. With a socket on the pinion nut and an inch lb. torque wrench, rotate the drive pinion several revolutions. Check and record the torque required to turn the drive pinion.

4. Remove the pinion nut. Use a flange holding tool to hold the flange while removing the pinion nut. Discard the pinion nut.

5. Mark the yoke and the drive pinion shaft for reassembly reference.

6. Remove the rear yoke with a puller.

7. Inspect the seal surface of the yoke and replace it with a new one if the seal surface is pitted, grooved, or otherwise damaged.

8. Remove the pinion oil seal using tool J-9233.

9. Before installing the new seal, coat the lip of the seal with rear axle lubricant.

10. Install the seal, driving it into place with tool J-22661.

11. Install the yoke on the pinion shaft. Align the marks made on the pinion shaft and yoke during disassembly.

12. Install a new pinion nut. Tighten nut until endplay is removed from the pinion bearing. Do not overtighten.

13. Check the torque required to turn the drive pinion. The pinion must be turned several revolutions to obtain an accurate reading.

14. Tighten the pinion nut to obtain the torque reading observed during disassembly (Step 3) plus 5 in.lb. Tighten the nut minutely each time, to avoid overtightening. Do not loosen and then retighten the nut.

NOTE: *If the desired torque is exceeded a new collapsible pinion spacer sleeve must be installed and the pinion gear preload reset.*

15. Install the driveshaft, aligning the index marks made during disassembly. Install the rear brake drums and wheels.

Semi-Floating Axles w/Flanged Shaft

1. Raise and support the vehicle.

2. Mark the driveshaft and yoke for reference during assembly and disconnect the driveshaft at the yoke.

3. Remove the pinion shaft nut and washer.

4. Remove the yoke from the pinion shaft, using a puller.

5. Remove the pinion shaft oil seal with tool J-25180.

6. Install the new seal with a suitable driver.

7. Install the pinion shaft washer and nut. Tighten the nut to 210 ft.lb.

8. Align the index marks on the driveshaft and yoke and install the driveshaft. Tighten the attaching bolts or nuts to 16 ft.lb.

9. Remove the supports and lower the vehicle.

Axle Shaft

REMOVAL AND INSTALLATION

Tapered Shaft

1. Jack up the vehicle and remove the hub cap.

2. Remove the wheel.

3. Remove the axle nut dust cap.

4. Remove the axle shaft cotter pin, castle nut and flat washer.

5. Back off the brake adjustment.

6. Use a puller to remove the wheel hub.

7. Remove the screws attaching the brake

Pulling off the wheel hub

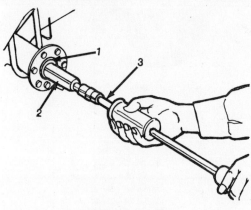

1. Cone and roller
2. Axle
3. Tool

Pulling the axle shaft

dust protector, grease and bearing retainers, brake assembly and shim to the housing.

8. Remove the hydraulic line from the brake assembly.

9. Remove the dust shield and oil seal.

NOTE: *If both shafts are being removed, keep the shims separated. Axle shaft endplay is adjusted at the left side only.*

10. Use a puller to remove the axle shaft.

11. Install the axle shaft in the reverse order of removal, using a new grease seal and installing the hub assembly before the woodruff key. Tighten the axle shaft nut to 150 ft.lb. Some axles have and inner oil seal fitted in the axle shaft housing, inboard of the bearing; some do not. If your axle does not have one, don't install one when replacing the bearing! Axles with an inner seal rely on chassis lube for bearing lubrication and must be prelubed prior to installation. Axles without an inner

seal rely on differential oil to lubricate the bearing.

NOTE: *Should the axle shaft be broken, the inner end can usually be drawn out of the housing with a wire loop after the outer oil seal is removed. However, if the broken end is less than 8" long, it usually is necessary to remove the differential assembly.*

Flanged Shaft

1. Jack up the vehicle and remove the wheels.

2. Remove the brake drum spring locknuts and remove the drum.

3. Remove the axle shaft flange cup plug by piercing the center with a sharp tool and prying it out.

4. Using the access hole in the axle shaft flange, remove the nuts which attach the backing plate and retainer to the axle tube flange.

5. Remove the axle shaft from the housing with an axle puller.

6. Install in reverse order of removal. Torque the bearing retainer bolts to 50 ft.lb. in a criss-cross pattern

NOTE: *Some axles have an inner oil seal fitted in the axle shaft housing, inboard of the bearing; some do not. If your axle does not have one, don't install one when replacing the bearing! Axles with an inner seal rely on chassis lube for bearing lubrication and must be prelubed prior to installation. Axles without an inner seal rely on differential oil to lubricate the bearing.*

Axle Shaft Bearing

REMOVAL AND INSTALLATION

Tapered Shaft Axles

NOTE: *An arbor press is necessary for this procedure.*

1. With the aid of an arbor press, remove the bearing from the axle shaft.

2. The new bearing must be installed with the use of the same press used for removal, or, bearing replacing tool J-2995.

FLANGE ADAPTER W-343

AXLE FLANGE

PULLER C-637

Removing the 1972–75 flanged axle shaft

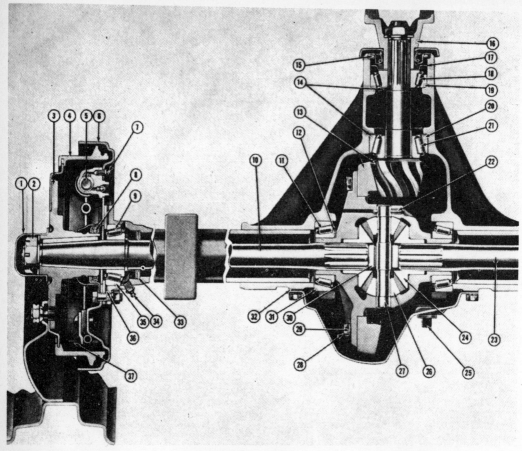

1. Hub cap
2. Hex nut
3. Rear wheel hub
4. Wheel brake drum
5. Brake wheel cylinder
6. Backing plate
7. Brake cylinder bleeder screw
8. Axle shaft outer grease retainer
9. Axle shaft bearing cone and roller
10. Axle shaft—left
11. Differential bearing cone and roller
12. Differential shims
13. Axle drive gear and pinion
14. Pinion bearing shims
15. Drive pinion oil seal
16. Universal joint end yoke
17. Drive pinion oil slinger
18. Drive pinion outer bearing cone and roller
19. Drive pinion outer bearing cup
20. Drive pinion inner bearing cup
21. Drive pinion inner bearing cone and roller
22. Pinion mate shaft pin and lock
23. Axle shaft—right
24. Side gear
25. Pipe plug (filler)
26. Pinion mate
27. Pinion mate shaft
28. Drive gear screw
29. Drive gear screw strap
30. Axle shaft spacer (center block)
31. Differential bearing cup
32. Axle housing cover gasket
33. Axle shaft oil seal (inboard)
34. Lubrication fitting
35. Axle shaft bearing cup
36. Rear axle shaft bearing shims
37. Brake shoe and lining

1945–71 rear axle cutaway

3. If an inner seal, in the axle housing, was there when you removed the shaft, replace it with a new inner seal and pack the bearing with wheel bearing grease, making sure the grease fills the cavities between the bearing rollers.

NOTE: *If there was no inner seal, don't install one. Don't pack the bearing with grease. The lack of an inner seal indicates that the bearing is lubed with axle lubricant.*

4. Axle shaft endplay can be measured by installing the hub retaining nut on the shaft so that it can be pushed and pulled with relative ease. Strike the end of each axle shaft with a lead hammer to seat the bearing cups against the support plate. Mount a dial indicator on the left side support plate with the stylus resting on the end of the axle shaft. Check the endplay while pushing and pulling on the axle shaft. Endplay should be within 0.004–0.008″ (0.1016–0.2032mm), with 0.006″ (0.1524mm) ideal. Add shims to increase endplay. Remove the hub retaining nut when finished checking endplay.

NOTE: *When a new axle shaft is installed, a new hub must also be installed. However, a new hub can be installed on an original axle shaft if the serrations on the shaft are not*

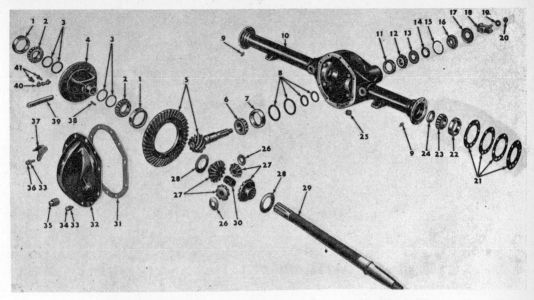

1. Bearing cup	15. Gasket	29. Axle shaft
2. Cone and rollers	16. Oil seal	30. Spacer
3. Shims	17. Dust shield	31. Gasket
4. Differential case	18. End yoke	32. Housing cover
5. Gear and pinion	19. Washer	33. Lockwasher
6. Cone and rollers	20. Pinion nut	34. Screw
7. Cup	21. Shims	35. Filler plug
8. Shims	22. Cup	36. Hex screw
9. Fitting	23. Cone and rollers	37. Tee bracket
10. Housing	24. Oil seal	38. Lock pin
11. Cup	25. Drain plug	39. Pinion shaft
12. Cone and rollers	26. Thrust washer	40. Lock strap
13. Oil slinger	27. Differential gears	41. Screw
14. Felt wick	28. Thrust washer	

1945–71 rear axle components

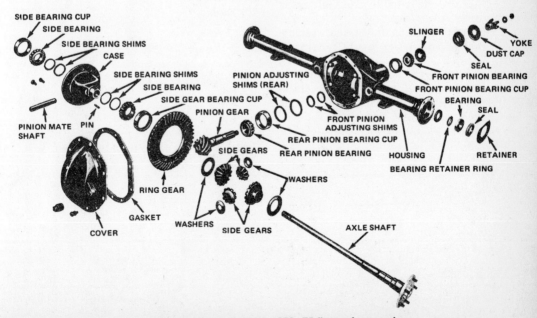

Component view of the 1972–75 flanged rear axle

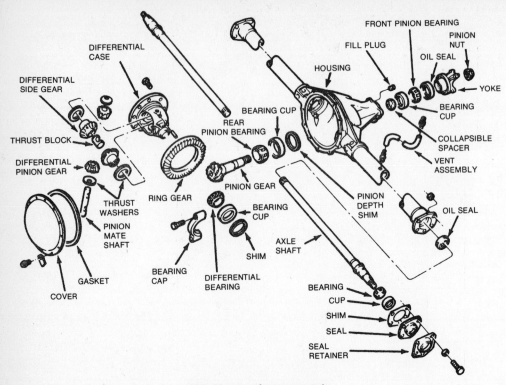

1976–86 rear axle components

worn or damaged. The procedures for install-ing an original hub and a new hub are different.

5. Install an original hub in the following manner:

a. Align the keyway in the hub with the axle shaft key;

b. Slide the hub onto the axle shaft as far as possible;

c. Install the axle shaft nut and washer;

d. Install the drum, drum retaining screws, and wheel;

e. Lower the vehicle onto its wheels and tighten the axle shaft nut to 250 ft.lb. If the cotter pin hole is not aligned, tighten the nut to the next castellation and install the pin. Do not loosen the nut to align the cotter pin hole.

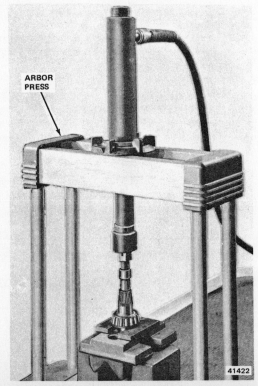

Removing the axle shaft bearing from a tapered axle shaft

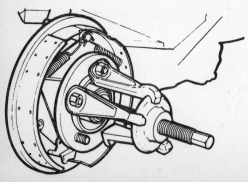

Using a puller to remove the hub on 1984–86 models

6. Install a new hub in the following manner:

a. Align the keyway in the hub with the axle shaft key.

b. Slide the hub onto the axle shaft as far as possible.

c. Install two well lubricated thrust washers and the axle shaft nut.

d. Install the brake drum, drum retaining screws, and wheel.

e. Lower the vehicle onto its wheels.

f. Tighten the axle shaft nut until the distance from the outer face of the hub to the outer end of the axle shaft is $1^5/_{16}''$ (33.3375mm). Pressing the hub onto the axle to the specified distance is necessary to form the hub serrations properly.

g. Remove the axle shaft nut and one thrust washer.

h. Install the axle shaft nut and tighten it to 250 ft.lb. If the cotter pin hole is not aligned, tighten the nut to the next castellation and install the pin. Do not loosen the nut to install the cotter pin.

7. Connect the brake line to the wheel cylinder and bleed the brake hydraulic system and adjust the brake shoes.

Flanged Shaft

NOTE: *An arbor press is necessary for this procedure.*

1. Position the axle shaft in a vise.

2. Remove the retaining ring by drilling a $1/4''$ (6.35mm) hole about $3/4$ of the way through the ring, then using a cold chisel over the hole, split the ring.

3. Remove the bearing with an arbor press, discard the seal and remove the retainer plate.

4. Installation is the reverse of removal. The new bearing must be pressed on. Make sure it is squarely seated.

Rear Axle Unit

REMOVAL AND INSTALLATION

1. Raise the vehicle and support it on jackstands.

2. Remove the rear wheels.

3. Place an indexing mark on the rear yoke and driveshaft, and disconnect the shaft.

4. Disconnect the shock absorbers from the axle tubes. Disconnect the track bar at the axle bracket, on vehicles so equipped.

5. Disconnect the brake hose from the tee fitting on the axle housing. Disconnect the vent tube at the axle.

6. Disconnect the parking brake cable at the frame mounting.

7. Remove the U-bolts. On vehicles with the spring mounted above the axle, disconnect the spring at the rear shackle.

Splitting the locking ring on the flanged shaft axle

Arbor press adapter on a flanged shaft bearing

8. Support the axle on a jack, remove the spring clips, and remove the axle assembly from under the vehicle.

9. Raise the axle on a jack and install the spring clips.

10. Install the U-bolts. On vehicles with the spring mounted above the axle, connect the spring at the rear shackle.

11. Connect the parking brake cable at the frame mounting.

12. Connect the brake hose at the tee fitting on the axle housing.

13. Connect the vent tube at the axle.

14. Connect the track bar at the axle bracket, on vehicles so equipped.

15. Connect the shock absorbers from the axle tubes.

16. Connect the driveshaft.

17. Install the rear wheels.

18. Lower the vehicle.

Wrangler

- Track bar bolts: 74 ft.lb.
- Shock absorber-to-axle nut: 44 ft.lb.
- Spring U-bolts: 90 ft.lb.

- Spring shackle bolts: 95 ft.lb.
- Spring-to-frame bracket bolts: 105 ft.lb.

CJ-2A, CJ-3A, CJ-3B
- $\frac{7}{16}$" spring U-bolt nut: 55 ft.lb.
- ½" spring U-bolt nut: 80 ft.lb.
- Spring pivot bolts: 30 ft.lb.

CJ-5, CJ-6, CJ-7 and Scrambler
- Shock absorber lower stud nut: 45 ft.lb.
- $\frac{9}{16}$" spring U-bolt nut: 100 ft.lb.
- ½" spring U-bolt nut: 55 ft.lb.
- Spring shackle nuts: 24 ft.lb.
- Spring pivot bolts: 100 ft.lb.

Utility Models
- $\frac{7}{16}$" spring U-bolt nut: 55 ft.lb.
- ½" spring U-bolt nut: 80 ft.lb.
- Spring pivot bolts: 30 ft.lb.

NOTE: *Bleed and adjust brakes accordingly.*

FRONT DRIVE AXLE

Axle Shaft, Bearing and Seal
REMOVAL AND INSTALLATION

Through 1971

The front axle shaft and universal joint assembly is removed as an assembly.

NOTE: *See the U-joint section of this chapter for a description of the three types used on these axles.*

1. Remove the wheel.
2. Remove the hub with a puller. If there are locking hubs, remove them as detailed in Chapter 1.
3. Remove the axle shaft driving flange bolts.

Front Drive Axle Application Chart

Axle Type	Years	Models
Spicer 25	1945–53	CJ-2A, CJ-3A
	1947–64	Utility Models
Dana 27	1954–71	CJ-3B, CJ-5, CJ-6
Dana 27A	1954–71	CJ-3B, CJ-5, CJ-6
Dana 30	1971–87	All models

Pulling the front drive hub

Pulling off axle shaft drive flange

4. Apply the foot brakes and remove the axle shaft flange with a puller.
5. Release the locking lip on the lockwasher and remove the outer nut, lockwasher, adjusting nut, and bearing lockwasher.
6. Remove the wheel hub and drum assembly with the bearings. Be careful not to damage the oil seal.
7. Remove the hydraulic brake tube and the brake backing plate screws.
8. Remove the spindle.

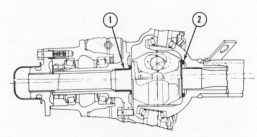

1. Bushing
2. Thrust washer

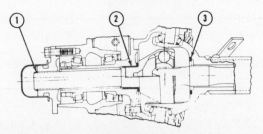

1. Snap ring
2. Bushing
3. Thrust washer

Bendix (top) and Rzeppa joint axle shafts

Wheel bearing nut wrench

9. Remove axle shaft and universal joint assembly.

10. Single cross cardan type installation is the reverse of the removal procedure.

11. Bendix type installation is as follows:

   a. Enter the U-joint and shaft assembly into the housing. Mesh the splined end of the shaft with the differential and push into place.

b. Install the wheel bearing spindle.

c. Install the brake tube and backing plate.

d. Grease and assemble the wheel bearings and hub and drum on the spindle. Install the bearing washer and adjusting nut. Tighten the nut until a slight drag is felt, then back off $\frac{1}{6}$ turn. Install remaining parts.

12. Early Rzeppa type type requires a shimming procedure. Installation is the same as the Bendix type except that a shim pack must be installed between the driving flange and the wheel hub to determine the proper operating clearance for the U-joint. To do this:

   a. Install the drive flange on the axle splines without shims.

   b. Install the axle nut and tighten it snugly.

   c. Install two opposite flange bolts snugly.

   d. Use a feeler gauge to measure the gap between the outer end of the hub and the inner face of the driving flange. This determines the amount of shimming to be used. It is necessary to install shims of a thickness equal to the measured gap plug 0.015–0.050″ (0.381–1.27mm). If no gap is found, install a 0.010″ (0.254mm) shim.

   e. Install the correct amount of shims, replace the flange and install the six bolts. Install the axle shaft nut and make sure that the proper end float has been obtained. To do

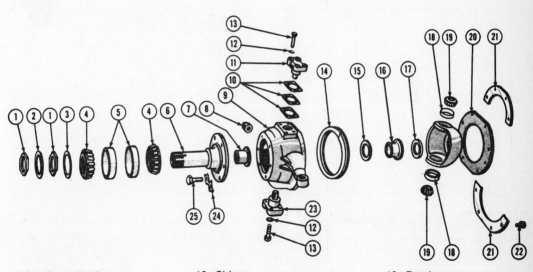

1. Bearing adjusting nut
2. Lockwasher
3. Lockwasher
4. Bearing cone and rollers
5. Bearing cup
6. Spindle
7. Bushing
8. Filler plug
9. Left knuckle
10. Shims
11. Upper bearing cap
12. Lockwasher
13. Bolt
14. Oil seal and backing ring
15. Thrust washer
16. Axle pilot
17. Oil seal
18. Bearing cup
19. Bearing cone and rollers
20. Oil seal
21. Retainer
22. Bolt
23. Lower bearing cap
24. Lockstrap
25. Bolt

Early model steering knuckle and spindle

this, back off the shaft nut so that a 0.050″ (1.27mm) feeler will fit between the nut and driving flange. Tap the end of the shaft with a soft mallet which will force in the shaft the amount of end float. Measure the clearance between the nut and driving flange. Clearance should be 0.015–0.050″ (0.381–1.27mm).

13. Late Rzeppa type installation is the same as the Bendix type except that a snapring is used to secure the outer end of the shaft controlling end float.

1972–86

NOTE: *On models with locking hubs, refer to Locking Hub Removal and Installation.*

1. Remove the locking hub or hub cap. On models with disc brakes, remove the caliper.

2. Remove the drive flange snapring.

3. On models with disc brakes, remove the rotor hub bolts, cover and gasket. On models with drum brakes, remove the axle flange bolts, lockwashers and flatwashers.

4. If the axle is on the vehicle, apply the foot brakes. Remove the axle flange with a puller.

5. Release the locking lip of the lockwasher, and remove the outer nut, lockwasher, adjusting nut, and bearing lockwasher.

6. On models with the disc brakes, remove the bearing and rotor. On models with drum brakes, back off on the brake adjusting star wheel adjusters and remove the brake drum assembly with the bearings. Be careful not to damage the oil seal.

7. On models with drum brakes, remove the brake backing plate. If the axle is on the vehicle, it will first be necessary to disconnect the brake hose between the front brake line and the flexible connection. On models with disc brakes, remove the adapter and splash shield.

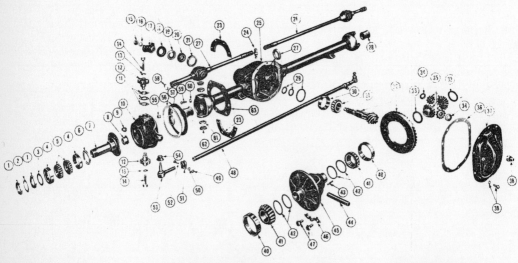

1. Nut	22. Right axle shaft with universal joint	43. Lock pin
2. Lockwasher	23. Knuckle oil seal retainer	44. Pinion shaft
3. Bearing lockwasher	24. Housing breather	45. Differential case
4. Wheel bearing cup	25. Front axle housing	46. Lock strap
5. Cone and rollers	26. Left axle shaft with universal joint	47. Bolts
6. Oil seal	27. Oil seal	48. Steering tie rod
7. Spindle	28. Axle shaft guide	49. Tie rod clamp nut
8. Spindle bushing	29. Shim pack	50. Lockwasher
9. Filler plug	30. Bearing cup	51. Tie rod socket clamp
10. Left knuckle and arm	31. Cone and rollers	52. Screw
11. Shims	32. Ring gear and pinion	53. Tie rod socket
12. Pivot pin	33. Thrust washer	54. Dust cover
13. Lockwasher	34. Thrust washer	55. Nut
14. Capscrew	35. Differential gears	56. Oil seal and backing ring
15. Nut	36. Housing cover gasket	57. Thrust washer
16. Washer	37. Housing cover	58. Snap ring
17. Universal joint yoke	38. Fill plug	59. Stop bolt
18. Oil seal	39. Screw and lockwasher	60. Nut
19. Oil slinger	40. Bearing cup	61. Bearing cup
20. Cone and rollers	41. Cone and rollers	62. Cone and rollers
21. Bearing cup	42. Shims	63. Gasket

Dana 27 front drive axle

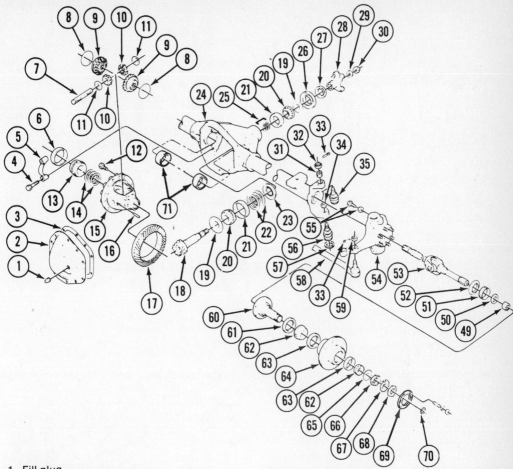

1. Fill plug
2. Axle housing cover
3. Axle housing cover gasket
4. Differential bearing cap bolt
5. Differential bearing cap
6. Differential bearing cup (2)
7. Pinion mate shaft
8. Thrust washer
9. Differential side gear
10. Differential pinion gear
11. Thrust washer
12. Ring gear mounting bolts
13. Differential bearing (2)
14. Differential bearing preload shims
15. Differential case
16. Pinion mate shaft pin
17. Ring gear
18. Pinion gear
19. Slinger
20. Pinion bearing
21. Pinion bearing cup
22. Pinion depth shims
23. Baffle
24. Axle housing
25. Pinion preload shims
26. Oil seal
27. Dust cap
28. Yoke
29. Washer
30. Pinion nut

31. Upper ball stud split ring seat
32. Upper ball stud nut
33. Cotter pin
34. Lower ball stud jamnut
35. Upper ball stud
49. Spindle bearing
50. Washer
51. Seal
52. Seal seat
53. Axle shaft
54. Steering knuckle
55. Steering stop bolt
56. Lower ball stud
57. Snap ring
58. Tie rod
59. Tie rod end nut
60. Spindle
61. Seal
62. Bearing
63. Bearing cup
64. Hub
65. Tabbed washer
66. Inner locknut
67. Lock washer
68. Outer locknut
69. Gasket
70. Snap ring
71. Inner oil seal

Dana 30 front axle assembly

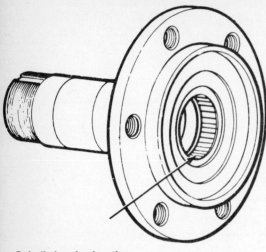

Spindle bearing location

8. Remove the spindle and spindle bushing.

9. Remove the axle shaft and universal joint assembly.

10. Clean all parts.

11. Insert the universal joint and axle shaft assembly into the axle housing, being careful not to knock out the inner seal. Insert the splined end of the axle shaft into the differential and push into place.

12. Install the wheel bearing spindle and bushing.

13. Install the brake backing plate, or adapter and splash shield.

14. Grease and assemble the wheel bearings and oil seal.

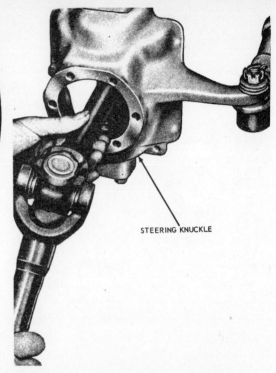

STEERING KNUCKLE

Typical front axle shaft removal on vehicles through 1979

15. Install the wheel hub and drum on the wheel bearing spindle. On disc brakes, install the rotor, hub, and caliper. Install the wheel bearing washer and adjusting nut. Tighten the nut to 50 ft.lb., and back it off $\frac{1}{6}$–$\frac{1}{4}$ turn while

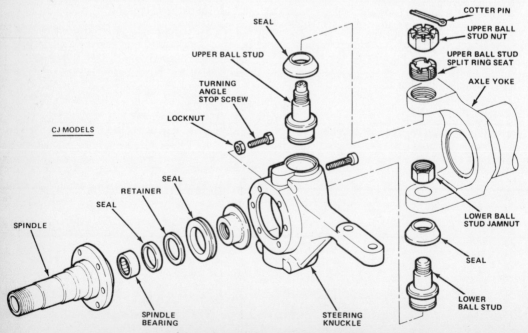

Late model spindle and knuckle assembly

rotating the hub. Install the lockwasher and nut, tighten the nut to 50 ft.lb. and then bend the lip of the lockwasher over onto the locknut.

16. Install the drive flange and gasket onto the hub and attach with six capscrews and lockwashers. Torque the capscrews to 30 ft.lb. in an alternate and even pattern. Install the snapring onto the outer end of the axle shaft.

17. Install the hub cap.

18. Install the wheel, lug nuts, and wheel disc.

19. If the tube was installed with the axle assembly on the vehicle, check the front wheel alignment, bleed the brakes and lubricate the front axle universal joints.

1987

1. Raise and support the vehicle safely.

2. Remove the wheels, calipers and rotors.

3. Remove the cotter pin, locknut and axle hub nut.

4. Remove the hub-to-knuckle attaching bolts.

5. Remove the hub and splash shield from the steering knuckle.

6. To remove the left shaft, remove the axle shaft from the housing.

7. To remove the right shaft:

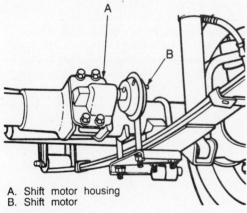

A. Shift motor housing
B. Shift motor

1987 front drive axle

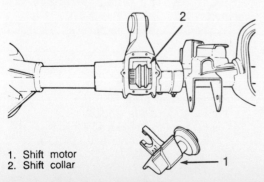

1. Shift motor
2. Shift collar

1987 right side front axle shaft

a. Disconnect the vacuum harness from the shift motor.

b. Remove the shift motor from the housing.

c. Remove the axle shaft from the housing.

8. To install the right axle shaft first be sure that the shift collar is in position on the intermediate shaft and that the axle shaft is fully engaged in the intermediate shaft end.

9. Install the shift motor, making sure that the fork engages with the collar. Tighten the bolts to 8 ft.lb.

10. On the left side, install the axle shaft in the housing.

11. Partially fill the hub cavity of the knuckle with chassis lube and install the hub and splash shield.

12. Tighten the hub bolts to 75 ft.lb.

13. Install the hub washer and nut. Torque the nut to 175 ft.lb. Install the locknut. Install a new cotter pin.

14. Install the rotor, caliper and wheel.

Pinion Seal and Yoke

REMOVAL AND INSTALLATION

All Models

1. Raise and support the front end on jackstands.

2. Matchmark the driveshaft and yoke and disconnect the driveshaft.

3. Using a holding tool, such as J-8614-01, on the yoke, remove the pinion nut.

4. Remove the yoke, using tools J-8614-01, -02, and -03, or their equivalents.

5. Using tool J-9233 or J-7583, or, on 1987 models, tool J-25180, or their equivalents, remove the seal.

6. Coat the outer rim of the new seal with sealer and intall it using a seal driver.

7. Install the yoke, pinion washer and a new pinion nut. Torque the nut to 210 ft.lb.

8. Connect the driveshaft.

Front Axle Unit

REMOVAL AND INSTALLATION

1945–86

1. Raise and support the vehicle safely. Remove the wheels.

2. Index the driveshaft to the differential yoke for the proper alignment upon installation. Disconnect the driveshaft at the axle yoke and secure the shaft to the frame rail.

3. Disconnect the steering linkage from the steering knuckles. Disconnect the shock absorbers at the axle housing.

4. If the vehicle is equipped with a stabilizer bar, remove the nuts attaching the stabilizer bar connecting links to the spring tie plates.

5. On vehicles equipped with sway bar, remove nuts attaching sway bar connecting links to spring tie plates.

6. Disconnect the breather tube from the axle housing. Disconnect the stabilizer bar link bolts at the spring clips.

7. Remove the brake calipers, or drums, hub and rotor, or brake shoes, and the brake shield.

8. Remove the U-bolts and the tie plates.

9. Support the assembly on a jack and loosen the nuts securing the rear shackles, but do not remove the bolts.

10. Remove the front spring shackle bolts. Lower the springs to the floor.

11. Pull the jack and axle housing from underneath the vehicle.

12. Raise the axle into position.

13. Install the front spring shackle bolts.

14. Tighten the nuts securing the rear shackles.

15. Install the U-bolts and the tie plates.

16. Install the brake calipers, or drums, hub and rotor, or brake shoes, and the brake shield.

17. Connect the breather tube to the axle housing.

18. Connect the stabilizer bar link bolts at the spring clips.

19. On vehicles equipped with a sway bar, install the nuts attaching sway bar connecting links to the spring tie plates.

20. If the vehicle is equipped with a stabilizer bar, install the nuts attaching the stabilizer bar connecting links to the spring tie plates.

21. Connect the steering linkage to the steering knuckles.

22. Connect the shock absorbers at the axle housing.

23. Connect the driveshaft at the axle yoke.

24. Install the wheels.

25. Lower the vehicle.

CJ-2A, CJ-3A, CJ-3B
- $7/16''$ spring U-bolt nuts: 55 ft.lb.
- All other spring U-bolt nuts: 80 ft.lb.
- Spring pivot bolts: 30 ft.lb.

CJ-5, CJ-6, CJ-7, Scrambler
- Connecting rod ball studs: 60 ft.lb. minimum.
- Spring shackle bolts: 24 ft.lb.
- Shock absorber lower mounting nut: 45 ft.lb.
- Spring pivot bolts: 100 ft.lb.
- $9/16''$ spring U-bolt nuts: 100 ft.lb.
- $1/2''$ spring U-bolt nuts: 55 ft.lb.

Utility Models
- $7/16''$ spring U-bolt nuts: 55 ft.lb.
- All other spring U-bolt nuts: 80 ft.lb.
- Spring pivot bolts: 30 ft.lb.

1987

1. Raise and support the vehicle safely. Remove the wheels.

2. Index the driveshaft to the differential yoke for the proper alignment upon installation. Disconnect the driveshaft at the axle yoke and secure the shaft to the frame rail.

3. Disconnect the vacuum harness from the shift motor.

4. Disconnect the vent hose from the axle housing.

5. Disconnect the center link at the right side of the tie rod.

6. Disconnect the shock absorbers at the axle.

7. Remove the steering damper.

8. Disconnect the track bar at the axle.

9. Loosen the stabilizer bar links at the bar and disconnect the stabilizer bar from the spring tie plates.

10. Loosen the bolts attaching the spring to the frame brackets.

11. Loosen the spring-to-shackle bolts.

12. Take up the weight of the axle with a floor jack.

13. Remove the spring U-bolts and tie plates.

14. Remove the front shackle bolts and remove the axle from the truck.

15. Raise the axle into position.

16. Install the front shackle bolts.

17. Install the spring U-bolts and tie plates.

18. Tighten the spring-to-shackle bolts.

19. Tighten the bolts attaching the spring to the frame brackets.

20. Connect the stabilizer bar from the spring tie plates.

21. Tighten the stabilizer bar links at the bar.

22. Connect the track bar at the axle.

23. Install the steering damper.

24. Connect the shock absorbers at the axle.

25. Connect the center link at the right side of the tie rod.

26. Connect the vent hose at the axle housing.

27. Connect the vacuum harness to the shift motor.

28. Connect the driveshaft at the axle yoke.

29. Install the wheels.

30. Lower the vehicle.
- Spring U-bolt nuts: 90 ft.lb.
- Tie rod-to-knuckle: 35 ft.lb
- Center link-to-knuckle: 35 ft.lb.
- Lower shock absorber bolt: 45 ft.lb.
- Track bar-to-axle: 74 ft.lb.
- Stabilizer bar link bolts: 45 ft.lb.
- Steering damper-to-axle: 55 ft.lb.

Shift Motor and Housing
REMOVAL AND INSTALLATION
Wrangler

1. Raise and support the front end on jackstands.
2. Place a drain pan under the shift motor.
3. Disconnect the vacuum harness at the motor.
4. Remove the attaching bolts and slowly lift off the motor and housing. Matchmark the shift fork and housing for installation reference.
5. Rotate the motor and remove the shift fork and motor snaprings.
6. Remove the motor from the housing and remove and discard the motor O-ring.
7. When installing the motor, always use a new O-ring. Install the motor in the housing and slide the shift fork on the shaft.
8. Position the housing and motor on the axle and add about 5 oz. of axle lubricant to the shift motor housing.
9. Engage the fork in the shift collar and install the attaching bolts. Torque the bolts to 8 ft.lb. (101 in.lb.).

Front Hub and Wheel Bearings
ADJUSTMENT

NOTE: *Sodium-based grease is not compatible with lithium-based grease. Read the package labels and be careful not to mix the two types. If there is any doubt as to the type of grease used, completely clean the old grease from the bearing and hub before replacing.*

Before handling the bearings, there are a few things that you should remember to do and not to do.

Remember to DO the following:
• Remove all outside dirt from the housing before exposing the bearing.
• Treat a used bearing as gently as you would a new one.
• Work with clean tools in clean surroundings.
• Use clean, dry canvas gloves, or at least clean, dry hands.
• Clean solvents and flushing fluids are a must.
• Use clean paper when laying out the bearings to dry.
• Protect disassembled bearings from rust and dirt. Cover them up.
• Use clean rags to wipe bearings.
• Keep the bearings in oil-proof paper when they are to be stored or are not in use.
• Clean the inside of the housing before replacing the bearing.

Do NOT do the following:
• Don't work in dirty surroundings.
• Don't use dirty, chipped or damaged tools.
• Try not to work on wooden work benches or use wooden mallets.
• Don't handle bearings with dirty or moist hands.
• Do not use gasoline for cleaning; use a safe solvent.
• Do not spin-dry bearings with compressed air. They will be damaged.
• Do not spin dirty bearings.
• Avoid using cotton waste or dirty cloths to wipe bearings.
• Try not to scratch or nick bearing surfaces.
• Do not allow the bearing to come in contact with dirt or rust at any time.

1945–86
4-WD

1. Raise the front of the vehicle and place jackstands under the axle.
2. Remove the wheel.
3. Remove the front hub grease cap and driving hub snapring. On models equipped with locking hubs, remove the retainer knob hub ring, agitator knob, snapring, outer clutch retaining ring and actuating cam body.
4. Remove the splined driving hub and the pressure spring. This may require slight prying with a screwdriver.
5. Remove the external snapring from the sindle shaft and remove the hub shaft drive gear.
6. Remove the wheel bearing locknut, lockring, adjusting nut and inner lockring.
7. On vehicles with drum brakes, remove the hub and drum assembly. This may require that the brake adjusting wheel be backed off a few turns. The outer wheel bearing and spring retainer will come off with the hub.
8. On vehicles with disc brakes, remove the caliper and suspend it out of the way by hanging it from a suspension or frame member with a length of wire. Do not disconnect the brake hose, and be careful to avoid stretching the hose. Remove the rotor and hub assembly. The outer wheel bearing and, on vehicles with locking hubs, the spring collar, will come off with the hub.
9. Carefully drive out the inner bearing and seal from the hub, using a wood block.
10. Inspect the bearing races for excessive wear, pitting or grooves. If they are cracked or grooved, or if pitting and excess wear is present, drive them out with a drift or punch.
11. Check the bearing for excess wear, pitting or cracks, or excess looseness.
NOTE: *If it is necessary to replace either the*

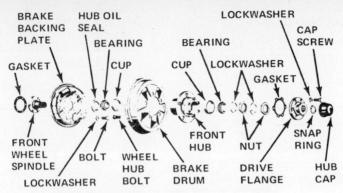

Front hub and wheel bearings with drum brakes

bearing or the race, replace both. *Never replace just a bearing or a race. These parts wear in a mating pattern. If just one is replaced, premature failure of the new part will result.*

12. If the old parts are retained, thoroughly clean them in a safe solvent and allow them to dry on a clean towel. Never spin dry them with compressed air.

13. On vehicles with drum brakes, cover the spindle with a cloth and thoroughly brush all dirt from the brakes. Never blow the dirt off the brakes, due to the presence of asbestos in the dirt, which is harmful to your health when inhaled.

14. Remove the cloth and thoroughly clean the spindle.

15. Thoroughly clean the inside of the hub.

16. Pack the inside of the hub with EP wheel bearing grease. Add grease to the hub until it is flush with the inside diameter of the bearing cup.

17. Pack the bearing with the same grease. A needle-shaped wheel bearing packer is best for this operation. If one is not available, place a large amount of grease in the palm of your hand and slide the edge of the bearing cage through the grease to pick up as much as possible, then work the grease in as best you can with your fingers.

18. If a new race is being installed, very carefully drive it into position until it bottoms all around, using a brass drift. Be careful to avoid scratching the surface.

19. Place the inner bearing in the race and install a new grease seal.

20. Place the hub assembly onto the spindle and install the inner lockring and outer bearing. Install the wheel bearing nut and torque it to 50 ft.lb. while turning the wheel back and forth to seat the bearings. Back off the nut about ¼ turn (90°) maximum.

21. Install the lockwasher with the tab aligned with the keyway in the spindle and turn the inner wheel bearing adjusting nut until the peg on the nut engages the nearest hole in the lockwasher.

22. Install the outer locknut and torque it to 50 ft.lb.

23. Install the spring collar, drive flange, snapring, pressure spring, and hub cap.

24. Install the caliper over the rotor.

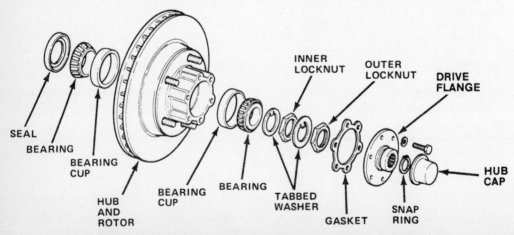

Front hub and wheel bearings with disc brakes, but without locking hubs

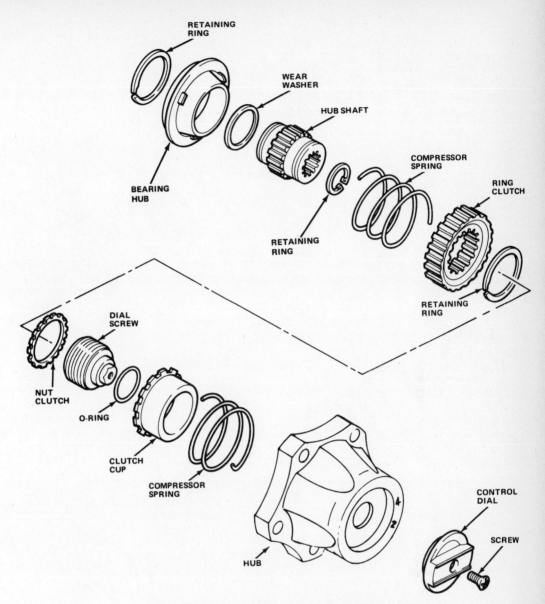

RETAINING
RING

WEAR
WASHER

HUB SHAFT

COMPRESSOR
SPRING

RING
CLUTCH

BEARING
HUB

RETAINING
RING

RETAINING
RING

DIAL
SCREW

NUT
CLUTCH

O-RING

CLUTCH
CUP

COMPRESSOR
SPRING

HUB

CONTROL
DIAL

SCREW

1980–83 front hub and wheel bearings with locking hubs

1947–64

2-WD

1. Raise the front of the vehicle and place jackstands under the axle.
2. Remove the wheel.
3. Remove the front hub grease cap.
4. Remove the cotter pin and locknut.
5. Pull out on the brake drum slightly to free the outer bearing and remove the bearing.
6. Remove the drum and hub.
7. Using an awl, puncture the inner seal and pry it out. Discard the seal.
8. Remove the inner bearing.
9. Inspect the bearing races for excessive

wear, pitting or grooves. If they are cracked or grooved, or if pitting and excess wear is present, drive them out with a drift or punch.
10. Check the bearing for excess wear, pitting or cracks, or excess looseness.

NOTE: *If it is necessary to replace either the bearing or the race, replace both. Never replace just a bearing or a race. These parts wear in a mating pattern. If just one is replaced, premature failure of the new part will result.*

11. If the old parts are retained, thoroughly clean them in a safe solvent and allow them to dry on a clean towel. Never spin dry them with compressed air.

1. Retaining ring
2. Bearing hub
3. Wear washer
4. Hub shaft
5. Retaining ring
6. Compressor spring
7. Ring clutch
8. Retaining ring
9. Nut clutch
10. Dial screw
11. O-ring
12. Clutch cup
13. Compressor spring
14. Hub
15. Control dial
16. Screw

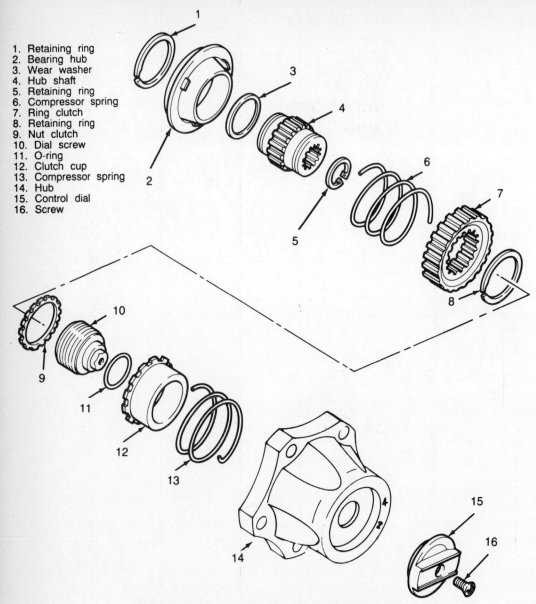

1984–86 front hub and wheel bearings with locking hubs

12. On vehicles with drum brakes, cover the spindle with a cloth and thoroughly brush all dirt from the brakes. Never blow the dirt off the brakes, due to the presence of asbestos in the dirt, which is harmful to your health when inhaled.

13. Remove the cloth and thoroughly clean the spindle.

14. Thoroughly clean the inside of the hub.

15. Pack the inside of the hub with EP wheel bearing grease. Add grease to the hub until it is flush with the inside diameter of the bearing cup.

16. Pack the bearing with the same grease. A needle-shaped wheel bearing packer is best for this operation. If one is not available, place a large amount of grease in the palm of your hand and slide the edge of the bearing cage through the grease to pick up as much as possible, then work the grease in as best you can with your fingers.

17. If a new race is being installed, very carefully drive it into position until it bottoms all around, using a brass drift. Be careful to avoid scratching the surface.

18. Place the inner bearing in the race and install a new grease seal.

19. Place the hub assembly onto the spindle

1. Spindle
2. Backing plate and brake assembly
3. Grease seal
4. Inner wheel bearing
5. Inner wheel bearing race
6. Brake drum
7. Outer wheel bearing race
8. Outer wheel bearing
9. Washer
10. Spindle nut
11. Cotter pin
12. Grease cap
13. Backing plate-to-spindle nut
14. Lockwasher
15. Backing plate-to-spindle bolt

2-wd front hub and bearings

and install the outer bearing. Install the wheel bearing nut and tighten it until the hub binds while turning. Back off the nut about $\frac{1}{6}$–$\frac{1}{4}$ turn to free the bearings. Install a new cotter pin.

20. Install the grease cap.
21. Install the wheel.
22. Lower the vehicle and install the hub cap.

1987

1. Raise and support the front end on jackstands.
2. Remove the wheel.
3. Dismount the caliper and suspend it out of the way.
4. Remove the rotor.
5. Remove the hub nut pin, cap and nut.
6. Remove the hub.
7. The hub and bearings are usually replaced as a unit. The hub and bearing carrier may, however, be disassembled and the bearings replaced as a set. Once the hub and bearing carrier have been separated, the bearings should not be reused.
8. Pack the hub cavity and bearings with wheel bearing grease and install the hub on the axle shaft. If the carrier was separated from the hub, make sure you install a new carrier seal and inner bearing seal.
9. Install the hub washer and nut. Torque the nut to 175 ft.lb. and instal the cap and new cotter pin.
10. Install the rotor, caliper and wheel.

2-WD FRONT AXLE

NOTE: *Early production Utility Models with the 4–134 engine were equipped with a Planar type, independent front suspension.*

All other 2-WD Utility Models are equipped with a solid I-beam type, reverse Elliot front suspension.

Pivot Pins

REMOVAL AND INSTALLATION

Solid I-Beam Front Axle

1. Raise and support the front end on jackstands.
2. Remove the hub and dust caps.
3. Remove the cotter pin, wheel retaining nut and washer.
4. Pull the wheel out slightly to free the outer bearing, remove the bearing and remove the wheel and hub assembly.
5. Disconnect the brake line at the wheel cylinder and cap the end.
6. Remove the brake shoes and springs.
7. Remove the brake backing plate.
8. Remove the pivot pin lock.
9. Remove the top expansion plug and drive out the pin through the bottom with the lower plug.
   NOTE: *There is a shim between the upper face of the axle and the spindle. Don't lose it!*
10. Remove the thrust bearing and bushings.
11. If new bushings are being installed, they must be reamed for a running fit with the pivot pins. Be sure that the oil holes in the bushings are aligned with their lubrication fittings.
12. If the thrust bearing shows any signs of wear, replace it.
13. Install the pivot pin, aligning the notch with the pin hole.
14. When assembling the knuckle, check for play between the axle and inner face of the knuckle. If play seems excessive, use a different size shim. Shims were available in 0.011"

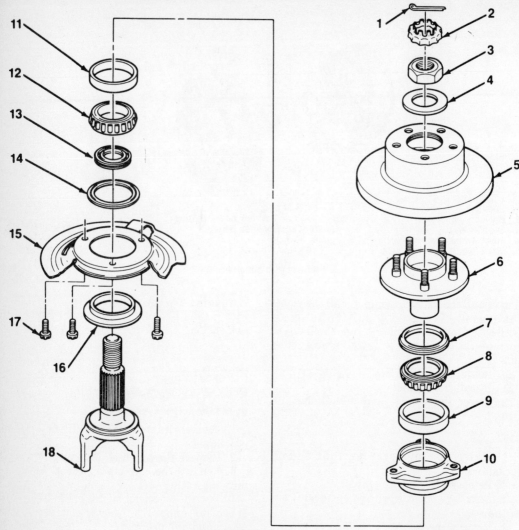

1. Cotter pin	7. Outer bearing seal	13. Inner bearing seal
2. Nut retainer	8. Outer bearing	14. Carrier seal
3. Nut	9. Outer bearing race	15. Rotor shield
4. Washer	10. Bearing carrier	16. Axle shaft dust slinger
5. Brake rotor	11. Inner bearing race	17. Bearing carrier bolts
6. Hub	12. Inner bearing	18. Axle shaft

1987 front hub and wheel bearings

(0.279mm), 0.033" (0.838mm) and 0.035" (0.889mm).

15. Install the top expansion plug and drive out the pin through the bottom with the lower plug.

16. Install the pivot pin lock.

17. Install the brake backing plate.

18. Install the brake shoes and springs.

19. Connect the brake line at the wheel cylinder.

20. Install the wheel and hub assembly.

21. Install the outer bearing.

22. Install the wheel retaining nut and washer.

23. While turning the wheel, tighten the nut until the wheel binds, then back off the nut 1/6–1/4 turn to free the bearing.

24. Install the cotter pin.

25. Install the hub and dust caps.

26. Bleed the brakes.

27. Lower the front end.

Planar Front Suspension

1. Raise and support the front end on jackstands.

2. Remove the hub and dust caps.

3. Remove the cotter pin, wheel retaining nut and washer.

4. Pull the wheel out slightly to free the out-

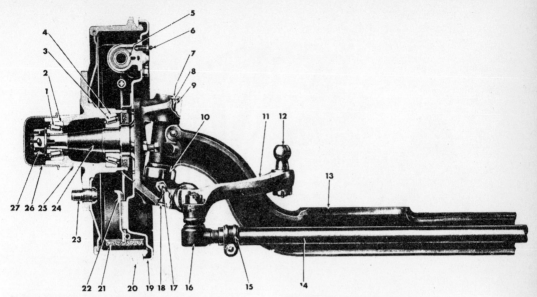

1. Outer front wheel bearing cone and rollers
2. Outer front wheel bearing race
3. Inner front wheel bearing cone and rollers
4. Inner front wheel bearing race
5. Wheel brake cylinder
6. Wheel brake cylinder bleeder screw
7. Pivot bolt expansion plug-upper
8. Pivot bolt
9. Steering knuckle bushing
10. Pivot bolt thrust bearing
11. Steering knuckle arm
12. Steering arm ball
13. Front axle I-beam
14. Steering tie rod

15. Steering tie rod clamp
16. Steering tie rod socket assembly
17. Lubrication fitting
18. Lower pivot bolt expansion plug
19. Brake backing plate assembly
20. Brake drum
21. Brake shoe assembly
22. Brake shoe retainer plate
23. Wheel hub bolt
24. Steering knuckle assembly
25. Front wheel hub
26. Hub cap
27. Front axle spindle nut

Solid I-beam, reverse Elliot type front axle

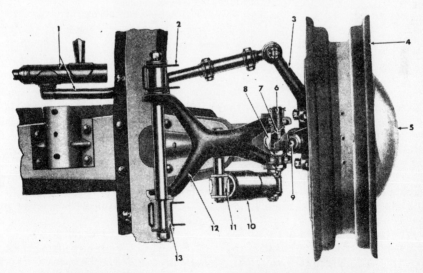

1. Tie rod
2. Frame bracket
3. Steering knuckle arm
4. Wheel
5. Hub cap
6. Control arm pin
7. Control arm pin bushing

8. Steering knuckle support
9. Hydraulic fitting
10. Shock absorber
11. Shock absorber bushing
12. Arm assembly
13. Control arm bushing

Planar type front suspension top view

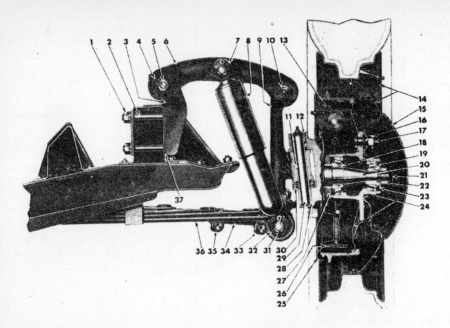

1. Frame bracket mounting nut
2. Frame bracket mounting screw
3. Frame bracket
4. Support arm mounting washer
5. Support arm mounting nut
6. Support arm assembly
7. Shock absorber mounting washer
8. Shock absorber
9. Knuckle support
10. Support arm pin
11. Pivot pin locking pin
12. Steering knuckle bearing
13. Wheel cylinder
14. Wheel
15. Hub cap
16. Lug nut
17. Lug bolt
18. Inner wheel bearing
19. Outer wheel bearing

20. Steering knuckle
21. Grease cap
22. Wheel retaining nut
23. Wheel nut tongue washer
24. Hub
25. Backing plate
26. Brake shoe
27. Dust washer
28. Knuckle bushing
29. Pivot pin
30. Pivot bearing
31. Shock absorber mounting washer
32. Shock absorber bushing
33. Tie rod clamp
34. Tie rod sleeve
35. Tie rod clamp
36. Front spring
37. Support arm shims

Planar type front suspension side view

er bearing, remove the bearing and remove the wheel and hub assembly.

5. Disconnect the brake line at the wheel cylinder and cap the end.

6. Remove the brake shoes and springs.

7. Remove the brake backing plate.

8. Remove the pivot pin lock.

9. Use a sharp drift to remove the pivot pin lower expansion plug.

10. Drive the pivot pin upward until the needle bearing assembly can be removed.

11. Drive the pivot pin out through the bottom.

12. Remove the bushings from the lower part of the spindle.

13. If new bushings are being installed, they must be reamed for a running fit with the pivot pins. Be sure that the oil holes in the bushings

are aligned with their lubrication fittings.

14. If the thrust bearing shows any signs of wear, replace it.

15. Drive the pivot pin in through the bottom.

16. Drive the pivot pin upward until the needle bearing assembly can be installed.

17. Install the pivot pin lower expansion plug.

18. Install the pivot pin lock.

19. Install the brake backing plate.

20. Install the brake shoes and springs.

21. Connect the brake line at the wheel cylinder.

22. Install the wheel and hub assembly.

23. Install the outer bearing.

24. Install the wheel retaining nut and washer.

25. While turning the wheel, tighten the nut until the wheel binds, then back off the nut $\frac{1}{6}$–$\frac{1}{4}$ turn to free the bearing.

26. Install a new cotter pin.

27. Install the hub and dust caps.
28. Bleed the brakes.
29. Lower the front end.

SPECIAL TOOLS

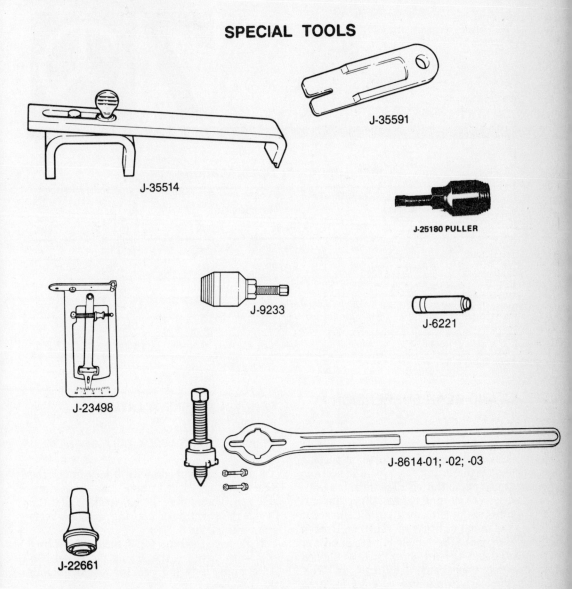

J-35591

J-35514

J-25180 PULLER

J-23498

J-9233

J-6221

J-8614-01; -02; -03

J-22661

Suspension and Steering

7

Wheel Alignment Specifications

Year	Caster (deg.)		Camber (deg.)		Toe-in (in.)	King Pin Incl. (deg.)
	Range	Pref.	Range	Pref.		
1945–73	2½P to 3½P	3P	1P to 2P	1½P*	³⁄₆₄ to ³⁄₃₂	7½
1974–80	2½P to 3½P	3P	1P to 2P	1½P	³⁄₆₄ to ³⁄₃₂	8½
1981	5½P to 6½P	6P	1¼P to 1¾P	1½P	³⁄₆₄ to ³⁄₃₂	8½
1982–83	5½P to 6½P	6P	½N to ½P	0	³⁄₆₄ to ³⁄₃₂	8½
1984–86	5½P to 6½P	6P	½N to ½P	0	0 to ³⁄₃₂	10
1987	7¾P to 8¼P	8P	½N to ½P	0	¹⁄₃₂ out to ¹⁄₃₂ in	10

*2-WD Utility Models: 1P

FRONT AND REAR SUSPENSION

Springs

All springs should be examined periodically for broken or shifted leaves, loose or missing clips, angle of the spring shackles, and position of the springs on the saddles. Springs with shifted leaves do not retain their normal strength. Missing clips may permit the spirit leaves to fan out or break on rebound. Broken leaves may make the vehicle hard to handle or permit the axle to shift out of line. Weakened springs may break causing difficulty in steering. Spring attaching clips or bolts must be tight. It is suggested that they be checked at each vehicle inspection.

All front springs on models through 1971, except as noted below, have shackles at the front of the springs. Model CJ-5 up to serial number 44437 and Model CJ-6 up to serial number 11981 have shackles at the rear of the front springs, and pivot bolts at the front.

All rear springs have shackles at the rear and pivot bolts at the front.

NOTE: *On 1972 and later models, all spring ends have silent block type rubber bushings. Never lubricate these rubber bushings.*

REMOVAL AND INSTALLATION

1945–1971

EXCEPT EARLY UTILITY MODELS WITH PLANAR FRONT SUSPENSION

1. Raise the vehicle with a jack under the axle and place a jackstand under the frame side rail. Then lower the axle jack so that the load is relieved from the spring and the wheels rest on the floor.

2. Remove the nuts which secure the spring clip bolts. Remove the spring plate and clip bolts. Free the spring from the axle by raising the axle jack.

3. Remove the pivot bolt nut and drive out the pivot bolt. Disconnect the shackle either by removing the lower nuts and bolts on the rubber bushed shackles, or by removing the threaded bushings on the U-shackles.

4. To replace, first install the pivot bolt. Then, connect the shackle using the following procedures.

5. On bronze bushed pivot bolts, install the bolt and nut and tighten the nut. Then back it off two cotter pin slots and install the cotter pin. The nut must be drawn up tightly but must be sufficiently loose to allow the spring to

Troubleshooting Basic Steering and Suspension Problems

Problem	Cause	Solution
Hard steering (steering wheel is hard to turn)	• Low or uneven tire pressure • Loose power steering pump drive belt • Low or incorrect power steering fluid • Incorrect front end alignment • Defective power steering pump • Bent or poorly lubricated front end parts	• Inflate tires to correct pressure • Adjust belt • Add fluid as necessary • Have front end alignment checked/adjusted • Check pump • Lubricate and/or replace defective parts
Loose steering (too much play in the steering wheel)	• Loose wheel bearings • Loose or worn steering linkage • Faulty shocks • Worn ball joints	• Adjust wheel bearings • Replace worn parts • Replace shocks • Replace ball joints
Car veers or wanders (car pulls to one side with hands off the steering wheel)	• Incorrect tire pressure • Improper front end alignment • Loose wheel bearings • Loose or bent front end components • Faulty shocks	• Inflate tires to correct pressure • Have front end alignment checked/adjusted • Adjust wheel bearings • Replace worn components • Replace shocks
Wheel oscillation or vibration transmitted through steering wheel	• Improper tire pressures • Tires out of balance • Loose wheel bearings • Improper front end alignment • Worn or bent front end components	• Inflate tires to correct pressure • Have tires balanced • Adjust wheel bearings • Have front end alignment checked/adjusted • Replace worn parts
Uneven tire wear	• Incorrect tire pressure • Front end out of alignment • Tires out of balance	• Inflate tires to correct pressure • Have front end alignment checked/adjusted • Have tires balanced

Troubleshooting the Steering Column

Problem	Cause	Solution
Will not lock	• Lockbolt spring broken or defective	• Replace lock bolt spring
High effort (required to turn ignition key and lock cylinder)	• Lock cylinder defective • Ignition switch defective • Rack preload spring broken or deformed • Burr on lock sector, lock rack, housing, support or remote rod coupling • Bent sector shaft • Defective lock rack • Remote rod bent, deformed • Ignition switch mounting bracket bent • Distorted coupling slot in lock rack (tilt column)	• Replace lock cylinder • Replace ignition switch • Replace preload spring • Remove burr • Replace shaft • Replace lock rack • Replace rod • Straighten or replace • Replace lock rack
Will stick in "start"	• Remote rod deformed • Ignition switch mounting bracket bent	• Straighten or replace • Straighten or replace
Key cannot be remove in "off-lock"	• Ignition switch is not adjusted correctly • Defective lock cylinder	• Adjust switch • Replace lock cylinder

Troubleshooting the Steering Column (cont.)

Problem	Cause	Solution
Lock cylinder can be removed without depressing retainer	• Lock cylinder with defective retainer • Burr over retainer slot in housing cover or on cylinder retainer	• Replace lock cylinder • Remove burr
High effort on lock cylinder between "off" and "off-lock"	• Distorted lock rack • Burr on tang of shift gate (automatic column) • Gearshift linkage not adjusted	• Replace lock rack • Remove burr • Adjust linkage
Noise in column	• One click when in "off-lock" position and the steering wheel is moved (all except automatic column) • Coupling bolts not tightened • Lack of grease on bearings or bearing surfaces • Upper shaft bearing worn or broken • Lower shaft bearing worn or broken • Column not correctly aligned • Coupling pulled apart • Broken coupling lower joint • Steering shaft snap ring not seated • Shroud loose on shift bowl. Housing loose on jacket—will be noticed with ignition in "off-lock" and when torque is applied to steering wheel.	• Normal—lock bolt is seating • Tighten pinch bolts • Lubricate with chassis grease • Replace bearing assembly • Replace bearing. Check shaft and replace if scored. • Align column • Replace coupling • Repair or replace joint and align column • Replace ring. Check for proper seating in groove. • Position shroud over lugs on shift bowl. Tighten mounting screws.
High steering shaft effort	• Column misaligned • Defective upper or lower bearing • Tight steering shaft universal joint • Flash on I.D. of shift tube at plastic joint (tilt column only) • Upper or lower bearing seized	• Align column • Replace as required • Repair or replace • Replace shift tube • Replace bearings
Lash in mounted column assembly	• Column mounting bracket bolts loose • Broken weld nuts on column jacket • Column capsule bracket sheared • Column bracket to column jacket mounting bolts loose • Loose lock shoes in housing (tilt column only) • Loose pivot pins (tilt column only) • Loose lock shoe pin (tilt column only) • Loose support screws (tilt column only)	• Tighten bolts • Replace column jacket • Replace bracket assembly • Tighten to specified torque • Replace shoes • Replace pivot pins and support • Replace pin and housing • Tighten screws
Housing loose (tilt column only)	• Excessive clearance between holes in support or housing and pivot pin diameters • Housing support-screws loose	• Replace pivot pins and support • Tighten screws
Steering wheel loose—every other tilt position (tilt column only)	• Loose fit between lock shoe and lock shoe pivot pin	• Replace lock shoes and pivot pin
Steering column not locking in any tilt position (tilt column only)	• Lock shoe seized on pivot pin • Lock shoe grooves have burrs or are filled with foreign material • Lock shoe springs weak or broken	• Replace lock shoes and pin • Clean or replace lock shoes • Replace springs
Noise when tilting column (tilt column only)	• Upper tilt bumpers worn • Tilt spring rubbing in housing	• Replace tilt bumper • Lubricate with chassis grease

Troubleshooting the Steering Column (cont.)

Problem	Cause	Solution
One click when in "off-lock" position and the steering wheel is moved	• Seating of lock bolt	• None. Click is normal characteristic sound produced by lock bolt as it seats.
High shift effort (automatic and tilt column only)	• Column not correctly aligned • Lower bearing not aligned correctly • Lack of grease on seal or lower bearing areas	• Align column • Assemble correctly • Lubricate with chassis grease
Improper transmission shifting—automatic and tilt column only	• Sheared shift tube joint • Improper transmission gearshift linkage adjustment • Loose lower shift lever	• Replace shift tube • Adjust linkage • Replace shift tube

Troubleshooting the Ignition Switch

Problem	Cause	Solution
Ignition switch electrically inoperative	• Loose or defective switch connector • Feed wire open (fusible link) • Defective ignition switch	• Tighten or replace connector • Repair or replace • Replace ignition switch
Engine will not crank	• Ignition switch not adjusted properly	• Adjust switch
Ignition switch wil not actuate mechanically	• Defective ignition switch • Defective lock sector • Defective remote rod	• Replace switch • Replace lock sector • Replace remote rod
Ignition switch cannot be adjusted correctly	• Remote rod deformed	• Repair, straighten or replace

Troubleshooting the Turn Signal Switch

Problem	Cause	Solution
Turn signal will not cancel	• Loose switch mounting screws • Switch or anchor bosses broken • Broken, missing or out of position detent, or cancelling spring	• Tighten screws • Replace switch • Reposition springs or replace switch as required
Turn signal difficult to operate	• Turn signal lever loose • Switch yoke broken or distorted • Loose or misplaced springs • Foreign parts and/or materials in switch • Switch mounted loosely	• Tighten mounting screws • Replace switch • Reposition springs or replace switch • Remove foreign parts and/or material • Tighten mounting screws
Turn signal will not indicate lane change	• Broken lane change pressure pad or spring hanger • Broken, missing or misplaced lane change spring • Jammed wires	• Replace switch • Replace or reposition as required • Loosen mounting screws, reposition wires and retighten screws
Turn signal will not stay in turn position	• Foreign material or loose parts impeding movement of switch yoke • Defective switch	• Remove material and/or parts • Replace switch
Hazard switch cannot be pulled out	• Foreign material between hazard support cancelling leg and yoke	• Remove foreign material. No foreign material impeding function of hazard switch—replace turn signal switch.

Troubleshooting the Turn Signal Switch (cont.)

Problem	Cause	Solution
No turn signal lights	• Inoperative turn signal flasher • Defective or blown fuse • Loose chassis to column harness connector • Disconnect column to chassis connector. Connect new switch to chassis and operate switch by hand. If vehicle lights now operate normally, signal switch is inoperative • If vehicle lights do not operate, check chassis wiring for opens, grounds, etc.	• Replace turn signal flasher • Replace fuse • Connect securely • Replace signal switch • Repair chassis wiring as required
Instrument panel turn indicator lights on but not flashing	• Burned out or damaged front or rear turn signal bulb • If vehicle lights do not operate, check light sockets for high resistance connections, the chassis wiring for opens, grounds, etc. • Inoperative flasher • Loose chassis to column harness connection • Inoperative turn signal switch • To determine if turn signal switch is defective, substitute new switch into circuit and operate switch by hand. If the vehicle's lights operate normally, signal switch is inoperative.	• Replace bulb • Repair chassis wiring as required • Replace flasher • Connect securely • Replace turn signal switch • Replace turn signal switch
Stop light not on when turn indicated	• Loose column to chassis connection • • Disconnect column to chassis connector. Connect new switch into system without removing old. Operate switch by hand. If brake lights work with switch in the turn position, signal switch is defective. • If brake lights do not work, check connector to stop light sockets for grounds, opens, etc.	• Connect securely • Replace signal switch • Repair connector to stop light circuits using service manual as guide
Turn indicator panel lights not flashing	• Burned out bulbs • High resistance to ground at bulb socket • Opens, ground in wiring harness from front turn signal bulb socket to indicator lights	• Replace bulbs • Replace socket • Locate and repair as required
Turn signal lights flash very slowly	• High resistance ground at light sockets • Incorrect capacity turn signal flasher or bulb • If flashing rate is still extremely slow, check chassis wiring harness from the connector to light sockets for high resistance • Loose chassis to column harness connection • Disconnect column to chassis connector. Connect new switch into system without removing old.	• Repair high resistance grounds at light sockets • Replace turn signal flasher or bulb • Locate and repair as required • Connect securely • Replace turn signal switch

Troubleshooting the Turn Signal Switch (Cont.)

Problem	Cause	Solution
	Operate switch by hand. If flashing occurs at normal rate, the signal switch is defective.	
Hazard signal lights will not flash—turn signal functions normally	• Blow fuse	• Replace fuse
	• Inoperative hazard warning flasher	• Replace hazard warning flasher in fuse panel
	• Loose chassis-to-column harness connection	• Conect securely
	• Disconnect column to chassis connector. Connect new switch into system without removing old. Depress the hazard warning lights. If they now work normally, turn signal switch is defective.	• Replace turn signal switch
	• If lights do not flash, check wiring harness "K" lead for open between hazard flasher and connector. If open, fuse block is defective	• Repair or replace brown wire or connector as required

pivot freely. Otherwise the spring might break.

6. On rubber bushed pivot bolts and locknuts (or lockwasher and nut) only tighten the bolt enough to hold the bushings in position until the vehicle is lowered from the jack.

7. Connect the shackle. On rubber bushed shackles install the bolts as in step 6 above. For U-shackles, insert the shackle through the frame bracket and eye of the spring. Holding the U-shackle tightly against the frame, start the upper bushing on the shackle, taking care that when it enters the thread in the frame it does not crossthread. Screw the bushing on the shackle tightly against the spring eye, and thread the bushing in approximately half way. Then, alternately from top bushing to lower bushing, turn them in until the head of the bushing is snug against the frame bracket and the bushing in the spring eye is $1/32''$ (0.79375mm) away from the spring as measured from the inside of the hexagon head in the spring. Lubricate the bushing and then try the flex of the shackle, which must be free. If a shackle is tight, rethread the bushings on the shackle.

8. Move the axle into position on the spring by lowering or raising the axle jack. Install the

1. Bracket and shaft
2. Axle bumper
3. Bolt and lockwasher
4. Bushing
5. Washer
6. Cotter pin
7. Bolt
8. Nut
9. Cotter pin
10. Bracket
11. Bushing
12. Bolt
13. Spring
14. Left plate and shaft
15. Lockwasher
16. Nut
17. Shock absorber
18. Bolt
19. Plate
20. Bushing
21. Bearing
22. Nut
23. Grease seal
24. Grease retainer
25. Spring shackle
26. Spring shackle bracket

2-wd front suspension, with the solid I-beam front axle

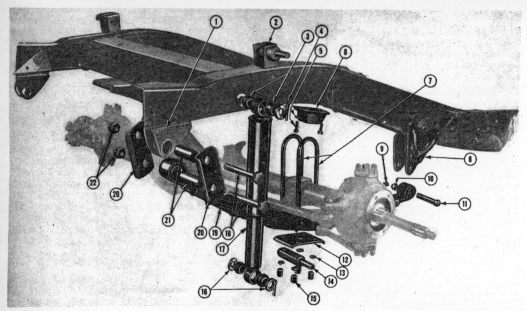

1. Bracket	9. Lubrication fitting	17. Front shock absorber
2. Bracket and shaft	10. Nut	18. Bolt
3. Bushing	11. Bolt	19. Front spring
4. Cotter pin	12. Plate	20. Spring shackle side plate
5. Bolt and lockwasher	13. Lockwasher	21. Silent-Bloc bushing
6. Axle bumper	14. Bracket	22. Nut
7. Clip	15. Nut	
8. Bracket and reinforcement	16. Special washer	

4-wd Utility front suspension

spring clip bolts, spring plate, lockwashers, and nuts. Torque the nuts to 50–55 ft.lb. Avoid overtightening. Be sure the spring is free to move at both ends.

9. Remove both jacks. On rubber bushed shackles and pivot bolts, allow the weight of the vehicle to seat the bushings in their operating positions. Then torque the nuts to 27–30 ft.lb.

EARLY UTILITY MODELS WITH PLANAR FRONT SUSPENSION

1. Raise and support the front end on jackstands.

2. Let the wheels hang to relieve spring tension.

3. Support the spring and disconnect the spring eyes at the knuckle supports.

4. Remove the spring.

5. Installation is the reverse of removal. Centralize the spring eye in the lower end of the knuckle support before starting the threaded pin. Torque the pivot bolts to 35 ft.lb.

1972–87

1. Raise the vehicle with a jack under the axle. Place a jackstand under the frame side rail. Then lower the axle jack so the load is re-lieved from the spring and the wheels just touch the floor.

2. Disconnect the shock absorber from the spring clip plate. On models through 1986, disconnect the stabilizer bar. On 1987 models, loosen, but don't remove, the front stabilizer bar link nut.

3. Remove the nuts which secure the spring clips (U-bolts). Remove the spring plate and spring clips. Free the spring from the axle by raising the axle.

4. Remove the pivot bolt nut and drive out the pivot bolt. Disconnect the shackle.

5. With the spring removed, the spring shackle and/or shackle plate may be removed from the spring.

6. Inspect the bushings in the eye of the main spring leaf and the bushings of the spring shackle for excessive wear. Replace if necessary.

7. The spring can be disassembled for replacing an individual spring leaf, by removing the clips and the center bolts.

8. To install the spring on the vehicle, with the bushings in place and the spring shackle attached to the springs, position the spring in the pivot hanger and install the pivot bolt and lock nut. Only tighten the lock nut enough to

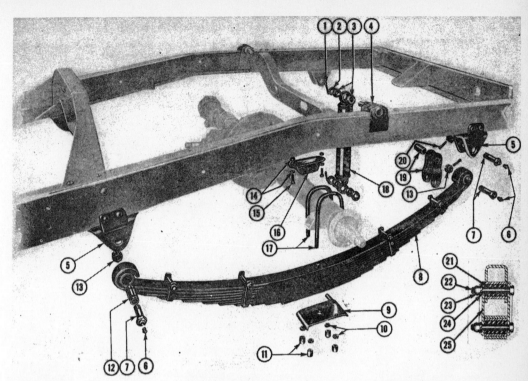

1. Cotter pin
2. Special washer
3. Bushing
4. Bracket and shaft
5. Rear spring hanger
6. Lubrication fitting
7. Bolt
8. Rear spring
9. Plate and shaft
10. Lockwasher
11. Nut
12. Rear spring eye bushing
13. Nut
14. Nut and lockwasher
15. Bolt
16. Axle bumper
17. Clip
18. Rear shock absorber
19. Rear spring shackle
20. Cotter pin
21. Silent-Bloc bushing
22. Bolt
23. Nut
24. Lockwasher
25. Spring shackle side plate

4-wd Utility rear suspension

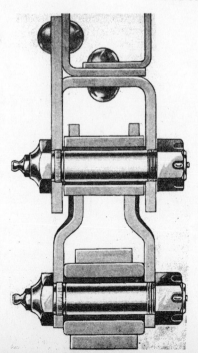

4-wd Utility rear shackle

hold the bushings in position until the vehicle is lowered from the jack.

9. Position the spring and install the shackle, shackle bolts, shackle plate if applicable, lockwasher, and nut. Only finger tighten the nuts at this time.

10. Move the axle into position on the spring by lowering the axle jack. Place the spring center bolt in the axle saddle hole. Install the spring clips, spring plate, lockwashers and nuts. Torque the $\frac{7}{16}$" (11.1125mm) nuts to 36–42 ft.lb. and the $\frac{1}{2}$" (12.7mm) nuts to 45–65 ft.lb. and the $\frac{9}{16}$" (14.2875mm) nuts to 100 ft.lb.

NOTE: *Be sure that the center bolt is properly centered in the axle saddle.*

11. Connect the shock absorber.

12. Remove the jack and allow the weight of the vehicle to seat the bushings in their operating positions. On models through 1976, torque the $\frac{7}{16}$" (11.1125mm) spring pivot bolt nuts and spring shackle nuts to 35–50 ft.lb. Torque the $\frac{5}{8}$" (15.875mm) shackle nuts 55–75 ft.lb. On 1977 and later models, tighten pivot bolts to 100 ft.lb., and shackle nuts to 24 ft.lb.

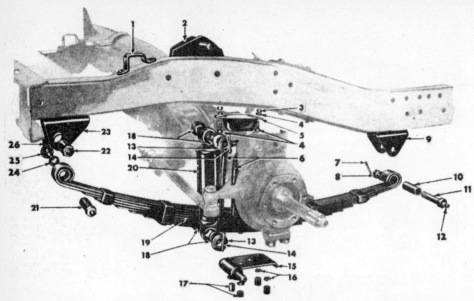

1. Bracket
2. Bracket and shaft
3. Nut
4. Screw and lockwasher
5. Axle bumper
6. Left clip
7. Cotter pin

8. Nut
9. Bracket
10. Eye bushing
11. Pivot bolt
12. Lubrication fitting
13. Washer
14. Cotter pin

15. Plate and shaft
16. Lockwasher
17. Nut
18. Bushing
19. Front spring
20. Shock absorber
21. Lower bushing

22. Upper bushing
23. Bracket
24. Grease seal retainer
25. Grease seal
26. U-bolt

CJ-2A, CJ-3A and early CJ-3B front spring assembly

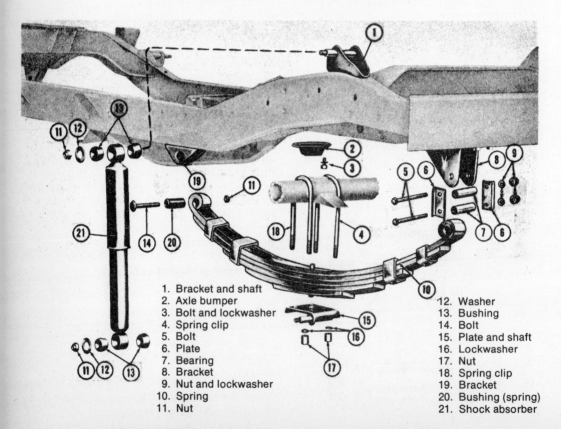

1. Bracket and shaft
2. Axle bumper
3. Bolt and lockwasher
4. Spring clip
5. Bolt
6. Plate
7. Bearing
8. Bracket
9. Nut and lockwasher
10. Spring
11. Nut

12. Washer
13. Bushing
14. Bolt
15. Plate and shaft
16. Lockwasher
17. Nut
18. Spring clip
19. Bracket
20. Bushing (spring)
21. Shock absorber

Front spring and shock absorber, late CJ-3B and early CJ-5 and CJ-6

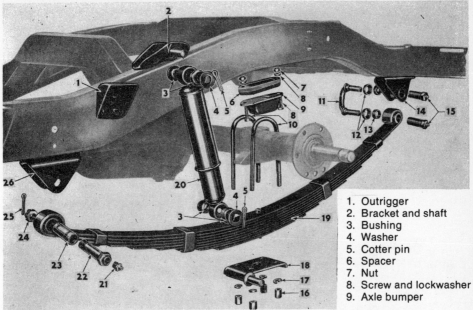

1. Outrigger
2. Bracket and shaft
3. Bushing
4. Washer
5. Cotter pin
6. Spacer
7. Nut
8. Screw and lockwasher
9. Axle bumper

10. Spring clip
11. Spring shackle "U" bolt
12. Grease seal retainer
13. Grease seal
14. Bracket
15. Bushing

16. Nut
17. Lockwasher
18. Plate and shaft
19. Rear spring
20. Shock absorber
21. Lubrication fitting

22. Pivot bolt
23. Eye bushing
24. Nut
25. Cotter pin
26. Bracket

Rear spring and shock absorber, CJ-2A, CJ-3A and CJ-3B

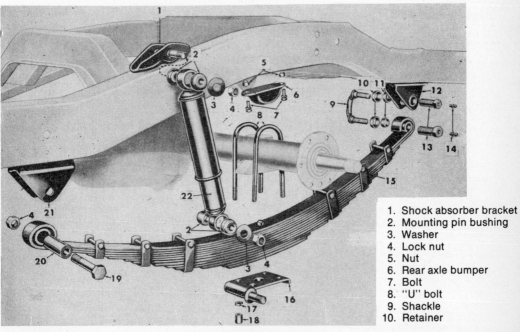

1. Shock absorber bracket
2. Mounting pin bushing
3. Washer
4. Lock nut
5. Nut
6. Rear axle bumper
7. Bolt
8. "U" bolt
9. Shackle
10. Retainer

11. Grease seal
12. Bracket
13. Threaded shackle bushing
14. Lube fitting

15. Rear spring assembly
16. Rear spring clip plate
17. Lockwasher
18. "U" bolt nut

19. Pivot bolt
20. Rubber bushing
21. Spring pivot bracket
22. Shock absorber assembly

Rear spring and shock absorber, CJ-5 and CJ-6 through 1971. Late models had no grease fittings in the shackle

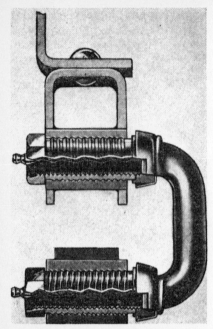

Front spring shackles with grease fittings used through early 1957. Right hand thread bushings have plain, hex heads. Left hand thread bushings have a groove around the heads

Shock Absorbers

REMOVAL AND INSTALLATION

All Except the Wrangler's Front Shocks

1. Remove the locknuts and washers. Utility, CJ-2A, CJ-3A and CJ-3B models have cotter pins instead of locknuts. Remove the cotter pins and washers on these models.

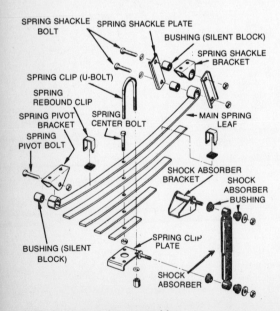

1972–75 front spring assembly

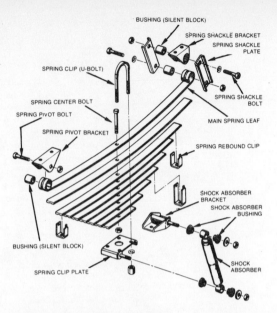

1972–75 rear spring assembly

2. Pull the shock absorber eyes and rubber bushings from the mounting pins.

3. Install the shocks in reverse order of the removal procedure. Torque the upper bolt to 35 ft.lb. (45 ft.lb. on the Wrangler), and the lower bolt to 45 ft.lb.

Wrangler Front Shock Absorbers

1. Remove the upper end nut, washer and grommet from the shock absorber stem.

2. Raise and support the front end on jackstands.

3. Unbolt the lower end and remove the shock absorber.

4. Remove the remaining upper grommet.

5. If the shock absorbers are being replaced, make sure that you use new grommets at the upper end. If you are reusing the shocks, it's a good idea to get new grommets if they show any signs of wear or are more than a year old.

6. Install the new lower grommet on the shock stem, with the shoulder facing upwards.

7. Mount the shock at the lower end, with the nut finger tight.

8. Guide the shock stem into the mounting hole in the frame bracket.

9. Torque the lower end nut to 45 ft.lb.

10. Lower the truck.

11. Install the new upper end grommet with the shoulder facing downwards.

12. Align the shoulders of the two upper end grommets in the frame mounting hole. Install the washer and nut. Torque the nut to 8 ft.lb. (96 in.lb.).

NOTE: *Squeaking usually occurs when movement takes place between the rubber bushings and the metal parts. The squeaking*

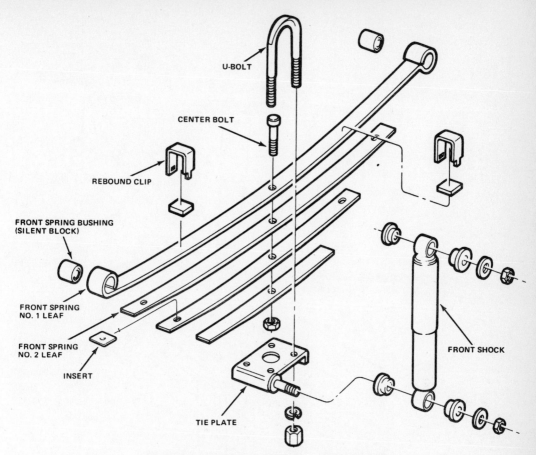

U-BOLT

CENTER BOLT

REBOUND CLIP

FRONT SPRING BUSHING
(SILENT BLOCK)

FRONT SPRING
NO. 1 LEAF

FRONT SPRING
NO. 2 LEAF

INSERT

TIE PLATE

FRONT SHOCK

Front spring and shock absorber, 1976–78 models

*may be eliminated by placing the bushings
under greater pressure. This is accomplished
either by adding additional washers where
the cotter pins are used or by tightening the
locknuts. Do not use mineral lubricant to stop
the squeaking as it will deteriorate the
rubber.*

Front Stabilizer Bar

REMOVAL AND INSTALLATION

1. Raise and support the front end on
jackstands.
2. Unbolt the stabilizer bar from the vertical links.
3. Unbolt the stabilizer bar from the frame
brackets.
4. Replace any worn or damaged rubber
parts.
5. Install the stabilizer bar at the links first,
hand tightening the fasteners.
6. Install the frame brackets, hand tightening the fasteners.
7. Make sure everything is aligned and
tighten the frame bracket bolts to 30 ft.lb. on

the Wrangler; 35 ft.lb. on the CJ-5, CJ-6, CJ-7
and Scrambler.
8. Tighten the link nuts to 45 ft.lb. on the
Wrangler; 55 ft.lb. on the CJ-5, CJ-6, CJ-7 and
Scrambler.

Track Bar

REMOVAL AND INSTALLATION

Wrangler

FRONT

1. Raise and support the front end on
jackstands.
2. Unbolt the bar from the frame bracket
and the axle bracket.
3. Installation is the reverse of removal.
Torque the bolts to 74 ft.lb.

REAR

1. Raise and support the rear end on
jackstands.
2. Unbolt the bar from the frame bracket.
3. Unbolt the bar from the axle bracket.
4. Remove the bar.
5. Installation is the reverse of removal.
Torque the bolts to 74 ft.lb.

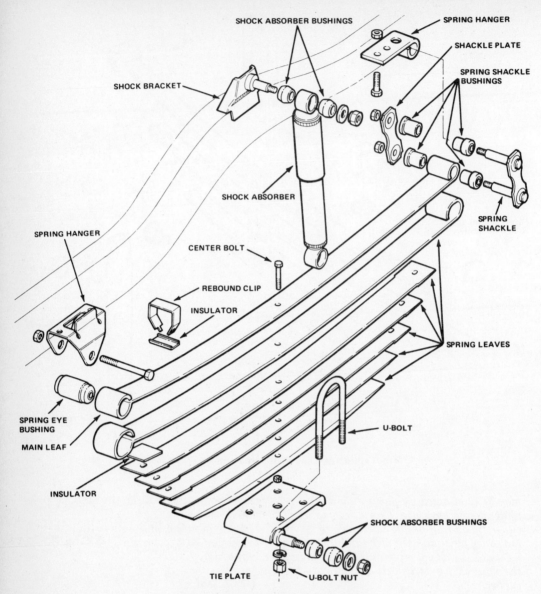

SHOCK ABSORBER BUSHINGS

SPRING HANGER

SHACKLE PLATE

SPRING SHACKLE BUSHINGS

SHOCK BRACKET

SHOCK ABSORBER

SPRING SHACKLE

SPRING HANGER

CENTER BOLT

REBOUND CLIP

INSULATOR

SPRING LEAVES

SPRING EYE BUSHING

MAIN LEAF

INSULATOR

U-BOLT

SHOCK ABSORBER BUSHINGS

TIE PLATE

U-BOLT NUT

Front suspension for 1979–86 models

STEERING

Steering Knuckle and Pivot Pins

REMOVAL AND INSTALLATION

1945–71

4-WD

1. Remove the eight screws that hold the oil seal retainer in place.

2. Remove the four screws which secure the lower pivot pin bearing cap.

3. Remove the four screws which hold the upper bearing cap in place. On CJ-2A models before serial number 22972, the nuts also hold the steering arm in place.

4. Remove the bearing cap. On CJ-2A and 3A, remove the brake hose shield.

5. The steering knuckle can now be removed from the axle.

6. Wash all of the parts in cleaning solvent.

7. Replace any worn or damaged parts. Inspect the bearings and races for scores, cracks, or chips. Should the bearing cups be damaged, they may be removed and installed with a driver.

8. To install, reverse the removal procedure. When reinstalling the steering knuckle sufficient shims must be installed under the top bearing cap to obtain the correct preload on the bearing. Shims are available in 0.003″

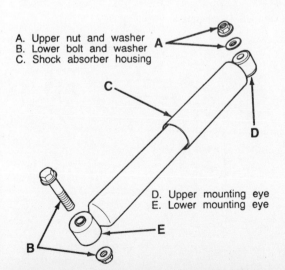

A. Shift motor
B. Shock absorber lower end
C. Link
D. Rear shackle bolt
E. Front shackle bolts
F. Spring tie plates
G. Differential housing
H. Driveshaft yoke

1987 front suspension

A. Upper nut and washer
B. Lower bolt and washer
C. Shock absorber housing
D. Upper mounting eye
E. Lower mounting eye

Shock absorber type used on the front and rear of all Jeep vehicles, except the front of Wrangler models

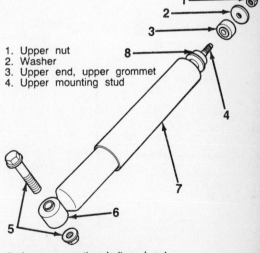

1. Upper nut
2. Washer
3. Upper end, upper grommet
4. Upper mounting stud
5. Lower mounting bolt and nut
6. Lower mounting eye
7. Shock absorber housing
8. Upper end, lower grommet

Shock absorber used on the front of Wrangler models

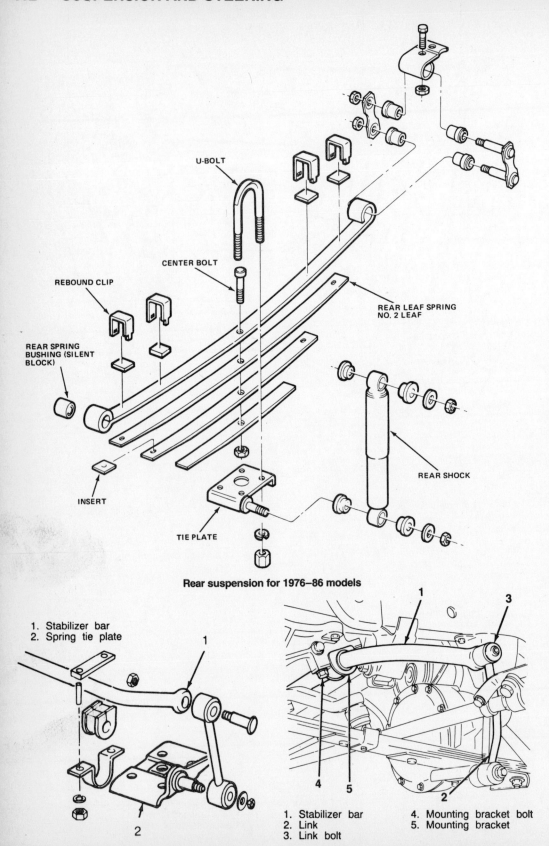

U-BOLT

CENTER BOLT

REBOUND CLIP

REAR LEAF SPRING NO. 2 LEAF

REAR SPRING BUSHING (SILENT BLOCK)

REAR SHOCK

INSERT

TIE PLATE

Rear suspension for 1976–86 models

1. Stabilizer bar
2. Spring tie plate

Front stabilizer bar used on all models through 1986

1. Stabilizer bar
2. Link
3. Link bolt
4. Mounting bracket bolt
5. Mounting bracket

Front stabilizer bar used on 1987 models

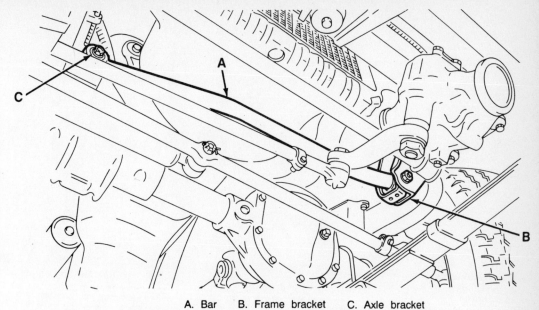

A. Bar   B. Frame bracket   C. Axle bracket
Front track bar on the Wrangler

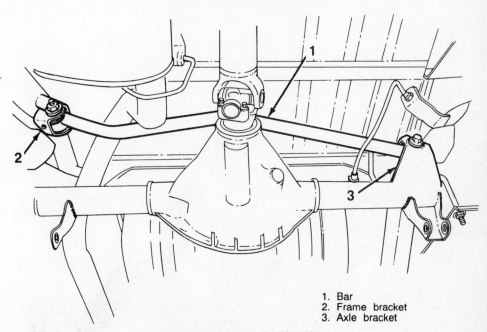

1. Bar
2. Frame bracket
3. Axle bracket

Rear track bar on the Wrangler

(0.0762mm), 0.005″ (0.127mm), 0.010″ (0.254mm), and 0.030″ (0.762mm). thicknesses. Install only one shim of the above thicknesses at the top only. Install the bearing caps, lockwashers, and screws, and tighten securely.

You can check the preload on the bearings by hooking a spring scale in the hole in the knuckle arm for the tie rod sprocket. Take the scale reading when the knuckle has just started its sweep.

The pivot pin bearing preload should be 12–16 lbs. with the oil seal removed. Remove or add shims to obtain a preload within these limits. If all shims are removed and adequate preload is still not obtained, a washer may be used under the top bearing cap to increase preload. When a washer is used, shims may have to be reinstalled to obtain proper adjustment.

2-WD w/SOLID I-BEAM FRONT AXLE

1. Raise and support the front end on jackstands.

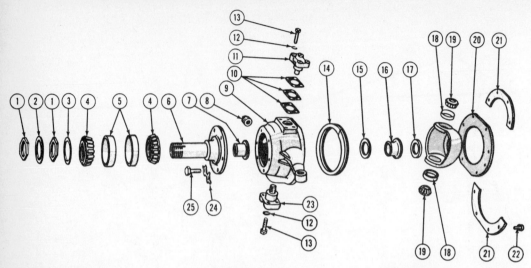

1. Bearing adjusting nut
2. Lockwasher
3. Lockwasher
4. Bearing cone and rollers
5. Bearing cup
6. Spindle
7. Bushing
8. Filler plug
9. Left knuckle and arm

10. Shims
11. Upper bearing cap
12. Lockwasher
13. Bolt
14. Oil seal and backing ring
15. Thrust washer
16. Axle pilot
17. Oil seal
18. Bearing cup

19. Bearing cone and rollers
20. Oil seal
21. Retainer
22. Bolt
23. Lower bearing cap
24. Lock strap
25. Bolt

1945–71 steering knuckle and wheel bearings

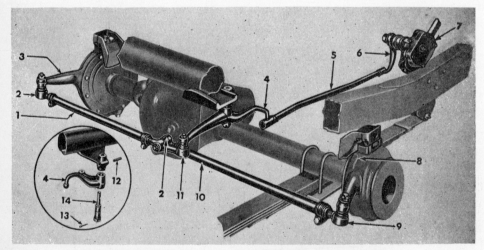

1. Tie rod—right
2. Tie rod socket—right
3. Knuckle and arm—right
4. Steering bell crank
5. Steering connecting rod
6. Steering gear arm
7. Steering gear housing

8. Knuckle and arm—left
9. Tie rod socket—left
10. Tie rod—left
11. Socket assembly
12. Steering bell crank pin
13. Steering bell crank cotter pin
14. Steering bell crank shaft

Steering system, CJ-2A models before serial number 22972

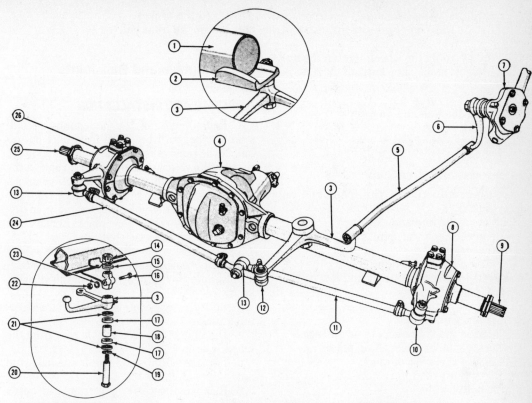

1. Frame cross tube (CJ-3B)
2. Steering bellcrank bracket
3. Steering bellcrank
4. Front axle assembly
5. Steering connecting rod
6. Steering gear arm
7. Steering gear
8. Left steering knuckle and arm
9. Left shaft and universal joint
10. Left tie rod socket
11. Left steering tie rod
12. Left tie rod socket
13. Right tie rod socket
14. Bellcrank nut
15. Washer
16. Bolt
17. Bellcrank bearing
18. Bearing spacer
19. Washer
20. Bellcrank shaft
21. Bearing seal
22. Nut
23. Lockwasher
24. Right steering tie rod
25. Right shaft and universal joint
26. Right steering knuckle and arm

Steering system on CJ-2A (ser. 22972 and up), CJ-3A, CJ-3B, and CJ-5 and CJ-6 through 1971

2. Remove the hub and dust caps.

3. Remove the cotter pin, wheel retaining nut and washer.

4. Pull the wheel out slightly to free the outer bearing, remove the bearing and remove the wheel and hub assembly.

5. Disconnect the brake line at the wheel cylinder and cap the end.

6. Remove the brake shoes and springs.

7. Remove the brake backing plate.

8. Remove the pivot pin lock.

9. Remove the top expansion plug and drive out the pin through the bottom with the lower plug.

NOTE: *There is a shim between the upper face of the axle and the spindle. Don't lose it!*

10. Remove the thrust bearing and bushings.

11. If new bushings are being installed, they must be reamed for a running fit with the pivot pins. Be sure that the oil holes in the bushings are aligned with their lubrication fittings.

12. If the thrust bearing shows any signs of wear, replace it.

13. Install the pivot pin, aligning the notch with the pin hole.

14. When assembling the knuckle, check for play between the axle and inner face of the knuckle. If play seems excessive, use a different size shim. Shims were available in 0.011" (0.279mm), 0.033" (0.838mm) and 0.035" (0.889mm).

15. Install the top expansion plug and drive out the pin through the bottom with the lower plug.

16. Install the pivot pin lock.

17. Install the brake backing plate.

18. Install the brake shoes and springs.

19. Connect the brake line at the wheel cylinder.

20. Install the wheel and hub assembly.

21. Install the outer bearing.
22. Install the wheel retaining nut and washer.
23. While turning the wheel, tighten the nut until the wheel binds, then back off the nut $\frac{1}{6}$–$\frac{1}{4}$ turn to free the bearing.
24. Install the cotter pin.
25. Install the hub and dust caps.
26. Bleed the brakes.
27. Lower the front end.

2-WD w/PLANAR FRONT SUSPENSION

1. Raise and support the front end on jackstands.
2. Remove the hub and dust caps.
3. Remove the cotter pin, wheel retaining nut and washer.
4. Pull the wheel out slightly to free the outer bearing, remove the bearing and remove the wheel and hub assembly.
5. Disconnect the brake line at the wheel cylinder and cap the end.
6. Remove the brake shoes and springs.
7. Remove the brake backing plate.
8. Remove the pivot pin lock.
9. Use a sharp drift to remove the pivot pin lower expansion plug.
10. Drive the pivot pin upward until the needle bearing assembly can be removed.
11. Drive the pivot pin out through the bottom.
12. Remove the bushings from the lower part of the spindle.
13. If new bushings are being installed, they must be reamed for a running fit with the pivot pins. Be sure that the oil holes in the bushings are aligned with their lubrication fittings.
14. If the thrust bearing shows any signs of wear, replace it.
15. Drive the pivot pin in through the bottom.
16. Drive the pivot pin upward until the needle bearing assembly can be installed.
17. Install the pivot pin lower expansion plug.
18. Install the pivot pin lock.
19. Install the brake backing plate.
20. Install the brake shoes and springs.
21. Connect the brake line at the wheel cylinder.
22. Install the wheel and hub assembly.
23. Install the outer bearing.
24. Install the wheel retaining nut and washer.
25. While turning the wheel, tighten the nut until the wheel binds, then back off the nut $\frac{1}{6}$–$\frac{1}{4}$ turn to free the bearing.
26. Install a new cotter pin.
27. Install the hub and dust caps.

28. Bleed the brakes.
29. Lower the front end.

Open Knuckle and Ball Joints 1972–86

REMOVAL AND INSTALLATION

1. Replacement of the ball joints, or ball stud, as they will be called from here on, requires the removal of the steering knuckle. To remove the steering knuckle, first remove the wheel, brake drum or disc, and hub as an assembly. Remove the brake assembly from the spindle. Position the brake assembly on the front axle in a convenient place. Remove the snapring from the axle shaft.
2. Remove the spindle and bearing assembly. It may be necessary to tap the spindle with a soft mallet to disengage it from the steering knuckle.
3. Slide the axle shaft out through the steering knuckle.
4. Disconnect the steering tie rods from the knuckle arm.
5. Remove and discard the lower ball stud nut.
6. Remove the cotter pin from the upper stud. Loosen the upper stud until the top edge of the nut is flush with the top end of the stud.
7. Use a lead hammer to unseat the upper and lower studs from the yoke. Remove the upper nut and the knuckle assembly.
8. Remove the ball stud seat from the upper hole in the axle yoke. It is threaded in the hole. There are special wrenches available for removing the seat. Remove the lower ball stud snapring.
9. Securely clamp the knuckle assembly in a vise with the upper ball stud pointed down.
10. Using a puller and adapters, or a large socket or drift, of approximately the same size as the ball stud, and a mallet, drive the lower stud out of the knuckle.

NOTE: *Throughout this procedure, where a ball stud is either removed or installed, a hydraulic press or a two jawed gear puller can be used and, if at all possible, should be used to make the job easier. However, it is possible to complete the job using a mallet, drift and a large socket the same size as the ball studs.*

11. Use a puller and adapters to remove the upper ball stud, or, place the socket on the bottom surface of the upper ball stud. Place the drift through the hole where the lower ball stud was and place in on the socket. Drive the upper ball stud out of the knuckle with a mallet.
12. Before installing the lower ball stud, run the lower ball stud nut onto the stud just far

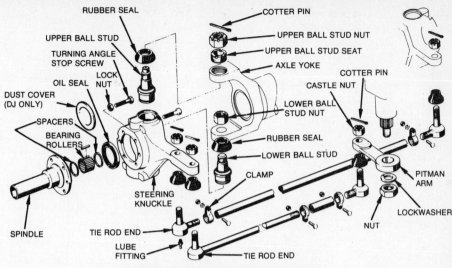

1972–77 steering knuckle and linkage

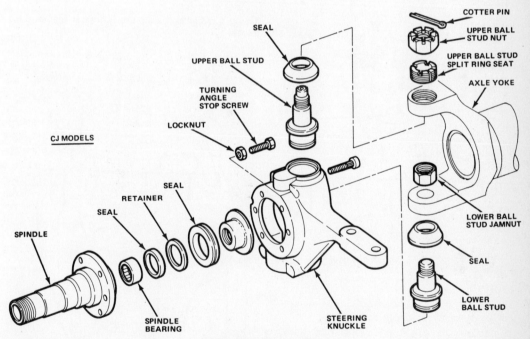

1978–86 steering knuckle

enough so the head of the stud is flush with the top edge of the nut.

13. Invert the knuckle in the vise. Position the lower ball stud in the knuckle with the nut in place. Use a puller to install the lower ball stud, or, place the same size socket over the nut and drive the ball stud into place with the drift and mallet.

14. Tighten the upper ball stud nut to 10–20 ft.lb. to draw the lower ball stud into the tapered hold in the yoke. Install the upper stud in the same manner as the lower. The drift will not be needed to install the upper ball stud.

15. Install the upper ball stud seat into the axle yoke. Use a new one if the old one shows evidence of wear. Torque the seat to 50 ft.lb.

16. Install the knuckle assembly onto the axle yoke. Install the lower stud nut. Tighten it to 70–90 ft.lb.

17. Install the upper stud nut and tighten it to 100 ft.lb. Install the cotter pin. If the cotter pin holes do not align, tighten the nut until the pin can be installed. Do not loosen the nut to align the holes.

18. Install the axle shaft.

19. Install the spindle and bearing assembly.

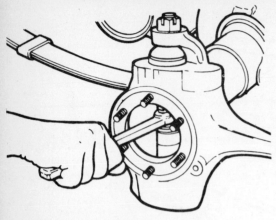

Removing lower ball stud nut

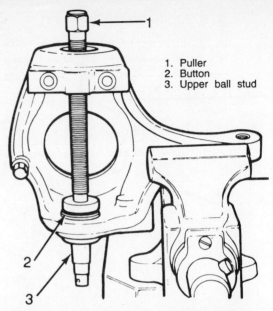

1. Puller
2. Button
3. Upper ball stud

Using a puller and adapters for upper ball stud removal

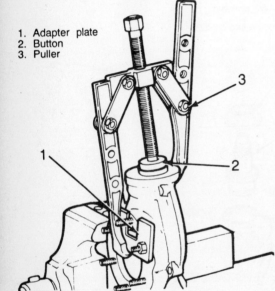

1. Adapter plate
2. Button
3. Puller

Using a puller for lower ball stud removal

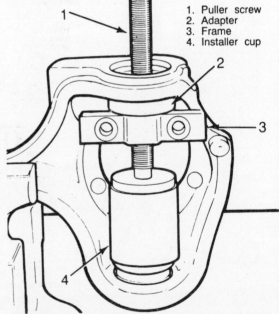

1. Puller screw
2. Adapter
3. Frame
4. Installer cup

20. Install the brake assembly.
21. Connect the steering rods.
22. Install the drum and hub, and wheel assembly.
23. Adjust the wheel bearings.

Steering Knuckle Oil Seal
REMOVAL AND INSTALLATION

Remove the old steering knuckle oil seal by removing the eight screws which hold it in place. Earlier production vehicles have two piece seals. Later production vehicles have a split oil seal and backing ring assembly, an oil seal felt, and two seal retainer plate halves.

Examine the spherical surface of the axle for scores or scratches which could damage the seal. Smooth any roughness with emery cloth.

Using a puller and adapters to install the lower ball stud

Before installing the oil seal felt, make a diagonal cut across the top side of the felt so that it may be slipped over the axle. Install the oil seal assembly in the sequence mentioned above, making sure the backing ring (of the oil seal and backing ring assembly) is toward the wheel.

After driving in wet, freezing weather swing the front wheels from side to side to remove

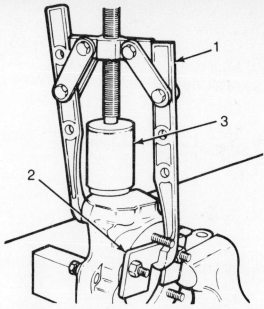

1. Puller   2. Plate   3. Installer cup

Using a puller and adapters to install the upper ball stud

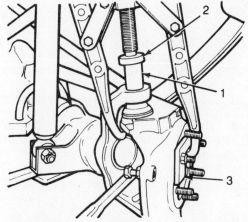

1. Nut socket   2. Button   3. Plate

Steering knuckle installation

moisture adhering to the oil seal and the spherical surface of the axle housing. This will prevent freezing with resultant damage to the seals. Should be vehicle be stored for any period of time, coat the surfaces with light grease to prevent rusting.

Steering Knuckle

REMOVAL AND INSTALLATION

Wrangler

1. Remove the outer axle shaft.
2. Remove the caliper anchor plate from the knuckle.

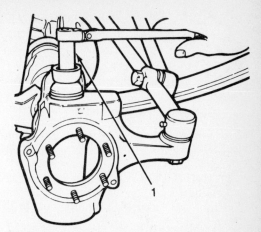

Tightening the upper ball stud seat. 1 is the nut wrench

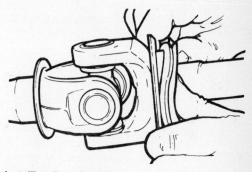

Installing the axle seal

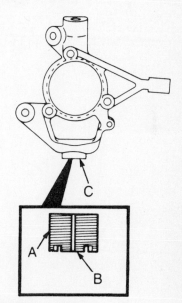

Split ring seat installation

3. Remove the knuckle-to-ball joint cotter pins and nuts.
4. Drive the knuckle out with a brass hammer.
NOTE: *A split ring seat is located in the bot-*

tom of the knuckle. During installation, this ring seat must be set to a depth of 5.23mm (0.206"). Measure the depth to the top of the ring seat (4).

5. Drive the knuckle in with a brass hammer.

NOTE: *A split ring seat is located in the bottom of the knuckle. During installation, this ring seat must be set to a depth of 5.23mm (0.206"). Measure the depth to the top of the ring seat (4).*

6. Install the knuckle-to-ball joint cotter pins and nuts.

7. Tighten the knuckle retaining nuts to 75 ft.lb.

8. Install the caliper anchor plate on the knuckle. Torque the caliper anchor bolts to 77 ft.lb.

9. Install the outer axle shaft.

Upper Ball Joint

REMOVAL AND INSTALLATION

Wrangler

NOTE: *This procedure requires the use of a special tool.*

1. Remove the steering knuckle.

2. Position a ball joint removal tool, J-34503-1 and 34503-3, in a C-clamp as shown, and on the upper ball joint.

3. Tighten the clamp screw to remove the joint.

4. Use tools J-34503-5 and J-34503-12, in a similar manner, as illustrated, to install the ball joint.

5. Install the knuckle.

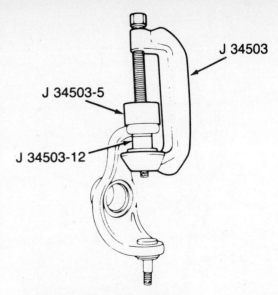

Wrangler upper ball joint installation

Lower Ball Joint

REMOVAL AND INSTALLATION

Wrangler

NOTE: *This procedure requires the use of a special tool.*

1. Remove the steering knuckle.

2. Position a ball joint removal tool, J-34503-1 and J-34503-3, as shown, on the lower ball joint.

3. Tighten the clamp screw to remove the joint.

4. Use tool J-34503-4 and J-34503-12 to install the ball joint by reversing the removal procedure.

5. Install the knuckle.

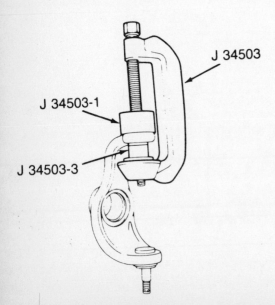

Wrangler upper ball joint removal

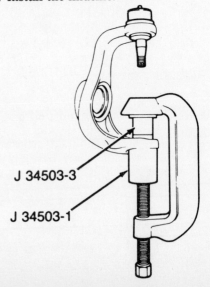

Wrangler lower ball joint removal

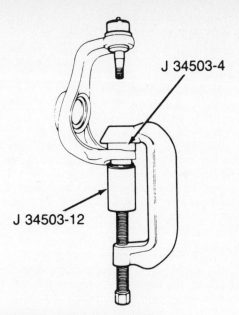

Wrangler lower ball joint installation

J 34503-4

J 34503-12

Upper Control Arm

REMOVAL AND INSTALLATION

Early Utility Models with the Planar Front Suspension

1. Raise and support the front end on jackstands.
2. Let the wheels hang to relieve spring tension.
3. Remove the wheels.
4. Remove the shock absorbers.
5. Remove the cotter pins, nuts and washers and disconnect the control arm at the knuckle support arm.
6. Rempove the control arm pin bushing.
7. Remove the nuts and remove the control arm and bushings from the frame brackets
8. Installation is the reverse of removal. When mounting the upper control arm pin bushing in the knuckle support, torque it to 175 ft.lb. Centralize the control arm assembly over the knuckle support before starting the threaded pin. This will provide the proper caster and equalize the clearance on each side for the dust seals.

Front End Alignment

Proper alignment of the front wheels must be maintained in order to ensure ease of steering and satisfactory tire life.

The most important factors of front wheel alignment are wheel camber, axle caster, and wheel toe-in.

Wheel toe-in is the distance by which the wheels are closer together at the front than at the rear.

1. Stop screw

1945–71 turning angle adjusting screw

Wheel camber is the amount the top of the wheels incline outward from the vertical.

Front axle caster is the amount in degrees that the steering pivot pins are tilted toward the rear of the vehicle. Positive caster is inclination of the top of the pivot pin toward the rear of the vehicle.

These points should be checked at regular intervals, particularly when the front axle has been subjected to a heavy impact. When check-

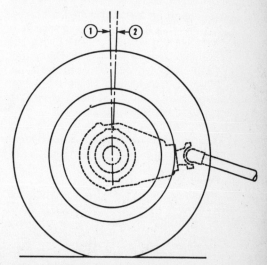

1. Vertical line   2. Caster angle

Caster

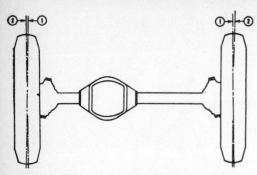

1. Vertical line   2. Camber angle

Camber

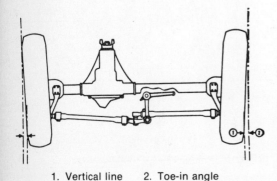

1. Vertical line   2. Toe-in angle

Toe-in

ing wheel alignment, it is important that wheel bearings and knuckle bearings (through 1971) be in proper adjustment. Loose bearings will affect instrument readings when checking the camber, pivot pin inclination, and toe-in.

Front wheel camber on 4-WD models, and solid I-beam 2-WD models is preset. Some alignment shops can correct camber to some extent by installing special tapered shims between the steering knuckle and the spindle.

Camber on early Utility models, with the Planar front suspension is controlled by a shim pack installed on each side, between the frame and the upper control arm support bracket. Shim thickness of 0.060″ (1.524mm) and 0.120″ (3.05mm) were used.

Caster is also preset, but can be altered by use of tapered shims between the axle pad and the springs. Wheel toe-in is adjustable.

TURNING ANGLE

To avoid damage to the U-joints, it is advisable to check the turning angle periodically. An adjustment turntable is advisable for properly determining the angle.

Correct turning angles are:

- CJ-2A and 3A, CJ-3B before ser. #57348-35326, CJ-5 before serial #57548-48284, CJ-6 before ser. #57748-12497: 23 degrees max.

- All models through 1971, after the above serial numbers: 27.5 degrees max.
- 1972–75 With standard (F78 x 15) tires: 34–35 degrees With larger optional tires: 31 degrees
- 1976: 31 degrees
- 1977: 29 degrees
- 1978–83: 31–32 degrees
- 1984–86: 30–31 degrees

To adjust the turning angle, loosen the lock-nut (on some early models, a securing weld will have to be broken) and turn the adjusting screw. The adjusting screw is located on the axle tube near the knuckle on early models, and on the knuckle, just below the axle center-line on later models.

CASTER ADJUSTMENT

Caster angle is established in the axle design by tilting the top of the kingpins forward so that an imaginary line through the center of the kingpins would strike the ground at a point ahead of the point of the contact.

The purpose of caster is to provide steering stability which will keep the front wheels in the straight ahead position and also assist in straightening up the wheels when coming out of a turn.

If the angle of caster, when accurately measured, is found to be incorrect, correct it to the specification given in this section by either installing new parts or installing caster shims between the axle pad and the springs.

If the camber and toe-in are correct and it is known that the axle is not twisted, a satisfactory check may be made by testing the vehicle on the road. Before road testing, make sure all tires are properly inflated, being particularly careful that both front tires are inflated to exactly the same pressure.

If the vehicle turns easily to either side but is hard to straighten out, insufficient caster for easy handling of the vehicle is indicated. If correction is necessary, it can usually be accomplished by installing shims between the springs and axle pads to secure the desired result.

CAMBER ADJUSTMENT

Except Early Utility Models with the Planar Front Suspension

The purpose of camber is to more nearly place the weight of the vehicle over the tire contact patch on the road to facilitate ease of steering. The result of excessive camber is irregular wear of the tires on the outside shoulders and is usually caused by bent axle parts.

The result of excessive negative or reverse camber will be hard steering and possibly a wandering condition. Tires will also wear on the inside shoulders. Negative camber is usually caused by excessive wear or looseness of the front wheel bearings, axle parts or the result of a sagging axle.

Unequal camber may cause any or a combination of the following conditions: unstable steering, wandering, kickback or road shock, shimmy or excessive tire wear. The cause of unequal camber is usually a bent steering knuckle or axle end.

Correct wheel camber is set in the axle at the time of manufacture. It is important that the camber be the same on both front wheels.

Planar Front Suspension

Camber is set by changing the shim pack thickness, located between the upper control arm bracket and the frame. Follow the procedure for upper control arm removal and installation, and change the shims as required.

TOE-IN ADJUSTMENT

Through 1971

The toe-in may be adjusted with a line or straight edge as the vehicle tread is the same in the front and rear. To set the adjustment both tie rods must be adjusted as outlined below: Set the tie rod end of the steering bellcrank at right angles with the front axle. Place a straight edge or line against the left rear wheel and left front wheel to determine if the wheel is in a straight ahead position. If the front wheel tire does not touch the straight edge at both the front and rear, it will be necessary to adjust the left tie rod by loosening the clamps on each end and turning the rod until the tire touches the straight edge.

Check the right hand side in the same manner, adjusting the tie rod if necessary making sure that the bellcrank remains at right angles to the axle. When it is determined that the front wheels are in the straight ahead position, set the toe-in by shortening each tie rod approximately ½ turn.

1972–87

First raise the front of the vehicle to free the front wheels. Turn the wheels to the straight ahead position. Use a Steadyrest® to scribe a pencil line in the center of each tire tread as the wheel is turned by hand. A good way to do this is to first coat a strip with chalk around the circumference of the tread at the center to form a base for a fine pencil line.

Measure the distance between the scribed lines at the front and rear of the wheels using care that both measurements are made at an equal distance from the floor. The distance be-

tween the lines should be greater at the rear than at the front by $\frac{3}{64}$" (1.19mm) to $\frac{3}{32}$" (2.238mm). To adjust, loosen the clamp bolts and turn the tie rod with a small pipe wrench. The tie rod is threaded with right and left hand threads to provide equal adjustment at both wheels. Do not overlook retightening the clamp bolts. It is common practice to measure between the wheel rims. This is satisfactory providing the wheels run true. By scribing a line on the tire tread, measurement is taken between the road contact points reducing error caused by wheel runout.

Steering Wheel
REMOVAL AND INSTALLATION
1945–75

1. Disconnect the negative battery cable.
2. Set the front tires in a straight ahead position.
3. Pull the horn button from the steering wheel.
4. Remove the steering wheel nut and horn button contact cup.
5. Scribe a line mark on the steering wheel and steering shaft if there is not one already. Release the turn signal assembly from the steering post and install a puller.
6. Remove the steering wheel and spring.
7. To install, align the scribe marks on the steering shaft with the steering wheel and secure the steering wheel spring, steering wheel, and horn button contact cup with the steering wheel nut.
8. Install the horn button.
9. Connect the battery cable and test the horn.

1976–87

NOTE: *Some steering shafts have metric threads. These are identified bu a groove cast into the shaft. See the accompanying illustration for an example.*

1. Disconnect the negative battery cable.
2. Place the front wheels in the straight ahead position.
3. Remove the horn button from the steering wheel. Turn the button until the locktabs on the button align with the notches in the contact cup and pull upward to remove it. With the sport wheel, just pull the button up.
4. Remove the steering wheel nut and washer.
5. If the Jeep is equipped with a sport style steering wheel, remove the horn button, nut and washer, bottom retaining ring, and horn contact ring.
6. Remove the plastic horn contact cup re-

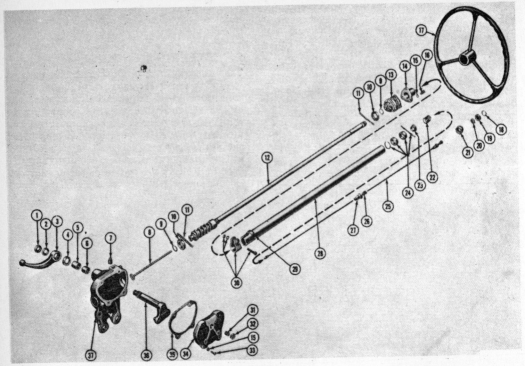

1. Nut	14. Upper cover	27. Spring cap
2. Lockwasher	15. Lockwasher	28. Steering column
3. Steering gear arm	16. Bolt	29. Oil hole cover
4. Lever shaft oil seal	17. Steering wheel	30. Clamp
5. Outer housing bushing	18. Horn button retainer	31. Adjusting screw
6. Inner housing bushing	19. Horn button	32. Nut
7. Filler plug	20. Horn button cap	33. Bolt
8. Cover and tube	21. Nut	34. Side cover
9. Ball retainer ring	22. Spring	35. Gasket
10. Cup	23. Spring seat	36. Shaft and lever
11. Ball (steel)	24. Bearing	37. Housing
12. Tube and cam	25. Horn cable	
13. Shims	26. Horn button spring	

1953–71 steering column and gear

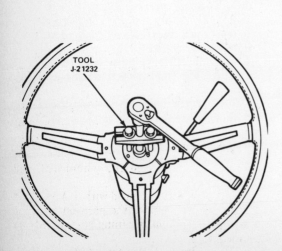

Steering wheel removal

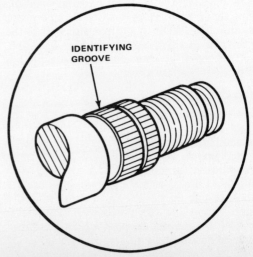

Metric steering shaft identification

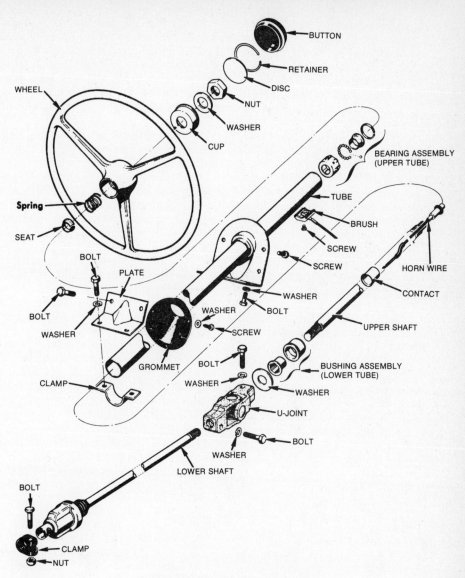

WHEEL

BUTTON

RETAINER

DISC

NUT

WASHER

CUP

Spring

SEAT

BOLT

PLATE

BOLT

WASHER

CLAMP

GROMMET

BOLT

WASHER

BOLT

WASHER

SCREW

BOLT

WASHER

BEARING ASSEMBLY
(UPPER TUBE)

TUBE

BRUSH

SCREW

SCREW

HORN WIRE

CONTACT

UPPER SHAFT

BUSHING ASSEMBLY
(LOWER TUBE)

WASHER

U-JOINT

BOLT

WASHER

LOWER SHAFT

BOLT

CLAMP

NUT

1972–75 steering column assembly

tainer and remove the cup and contact plate from the steering wheel.

7. Remove the horn contact pin and bushing from the steering wheel.

8. Paint or scribe alignment marks on the steering wheel and shaft for reference during assembly.

9. Remove the steering wheel using a puller.

10. Position the steering wheel on the shaft, aligning the scribed marks.

11. Install the horn contact pin and bushing.

12. Install the plastic horn contact cup retainer and install the cup and contact plate.

13. If the Jeep is equipped with a sport style steering wheel, install the horn button, nut and washer, bottom retaining ring, and horn contact ring.

14. Install the steering wheel nut and washer. Tighten the nut to 20 ft.lb. for 1976–77; 30 ft.lb. for 1978–86; 25 ft.lb. for 1987.

15. Install the horn button. Turn the button until the locktabs on the button align with the notches in the contact cup. With the sport wheel, just push the button on.

16. Connect the negative battery cable.

Turn Signal Switch
REPLACEMENT

1945–75

The turn signal switch is attached to the steering column; the whole unit is mounted externally. To remove the switch assembly, remove the attaching screws, unfasten the wires and remove the unit from the steering column. The most frequent causes of failure in the directional signal system are loose connections and burned out bulbs. A flashing rate of approximately twice normal usually indicates a burned out bulb in the circuit. When trouble in the signal switch is suspected, it is advisable to make a few checks to definitely locate the trouble before going tot he effort of removing the signal switch. First check the fuse. There is an inline fuse located between the ignition switch and the turn signal flasher. If the fuse checks out OK, next eliminate the flasher unit by substituting a known good flasher. If a new flasher does not cure the trouble, check the signal system wiring connections at the fuse and at the steering column connector.

NOTE: *If the right front parking light and the right rear stop light are inoperative, switch failure is indicated. If the brake lights function properly, the rear signal lights are OK.*

To check the switch on models through 1971, first put the control lever in the neutral position. Then disconnect the wire to the right side circuit and bridge it to the "L" terminal, thus by-passing the signal switch. If the right side circuit lights, the signal switch is inoperative and must be replaced.

To check out the switch on the 1972 and 1973 models, disconnect the switch at the six wire connector. Use a jumper wire from the white (battery feed) wire to the other wires. Circuitry is as follows:

- White to Orange: Right rear
- White to Black: Right front
- White to Yellow: Left front
- White to Blue: Left rear

If the lights in any of these circuits light then the switch is bad and must be replaced.

1976–79

1. Disconnect the negative battery cable.
2. Remove the steering wheel.
3. Loosen the anti-theft cover retaining screws on 1976 models and lift the cover from the steering column. It is not necessary to completely remove these screws.
4. Depress the lockplate and pry the round wire snapring from the steering shaft groove. A lockplate compressor tool is available for compressing the lockplate.
5. Remove the lockplate, directional signal canceling cam, upper bearing preload spring, and thrust washer from the steering shaft.
6. Move the directional signal actuating lever to the right turn position and remove the lever.
7. Depress the hazard warning light switch and remove the button by turning it counterclockwise.

8. Remove the directional signal wiring harness connector block from its mounting bracket on the right side of the lower column.
9. On vehicles equipped with an automatic transmission, use a stiff wire, such as a paper clip, to depress the lock tab which retains the shift quadrant light wire in the connector block.
10. Remove the directional signal switch retaining screws and pull the switch and wiring harness from the steering column.
11. Guide the wiring harness of the new switch into position and carefully align the switch assembly. make sure that the actuating lever pivot is correctly aligned and seated in the upper housing pivot boss prior to installing the retaining screws.
12. Install the directional signal lever and actuate the directional signal switch to assure correct operation.
13. Place the thrust washer, spring, and directional signal canceling cam on the upper end of the steering shaft.
14. Align the lockplate splines with the steering shaft splines and place the lockplate in position with the directional signal canceling cam shaft protruding through the dogleg opening in the lockplate.
15. Install the snapring.
16. Install the anti-theft cover.
17. Install the steering wheel and connect the negative battery cable.
18. Check the operation of the turn signal switch.

1980–87

1. Disconnect the battery ground.
2. Cover the painted areas of the column.
3. Remove the column-to-dash bezel.
4. Loosen the toe plate screws.
5. With tilt columns, place the column in the non-tilt position.
6. Remove the steering wheel.
7. Remove the lock plate cover.
8. Compress the lock plate and unseat the steering shaft snapring as follows:
   a. Check the steering shaft nut threads. Metric threads have an identifying groove in the steering wheel splines. SAE threads do not.
   b. With SAE threads use a compressor tool such as tool J-23653 to compress the lock plate and remove the snapring.
   c. If the shaft has metric threads, replace the forcing screw in the compressor with metric forcing screw J-23653-4 before using.
9. Remove the compressor and snapring.
10. Remove the lock plate, canceling cam and upper bearing preload spring.

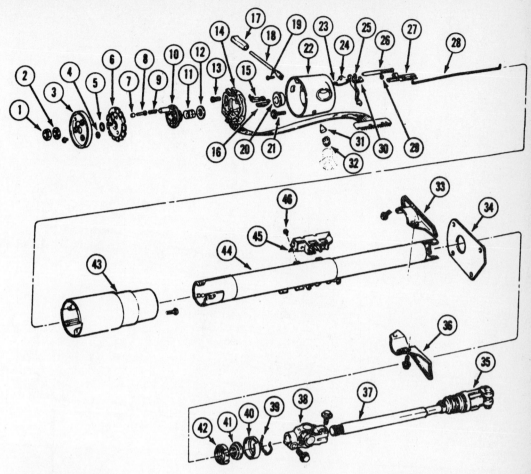

1. Steering wheel nut
2. Washer
3. Anti-theft cover
4. Anti-theft cover screw and retainer
5. Steering shaft snap-ring
6. Lockplate
7. Bushing
8. Horn contact pin
9. Spring
10. Concelling cam
11. Upper bearing preload spring
12. Thrust washer
13. Turn signal switch screw
14. Turn signal switch
15. Buzzer switch
16. Buzzer switch spring

17. Turn signal lever knob
18. Turn signal lever
19. Turn signal lever screw
20. Upper bearing
21. Housing retaining screw
22. Housing
23. Rack preload spring
24. Key release lever spring
25. Wave washer
26. Lockbolt
27. Lock rack
28. Remote rod
29. Spring washer
30. Key release lever
31. Hazard warning switch knob
32. Sector

33. Upper half of toe plate
34. Seal
35. Intermediate shaft coupling
36. Lower half of toe plate
37. Intermediate shaft
38. U-joint
39. Snap-ring
40. Retainer
41. Lower bearing
42. Lower bearing adapter
43. Shroud
44. Jacket
45. Ignition switch
46. Ignition switch screw

1976–79 steering column

11. Place the turn signal lever in the right turn position and remove the lever.

12. Remove the hazard warning knob. Press the knob inward and turn counterclockwise to remove it.

13. Remove the wiring harness protectors.

14. Disconnect the wiring harness connectors.

15. Remove the turn signal switch attaching screws and lift out the switch.

16. Install the turn signal switch and attaching screws. Torque the screws to 35 in.lb.

17. Connect the wiring harness connectors.

18. Install the wiring harness protectors.

19. With the turn signal switch in the neutral position, install the hazard warning knob. Press the knob inward and turn clockwise to install it.

20. Install the lever. Torque the attaching screws to 35 in.lb.

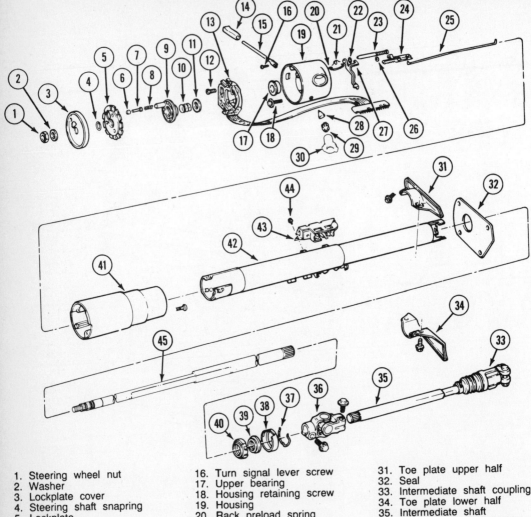

1. Steering wheel nut
2. Washer
3. Lockplate cover
4. Steering shaft snapring
5. Lockplate
6. Retainer
7. Horn contact pin
8. Spring
9. Canceling cam
10. Upper bearing preload spring
11. Thrust washer
12. Turn signal switch screw
13. Turn signal switch
14. Turn signal lever knob
15. Turn signal lever

16. Turn signal lever screw
17. Upper bearing
18. Housing retaining screw
19. Housing
20. Rack preload spring
21. Key release lever spring
22. Wave washer
23. Lock bolt
24. Lock rack
25. Remote rod
26. Spring washer
27. Key release lever
28. Hazard warning switch knob
29. Lock sector
30. Lock cylinder

31. Toe plate upper half
32. Seal
33. Intermediate shaft coupling
34. Toe plate lower half
35. Intermediate shaft
36. Intermediate shaft U-joint
37. Snapring
38. Retainer
39. Lower bearing
40. Lower bearing adapter
41. Shroud
42. Jacket
43. Ignition switch
44. Ignition switch screw
45. Steering shaft

1980–86 steering column, with manual transmission

21. Install the upper bearing preload spring.
22. Install the canceling cam.
23. Install the lock plate.
24. Using the compressor, install the snapring.
25. Install the lock plate cover.
26. Install the steering wheel.
27. Loosen the toe plate screws.
28. Install the column-to-dash bezel.
29. Connect the battery ground.

Ignition Switch

REPLACEMENT

1945–75

1. Disconnect the battery ground cable.
2. On models through 1972, unscrew the nut from the front of the instrument panel and remove the switch. Some early production Utility models had a switch held in place by a bezel

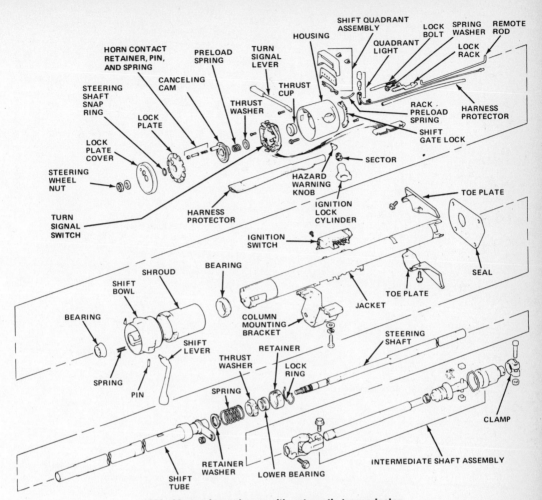

1980–86 steering column, with automatic transmission

Lockplate components

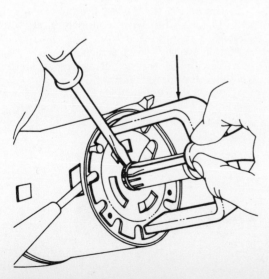

Using lockplate spring compressor

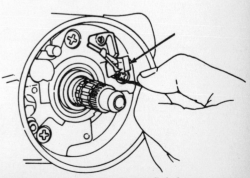

Removing the key warning switch buzzer components

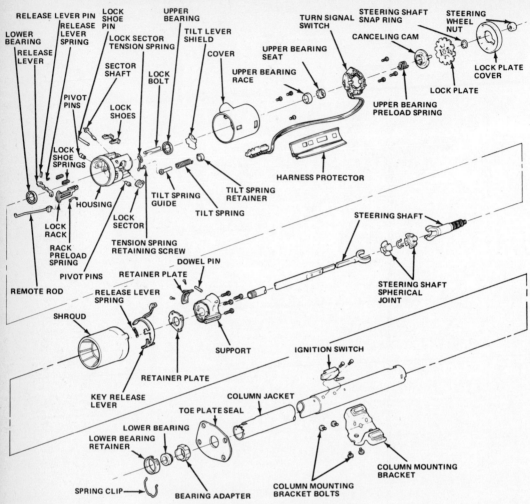

1980–86 steering column, with tilt wheel

and tension spring, rather than a threaded bezel.

3. On 1973–75 models, reach behind the panel and press the switch in against the spring. Turn the bezel counterclockwise to release.

4. Lower the switch and detach the wiring.

5. Reverse the procedure for installation.

1975–86

The ignition switch is on top of the lower part of the steering column, inside the vehicle.

1. Put the key in the lock and turn to the OFF/UNLOCKED position.

2. Disconnect the battery ground cable.

3. Detach the wire connectors at the switch.

4. Remove the switch screws.

5. Disconnect the actuating rod from the switch and remove the switch.

6. Move the switch slider all the way down the column. Move it back toward the steering wheel two clicks to the center OFF/UN-LOCKED position.

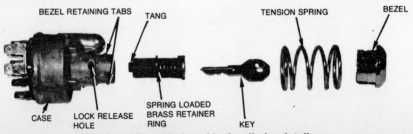

1973–75 ignition switch and lock cylinder details

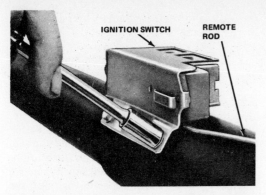

IGNITION SWITCH   **REMOTE ROD**

Ignition switch removal or installation, column mounted switches

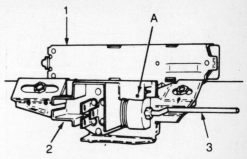

A. ³⁄₃₂" diameter hole
1. Ignition switch
2. Dimmer switch
3. Actuator rod

1987 dimmer switch

7. Engage the column actuating rod in the switch slider and fasten the switch down.

8. Connect the wire connectors, then the battery ground cable.

1987

1. Disconnect the battery ground.

2. Tape the dimmer switch actuator rod to the column to keep it from disengaging.

3. Remove the dimmer switch.

4. Unplug the wiring connector at the ignition switch.

5. Remove the attaching screws and lift the switch off of the column until it clears the actuator rod. Remove the switch.

6. When installing the ignition switch, engage the actuator rod in the bottom of the switch. Install the switch on the column and tighten the screws.

7. Adjust the ignition switch as follows:

   a. Insert the key and turn the lock cylinder to the OFF/UNLOCK position.

   b. Loosen the switch mounting screws.

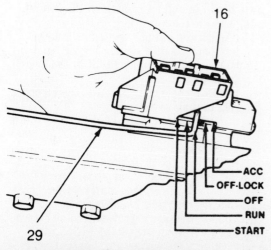

16

ACC
OFF-LOCK
OFF
RUN
START

29

1. Switch   2. Actuator rod

1987 ignition switch

   c. Move the switch down the column to eliminate any play and tighten the screws to 35 in.lb.

   d. Connect the wiring to the switch.

8. Engage the actuator rod in the dimmer switch and install the switch on the column.

9. Untape the rod.

10. Adjust the dimmer switch as follows:

   a. Compress the switch slightly and insert a ³⁄₃₂" (2.238mm) drill bit in the switch adjusting hole.

   b. Move the switch towards the steering wheel to remove any play.

   c. Tighten the attaching screws to 35 in.lb.

   d. Connect the battery ground.

   e. Remove the drill bit.

   f. Check the operation of the switch.

NOTE: *If your Jeep has a tilt column, check the switch operation in all positions.*

Ignition Lock Cylinder

REPLACEMENT

1945–75

CJ MODELS

1. Remove the ignition switch.

2. Put the key in the lock and turn it to the ON position.

3. Insert a heavy paper clip wire or something similar through the release hole in the side of the switch. Push in the retaining ring until the lock cylinder can be pulled out.

4. To install the new lock cylinder, line up the tang on the cylinder with the slot in the case and push the cylinder in.

5. Replace the switch.

UTILITY MODELS

1. Turn the key to the left, to the AUXILIARY position.

2. Insert a piece of heavy wire or unbent paper clip into the release hole in the lock cylin-

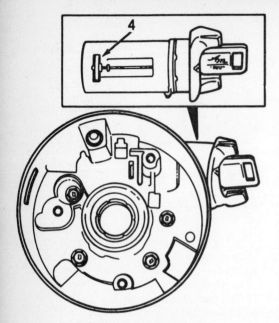

4. Lock cylinder retaining tab

1976–86 lock cylinder

der. This will compress the cylinder retainer.

3. Pull the cylinder out with the key.

4. Installation is the reverse of removal.

1976–86

1. Disconnect the battery ground cable.

2. Remove the turn signal switch as described earlier in this chapter. You don't have to remove the switch completely, just set it aside.

3. Insert the key. Position the key as follows.

• 1976–83: With manual transmission, put it in the ON position; with automatic, put it in OFF/LOCK.

• 1984–86: Two detent positions, clockwise, beyond OFF/LOCK.

4. Working through the slot next to the turn signal switch mounting boss, use a thin screwdriver to release the lock cylinder.

5. To install, insert the key in the new lock cylinder. Hold the sleeve and turn the key clockwise until it stops. Align the cylinder retaining tab with the housing slot and insert the cylinder. Push the cylinder in, rotate to engage, then push in until the retaining tab engages the housing groove.

6. The rest of the procedure is the reverse of removal.

1987

1. Disconnect the battery ground cable.

2. Remove the turn signal switch as described earlier in this chapter. You don't have to remove the switch completely, just set it aside.

3. Remove the wiper switch harness and any additional harnesses from the column.

4. Insert the key and turn it to the ON position.

5. Remove the key warning buzzer and clip, with needle nosed pliers, or a paper clip with a 90° bend. Don't remove the buzzer and clip separately, since the clip will fall into the column.

6. Using a thin bladed screwdriver, remove the lock cylinder retaining screw and pull the lock cylinder out of the column housing.

7. Before installation, insert the key into the cylinder. Hold the cylinder sleeve so it won't turn and rotate the key clockwise until it stops. This retracts the cylinder actuator.

8. Align the lock cylinder tab with the housing keyway.

9. Push the cylinder into the housing unti it bottoms.

10. Install the cylinder retaining screw and torque it to 40 in.lb.

11. Turn the key to ON.

12. Install the key warning buzzer switch and clip.

13. When installing the ignition switch, engage the actuator rod in the bottom of the switch. Install the switch on the column and tighten the screws.

14. Adjust the ignition switch as follows:

  a. Insert the key and turn the lock cylinder to the OFF/UNLOCK position.

  b. Loosen the switch mounting screws.

  c. Move the switch down the column to eliminate any play and tighten the screws to 35 in.lb.

  d. Connect the wiring to the switch.

15. Engage the actuator rod in the dimmer switch and install the switch on the column.

16. Untape the rod.

17. Adjust the dimmer switch as follows:

  a. Compress the switch slightly and insert a $\frac{3}{32}$" (2.238mm) drill bit in the switch adjusting hole.

  b. Move the switch towards the steering wheel to remove any play.

  c. Tighten the attaching screws to 35 in.lb.

  d. Connect the battery ground.

  e. Remove the drill bit.

  f. Check the operation of the switch.

NOTE: *If your Jeep has a tilt column, check the switch operation in all positions.*

18. Install the turn signal switch and attaching screws. Torque the screws to 35 in.lb.

19. Connect the wiring harness connectors.

20. Install the wiring harness protectors.

21. With the turn signal switch in the neutral position, install the hazard warning knob.

Press the knob inward and turn clockwise to install it.

22. Install the lever. Torque the attaching screws to 35 in.lb.
23. Install the upper bearing preload spring.
24. Install the canceling cam.
25. Install the lock plate.
26. Using the compressor, install the snapring.
27. Install the lock plate cover.
28. Install the steering wheel.
29. Loosen the toe plate screws.
30. Install the column-to-dash bezel.
31. Connect the battery ground.

Steering Column
REMOVAL AND INSTALLATION
1945–86

1. Disconnect the battery ground.
2. Remove the column cover plate at the floorboards.
3. On early CJ-2A and DJ-3A with remote control, remove the two screws attaching the remote control housing to the steering column.
4. On later models, remove the column-to-dash lower bezel. On models with automatic transmission, disconnect the shift rod at the column. On CJ-7 and Scrambler with air conditioning, it will be necessary to remove the left side air conditioning duct.
5. Remove the column-to-dash bracket and lower the column.
NOTE: *Later models have breakaway capsules in the bracket. Remove the bracket and put it in a safe place to avoid damage to the capsules.*
6. Disconnect any wiring attached to column components.
7. Remove the steering column-to-gear shaft coupling and pull the column out of the Jeep.
8. On models with energy absorbing columns, it is extremely important that only specified fasteners be used. Fasteners which are not of the exact length or hardness may impair the energy absorbing action of the column. Bolts securing the column mounting bracket to the dash must be torqued exactly.
9. Connect the column to the gear shaft and tighten the coupling pinch bolt to 45 ft.lb.
10. Connect all wiring. If you have Cruise Command, connect the white wire first, then the black one.
11. Install the toe plates, but don't fully tighten the fasteners.
12. Install the bracket on the column and torque the bolts to 20 ft.lb.
13. Align the bracket and dash and loosely install the mounting bolts.
14. While applying a constant upward pres-

sure on the column, torque the bracket-to-dash bolts to 20 ft.lb.
15. Torque the toe plate bolts to 10 ft.lb.
16. Install the bezel.
17. Connect the transmission linkage and check its operation.

1987

1. Disconnect the battery ground.
2. Set the parking brake.
3. Remove the steering wheel.
4. Matchmark the steering shaft and the U-joint.
5. Remove the column cover plate at the floorboards.
6. On models with automatic transmission, disconnect the shift rod at the column.
7. Remove the pinch bolt from the U-joint.
NOTE: *Do not separate the steering shaft and inetrmediate shaft at this time. To do so would damage the components*
8. Remove the speedometer/tachometer trim cover.
9. Remove the column-to-dash bracket and lower the column.
NOTE: *Later models have breakaway capsules in the bracket. Remove the bracket and put it in a safe place to avoid damage to the capsules.*
10. Disconnect any wiring attached to column components.
11. Pull the column from the Jeep.
12. It is extremely important that only specified fasteners be used. Fasteners which are not of the exact length or hardness may impair the energy absorbing action of the column. Bolts securing the column mounting bracket to the dash must be torqued exactly.
13. Connect the column to the gear shaft and tighten the coupling pinch bolt to 45 ft.lb.
14. Connect all wiring.
15. Install the toe plates, but don't fully tighten the fasteners.
16. Install the bracket on the column and torque the bolts to 20 ft.lb.
17. Align the bracket and dash and loosely install the mounting bolts.
18. While applying a constant upward pressure on the column, torque the bracket-to-dash bolts to 20 ft.lb.
19. Torque the toe plate bolts to 10 ft.lb.
20. Install the trim plate.
21. Connect the transmission linkage and check its operation.

Manual Steering Gear
REMOVAL AND INSTALLATION
1945–71

The steering gear has to be removed down through the floor pan.

Troubleshooting the Manual Steering Gear

Problem	Cause	Solution
Hard or erratic steering	• Incorrect tire pressure	• Inflate tires to recommended pressures
	• Insufficient or incorrect lubrication	• Lubricate as required (refer to Maintenance Section)
	• Suspension, or steering linkage parts damaged or misaligned	• Repair or replace parts as necessary
	• Improper front wheel alignment	• Adjust incorrect wheel alignment angles
	• Incorrect steering gear adjustment	• Adjust steering gear
	• Sagging springs	• Replace springs
Play or looseness in steering	• Steering wheel loose	• Inspect shaft spines and repair as necessary. Tighten attaching nut and stake in place.
	• Steering linkage or attaching parts loose or worn	• Tighten, adjust, or replace faulty components
	• Pitman arm loose	• Inspect shaft splines and repair as necessary. Tighten attaching nut and stake in place
	• Steering gear attaching bolts loose	• Tighten bolts
	• Loose or worn wheel bearings	• Adjust or replace bearings
	• Steering gear adjustment incorrect or parts badly worn	• Adjust gear or replace defective parts
Wheel shimmy or tramp	• Improper tire pressure	• Inflate tires to recommended pressures
	• Wheels, tires, or brake rotors out-of-balance or out-of-round	• Inspect and replace or balance parts
	• Inoperative, worn, or loose shock absorbers or mounting parts	• Repair or replace shocks or mountings
	Loose or worn steering or suspension parts	• Tighten or replace as necessary
	• Loose or worn wheel bearings	• Adjust or replace bearings
	• Incorrect steering gear adjustments	• Adjust steering gear
	• Incorrect front wheel alignment	• Correct front wheel alignment
Tire wear	• Improper tire pressure	• Inflate tires to recommended pressures
	• Failure to rotate tires	• Rotate tires
	• Brakes grabbing	• Adjust or repair brakes
	• Incorrect front wheel alignment	• Align incorrect angles
	• Broken or damaged steering and suspension parts	• Repair or replace defective parts
	• Wheel runout	• Replace faulty wheel
	• Excessive speed on turns	• Make driver aware of conditions
Vehicle leads to one side	• Improper tire pressures	• Inflate tires to recommended pressures
	• Front tires with uneven tread depth, wear pattern, or different cord design (i.e., one bias ply and one belted or radial tire on front wheels)	• Install tires of same cord construction and reasonably even tread depth, design, and wear pattern
	• Incorrect front wheel alignment	• Align incorrect angles
	• Brakes dragging	• Adjust or repair brakes
	• Pulling due to uneven tire construction	• Replace faulty tire

1. Remove the left front fender.
2. On early CJ-2A and Utility models with remote control steering linkage, disconnect the control rods at the transmission.
3. Remove the steering wheel.
4. Unbolt the steering column bracket from the instrument panel.
5. Disconnect the exhaust pipe at the manifold.
6. Remove the steering column cover plate from the floorboard.
7. On early CJ-2A and Utility models, remove the two screws holding the shift control rods housing to the steering column.

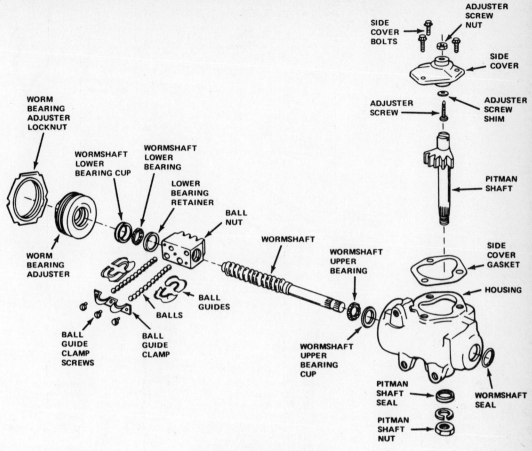

WORM BEARING ADJUSTER LOCKNUT

WORMSHAFT LOWER BEARING CUP

WORMSHAFT LOWER BEARING

LOWER BEARING RETAINER

BALL NUT

WORM BEARING ADJUSTER

WORMSHAFT

WORMSHAFT UPPER BEARING

BALL GUIDES

BALLS

BALL GUIDE CLAMP SCREWS

BALL GUIDE CLAMP

WORMSHAFT UPPER BEARING CUP

SIDE COVER BOLTS

ADJUSTER SCREW NUT

SIDE COVER

ADJUSTER SCREW

ADJUSTER SCREW SHIM

PITMAN SHAFT

SIDE COVER GASKET

HOUSING

PITMAN SHAFT SEAL

WORMSHAFT SEAL

PITMAN SHAFT NUT

1972–83 manual steering gear

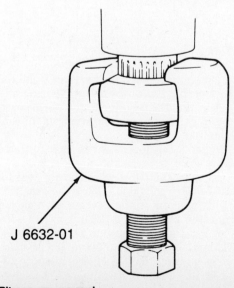

J 6632-01

Pitman arm removal

8. On CJ-2A models, remove the horn wire contact. On all other models, disconnect the horn wire.

9. On early CJ-2A and Utility models, lower the shift linkage through the floor.

10. Remove the drag link from the steering gear arm ball.

11. Unbolt the steering gear housing from the frame.

12. Lower the steering gear through the floor pan and over the outside of the frame rail.

13. Lift the steering gear through the floor pan and into position on the frame rail.

14. Install the bolts attaching the steering gear housing to the frame. Torque the 3/8" bolts to 40 ft.lb.; the 7/16" bolts to 55 ft.lb.

15. Install the drag link on the steering gear arm ball.

16. On early CJ-2A and Utility models, install the shift linkage.

17. On CJ-2A models, install the horn wire

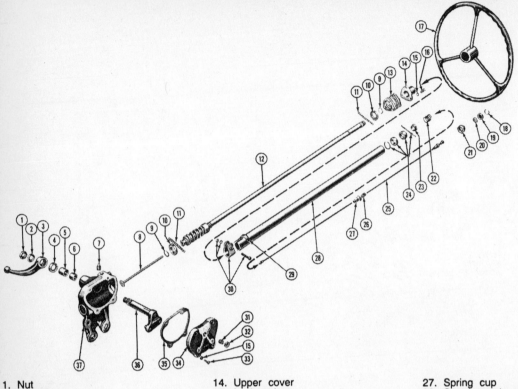

1. Nut	14. Upper cover	27. Spring cup
2. Lockwasher	15. Lockwasher	28. Steering column
3. Steering gear arm	16. Bolt	29. Oil hole cover
4. Lever shaft oil seal	17. Steering wheel	30. Clamp
5. Outer housing bushing	18. Horn button retainer	31. Adjusting screw
6. Inner housing bushing	19. Horn button	32. Nut
7. Filler plug	20. Horn button cap	33. Bolt
8. Cover and tube	21. Nut	34. Side cover
9. Ball retaining ring	22. Spring	35. Gasket
10. Cup	23. Spring seat	36. Shaft and lever
11. Ball (steel)	24. Bearing	37. Housing
12. Tube and cam	25. Horn cable	
13. Shims	26. Horn buton spring	

1945–71 steering gear and column

contact. On all other models, Connect the horn wire.

18. On early CJ-2A and Utility models, install the two screws holding the shift control rods housing to the steering column.

19. Install the steering column cover plate on the floorboard.

20. Connect the exhaust pipe at the manifold.

21. Bolt the steering column bracket to the instrument panel.

22. Install the steering wheel.

23. On early CJ-2A and Utility models with remote control steering linkage, connect the control rods at the transmission.

24. Install the left front fender.

25. Adjust the shifting linkage on early CJ-2A and Utility models.

1972–75

1. Disconnect the steering gear from the lower steering shaft by removing the bolt and nut attaching the coupling to the worm shaft.

2. Disconnect the steering arm from the connecting rod.

3. Remove the upper steering gear-to-frame bracket bolt.

4. Remove the two lower steering gear-to-frame bracket bolts and remove the gear.

5. Installation is the reverse of removal. Torque the pitman arm-to-shaft nut to 160–250 ft.lb.; the steering bracket-to-frame ⅜" (9.525mm) bolt to 35–45 ft.lb.; the steering bracket-to-frame ⁷⁄₁₆" (11.1125mm) bolt to 60–70 ft.lb.; the steering gear-to-bracket bolts to 60–80 ft.lb.

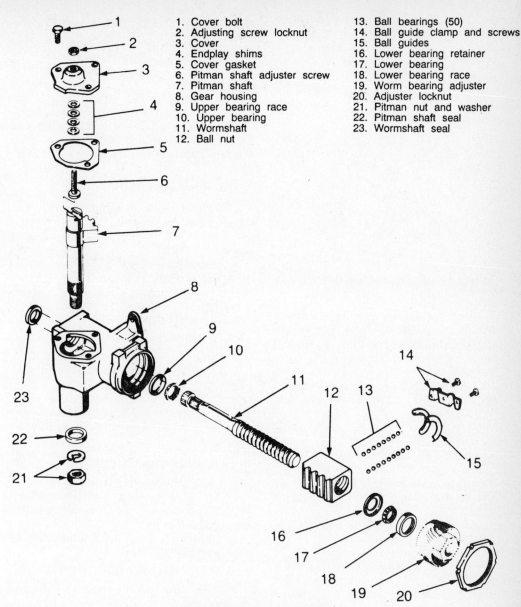

1. Cover bolt
2. Adjusting screw locknut
3. Cover
4. Endplay shims
5. Cover gasket
6. Pitman shaft adjuster screw
7. Pitman shaft
8. Gear housing
9. Upper bearing race
10. Upper bearing
11. Wormshaft
12. Ball nut
13. Ball bearings (50)
14. Ball guide clamp and screws
15. Ball guides
16. Lower bearing retainer
17. Lower bearing
18. Lower bearing race
19. Worm bearing adjuster
20. Adjuster locknut
21. Pitman nut and washer
22. Pitman shaft seal
23. Wormshaft seal

1984–87 manual steering gear

1976–86

1. Remove the intermediate shaft-to-wormshaft coupling clamp bolt and disconnect the intermediate shaft.

2. Remove the pitman arm nut and lockwasher.

3. Using a puller, remove the Pitman arm from the shaft.

4. Raise the left side of the vehicle slightly to relieve tension on the left front spring and rest the frame on a jackstand.

5. Remove the steering gear lower bracket-to-frame bolts.

6. Remove the bolts attaching the steering gear upper bracket to the crossmember. Begin-ning in 1979, one of these bolts is a Torx® head bolt. This bolt, and some others may be removed with the aid of a 9 inch extension. Remove the gear.

NOTE: *Loctite® 271 or similar material must be applied to all attaching bolt threads prior to installation.*

7. Position the tie plate upper and lower mounting brackets on the gear and install the bolts. Torque the bracket-to-gear bolts to 70 ft.lb. and the bracket-to-tie plate bolt to 55 ft.lb.

8. Align and engage the intermediate shaft coupling with the steering gear wormshaft splines.

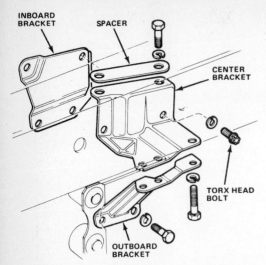

Steering gear mounting brackets on 1972 and later models

9. Position the steering gear on the frame and install the mounting bolts. Torque the bolts to 55 ft.lb. Install the Pitman arm and torque the nut to 185 ft.lb.

NOTE: *The steering gear may produce a slight roughness, this can be eliminated by turning the steering wheel full left and right 10–15 times.*

1987

1. Remove the intermediate shaft-to-wormshaft coupling clamp bolt and disconnect the intermediate shaft.
2. Raise and support the front end on jackstands.
3. Disconnect the center link from the pitman arm.
4. Remove the front stabilizer bar.
5. Remove the pitman arm nut and washer.
6. Matchmark the pitman arm and shaft and, with a puller, such as J-6632-01, remove the pitman arm.
7. Remove the mounting bolts and the gear.
8. Position the gear on the frame and install the mounting bolts. Torque the gear-to-frame bolts to 75 ft.lb.
9. Install the pitman arm. Torque the pitman arm nut to 185 ft.lb. and stake it in two places.
10. Install the front stabilizer bar. Torque the stabilizer bar-to-frame bolts to 55 ft.lb. Torque the stabilizer bar-to-link bolts to 27 ft.lb.
11. Connect the center link to the pitman arm. Torque the center link-to-pitman arm nut to 35 ft.lb.
12. Install the intermediate shaft-to-wormshaft coupling clamp bolt. Torque the bolt to 33 ft.lb.

MANUAL STEERING GEAR ADJUSTMENT

NOTE: *Adjustments must be made in the order given. Failure to following sequence could result in damage to the gear.*

1945–71

Before adjusting, remove all load from the system by disconnect the drag link from the steering arm and loosening the instrument panel bracket bolts and the steering gear-to-frame bolts.

STEERING SHAFT PLAY ADJUSTMENT

1. Remove the shims installed between the steering gear housing and the upper cover.
2. Loosen the housing side cover adjusting screw.
3. Loosen the housing cover to cut and remove one or more shims as required. Proper adjustment allows a slight drag and free operation.
4. Tighten the cover.

BACKLASH ADJUSTMENT

1. Loosen the adjusting screw locknut.
2. Turn the adjusting screw in until a very slight drag is felt through the mid-point in steering wheel travel. This procedure is done with the wheels in the straight-ahead position.
3. Tighten the adjusting screw locknut.

1972–75

WORM BEARING PRELOAD ADJUSTMENT

1. Loosen the steering gear end cover.
2. Add to or subtract from the number of shims under the cover to obtain a rolling torque of 2–5 in.lb.
3. Tighten the cover bolts alternately and evenly to 18–22 ft.lb.

STEERING GEAR CLEARANCE ADJUSTMENT

1. Loosen the locknut and turn the adjusting screw on the side cover, counterclockwise until the worm gear shaft turns freely through its entire range of travel.
2. Count the number of turns necessary to rotate the worm gear shaft through its travel.
3. Turn the shaft to center point.
4. Rotate the shaft back and forth over center, and tighten the adjusting screw until the shaft binds slightly at the center point.
5. Adjust the screw to obtain a rolling torque of 7–12 in.lb. through the center.
6. Hold the adjusting screw and tighten the locknut to 16–20 ft.lb.

1976–79

WORM BEARING PRELOAD ADJUSTMENT

1. Check that the steering gear mounting bolts are properly torqued.

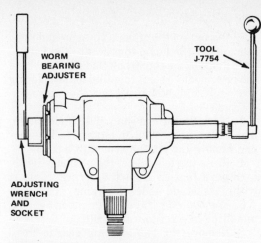

Adjusting worm bearing preload

2. Matchmark and remove the pitman arm.

3. Attach an inch-pound torque wrench and socket to the pitman shaft and turn the shaft to the extreme right and left, without hitting the travel stops.

4. Loosen the adjuster locknut. Tighten the worm bearing adjuster until the torque wrench shows 8 in.lb. within ½ turn of either extreme.

5. Tighten the adjuster locknut to 90 ft.lb. and recheck the torque reading on the shaft.

PITMAN SHAFT OVERCENTER ADJUSTMENT

1. Rotate the wormshaft from stop-to-stop and count the number of turns.

Adjusting Pitman shaft overcenter torque drag

2. Rotate the wormshaft back from the stop, ½ the total number of turns.

3. Install an inch-pound torque wrench and socket J-7754 on the splined end of the wormshaft. Check the rotating torque as the shaft passes over the center point of travel. Overcenter torque should be 4–10 in.lb. If not, proceed with steps 4–6.

4. Loosen the adjuster locknut.

5. Rotate the shaft over center and tighten the adjuster as necessary. Do not exceed 16 in.lb. combined total drag (overcenter + worm bearing preload.

6. Hold the adjuster screw and tighten the locknut to 23 ft.lb. Do not allow the adjuster to turn, or the adjustment will have to be made over again!

7. Install the pitman arm, torque it to 185 ft.lb. and stake it in two places.

1980–87

WORM BEARING PRELOAD ADJUSTMENT

1. Check that the steering gear mounting bolts are properly torqued.

2. Matchmark and remove the pitman arm.

3. Remove the horn button and cover. Attach an inch-pound torque wrench and socket to steering wheel nut and turn the shaft to the extreme right or left, gently, until you hit the stop. Then, turn it back ½ turn.

4. Turn the torque wrench through a 90° arc and check the torque reading. Torque should be 5–8 in.lb. If not, proceed with steps 4 and 5.

5. Loosen the adjuster locknut. Tighten the worm bearing adjuster until the torque wrench shows 5–8 in.lb. within ½ turn of either extreme.

6. Tighten the adjuster locknut to 90 ft.lb. and recheck the torque reading on the shaft.

PITMAN SHAFT OVERCENTER ADJUSTMENT

1. With the pitman shaft removed, rotate the wormshaft from stop-to-stop and count the number of turns.

2. Rotate the wormshaft back from the stop, ½ the total number of turns.

3. Install an inch-pound torque wrench and socket on the steering wheel nut. Check the rotating torque as the shaft passes over the center point of travel. Overcenter torque should be equal to the worm bearing preload plus 4–10 in.lb., but not more than 18 in.lb. If not, proceed with steps 4–6.

4. Loosen the adjuster locknut.

5. Rotate the shaft over center and tighten the adjuster as necessary.

6. Hold the adjuster screw and tighten the locknut to 25 ft.lb. Do not allow the adjuster to turn, or the adjustment will have to be made over again!

7. Install the pitman arm, torque it to 185 ft.lb. and stake it in two places.

Power Steering Gear

REMOVAL AND INSTALLATION

1972–75

1. Disconnect the hoses at the gear and raise them above the pump to prevent fluid loss.
2. Remove the pinch bolt from the lower flange.
3. Remove the pitman arm nut and lockwasher, and remove the pitman arm with a puller.
4. Unbolt and remove the pump.
5. Installation is the reverse of removal. Torque the pitman arm nut to 160–210 ft.lb. and the gear-to-frame bolts to 55 ft.lb.

1976–86

1. Disconnect the hoses at the gear and raise them above the pump to prevent fluid loss.
2. Remove the clamp bolt and nut attaching the intermediate shaft coupling to the steering gear stub shaft and disconnect the intermediate shaft.
3. Mark the pitman shaft and arm for alignment. Remove the pitman nut and lockwasher and remove the pitman arm with a puller.
4. Raise the left side of the vehicle slightly to relieve tension from the spring. Support with a jackstand under the frame.
5. Remove the three lower steering gear mounting bracket-to-frame bolts.
6. Remove the two steering gear-to-crossmember upper bolts. Remove the gear and brackets as an assembly.
7. Remove the brackets from the gear.

Troubleshooting the Power Steering Gear

Problem	Cause	Solution
Hissing noise in steering gear	• There is some noise in all power steering systems. One of the most common is a hissing sound most evident at standstill parking. There is no relationship between this noise and performance of the steering. Hiss may be expected when steering wheel is at end of travel or when slowly turning at standstill	• Slight hiss is normal and in no way affects steering. Do not replace valve unless hiss is extremely objectionable. A replacement valve will also exhibit slight noise and is not always a cure. Investigate clearance around flexible coupling rivets. Be sure steering shaft and gear are aligned so flexible coupling rotates in a flat plane and is not distorted as shaft rotates. Any metal-to-metal contacts through flexible coupling will transmit valve hiss into passenger compartment through the steering column.
Rattle or chuckle noise in steering gear	• Gear loose on frame	• Check gear-to-frame mounting screws. Tighten screws to 88 N·m (65 foot pounds) torque.
	• Steering linkage looseness	• Check linkage pivot points for wear. Replace if necessary.
	• Pressure hose touching other parts of car	• Adjust hose position. Do not bend tubing by hand.
	• Loose pitman shaft over center adjustment	• Adjust to specifications
	NOTE: A slight rattle may occur on turns because of increased clearance off the "high point." This is normal and clearance must not be reduced below specified limits to eliminate this slight rattle.	
	• Loose pitman arm	• Tighten pitman arm nut to specifications
Squawk noise in steering gear when turning or recovering from a turn	• Damper O-ring on valve spool cut	• Replace damper O-ring
Poor return of steering wheel to center	• Tires not properly inflated • Lack of lubrication in linkage and ball joints	• Inflate to specified pressure • Lube linkage and ball joints

Troubleshooting the Power Steering Gear (cont.)

Problem	Cause	Solution
	• Lower coupling flange rubbing against steering gear adjuster plug	• Loosen pinch bolt and assemble properly
	• Steering gear to column misalignment	• Align steering column
	• Improper front wheel alignment	• Check and adjust as necessary
	• Steering linkage binding	• Replace pivots
	• Ball joints binding	• Replace ball joints
	• Steering wheel rubbing against housing	• Align housing
	• Tight or frozen steering shaft bearings	• Replace bearings
	• Sticking or plugged valve spool	• Remove and clean or replace valve
	• Steering gear adjustments over specifications	• Check adjustment with gear out of car. Adjust as required.
	• Kink in return hose	• Replace hose
Car leads to one side or the other (keep in mind road condition and wind. Test car in both directions on flat road)	• Front end misaligned • Unbalanced steering gear valve **NOTE:** If this is cause, steering effort will be very light in direction of lead and normal or heavier in opposite direction	• Adjust to specifications • Replace valve
Momentary increase in effort when turning wheel fast to right or left	• Low oil level • Pump belt slipping • High internal leakage	• Add power steering fluid as required • Tighten or replace belt • Check pump pressure. (See pressure test)
Steering wheel surges or jerks when turning with engine running especially during parking	• Low oil level • Loose pump belt • Steering linkage hitting engine oil pan at full turn • Insufficient pump pressure • Pump flow control valve sticking	• Fill as required • Adjust tension to specification • Correct clearance • Check pump pressure. (See pressure test). Replace relief valve if defective. • Inspect for varnish or damage, replace if necessary
Excessive wheel kickback or loose steering	• Air in system • Steering gear loose on frame • Steering linkage joints worn enough to be loose • Worn poppet valve • Loose thrust bearing preload adjustment • Excessive overcenter lash	• Add oil to pump reservoir and bleed by operating steering. Check hose connectors for proper torque and adjust as required. • Tighten attaching screws to specified torque • Replace loose pivots • Replace poppet valve • Adjust to specification with gear out of vehicle • Adjust to specification with gear out of car
Hard steering or lack of assist	• Loose pump belt • Low oil level **NOTE:** Low oil level will also result in excessive pump noise • Steering gear to column misalignment • Lower coupling flange rubbing against steering gear adjuster plug • Tires not properly inflated	• Adjust belt tension to specification • Fill to proper level. If excessively low, check all lines and joints for evidence of external leakage. Tighten loose connectors. • Align steering column • Loosen pinch bolt and assemble properly • Inflate to recommended pressure

Troubleshooting the Power Steering Gear (cont.)

Problem	Cause	Solution
Foamy milky power steering fluid, low fluid level and possible low pressure	• Air in the fluid, and loss of fluid due to internal pump leakage causing overflow	• Check for leak and correct. Bleed system. Extremely cold temperatures will cause system aeriation should the oil level be low. If oil level is correct and pump still foams, remove pump from vehicle and separate reservoir from housing. Check welsh plug and housing for cracks. If plug is loose or housing is cracked, replace housing.
Low pressure due to steering pump	• Flow control valve stuck or inoperative • Pressure plate not flat against cam ring	• Remove burrs or dirt or replace. Flush system. • Correct
Low pressure due to steering gear	• Pressure loss in cylinder due to worn piston ring or badly worn housing bore • Leakage at valve rings, valve body-to-worm seal	• Remove gear from car for disassembly and inspection of ring and housing bore • Remove gear from car for disassembly and replace seals

NOTE: *Prior to installation, all bolts must be coated with Loctite® 271 or its equivalent.*

8. Position the mounting brackets on the gear and torque the bolts to 70 ft.lb.

9. Align and connect the intermediate shaft coupling to the steering gear stub shaft.

10. Position the steering gear on the frame and crossmember. Install and tighten the bolts to 55 ft.lb.

11. Lower the vehicle.

12. Install the intermediate shaft coupling-to-steering gear stub shaft clamp bolt and nut. Tighten the nut to 45 ft.lb.

13. Align and install the pitman arm, nut and lockwasher. Torque the nut to 185 ft.lb. Stake the nut in two places.

14. Connect the hoses. Torque the hose connections to 25 ft.lb.

1987

1. Place the wheels in a straight ahead position.

2. Place a drain pan under the steering gear.

3. Disconnect the hoses at the gear. Secure the hose ends in an upward position, higher than the gear. Cap the open ends.

4. Disconnect the intermediate shaft from the steering gear shaft.

5. Raise and support the front end on jackstands.

6. Matchmark the pitman arm and shaft.

7. Disconnect the center link from the pitman arm.

8. Remove the stabilizer bar.

9. Remove the pitman arm nut and washer. Using a puller, remove the pitman arm.

10. Remove the mounting bolts and remove the gear.

11. Position the gear and install the mounting bolts. Torque the steering gear-to-frame bolts to 75 ft.lb.

12. Install the pitman arm, nut, and washer. Torque the pitman arm nut to 185 ft.lb.

13. Install the stabilizer bar. Torque the stabilizer bar-to-frame bolts to 30 ft.lb.; the stabilizer bar-to-link nuts to 45 ft.lb.

14. Connect the center link to the pitman arm. Torque the center link-to-pitman arm nuts to 35 ft.lb.

15. Connect the intermediate shaft to the steering gear shaft. Torque the intermediate shaft pinch bolt to 45 ft.lb.

16. Connect the hoses at the gear.

POWER STEERING GEAR ADJUSTMENTS

NOTE: *The gear must be adjusted off the vehicle. All adjustments must be made in the sequence described below. Worm bearing preload is always adjusted first!*

Worm Bearing Preload Adjustment

1. Mount the gear assembly in a vise.

2. Torque the adjuster plug to 20 ft.lb.

3. Mark the gear housing in line with one of the adjuster plug holes.

4. Measure counterclockwise $^3/_{16}$–$^1/_4$" (4.7625–6.35mm) from the first mark on models through 1979; $^1/_2$" (12.7mm) from the first mark on 1980–86 models; $^3/_{16}$–$^1/_4$" (4.7625–

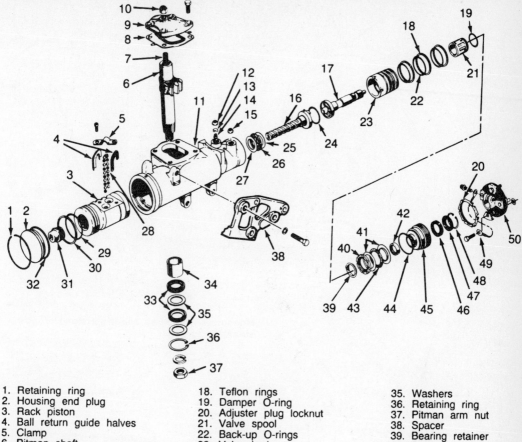

1. Retaining ring
2. Housing end plug
3. Rack piston
4. Ball return guide halves
5. Clamp
6. Pitman shaft
7. Adjusting screw
8. Gasket
9. Side cover
10. Locknut
11. Housing
12. Pressure port seat
13. Poppet valve
14. Spring
15. Return port seat
16. Worm
17. Stub shaft

18. Teflon rings
19. Damper O-ring
20. Adjuster plug locknut
21. Valve spool
22. Back-up O-rings
23. Valve body
24. O-ring
25. Race
26. Thrust bearing
27. Race
28. Ball bearings (24)
29. Back-up O-ring
30. Piston ring
31. Rack piston end plug
32. O-ring
33. Oil seals
34. Needle bearings

35. Washers
36. Retaining ring
37. Pitman arm nut
38. Spacer
39. Bearing retainer
40. Spacer
41. Races
42. Bearing
43. Thrust bearing
44. O-ring
45. Adjuster plug
46. Oil seal
47. Washer and dust seal
48. Retaining ring
49. Ground wire
50. Flexible coupling

Power steering gear

6.35mm) for 1987 models, and make another mark.

5. Turn the adjuster plug counterclockwise to align the hole with the second mark.

6. Hold the adjuster plug and torque the locknut to 85 ft.lb. Do not allow the adjuster to turn.

7. Turn the stubshaft clockwise to its stop, then back ¼ turn.

8. Using a torque wrench of no more than 50 in.lb. capacity and a 12 point deep socket, check the rotating torque at the splined end of the stub shaft at or near a vertical position. Torque should be 4–10 in.lb.

9. If the torque cannot be adjusted within these limits, the gear will have to be rebuilt.

Pitman Shaft Overcenter Adjustment

1. Loosen the adjuster screw locknut.

2. Turn the adjuster screw counterclockwise until the screw is fully extended. Turn the screw back in one full turn.

3. Count the number of turns to rotate the stubshaft from stop-to-stop.

4. Turn the shaft back ½ the number of turns. At this point the flat surface of the stubshaft should be upward and the master spline on the pitman shaft should be aligned with the adjuster screw.

5. Install a 50 in.lb. torque wrench and deep 12 point socket on the splined end of the stub shaft. Place the torque wrench in a vertical position.

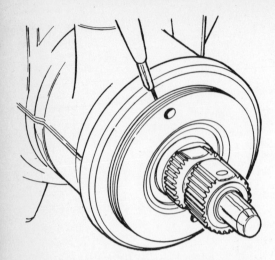

Marking power steering gear housing adjacent to the hole in the adjuster

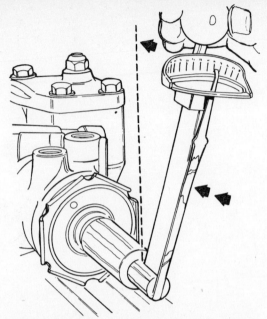

Measuring wormshaft bearing preload on power steering gears

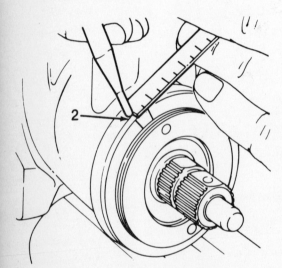

Making the second mark on the housing

6. Rotate the torque wrench 45 degrees to each side and record the highest torque at or near center. Record this reading.

7. Adjust the torque by turning the adjuster screw clockwise. Adjustment is: the recorded reading plus 4–8 in.lb. for new gears, but not exceeding 14. in.lb. total; the previously recorded reading plus 4–5 in.lb. for used gears, but not exceeding 14 in.lb. combined total.

8. Tighten the adjuster screw locknut to 35 ft.lb. while holding the adjuster screw.

9. Install the gear.

Power Steering Pump

REMOVAL AND INSTALLATION

If the power steering pump has to be removed to service another component, it is not neces-

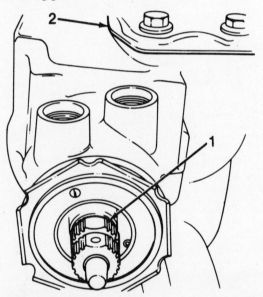

Stubshaft (1) position with gear centered. 2 is the gear housing

sary to remove the hoses from the pump. Just disconnect the mounting fixtures and lift the pump away from the engine and lay it out of the way. The only time the power steering hoses have to be removed from the pump is when the pump has to be removed from the vehicle for service or replacement.

1. Remove the pump drive belt tension adjusting bolt. Disconnect the belt from the pump.

2. Disconnect the return and pressure hoses

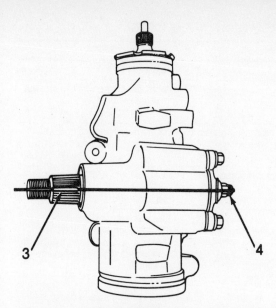

Pitman shaft master spline (3) position with the gear centered. 4 is the adjusting screw

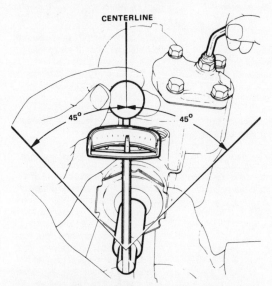

Measuring Pitman shaft overcenter torque drag on power steering gears

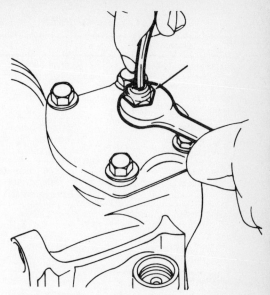

Holding the locknut while turning the adjusting nut

- 1972–83
   Pump adjusting bolts: 35 ft.lb.
   Pump-to-bracket bolts: 35 ft.lb.
   Bracket-to-engine bolts: 35 ft.lb.
   Hose-to-pump connection: 30 ft.lb.
- 1984–86
   Pump adjusting bolts: 35 ft.lb.
   Pump-to-bracket bolts: 35 ft.lb.
   Bracket-to-engine bolts: 35 ft.lb.
   Hose-to-pump connection: 20 ft.lb.
- 1987
   Pump-to-bracket bolts: 28 ft.lb.
   Bracket-to-engine bolts: 33 ft.lb.
   Pump pivot stud nut: 21 ft.lb.
   Pump adjusting bolt: 21 ft.lb.
   Hose-to-pump connection: 21 ft.lb.

7. Adjust the drive belt tension.

8. Fill the pump reservoir to the correct level.

9. Start the engine and wait for at least three minutes before turning the steering wheel. Check the lever frequently during this time.

10. Slowly turn the steering wheel through its entire range a few times with the engine running. Recheck the level and inspect for possible leaks.

NOTE: *If air becomes trapped in the fluid, the pump may become noisy until all of the air is out. This may take some time since trapped air does not bleed out rapidly.*

Tie Rod End

REMOVAL AND INSTALLATION

1945–71

NOTE: *Early production CJ models and early production 2-WD Utility models with*

from the pump. Cover the hose connector and union on the pump and open ends of the hoses to avoid the entrance of dirt.

3. On the 8–304, remove the front bracket from the engine.

4. Remove the two nuts which secure the rear of the pump to the bracket, and the two bolts which secure the front of the pump to the bracket and remove the pump.

5. To install, position the pump in the bracket and install the rear attaching screws. On the 8–304, install the front bracket.

6. Connect the hydraulic hoses.

Observe the following torques:

Troubleshooting the Power Steering Pump

Problem	Cause	Solution
Chirp noise in steering pump	• Loose belt	• Adjust belt tension to specification
Belt squeal (particularly noticeable at full wheel travel and stand still parking)	• Loose belt	• Adjust belt tension to specification
Growl noise in steering pump	• Excessive back pressure in hoses or steering gear caused by restriction	• Locate restriction and correct. Replace part if necessary.
Growl noise in steering pump (particularly noticeable at stand still parking)	• Scored pressure plates, thrust plate or rotor • Extreme wear of cam ring	• Replace parts and flush system • Replace parts
Groan noise in steering pump	• Low oil level • Air in the oil. Poor pressure hose connection.	• Fill reservoir to proper level • Tighten connector to specified torque. Bleed system by operating steering from right to left—full turn.
Rattle noise in steering pump	• Vanes not installed properly • Vanes sticking in rotor slots	• Install properly • Free up by removing burrs, varnish, or dirt
Swish noise in steering pump	• Defective flow control valve	• Replace part
Whine noise in steering pump	• Pump shaft bearing scored	• Replace housing and shaft. Flush system.
Hard steering or lack of assist	• Loose pump belt • Low oil level in reservoir **NOTE:** Low oil level will also result in excessive pump noise • Steering gear to column misalignment • Lower coupling flange rubbing against steering gear adjuster plug • Tires not properly inflated	• Adjust belt tension to specification • Fill to proper level. If excessively low, check all lines and joints for evidence of external leakage. Tighten loose connectors. • Align steering column • Loosen pinch bolt and assemble properly • Inflate to recommended pressure
Foaming milky power steering fluid, low fluid level and possible low pressure	• Air in the fluid, and loss of fluid due to internal pump leakage causing overflow	• Check for leaks and correct. Bleed system. Extremely cold temperatures will cause system aeration should the oil level be low. If oil level is correct and pump still foams, remove pump from vehicle and separate reservoir from body. Check welsh plug and body for cracks. If plug is loose or body is cracked, replace body.
Low pump pressure	• Flow control valve stuck or inoperative • Pressure plate not flat against cam ring	• Remove burrs or dirt or replace. Flush system. • Correct
Momentary increase in effort when turning wheel fast to right or left	• Low oil level in pump • Pump belt slipping • High internal leakage	• Add power steering fluid as required • Tighten or replace belt • Check pump pressure. (See pressure test)
Steering wheel surges or jerks when turning with engine running especially during parking	• Low oil level • Loose pump belt • Steering linkage hitting engine oil pan at full turn • Insufficient pump pressure	• Fill as required • Adjust tension to specification • Correct clearance • Check pump pressure. (See pressure test). Replace flow control valve if defective.

Troubleshooting the Power Steering Pump (cont.)

Problem	Cause	Solution
Steering wheel surges or jerks when turning with engine running especially during parking (cont.)	• Sticking flow control valve	• Inspect for varnish or damage, replace if necessary
Excessive wheel kickback or loose steering	• Air in system	• Add oil to pump reservoir and bleed by operating steering. Check hose connectors for proper torque and adjust as required.
Low pump pressure	• Extreme wear of cam ring	• Replace parts. Flush system.
	• Scored pressure plate, thrust plate, or rotor	• Replace parts. Flush system.
	• Vanes not installed properly	• Install properly
	• Vanes sticking in rotor slots	• Freeup by removing burrs, varnish, or dirt
	• Cracked or broken thrust or pressure plate	• Replace part

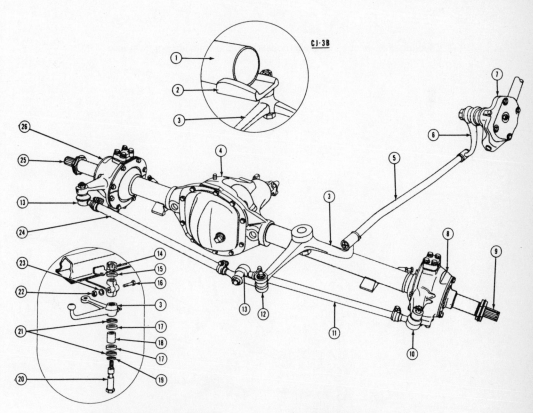

1. Frame cross tube (CJ-3B)
2. Steering bellcrank bracket (CJ-3B)
3. Steering bellcrank
4. Front axle
5. Connecting rod (drag link)
6. Steering gear arm
7. Steering gear
8. Left steering knuckle and arm
9. Left shaft and U-joint
10. Left tie rod socket
11. Left tie rod
12. Left tie rod socket
13. Right tie rod socket
14. Bellcrank nut
15. Washer
16. Bolt
17. Bellcrank bearing
18. Bearing spacer (early models)
19. Washer
20. Bellcrank shaft
21. Bearing seal
22. Nut
23. Lockwasher
24. Right steering tie rod
25. Right shaft and U-joint
26. Right steering knuckle and arm

1945–71 4-wd steering linkage

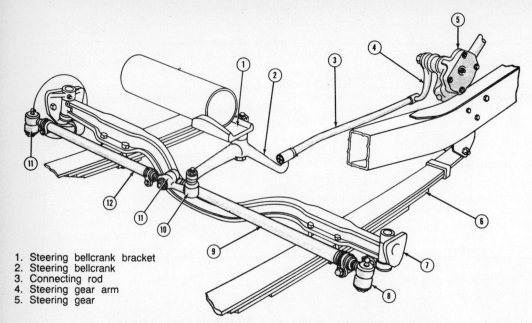

1. Steering bellcrank bracket
2. Steering bellcrank
3. Connecting rod
4. Steering gear arm
5. Steering gear

Steering linkage used on 2-wd models with the solid I-beam front axle

1. Cotter pin
2. Nut
3. Dust cover
4. Left socket
5. Nut
6. Lockwasher
7. Left tie rod
8. Lubrication fitting
9. Left socket (for right tie rod)
10. Right tie rod
11. Right socket
12. Bolt
13. Tie rod clamp

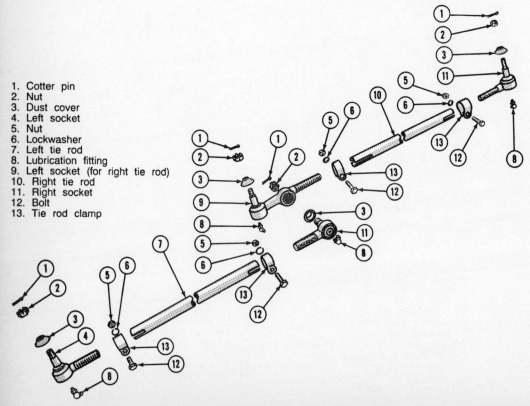

Tie rod used on the CJ-3B, Cj-5, CJ-6 through 1971

the 4–134 engine have 2-piece tie rods. All others have a one-piece rod.

1. Raise and support the front end on jackstands.

2. Remove the cotter pin and nut and disconnect the right tie rod section from the bell crank.

3. Remove the cotter pins and nuts, and, using a puller or separator, disconnect the outer ends from the knuckles.

4. Where applicable, the left and right tie rod sections can now be spearated.

5. The tie rod ends can be removed by loosening the clamps and unscrewing the ends. Before unscrewing the ends, note the exact number of threads visible, as an installation reference.

6. All seals that show any sign of wear should be replaced. New tie rod ends should be installed if the old ones show any play or roughness of movement.

7. Install the new tie rod ends, leaving the exact number of threads exposed, as previously noted. On CJ models, torque all nuts to 38–42 ft.lb. On Utility models, torque the $5/16$" clamp bolts to 10–15 ft.lb.; the $7/16$" clamp bolts to 35–45 ft.lb.

1972–79

1. Remove the cotter pins and retaining nuts at both ends of the tie rod and from the end of the connecting rod where it attaches to the tie rod.

2. Remove the nut attaching the steering damper push rod to the tie rod bracket and move the damper aside.

3. Remove the tie rod ends from the steering arms and connecting rod with a puller.

4. Count the number of threads showing on the tie rod before removing the ends, as a guide to installation.

5. Loosen the adjusting tube clamp bolts and unthread the ends.

6. Installation is the reverse of removal. Torque the connecting rod-to-tie rod nut to 40 ft.lb. on models through 1971 and to 70 ft.lb. on 1972 and later models.

7. Adjust toe-in, if necessary.

1980–86

1. Raise and support the front end on jackstands.

2. Remove the cotter pins and nuts attaching the tie rod to the knuckles.

3. Remove the steering damper to tie rod nut and move the damper aside.

4. Using a separator, remove the tie rod from the knuckles.

5. The tie rod ends can be removed from the tie rod by loosening the clamp and unscrewing them. Before unscrewing them, note the exact number of threads visible for installation reference.

6. Install the new ends leaving the correct number of threads visible. Torque the clamp bolts to 12 ft.lb.

7. Connect the tie rod to the knuckles and torque the nuts to 50 ft.lb. Install new cotter pins.

8. Connect the steering damper and torque the nut to 22 ft.lb.

1987

1. Remove the cotter pins and retaining nuts at both ends of the tie rod and from the end of the connecting rod where it attaches to the tie rod.

2. Remove the nut attaching the steering damper push rod to the tie rod bracket and move the damper aside.

3. Remove the tie rod ends from the steering arms and connecting rod with a puller.

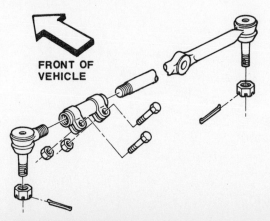

FRONT OF VEHICLE

1972–86 tie rod assembly

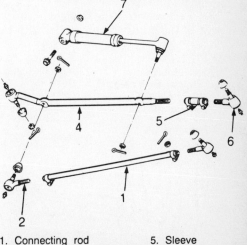

1. Connecting rod
2. Connecting rod ball stud
4. Tie rod
5. Sleeve
6. Tie rod end
7. Steering damper

1987 steering linkage

4. Count the number of threads showing on the tie rod before removing the ends, as a guide to installation.

5. Loosen the adjusting tube clamp bolts and unthread the ends.

6. Installation is the reverse of removal. Torque the steering damper-to-tie rod nut to 53 ft.lb.; all other nuts to 35 ft.lb.

7. Adjust toe-in, if necessary.

Center Link/Connecting Rod/Drag Link

REMOVAL AND INSTALLATION

1945–71

1. Raise and support the front end on jackstands.

2. Remove the cotter pins at each end of the link.

3. Remove the adjusting plugs, ball seats and spring from each end.

4. Disconnect the link and remove the dust cover and dust shield.

5. Replacement kits are available which contain all the above parts. Its best to replace all these parts at once.

6. Install the dust cover and shield at each end and connect the link at the steering arm and bell crank.

7. Install the ball seat and spring at each end and turn the adjusting plugs in until they firmly contact the ball. At the front end, back off the adjusting plug ½ turn and insert a new cotter pin. At the steering arm end, back off the plug one full turn and insert a new cotter pin.

1972–79

1. Raise and support the front end on jackstands.

2. Place the wheels in the straight ahead position with the pitman arm parallel with the

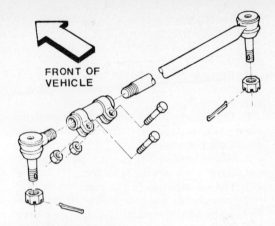

FRONT OF VEHICLE

1972–86 connecting rod

vehicle centerline. Matchmark the pitman arm and gear housing to be sure that the wheels don't move.

3. Remove the cotter pins and nuts at each end of the link.

4. Using a separator, disconnect the link from the pitman arm and tie rod.

5. With everything aligned, install the link. Torque the nuts to 70 ft.lb., minimum, and install new cotter pins.

1980–86

1. Raise and support the front end on jackstands.

2. Place the wheels in the straight ahead position with the pitman arm parallel with the vehicle centerline. Matchmark the pitman arm and gear housing to be sure that the wheels don't move.

3. Remove the cotter pins and nuts at each end of the link.

4. Using a separator, disconnect the link from the knuckle and pitman arm.

5. With everything aligned, install the link.

1. Cotter pin
2. Adjusting plug
3. Ball seat
4. Ball seat spring
5. Plug spring
6. Draglink
7. Adjusting plug
8. Dust cover
9. Dust cover shield
10. Lubricating fitting

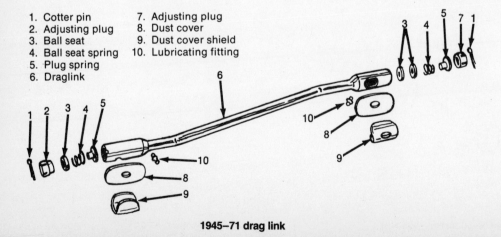

1945–71 drag link

Torque the nuts to 60 ft.lb., minimum, and install new cotter pins.

1987

1. Raise and support the front end on jackstands.

2. Place the wheels in the straight ahead position with the pitman arm parallel with the vehicle centerline. Matchmark the pitman arm and gear housing to be sure that the wheels don't move.

3. Remove the cotter pins and nuts at each end of the link.

4. Using a separator, disconnect the link from the pitman arm and tie rod.

5. With everything aligned, install the link. Torque the nuts to 35 ft.lb., minimum, and install new cotter pins.

Steering Damper

REMOVAL AND INSTALLATION

1. Raise and support the front end on jackstands.

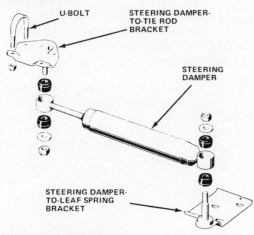

U-BOLT   STEERING DAMPER-TO-TIE ROD BRACKET

STEERING DAMPER

STEERING DAMPER-TO-LEAF SPRING BRACKET

1972–79 steering damper

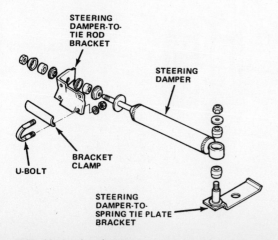

STEERING DAMPER-TO-TIE ROD BRACKET

STEERING DAMPER

BRACKET CLAMP

U-BOLT

STEERING DAMPER-TO-SPRING TIE PLATE BRACKET

1980–86 steering damper

2. Place the wheels in a straight ahead position.

3. Remove the attaching nut at each end of the damper and remove the damper.

4. Install the damper, making sure that the wheels are still in the straight ahead position. Torque the nuts as follows.

- Through 1986
  ⅜" nut: 22 ft.lb.
  ⁷⁄₁₆" nut: 30 ft.lb.
- 1987
  Tie rod end: 53 ft.lb.
  Axle end: 55 ft.lb.

Pitman Arm

REMOVAL AND INSTALLATION

1. Raise and support the front end on jackstands.

2. Place the wheels in a straight ahead position.

3. Matchmark the pitman arm and gear housing.

4. Disconnect the connecting rod/drag link from the arm or, on Utility models, the knuckle.

5. Matchmark the pitman arm and shaft.

6. Remove the pitman arm nut and washer.

7. Using a puller, remove the pitman arm from the gear. Never hammer on the arm or use a wedge tool to remove it!

8. Install the pitman arm aligning the matchmarks on the arm and shaft.

9. Install the washer and nut. Torque the nut to:

- 1945–71:
  Ross gear, except Utility models: 70–90 ft.lb.
  Ross gear, Utility models: 95–115 ft.lb.
  Saginaw gear: 120–160 ft.lb.
- 1972–87: 185 ft.lb.

10. Connect the connecting rod/drag link, or knuckle, to the pitman arm. Torque the pitman arm-to-knuckle nut to 65 ft.lb. Torque the pitman arm-to-link nut to 70 ft.lb. on models through 1979; 60 ft.lb. on 1980–86 models; 35 ft.lb. on 1987 models.

Bellcrank

REMOVAL AND INSTALLATION

1945–71

1. Raise and support the front end on jackstands.

2. Place the wheels in a straight ahead position.

3. Disconnect the connecting rod and tir rod from the bellcrank.

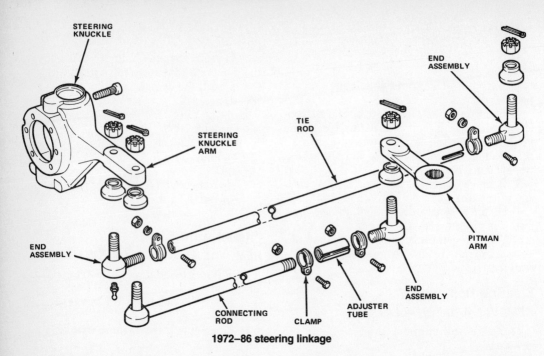

1972–86 steering linkage

4. Remove the bellcrank-to-support bracket nut and washers.

5. Remove the bellcrank from the support bracket. It may be necessary to drive it out of the bracket with a soft drift.

6. To disassemble the bellcrank, drive out the pin and remove the parts. Service kits are available for rebuiding the bellcrank. CJ-2A models, starting with serial number 199079, and all CJ models using bellcranks after that, have a new bellcrank assembly. Most notably,

the pin size was increased from 3/4″ (19.05mm) to 7/8″ (22.225mm), a floating hardened sleeve was installed between the pin and needle bearings, and a new arm, with upward facing bearings was used.

7. When assembling the parts, make sure that the new bearings in the bellcrank are installed 1/8″ (3.175mm) below the surface of the bellcrank face. When installing the washers, make sure that the chamfer on the washers face the bellcrank.

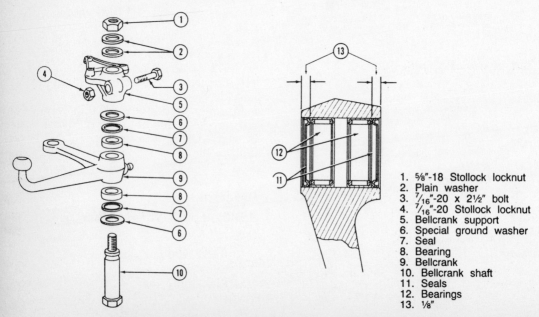

1. 5/8″-18 Stollock locknut
2. Plain washer
3. 7/16″-20 x 2½″ bolt
4. 7/16″-20 Stollock locknut
5. Bellcrank support
6. Special ground washer
7. Seal
8. Bearing
9. Bellcrank
10. Bellcrank shaft
11. Seals
12. Bearings
13. 1/8″

Bellcrank assembly used on early model CJ and Utility vehicles

8. After assembling the parts, install the bellcrank in the Jeep, but don't connect the linkage. Torque the bellcrank pin nut to:

• CJ-2A, before serial number 199079, and Utility Models: 70–90 ft.lb.

• All other models: 14–19 ft.lb.

9. Loosen the $\frac{7}{16}$" clamp bolt and adjust the locknut on the end of the bellcrank shaft until the bellcrank just rotates freely, without binding.

10. Torque the $\frac{7}{16}$" clamp nut to 50–70 ft.lb.

11. Connect the tie rod to the bellcrank and torque the nut to 38–45 ft.lb.

12. Connect the connecting rod to the bellcrank and adjust is as explained above.

SPECIAL TOOLS

J-34503

J-23653

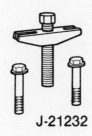

J-21232

Brakes

8

Brake Specifications

Years	Master Cyl. Bore	Brake Disc				Brake Drum		Wheel Cyl. or Caliper Bore	
		Original Thickness	Minimum Thickness	Maximum Run-out	Diameter	Orig. Inside Dia.	Max. Wear Limit	Front	Rear
1945–71 CJ models	1.000	—	—	—	—	9.000	9.060	1.000	0.750
1947–64 Utility	1.000	—	—	—	—	11.000	11.060	1.125	1.000
1972–73	1.000	—	—	—	—	11.000	11.060	1.125	0.975
1974–76*	1.000	—	—	—	—	11.000	11.060	1.125	0.975
1977	1.000	1.200	1.120	0.005	12.000	11.000	11.060	3.100	0.975
1978	1.000	1.200	1.120	0.005	12.000	11.000	11.060	3.100	0.875
1979–83	1.000	1.000	0.815	0.005	12.000	10.000	10.060	2.600	0.875
1984–86	1.000	1.000	0.815	0.005	11.690	10.000	10.060	2.600	0.875
1987	0.937	0.884	0.815	0.005	11.040	10.000	10.060	2.600	0.875

*Includes 1977 models with front drum brakes

BASIC OPERATING PRINCIPLES

Hydraulic systems are used to actuate the brakes of all modern automobiles. The system transports the power required to force the frictional surfaces of the braking system together from the pedal to the individual brake units at each wheel. A hydraulic system is used for two reasons. First, fluid under pressure can be carried to all parts of an automobile by small hoses, some of which are flexible, without taking up a significant amount of room or posing routing problems. Second, a great mechanical advantage can be given to the brake pedal end of the system, and the foot pressure required to actuate the brakes can be reduced by making the surface area of the master cylinder pistons smaller than that of any of the pistons in the wheel cylinders or calipers.

The master cylinder consists of a fluid reservoir and either a single or double cylinder and piston assembly. Double type master cylinders are designed to separate the front and rear braking systems hydraulically in case of a leak.

Steel lines carry the brake fluid to a point on the vehicle's frame near each of the vehicle's wheels. The fluid is then carried to the wheel cylinders by flexible tubes in order to allow for suspension and steering movements.

Each wheel cylinder contains two pistons, one at either end, which push outward in opposite directions. In disc brake systems, the cylinders are part of the calipers. One or four cylinders are used to force the brake pads against the disc, but all cylinders contain one piston only. All pistons employ some type of seal, usually made of rubber, to minimize fluid leakage.

A rubber dust boot seals the outer end of the cylinder against dust and dirt. The boot fits around the outer end of the piston on disc brake calipers, and around the brake actuating rod on wheel cylinders.

The hydraulic system operates as follows: When at rest, the entire system, from the piston(s) in the master cylinder to those in the wheel cylinders or calipers, is full of brake fluid. Upon application of the brake pedal, fluid trapped in front of the master cylinder piston(s) is forced through the lines to the wheel cylinders. Here, it forces the pistons outward, in the case of drum brakes, and inward toward the disc, in the case of disc brakes. The motion of the pistons is opposed by return springs mounted outside the cylinders in drum brakes, and by internal springs or spring seals, in disc brakes.

Upon release of the brake pedal, a spring located inside the master cylinder immediately returns the master cylinder pistons to the normal position. The pistons contain check valves and the master cylinder has compensating ports drilled in it. These are uncovered as the pistons reach their normal position. The piston check valves allow fluid to flow toward the wheel cylinders or calipers as the pistons withdraw. Then, as the return springs force the brake pads or shoes into the released position, the excess fluid reservoir through the compensating ports. It is during the time the pedal is in the released position that any fluid that has leaked out of the system will be replaced through the compensating ports.

Dual circuit master cylinders employ two pistons, located one behind the other, in the same cylinder. The primary piston is actuated directly by mechanical linkage from the brake pedal. The secondary piston is actuated by fluid trapped between the two pistons. If a leak develops in front of the secondary piston, it moves forward until it bottoms against the front of the master cylinder, and the fluid trapped between the pistons will operate the rear brakes. If the rear brakes develop a leak, the primary piston will move forward until direct contact with the secondary piston takes place, and it will force the secondary piston to actuate the front brakes. In either case, the brake pedal moves farther when the brakes are applied, and less braking power is available.

All dual circuit systems use a switch to warn the driver when only half of the brake system is operational. This switch is located in a valve body which is mounted on the firewall or the frame below the master cylinder. A hydraulic piston receives pressure from both circuits, each circuit's pressure being applied to one end of the piston. When the pressures are in balance, the piston remains stationary. When one circuit has a leak, however, the greater pressure in that circuit during application of the brakes will push the piston to one side, closing the switch and activating the brake warning light.

In disc brake systems, this valve body also contains a metering valve and, in some cases, a proportioning valve. The metering valve keeps pressure from traveling to the disc brakes on the front wheels until the brake shoes on the rear wheels have contacted the drums, ensuring that the front brakes will never be used alone. The proportioning valve controls the pressure to the rear brakes to avoid rear wheel lock-up during very hard braking.

Warning lights may be tested by depressing the brake pedal and holding it while opening one of the wheel cylinder bleeder screws. If this does not cause the light to go on, substitute a new lamp, make continuity checks, and, finally, replace the switch as necessary.

The hydraulic system may be checked for leaks by applying pressure to the pedal gradually and steadily. If the pedal sinks very slowly to the floor, the system has a leak. This is not to be confused with a springy or spongy feel due to the compression of air within the lines. If the system leaks, there will be a gradual change in the position of the pedal with a constant pressure.

Check for leaks along all lines and at wheel cylinders. If no external leaks are apparent, the problem is inside the master cylinder.

Disc Brakes
BASIC OPERATING PRINCIPLES

Instead of the traditional expanding brakes that press outward against a circular drum, disc brake systems utilize a disc (rotor) with brake pads positioned on either side of it. Braking effect is achieved in a manner similar to the way you would squeeze a spinning phonograph record between your fingers. The disc (rotor) is a casting with cooling fins between the two braking surfaces. This enables air to circulate between the braking surfaces making them less sensitive to heat buildup and more resistant to fade. Dirt and water do not affect braking action since contaminants are thrown off by the centrifugal action of the rotor or scraped off the by the pads. Also, the equal clamping action of the two brake pads tends to ensure uniform, straightline stops. Disc brakes are inherently self-adjusting.

There are three general types of disc brake:
1. A fixed caliper.
2. A floating caliper.

3. A sliding caliper.

The fixed caliper design uses two pistons mounted on either side of the rotor (in each side of the caliper). The caliper is mounted rigidly and does not move.

The sliding and floating designs are quite similar. In fact, these two types are often lumped together. In both designs, the pad on the inside of the rotor is moved into contact with the rotor by hydraulic force. The caliper, which is not held in a fixed position, moves slightly, bringing the outside pad into contact with the rotor. There are various methods of attaching floating calipers. Some pivot at the bottom or top, and some slide on mounting bolts. In any event, the end result is the same.

Drum Brakes

BASIC OPERATING PRINCIPLES

Drum brakes employ two brake shoes mounted on a stationary backing plate. These shoes are positioned inside a circular drum which rotates with the wheel assembly. The shoes are held in place by springs. This allows them to slide toward the drums (when they are applied) while keeping the linings and drums in alignment. The shoes are actuated by a wheel cylinder which is mounted at the top of the backing plate. When the brakes are applied, hydraulic pressure forces the wheel cylinder's actuating links outward. Since these links bear directly against the top of the brake shoes, the tops of the shoes are then forced against the inner side of the drum. This action forces the bottoms of the two shoes to contact the brake drum by rotating the entire assembly slightly (known as servo action). When pressure within the wheel cylinder is relaxed, return springs pull the shoes back away from the drum.

Most modern drum brakes are designed to self-adjust themselves during application when the vehicle is moving in reverse. This motion causes both shoes to rotate very slightly with the drum, rocking an adjusting lever, thereby causing rotation of the adjusting screw.

Power Boosters

Power brakes operate just as standard brake systems except in the actuation of the master cylinder pistons. A vacuum diaphragm is located on the front of the master cylinder and assists the driver in applying the brakes, reducing both the effort and travel he must put into moving the brake pedal.

The vacuum diaphragm housing is connected to the intake manifold by a vacuum hose. A check valve is placed at the point where the hose enters the diaphragm housing, so that during periods of low manifold vacuum brake assist vacuum will not be lost.

Depressing the brake pedal closes off the vacuum source and allows atmospheric pressure to enter on one side of the diaphragm. This causes the master cylinder pistons to move and apply the brakes. When the brake pedal is released, vacuum is applied to both sides of the diaphragm, and return springs return the diaphragm and master cylinder pistons to the released position. If the vacuum fails, the brake pedal rod will butt against the end of the master cylinder actuating rod, and direct mechanical application will occur as the pedal is depressed.

The hydraulic and mechanical problems that apply to conventional brake systems also apply to power brakes, and should be checked for if the tests below do not reveal the problem. Test for a system vacuum leak as described below:

1. Operate the engine at idle without touching the brake pedal for at least one minute.

2. Turn off the engine, and wait one minute.

3. Test for the presence of assist vacuum by depressing the brake pedal and releasing it several times. Light application will produce less and less pedal travel, if vacuum was present. If there is no vacuum, air is leaking into the system somewhere.

Test for system operation as follows:

1. Pump the brake pedal (with engine off) until the supply vacuum is entirely gone.

2. Put a light, steady pressure on the pedal.

3. Start the engine, and operate it at idle. If the system is operating, the brake pedal should fall toward the floor if constant pressure is maintained on the pedal.

Power brake systems may be tested for hydraulic leaks just as ordinary systems are tested.

CAUTION: *Brake linings contain asbestos. Asbestos is a known cancer-causing agent. When working on brakes, remember that the dust which accumulates on the brake parts and/or in the drum contains asbestos. Always wear a protective face covering, such as a painter's mask, when working on the brakes. NEVER blow the dust from the brakes or drum! There are solvents made for the purpose of cleaning brake parts. Use them!*

Adjustment of Drum Brakes Only

The method of brake adjustment varies depending on whether the vehicle is equipped with cam adjustment brakes or star wheel adjustment brakes with self adjusters. When the

Troubleshooting the Brake System

Problem	Cause	Solution
Low brake pedal (excessive pedal travel required for braking action.)	• Excessive clearance between rear linings and drums caused by inoperative automatic adjusters	• Make 10 to 15 alternate forward and reverse brake stops to adjust brakes. If brake pedal does not come up, repair or replace adjuster parts as necessary.
	• Worn rear brakelining	• Inspect and replace lining if worn beyond minimum thickness specification
	• Bent, distorted brakeshoes, front or rear	• Replace brakeshoes in axle sets
	• Air in hydraulic system	• Remove air from system. Refer to Brake Bleeding.
Low brake pedal (pedal may go to floor with steady pressure applied.)	• Fluid leak in hydraulic system	• Fill master cylinder to fill line; have helper apply brakes and check calipers, wheel cylinders, differential valve tubes, hoses and fittings for leaks. Repair or replace as necessary.
	• Air in hydraulic system	• Remove air from system. Refer to Brake Bleeding.
	• Incorrect or non-recommended brake fluid (fluid evaporates at below normal temp).	• Flush hydraulic system with clean brake fluid. Refill with correct-type fluid.
	• Master cylinder piston seals worn, or master cylinder bore is scored, worn or corroded	• Repair or replace master cylinder
Low brake pedal (pedal goes to floor on first application—o.k. on subsequent applications.)	• Disc brake pads sticking on abutment surfaces of anchor plate. Caused by a build-up of dirt, rust, or corrosion on abutment surfaces	• Clean abutment surfaces
Fading brake pedal (pedal height decreases with steady pressure applied.)	• Fluid leak in hydraulic system	• Fill master cylinder reservoirs to fill mark, have helper apply brakes, check calipers, wheel cylinders, differential valve, tubes, hoses, and fittings for fluid leaks. Repair or replace parts as necessary.
	• Master cylinder piston seals worn, or master cylinder bore is scored, worn or corroded	• Repair or replace master cylinder
Decreasing brake pedal travel (pedal travel required for braking action decreases and may be accompanied by a hard pedal.)	• Caliper or wheel cylinder pistons sticking or seized	• Repair or replace the calipers, or wheel cylinders
	• Master cylinder compensator ports blocked (preventing fluid return to reservoirs) or pistons sticking or seized in master cylinder bore	• Repair or replace the master cylinder
	• Power brake unit binding internally	• Test unit according to the following procedure: (a) Shift transmission into neutral and start engine (b) Increase engine speed to 1500 rpm, close throttle and fully depress brake pedal (c) Slow release brake pedal and stop engine (d) Have helper remove vacuum check valve and hose from power unit. Observe for backward movement of brake pedal. (e) If the pedal moves backward, the power unit has an internal bind—replace power unit

Troubleshooting the Brake System (cont.)

Problem	Cause	Solution
Spongy brake pedal (pedal has abnormally soft, springy, spongy feel when depressed.)	• Air in hydraulic system • Brakeshoes bent or distorted • Brakelining not yet seated with drums and rotors • Rear drum brakes not properly adjusted	• Remove air from system. Refer to Brake Bleeding. • Replace brakeshoes • Burnish brakes • Adjust brakes
Hard brake pedal (excessive pedal pressure required to stop vehicle. May be accompanied by brake fade.)	• Loose or leaking power brake unit vacuum hose • Incorrect or poor quality brake-lining • Bent, broken, distorted brakeshoes • Calipers binding or dragging on mounting pins. Rear brakeshoes dragging on support plate. • Caliper, wheel cylinder, or master cylinder pistons sticking or seized • Power brake unit vacuum check valve malfunction • Power brake unit has internal bind • Master cylinder compensator ports (at bottom of reservoirs) blocked by dirt, scale, rust, or have small burrs (blocked ports prevent fluid return to reservoirs). • Brake hoses, tubes, fittings clogged or restricted • Brake hoses, tubes, fittings clogged or restricted • Brake fluid contaminated with improper fluids (motor oil, transmission fluid, causing rubber	• Tighten connections or replace leaking hose • Replace with lining in axle sets • Replace brakeshoes • Replace mounting pins and bushings. Clean rust or burrs from rear brake support plate ledges and lubricate ledges with molydisulfide grease. **NOTE:** If ledges are deeply grooved or scored, do not attempt to sand or grind them smooth—replace support plate. • Repair or replace parts as necessary • Test valve according to the following procedure: (a) Start engine, increase engine speed to 1500 rpm, close throttle and immediately stop engine (b) Wait at least 90 seconds then depress brake pedal (c) If brakes are not vacuum assisted for 2 or more applications, check valve is faulty • Test unit according to the following procedure: (a) With engine stopped, apply brakes several times top exhaust all vacuum in system (b) Shift transmission into neutral, depress brake pedal and start engine (c) If pedal height decreases with foot pressure and less pressure is required to hold pedal in applied position, power unit vacuum system is operating normally. Test power unit. If power unit exhibits a bind condition, replace the power unit. • Repair or replace master cylinder **CAUTION:** Do not attempt to clean blocked ports with wire, pencils, or similar implements. Use compressed air only. • Use compressed air to check or unclog parts. Replace any damaged parts. • Use compressed air to check or unclog parts. Replace any damaged parts. • Replace all rubber components, combination valve and hoses. Flush entire brake system with

Troubleshooting the Brake System (cont.)

Problem	Cause	Solution
	components to swell and stick in bores	DOT 3 brake fluid or equivalent.
	• Low engine vacuum	• Adjust or repair engine
Grabbing brakes (severe reaction to brake pedal pressure.)	• Brakelining(s) contaminated by grease or brake fluid	• Determine and correct cause of contamination and replace brakeshoes in axle sets
	• Parking brake cables incorrectly adjusted or seized	• Adjust cables. Replace seized cables.
	• Incorrect brakelining or lining loose on brakeshoes	• Replace brakeshoes in axle sets
	• Caliper anchor plate bolts loose	• Tighten bolts
	• Rear brakeshoes binding on support plate ledges	• Clean and lubricate ledges. Replace support plate(s) if ledges are deeply grooved. Do not attempt to smooth ledges by grinding.
	• Incorrect or missing power brake reaction disc	• Install correct disc
	• Rear brake support plates loose	• Tighten mounting bolts
Dragging brakes (slow or incomplete release of brakes)	• Brake pedal binding at pivot	• Loosen and lubricate
	• Power brake unit has internal bind	• Inspect for internal bind. Replace unit if internal bind exists.
	• Parking brake cables incorrrectly adjusted or seized	• Adjust cables. Replace seized cables.
	• Rear brakeshoe return springs weak or broken	• Replace return springs. Replace brakeshoe if necessary in axle sets.
	• Automatic adjusters malfunctioning	• Repair or replace adjuster parts as required
	• Caliper, wheel cylinder or master cylinder pistons sticking or seized	• Repair or replace parts as necessary
	• Master cylinder compensating ports blocked (fluid does not return to reservoirs).	• Use compressed air to clear ports. Do not use wire, pencils, or similar objects to open blocked ports.
Vehicle moves to one side when brakes are applied	• Incorrect front tire pressure	• Inflate to recommended cold (reduced load) inflation pressure
	• Worn or damaged wheel bearings	• Replace worn or damaged bearings
	• Brakelining on one side contaminated	• Determine and correct cause of contamination and replace brakelining in axle sets
	• Brakeshoes on one side bent, distorted, or lining loose on shoe	• Replace brakeshoes in axle sets
	• Support plate bent or loose on one side	• Tighten or replace support plate
	• Brakelining not yet seated with drums or rotors	• Burnish brakelining
	• Caliper anchor plate loose on one side	• Tighten anchor plate bolts
	• Caliper piston sticking or seized	• Repair or replace caliper
	• Brakelinings water soaked	• Drive vehicle with brakes lightly applied to dry linings
	• Loose suspension component attaching or mounting bolts	• Tighten suspension bolts. Replace worn suspension components.
	• Brake combination valve failure	• Replace combination valve
Chatter or shudder when brakes are applied (pedal pulsation and roughness may also occur.)	• Brakeshoes distorted, bent, contaminated, or worn	• Replace brakeshoes in axle sets
	• Caliper anchor plate or support plate loose	• Tighten mounting bolts
	• Excessive thickness variation of rotor(s)	• Refinish or replace rotors in axle sets

Troubleshooting the Brake System (cont.)

Problem	Cause	Solution
Noisy brakes (squealing, clicking, scraping sound when brakes are applied.)	• Bent, broken, distorted brakeshoes • Excessive rust on outer edge of rotor braking surface • Brakelining worn out—shoes contacting drum of rotor • Broken or loose holdown or return springs • Rough or dry drum brake support plate ledges • Cracked, grooved, or scored rotor(s) or drum(s) • Incorrect brakelining and/or shoes (front or rear).	• Replace brakeshoes in axle sets • Remove rust • Replace brakeshoes and lining in axle sets. Refinish or replace drums or rotors. • Replace parts as necessary • Lubricate support plate ledges • Replace rotor(s) or drum(s). Replace brakeshoes and lining in axle sets if necessary. • Install specified shoe and lining assemblies
Pulsating brake pedal	• Out of round drums or excessive lateral runout in disc brake rotor(s)	• Refinish or replace drums, re-index rotors or replace

brake linings become worn, effective brake pedal travel is reduced. Adjusting the brake shoes will restore the necessary travel.

Before adjusting the brakes, check the spring nuts, brake dust shield to axle flange bolts, and wheel bearing adjustments. Any looseness in these parts will cause erratic brake operation. Also on models through 1971 make sure that the brake pedal has the correct amount of free travel without moving the master cylinder piston (free play). There should be about ½" of free play at the master cylinder eye bolt. Turn the eye bolt to adjust free play. On models from 1972 on, the pedal free travel is determined by the pedal pushrod length and is not adjustable. If pedal free travel is less than $\frac{1}{16}$" replace the pushrod.

Release the parking brakes and centralize the brake shoes in the drums by depressing the brake pedal hard and then releasing it. It is best to have all four wheels off the ground when the brakes are adjusted so that you can go back to each wheel to double check your adjustments.

INITIAL BRAKE SHOE ADJUSTMENT

If the brake assemblies have been disassembled, an initial adjustment must be made before the drum is installed. It may also be necessary to back off the adjustment to remove the drums.

When the brake parts have been installed in their correct position, adjust the adjusting screw assemblies to a point where approximately ⅜" of threads are exposed between the star wheel and the star wheel nut.

CAM ADJUSTMENT BRAKES

1. Jack up the vehicle until all of the wheels, or at least the one to be adjusted first, are off the ground.

2. Turn the forward shoe adjusting cams on the left side of the vehicle clockwise until the shoes are tight against the drums. Then turn the cams in the opposite direction until the wheels rotate freely without brake drag.

3. Turn the rear adjusting cams on the left side counterclockwise until the shoes are tight against the drums. Then turn the cams in the opposite direction until the wheels rotate freely without brake drag.

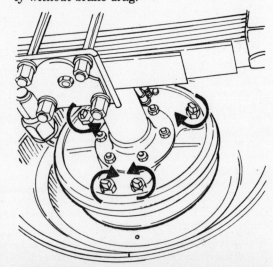

Brake adjustment points on CJ-2A and CJ-3A models. Note the anchor pin adjusters at the bottom of the backing plate

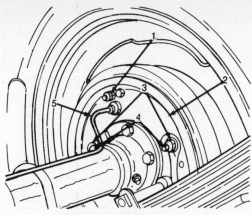

1. Bleeder screw
2. Brake backing plate
3. Eccentric lock nut
4. Eccentric adjusting screw
5. Brake fluid line

Brake adjustments on all CJ-3B models and CJ-5 and CJ-6 models with cam adjusters

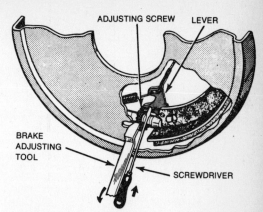

To loosen the self-adjusting drum brake, you have to hold the adjusting lever away from the star wheel

4. Repeat the two steps given above on the right side of the vehicle, turning the forward shoe adjusting cams counterclockwise and the rear shoe adjusting clockwise to tighten.

In CJ-2A and CJ-3A models, if additional adjustment is required or when installing new brakes, reset the anchor pins as follows:

a. With the brakes installed and the drum in place, loosen the anchor pin locknuts at the bottom of the backing plate.

b. Turn the anchor pins in toward each other until a brake shoe-to-drum clearance is 0.005″ at the lower end of the shoe and 0.008″ at the upper end. On early models, a slot in the brake drum was provided to measure this clearance. The slot was eliminated on later models.

STAR WHEEL ADJUSTING TYPE BRAKES (WITH SELF ADJUSTERS)

1. Raise and support the vehicle on jackstands.

2. Remove the access slot cover and using a brake adjusting tool or screwdriver, rotate the star wheel until the wheel is locked and can't be turned in the clockwise direction.

3. Back off the star wheel until the wheel rotates freely. To back off the star wheel on the brake, insert an ice pick or thin screw driver in the adjusting screw slot to hold the automatic adjusting lever away from the star wheel. Do not attempt to back off on the adjusting screw without holding the adjusting lever away from the star wheel as the adjuster will be damaged.

HYDRAULIC SYSTEM

Master Cylinder

REMOVAL AND INSTALLATION

To remove the master cylinder, disconnect and plug the brake lines, disconnect the wires from the stoplight switch, disconnect the master cylinder pushrod at the brake pedal (non-power brakes only), remove all attaching bolts and nuts and lift the assembly from the vehicle.

Installation is the reverse of the removal procedure. Torque the mounting bolts to 30 ft.lb. on 1945–86 models; 18 ft.lb. on 1987 models. Bleed the hydraulic system.

OVERHAUL

Single System

1. After the master cylinder has been removed it should be dismantled and washed in alcohol. Never wash any part of the hydraulic braking system in gasoline or kerosene.

2. After all the parts have been thoroughly cleaned with alcohol, make a careful inspection, replacing those parts which show signs of deterioration.

3. Inspect the cylinder bore. If it is rough, it should be honed out or a new cylinder installed.

4. Clean out the cylinder with alcohol. Pass a wire through the ports that open from the supply reservoir into the cylinder bore to make sure that these passages are free of any foreign matter.

5. Install a new piston, primary cup, valve, and valve seat when rebuilding the master cylinder.

6. When reassembling the master cylinder, dip all internal parts in clean brake fluid. Install the valve seat in the end of the cylinder with the flat surface toward the valve.

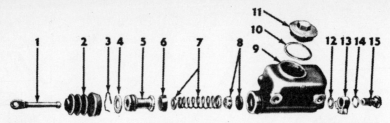

1. Pushrod
2. Boot
3. Piston stop lock wire
4. Stop plate
5. Piston
6. Master cylinder cup
7. Valve spring assembly
8. Valve seat
9. Supply tank
10. Filler cap gasket
11. Filler cap
12. Outlet fitting gasket
13. Outlet fitting
14. Outlet fitting bolt
15. Outlet fitting bolt

Single system master cylinder

7. Install the valve assembly.

8. Install the return spring and primary cup. The flat side of the cup goes toward the piston.

9. Install the piston and the piston stop snapring.

10. Install the fitting connection.

11. Fill the reservoir half full with brake fluid and operate the piston with the piston rod until fluid is ejected at the fitting.

12. Install the master cylinder to the firewall or in position under the floor pan. Fill it to a level ½" below the top of the fill hole.

13. Make the necessary connections and adjust the pedal clearance.

14. Bleed the brake lines.

15. Recheck the entire hydraulic brake system to make sure there are no leaks.

Dual System Through 1975

1. Remove the filler cap and empty all the fluid.

2. The stop light switch and primary piston stop, located in the stop light switch outlet hole, must be removed before removing the snapring from the piston bore. Remove the snapring, pushrod assembly and the primary and secondary piston assemblies. Air pressure applied in the piston stop hole will help facili-

1. Boot
2. Snapring
3. Piston assembly
4. Backing ring
5. Master cylinder cup
6. Master cylinder cup
7. Piston
8. Master cylinder cup
9. Cup protector
10. Spring
11. Cylinder housing
12. Cover gasket
13. Cover
14. Washer gasket
15. Washer
16. Cover bolt
17. Check valve spring
18. Check valve
19. Tube seat
20. Piston stop

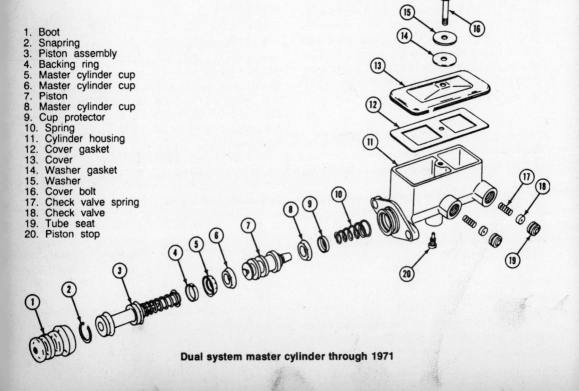

Dual system master cylinder through 1971

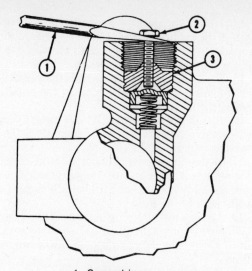

1. Screwdriver
2. Self-tapping screw
3. Tube seat

Removing tube seats

tate the removal of the secondary piston assembly.

3. The residual check valves are located under the front and rear fluid outlet tube seats.

4. The tube seats must be removed with self tapping screws to permit the removal of the check valves. Screw the self-tapping screws into the tube seats and place two screw driver tips under the screw head and force the screw upward.

5. Remove the expander in the rear secondary cup, secondary cups, return spring cup protector, primary cup, and washer from the secondary piston.

6. Immerse all of the metal parts in clean brake fluid and clean them. Use an air hose to blow out dirt and cleaning solvent from recesses and internal passages.

7. After cleaning, place all of the parts on clean paper or in a clean pan.

8. Inspect all parts for damage or excessive wear. Replace any damaged, worn, or chipped

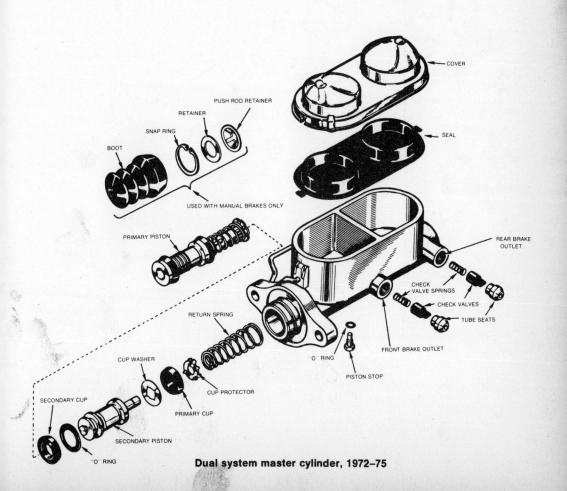

Dual system master cylinder, 1972–75

parts. Inspect the hydraulic cylinder bore for signs of scoring, rust, pitting, or etching. Any of these will require replacement of the hydraulic cylinder.

9. Prior to assembling the master cylinder, dip all of the components in clean brake fluid and place them on clean paper or in a clean pan.

10. Install the primary cup washer, primary cup, cup protector, and return spring in the secondary position.

11. Install the piston cups in the double groove end of the secondary piston, so the flat side of the cups face each other (lip of the cups away from each other). Install the cup expander in the lip groove of the end cup.

12. Coat the cylinder bore and piston assemblies with clean brake fluid before installing any parts in the cylinder.

13. Install the secondary piston assembly first and then the primary piston.

14. Install the pushrod assembly, which includes the pushrod, boot, and rod retainer, and secure with the snapring. Install the primary piston stop and stop light switch.

15. Place new rubber check valves over the check valve springs and install in the outlet holes, spring first.

16. Install the tube seats, flat side toward the check valve, and press in with tube nuts or the master cylinder brake tube nuts.

17. Before the master cylinder is installed on the vehicle it must be bled. Support the cylinder assembly in a vise and fill both fluid reservoirs with brake fluid.

18. Loosely install a plug in each outlet of the cylinder. Depress the push rod several times until air bubbles cease to appear in the brake fluid.

19. Tighten the plugs and attempt to depress the piston. The piston travel should be restricted after all of the air is expelled.

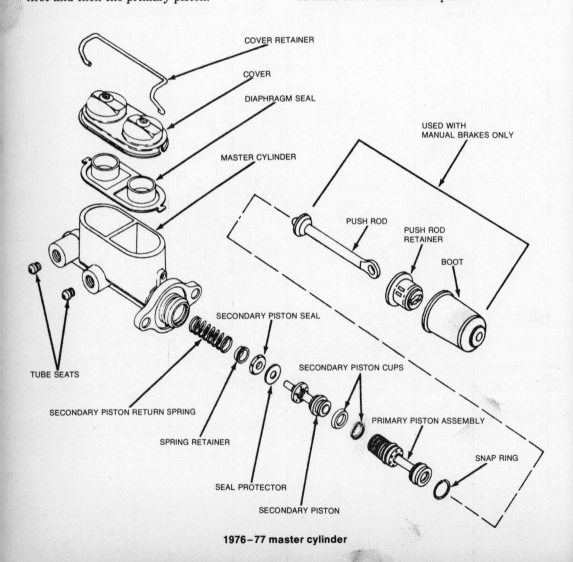

1976–77 master cylinder

20. Install the master cylinder in the vehicle and bleed all the hydraulic lines at the wheel cylinders.

Dual System 1976–87

1. Remove the master cylinder from the vehicle and remove the cover and diaphragm seal. Drain the brake fluid from the reservoir and mount it in a vise.

2. With non-power brakes, slide the boot back on the pushrod. Push the pushrod in and unseat the primary piston snapring. Remove the pushrod, boot, snapring, and pushrod retainer as an assembly. With power brakes, push the primary piston in with a wooden dowel and remove the piston snapring.

3. Remove the primary and secondary piston assemblies. Air pressure applied through the piston stop hole will help in the removal of the secondary piston.

4. Clamp the primary piston pushrod in a vise, with the brake pedal eyelet facing down-

ward and the rear face of the primary piston positioned just above the jaws of the vise.

5. Remove the rubber insert from the primary piston and discard it. NEVER ATTEMPT TO REUSE THIS INSERT! A REPLACEMENT INSERT MUST BE OBTAINED!!

6. Remove the piston seal and piston cups from the secondary piston. It is not necessary to disassemble the primary piston because a new complete primary piston assembly is supplied in the rebuilding kit.

7. Clean and inspect the master cylinder. Replace the master cylinder body if the bore is severely scored, corroded, or pitted, cracked, porous, or is otherwise damaged. Check the bypass and compensator ports to make sure that they are open and not plugged or dirty. Use brake fluid and air pressure to open these passages. Do not use wire.

NOTE: *Use only clean brake fluid or an approved cleaning solvent to wash the master cylinder. Do not use any solvent containing*

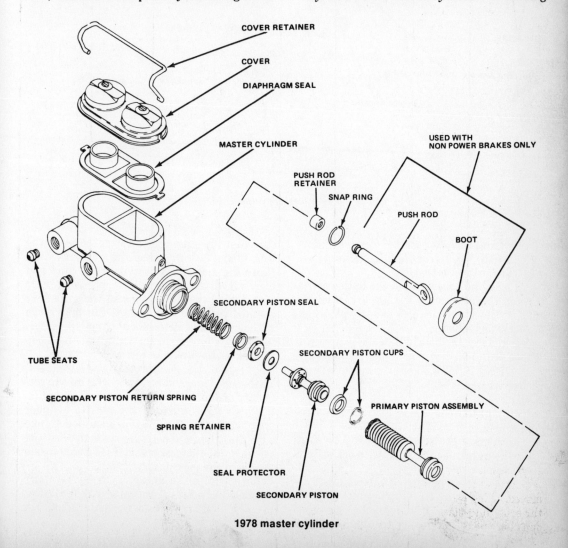

1978 master cylinder

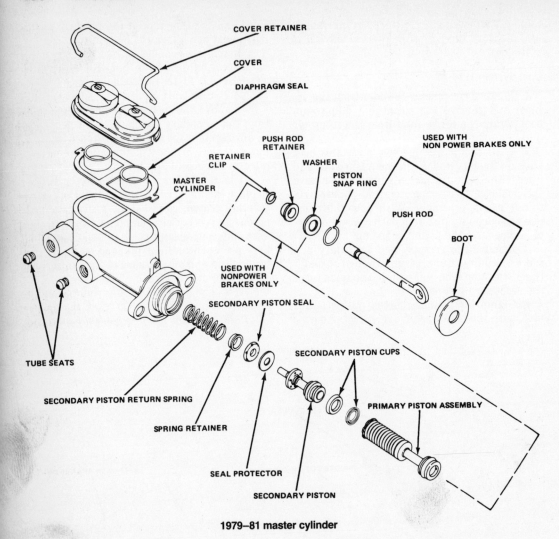

1979–81 master cylinder

mineral oil such as gasoline, kerosene, alcohol, or carbon tetrachloride. Mineral oil harms rubber components.

8. Check the tube seats in the outlet ports. Replace the seats only if they are cracked, scored, cocked in the bore, or loose. Replace the tube seats as follows:

a. Enlarge the hole in the tube seat with a $^{13}/_{64}$" drill bit.

b. Place a flat washer on each outlet port and thread a ¼"–20 x ¾" long screw into the seat.

c. Tighten the screw until the seat is loosened.

d. Remove the seat, screw, and washer. Flush any metal chips away with brake fluid and compressed air.

9. Install the replacement tube seats, if removed, using spare tube fitting nuts to press the seats into place. Be careful that the seats don't become cocked during installation. Make

sure that the seats are bottomed. Remove the tube fitting nuts and check for burrs or chips. Rinse the master cylinder in brake fluid and blow out all passages with compressed air.

10. Install the piston cups on the secondary piston. The piston cup installed in the groove at the end of the piston should have its lip facing away from the piston. Install the next cup so that its lip faces the piston.

11. Install the seal protector, piston seal, spring retainer, and return spring on the secondary piston. Install the piston seal so that its lip faces the interior of the master cylinder bore when the assembly is installed. Make sure that the return spring seats against the retainer and that the retainer is located inside the lip of the piston seal.

12. Lubricate the master cylinder bore and secondary piston seal and cups with brake fluid and install the secondary piston assembly in the cylinder bore.

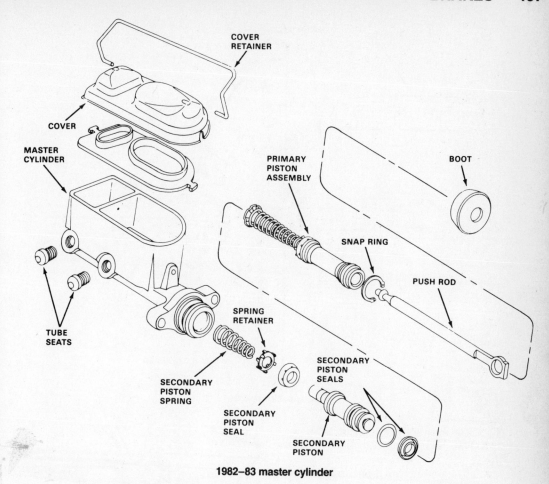

1982–83 master cylinder

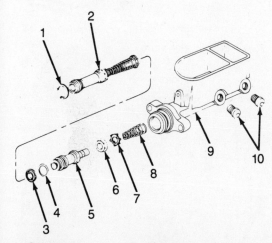

1984–87 master cylinder

1. Snapring
2. Primary piston
3. Seal
4. Seal
5. Secondary piston
6. Rear seal
7. retainer
8. Spring
9. Master cylinder body
10. Outlet port tube seats

13. Lubricate the seals on the primary piston assembly with brake fluid and install the assembly in the master cylinder bore.

14. With power brakes, push the primary piston inward with a wooden bowel and install the retaining snapring in the groove of the master cylinder bore.

15. With non-power brakes, install the pushrod, pushrod retainer, and boot. Push in and install the piston snapring.

16. Install the diaphragm seal on the master cylinder cover.

17. Install the master cylinder in the vehicle. Bleed the system.

Power Brake Booster

REMOVAL AND INSTALLATION

1. Disconnect the power unit pushrod at the pedal.

2. Disconnect the vacuum line at the power unit check valve.

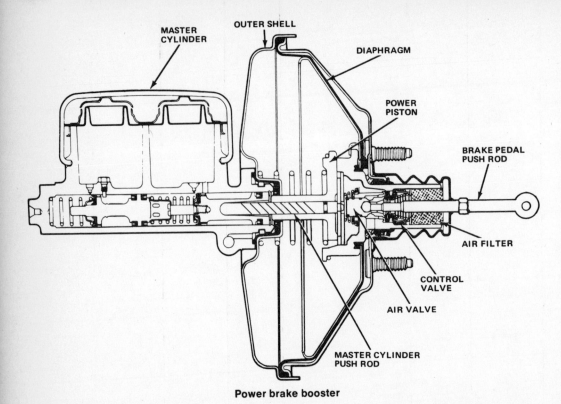

Power brake booster

3. Unbolt the master cylinder from the power unit and push the master cylinder aside carefully.

4. Unbolt the power unit bellcrank at the dash panel and remove the power unit and bellcrank as an assembly. If the power unit is being discarded, save the bellcrank for the new unit.

5. Installation is the reverse of removal. Torque the bellcrank-to-dash panel bolts to 35 ft.lb.; the master cylinder-to-power unit bolts to 30 ft.lb. on models through 1986, or 18 ft.lb. on 1987 models; the pushrod-to-pedal bolt and nut to 35 ft.lb.

Proportioning Valve

The proportioning valve is actually a three part unit, containing a metering valve, pressure differential valve and brake pressure warning switch. If any of these functions fails, the unit must be replaced. It is not repairable. Two different types of valves were used. On models in the early 1970s, a D-type valve was used, in the late 1970's, a Type W was also used. They are similar in appearance and the only significant difference is in the method of holding open the valve during bleeding. Type W uses tool J-26869; type D uses tool J-23709. The valves are not interchangeable, however. In late 1983, the W-type became the only type used.

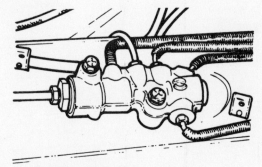

Type D combination valve

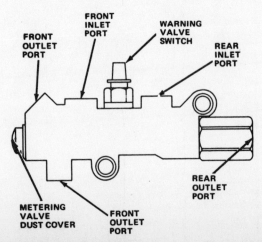

Type W combination valve

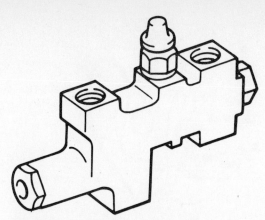

Proportioning valve used on 1987 models

The valve is located on the frame rail, directly under the driver's position on models through 1986 and on the left fender panel just below the master cylinder, on 1987 models.

REMOVAL AND INSTALLATION

1. Disconnect the brake lines at the valve and plug them.
2. Unbolt and remove the valve.
3. Installation is the reverse of removal. Bleed the system.

Brake Hoses and Lines

INSPECTION

1. Inspect all connections for signs of leakage.
2. Replace any hose that shows signs of wear, scuffing or loss of rubber coating.
3. Replace any hose or line that becomes kinked or creased.
4. Replace any hose that shows signs of cracking or cutting.
5. Replace any hose that appears swollen.
6. Replace any line that shows signs of corrosion.

REMOVAL AND INSTALLATION

1. Clean the connections thoroughly before opening them.
2. Hane handy some means of capping the line remaining in the vehicle so as to prevent excessive fluid loss.
3. Use a wrench of the exact size necessary to loosen the fitting. Avoid using an adjustable wrench or pliers, as brake line fittings are easily rounded off.
4. When replacing a brake hose connected to a brake caliper, always replace the copper gasket under the union.
5. Front brake hoses are usually connected to the metal line at a junction attached to the frame or a suspension member. In many cases,

there is a U-shaped clip which must be driven out to free the junction.
6. When installing a brake hose or line, observe the following torques, where possible:
• Brake hose union-to-disc brake caliper bolt: 25 ft.lb.
• Brake line-to-wheel cylinder connection: 160 in.lb.

Bleeding the Brakes

The hydraulic brake system must be bled whenever a fluid line has been disconnected because air gets into the system. A leak in the system may sometimes be indicated by a spongy brake pedal. Air trapped in the system is compressible and does not permit the pressure applied to the brake pedal to be transmitted solidly through the brakes. The system must be absolutely free from air at all times. When bleeding brakes, bleed at the wheel most distant from the master cylinder first, the next most distant second, and so on. During the bleeding operation the master cylinder must be kept at least ¾ full of brake fluid.

NOTE: *On 1974 and later models, there is a combination pressure differential (failure warning) and proportioning valve in the hy-*

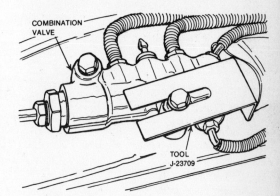

Metering valve tool installation on the Type D valve

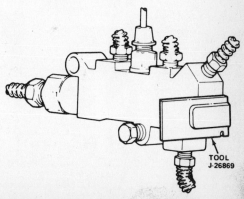

Metering valve tool installed on a type W combination valve

draulic system. *It is in the engine compart-*
ment on the inner side of the left frame rail.
When bleeding the brake system, the meter-
ing section of the valve must be held open. On
1974–76 models, remove the warning switch
wire, switch terminal, plunger, and spring
from the valve. On all 1977 models and
1978–79 models using a valve assembly with
a flat exterior surface, remove the plastic dust
cover at the end of the valve and hold the
valve stem OUT. On 1978–79 models using a
valve assembly with a rounded exterior sur-
face, hold the valve stem IN by pressing
against the dust cover boot. Tools are avail-
able to hold the valve stem in the proper loca-
tion or can be fabricated.

To bleed the brakes, first carefully clean all
dirt from around the master cylinder filler cap.
If a bleeder tank is used follow the manufac-

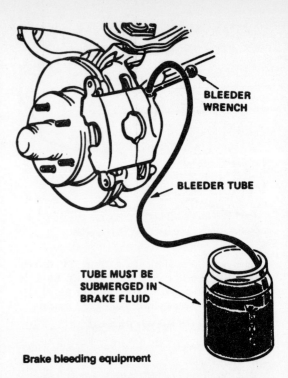

Brake bleeding equipment

Bleeding the brakes on early models

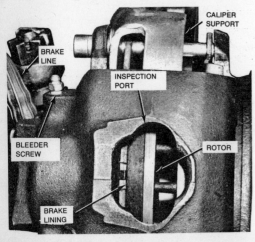

The thickness of the disc brake pad linings can
be checked visually. Minimum safe thickness is
¹/₁₆ in. with bonded linings and ¹/₃₂ in. above the
rivet heads with riveted lining

turer's instructions. Remove the filler cap and
fill the master cylinder to the lower edge of the
filler neck. Clean off the bleeder connections at
all four wheel cylinders. Attach the bleeder
hose to the right rear wheel cylinder bleeder
screw and place the end of the tube in a glass
jar, submerged in brake fluid. Open the bleeder valve ½–¾ of a turn. Have an assistant depress the brake pedal slowly and allow it to return. Continue this pumping action to force
any air out of the system. When bubbles cease
to appear at the end of the bleeder hose, close
the bleeder valve and remove the hose.

Check the level of fluid in the master cylinder reservoir and replenish as necessary.

After the bleeding operation at each wheel
cylinder has been completed, fill the master
cylinder reservoir and replace the filler plug.

Do not reuse the fluid which has been removed from the lines through the bleeding process because it contains air bubbles and dirt.

Stop Light Switch

Two types of switches have been used on Jeep
vehicles. One type is attached to the brake pedal rod end of the push rod, and cannot be adjusted. The other type is mounted on a flange
attached to the brake pedal support bracket
and is held in the off position by the brake pedal's being in its released position. Upon depressing the brake pedal, the switch plunger is
allowed to move outward and contact is made
within the switch to allow current to pass and
operate the stop lights.

SWITCH ADJUSTMENT

NOTE: *On some vehicles equipped with air conditioning, remove the screws attaching the evaporator housing to the instrument panel and move the housing away from the panel.*

1. Hold the brake pedal in the applied position.

2. Push the stop light switch through the mounting bracket until it stops against the brake pedal bracket. Release the pedal to set the switch in the proper position.

3. Check the position of the switch. The switch plunger should be in the ON position and activate the brake lights after a brake pedal travel of 3/8–5/8".

DISC BRAKES

The front disc brake consists of 3 assemblies, the caliper assembly, the hub and rotor assembly, and the support and shield assembly.

The caliper is a single piston sliding type, of one piece casting construction with the inboard side containing the single piston, piston bore and the bleeder screw and fluid inlet holes. There are two brake pads within the caliper, positioned on either side of the rotor. The brake pads take the place of brake shoes on drum brakes and the rotor takes the place of brake drums. The pads themselves actually consist of two parts: the metal shoe and the composition lining which is bonded or riveted to the shoe.

The significant operating feature of the single piston caliper is that it is free to slide laterally on the anchor plate. The pressure applied to the piston is transmitted to the inboard brake pad, forcing the lining of the pad against the inboard rotor surface. The pressure applied to the inboard end or bottom of the piston bore forces the caliper to slide toward the inboard side. This inward movement of the caliper causes the outboard section of the caliper to apply pressure against the lining of the outboard pad, forcing the lining of the outboard pad, forcing the lining against the outboard surface of the rotor. As hydraulic pressure builds within the brake lines, due to the increased application of pressure at the brake pedal, the brake pad assemblies press against the rotor surfaces with increasing force, thus slowing the rotation of the rotor.

Brake Pads

REMOVAL AND INSTALLATION

Through 1981

CAUTION: *Brake shoes contain asbestos, which has been determined to be a cancer*

causing agent. Never clean the brake surfaces with compressed air! Avoid inhaling any dust from any brake surface! When cleaning brake surfaces, use a commercially available brake cleaning fluid.*

1. Remove 2/3 of the brake fluid from the front reservoir.

2. Raise the vehicle so that the wheel to be worked on is off the ground. Support the vehicle with jackstands.

3. Remove the front wheels.

4. Place a C-clamp on the caliper so that the solid end contacts the back of the caliper and the screw end contacts the metal part of the outboard brake pad.

5. Tighten the clamp until the caliper moves far enough to force the piston to the bottom of the piston bore. This will back the brake pads off the rotor surface to facilitate the removal and installation of the caliper assembly.

6. Remove the C-clamp.

NOTE: *Do not push down on the brake pedal or the piston and brake pads will return to their original positions up against the rotor.*

7. Remove the caliper support key retaining screw with a 1/4" Allen wrench. Drive the support key and spring out with a punch.

NOTE: *If just the brake pads are being replaced, it is not necessary to remove the caliper assembly entirely from the vehicle. Do not remove the brake line. Rest the caliper on the front spring or other suitable support. Do not allow the brake hose to support the weight of the caliper.*

8. Remove the brake pad assemblies. Remove the anti-rattle spring from the inboard pad. Note the position of the spring before removing it for correct installation later.

9. Wipe the inside of the caliper clean, including the exterior of the dust boot. Inspect the dust boot for cuts or cracks and for proper seating in the piston bore. If evidence of fluid leakage is noted, the caliper should be rebuilt.

10. Check the sliding surface of the caliper and anchor plate for rust or corrosion. Clean them with a wire brush and fine sandpaper; lubricate with molybdenum disulphide grease.

11. Install the inboard pad anti-rattle spring on the rear flange of the pad. Make sure the looped section of the spring is away from the rotor.

12. Install the inboard pad with spring attached in the caliper anchor plate.

13. Install the outboard pad in the caliper.

14. Place the caliper over the rotor and on the anchor plate.

NOTE: *Be careful not to damage or dislodge the dust boot.*

15. Insert the support key and spring between the sliding surfaces at the rear of the caliper. Drive them into place with a punch.

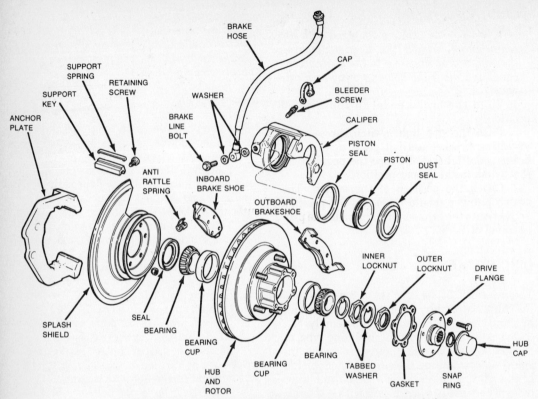

Disc brake unit used on models through 1981, without locking hubs

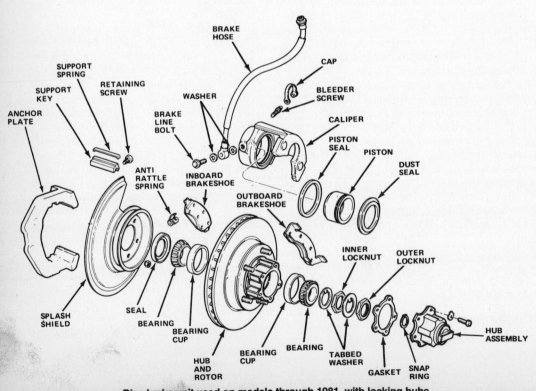

Disc brake unit used on models through 1981, with locking hubs

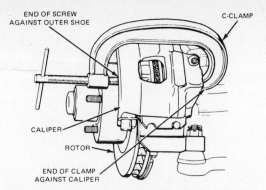

Bottoming the caliper piston on models through 1981

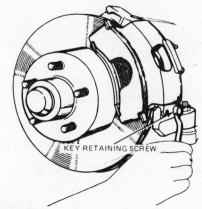

Removing the caliper retaining screw on models through 1981

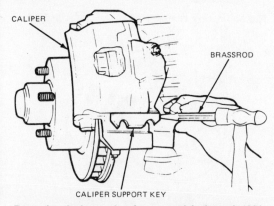

Removing the key and spring on models through 1981

16. Install the key retaining screw and torque it to 15 ft.lb.

17. Fill the master cylinder to within ¼" of the rim.

18. Press firmly on the brake pedal several times till the pedal is firm.

19. Recheck the master cylinder level.

1984–86

CAUTION: *Brake shoes contain asbestos, which has been determined to be a cancer*

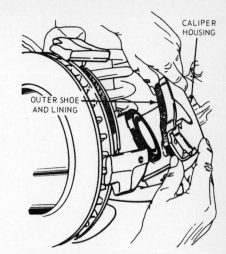

Removing the outer pad on models through 1981

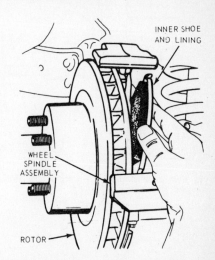

Removing the inner pad on models through 1981

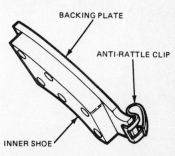

Installing the anti-rattle clip on the inner pad on models through 1981

causing agent. Never clean the brake surfaces with compressed air! Avoid inhaling any dust from any brake surface! When cleaning brake surfaces, use a commercially available brake cleaning fluid.

1. Remove ⅔ of the brake fluid from the front reservoir.

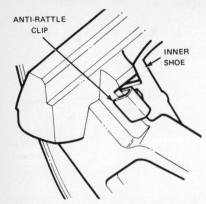

Installing the inner pad on the caliper support on models through 1981

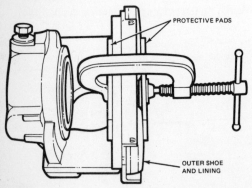

Installing the outer pad in the caliper on models through 1981

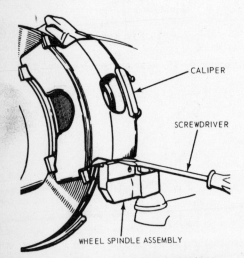

Installing the caliper on models through 1981

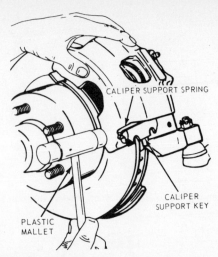

Installing the caliper support key and spring on models through 1981

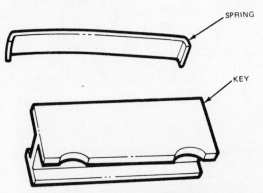

Key and spring assembly on models through 1981

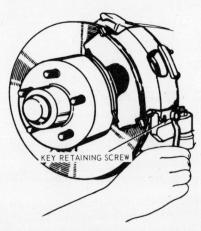

Installing the key retaining screw on models through 1981

2. Raise the vehicle so that the wheel to be worked on is off the ground. Support the vehicle with jackstands.

3. Remove the front wheels.

4. Place a C-clamp on the caliper so that the solid end contacts the back of the caliper and the screw end contacts the metal part of the outboard brake pad.

5. Tighten the clamp until the caliper moves far enough to force the piston to the bottom of the piston bore. This will back the brake pads

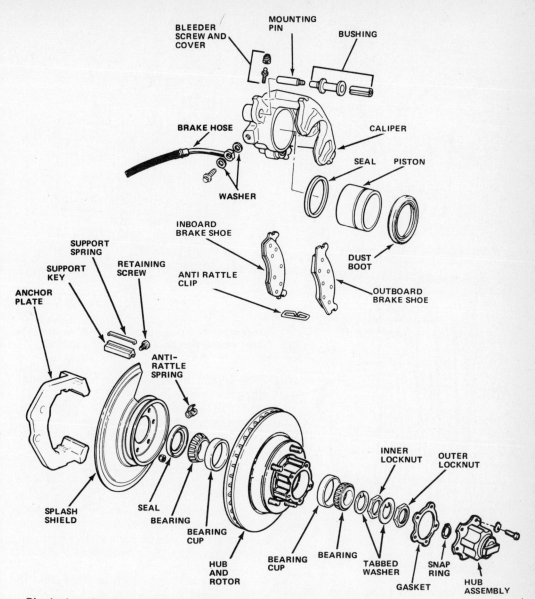

Disc brake unit used on 1982–87 models. The 1987 models have an upper and lower anti-rattle spring

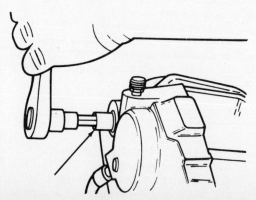

Removing the caliper mounting pins on 1982–87 models

off the rotor surface to facilitate the removal and installation of the caliper assembly.

6. Remove the C-clamp.

NOTE: *Do not push down on the brake pedal or the piston and brake pads will return to their original positions up against the rotor.*

7. Remove the caliper mounting pins and lift off the caliper. Don't disconnect the brake line! Don't allow the brake line to support the weight of the caliper!

8. Hold the anti-rattle clip against the caliper anchor plate and remove the outboard pad.

9. Remove the inboard pad and anti-rattle clip.

10. Clean the caliper with a rag and solvent

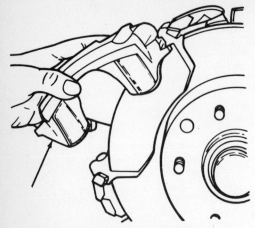

Lifting off the caliper on 1982–87 models

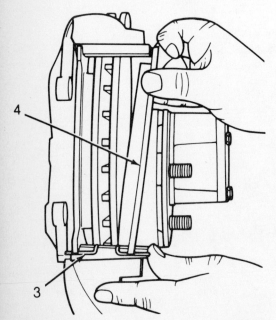

Anti-rattle clip (3); outboard pad (4) on 1982–87 models. The 1987 models also have an upper anti-rattle clip

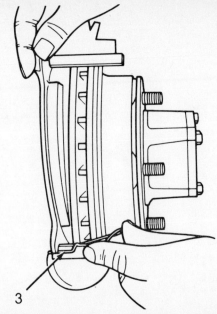

Removing the inboard pad on 1982–87 models. The 1987 models also have an upper anti-rattle clip

16. Install the caliper and tighten the mounting pins to 30 ft.lb.

17. Fill the master cylinder and press firmly on the brake pedal to seat the pads.

18. Install the wheels, and lower the truck.

1987

CAUTION: *Brake shoes contain asbestos, which has been determined to be a cancer causing agent. Never clean the brake surfaces with compressed air! Avoid inhaling any dust from any brake surface! When cleaning brake surfaces, use a commercially available brake cleaning fluid.*

1. Remove ⅔ of the brake fluid from the front reservoir.

2. Raise the vehicle so that the wheel to be worked on is off the ground. Support the vehicle with jackstands.

3. Remove the front wheels.

4. Place a C-clamp on the caliper so that the solid end contacts the back of the caliper and the screw end contacts the metal part of the outboard brake pad.

5. Tighten the clamp until the caliper moves far enough to force the piston to the bottom of the piston bore. This will back the brake pads off the rotor surface to facilitate the removal and installation of the caliper assembly.

6. Remove the C-clamp.

NOTE: *Do not push down on the brake pedal or the piston and brake pads will return to their original positions up against the rotor.*

7. Remove the caliper mounting pins and

made for cleaning brake surfaces. Avoid disturbing the dust boot.

11. If there are any indications of fluid leakage, the caliper must be rebuilt.

12. Clean the anchor plate and caliper mounting surfaces with a wire brush.

13. Cloat the mounting surfaces with a light coating of caliper lubricant.

14. Install the anti-rattle clip on the trailing edge of the anchor plate. The split end of the clip must face away from the rotor.

15. Install the inboard, then the outboard pads, while holding the clip.

CAUTION: *Avoid damaging the caliper piston dust boot while installing the pads!*

lift off the caliper. Don't disconnect the brake line! Don't allow the brake line to support the weight of the caliper!

8. Push the top anti-rattle spring aside and remove the outboard pad.

9. Remove the inboard pad and the top and bottom anti-rattle springs.

10. Clean the caliper with a rag and solvent made for cleaning brake surfaces. Avoid disturbing the dust boot.

11. If there are any indications of fluid leakage, the caliper must be rebuilt.

12. Clean the anchor plate and caliper mounting surfaces with a wire brush.

13. Cloat the mounting surfaces with a light coating of caliper lubricant.

14. Install the top and bottom anti-rattle springs.

15. Install the inboard, then the outboard pads. Check the position of the springs. Make sure that they are seated properly and that the spring ends are in contact with the pad mounting ears.

CAUTION: *Avoid damaging the caliper piston dust boot while installing the pads!*

16. Install the caliper and tighten the mounting pins to 30 ft.lb.

17. Fill the master cylinder and press firmly on the brake pedal to seat the pads.

18. Install the wheels, and lower the truck.

Caliper
REMOVAL AND INSTALLATION
Through 1981

CAUTION: *Brake shoes contain asbestos, which has been determined to be a cancer causing agent. Never clean the brake surfaces with compressed air! Avoid inhaling any dust from any brake surface! When cleaning brake surfaces, use a commercially available brake cleaning fluid.*

1. Remove ⅔ of the brake fluid from the front reservoir.

2. Raise the vehicle so that the wheel to be worked on is off the ground. Support the vehicle with jackstands.

3. Remove the front wheels.

4. Place a C-clamp on the caliper so that the solid end contacts the back of the caliper and the screw end contacts the metal part of the outboard brake pad.

5. Tighten the clamp until the caliper moves far enough to force the piston to the bottom of the piston bore. This will back the brake pads off the rotor surface to facilitate the removal and installation of the caliper assembly.

6. Remove the C-clamp.

NOTE: *Do not push down on the brake pedal or the piston and brake pads will return to*

their original positions up against the rotor.

7. Remove the caliper support key retaining screw with a ¼" Allen wrench. Drive the support key and spring out with a punch.

NOTE: *If just the brake pads are being replaced, it is not necessary to remove the caliper assembly entirely from the vehicle. Do not remove the brake line. Rest the caliper on the front spring or other suitable support. Do not allow the brake hose to support the weight of the caliper.*

8. If the caliper is being removed in order to be rebuilt, then it is necessary to disconnect the brake fluid hose. Clean the brake fluid hose-to-caliper connection thoroughly. Remove the hose-to-caliper bolt. Cap or tape the open ends to keep dirt out. Discard the copper gaskets.

9. Wipe the inside of the caliper clean, including the exterior of the dust boot. Inspect the dust boot for cuts or cracks and for proper seating in the piston bore. If evidence of fluid leakage is noted, the caliper should be rebuilt.

10. Check the sliding surface of the caliper and anchor plate for rust or corrosion. Clean them with a wire brush and fine sandpaper; lubricate with molybdenum disulphide grease.

11. Place the caliper over the rotor and on the anchor plate.

NOTE: *Be careful not to damage or dislodge the dust boot.*

12. Insert the support key and spring between the sliding surfaces at the rear of the caliper. Drive them into place with a punch.

13. Install the key retaining screw and torque it to 15 ft.lb..

14. Connect the hose to the caliper, using a new copper gasket under the hose union. Torque the bolt to 25 ft.lb.

15. Fill the master cylinder to within ¼" of the rim.

16. Press firmly on the brake pedal several times till the pedal is firm.

17. Recheck the master cylinder level.

NOTE: *If the brake fluid hose was disconnected, it will be necessary to bleed the hydraulic system.*

1983–87

CAUTION: *Brake shoes contain asbestos, which has been determined to be a cancer causing agent. Never clean the brake surfaces with compressed air! Avoid inhaling any dust from any brake surface! When cleaning brake surfaces, use a commercially available brake cleaning fluid.*

1. Remove ⅔ of the brake fluid from the front reservoir.

2. Raise the vehicle so that the wheel to be

worked on is off the ground. Support the vehicle with jackstands.

3. Remove the front wheels.

4. Place a C-clamp on the caliper so that the solid end contacts the back of the caliper and the screw end contacts the metal part of the outboard brake pad.

5. Tighten the clamp until the caliper moves far enough to force the piston to the bottom of the piston bore. This will back the brake pads off the rotor surface to facilitate the removal and installation of the caliper assembly.

6. Remove the C-clamp.

NOTE: *Do not push down on the brake pedal or the piston and brake pads will return to their original positions up against the rotor.*

7. Remove the caliper mounting pins and lift off the caliper. Don't disconnect the brake line unless the caliper is being removed for service! Don't allow the brake line to support the weight of the caliper! If you disconnect the brake line, cap it to prevent fluid loss.

8. Clean the caliper with a rag and solvent made for cleaning brake surfaces. Avoid disturbing the dust boot.

9. If there are any indications of fluid leakage, the caliper must be rebuilt.

10. Clean the anchor plate and caliper mounting surfaces with a wire brush.

11. Cloat the mounting surfaces with a light coating of caliper lubricant.

12. Install the caliper and tighten the mounting pins to 30 ft.lb.

13. Connect the hose to the caliper, using a new copper gasket under the hose union. Torque the bolt to 25 ft.lb.

14. Fill the master cylinder and press firmly on the brake pedal to seat the pads.

15. Install the wheels, and lower the truck.

NOTE: *If the brake fluid hose was disconnected, it will be necessary to bleed the hydraulic system.*

OVERHAUL

CAUTION: *Brake shoes contain asbestos, which has been determined to be a cancer causing agent. Never clean the brake surfaces with compressed air! Avoid inhaling any dust from any brake surface! When cleaning brake surfaces, use a commercially available brake cleaning fluid.*

1. Remove the caliper assembly and remove the brake pads. If the pads are to be reused, mark their location in the caliper.

2. Clean the caliper exterior with clean brake fluid. Drain any residual fluid from the caliper and place it on a clean work surface.

NOTE: *Removal of the caliper piston requires the use of compressed air. Do not, under any circumstances, place your fingers in*

Removing the piston with compressed air

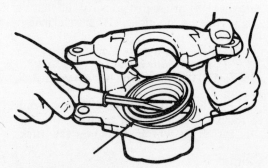

Removing the dust seal

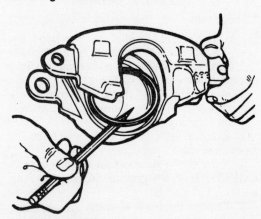

Removing the O-ring

front of the piston in an attempt to catch or protect it when applying compressed air to remove the piston.

3. Pad the interior of the caliper with clean cloths. Use several cloths and pad the interior well to avoid damaging the piston when it comes out of the bore.

4. Insert an air nozzle into the inlet hole in the caliper and gently apply air pressure on

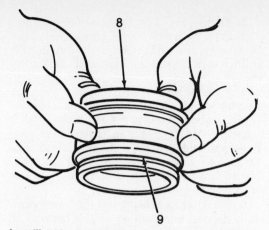

Installing the metal retainer (8) in the groove (9)

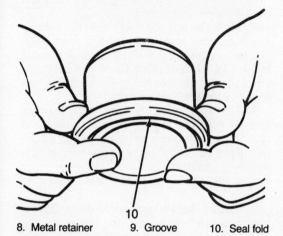

| 8. Metal retainer | 9. Groove | 10. Seal fold |

Dust seal installation

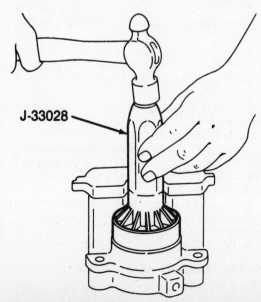

Seating the metal retainer

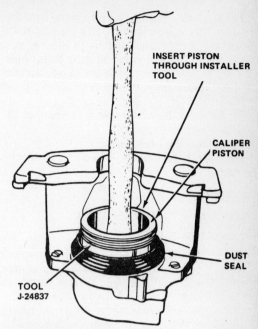

INSERT PISTON THROUGH INSTALLER TOOL

CALIPER PISTON

DUST SEAL

TOOL J-24837

Caliper piston installation

the piston to push it out of the bore. Use only enough air pressure to ease the piston out of the bore.

5. Pry the dust boot out of the bore with a screwdriver. Use caution during this operation to prevent scratching the bore. Discard the dust boot.

6. Remove the piston seal from the piston bore and discard the seal. Use only non-scratching implements such as a wooden stick or a piece of plastic to remove the seal. Do not use a metal tool as it could very easily scratch the bore.

7. Remove the bleeder screw. Remove and discard the sleeves and rubber bushings from the mounting ears.

8. Clean all parts with clean brake fluid. Blow out all of the passages in the caliper and bleeder valve. Use only dry and filtered compressed air.

9. Examine the piston for defects. Replace the piston if it is nicked, scratched, corroded. Examine the caliper piston bore for the same defects as the piston. Minor stains or corrosion can be polished with a fiber brush.

10. Lubricate the bore and new seal with brake fluid and install the seal in the groove in the bore.

11. Lubricate the piston with brake fluid and install the new dust boot into the piston groove so that the fold in the boot faces the open end of the piston. Slide the metal portion of the dust boot over the open end of the piston and push the retainer toward the back of the piston until the lip on the fold seats in the piston groove.

Then push the retainer portion of the boot forward until the boot is flush with the rim at the open end of the piston and snaps into place.

12. Insert the piston in the bore, being careful not to unseat the piston seal. Push the piston to the bottom of the bore.

13. Install the bleeder screw.

14. Connect the brake line to the caliper using new copper gaskets.

15. Install the brake pads.

16. Install the caliper. Bleed the hydraulic system.

Rotor (Disc)

REMOVAL AND INSTALLATION

Through 1986

CAUTION: *Brake shoes contain asbestos, which has been determined to be a cancer causing agent. Never clean the brake surfaces with compressed air! Avoid inhaling any dust from any brake surface! When cleaning brake surfaces, use a commercially available brake cleaning fluid.*

1. Loosen the front wheel lug nuts. Raise and support the front end on jackstands.

2. Remove the wheels.

3. Remove the front hub grease cap and driving hub snapring. On models equipped with locking hubs, remove the retainer knob hub ring, agitator knob, snapring, outer clutch retaining ring and actuating cam body.

4. Remove the splined driving hub and the pressure spring. This may require slight prying with a screwdriver.

5. Remove the external snapring from the sindle shaft and remove the hub shaft drive gear.

6. Remove the wheel bearing locknut, lockring, adjusting nut and inner lockring.

7. Remove the caliper and suspend it out of the way by hanging it from a suspension or frame member with a length of wire. Do not disconnect the brake hose, and be careful to avoid stretching the hose. Remove the rotor and hub assembly. The outer wheel bearing and, on vehicles with locking hubs, the spring collar, will come off with the hub.

8. If the old parts are retained, thoroughly clean them in a safe solvent and allow them to dry on a clean towel. Never spin dry them with compressed air.

9. On vehicles with drum brakes, cover the spindle with a cloth and thoroughly brush all dirt from the brakes. Never blow the dirt off the brakes, due to the presence of asbestos in the dirt, which is harmful to your health when inhaled.

10. Remove the cloth and thoroughly clean the spindle.

11. Thoroughly clean the inside of the hub.

12. Pack the inside of the hub with EP wheel bearing grease. Add grease to the hub until it is flush with the inside diameter of the bearing cup.

13. Pack the bearing with the same grease. A needle-shaped wheel bearing packer is best for this operation. If one is not available, place a large amount of grease in the palm of your hand and slide the edge of the bearing cage through the grease to pick up as much as possible, then work the grease in as best you can with your fingers.

14. If a new race is being installed, very carefully drive it into position until it bottoms all around, using a brass drift. Be careful to avoid scratching the surface.

15. Place the inner bearing in the race and install a new grease seal.

16. Place the hub assembly onto the spindle and install the inner lockring and outer bearing. Install the wheel bearing nut and torque it to 50 ft.lb. while turning the wheel back and forth to seat the bearings. Back off the nut about ¼ turn (90°) maximum.

17. Install the lockwasher with the tab aligned with the keyway in the spindle and turn the inner wheel bearing adjusting nut until the peg on the nut engages the nearest hole in the lockwasher.

18. Install the outer locknut and torque it to 50 ft.lb.

19. Install the spring collar, drive flange, snapring, pressure spring, and hub cap.

20. Install the caliper over the rotor.

1987

CAUTION: *Brake shoes contain asbestos, which has been determined to be a cancer causing agent. Never clean the brake surfaces with compressed air! Avoid inhaling any dust from any brake surface! When cleaning brake surfaces, use a commercially available brake cleaning fluid.*

1. Raise and support the front end on jackstands.

2. Remove the wheels.

3. Remove the caliper as outlined earlier, but don't disconnect the brake line. Suspend the caliper out of the way by wiring it to the front spring.

4. Remove the rotor from the hub.

5. Inspect the rotor, clean the mounting surfaces and install it on the hub.

6. Install the caliper and wheel.

INSPECTION AND MEASUREMENT

Check the rotor for surface cracks, nicks, broken cooling fins and scoring of both contact surfaces. Some scoring of the surfaces may oc-

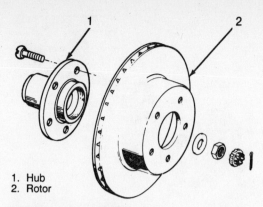

1. Hub
2. Rotor

1987 hub and rotor (disc)

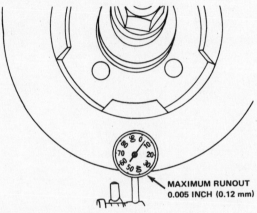

MAXIMUM RUNOUT
0.005 INCH (0.12 mm)

Checking rotor lateral runout

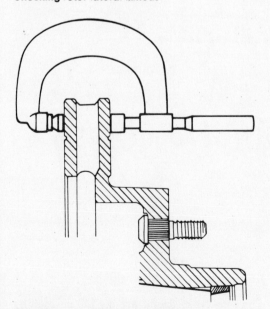

Checking rotor thickness variation

cur during normal use. Scoring that is 0.009"
deep or less is not detrimental to the operation
of the brakes.

If the rotor surface is heavily rusted or
scaled, clean both surfaces on a disc brake
lathe using flat sanding discs before attempting any measurements.

With the hub and rotor assembly mounted
on the spindle of the vehicle or a disc brake
lathe and all play removed from the wheel
bearings, assemble a dial indicator so that the
stem contacts the center of the rotor braking
surface. Zero the dial indicator before taking
any measurements. Lateral runout must not
exceed 0.005" with a maximum rate of change
not to exceed 0.001" in 30 degrees of rotation.
Excessive runout will cause the rotor to wobble
and knock the piston back into the caliper
causing increased pedal travel, noise and
vibration.

After the rotor has been refinished, the
minimum thickness of 1.1207" is acceptable for
models through 1978; 0.815" for 1979–87 models. Discard the rotor if the thickness is less.

NOTE: *Remember to adjust the wheel bearings after the runout measurement has been
taken.*

DRUM BRAKES

Brake Drum

REMOVAL AND INSTALLATION

CAUTION: *Brake shoes contain asbestos,
which has been determined to be a cancer
causing agent. Never clean the brake surfaces
with compressed air! Avoid inhaling any
dust from any brake surface! When cleaning
brake surfaces, use a commercially available
brake cleaning fluid.*

Front

The front brake drums are attached to the
wheel hubs by five bolts. These bolts are also
used for mounting the wheels on the hub.
Press or drive out the bolts to remove the drum
from the hub.

When placing the drum on the hub, make
sure that the contacting surfaces are clean and
flat. Line up the holes in the drum with those
in the hub and put the drum over the shoulder
on the hub. Insert five new bolts through the
drum and hub and drive the bolts into place
solidly. Place a round piece of stock approximately the diameter of the head of the bolt, in
a vise. Next place the hub and drum assembly
over it so that the bolt head rests on it. Then
flatten the bolt head into the countersunk section of the hub with a punch.

The runout of the drum face should be within 0.030". If the runout is found to be greater
than 0.030", it will be necessary to reset the
bolts to correct the condition.

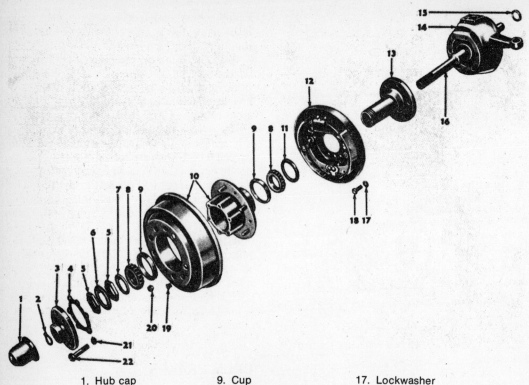

1. Hub cap
2. Snap ring
3. Drive flange
4. Gasket
5. Nut
6. Lockwasher
7. Lockwasher
8. Cone and rollers
9. Cup
10. Hub and drum
11. Oil seal
12. Left front brake
13. Spindle and bushing
14. Left knuckle and arm
15. Thrust washer
16. Universal joint shaft
17. Lockwasher
18. Bolt
19. Screw
20. Nut
21. Lockwasher
22. Bolt

1945–71 front hub, drum and brake assembly

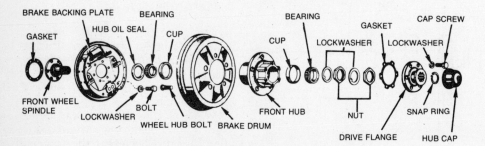

1972 and later front hub and drum brake assembly

The left hand hub bolts have an L stamped on the head of the bolt. The left hand threaded nuts may have a groove cut around the hexagon faces, or the word LEFT stamped on the face.

Hubs with left hand threaded hub bolts are installed on the left hand side of the vehicle. Late production vehicles are equipped with right hand bolts and nuts on all four bolts.

Rear

The rear brake drums are held in position by spring clip type locknuts or by three drum-to-hub retaining screws, depending on the model and year. After the spring type locknuts or retaining screws are removed, the drum can be slid off the axle shaft or hub and brake shoes. It may be necessary to back off the brake shoe ad-

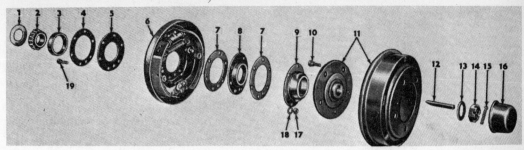

1. Oil seal
2. Cone and rollers
3. Cup
4. Shims
5. Bearing retainer
6. Brake
7. Gasket
8. Grease retainer
9. Grease protecter
10. Bolt
11. Hub and drum
12. Shaft key
13. Oil seal
14. Nut
15. Cotter pin
16. Hub cap
17. Nut
18. Lockwasher
19. Bolt

1945–71 rear brake and hub assembly

justment so that any lip on the inside of the brake drum clears the brake shoes.

INSPECTION

Using a brake drum micrometer, check all drums. Should a brake drum be scored or rough, it may be reconditioned by grinding or turning on a lathe. Do not remove more than 0.030″ thickness of metal.

Use a clean cloth to clean dirt from the brake drums. If further cleaning is required, use soap and water. Do not use brake fluid, gasoline, kerosene or any other similar solvents.

Brake Shoes
REMOVAL AND INSTALLATION

CAUTION: *Brake shoes contain asbestos, which has been determined to be a cancer causing agent. Never clean the brake surfaces with compressed air! Avoid inhaling any dust from any brake surface! When cleaning*

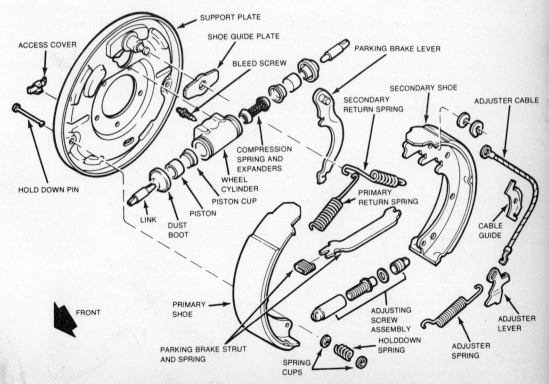

1972 and later self-adjusting rear drum brake components

brake surfaces, use a commercially available brake cleaning fluid.

1. Jack up the vehicle so that all four wheels are off the ground.

2. On vehicles equipped with cam adjustment brakes, turn all eccentrics to the lower side of the cam. On vehicles equipped with star wheel adjustment, turn the star adjuster all the way in.

3. Remove the wheels and the hubs and drums to give access to the brake shoes.

4. Install wheel cylinder clamps to retain the wheel cylinder pistons in place and prevent leakage of brake fluid while replacing the shoes.

5. Remove the return springs with a brake spring removed tool.

6. On models with self adjusters, remove the adjuster cable, cable guide, adjuster lever and adjuster springs.

7. Remove the hold down clips or springs and remove the brake shoes.

8. Before installing the new shoes, now would be a good time to inspect the oil seals in the hubs. If the condition of the seals i doubtful, replace them. Also check the wheel cylinders for leakage. Pull back the dust covers. If there is fluid present behind the dust cover the wheel cylinder must be rebuilt or replaced.

9. Clean the backing plate with a brush or cloth. Place a dab of molybdenum disulphide grease on each spot where the shoes rub the backing plate.

NOTE: *Always replace brake lining in axle sets. Never replace linings on one side or just on one wheel.*

10. Install the parking brake cable and lever on the secondary shoe. Secure the lever with a washer and new U-clip.

11. Install the guide and self-adjuster cable on the anchor pin.

12. Install the shoes, one at a time, on the backing plate and secure them with the holddown springs, pins and retainers.

13. Install the cross-strut and spring.

14. Install the star wheel adjuster, spring and lever.

15. Install the return springs.

16. Make sure that the brake shoe surfaces are clean and free from any contamination.

17. Perform the initial brake shoe adjustment, outlined at the beginning of this chapter.

18. Install the drums and wheels, lower the truck and check brake operation. On Jeep vehicles without self-adjusters, see the Adjustment procedures at the beginning of this chapter. On vehicles with self-adjusters, drive the Jeep in a series of alternating forward and reverse stops. Usually 10–15 full stops in reverse are sufficient.

Wheel Cylinders

CAUTION: *Brake shoes contain asbestos, which has been determined to be a cancer causing agent. Never clean the brake surfaces with compressed air! Avoid inhaling any dust from any brake surface! When cleaning brake surfaces, use a commercially available brake cleaning fluid.*

OVERHAUL

Wheel cylinder rebuilding kits are available for reconditioning wheel cylinders. The kits usually contain new cup springs, cylinder cups and in some, new boots. The most important factor to keep in mind when rebuilding wheel cylinders is cleanliness. Keep all dirt away from the wheel cylinders when you are reassembling them.

1. To remove the wheel cylinder, jack up the vehicle and remove the wheel, hub, and drum.

2. Disconnect the brake line at the fitting on the brake backing plate.

3. Remove the brake assemblies.

4. Remove the screws or nuts that hold the

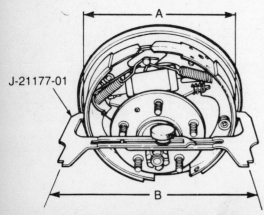

Measure the assembled shoes at A and the drum at B to obtain the initial brake shoe-to-drum clearance. The tool shown is preset for proper adjustment

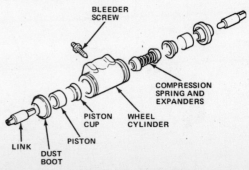

Wheel cylinder used on all Jeep vehicles

wheel cylinder to the backing plate and remove the wheel cylinder from the vehicle.

5. Remove the rubber dust covers on the ends of the cylinder. Remove the pistons and piston cups and the spring. Remove the bleeder screw and make sure it is not plugged.

6. Discard all of the parts that the rebuilding kit will replace.

7. Examine the inside of the cylinder. If it is severely rusted, pitted or scratched, then the cylinder must be replaced as the piston cups won't be able to seal against the walls of the cylinder.

8. Using emery cloth or crocus cloth, polish the inside of the cylinder. Do not polish in a lengthwise direction. Polish by rotating the wheel cylinder around the polishing cloth supported on your fingers. The purpose of this is to put a new surface on the inside of the cylinder. Keep the inside of the cylinder coated with brake fluid while polishing.

NOTE: *Honing the wheel cylinders is not recommended due to the possibility of removing too much material from the bore, making it too large to seal.*

9. Wash out the cylinder with clean brake fluid after polishing.

10. When reassembling the cylinder dip all of the parts in clean brake fluid. Reassemble in the reverse order of removal. Torque the wheel cylinder-to-backing plate fasteners to 18 ft.lb. through 1983; 15 ft.lb. for 1984–86 models; 90 in.lb. (7.5 ft.lb.) for 1987 models. Torque the brake line-to-wheel cylinder connection to 160 in.lb.

Front Wheel Bearings

See the section above, under disc brakes, for full details on front wheel bearing removal, service, and adjustment.

TRANSMISSION BRAKE

Brake Shoe

REPLACEMENT

CAUTION: *Brake shoes contain asbestos, which has been determined to be a cancer causing agent. Never clean the brake surfaces with compressed air! Avoid inhaling any dust from any brake surface! When cleaning brake surfaces, use a commercially available brake cleaning fluid.*

1. Remove the driveshaft.

1. Cable and conduit	9. Backing plate
2. Tube fastener	10. Shoe and lining
3. Spring	11. Return spring
4. Bracket	12. Drum
5. Rear cap	13. Hex bolt
6. Bushing	14. Rear flange
7. Driven gear	15. Plain washer
8. Sleeve	16. Nut

17. Yoke
18. Yoke and plug
19. Adjusting spring
20. Bracket
21. Operating lever
22. Adjusting clevis
23. Spring clip
24. spring link

Driveshaft mounted hand brake

2. Remove the retracting spring clevis pin and the spring clip.

3. Remove the hub locknut, the nut and washer from the transfer case output shaft.

4. Using a puller, remove the brake drum and companion flange.

5. Remove the retracting springs and shoes from the backing plate.

6. Clean all parts with a safe solvent.

7. Installation is the reverse of removal. Replace any weak springs and clean the adjuster threads. Coat the threads with a LIGHT film of oil. It will be necessary to back off the adjusting screw wheels to allow drum installation.

6. Adjust the brake.

PARKING BRAKE

Adjustment

Through 1971, Transmission Brake

Make sure that the brake handle on the instrument panel is fully released. Check the operat-

1. Tool W-172   2. Adapter   3. Brake drum

Removing transmission brake drum

1. Ball nut
2. ³⁄₃₂″ [2,38 mm.] clearance
3. Adjusting screw

Transmission brake adjustment

ing linkage and the cable to make sure that they don't bind. If necessary, free the cable and lubricate it. Rotate the brake drum until one paid of the three sets of holes are over the shoe adjusting screw wheels in the brake drum. Use the edge of the holes in the brake drum as a fulcrum for the brake adjusting tool or a screwdriver. Rotate each notched adjusting screw by moving the handle of the tool away from the center of the driveshaft until the shoes are snug against the drum. Back off seven notches on the adjusting screw wheels to secure the proper running clearance between the shoes and the drum.

1972–86

1. Make sure that the hydraulic brakes are in satisfactory adjustment.

2. Raise the rear wheels off the ground and disengage the parking brake.

3. Loosen the locknut on the brake cable adjusting rod, located directly behind the frame center crossmember.

4. Spin the wheels and tighten the adjustment until the rear wheels drag slightly. Loosen the adjustment until there is no drag and the wheels spin freely.

5. Tighten the locknut to lock the adjusting nut.

1987

NOTE: *This procedure requires the use of a special tool. If the special tool cannot be obtained, follow the procedure given for 1972-86 models.*

1. Make sure that the hydraulic brakes are properly adjusted. Fully apply and release the parking brake five times.

2. Raise and support the truck on jackstands. Loosen the cable adjusting nuts.

3. Using an inch pound torque wrench and adjustment adapter J-34651, apply a torque of 45–50 in.lb.

4. Adjust the equalizer adjusting nut so that the gauge pointer is in the blue band on the tool. Tighten the adjusting nuts.

5. Apply and release the brake lever fully, five times, and recheck the adjustment.

6. When adjustment is correct, stake the adjusting nuts.

REMOVAL AND INSTALLATION

Rear Wheel Type Hand Brake

FRONT CABLE

1. Disconnect the cable at the equalizer Disconnect the return spring, if equipped.

2. Disconnect the other end of the cable at the equalizer adjusting rod.

3. Disconnect the cable at any retaining clip

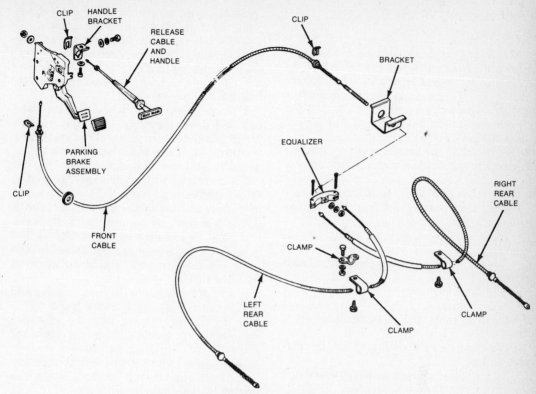

1972 and later parking brake system components

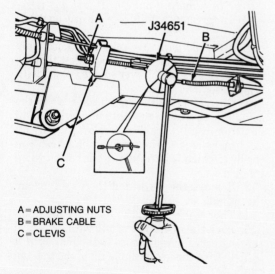

A = ADJUSTING NUTS
B = BRAKE CABLE
C = CLEVIS

Using a special tool to adjust the parking brake on 1987 models

on the body. On later models, through 1986, roll the carpet back and remove the front cable ferrule-to-lever retaining clip. On 1987 models, compress the lock tabs that retain the cable in the parking brake pedal. A small hose clamp is good for this purpose.

4. Remove the cable.

5. Installation is the reverse of removal. On 1987 models, retain the grommet from the pedal end, if the cable is being replaced.

REAR CABLES

1. Back off the adjuster at the equalizer and disconnect the cable.

2. Raise and support the rear end on jackstands. Detach the cables from any body clips.

3. Remove the wheel and brake drums.

4. Remove the brake shoes and disconnect the cable ends at the actuating levers.

5. Compress the locking tabs that secure the cables to the backing plates and slide the cable from the plates.

6. Installation is the reverse of removal. Adjust the parking brake.

Transmission Type Hand Brake

1. Fully release the hand brake.

2. Disconnect the cable at the hand brake lever.

3. Disconnect the hook from the spring at the actuating lever.

4. Installation is the reverse of removal.

Front Hub and Wheel Bearings
ADJUSTMENT

NOTE: *Sodium-based grease is not compatible with lithium-based grease. Read the package labels and be careful not to mix the two types. If there is any doubt as to the type of grease used, completely clean the old grease from the bearing and hub before replacing.*

Before handling the bearings, there are a few things that you should remember to do and not to do.

Remember to DO the following:
• Remove all outside dirt from the housing before exposing the bearing.
• Treat a used bearing as gently as you would a new one.
• Work with clean tools in clean surroundings.
• Use clean, dry canvas gloves, or at least clean, dry hands.
• Clean solvents and flushing fluids are a must.
• Use clean paper when laying out the bearings to dry.
• Protect disassembled bearings from rust and dirt. Cover them up.
• Use clean rags to wipe bearings.
• Keep the bearings in oil-proof paper when they are to be stored or are not in use.
• Clean the inside of the housing before replacing the bearing.

Do NOT do the following:
• Don't work in dirty surroundings.
• Don't use dirty, chipped or damaged tools.
• Try not to work on wooden work benches or use wooden mallets.
• Don't handle bearings with dirty or moist hands.
• Do not use gasoline for cleaning. Use a safe solvent.
• Do not spin-dry bearings with compressed air. They will be damaged.
• Do not spin dirty bearings.
• Avoid using cotton waste or dirty cloths to wipe bearings.
• Try not to scratch or nick bearing surfaces.
• Do not allow the bearing to come in contact with dirt or rust at any time.

1945–86
4-WD

1. Raise the front of the vehicle and place jackstands under the axle.
2. Remove the wheel.
3. Remove the front hub grease cap and driving hub snapring. On models equipped with locking hubs, remove the retainer knob hub ring, agitator knob, snapring, outer clutch retaining ring and actuating cam body.
4. Remove the splined driving hub and the pressure spring. This may require slight prying with a screwdriver.
5. Remove the wheel bearing locknut, lockring and adjusting nut.
6. On vehicle with drum brakes, remove the hub and drum assembly. This may require that the brake adjusting wheel be backed off a few turns. The outer wheel bearing and spring retainer will come off with the hub.
7. On vehicles with disc brakes, remove the caliper and suspend it out of the way by hanging it from a suspension or frame member with a length of wire. Do not disconnect the brake hose, and be careful to avoid stretching the hose. Remove the rotor and hub assembly. The outer wheel bearing and spring will come off with the hub.
8. Carefully drive out the inner bearing and seal from the hub, using a wood block.
9. Inspect the bearing races for excessive wear, pitting or grooves. If they are cracked or grooved, or if pitting and excess wear is present, drive them out with a drift or punch.
10. Check the bearing for excess wear, pitting or cracks, or excess looseness.

NOTE: *If it is necessary to replace either the bearing or the race, replace both. Never replace just a bearing or a race. These parts wear in a mating pattern. If just one is replaced, premature failure of the new part will result.*

11. If the old parts are retained, thoroughly clean them in a safe solvent and allow them to dry on a clean towel. Never spin dry them with compressed air.
12. On vehicles with drum brakes, cover the spindle with a cloth and thoroughly brush all dirt from the brakes. Never blow the dirt off the brakes, due to the presence of asbestos in the dirt, which is harmful to your health when inhaled.
13. Remove the cloth and thoroughly clean the spindle.
14. Thoroughly clean the inside of the hub.
15. Pack the inside of the hub with EP wheel bearing grease. Add grease to the hub until it is flush with the inside diameter of the bearing cup.
16. Pack the bearing with the same grease. A needle-shaped wheel bearing packer is best for this operation. If one is not available, place a large amount of grease in the palm of your hand and slide the edge of the bearing cage through the grease to pick up as much as possible, then work the grease in as best you can with your fingers.
17. If a new race is being installed, very care-

fully drive it into position until it bottoms all around, using a brass drift. Be careful to avoid scratching the surface.

18. Place the inner bearing in the race and install a new grease seal.

19. Place the hub assembly onto the spindle and install the outer bearing. Install the wheel bearing nut and torque it to 50 ft.lb. while turning the wheel back and forth to seat the bearings. Back off the nut about ¼ turn maximum.

20. Install the lockwasher with the inner tab aligned with the keyway in the spindle and turn the inner wheel bearing adjusting nut until the peg engages the nearest hole in the lockwasher.

21. Install the outer locknut and torque it to 50 ft.lb.

22. Install the pressure spring, drive flange, snapring and hub cap.

23. Install the caliper over the rotor.

1947–64

2-WD

1. Raise the front of the vehicle and place jackstands under the axle.

2. Remove the wheel.

3. Remove the front hub grease cap.

4. Remove the cotter pin and locknut.

5. Pull out on the brake drum slightly to free the outer bearing and remove the bearing.

6. Remove the drum and hub.

7. Using an awl, puncture the inner seal and pry it out. Discard the seal.

8. Remove the inner bearing.

9. Inspect the bearing races for excessive wear, pitting or grooves. If they are cracked or grooved, or if pitting and excess wear is present, drive them out with a drift or punch.

10. Check the bearing for excess wear, pitting or cracks, or excess looseness.

NOTE: *If it is necessary to replace either the bearing or the race, replace both. Never replace just a bearing or a race. These parts wear in a mating pattern. If just one is replaced, premature failure of the new part will result.*

11. If the old parts are retained, thoroughly clean them in a safe solvent and allow them to dry on a clean towel. Never spin dry them with compressed air.

12. On vehicles with drum brakes, cover the spindle with a cloth and thoroughly brush all dirt from the brakes. Never blow the dirt off the brakes, due to the presence of asbestos in the dirt, which is harmful to your health when inhaled.

13. Remove the cloth and thoroughly clean the spindle.

14. Thoroughly clean the inside of the hub.

15. Pack the inside of the hub with EP wheel bearing grease. Add grease to the hub until it is flush with the inside diameter of the bearing cup.

16. Pack the bearing with the same grease. A needle-shaped wheel bearing packer is best for this operation. If one is not available, place a large amount of grease in the palm of your hand and slide the edge of the bearing cage through the grease to pick up as much as possible, then work the grease in as best you can with your fingers.

17. If a new race is being installed, very carefully drive it into position until it bottoms all around, using a brass drift. Be careful to avoid scratching the surface.

18. Place the inner bearing in the race and install a new grease seal.

19. Place the hub assembly onto the spindle and install the outer bearing. Install the wheel bearing nut and tighten it until the hub binds while turning. Back off the nut about ⅙–¼ turn to free the bearings. Install a new cotter pin.

20. Install the grease cap.

21. Install the wheel.

22. Lower the vehicle and install the hub cap.

1987

1. Raise and support the front end on jackstands.

2. Remove the wheel.

3. Dismount the caliper and suspend it out of the way.

4. Remove the rotor.

5. Remove the hub nut pin, cap and nut.

6. Remove the hub.

7. The hub and bearings are usually replaced as a unit. The hub and bearing carrier may, however, be disassembled and the bearings replaced as a set. Once the hub and bearing carrier have been separated, the bearings should not be reused.

8. Pack the hub cavity and bearings with wheel bearing grease and install the hub on the axle shaft. If the carrier was separated from the hub, make sure you install a new carrier seal and inner bearing seal.

9. Install the hub washer and nut. Torque the nut to 175 ft.lb. and instal the cap and new cotter pin.

10. Install the rotor, caliper and wheel.

SPECIAL TOOLS

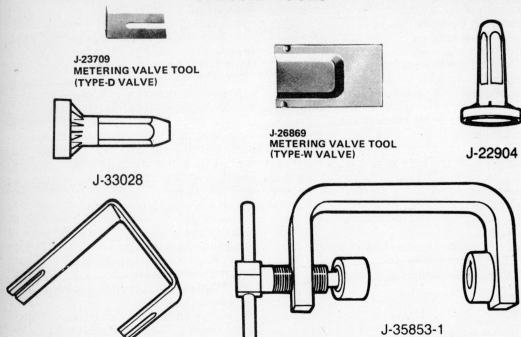

J-23709
METERING VALVE TOOL
(TYPE-D VALVE)

J-26869
METERING VALVE TOOL
(TYPE-W VALVE)

J-22904

J-33028

J-35853-2

J-35853-1

Body and Trim

EXTERIOR

Windshield Frame

REMOVAL AND INSTALLATION

1945–71

FOLDING WINDSHIELD

1. On early models, disconnect the wiper vacuum hose from the vacuum motor.
2. On later models, disconnect the wiring from the electric wiper motor.
3. Unlatch the clamps on each side of the windshield.
4. Tilt the windshield forward until the slot in each hinge aligns with the flat side of the pin in the body hinges.
5. Pull the windshield frame of the pins and remove it from the body.

1972–86

1. Disengage the top from the frame.
2. Disconnect the wiper motor wiring harness from the switch.
3. Remove the hinge-to-frame bolts.
4. Remove the holddown knobs and lift off the frame.
5. Installation is the reverse of removal.

Windshield Glass

REMOVAL AND INSTALLATION

Utility Models with 2-Piece Windshield

NOTE: *To replace either side of the glass, both glass sections, in their common frame, must first be removed.*

1. Remove the cover plate from the center bar garnish molding.
2. Remove the mirror bracket plate.
3. Remove the center bar.
4. Remove the outer cover panel.
5. Remove the two garnish moldings.
6. Have an assistant support the windshield assembly from the inside, while you, working on the outside, force the rubber molding off the body flange with a wood spatula. Start at the top center and press inward while prying off the molding, to prevent it from slipping back over the flange.
7. Replace the pane of glass to be removed, by working the rubber channel over the edge of the glass. It may be necessary to break the cement seal with a screwdriver.
8. Thoroughly clean and inspect the weatherstripping. Replace it if it is worn, cracked or brittle.
9. Apply a $\frac{1}{16}''$ (1.5mm) bead of 3M Auto Bedding and Glazing Compound, or equivalent, completely around the weatherstripping in the glass cavity.
10. Install the weatherstripping on the glass.
11. Install the glass in the frame, working the rubber wetaherstripping into position.
12. Make up a slippery soap and water solution and thoroughly coat the body flange and the rubber weatherstripping.
13. Place a $\frac{1}{16}''$ (at least) to $\frac{1}{8}''$ (at most) cord in the flange cavity of the weatherstripping, completely around the circumference. You'll need at leats 8' of string. Let the ends of the cord hang outside the glass at the upper center.
14. Position the glass frame and weatherstripping in the opening. Pull on the ends of the cord to pull the lip of the weatherstripping over the body flange.
15. Use a wood spatula to lock the weatherstripping.
16. Apply a bead of 3M Windshield Sealer, or equivalent, between the weatherstripping and the body flange, around its entire perimeter. Clean off the excess.

Utility Models with 1-Piece Windshield

1. Unscrew and remove the garnish molding covers.

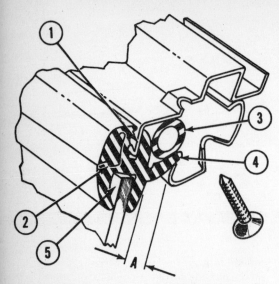

1. Hem flange groove
2. Weatherstripping lock
3. Filler tubing
4. Weatherstripping lip
5. Glass groove

One-piece windshield weatherstripping used on Utility models

2. Remove the garnish moldings.

3. If the vehicle has a heater, there are rubber plugs under the garnish molding at each side of the defroster openings. Save the plugs.

4. Using a wood spatula, unlock the rubber weatherstripping.

5. Carefully remove the windshield and discard the weatherstripping.

6. Apply a $\frac{1}{16}''$ (1.5mm) bead of 3M Auto Bedding and Glazing Compound, or equivalent, completely around hem flange groove of the new weatherstripping.

7. Install the weatherstripping on the hem flange with the weatherstripping lock facing outside.

8. Install the filler tubing beneath the weatherstripping lip, facing inside. Locate the 6" (152mm) long pice of tubing at the top center of the windshield opening. Locate the 32" (813mm) long piece of tubing along the bottom edge of the windshield opening with the ends of the tubing extending beyond the defroster openings in the instrument panel. Install these pieces of tubing *before* installing the windshield glass.

9. With the weatherstipping unlocked, install the windshield glass in the glass groove of the weatherstripping. Fill the glass groove with a $\frac{1}{16}''$ (1.5mm) bead of 3M Auto Bedding and Glazing Compound, or equivalent.

10. Lock the weatherstripping into place with a wood spatula. Remove all excess sealer.

11. Install the garnish moldings, molding covers and defroster rubber plugs. The 1½" (38mm) long screws are used along the top; the

1¼" (32mm) long screws along the sides and bottom.

If a different type of garnish molding was used, new garnish molding screw holes must be drilled before the molding can be installed. Use the new moldings as templates.

   a. Position the moldings on the door pillars with the the moldings as far as possible to the rear.

   b. Drill three ⅛" (3mm) holes in each pillar and loosely attach the moldings with screws.

   c. Position the ends of the moldings at both the top and bottom center of the windshield opening with dimension A, in the accompanying illustration, ⅛"–³⁄₁₆" (3–5mm)

   d. Drill seven ⅛" (3mm) holes in the header rail and nine ⅛" (3mm) holes in the instrument panel.

   e. Install the garnish moldings as instructed in Step 11.

1945–53 CJ-2A, CJ-3A

1. Remove the screws on each side of the windshield adjusting bracket at the top.

2. Bend down the lip on the left hand outer end of the hinge at the top.

3. Open the windshield just enough to clear the frame and slide the assembly out of the hinge to the left.

4. Unbolt the upper glass channel from the frame and remove it.

5. Remove the glass from the frame.

6. Installation is the reverse of removal. Use new tape on the glass.

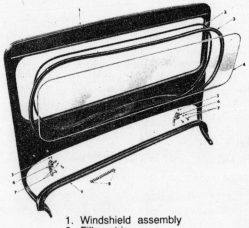

1. Windshield assembly
2. Filler strip
3. Weatherstripping
4. Glass
5. Screw
6. Clamp
7. Screw and lockwasher
8. Screw
9. Weatherstripping

CJ-3B, CJ-5, CJ-6 windshield through 1971

1953–86

1. Cover all adjoining painted surfaces.
2. Remove the wiper arms.
3. Remove the rear view mirror from its bracket.
4. Remove the sun visors.
5. Disconnect the defroster ducts.
6. Have someone support the glass from the outside. Starting at the top, pull the weatherstripping away from the flange while gently pushing out on the glass. It may be necessary to break the sealer by prying with a wood spatula.
7. Work the entire weatherstripping from the flange to remove the glass.
8. Thoroughly clean and inspect the weatherstripping. Replace it if it is worn, cracked or brittle.
9. Apply a $\frac{1}{16}$" (1.5mm) bead of 3M Auto Bedding and Glazing Compound, or equivalent, completely around the weatherstripping in the flange cavity.
10. Install the weatherstripping on the glass. The split should be at the bottom center.
11. Position the glass and weatherstripping in the frame, and, beginning at the bottom, work the weatherstripping over the flange with a wood spatula or fiber stick.
12. When the glass is installed, apply a bead of 3M Windshield Sealer, or equivalent, be-

Unlocking the weatherstripping with a wood spatula

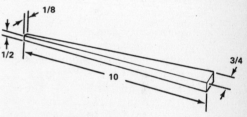

Wood spatula dimensions

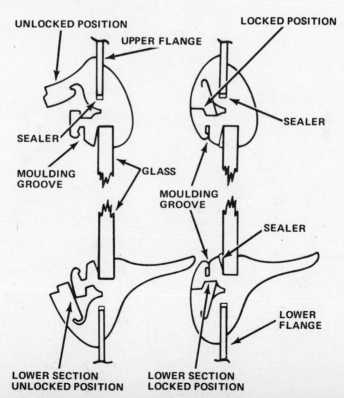

Cross-section of the windshield weatherstripping, with the molding removed, on 1953–86 models

tween the glass and the weatherstripping on the outside. Clean off the excess.

13. Install the mirror.
14. Install the wiper arms.
15. Install the defroster ducts.
16. Install the sun visors.

1987

NOTE: *These vehicles employ a bonded windshield system. If the windshield to be replaced has not suffered major damage, either to the glass or frame, and can be removed intact, then a do-it-yourselfer can perform the job. Even so, a special tool, called an electric hot knife must be used. If, however, the glass has been extensively damaged, or the frame and molding damaged so that a loss of adhesion has occurred, then the job should be left to a professional. The following procedure is a do-it-yourselfer procedure, assuming a simple replacement of an intact glass and good seal-to-glass adhesion.*

1. Remove the wiper arms.
2. Remove the sun visors.
3. Remove the molding cap and molding.
4. Cover all adjacent painted surfaces.
5. Using an electric hot knife under the edge of the glass, cut the adhesive material as close to the inside surface of the glass as possible.

NOTE: *Make sure that an even, uniform bead of sealer remains on the body for installation purposes. NEVER ALLOW THE HOT KNIFE TO STOP DURING THE CUT-*

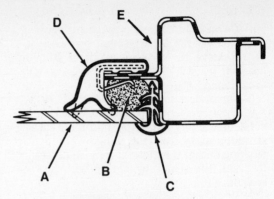

A. Glass
B. Urethane adhesive
C. Windshield reveal molding
D. Garnish molding
E. Windshield frame

Cross-section of a 1987 windshield, installed

TING PROCESS! Allowing the knife to stop will cause permanent damage to the adhesive material.

6. Clean old sealant from the windshield opening with Kent Acrysol®, or equivalent.
7. Clean the glass with a glass cleaner that DOES NOT contain silicone.
8. Apply a smooth, continuous bead of approved urethane windshield bonding adhesive material around the entire perimeter of the windshield opening flange.
9. Carefully position the glass in the windshield opening. and press down to set the adhe-

A. Glass
B. Urethane
C. Windshield reveal molding
D. Garnish molding
E. Frame

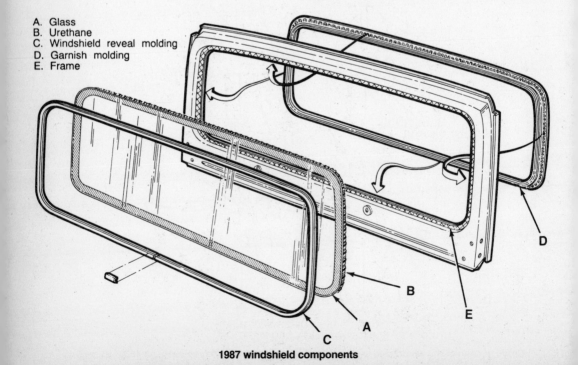

1987 windshield components

sive. Don't press too hard or too much adhesive will be lost.

10. Remove any sheet metal masking that you applied.

11. Install the windshield molding and cap.

12. Install the sun visors.

13. Install the wiper arms.

Hardtop

REMOVAL AND INSTALLATION

1. Remove the hardtop-to-windshield frame screws.

2. Remove the hardtop-to-rear quarter panel bolts.

3. Disconnect the dome lamp.

4. Lift the top from the Jeep, being careful to avoid damage to the foam seals.

5. Installation is the reverse of removal.

Grille

REMOVAL AND INSTALLATION

Except Utility Models

1. Remove the front crossmember cover, if so equipped.

2. Remove the screws securing the radiator and shroud to the radiator grille guard panel.

3. Remove the bolts securing the guard panel to the fenders.

4. Remove the grille-to-frame crossmember holddown assembly, keeping track of the sequence of parts.

5. Loosen the radiator support rods-to-grille guard support bracket nuts.

6. Remove the rods from the brackets.

7. Tilt the grille panel forward and disconnect the electrical wiring at the headlamp sealed beam unit and parking lamp assembly wiring harness at the connectors.

8. If your Jeep has air conditioning:

   a. Discharge the system as described in Chapter 1.

   b. Disconnect the high pressure hose at the sight glass. Immediately cap both openings!

   c. Connect the high pressure hose at the compressor. Immediately cap both openings!

9. Lift the grille from the vehicle.

10. Position the grille panel and connect the electrical wiring at the headlamp sealed beam

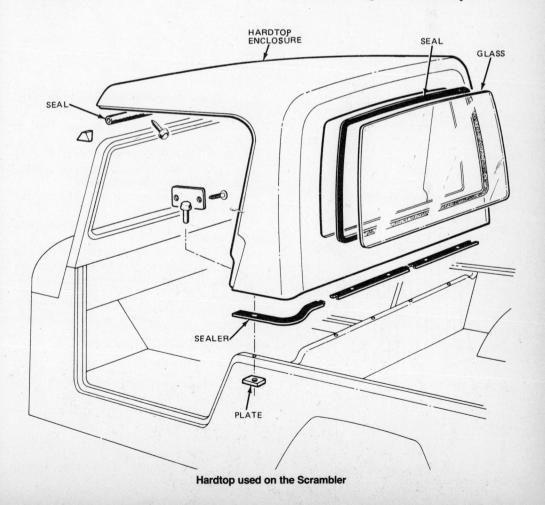

Hardtop used on the Scrambler

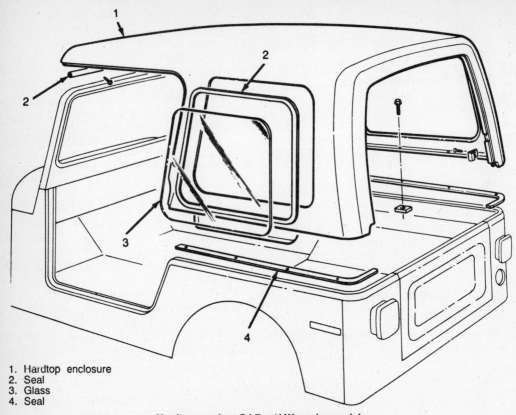

1. Hardtop enclosure
2. Seal
3. Glass
4. Seal

Hardtop used on CJ-7 and Wrangler models

unit and parking lamp assembly wiring harness at the connectors.

11. If your Jeep has air conditioning:

a. Connect the high pressure hose at the compressor.

b. Connect the high pressure hose at the sight glass.

c. Charge the system as described in Chapter 1.

12. Install the rods on the brackets.

13. Tighten the radiator support rods-to-grille guard support bracket nuts.

14. Install the grille-to-frame crossmember holddown assembly.

15. Install the bolts securing the guard panel to the fenders.

16. Install the screws securing the radiator and shroud to the radiator grille guard panel.

17. Install the front crossmember cover, if so equipped.

Fenders

REMOVAL AND INSTALLATION

Except Utility Models

1. Remove or disconnect all items attached to the fender apron.

2. Disconnect the wiring at the marker light.

3. Remove the rocker panel molding on models through 1986.

4. On 1987 models, remove the antenna where necessary.

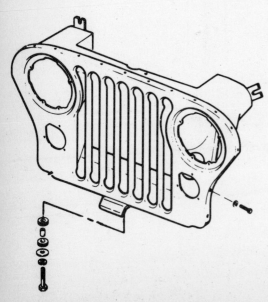

CJ grille components

CJ-3B body

1. Rear passenger's seat
2. Left side panel
3. Driver's seat
4. Rear view mirror
5. Windshield
6. Cowl
7. Step
8. Front passenger's seat
9. Right side panel
10. Spare tire bracket
11. Right tailgate chain
12. Tailgate
13. Left tailgate chain

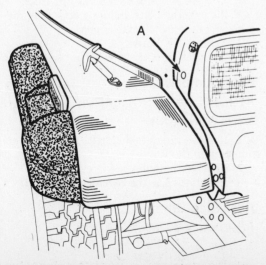

Removing the grill-to-frame crossmember holddown assembly. A are the guard panel-to-fender bolts

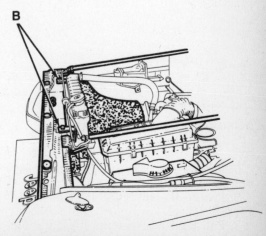

B are the radiator support rods-to-grille guard support bracket nuts

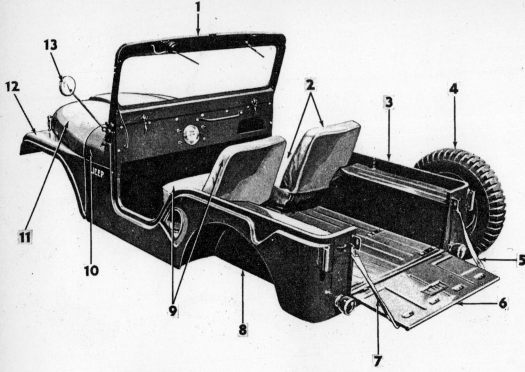

1. Windshield
2. Front passenger seat
3. Right side panel
4. Spare tire
5. Right tailgate chain
6. Tailgate
7. Left tailgate chain
8. Left side panel
9. Driver's seat
10. Cowl
11. Hood
12. Left front fender
13. Rear view mirror

Early CJ-5 body

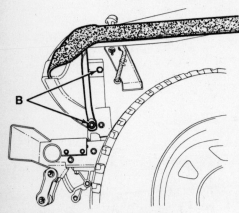

B are the radiator-to-grill panel bolts

5. Remove the bolts attaching the fender and brace to the firewall.
6. Remove the bolts attaching the fender to the grille panel.
7. Pull the fender out and lift it from the Jeep.
8. Installation is the reverse of removal.

Front Bumper
REMOVAL AND INSTALLATION
Except Utility Models
1. Remove any auxiliary lighting.
2. Remove the bolts and nuts attaching the bumper to the frame extensions.
3. Remove the bumper.
4. Installation is the reverse of removal.

Rear Bumpers
REMOVAL AND INSTALLATION
Except Utility Models
1. Remove the nuts and bolts attaching the bumpers to the frame.
2. Remove the bumpers.
3. Installation is the reverse of removal.

Rear Step Bumper
REMOVAL AND INSTALLATION
Scrambler
1. Disconnect the license plate wiring at the connectors.

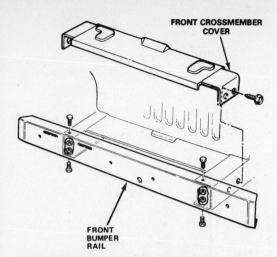

Front bumper typical of CJ models and Wrangler

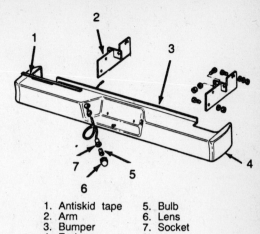

1. Antiskid tape 5. Bulb
2. Arm   6. Lens
3. Bumper   7. Socket
4. End cap

Rear step bumper used on the CJ-7

2. Unbolt and remove the bumper from the mounting arms.

3. Unbolt and remove the mounting arms from the frame.

Front Crossmember Cover
REMOVAL AND INSTALLATION
Except Utility Models

1. Remove the nuts and bolts attaching the crossmember to the frame.

2. Remove the crossmember.

3. Installation is the reverse of removal.

Swingout Spare Tire Carrier
REMOVAL AND INSTALLATION

1. Remove the tire from the carrier.

2. Remove the hinge pin nuts and bolts.

3. Support the carrier. Unlatch the handle from the latch bracket and remove the carrier and hinge spacer washers.

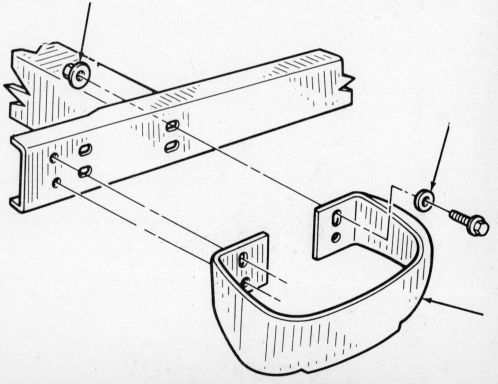

Rear bumper used on CJ and Wranger

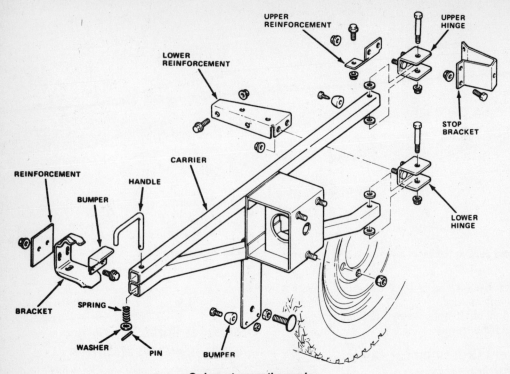

Swingout spare tire carrier

4. Remove the pin attaching the latch handle to the carrier and remove the handle, spring and washer.

5. Installation is the reverse of removal.

Roll Bar

REMOVAL AND INSTALLATION

Through 1986

NOTE: *Torx fasteners are used.*

1. Remove the left front seat.

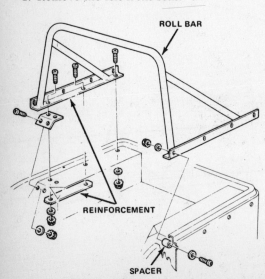

Roll bar used through 1986

2. Remove the hardtop, or, fold the soft top back.

3. Tilt the right front seat forward.

4. Remove any carpeting.

5. Remove the roll bar-to-body bolts.

6. Using a heat gun, such as tool J-25070 or equivalent, heat the area around the mounting brackets to soften the sealer.

7. Align the bolt holes before installation. Use new sealer. Don't tighten any of the bolts until they all are installed and the assembly is aligned.

1987

1. Remove the bolts from the roll bar end of the extension bars.

2. Remove the bolts from the windshield end of the extension bars and remove the bars.

3. Unbolt the seatbelts from the roll bar.

4. Unbolt the roll bar from the floor pan and lift it from the Jeep.

5. Installation is the reverse of removal. Use new sealer under the roll bar legs. Torque the roll bar-to-floor pan bolts to 66 ft.lb.; the seatbelt-to-roll bar bolts to 46 ft.lb.; the extension bar bolts to 45 ft.lb.

Soft Top

ADJUSTMENT

Tops With Metal Doors

1. Unsnap the top from the vertical support blade.

A. Bolts
B. Bolts
C. Seat belt anchor hole
D. Floor anchor bolt
E. Rear leg bolt

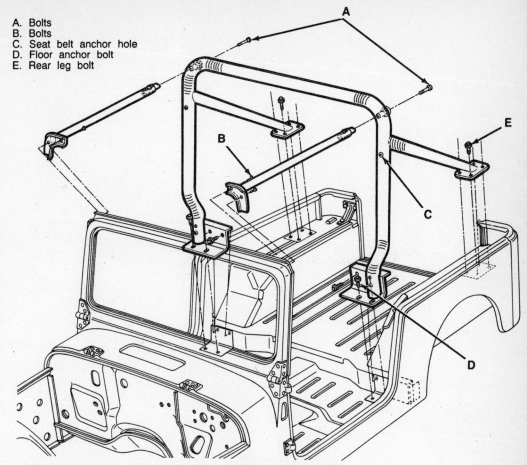

1987 roll bar

2. Loosen the adjusting screws.
3. Reposition the vertical support blade.
4. Tighten the adjusting screws.
5. Reposition and snap the soft top into place.

Hood

REMOVAL AND INSTALLATION

All Models

1. Matchmark the hinges and mounting panels.
2. Disconnect the underhood light wire.
3. Unbolt the hood from the hinges.
4. Remove the hood prop rod, prop rod retainer clip, side catch brackets, windshield bumpers and footman loop.
5. Assembly and installation is the reverse of removal and disassembly. Check hood alignment

ALIGNMENT

All Models

1. Loosen the hinge mounting screws on one side and tap the hinge in the direction opposite to which the hood is to be moved.

2. Tighten the screws.
3. Repeat this procedure on the opposite hinge.

Liftgate

REMOVAL AND INSTALLATION

CJ-7 and Wrangler

NOTE: *Torx fasteners are used in this procedure.*
CAUTION: *Never remove the liftgate supports with the liftgate closed. The support are under considerable spring tension! After removal, never attempt to disassemble the supports!*
1. Open and support the liftgate.
2. Disconnect the defogger wiring.
2. Remove the liftgate-to-supports screws and fold the supports downward.
3. Remove the hinges-to-liftgate screws and lift off the liftgate.
4. Installation is the reverse of removal. Check alignment.

Utility Wagons

1. Matchmark the support prop-to-liftgate position.

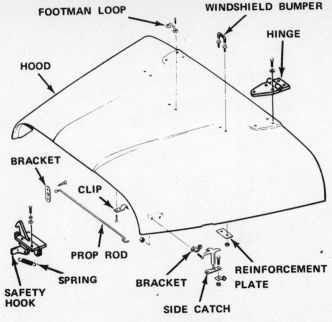

FOOTMAN LOOP

WINDSHIELD BUMPER

HINGE

HOOD

BRACKET

CLIP

PROP ROD

SPRING

SAFETY HOOK

BRACKET

SIDE CATCH

REINFORCEMENT PLATE

CJ hood through 1986

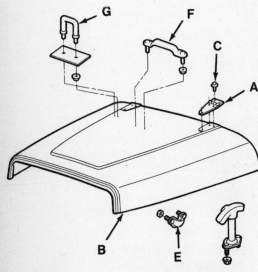

A. Hinge
B. Hood
C. Bolts
D. Light
E. Catch brackets
F. Footman loop
G. Windshield bumpers

1987 hood

2. Unbolt the support props from the liftgate.

3. Unbolt the liftgate hinge from the body.

4. Installation is the reverse of removal.

ALIGNMENT

CJ-7 and Wrangler

NOTE: *Torx fasteners are used in this procedure.*

CAUTION: *Never remove the liftgate sup-*

ports with the liftgate closed. The support are under considerable spring tension! After removal, never attempt to disassemble the supports!

1. Open and support the liftgate.

2. Remove the liftgate-to-supports screws and fold the supports downward.

3. Remove the hinges-to-liftgate screws and lift off the liftgate.

NOTE: *Don't disconnect the release cables from the latches.*

4. Loosen the hinge attaching screws.

5. Close the liftgate and move it to obtain a satisfactory fit.

6. Open the liftgate and tighten the liftgate-to-hinge screws.

7. Install the latches and supports.

Utility Wagons

No adjustment is possible on the piano hinge type liftgate hinges. However, both upper and lower lock catches mounted on the body pillars are adjustable vertically. Loosen the mounting screws and move the catches to obatin a satifactory fit.

Tailgate

REMOVAL AND INSTALLATION

CJ-2A, -3A, -3B, -5, -6, and Utility Pick-Ups

1. Open the tailgate to the 45° position and disengage the right hinge.

2. Open it a bit more and disengage the left hinge.

3. Installation is the reverse of removal.

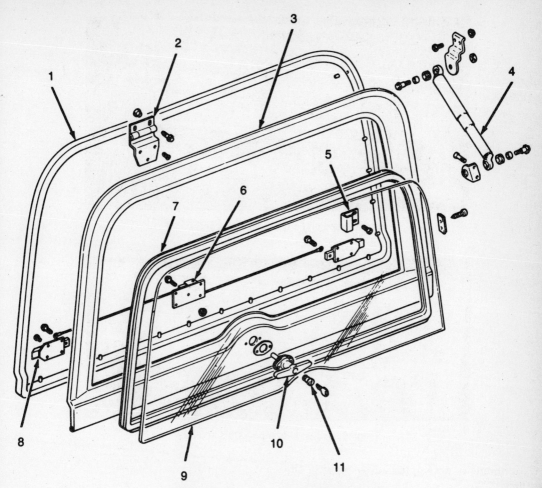

1. Rubber seal
2. Hinge
3. Liftgate
4. Support
5. Striker
6. Remote control
7. Weatherstripping
8. Latch
9. Glass
10. Outside handle
11. Lock cylinder

CJ-7 liftgate

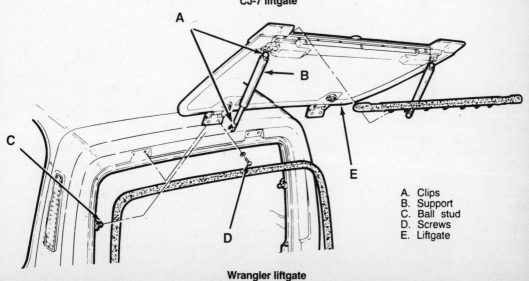

A. Clips
B. Support
C. Ball stud
D. Screws
E. Liftgate

Wrangler liftgate

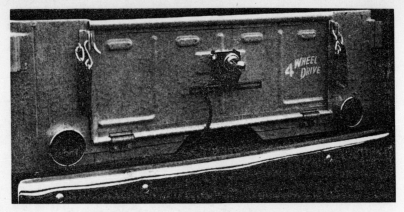

Tailgate used on early model CJ-5A and CJ-6A

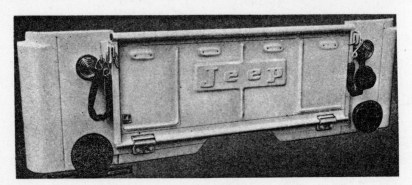

Tailgate used on later model CJ-5 and CJ-6

Alignment is accomplished by moving the hinges.

Utility Wagons

1. Matchmark the support prop-to-tailgate position.
2. Unbolt the support props from the liftgate.
3. Unbolt the liftgate hinge from the body.
4. Installation is the reverse of removal. Alignment is accomplished by loosening the catches and moving them to obtain a satisfactory fit.

CJ-7 and Scrambler

1. Unbolt the support cables from the tailgate.
2. With the tailgate closed, remove the hinge-to-tailgate bolts and remove the tailgate.
3. Installation is the reverse of removal. Alignment is accomplished by moving the hinges.

Wrangler

1. Open the tailgate.
2. Unbolt and remove the tailgate stop swing cover.

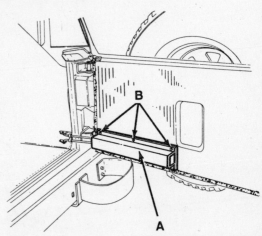

A. Shield   B. Fasteners

A is the cover; B are the screws, on the Wrangler tailgate

3. Pry out the retainer spacer that secure the tailgate tension spring in the bracket.
4. Squeeze the spring and remove it from the bracket.
5. Remove the plastic isolator.
6. Close the tailgate.
7. Remove the tailgate hinge bolts.

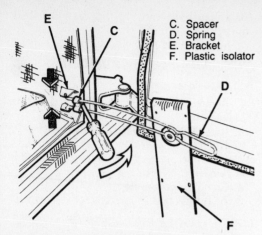

C. Spacer
D. Spring
E. Bracket
F. Plastic isolator

Removing the spring from the Wrangler tailgate

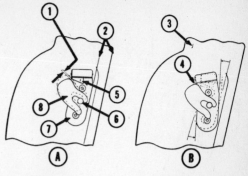

A - Incorrect
B - Correct
1. Clearance
2. Parallel
3. Pillar

4. No clearance
5. Wedge
6. Striker plate pin
7. Striker plate
8. Door lock toggle

Lock toggle and striker plate positioning for Utility models

8. Release the latch and lift out the tailgate.
9. Installation is the reverse of removal. Alignment is accomplished by loosening the hinge bolts and moving the closed tailgate to obtain a satisfactory fit.

Doors
REMOVAL AND INSTALLATION
CJ and Wrangler with Hardtop, and Utility Models

1. Matchmark the hinge-to-door position.
2. Remove the hinge-to-door screws and lift off the door.
3. When installing the door, install the fasteners but don't fully tighten them. Move the door to obtain a satisfactory fit when closed, then tighten the screws.

Striker Plate
ADJUSTMENT

To prevent the door's opening in the safety latched position, the door striker wedge must be properly positioned in relation to the cam surface of the lock toggle. Improper safely latch positioning will permit the toggle to override the striker pin, causing the door to open. The striker must be positioned so that the door lock toggle will be held securely in engagement with the striker pin.
1. Position a brass drift against the upper inside edge of the striker plate.
2. Using a heavy hammer, drive the striker plate outward until the wedge end of the plate firmly contacts the cam surface of the lock toggle, extering enough pressure to prevent the toggle from overriding the striker pin.
3. Make several checks of the safety latch operation until it is satisfactory.

4. Securely tighten the striker plate-to-pillar screws after the adjustment.

Door Hinges
REMOVAL AND INSTALLATION
CJ and Wrangler with Hardtop Door

NOTE: *Plastic shims are used at the hinge pins. Don't lose them!*
1. Matchmark the hinge-to-body position and the hinge-to-door position.
2. Remove the hinge-to-body screws and lift off the door assembly.
NOTE: *The upper hinge is part of the windshield hinge assembly, so support the windshield before removing the door.*
3. Remove the hinges from the door.
4. When installing the door and hinges, don't fully tighten any fasteners until door, hinge and windshield alignment is satisfactory.

Door Lock
LOCK CYLINDER AND OUTSIDE HANDLE REPLACEMENT
CJ Hardtop

NOTE: *Replacement outside handles come without the lock cylinder. Replacement lock cylinders come uncoded, without keys.*
1. Unbolt and remove the handle from the door.
2. To code your existing key to a replacement cylinder:
   a. Insert your key in the new cylinder.
   b. File the tumblers until they are flush with the cylinder body.
   c. Remove and install the key, making sure that ll the tumblers are flush with the cylinder body with the key installed.

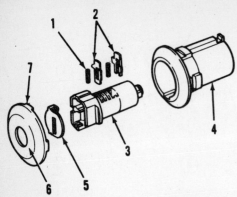

1. Spring
2. Tumblers
3. Lock cylinder
4. Lock casing
5. Door
6. Key hole
7. Bezel

CJ-7, Scrambler and Wrangler door lock, with hard-top

3. Install the new cylinder in the new handle.

4. Install the handle on the door.

OUTSIDE HANDLE REPLACEMENT

Utility Models

1. Remove the handle retaining screw from the door edge.

2. Raise the glass to the full up position.

3. Unsnap the door trim panel from the corner of the door, just enough to reach behind it and remove the retaining nut.

4. Remove the handle.

5. Installation is the reverse of removal.

LOCK CYLINDER REPLACEMENT

Utility Models

1. Raise the glass to the full up position.

2. Press inward on the window handle trim ring and remove the handle retaining pin.

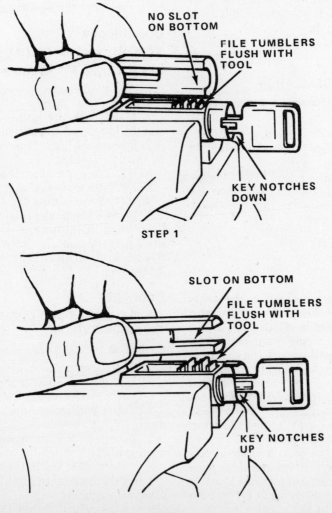

Filing the lock tumblers

3. Remove the crank handle.

4. Remove the arm rest.

5. Unsnap the trim panel. Be very careful! The trim panel is easily torn when prying at the retaining snaps.

6. Unscrew the lock button.

7. Remove the two lower glass channel screws from the door edge.

8. Lock the door by truning the forked latch to the vertical position.

9. Remove the three lock control attaching screws from the door panel.

10. Remove the four lock assembly-to-door edge screws and remove the lock assembly.

11. Installation is the reverse of removal.

DOOR LOCK ADJUSTMENT

Utility Models

Should the outside door handle fail to release the lock easily, it is usually due to the trigger in the handle failing to release the lock until it is nearly flush with the handle. This is due to wear or a bent release lever on the lock assembly. To correct this problem:

1. Remove the door trim panel.

2. Remove the outside door handle.

3. Close and lock the door with the button.

4. Working through the door handle hole, measure the distance from the outside face of the sheet metal to the lock release lever.

5. On the door handle, measure the distance from the edge of the handle casing to the tip of the boss on the trigger striker lever.

6. Subtract the two measurements. The result will be the amount that the lever boss must be built up. Brazing is an acceptable way to restore the lost metal. Add slightly more than necessary and file it down to the correct dimension.

7. Lubricate the working parts, install the handle and check lock operation.

Liftgate Lock

OUTSIDE HANDLE REPLACEMENT

CJ-7 Hardtop

NOTE: *Replacement outside handles come without the lock cylinder. Replacement lock cylinders come uncoded, without keys.*

1. Unbolt and remove the remote linkage from the inside of the liftgate.

2. Unbolt and remove the handle from the door.

3. To code your existing key to a replacement cylinder:

   a. Insert your key in the new cylinder.

   b. File the tumblers until they are flush with the cylinder body.

   c. Remove and install the key, making

Door handle adjustment on Utility models

sure that the tumblers are flush with the cylinder body with the key installed.

4. Install the new cylinder in the new handle.

5. Install the handle on the door.

6. Install the remote linkage.

Tailgate Lock

LATCH MECHANISM REMOVAL AND INSTALLATION

Wrangler

1. Open the tailgate and remove the screw from the latch mechanism housing.

2. Disconnect the latch linkage.

3. Remove the latch-to-tailgate screws.

4. Remove the retaining clip from the lock cylinder.

5. Remove the handle retaining screw and lift out the handle.

6. Remove the latch from the tailgate.

7. Installation is the reverse of removal.

LOCK CYLINDER REMOVAL AND INSTALLATION

CJ-7

1. Remove the plastic cover.

2. Remove the retaining clip.

3. Remove the snapring.

4. Disconnect the lock cylinder from the linkage.

5. Installation is the reverse of removal.

INTERIOR

Door Trim Panel

REMOVAL AND INSTALLATION

Utility and Hardtop

1. Remove the door handle.

2. Remove the window crank handle.

3. Carefully pry the trim panel clips from the door. Be very careful! It's very easy to tear the trim panel or tear loose the clip from the panel. Inexpensive tools are made for this job and are available at most auto parts stores.

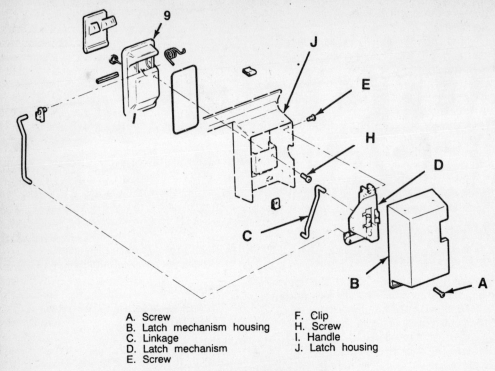

A. Screw
B. Latch mechanism housing
C. Linkage
D. Latch mechanism
E. Screw

F. Clip
H. Screw
I. Handle
J. Latch housing

Wrangler tailgate latch mechanism

4. Remove the watershield.
5. Installation is the reverse of removal.

Door Glass

REMOVAL AND INSTALLATION

Hardtop

1. Remove the door handle.
2. Remove the window crank handle.
3. Carefully pry the trim panel clips from the door. Be very careful! It's very easy to tear the trim panel or tear loose the clip from the panel. Inexpensive tools are made for this job and are available at most auto parts stores.
4. Remove the watershield.
5. Remove the glass down-stop.
6. Remove the guide panel-to-plastic fastener screws.
7. Remove the guide channel and plastic fasteners.
8. Remove the division channel upper attaching screw and lower adjusting screw.
9. Disengage the front three inches of weatherstripping from the upper door frame.
10. Remove the division channel.
11. Tilt the glass toward the hinge side of the door and disengage it from the rear channel.
12. Pull the glass up and out of the door.
13. Insert the glass into the door with the front tilted down, while engaging the rear channel.
14. Install the plastic fasteners on the glass.
15. Lower the glass to the bottom of the door.
16. Lower the division channel into the door and position the glass in the channel.
17. Install the upper attaching screw and lower adjusting screw.
18. Install the weatherstripping.
19. Slide the guide channel on the regulator arm and position the channel on the glass. Install the screws.
20. Install the glass down-stop.
21. Make sure that the window works properly.
22. Install the watershield.
23. Install the trim panel and handles.

Utility Models

1. Remove the door trim panel.
2. Remove the garnish molding from around the glass.
3. Loosen the glass run channel and remove the regulator control arms from the channel., mounted on the bottom of the glass, by removing the two hair pin type locks which retain the control arm buttons.
4. Remove the glass and runway as an assembly, through the window opening.
5. Installation is the reverse of removal.

CHILTON'S
AUTO BODY
REPAIR TIPS

Tools and Materials • Step-by-Step Illustrated Procedures
How To Repair Dents, Scratches and Rust Holes
Spray Painting and Refinishing Tips

EASY
STEP-BY-STEP
TIPS FROM PROS

With a little practice, basic body repair procedures can be mastered by any do-it-yourself mechanic. The step-by-step repairs shown here can be applied to almost any type of auto body repair.

TOOLS & MATERIALS

You may already have basic tools, such as hammers and electric drills. Other tools unique to body repair — body hammers, grinding attachments, sanding blocks, dent puller, half-round plastic file and plastic spreaders — are relatively inexpensive and can be obtained wherever auto parts or auto body repair parts are sold. Portable air compressors and paint spray guns can be purchased or rented.

Auto Body Repair Kits

The best and most often used products are available to the do-it-yourselfer in kit form, from major manufacturers of auto body repair products. The same manufacturers also merchandise the individual products for use by pros.

Kits are available to make a wide variety of repairs, including holes, dents and scratches and fiberglass, and offer the advantage of buying the materials you'll need for the job. There is little waste or chance of materials going bad from not being used. Many kits may also contain basic body-working tools such as body files, sanding blocks and spreaders. Check the contents of the kit before buying your tools.

BODY REPAIR TIPS

Safety

Many of the products associated with auto body repair and refinishing contain toxic chemicals. Read all labels before opening containers and store them in a safe place and manner.

• Wear eye protection (safety goggles) when using power tools or when performing any operation that involves the removal of any type of material.

• Wear lung protection (disposable mask or respirator) when grinding, sanding or painting.

Sanding

1 Sand off paint before using a dent puller. When using a non-adhesive sanding disc, cover the back of the disc with an overlapping layer or two of masking tape and trim the edges. The disc will last considerably longer.

2 Use the circular motion of the sanding disc to grind *into* the edge of the repair. Grinding or sanding away from the jagged edge will only tear the sandpaper.

3 Use the palm of your hand flat on the panel to detect high and low spots. Do not use your fingertips. Slide your hand slowly back and forth.

WORKING WITH BODY FILLER

Mixing The Filler

Cleanliness and proper mixing and application are extremely important. Use a clean piece of plastic or glass or a disposable artist's palette to mix body filler.

1 Allow plenty of time and follow directions. No useful purpose will be served by adding more hardener to make it cure (set-up) faster. Less hardener means more curing time, but the mixture dries harder; more hardener means less curing time but a softer mixture.

2 Both the hardener and the filler should be thoroughly kneaded or stirred before mixing. Hardener should be a solid paste and dispense like thin toothpaste. Body filler should be smooth, and free of lumps or thick spots.

Getting the proper amount of hardener in the filler is the trickiest part of preparing the filler. Use the same amount of hardener in cold or warm weather. For contour filler (thick coats), a bead of hardener twice the diameter of the filler is about right. There's about a 15% margin on either side, but, if in doubt use less hardener.

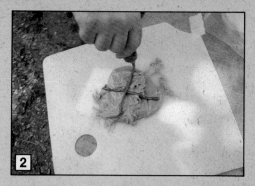

3 Mix the body filler and hardener by wiping across the mixing surface, picking the mixture up and wiping it again. Colder weather requires longer mixing times. Do not mix in a circular motion; this will trap air bubbles which will become holes in the cured filler.

Applying The Filler

1 For best results, filler should not be applied over ¼″ thick.

Apply the filler in several coats. Build it up to above the level of the repair surface so that it can be sanded or grated down.

The first coat of filler must be pressed on with a firm wiping motion.

Apply the filler in one direction only. Working the filler back and forth will either pull it off the metal or trap air bubbles.

REPAIRING DENTS

Before you start, take a few minutes to study the damaged area. Try to visualize the shape of the panel before it was damaged. If the damage is on the left fender, look at the right fender and use it as a guide. If there is access to the panel from behind, you can reshape it with a body hammer. If not, you'll have to use a dent puller. Go slowly and work the metal a little at a time. Get the panel as straight as possible before applying filler.

1 This dent is typical of one that can be pulled out or hammered out from behind. Remove the headlight cover, headlight assembly and turn signal housing.

2 Drill a series of holes ½ the size of the end of the dent puller along the stress line. Make some trial pulls and assess the results. If necessary, drill more holes and try again. Do not hurry.

3 If possible, use a body hammer and block to shape the metal back to its original contours. Get the metal back as close to its original shape as possible. Don't depend on body filler to fill dents.

4 Using an 80-grit grinding disc on an electric drill, grind the paint from the surrounding area down to bare metal. Use a new grinding pad to prevent heat buildup that will warp metal.

5 The area should look like this when you're finished grinding. Knock the drill holes in and tape over small openings to keep plastic filler out.

6 Mix the body filler (see Body Repair Tips). Spread the body filler evenly over the entire area (see Body Repair Tips). Be sure to cover the area completely.

7 Let the body filler dry until the surface can just be scratched with your fingernail. Knock the high spots from the body filler with a body file ("Cheesegrater"). Check frequently with the palm of your hand for high and low spots.

8 Check to be sure that trim pieces that will be installed later will fit exactly. Sand the area with 40-grit paper.

9 If you wind up with low spots, you may have to apply another layer of filler.

10 Knock the high spots off with 40-grit paper. When you are satisfied with the contours of the repair, apply a thin coat of filler to cover pin holes and scratches.

11 Block sand the area with 40-grit paper to a smooth finish. Pay particular attention to body lines and ridges that must be well-defined.

12 Sand the area with 400 paper and then finish with a scuff pad. The finished repair is ready for priming and painting (see Painting Tips).

Materials and photos courtesy of Ritt Jones Auto Body, Prospect Park, PA.

REPAIRING RUST HOLES

There are many ways to repair rust holes. The fiberglass cloth kit shown here is one of the most cost efficient for the owner because it provides a strong repair that resists cracking and moisture and is relatively easy to use. It can be used on large and small holes (with or without backing) and can be applied over contoured areas. Remember, however, that short of replacing an entire panel, no repair is a guarantee that the rust will not return.

1 Remove any trim that will be in the way. Clean away all loose debris. Cut away all the rusted metal. But be sure to leave enough metal to retain the contour or body shape.

2 Grind away all traces of rust with a 24-grit grinding disc. Be sure to grind back 3-4 inches from the edge of the hole down to bare metal and be sure all traces of paint, primer and rust are removed.

3 Block sand the area with 80 or 100 grit sandpaper to get a clear, shiny surface and feathered paint edge. Tap the edges of the hole inward with a ball peen hammer.

4 If you are going to use release film, cut a piece about 2-3″ larger than the area you have sanded. Place the film over the repair and mark the sanded area on the film. Avoid any unnecessary wrinkling of the film.

5 Cut 2 pieces of fiberglass matte to match the shape of the repair. One piece should be about 1″ smaller than the sanded area and the second piece should be 1″ smaller than the first. Mix enough filler and hardener to saturate the fiberglass material (see Body Repair Tips).

6 Lay the release sheet on a flat surface and spread an even layer of filler, large enough to cover the repair. Lay the smaller piece of fiberglass cloth in the center of the sheet and spread another layer of filler over the fiberglass cloth. Repeat the operation for the larger piece of cloth.

7 Place the repair material over the repair area, with the release film facing outward. Use a spreader and work from the center outward to smooth the material, following the body contours. Be sure to remove all air bubbles.

8 Wait until the repair has dried tack-free and peel off the release sheet. The ideal working temperature is 60°-90° F. Cooler or warmer temperatures or high humidity may require additional curing time. Wait longer, if in doubt.

9 Sand and feather-edge the entire area. The initial sanding can be done with a sanding disc on an electric drill if care is used. Finish the sanding with a block sander. Low spots can be filled with body filler; this may require several applications.

10 When the filler can just be scratched with a fingernail, knock the high spots down with a body file and smooth the entire area with 80-grit. Feather the filled areas into the surrounding areas.

11 When the area is sanded smooth, mix some topcoat and hardener and apply it directly with a spreader. This will give a smooth finish and prevent the glass matte from showing through the paint.

12 Block sand the topcoat smooth with finishing sandpaper (200 grit), and 400 grit. The repair is ready for masking, priming and painting (see Painting Tips).

Materials and photos courtesy Marson Corporation, Chelsea, Massachusetts

PAINTING TIPS

Preparation

1 SANDING — Use a 400 or 600 grit wet or dry sandpaper. Wet-sand the area with a ¼ sheet of sandpaper soaked in clean water. Keep the paper wet while sanding. Sand the area until the repaired area tapers into the original finish.

2 CLEANING — Wash the area to be painted thoroughly with water and a clean rag. Rinse it thoroughly and wipe the surface dry until you're sure it's completely free of dirt, dust, fingerprints, wax, detergent or other foreign matter.

3 MASKING — Protect any areas you don't want to overspray by covering them with masking tape and newspaper. Be careful not get fingerprints on the area to be painted.

4 PRIMING — All exposed metal should be primed before painting. Primer protects the metal and provides an excellent surface for paint adhesion. When the primer is dry, wet-sand the area again with 600 grit wet-sandpaper. Clean the area again after sanding.

Painting Techniques

P aint applied from either a spray gun or a spray can (for small areas) will provide good results. Experiment on an old piece of metal to get the right combination before you begin painting.

SPRAYING VISCOSITY (SPRAY GUN ONLY) — Paint should be thinned to spraying viscosity according to the directions on the can. Use only the recommended thinner or reducer and the same amount of reduction regardless of temperature.

AIR PRESSURE (SPRAY GUN ONLY) — This is extremely important. Be sure you are using the proper recommended pressure.

TEMPERATURE — The surface to be painted should be approximately the same temperature as the surrounding air. Applying warm paint to a cold surface, or vice versa, will completely upset the paint characteristics.

THICKNESS — Spray with smooth strokes. In general, the thicker the coat of paint, the longer the drying time. Apply several thin coats about 30 seconds apart. The paint should remain wet long enough to flow out and no longer; heavier coats will only produce sags or wrinkles. Spray a light (fog) coat, followed by heavier color coats.

DISTANCE — The ideal spraying distance is 8"-12" from the gun or can to the surface. Shorter distances will produce ripples, while greater distances will result in orange peel, dry film and poor color match and loss of material due to overspray.

OVERLAPPING — The gun or can should be kept at right angles to the surface at all times. Work to a wet edge at an even speed, using a 50% overlap and direct the center of the spray at the lower or nearest edge of the previous stroke.

RUBBING OUT (BLENDING) FRESH PAINT — Let the paint dry thoroughly. Runs or imperfections can be sanded out, primed and repainted.

Don't be in too big a hurry to remove the masking. This only produces paint ridges. When the finish has dried for at least a week, apply a small amount of fine grade rubbing compound with a clean, wet cloth. Use lots of water and blend the new paint with the surrounding area.

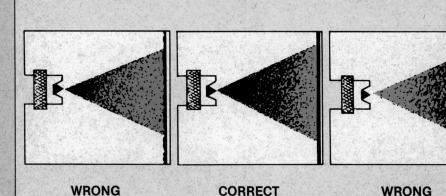

WRONG

Thin coat. Stroke too fast, not enough overlap, gun too far away.

CORRECT

Medium coat. Proper distance, good stroke, proper overlap.

WRONG

Heavy coat. Stroke too slow, too much overlap, gun too close.

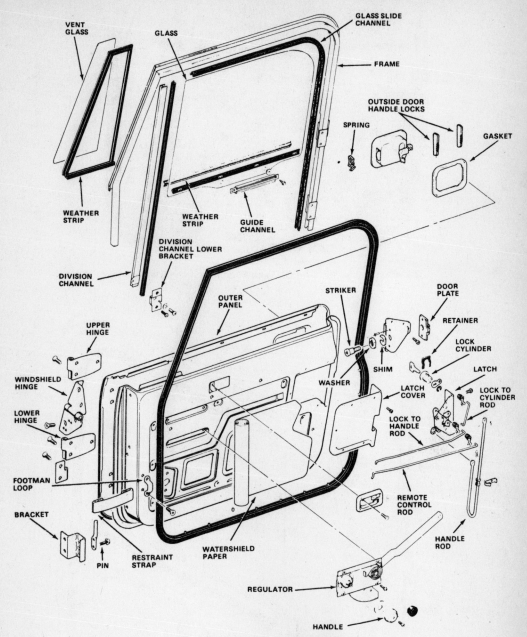

CJ-7 and Scrambler hardtop door

Window Regulator

REMOVAL AND INSTALLATION

Hardtop

1. Remove the door handle.
2. Remove the window crank handle.
3. Carefully pry the trim panel clips from the door. Be very careful! It's very easy to tear the trim panel or tear loose the clip from the panel. Inexpensive tools are made for this job and are available at most auto parts stores.
4. Remove the watershield.

5. Lower the glass to gain access to the guide channel fasteners.
6. Remove the fasteners and guide channel.
7. Raise the window to thew full up position and secure it in position by using masking tape to tape it to the door frame.
8. Remove the division channel lower adjusting screw.
9. Remove the regulator attaching screws.
10. Push the division channel outward and remove the regulator through the access hole.
11. Installation is the reverse of removal.

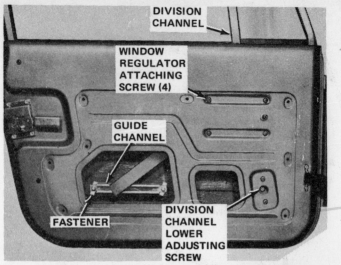

Door glass replacement on CJ-7 and Scrambler models with hardtop

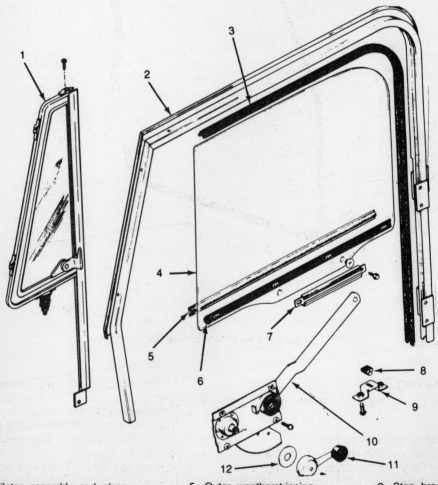

1. Ventilator assembly and glass	5. Outer weatherstripping
2. Top door frame	6. Inner weatherstripping
3. Channel	7. Window regulator arm
4. Glass	8. Stop bumper

9. Stop bracket
10. Window regulator
11. Handle
12. Washer

Door glass replacement on CJ-7 and Scrambler models with moveable vent windows

Stationary Window Glass
REMOVAL AND INSTALLATION
Utility and Hardtop

1. Unlock the weatherstripping from the hardtop with a wood spatula or fiber stick.
2. Using a fiber stick, break the seal between the glass and weatherstripping.
3. Push the glass and weatherstripping outward and remove it.
4. Inspect the weatherstripping. Replace it if cracked or otherwise damaged. Clean all old sealer from the glass and weatherstripping.
5. Apply a $^3/_{16}$" (4.7mm) bead of 3M Auto Bedding and Glazing Compound, or equivalent, in the weatherstripping glass cavity, using a pressure applicator.
6. Install the glass in the weatherstripping.
7. Place a ¼" (6.35mm) cord in the flange cavity of the weatherstripping, completely around the circumference. Let the ends of the cord hang outside the glass at the upper center.
8. Position the glass and weatherstripping in the opening. Pull on the ends of the cord to pull the lip of the weatherstripping over the hardtop flange.
9. Use a wood spatula to lock the weatherstripping.
10. Apply a bead of 3M Windshield Sealer, or equivalent, between the weatherstripping and the glass, around its entire perimeter. Clean off the excess.

Liftgate Glass
REMOVAL AND INSTALLATION
Utility and CJ-7 Hardtop

1. Unlock the weatherstripping from the hardtop with a wood spatula or fiber stick.
2. Using a fiber stick, break the seal between the glass and weatherstripping.
3. Push the glass and weatherstripping outward and remove it.
4. Inspect the weatherstripping. Replace it if cracked or otherwise damaged. Clean all old sealer from the glass and weatherstripping.
5. Apply a $^3/_{16}$" (4.7mm) bead of 3M Auto Bedding and Glazing Compound, or equivalent, in the weatherstripping glass cavity, using a pressure applicator.

6. Install the glass in the weatherstripping.
7. Place a ¼" (6.35mm) cord in the flange cavity of the weatherstripping, completely around the circumference. Let the ends of the cord hang outside the glass at the upper center.
8. Position the glass and weatherstripping in the opening. Pull on the ends of the cord to pull the lip of the weatherstripping over the hardtop flange.
9. Use a wood spatula to lock the weatherstripping.
10. Apply a bead of 3M Windshield Sealer, or equivalent, between the weatherstripping and the glass, around its entire perimeter. Clean off the excess.

Seats
REMOVAL AND INSTALLATION
Front or Rear

1. Unbolt the seat frame from the floor pan.
2. Remove the seat.
3. Installation is the reverse of removal. Torque the bolts to 15 ft.lb.

NOTE: *The seat pivot bolts on Utility models may work loose unless they are properly installed. Proper installation is with the bolt head next to the seat leg, not the pivot bracket. The flat washer should be next to the seat leg.*

1. Location holes
2. Spacer

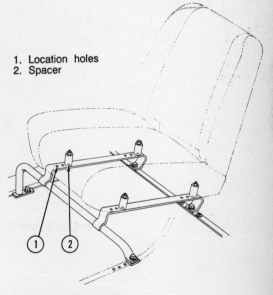

Utility model front seat

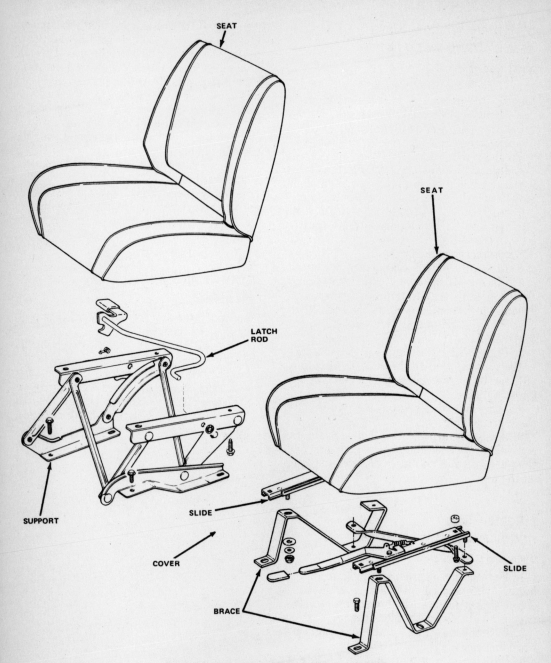

SEAT

SEAT

LATCH
ROD

SUPPORT

SLIDE

COVER

SLIDE

BRACE

Bucket seats used on all models through 1986

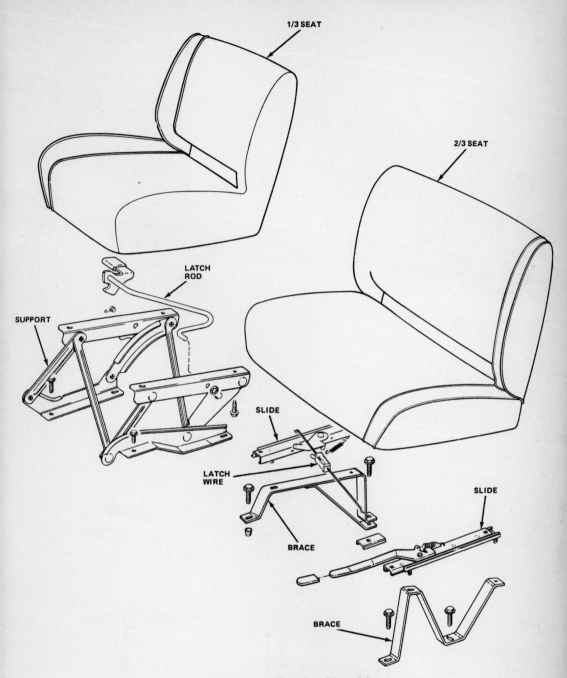

1/3 SEAT

2/3 SEAT

LATCH
ROD

SUPPORT

SLIDE

LATCH
WIRE

SLIDE

BRACE

BRACE

⅓–⅔ style seat, optional on CJ models

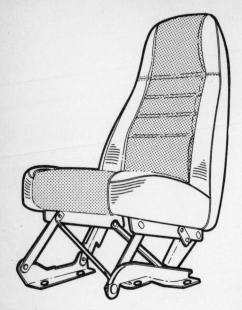

Wrangler front seat

Rear seat used on all CJ and Wrangler models

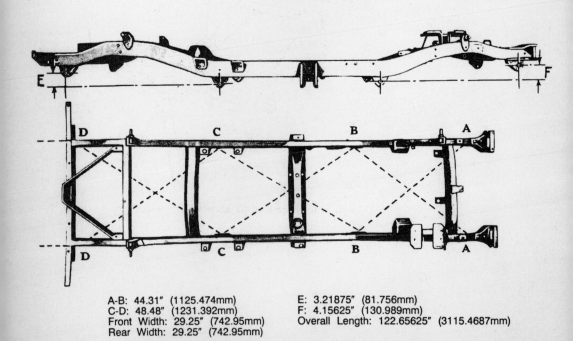

A-B: 44.31″ (1125.474mm)
C-D: 48.48″ (1231.392mm)
Front Width: 29.25″ (742.95mm)
Rear Width: 29.25″ (742.95mm)

E: 3.21875″ (81.756mm)
F: 4.15625″ (130.989mm)
Overall Length: 122.65625″ (3115.4687mm)

Frame dimensions for the CJ-2A, CJ-3A, DJ-3A, CJ-3B

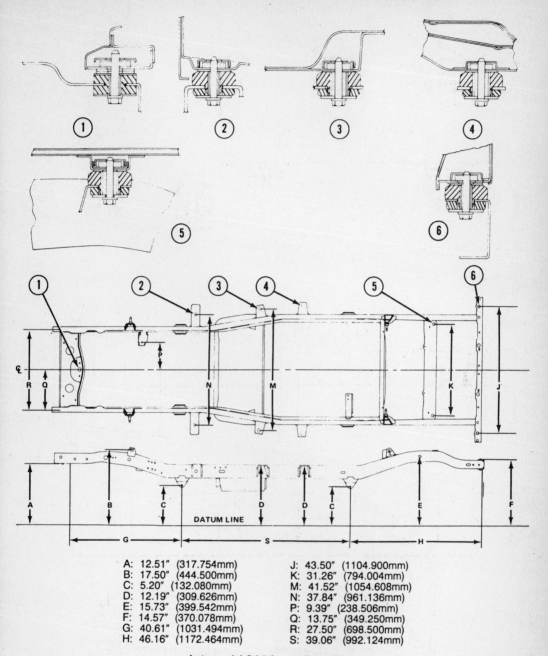

A: 12.51″ (317.754mm)
B: 17.50″ (444.500mm)
C: 5.20″ (132.080mm)
D: 12.19″ (309.626mm)
E: 15.73″ (399.542mm)
F: 14.57″ (370.078mm)
G: 40.61″ (1031.494mm)
H: 46.16″ (1172.464mm)

J: 43.50″ (1104.900mm)
K: 31.26″ (794.004mm)
M: 41.52″ (1054.608mm)
N: 37.84″ (961.136mm)
P: 9.39″ (238.506mm)
Q: 13.75″ (349.250mm)
R: 27.50″ (698.500mm)
S: 39.06″ (992.124mm)

Late model CJ-5 frame dimensions

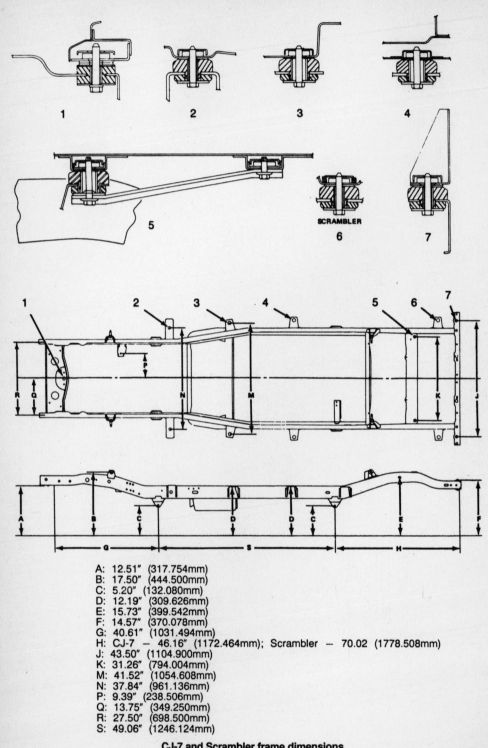

A: 12.51″ (317.754mm)
B: 17.50″ (444.500mm)
C: 5.20″ (132.080mm)
D: 12.19″ (309.626mm)
E: 15.73″ (399.542mm)
F: 14.57″ (370.078mm)
G: 40.61″ (1031.494mm)
H: CJ-7 — 46.16″ (1172.464mm); Scrambler — 70.02 (1778.508mm)
J: 43.50″ (1104.900mm)
K: 31.26″ (794.004mm)
M: 41.52″ (1054.608mm)
N: 37.84″ (961.136mm)
P: 9.39″ (238.506mm)
Q: 13.75″ (349.250mm)
R: 27.50″ (698.500mm)
S: 49.06″ (1246.124mm)

CJ-7 and Scrambler frame dimensions

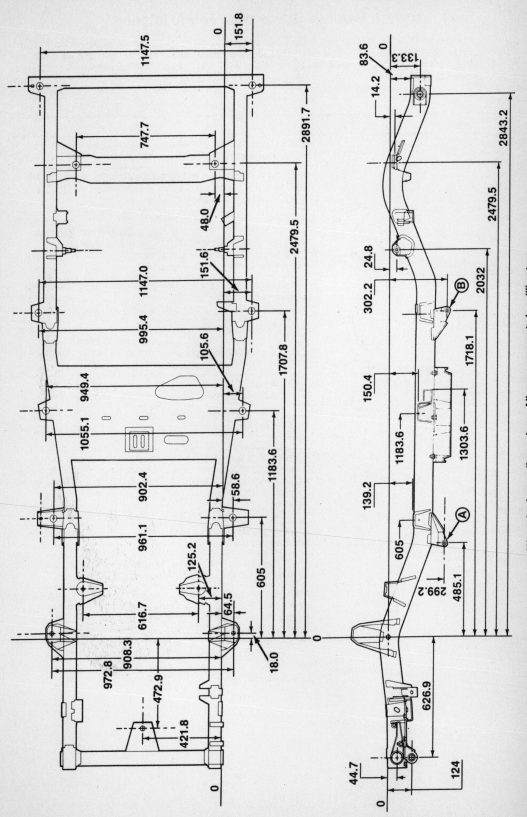

Wrangler frame dimensions. All measurements in millimeters

How to Remove Stains from Fabric Interior

For rest results, spots and stains should be removed as soon as possible. Never use gasoline, lacquer thinner, acetone, nail polish remover or bleach. Use a 3′ x 3″ piece of cheesecloth. Squeeze most of the liquid from the fabric and wipe the stained fabric from the outside of the stain toward the center with a lifting motion. Turn the cheesecloth as soon as one side becomes soiled. When using water to remove a stain, be sure to wash the entire section after the spot has been removed to avoid water stains. Encrusted spots can be broken up with a dull knife and vacuumed before removing the stain.

Type of Stain	How to Remove It
Surface spots	Brush the spots out with a small hand brush or use a commercial preparation such as K2R to lift the stain.
Mildew	Clean around the mildew with warm suds. Rinse in cold water and soak the mildew area in a solution of 1 part table salt and 2 parts water. Wash with upholstery cleaner.
Water stains	Water stains in fabric materials can be removed with a solution made from 1 cup of table salt dissolved in 1 quart of water. Vigorously scrub the solution into the stain and rinse with clear water. Water stains in nylon or other synthetic fabrics should be removed with a commercial type spot remover.
Chewing gum, tar, crayons, shoe polish (greasy stains)	Do not use a cleaner that will soften gum or tar. Harden the deposit with an ice cube and scrape away as much as possible with a dull knife. Moisten the remainder with cleaning fluid and scrub clean.
Ice cream, candy	Most candy has a sugar base and can be removed with a cloth wrung out in warm water. Oily candy, after cleaning with warm water, should be cleaned with upholstery cleaner. Rinse with warm water and clean the remainder with cleaning fluid.
Wine, alcohol, egg, milk, soft drink (non-greasy stains)	Do not use soap. Scrub the stain with a cloth wrung out in warm water. Remove the remainder with cleaning fluid.
Grease, oil, lipstick, butter and related stains	Use a spot remover to avoid leaving a ring. Work from the outisde of the stain to the center and dry with a clean cloth when the spot is gone.
Headliners (cloth)	Mix a solution of warm water and foam upholstery cleaner to give thick suds. Use only foam—liquid may streak or spot. Clean the entire headliner in one operation using a circular motion with a natural sponge.
Headliner (vinyl)	Use a vinyl cleaner with a sponge and wipe clean with a dry cloth.
Seats and door panels	Mix 1 pint upholstery cleaner in 1 gallon of water. Do not soak the fabric around the buttons.
Leather or vinyl fabric	Use a multi-purpose cleaner full strength and a stiff brush. Let stand 2 minutes and scrub thoroughly. Wipe with a clean, soft rag.
Nylon or synthetic fabrics	For normal stains, use the same procedures you would for washing cloth upholstery. If the fabric is extremely dirty, use a multi-purpose cleaner full strength with a stiff scrub brush. Scrub thoroughly in all directions and wipe with a cotton towel or soft rag.

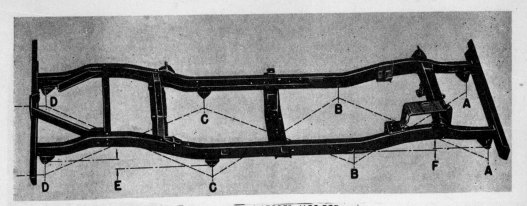

A-B: 47.08" (1195.832mm)
C-D: 52.37" (1330.198mm)
Front Width: 29.25" (742.95mm)
Rear Width: 29.25" (742.95mm)
E: 3.21875" (81.756mm)

F: 4.15625" (130.989mm)
Overall Length:
    CJ-5, CJ-5A -- 128.4375" (3262.3125mm)
    CJ-6, CJ-6A -- 148.4375" (3770.3125mm)

Frame dimensions for early model CJ-5, CJ-5A, CJ-6, CJ-6A with the F4-134 engine

Mechanic's Data

General Conversion Table

Multiply By	To Convert	To	
		LENGTH	
2.54	Inches	Centimeters	.3937
25.4	Inches	Millimeters	.03937
30.48	Feet	Centimeters	.0328
.304	Feet	Meters	3.28
.914	Yards	Meters	1.094
1.609	Miles	Kilometers	.621
		VOLUME	
.473	Pints	Liters	2.11
.946	Quarts	Liters	1.06
3.785	Gallons	Liters	.264
.016	Cubic inches	Liters	61.02
16.39	Cubic inches	Cubic cms.	.061
28.3	Cubic feet	Liters	.0353
		MASS (Weight)	
28.35	Ounces	Grams	.035
.4536	Pounds	Kilograms	2.20
—	To obtain	From	Multiply by

Multiply By	To Convert	To	
		AREA	
.645	Square inches	Square cms.	.155
.836	Square yds.	Square meters	1.196
		FORCE	
4.448	Pounds	Newtons	.225
.138	Ft./lbs.	Kilogram/meters	7.23
1.36	Ft./lbs.	Newton-meters	.737
.112	In./lbs.	Newton-meters	8.844
		PRESSURE	
.068	Psi	Atmospheres	14.7
6.89	Psi	Kilopascals	.145
		OTHER	
1.104	Horsepower (DIN)	Horsepower (SAE)	.9861
.746	Horsepower (SAE)	Kilowatts (KW)	1.34
1.60	Mph	Km/h	.625
.425	Mpg	Km/1	2.35
—	To obtain	From	Multiply by

Tap Drill Sizes

National Coarse or U.S.S.

Screw & Tap Size	Threads Per Inch	Use Drill Number
No. 5	40	.39
No. 6	32	.36
No. 8	32	.29
No. 10	24	.25
No. 12	24	.17
1/4	20	8
5/16	18	.F
3/8	16	5/16
7/16	14	.U
1/2	13	27/64
9/16	12	31/64
5/8	11	17/32
3/4	10	21/32
7/8	9	49/64

National Coarse or U.S.S.

Screw & Tap Size	Threads Per Inch	Use Drill Number
1	8	7/8
1 1/8	7	63/64
1 1/4	7	1 7/64
1 1/2	6	1 11/32

National Fine or S.A.E.

Screw & Tap Size	Threads Per Inch	Use Drill Number
No. 5	44	.37
No. 6	40	.33
No. 8	36	.29
No. 10	32	.21

National Fine or S.A.E.

Screw & Tap Size	Threads Per Inch	Use Drill Number
No. 12	28	.15
1/4	28	3
6/16	24	1
3/8	24	.Q
7/16	20	.W
1/2	20	29/64
9/16	18	33/64
5/8	18	37/64
3/4	16	11/16
7/8	14	13/16
1 1/8	12	1 3/64
1 1/4	12	1 11/64
1 1/2	12	1 27/64

Drill Sizes In Decimal Equivalents

Inch	Decimal	Wire	mm	Inch	Decimal	Wire	mm	Inch	Decimal	Wire & Letter	mm	Inch	Decimal	Letter	mm	Inch	Decimal	mm
1/64	.0156		.39		.0730	49			.1614		4.1		.2717		6.9		.4331	11.0
	.0157		.4		.0748		1.9		.1654		4.2		.2720	I		7/16	.4375	11.11
	.0160	78			.0760	48			.1660	19			.2756		7.0		.4528	11.5
	.0165		.42		.0768		1.95		.1673		4.25		.2770	J		29/64	.4531	11.51
	.0173		.44	5/64	.0781		1.98		.1693		4.3		.2795		7.1	15/32	.4688	11.90
	.0177		.45		.0785	47			.1695	18			.2810	K			.4724	12.0
	.0180	77			.0787		2.0	11/64	.1719		4.36	9/32	.2812		7.14	31/64	.4844	12.30
	.0181		.46		.0807		2.05		.1730	17			.2835		7.2		.4921	12.5
	.0189		.48		.0810	46			.1732		4.4		.2854		7.25	1/2	.5000	12.70
	.0197		.5		.0820	45			.1770	16			.2874		7.3		.5118	13.0
	.0200	76			.0827		2.1		.1772		4.5		.2900	L		33/64	.5156	13.09
	.0210	75			.0846		2.15		.1800	15			.2913		7.4	17/32	.5312	13.49
	.0217		.55		.0860	44			.1811		4.6		.2950	M			.5315	13.5
	.0225	74			.0866		2.2		.1820	14			.2953		7.5	35/64	.5469	13.89
	.0236		.6		.0886		2.25		.1850	13		19/64	.2969		7.54		.5512	14.0
	.0240	73			.0890	43			.1850		4.7		.2992		7.6	9/16	.5625	14.28
	.0250	72			.0906		2.3		.1870		4.75		.3020	N			.5709	14.5
	.0256		.65		.0925		2.35	3/16	.1875		4.76		.3031		7.7	37/64	.5781	14.68
	.0260	71			.0935	42			.1890		4.8		.3051		7.75		.5906	15.0
	.0276		.7	3/32	.0938		2.38		.1890	12			.3071		7.8	19/32	.5938	15.08
	.0280	70			.0945		2.4		.1910	11			.3110		7.9	39/64	.6094	15.47
	.0292	69			.0960	41			.1929		4.9	5/16	.3125		7.93		.6102	15.5
	.0295		.75		.0965		2.45		.1935	10			.3150		8.0	5/8	.6250	15.87
	.0310	68			.0980	40			.1960	9			.3160	O			.6299	16.0
1/32	.0312		.79		.0981		2.5		.1969		5.0		.3189		8.1	41/64	.6406	16.27
	.0315		.8		.0995	39			.1990	8			.3228		8.2		.6496	16.5
	.0320	67			.1015	38			.2008		5.1		.3230	P		21/32	.6562	16.66
	.0330	66			.1024		2.6		.2010	7			.3248		8.25		.6693	17.0
	.0335		.85		.1040	37		13/64	.2031		5.16		.3268		8.3	43/64	.6719	17.06
	.0350	65			.1063		2.7		.2040	6		21/64	.3281		8.33	11/16	.6875	17.46
	.0354		.9		.1065	36			.2047		5.2		.3307		8.4		.6890	17.5
	.0360	64			.1083		2.75		.2055	5			.3320	Q		45/64	.7031	17.85
	.0370	63		7/64	.1094		2.77		.2067		5.25		.3346		8.5		.7087	18.0
	.0374		.95		.1100	35			.2087		5.3		.3386		8.6	23/32	.7188	18.25
	.0380	62			.1102		2.8		.2090	4			.3390	R			.7283	18.5
	.0390	61			.1110	34			.2126		5.4		.3425		8.7	47/64	.7344	18.65
	.0394		1.0		.1130	33			.2130	3		11/32	.3438		8.73		.7480	19.0
	.0400	60			.1142		2.9		.2165		5.5		.3445		8.75	3/4	.7500	19.05
	.0410	59			.1160	32		7/32	.2188		5.55		.3465		8.8	49/64	.7656	19.44
	.0413		1.05		.1181		3.0		.2205		5.6		.3480	S			.7677	19.5
	.0420	58			.1200	31			.2210	2			.3504		8.9	25/32	.7812	19.84
	.0430	57			.1220		3.1		.2244		5.7		.3543		9.0		.7874	20.0
	.0433		1.1	1/8	.1250		3.17		.2264		5.75		.3580	T		51/64	.7969	20.24
	.0453		1.15		.1260		3.2		.2280	1			.3583		9.1		.8071	20.5
3/64	.0465	56			.1280		3.25		.2283		5.8	23/64	.3594		9.12	13/16	.8125	20.63
	.0469		1.19		.1285	30			.2323		5.9		.3622		9.2		.8268	21.0
	.0472		1.2		.1299		3.3		.2340	A			.3642		9.25	53/64	.8281	21.03
	.0492		1.25		.1339		3.4	15/64	.2344		5.95		.3661		9.3	27/32	.8438	21.43
	.0512		1.3		.1360	29			.2362		6.0		.3680	U			.8465	21.5
	.0520	55			.1378		3.5		.2380	B			.3701		9.4	55/64	.8594	21.82
	.0531		1.35		.1405	28			.2402		6.1		.3740		9.5		.8661	22.0
	.0550	54		9/64	.1406		3.57		.2420	C		3/8	.3750		9.52	7/8	.8750	22.22
	.0551		1.4		.1417		3.6		.2441		6.2		.3770	V			.8858	22.5
	.0571		1.45		.1440	27			.2460	D			.3780		9.6	57/64	.8906	22.62
	.0591		1.5		.1457		3.7		.2461		6.25		.3819		9.7		.9055	23.0
	.0595	53			.1470	26			.2480		6.3		.3839		9.75	29/32	.9062	23.01
	.0610		1.55		.1476		3.75	1/4	.2500	E	6.35		.3858		9.8	59/64	.9219	23.41
1/16	.0625		1.59		.1495	25			.2520		6.		.3860	W			.9252	23.5
	.0630		1.6		.1496		3.8		.2559		6.5		.3898		9.9	15/16	.9375	23.81
	.0635	52			.1520	24			.2570	F		25/64	.3906		9.92		.9449	24.0
	.0650		1.65		.1535		3.9		.2598		6.6		.3937		10.0	61/64	.9531	24.2
	.0669		1.7		.1540	23			.2610	G			.3970	X			.9646	24.5
	.0670	51		5/32	.1562		3.96		.2638		6.7		.4040	Y		31/32	.9688	24.6
	.0689		1.75		.1570	22		17/64	.2656		6.74	13/32	.4062		10.31		.9843	25.0
	.0700	50			.1575		4.0		.2657		6.75		.4130	Z		63/64	.9844	25.0
	.0709		1.8		.1590	21			.2660	H			.4134		10.5	1	1.0000	25.4
	.0728		1.85		.1610	20			.2677		6.8	27/64	.4219		10.71			

GLOSSARY OF TERMS

AIR/FUEL RATIO: The ratio of air to gasoline by weight in the fuel mixture drawn into the engine.

AIR INJECTION: One method of reducing harmful exhaust emissions by injecting air into each of the exhaust ports of an engine. The fresh air entering the hot exhaust manifold causes any remaining fuel to be burned before it can exit the tailpipe.

ALTERNATOR: A device used for converting mechanical energy into electrical energy.

AMMETER: An instrument, calibrated in amperes, used to measure the flow of an electrical current in a circuit. Ammeters are always connected in series with the circuit being tested.

AMPERE: The rate of flow of electrical current present when one volt of electrical pressure is applied against one ohm of electrical resistance.

ANALOG COMPUTER: Any microprocessor that uses similar (analogous) electrical signals to make its calculations.

ARMATURE: A laminated, soft iron core wrapped by a wire that converts electrical energy to mechanical energy as in a motor or relay. When rotated in a magnetic field, it changes mechanical energy into electrical energy as in a generator.

ATMOSPHERIC PRESSURE: The pressure on the Earth's surface caused by the weight of the air in the atmosphere. At sea level, this pressure is 14.7 psi at 32°F (101 kPa at 0°C).

ATOMIZATION: The breaking down of a liquid into a fine mist that can be suspended in air.

AXIAL PLAY: Movement parallel to a shaft or bearing bore.

BACKFIRE: The sudden combustion of gases in the intake or exhaust system that results in a loud explosion.

BACKLASH: The clearance or play between two parts, such as meshed gears.

BACKPRESSURE: Restrictions in the exhaust system that slow the exit of exhaust gases from the combustion chamber.

BAKELITE: A heat resistant, plastic insulator material commonly used in printed circuit boards and transistorized components.

BALL BEARING: A bearing made up of hardened inner and outer races between which hardened steel ball roll.

BALLAST RESISTOR: A resistor in the primary ignition circuit that lowers voltage after the engine is started to reduce wear on ignition components.

BEARING: A friction reducing, supportive device usually located between a stationary part and a moving part.

BIMETAL TEMPERATURE SENSOR: Any sensor or switch made of two dissimilar types of metal that bend when heated or cooled due to the different expansion rates of the alloys. These types of sensors usually function as an on/off switch.

BLOWBY: Combustion gases, composed of water vapor and unburned fuel, that leak past the piston rings into the crankcase during normal engine operation. These gases are removed by the PCV system to prevent the buildup of harmful acids in the crankcase.

BRAKE PAD: A brake shoe and lining assembly used with disc brakes.

BRAKE SHOE: The backing for the brake lining. The term is, however, usually applied to the assembly of the brake backing and lining.

BUSHING: A liner, usually removable, for a bearing; an anti-friction liner used in place of a bearing.

BYPASS: System used to bypass ballast resistor during engine cranking to increase voltage supplied to the coil.

CALIPER: A hydraulically activated device in a disc brake system, which is mounted straddling the brake rotor (disc). The caliper contains at least one piston and two brake pads. Hydraulic pressure on the piston(s) forces the pads against the rotor.

CAMSHAFT: A shaft in the engine on which are the lobes (cams) which operate the valves. The camshaft is driven by the crankshaft, via a belt, chain or gears, at one half the crankshaft speed.

CAPACITOR: A device which stores an electrical charge.

CARBON MONOXIDE (CO): a colorless, odorless gas given off as a normal byproduct of combustion. It is poisonous and extremely dangerous in confined areas, building up slowly to toxic levels without warning if adequate ventilation is not available.

CARBURETOR: A device, usually mounted on the intake manifold of an engine, which mixes the air and fuel in the proper proportion to allow even combustion.

CATALYTIC CONVERTER: A device installed in the exhaust system, like a muffler, that converts harmful byproducts of combustion into carbon dioxide and water vapor by means of a heat-producing chemical reaction.

CENTRIFUGAL ADVANCE: A mechanical method of advancing the spark timing by using flyweights in the distributor that react to centrifugal force generated by the distributor shaft rotation.

CHECK VALVE: Any one-way valve installed to permit the flow of air, fuel or vacuum in one direction only.

CHOKE: A device, usually a moveable valve, placed in the intake path of a carburetor to restrict the flow of air.

CIRCUIT: Any unbroken path through which an electrical current can flow. Also used to describe fuel flow in some instances.

CIRCUIT BREAKER: A switch which protects an electrical circuit from overload by opening the circuit when the current flow exceeds a predetermined level. Some circuit breakers must be reset manually, while other reset automatically

COIL (IGNITION): A transformer in the ignition circuit which steps of the voltage provided to the spark plugs.

COMBINATION MANIFOLD: An assembly which includes both the intake and exhaust manifolds in one casting.

COMBINATION VALVE: A device used in some fuel systems that routes fuel vapors to a charcoal storage canister instead of venting them into the atmosphere. The valve relieves fuel tank pressure and allows fresh air into the tank as fuel level drops to prevent a vapor lock situation.

COMPRESSION RATIO: The comparison of the total volume of the cylinder and combustion chamber with the piston at BDC and the piston at TDC.

CONDENSER: 1. An electrical device which acts to store an electrical charge, preventing voltage surges.
2. A radiator-like device in the air conditioning system in which refrigerant gas condenses into a liquid, giving off heat.

CONDUCTOR: Any material through which an electrical current can be transmitted easily.

CONTINUITY: Continuous or complete circuit. Can be checked with an ohmmeter.

COUNTERSHAFT: An intermediate shaft which is rotated by a mainshaft and transmits, in turn, that rotation to a working part.

CRANKCASE: The lower part of an engine in which the crankshaft and related parts operate.

CRANKSHAFT: The main driving shaft of an engine which receives reciprocating motion from the pistons and converts it to rotary motion.

CYLINDER: In an engine, the round hole in the engine block in which the piston(s) ride.

CYLINDER BLOCK: The main structural member of an engine in which is found the cylinders, crankshaft and other principal parts.

CYLINDER HEAD: The detachable portion of the engine, fastened, usually, to the top of the cylinder block, containing all or most of the combustion chambers. On overhead valve engines, it contains the valves and their operating parts. On overhead cam engines, it contains the camshaft as well.

DEAD CENTER: The extreme top or bottom of the piston stroke.

DETONATION: An unwanted explosion of the air fuel mixture in the combustion chamber caused by excess heat and compression, advanced timing, or an overly lean mixture. Also referred to as "ping".

DIAPHRAGM: A thin, flexible wall separating two cavities, such as in a vacuum advance unit.

DIESELING: A condition in which hot spots in the combustion chamber cause the engine to run on after the key is turned off.

DIFFERENTIAL: A geared assembly which allows the transmission of motion between drive axles, giving one axle the ability to turn faster than the other.

DIODE: An electrical device that will allow current to flow in one direction only.

DISC BRAKE: A hydraulic braking assembly consisting of a brake disc, or rotor, mounted on an axle, and a caliper assembly containing, usually two brake pads which are activated by hydraulic pressure. The pads are forced against the sides of the disc, creating friction which slows the vehicle.

DISTRIBUTOR: A mechanically driven device on an engine which is responsible for electrically firing the spark plug at a predetermined point of the piston stroke.

DOWEL PIN: A pin, inserted in mating holes in two different parts allowing those parts to maintain a fixed relationship.

DRUM BRAKE: A braking system which consists of two brake shoes and one or two wheel cylinders, mounted on a fixed backing plate, and a brake drum, mounted on an axle, which revolves around the assembly. Hydraulic action applied to the wheel cylinders forces the shoes outward against the drum, creating friction and slowing the vehicle.

DWELL: The rate, measured in degrees of shaft rotation, at which an electrical circuit cycles on and off.

ELECTRONIC CONTROL UNIT (ECU): Ignition module, module, amplifier or igniter. See Module for definition.

ELECTRONIC IGNITION: A system in which the timing and firing of the spark plugs is controlled by an electronic control unit, usually called a module. These systems have not points or condenser.

ENDPLAY: The measured amount of axial movement in a shaft.

ENGINE: A device that converts heat into mechanical energy.

EXHAUST MANIFOLD: A set of cast passages or pipes which conduct exhaust gases from the engine.

FEELER GAUGE: A blade, usually metal, of precisely predetermined thickness, used to measure the clearance between two parts. These blades usually are available in sets of assorted thicknesses.

F-Head: An engine configuration in which the intake valves are in the cylinder head, while the camshaft and exhaust valves are located in the cylinder block. The camshaft operates the intake valves via lifters and pushrods, while it operates the exhaust valves directly.

FIRING ORDER: The order in which combustion occurs in the cylinders of an engine. Also the order in which spark is distributed to the plugs by the distributor.

FLATHEAD: An engine configuration in which the camshaft and all the valves are located in the cylinder block.

FLOODING: The presence of too much fuel in the intake manifold and combustion chamber which prevents the air/fuel mixture from firing, thereby causing a no-start situation.

FLYWHEEL: A disc shaped part bolted to the rear end of the crankshaft. Around the outer perimeter is affixed the ring gear. The starter drive engages the ring gear, turning the flywheel, which rotates the crankshaft, imparting the initial starting motion to the engine.

FOOT POUND (ft.lb. or sometimes, ft. lbs.): The amount of energy or work needed to raise an item weighing one pound, a distance of one foot.

FUSE: A protective device in a circuit which prevents circuit overload by breaking the circuit when a specific amperage is present. The device is constructed around a strip or wire of a lower amperage rating than the circuit it is designed to protect. When an amperage higher than that stamped on the fuse is present in the circuit, the strip or wire melts, opening the circuit.

GEAR RATIO: The ratio between the number of teeth on meshing gears.

GENERATOR: A device which converts mechanical energy into electrical energy.

HEAT RANGE: The measure of a spark plug's ability to dissipate heat from its firing end. The higher the heat range, the hotter the plug fires.

HUB: The center part of a wheel or gear.

HYDROCARBON (HC): Any chemical compound made up of hydrogen and carbon. A major pollutant formed by the engine as a byproduct of combustion.

HYDROMETER: An instrument used to measure the specific gravity of a solution.

INCH POUND (in.lb. or sometimes, in. lbs.): One twelfth of a foot pound.

INDUCTION: A means of transferring electrical energy in the form of a magnetic field. Principle used in the ignition coil to increase voltage.

INJECTION PUMP: A device, usually mechanically operated, which meters and delivers fuel under pressure to the fuel injector.

INJECTOR: A device which receives metered fuel under relatively low pressure and is activated to inject the fuel into the engine under relatively high pressure at a predetermined time.

INPUT SHAFT: The shaft to which torque is applied, usually carrying the driving gear or gears.

INTAKE MANIFOLD: A casting of passages or pipes used to conduct air or a fuel/air mixture to the cylinders.

JOURNAL: The bearing surface within which a shaft operates.

KEY: A small block usually fitted in a notch between a shaft and a hub to prevent slippage of the two parts.

MANIFOLD: A casting of passages or set of pipes which connect the cylinders to an inlet or outlet source.

MANIFOLD VACUUM: Low pressure in an engine intake manifold formed just below the throttle plates. Manifold vacuum is highest at idle and drops under acceleration.

MASTER CYLINDER: The primary fluid pressurizing device in a hydraulic system. In automotive use, it is found in brake and hydraulic clutch systems and is pedal activated, either directly or, in a power brake system, through the power booster.

MODULE: Electronic control unit, amplifier or igniter of solid state or integrated design which controls the current flow in the ignition primary circuit based on input from the pickup coil. When the module opens the primary circuit, the high secondary voltage is induced in the coil.

NEEDLE BEARING: A bearing which consists of a number (usually a large number) of long, thin rollers.

OHM: (Ω) The unit used to measure the resistance of conductor to electrical flow. One ohm is the amount of resistance that limits current flow to one ampere in a circuit with one volt of pressure.

OHMMETER: An instrument used for measuring the resistance, in ohms, in an electrical circuit.

OUTPUT SHAFT: The shaft which transmits torque from a device, such as a transmission.

OVERDRIVE: A gear assembly which produces more shaft revolutions than that transmitted to it.

OVERHEAD CAMSHAFT (OHC): An engine configuration in which the camshaft is mounted on top of the cylinder head and operates the valve either directly or by means of rocker arms.

OVERHEAD VALVE (OHV): An engine configuration in which all of the valves are located in the cylinder head and the camshaft is located in the cylinder block. The camshaft operates the valves via lifters and pushrods.

OXIDES OF NITROGEN (NOx): Chemical compounds of nitrogen produced as a byproduct of combustion. They combine with hydrocarbons to produce smog.

OXYGEN SENSOR: Used with the feedback system to sense the presence of oxygen in the exhaust gas and signal the computer which can reference the voltage signal to an air/fuel ratio.

PINION: The smaller of two meshing gears.

PISTON RING: An open ended ring which fits into a groove on the outer diameter of the piston. Its chief function is to form a seal between the piston and cylinder wall. Most automotive pistons have three rings: two for compression sealing; one for oil sealing.

PRELOAD: A predetermined load placed on a bearing during assembly or by adjustment.

PRIMARY CIRCUIT: Is the low voltage side of the ignition system which consists of the ignition switch, ballast resistor or resistance wire, bypass, coil, electronic control unit and pick-up coil as well as the connecting wires and harnesses.

PRESS FIT: The mating of two parts under pressure, due to the inner diameter of one being smaller than the outer diameter of the other, or vice versa; an interference fit.

RACE: The surface on the inner or outer ring of a bearing on which the balls, needles or rollers move.

REGULATOR: A device which maintains the amperage and/or voltage levels of a circuit at predetermined values.

RELAY: A switch which automatically opens and/or closes a circuit.

RESISTANCE: The opposition to the flow of current through a circuit or electrical device, and is measured in ohms. Resistance is equal to the voltage divided by the amperage.

RESISTOR: A device, usually made of wire, which offers a preset amount of resistance in an electrical circuit.

RING GEAR: The name given to a ring-shaped gear attached to a differential case, or affixed to a flywheel or as part a planetary gear set.

ROLLER BEARING: A bearing made up of hardened inner and outer races between which hardened steel rollers move.

ROTOR: 1. The disc-shaped part of a disc brake assembly, upon which the brake pads bear; also called, brake disc.
2. The device mounted atop the distributor shaft, which passes current to the distributor cap tower contacts.

SECONDARY CIRCUIT: The high voltage side of the ignition system, usually above 20,000 volts. The secondary includes the ignition coil, coil wire, distributor cap and rotor, spark plug wires and spark plugs.

SENDING UNIT: A mechanical, electrical, hydraulic or electromagnetic device which transmits information to a gauge.

SENSOR: Any device designed to measure engine operating conditions or ambient pressures and temperatures. Usually electronic in nature and designed to send a voltage signal to an on-board computer, some sensors may operate as a simple on/off switch or they may provide a variable voltage signal (like a potentiometer) as conditions or measured parameters change.

SHIM: Spacers of precise, predetermined thickness used between parts to establish a proper working relationship.

SLAVE CYLINDER: In automotive use, a device in the hydraulic clutch system which is activated by hydraulic force, disengaging the clutch.

SOLENOID: A coil used to produce a magnetic field, the effect of which is produce work.

SPARK PLUG: A device screwed into the combustion chamber of a spark ignition engine. The basic construction is a conductive core inside of a ceramic insulator, mounted in an outer conductive base. An electrical charge from the spark plug wire travels along the conductive core and jumps a preset air gap to a grounding point or points at the end of the conductive base. The resultant spark ignites the fuel/air mixture in the combustion chamber.

SPLINES: Ridges machined or cast onto the outer diameter of a shaft or inner diameter of a bore to enable parts to mate without rotation.

TACHOMETER: A device used to measure the rotary speed of an engine, shaft, gear, etc., usually in rotations per minute.

THERMOSTAT: A valve, located in the cooling system of an engine, which is closed when cold and opens gradually in response to engine heating, controlling the temperature of the coolant and rate of coolant flow.

TOP DEAD CENTER (TDC): The point at which the piston reaches the top of its travel on the compression stroke.

TORQUE: The twisting force applied to an object.

TORQUE CONVERTER: A turbine used to transmit power from a driving member to a driven member via hydraulic action, providing changes in drive ratio and torque. In automotive use, it links the driveplate at the rear of the engine to the automatic transmission.

TRANSDUCER: A device used to change a force into an electrical signal.

TRANSISTOR: A semi-conductor component which can be actuated by a small voltage to perform an electrical switching function.

TUNE-UP: A regular maintenance function, usually associated with the replacement and adjustment of parts and components in the electrical and fuel systems of a vehicle for the purpose of attaining optimum performance.

TURBOCHARGER: An exhaust driven pump which compresses intake air and forces it into the combustion chambers at higher than atmospheric pressures. The increased air pressure allows more fuel to be burned and results in increased horsepower being produced.

VACUUM ADVANCE: A device which advances the ignition timing in response to increased engine vacuum.

VACUUM GAUGE: An instrument used to measure the presence of vacuum in a chamber.

VALVE: A device which control the pressure, direction of flow or rate of flow of a liquid or gas.

VALVE CLEARANCE: The measured gap between the end of the valve stem and the rocker arm, cam lobe or follower that activates the valve.

VISCOSITY: The rating of a liquid's internal resistance to flow.

VOLTMETER: An instrument used for measuring electrical force in units called volts. Voltmeters are always connected parallel with the circuit being tested.

WHEEL CYLINDER: Found in the automotive drum brake assembly, it is a device, actuated by hydraulic pressure, which, through internal pistons, pushes the brake shoes outward against the drums.

ABBREVIATIONS AND SYMBOLS

A: Ampere

AC: Alternating current

A/C: Air conditioning

A-h: Ampere hour

AT: Automatic transmission

ATDC: After top dead center

μA: Microampere

bbl: Barrel

BDC: Bottom dead center

bhp: Brake horsepower

BTDC: Before top dead center

BTU: British thermal unit

C: Celsius (Centigrade)

CCA: Cold cranking amps

cd: Candela

cm^2: Square centimeter

cm^3, cc: Cubic centimeter

CO: Carbon monoxide

CO_2: Carbon dioxide

cu.in., in^3: Cubic inch

CV: Constant velocity

Cyl.: Cylinder

DC: Direct current

ECM: Electronic control module

EFE: Early fuel evaporation

EFI: Electronic fuel injection

EGR: Exhaust gas recirculation

Exh.: Exhaust

F: Fahrenheit

F: Farad

pF: Picofarad

μF: Microfarad

FI: Fuel injection

ft.lb., ft. lb., ft. lbs.: foot pound(s)

gal: Gallon

g: Gram

HC: Hydrocarbon

HEI: High energy ignition

HO: High output

hp: Horsepower

Hyd.: Hydraulic

Hz: Hertz

ID: Inside diameter

in.lb.; in. lb.; in. lbs: inch pound(s)

Int.: Intake

K: Kelvin

kg: Kilogram

kHz: Kilohertz

km: Kilometer

km/h: Kilometers per hour

kΩ: Kilohm

kPa: Kilopascal

kV: Kilovolt

kW: Kilowatt

l: Liter

l/s: Liters per second

m: Meter

mA: Milliampere

mg: Milligram

mHz: Megahertz

mm: Millimeter

mm^2: Square millimeter

m^3: Cubic meter

$M\Omega$: Megohm

m/s: Meters per second

MT: Manual transmission

mV: Millivolt

μm: Micrometer

N: Newton

N-m: Newton meter

NOx: Nitrous oxide

OD: Outside diameter

OHC: Over head camshaft

OHV: Over head valve

Ω: Ohm

PCV: Positive crankcase ventilation

psi: Pounds per square inch

pts: Pints

qts: Quarts

rpm: Rotations per minute

rps: Rotations per second

R-12: A refrigerant gas (Freon)

SAE: Society of Automotive Engineers

SO_2: Sulfur dioxide

T: Ton

t: Megagram

TBI: Throttle Body Injection

TPS: Throttle Position Sensor

V: 1. Volt; 2. Venturi

μV: Microvolt

W: Watt

∞: Infinity

‹: Less than

›: Greater than

Index

A

Air cleaner, 19
Air conditioning
  Blower, 292
  Compressor, 173
  Control panel, 296
  Discharging, evacuating, charging and leak
      testing, 38-39
  Gauge sets, 35
  General service, 32
  Evaporator, 296
  Inspection, 36
  Isolating the compressor, 38
  Operation, 32
  Preventive maintenance, 34
  Safety precautions, 35
  Sight glass check, 37
  System tests, 37
  Troubleshooting, 33, 40
Air pump, 236, 243
Alternator
  Alternator precautions, 129
  Operation, 127
  Removal and installation, 129
  Troubleshooting, 127
Antifreeze, 57
Automatic transfer case
  Application chart, 18, 357
  Removal and installation, 367
Automatic transmission
  Adjustments, 353
  Application chart, 19, 349
  Auxiliary oil cooler, 350
  Back-up light switch, 355
  Filter change, 347
  Fluid change, 54, 347
  Linkage adjustments, 353
  Neutral safety switch, 355
  Operation, 345
  Pan removal, 347
  Removal and installation, 355
  Troubleshooting, 348

B

Back-up light switch
  Automatic transmission, 355
  Manual transmission, 331
Ball joints
  Except Wrangler, 416
  Wrangler, 420
Battery
  Fluid level and maintenance, 24
  Jump starting, 26
  Removal and installation, 144
Bellcrank, 451
Belts, 29, 129
Brakes
  Bleeding, 469
  Brake light switch, 470

Disc brakes
  Caliper, 477
  Description, 471
  Operating principals, 455
  Pads, 471
  Rotor (Disc), 515
Drum brakes
  Adjustment, 456
  Drum, 481
  Operating principals, 456
  Shoes, 483
  Wheel cylinder, 484
Fluid level, 57
Hoses and lines, 469
Master cylinder, 461
Operation, 454
Parking brake
  Adjustment, 486
  Removal and installation, 486
Power booster
  Operating principals, 456
  Removal and installation, 467
Proportioning valve, 468
Specifications, 454
Transmission brake, 485
Troubleshooting, 457
Breaker points, 86
Bulbs, 304
Bumpers, 498

C

Calipers
  Overhaul, 478
  Removal and installation, 477
Camber, 422
Camshaft and bearings
  4-134 engine, 214
  4-150 engine, 214
  4-151 engine, 215
  6-225 engine, 216
  6-226 engine, 217
  6-230 engine, 218
  6-232, 258 engine, 219
  8-304 engine, 220
Capacities Chart, 67
Carburetor
  Adjustments, 106-113, 267-281
  Overhaul, 255-281
  Removal and installation, 254
  Specifications, 252
Caster, 422
Center link/Connecting rod/Drag link, 450
Chassis electrical system
  Circuit protection, 302
  Heater and air conditioning, 292
  Instrument panel, 299
  Lighting, 301
  Troubleshooting, 287-291
  Windshield wipers, 296
Chassis lubrication, 60

Charging system, 127
Choke, 276-278
Circuit breakers, 304
Clutch
  Adjustment, 336
  Hydraulic system bleeding, 344
  Master cylinder, 337
  Operation, 305
  Removal and installation, 332
  Slave cylinder, 343
  Troubleshooting, 332
Coil (ignition), 120
Combination manifold, 167
Combination switch, 426
Compression testing, 153
Compressor
  Isolating, 38
  Removal and installation, 173
Condenser, 86
Connecting rods and bearings, 220, 221
Constant velocity (CV) joints
Control arm, 421
Cooling system, 57
Crankcase ventilation valve, 22
Crankshaft, 229
Crankshaft damper, 200
Cylinder head
  Removal, inspection and installation
    4-134 engine, 182
    4-150 engine, 182
    4-151 engine, 184
    6-225 engine, 184
    6-226 engine, 185
    6-230 engine, 186
    6-232, 258 engine, 186
    8-304 engine, 187
Cylinders
  Inspection, 221
  Reboring, 224
  Refinishing, 223

D

Disc brakes, 471
Distributor
  Breaker points, 86
  Condenser, 86
  Removal and installation, 121-127
Door glass, 508
Door locks, 505
Doors, 505
Door trim panel, 507
Drive axle (front)
  Application chart, 382
  Axle shaft, bearing and seal, 382
  Fluid recommendations, 59
  Front hub and wheel bearings, 39, 389
  Lubricant level, 59
  Pinion seal and yoke, 387
  Removal and installation, 387
  Shift motor and housing, 389
Drive axle (rear)
  Axle shaft, 376

Axle shaft bearing, 377
Fluid recommendations, 59
Identification, 375
Lubricant level, 59
Operation, 374
Pinion oil seal, 375
Ratios, 375
Removal and installation, 381
Driveshaft
  Front, 370
  Rear, 370
Drive Train, 305
Drum brakes, 481
Dwell angle, 91

E

EGR valve, 243
Electrical
  Chassis, 287
  Engine, 120
Electronic Ignition
  AMC BID System, 91
  AMC SSI System, 93
  AMC/Renault System, 95
  Delco HEI System, 96
Emission controls
  Air pump, 236, 243
  Applications chart, 235
  Catalytic Converter, 248
  Choke Heat By-pass Valve, 249
  Electrically Assisted Choke, 245
  Exhaust Gas Recirculation (EGR) system, 243
  Feedback system, 248
  Fuel Return system, 249
  Fuel Tank Vapor Control system, 245
  PCV valve, 235
  Thermostatically controlled air cleaner, 240
  Transmission controlled spark system, 240
  Troubleshooting, 249ff
  Vacuum Throttle Modulating (VTM) system, 248
Engine
  Camshaft, 214
  Combination manifold, 167
  Compression testing, 153
  Connecting rods and bearings, 220
  Crankshaft, 229
  Crankshaft damper, 200
  Cylinder head, 182-187
  Cylinders, 21
  Design, 145
  Exhaust manifold, 171
  Fluids and lubricants, 51
  Flywheel, 232
  Front (timing) cover, 200
  Front seal, 200ff
  Identification, 14, 18
  Intake manifold, 167
  Main bearings, 229
  Oil pan, 194
  Oil pump, 197
  Overhaul, 151
  Piston pin, 221

Engine (*continued*)
  Pistons, 220
  Rear main seal, 227
  Removal and installation
      4-134 engine, 154
      4-150 engine, 156
      4-151 engine, 158
      6-225 engine, 158
      6-226 engine, 159
      6-230 engine, 161
      6-232 engine, 161
      6-258 engine, 161
      8-304 engine, 161
  Rings, 224
  Rocker shafts and studs, 162
  Specifications, 116ff
  Thermostat, 167
  Timing chain and gears, 206-213
  Tools, 152
  Troubleshooting, 146
  Valve guides, 192
  Valves, 188
  Valve seats, 193
  Valve springs, 191
  Valve timing, 213
  Water pump, 175
Evaporative canister, 23
Evaporator, 296
Exhaust Manifold, 171
Exhaust system, 232

F

Fan, 175
Fenders, 496
Firing orders, 83-84
Fluids and lubricants
  Automatic transmission, 54
  Battery, 24
  Chassis greasing, 60
  Coolant, 57
  Drive axle, 59
  Engine oil, 51
  Fuel, 51
  Manual transmission, 53
  Master cylinder
      Brake, 57
      Clutch, 57
  Power steering pump, 59
  Steering gear, 59
  Steering knuckle, 60
  Transfer case, 56
Flywheel and ring gear, 232
Front axle (2-wd)
      Identification, 393
      Pivot pins, 393
Front bumper, 498
Front crossmember cover, 499
Front drive axle
      Application chart, 382
      Axle shaft, bearing and seal, 382
      Fluid recommendations, 59
      Front hub and wheel bearings, 39, 389

      Lubricant level, 59
      Pinion seal and yoke, 387
      Removal and installation, 387
      Shift motor and housing, 389
Front brakes, 471, 481
Front hubs, 39, 389
Front suspension
  Ball joints
      Exc. Wrangler, 416
      Wrangler, 420
  Knuckles, 410, 416
  Shock absorbers, 408
  Springs, 398
  Stabilizer bar, 409
  Steering damper, 451
  Track bar, 409
  Troubleshooting, 399
  Upper control arm, 421
  Wheel alignment, 421
Front wheel bearings, 389, 488
Fuel injection
  Fuel body, 284
  Fuel pressure regulator, 284
  Fuel pump, 282
  Idle speed actuator motor, 285
  Injectors, 284
  Throttle body, 282
  Throttle position sensor, 285
Fuel filter, 21
Fuel pump, 251, 282
Fuel system
  Carbureted, 251
  Fuel injection, 281
  Troubleshooting, 251
Fuel tank, 285
Fuses and circuit breakers, 304
Fusible links, 302

G

Gearshift linkage adjustment
  Automatic, 385
  Manual, 331
Generator
  Operation, 127
  Removal and installation, 129
  Troubleshooting, 127
Glossary, 522
Governor, 281
Grille, 495

H

Hardtop, 495
Headlights, 301
Heater
  Blower, 292
  Control panel, 296
  Core, 294
Heat riser, 23
Hinges, 505
History, 6
Hoisting, 63

Hood, 501
Hoses, 30
How to Buy a Used Truck, 63
How to Use This Book, 1
Hubs, 39, 44, 389, 488

I

Identification
  Axle, 19
  Engine, 14, 18
  Model, 6
  Serial number, 12
  Transfer case, 18
  Transmission
    Automatic, 19, 349
    Manual, 18, 343
  Vehicle, 12
Idle speed and mixture adjustment, 106-113
Ignition lock cylinder, 431
Ignition module, 121
Ignition switch, 428
Ignition timing, 99
Injectors, 284
Instrument cluster, 299
Instrument panel
  Cluster, 299
  Radio, 301
  Speedometer cable, 300
Intake manifold
  4-134 engine, 167
  4-150 engine, 167
  4-151 engine, 168
  6-225 engine, 169
  6-226 engine, 169
  6-230 engine, 169
  6-232, 258 engine, 170
  8-304 engine, 170

J

Jacking points, 63
Jump starting, 26

K

King pins, 393, 410
Knuckles, 410, 416
Knuckle oil seal, 418

L

Light bulb charts, 304
Liftgate, 501
Liftgate glass, 511
Liftgate lock, 507
Locking hubs, 44, 389
Lubrication
  Automatic transmission, 54
  Chassis, 60
  Differential, 59
  Engine, 51
  Manual transmission, 53
  Transfer case, 56

M

Main bearings, 229
Maintenance intervals, 69
Manifolds
  Combination, 167
  Intake, 167
  Exhaust, 171
Manual steering gear
  Adjustments, 438
  Removal and installation, 433
  Troubleshooting, 434
Manual transfer case
  Application chart, 357
  Linkage adjustment, 366
  Removal and installation, 356
Manual transmission
  Adjustments, 331
  Application chart, 18, 308
  Operation, 305
  Removal and installation, 306
  Troubleshooting, 306
Master cylinder
  Brake, 461
  Clutch, 337
Mechanic's data, 520
Model identification, 6
Module (ignition), 121

N

Neutral safety switch, 355

O

Oil and fuel recommendations, 51
Oil and filter change (engine), 52
Oil level check
  Differential, 59
  Engine, 51
  Transfer case, 56
  Transmission
    Automatic, 54
    Manual, 53
Oil pan, 194
Oil pump, 197
Outside vehicle maintenance
  Lock cylinders, 60
  Door hinges, 60
  Tailgate, 60
  Body drain holes, 60
Overdrive, 379

P

Parking brake, 486
Piston pin, 221
Pistons, 220-227
Pitman arm, 451
Pivot pins, 393, 410
PCV valve, 22
Points, 86
Power brake booster, 467

Power steering gear
    Adjustments, 442
    Removal and installation, 440
    Troubleshooting, 440
Power steering pump
    Removal and installation, 444
    Troubleshooting, 446
Power take-off
    Operation, 368
    Pulley drive unit, 370
    Shaft drive unit, 369
    Shift unit, 368
    Specification chart, 371
Preventive Maintenance Charts, 69
Pushing, 60

Q

Quick Reference Specifications, iv

R

Radiator, 174
Radiator cap, 58
Radio, 301
Rear axle
    Axle shaft, 376
    Axle shaft bearing, 377
    Fluid recommendations, 59
    Identification, 375
    Lubricant level, 59
    Operation, 374
    Pinion oil seal, 375
    Ratios, 375
    Removal and installation, 416
Rear brakes, 516
Rear bumper, 533
Rear main oil seal, 227
Rear suspension
    Shock absorbers, 443
    Springs, 433
    Track bar, 444
    Troubleshooting, 434
Rear wheel bearings, 412
Regulator
    Operation, 130
    Removal and installation, 133
    Testing and adjustment, 130-133
Rings, 224
Rocker arms or shaft, 162
Roll bar, 535
Rotor (Brake disc), 515
Routine maintenance, 17

S

Safety notice, ii, 5
Seats, 546
Serial number location, 12
Shock absorbers, 443
Solenoid, 138
Slave cylinder, 378

Soft top, 535
Spare tire carrier, 534
Spark plugs, 84
Spark plug wires, 86
Special tools, 3
Specifications Charts
    Alternator and regulator, 114
    Brakes, 489
    Camshaft, 116
    Carburetor, 252-254
    Crankshaft and connecting rod, 118
    Fastener markings and torque standards, 155
    Fuses and Circuit Breakers, 304
    General engine, 116
    Generator and regulator, 114
    Light bulbs, 304
    Piston and ring, 119
    Power take-off, 406
    Preventive Maintenance, 69-77
    Starter, 115
    Torque, 119
    Tune-up, 81
    Valves, 117
    Wheel alignment, 433
Speedometer cable, 300
Springs, 433
Stain removal, 554
Starter
    Drive replacement, 133-138
    Overhaul, 139-144
    Removal and installation, 133
    Solenoid or relay replacement, 138
    Troubleshooting, 134
Steering column, 468
Steering damper, 486
Steering gear
    Manual, 468
    Power, 475
Steering knuckles
    exc. Wrangler, 445, 451
    Wrangler only, 454
Steering knuckle oil seal, 453
Steering linkage
    Bellcrank, 486
    Center link/Connecting rod/Drag link, 485
    Pitman arm, 486
    Steering damper, 486
    Tie rod ends, 480
Steering wheel, 458
Striker plate, 540
Stripped threads, 152
Suspension, 433

T

Tailgate, 537
Tailgate lock, 542
Thermostat, 167
Throttle body, 282
Tie rod ends, 480
Timing (ignition)
    Point type systems, 99

Electronic systems, 103
Timing chain and gears
    L4-134 engine, 206
    F4-134 engine, 207
    4-150 engine, 207
    4-151 engine, 208
    6-225 engine, 209
    6-226 engine, 209
    6-230 engine, 210
    6-232, 258 engine, 211
    8-304 engine, 211
Timing gear cover
    4-134 engine, 200
    4-150 engine, 200
    4-151 engine, 202
    6-225 engine, 202
    6-226 engine, 202
    6-230 engine, 203
    6-232, 258 engine, 204
    8-304 engine, 205
Tires
    Description, 46
    Rotation, 50
    Troubleshooting, 48
    Wear problems, 49
Toe-in, 458
Tools, 2
Towing, 60
Trailer towing, 61
Transfer Case
    Application chart, 392
    Automatic, 402
    Manual, 391
Transmission
    Automatic, 380
    Manual, 341
    Routine maintenance, 53
Transmission brake, 520
Troubleshooting Charts
    Air conditioning, 33, 40-41
    Automatic transmission, 383
    Brakes, 492
    Charging system, 127
    Clutch, 367
    Cooling system, 148
    Drive belts, 150
    Driveshaft, 405
    Emission control systems, 249ff
    Engine mechanical, 146
    Engine performance, 78
    Fuel system, 251
    Gauges, 290
    Heater, 291
    Ignition switch, 436
    Ignition system
        Electronic, 92, 94, 95, 97
        Point type, 87
    Lights, 289
    Lockup torque converter, 383
    Manual steering gear, 469
    Manual transmission, 341
    Power steering gear, 475

Power steering pump, 481
Rear axle, 406
Starting system, 134
Steering and suspension, 434
Steering column, 434
Tires, 48
Transfer case, 341
Transmission fluid indications, 385
Turn signals and flashers, 288
Turn signal switch, 436
Wheels, 48
Windshield wipers, 291
Tune-up
    Procedures, 83
    Specifications, 81
    Troubleshooting, 78
Turning angle, 457
Turn signal switch, 460

U
U-joints
    Identification, 406
    Overhaul
        Bendix joint, 407
        Constant velocity joint, 409
        Rzeppa joint, 407
        Single cross Cardan joint, 408
        Understanding the manual transmission and
            clutch, 340
Upper control arm, 456

V
Valve guides, 192
Valve lash adjustment
    4-134 engine, 103
    6-226 engine, 104
    6-230 engine, 105
Valve seats, 193
Valve service, 188
Valve specifications, 117
Valve springs, 191
Valve timing, 213
Vehicle identification, 12

W
Water pump
    4-134 engine, 175
    4-150 engine, 175
    4-151 engine, 175
    6-225 engine, 177
    6-226 engine, 178
    6-230 engine, 178
    6-232, 258 engine, 180
    8-304 engine, 178
Wheel alignment, 456
Wheel bearings
    Front drive axle, 39, 424
Wheel cylinders, 519

Wheels, 46
Window glass, 546
Window regulator, 544
Windshield, 526
Windshield wipers
Arm, 296
Blade, 27, 296
Linkage, 298
Motor, 297
Wiring diagrams, 305–339

Chilton's Repair & Tune-Up Guides

The Complete line covers domestic cars, imports, trucks, vans, RV's and 4-wheel drive vehicles.

RTUG Title	Part No.	RTUG Title	Part No.
AMC 1975-82	7199	**Corvair 1960-69**	6691
Covers all U.S. and Canadian models		Covers all U.S. and Canadian models	
Aspen/Volare 1976-80	6637	**Corvette 1953-62**	6576
Covers all U.S. and Canadian models		Covers all U.S. and Canadian models	
Audi 1970-73	5902	**Corvette 1963-84**	6843
Covers all U.S. and Canadian models.		Covers all U.S. and Canadian models	
Audi 4000/5000 1978-81	7028	**Cutlass 1970-85**	6933
Covers all U.S. and Canadian models including turbocharged and diesel engines		Covers all U.S. and Canadian models	
Barracuda/Challenger 1965-72	5807	**Dart/Demon 1968-76**	6324
Covers all U.S. and Canadian models		Covers all U.S. and Canadian models	
Blazer/Jimmy 1969-82	6931	**Datsun 1961-72**	5790
Covers all U.S. and Canadian 2- and 4-wheel drive models, including diesel engines		Covers all U.S. and Canadian models of Nissan Patrol; 1500, 1600 and 2000 sports cars; Pick-Ups; 410, 411, 510, 1200 and 240Z	
BMW 1970-82	6844	**Datsun 1973-80 Spanish**	7083
Covers all U.S. and Canadian models		**Datsun/Nissan F-10, 310, Stanza, Pulsar 1977-86**	7196
Buick/Olds/Pontiac 1975-85	7308	Covers all U.S. and Canadian models	
Covers all U.S. and Canadian full size rear wheel drive models		**Datsun/Nissan Pick-Ups 1970-84**	6816
Cadillac 1967-84	7462	Covers all U.S and Canadian models	
Covers all U.S. and Canadian rear wheel drive models		**Datsun/Nissan Z & ZX 1970-86**	6932
Camaro 1967-81	6735	Covers all U.S. and Canadian models	
Covers all U.S. and Canadian models		**Datsun/Nissan 1200, 210, Sentra 1973-86**	7197
Camaro 1982-85	7317	Covers all U.S. and Canadian models	
Covers all U.S. and Canadian models		**Datsun/Nissan 200SX, 510, 610, 710, 810, Maxima 1973-84**	7170
Capri 1970-77	6695	Covers all U.S. and Canadian models	
Covers all U.S. and Canadian models		**Dodge 1968-77**	6554
Caravan/Voyager 1984-85	7482	Covers all U.S. and Canadian models	
Covers all U.S. and Canadian models		**Dodge Charger 1967-70**	6486
Century/Regal 1975-85	7307	Covers all U.S. and Canadian models	
Covers all U.S. and Canadian rear wheel drive models, including turbocharged engines		**Dodge/Plymouth Trucks 1967-84**	7459
Champ/Arrow/Sapporo 1978-83	7041	Covers all $1/2$, $3/4$, and 1 ton 2- and 4-wheel drive U.S. and Canadian models, including diesel engines	
Covers all U.S. and Canadian models		**Dodge/Plymouth Vans 1967-84**	6934
Chevette/1000 1976-86	6836	Covers all $1/2$, $3/4$, and 1 ton U.S. and Canadian models of vans, cutaways and motor home chassis	
Covers all U.S. and Canadian models		**D-50/Arrow Pick-Up 1979-81**	7032
Chevrolet 1968-85	7135	Covers all U.S. and Canadian models	
Covers all U.S. and Canadian models		**Fairlane/Torino 1962-75**	6320
Chevrolet 1968-79 Spanish	7082	Covers all U.S. and Canadian models	
Chevrolet/GMC Pick-Ups 1970-82 Spanish	7468	**Fairmont/Zephyr 1978-83**	6965
Chevrolet/GMC Pick-Ups and Suburban 1970-86	6936	Covers all U.S. and Canadian models	
Covers all U.S. and Canadian $1/2$, $3/4$ and 1 ton models, including 4-wheel drive and diesel engines		**Fiat 1969-81**	7042
		Covers all U.S. and Canadian models	
Chevrolet LUV 1972-81	6815	**Fiesta 1978-80**	6846
Covers all U.S. and Canadian models		Covers all U.S. and Canadian models	
Chevrolet Mid-Size 1964-86	6840	**Firebird 1967-81**	5996
Covers all U.S. and Canadian models of 1964-77 Chevelle, Malibu and Malibu SS; 1974-77 Laguna; 1978-85 Malibu; 1970-86 Monte Carlo; 1964-84 El Camino, including diesel engines		Covers all U.S. and Canadian models	
		Firebird 1982-85	7345
		Covers all U.S. and Canadian models	
		Ford 1968-79 Spanish	7084
Chevrolet Nova 1986	7658	**Ford Bronco 1966-83**	7140
Covers all U.S. and Canadian models		Covers all U.S. and Canadian models	
Chevy/GMC Vans 1967-84	6930	**Ford Bronco II 1984**	7408
Covers all U.S. and Canadian models of $1/2$, $3/4$, and 1 ton vans, cutaways, and motor home chassis, including diesel engines		Covers all U.S. and Canadian models	
		Ford Courier 1972-82	6983
		Covers all U.S. and Canadian models	
Chevy S-10 Blazer/GMC S-15 Jimmy 1982-85	7383	**Ford/Mercury Front Wheel Drive 1981-85**	7055
Covers all U.S. and Canadian models		Covers all U.S. and Canadian models Escort, EXP, Tempo, Lynx, LN-7 and Topaz	
Chevy S-10/GMC S-15 Pick-Ups 1982-85	7310	**Ford/Mercury/Lincoln 1968-85**	6842
Covers all U.S. and Canadian models		Covers all U.S. and Canadian models of FORD Country Sedan, Country Squire, Crown Victoria, Custom, Custom 500, Galaxie 500, LTD through 1982, Ranch Wagon, and XL; MERCURY Colony Park, Commuter, Marquis through 1982, Gran Marquis, Monterey and Park Lane; LINCOLN Continental and Towne Car	
Chevy II/Nova 1962-79	6841		
Covers all U.S. and Canadian models			
Chrysler K- and E-Car 1981-85	7163		
Covers all U.S. and Canadian front wheel drive models			
Colt/Challenger/Vista/Conquest 1971-85	7037		
Covers all U.S. and Canadian models			
Corolla/Carina/Tercel/Starlet 1970-85	7036	**Ford/Mercury/Lincoln Mid-Size 1971-85**	6696
Covers all U.S. and Canadian models		Covers all U.S. and Canadian models of FORD Elite, 1983-85 LTD, 1977-79 LTD II, Ranchero, Torino, Gran Torino, 1977-85 Thunderbird; MERCURY 1972-85 Cougar,	
Corona/Cressida/Crown/Mk.II/Camry/Van 1970-84	7044		
Covers all U.S. and Canadian models			

continued on next page

RTUG Title	Part No.	RTUG Title	Part No.
1983-85 Marquis, Montego, 1980-85 XR-7; LINCOLN 1982-85 Continental, 1984-85 Mark VII, 1978-80 Versailles		Mercedes-Benz 1974-84 Covers all U.S. and Canadian models	6809
Ford Pick-Ups 1965-86 Covers all 1/2, 3/4 and 1 ton, 2- and 4-wheel drive U.S. and Canadian pick-up, chassis cab and camper models, including diesel engines	6913	Mitsubishi, Cordia, Tredia, Starion, Galant 1983-85 Covers all U.S. and Canadian models	7583
		MG 1961-81 Covers all U.S. and Canadian models	6780
Ford Pick-Ups 1965-82 Spanish	7469	Mustang/Capri/Merkur 1979-85 Covers all U.S. and Canadian models	6963
Ford Ranger 1983-84 Covers all U.S. and Canadian models	7338	Mustang/Cougar 1965-73 Covers all U.S. and Canadian models	6542
Ford Vans 1961-86 Covers all U.S. and Canadian 1/2, 3/4 and 1 ton van and cutaway chassis models, including diesel engines	6849	Mustang II 1974-78 Covers all U.S. and Canadian models	6812
		Omni/Horizon/Rampage 1978-84 Covers all U.S. and Canadian models of DODGE Omni, Miser, 024, Charger 2.2; PLYMOUTH Horizon, Miser, TC3, TC3 Tourismo; Rampage	6845
GM A-Body 1982-85 Covers all front wheel drive U.S. and Canadian models of BUICK Century, CHEVROLET Celebrity, OLDSMOBILE Cutlass Ciera and PONTIAC 6000	7309	
		Opel 1971-75 Covers all U.S. and Canadian models	6575
GM C-Body 1985 Covers all front wheel drive U.S. and Canadian models of BUICK Electra Park Avenue and Electra T-Type, CADILLAC Fleetwood and deVille, OLDSMOBILE 98 Regency and Regency Brougham	7587	Peugeot 1970-74 Covers all U.S. and Canadian models	5982
		Pinto/Bobcat 1971-80 Covers all U.S. and Canadian models	7027
		Plymouth 1968-76 Covers all U.S. and Canadian models	6552
		Pontiac Fiero 1984-85 Covers all U.S. and Canadian models	7571
GM J-Car 1982-85 Covers all U.S. and Canadian models of BUICK Skyhawk, CHEVROLET Cavalier, CADILLAC Cimarron, OLDSMOBILE Firenza and PONTIAC 2000 and Sunbird	7059	Pontiac Mid-Size 1974-83 Covers all U.S. and Canadian models of Ventura, Grand Am, LeMans, Grand LeMans, GTO, Phoenix, and Grand Prix	7346
		Porsche 924/928 1976-81 Covers all U.S. and Canadian models	7048
GM N-Body 1985-86 Covers all U.S. and Canadian models of front wheel drive BUICK Somerset and Skylark, OLDSMOBILE Calais, and PONTIAC Grand Am	7657	Renault 1975-85 Covers all U.S. and Canadian models	7165
		Roadrunner/Satellite/Belvedere/GTX 1968-73 Covers all U.S. and Canadian models	5821
GM X-Body 1980-85 Covers all U.S. and Canadian models of BUICK Skylark, CHEVROLET Citation, OLDSMOBILE Omega and PONTIAC Phoenix	7049	RX-7 1979-81 Covers all U.S. and Canadian models	7031
		SAAB 99 1969-75 Covers all U.S. and Canadian models	5988
		SAAB 900 1979-85 Covers all U.S. and Canadian models	7572
GM Subcompact 1971-80 Covers all U.S. and Canadian models of BUICK Skyhawk (1975-80), CHEVROLET Vega and Monza, OLDSMOBILE Starfire, and PONTIAC Astre and 1975-80 Sunbird	6935	Snowmobiles 1976-80 Covers Arctic Cat, John Deere, Kawasaki, Polaris, Ski-Doo and Yamaha	6978
		Subaru 1970-84 Covers all U.S. and Canadian models	6982
Granada/Monarch 1975-82 Covers all U.S. and Canadian models	6937	Tempest/GTO/LeMans 1968-73 Covers all U.S. and Canadian models	5905
Honda 1973-84 Covers all U.S. and Canadian models	6980	Toyota 1966-70 Covers all U.S. and Canadian models of Corona, MkII, Corolla, Crown, Land Cruiser, Stout and Hi-Lux	5795
International Scout 1967-73 Covers all U.S. and Canadian models	5912	
Jeep 1945-87 Covers all U.S. and Canadian CJ-2A, CJ-3A, CJ-3B, CJ-5, CJ-6, CJ-7, Scrambler and Wrangler models	6817	Toyota 1970-79 Spanish	7467
		Toyota Celica/Supra 1971-85 Covers all U.S. and Canadian models	7043
Jeep Wagoneer, Commando, Cherokee, Truck 1957-86 Covers all U.S. and Canadian models of Wagoneer, Cherokee, Grand Wagoneer, Jeepster, Jeepster Commando, J-100, J-200, J-300, J-10, J20, FC-150 and FC-170	6739	Toyota Trucks 1970-85 Covers all U.S. and Canadian models of pickups, Land Cruiser and 4Runner	7035
		Valiant/Duster 1968-76 Covers all U.S. and Canadian models	6326
		Volvo 1956-69 Covers all U.S. and Canadian models	6529
Laser/Daytona 1984-85 Covers all U.S. and Canadian models	7563	Volvo 1970-83 Covers all U.S. and Canadian models	7040
Maverick/Comet 1970-77 Covers all U.S. and Canadian models	6634	VW Front Wheel Drive 1974-85 Covers all U.S. and Canadian models	6962
Mazda 1971-84 Covers all U.S. and Canadian models of RX-2, RX-3, RX-4, 808, 1300, 1600, Cosmo, GLC and 626	6981	VW 1949-71 Covers all U.S. and Canadian models	5796
		VW 1970-79 Spanish	7081
Mazda Pick-Ups 1972-86 Covers all U.S. and Canadian models	7659	VW 1970-81 Covers all U.S. and Canadian Beetles, Karmann Ghia, Fastback, Squareback, Vans, 411 and 412	6837
Mercedes-Benz 1959-70 Covers all U.S. and Canadian models	6065	
Mercedes-Benz 1968-73 Covers all U.S. and Canadian models	5907	

Chilton's Repair Manuals are available at your local retailer or by mailing a check or money order for **$15.95** per book plus **$3.50** for 1st book and **$.50** for each additional book to cover postage and handling ?:

Chilton Book Company
Dept. DM
Radnor, PA 19089

NOTE: When ordering be sure to include your name & address, book part No. & title.